COMPARATIVE ECONOMICS IN A TRANSFORMING WORLD ECONOMY

THE IRWIN SERIES IN ECONOMICS

COMPARATIVE ECONOMICS IN A TRANSFORMING WORLD ECONOMY

J. Barkley Rosser, Jr.
James Madison University

Marina V. Rosser
James Madison University

Chicago • Bogotá • Boston • Buenos Aires • Caracas
London • Madrid • Mexico City • Sydney • Toronto

IRWIN **Concerned about Our Environment**
In recognition of the fact that our company is a large end-user of fragile yet replenishable resources, we at IRWIN can assure you that every effort is made to meet or exceed Environmental Protection Agency (EPA) recommendations and requirements for a "greener" workplace.

To preserve these natural assets, a number of environmental policies, both companywide and department-specific, have been implemented. From the use of 50% recycled paper in our textbooks to the printing of promotional materials with recycled stock and soy inks to our office paper recycling program, we are committed to reducing waste and replacing environmentally unsafe products with safer alternatives.

Irwin Book Team

Senior sponsoring editor: *Gary Nelson*
Editorial assistant: *Tracey Douglas*
Senior marketing manager: *Ron Bloecher*
Production supervisor: *Lara Feinberg*
Manager, graphics and desktop services: *Kim Meriwether*
Project editor: *Maggie Rathke*
Designer: *Matthew Baldwin*
Compositor: *Times Mirror Higher Education Group, Inc., Imaging Group*
Typeface: *10/12 Times Roman*
Printer: *R. R. Donnelley & Sons, Company*

Cover illustration: © 1995 M. C. Escher/Cordon Art-Baarn-Holland. All rights reserved.

Times Mirror
Higher Education Group

Library of Congress Cataloging-in-Publication Data

Rosser, John Barkley
    Comparative economics in a transforming world economy / J. Barkley
Rosser, Jr., Marina Vschernaya Rosser
        p. cm.
    Includes bibliographical references and index.
        ISBN 0–256–13095–7
        1. Comparative economics. 2. International economic relations.
    I. Rosser, Marina Vschernaya. II. Title.
    HB90.R67   1966
    337—dc20   95–23362

Printed in the United States of America
1 2 3 4 5 6 7 8 9 0 DO 21 0 9 8 7 6 5

We wish to dedicate this book to our loving mothers,
Annetta Hamilton Rosser and Nata Borisovna Vcherashnaya.

PREFACE

The transformation of the world economy is in turn transforming the field of comparative economics. The classic confrontation of capitalism and socialism has largely dissolved with the dissolution of the Soviet Union, its empire, and the end of the Cold War. Most of the formerly socialist economies, even those that remain ruled by Communist Parties such as the Peoples' Republic of China, are now in various transitions towards mostly market forms of economic systems. New forms arise out of these processes and other forms arise on the world scene such as the Islamic economy.

This book seeks to be a part of this transformation of the field of comparative economics. Just as the economies in transition continue to retain elements of their old systems, so this book retains elements of the ''old comparative economics,'' with a comparison of the theory and practice of market capitalism and command socialism as a central organizing feature. Although only a few economies in the world still practice command socialism, study of it reveals the background of the economies involved in attempting transitions, and also highlights important aspects of market capitalist economies. Thus one aspect of this book which is old and new at the same time is the comparison of the North and South Korean economies presented in Chapter 18—a case not presented in any previous comparative economics book.

However, this book moves in directions that we think will increasingly mark and define the field as it is transformed. Probably the single most important innovation of this book is its definition and examination of the *new traditional economy*. We see this as a new ideological and systemic movement that is increasingly influential around the world. It involves an economy that seeks to combine the custom-and-family-based orientation of a classic traditional economy with modern technology and involvement in the modern world economy.

The most obvious manifestation of this phenomenon is the spreading of Islamic economics into more and more countries. However, the new traditional economy concept applies in other religious and cultural arenas as well, such as the neo-Confucian one in East Asia. Indeed, much of what distinguishes largely market capitalist Japan from the U.S. and Western European economic systems is the "familistic groupism" of its society and economy which can be viewed as exhibiting new traditional elements. Our most clear-cut case study of such an economy is that of the Islamic Republic of Iran in Chapter 16, which has never been presented in any comparative economics book before.

Another unique element of this book is its much more detailed consideration of the various paths taken by the successor states to the former Soviet Union. This reflects the unique perspective of one of the coauthors of this book as a former citizen and professional economist working within the former Soviet Union. We feel the variety of the successor states' paths reflects the variety of possible outcomes facing the world economy as a whole. The Central Asian former republics in particular face virtually all modern forms of change, with existing systems retaining strong elements of the old command socialist model while they face the alternatives of market capitalism, Islamic economics, and even East Asian models. We emphasize Asian cases more strongly in this book than is done in most other books.

In many areas we cover material common to most books of comparative economics. These include comparisons among the variations of market capitalism; discussion of the issues of global economic integration in the European Union (EU), the North American Free Trade Agreement (NAFTA), and the new World Trade Organization (WTO) as contrasted with the tendency toward disintegration as in the breakup of the old Soviet-dominated Council of Mutual Economic Assistance (CMEA), the problems facing developing economies, and a variety of special policy topics of global significance with an emphasis on varying approaches to environmental policy. We also attempt to present cases covering most regions of the world.

In the spectrum of theoretical versus institutional approaches we attempt to strike a reasonable balance between the two, although we probably tilt somewhat in favor of the latter. Theoretical issues related to the various types of economic systems are thoroughly aired in the first part of the book, taking account of recent theoretical developments in neoclassical economics such as information economics and principal-agent problems, as well as a presentation of Marxian economic theory. However our full-chapter case studies are done in depth, always beginning with a presentation of the specific historical, political, cultural, and other factors which shape the institutional frameworks and tendencies within the society under study. Theory is accounted for, but it is never applied without a clear accounting of historical/institutional context.

Like all economists, we have our normative and ideological biases which inevitably reveal themselves from time to time in this book. However, we have made a sincere effort to be objective and fair-minded about both theories and facts as much as this is possible. Thus, we have made an effort to present a variety of perspectives, with each being presented at least somewhere in its strongest possible light. We have not attempted to shy away from ''uncomfortable facts'' that do not fit with our own preconceptions. Indeed, although there are many generalizations that can be found in this book, the careful reader will also usually find exceptions to most of them somewhere. A good generalization is that most generalizations must be taken with several rather large grains of salt, given what a complicated and peculiar place the world really is.

This book is in four parts. Part I presents a general theoretical overview. Chapter 1 presents a broad empirical comparison of many different economies after initially defining various categories. Chapter 2 discusses the fundamentals of market capitalism and its variations with a special emphasis on the case of the United States. Chapter 3 does the same for command socialism and its variations. The fourth chapter is more unusual for a comparative economics book and presents the theory of the old traditional economy as well as delving into certain deeper issues of comparing economies. Chapter 4 prepares the framework for the discussion of the new traditional economy in Chapter 5, where specifically the Islamic economy as well as systems associated with various other religions are examined. There is some discussion of several economies including Burma, India, and Israel.

Part II presents case studies of market capitalism, in particular Japan, France, Sweden, and Germany. The chapter on France includes a special discussion of the European Union and its prospects. The chapter on Germany includes a discussion of the former East German economy and the problems of reunification of the two Germanies. Although it does not have a chapter to itself, considerable discussion of and data on the U.S. economy is presented in the first part of chapter 2. The U.S. economy is thus presented throughout Part II and indeed the whole book as the touchstone case of market capitalism. There is also considerable discussion of the case of Great Britain in the last chapter of the book, 19, which especially focuses on the privatization issue.

Part III focuses on the transitions of the various previously socialist economies. Chapter 10 presents the Soviet model as it developed up to its collapse at the end of 1991. The following chapters cover the successor states to the USSR, Poland, Hungary, the former Yugoslavia, and China. The chapter on Poland includes an extended discussion on the Czech Republic as well. The chapter on China also contains extended discussions of the economies of Hong Kong and Taiwan.

Part IV presents alternative models among developing economies. Iran is the example of a new traditional economy. Material on Pakistan and Saudi Arabia is also presented. Mexico is a case of a complexly mixed economy in transition from an insular state orientation to a more open and market orientation. Comparative material on a number of other Latin American economies is also included at the end of the chapter. The two Koreas then present a sharp contrast of alternatives. Chapter 19 discusses broader questions of global trends of various sorts but includes a discussion of the sub-Saharan African success story of Botswana, as well as of British privatization.

We began writing this book in the summer of 1992. This preface is being written at the completion of its final revisions in July 1995. We have done our best to be current and up-to-date, but certainly any reader must understand that one of the challenges facing comparative economics now is the very rapidity of change that is going on. Thus almost certainly some of the assertions and facts presented herein will be out-of-date and possibly looking rather ridiculous by the time you read this. We beg your indulgence and understanding on this point.

Numerous individuals have contributed to the writing and production of this book in a variety of ways. Almost certainly we shall fail to recognize somebody and request forgiveness in advance for doing so. However we do wish to acknowledge and thank by name as many as we reasonably can. None of these parties should be held responsible for any factual errors or questionable interpretations contained in this book.

The following individuals participated in formally reviewing this book:

Professor Nora Ann Colton, Drew University

Professor Barry Duman, West Texas A&M University

Professor Thomas Grooms, Northwood Institute

Professor James Kuhlman, University of South Carolina

Professor Susan Linz, Michigan State University

Professor Ding Lu, University of Nebraska

Professor Robert Smith, University of Oregon

Professor James Stodder, Rensselaer Polytechnic Institute

Professor Edward Stuart, Northeastern Illinois University.

Two other individuals who read the entire first draft of the manuscript and made numerous important and useful suggestions are David Colander and Lynn Turgeon. We especially want to thank Lynn, without whose input this book would not have been written at all.

Other individuals who read at least some portion of the manuscript and made suggestions include Ehsan Ahmed, Ralph Andreano, the late Jack Barbash, Sohrab Behdad, Cyrus Bina, Warren Braun, Bruce Brunton, Alain Chaboud, Lee Congdon, William Duddleston, Éva Ehrlich, Edward Friedman, Huang Qiang, Evan Kraft, Bozena Leven, Fatima Moghadam, Paul Phillips, Frederic Pryor, Kenneth Roberts, Annetta Rosser, Linda Seligmann, Charles Simon, Zoltan Tarr, Mehrdad Valibeigi, Mark White, James Whitman, Hamid Zanganeh, and Wei-Bin Zhang.

Besides many of the above, others who have either made research materials available to us or have otherwise assisted with support or suggestions include Michael Alexeev, Leszek Balcerowicz, Daniel Berkowitz, Oleg Bogomolov, Daniel Bromley, John Clayton, Harry Cleaver, Peter Dorman,

Gregory Dow, Dietrich Earnhart, Edgar Feige, Fang Fukang, Carl Folke, Shirley Gedeon, Marshall Goldman, the late David Granick, Gertrude Schroeder Greenslade, Roger Guesnerie, Folke Günther, Robert Horn, David Iaquinta, Mark Knell, Francis Kramarz, Timur Kuran, Karl-Gustar Lofgren, Nora Lustig, Mikhail Lyugachov, Jacques Mairesse, Victor Makarov, Karl-Goran Mäler, Claire Mangasarian, Caroline Marshall, Anne Mayhew, Woodford McClellan, Robert McIntyre, Stanislav Menshikov, William Mitchell, Donald Nichols, Charles Perrings, Louis Putterman, Tönu Puu, Gábor Révész, Dorothy Rosenberg, Mark Selden, Thomas Selden, Charles Sweet, Alexander Tsapin, Atsuko Ueda, Chong Yoon, Andrew Zimbalist, and Tomasz Żylicz.

We especially thank Mohammed Elshentenawy, Loretta Grunewald, and William Wood for technical assistance.

We wish to acknowledge the capable staff at Richard D. Irwin, Inc. including Chad Douglas who originally connected us with this fine company; Ellen Cleary, Tracey Douglas, and Tia Schultz who were development editors; Rita McMullen, Maggie Rathke, and Susan Trentacosti, who were project editors; Ginger Rodriguez who was copy editor, and Times Mirror Higher Education Group, Inc., Imaging Group who was compositor. Finally we wish to thank Senior Economics Editor Gary Nelson for his firm guidance and wise counsel throughout this project.

This book is dedicated to our beloved mothers, Annetta Hamilton Rosser and Nata Borisovna Vcherashnaya.

J. Barkley Rosser, Jr.
Marina V. Rosser

CONTENTS

OVERVIEW OF COMPARATIVE ECONOMICS

Part I of this book presents the theoretical and conceptual framework used in the remaining parts, which consist mostly of sets of country case studies grouped in broad categories. It contains five chapters.

The first chapter presents definitions and basic examples of the categories used in this book, *tradition, market,* and *command* for allocative mechanisms, and *capitalism* and *socialism* for ownership systems. Broad trends in the world economy and in these systems are laid out. A major comparison of 26 countries on a number of basic economic characteristics also is presented.

Chapter 2 lays out the theory of market capitalism, the world's increasingly dominant economic system. It also discusses problems in its practice with a special emphasis on the case of the U.S. economy, the world's largest and also the most clear-cut market capitalist example. The U.S. economy and the market capitalist system are the touchstone cases for comparison with all other models and cases.

Chapter 3 examines the theory and history of socialism in its various forms, of which command socialism has been the most important. However it has now largely disappeared and the future importance of socialism is likely to come from its other forms.

Chapter 4 looks at the old traditional economy in its primitive form, mostly found now in rural parts of less developed countries. This chapter examines more deeply issues raised in Chapter 1 regarding how to think about economic systems and their classification.

Chapter 5 considers the new traditional economy, a system that seeks to combine a traditional approach, usually based on a traditional religion, with modern technology. The Islamic economy is the most developed example of this emerging form and is discussed in detail, but it also plays a role in East Asia in the neo-Confucian societies.

A central issue running through all these systems is the role of government in the economy. How much should it be involved and in what ways? Certainly in the contrast between market capitalism and command socialism in their pure forms this issue is highlighted. But in examining the variations within each of those forms the varying role of government plays a critical part. Also government plays a role in the traditional economies, especially the new traditional economies. The Islamic economic system only becomes established if a government causes it to be by passing laws mandating it.

Market Capitalist
Planned Market Capitalist
Social Market Capitalist
Market Socialist
Command Socialist
New Traditional

1

How Do We Compare Economies?

*As mankind approaches the end of the millennium, the twin crises of
authoritarianism and socialist central planning have left only one
competitor standing in the ring as an ideology of potentially universal
validity: liberal democracy, the doctrine of individual freedom and popular
sovereignty . . . In its economic manifestation, liberalism is the recognition
of the right of free economic activity and economic exchange based on
private property and markets.*

Francis Fukuyama, The End of History and the Last Man

Introduction

We have witnessed a profound transformation of the world political and economic order, the ultimate outcome of which is impossible to foresee. The
former Soviet Union (FSU) has broken up,[1] its empire of satellite states has
dissolved, and most of the former constituent parts are trying to fulfill the
above prophecy of Francis Fukuyama. In his view, the end of the Cold War
means the convergence of the entire world on the American model of political
economy and the end of any significant competition between alternative forms
of political or economic systems.

Is this true? We beg to differ. For one thing the economic crisis of the
former Soviet empire has spilled into the advanced capitalist world, partly
through the conduit of reunified Germany, which drained money from its

---

[1]Prior to 1917 the Russian Empire included many nationalities ruled by a tsar. With the
Bolshevik Revolution, several nationalities gained independence, some permanently like the
Finns and the Poles, and some only briefly like the Ukrainians. Then there was Soviet Russia.
In 1922 it became the Union of Soviet Socialist Republics (USSR) or Soviet Union, which
ceased to exist at the end of 1991. Now there is a loose confederation of 12 of the former 15
republics of the USSR called the Commonwealth of Independent States (CIS). When referring
in the present to all of the 15 republics as a group we shall use the term ''former Soviet
Union'' or FSU.

neighbors to pay for the costs of unification. Unpopular incumbent governments and serious questions about economic policy resound throughout the supposedly victorious market capitalist nations.

Furthermore, the collapse of Soviet Communism has coincided with a surge of missionary activity in the formerly Soviet Central Asian republics by advocates of fundamentalist Islam. They present their view as not just a change in personal moral codes, but a total system of economic and political organization of society, a possible "third way" between capitalism and socialism. Throughout the Islamic world fundamentalist groups either have taken control of governments or are the leading opposition to existing governments. In other nations, movements based upon fundamentalist versions of local religions have emerged and become prominent. In East Asia many see the cultural heritage of Confucianism creating a special economic environment. This appeal to economic systems based on traditional religions is the *new traditional economy* and it presents a serious alternative on the world stage. The Islamic version is the most fully worked out and influential.

Fukuyama recognizes that the rise of Islamic fundamentalism constitutes a potential exception to his thesis, but responds that it will be limited to the zone of existing Islamic predominance, thus ruling it out as a "potentially universal ideology." But the emergence of similar movements in other religions offers the possibility that the new traditional economy concept could be universal even while differing in significant details across religions. Cold War could give way to Holy War.

Even if Fukuyama is right that the socialist alternative will shortly be dead and that fundamentalism will be limited in its appeal, economic tensions between the United States, Japan, and Western Europe have focused attention upon deep structural differences between these and other market capitalist economies. There are many varieties of market capitalism, and as stagnation and increasing income inequality threaten the world economy the significance of these differences increases and the global search for efficient and humane economic systems accelerates. Many countries have sought to emulate some aspects of the Japanese economic system, but even Japan is now experiencing considerable economic and political difficulties.

Indeed the socialist alternative continues both as an existing system and as a possibility in some form as yet unseen. The purest existence of classical socialism persists in relatively obscure corners of the globe such as North Korea and Cuba. But despite general dismantling of central planning bureaucracies, legalization of market activities, and privatization drives, large portions of the former Soviet bloc remain actually socialist in the sense of widespread state ownership of the means of production. In the most populous nation on earth, China, a grand drama unfolds as the system remains officially socialist while engaging in a piecemeal marketization and spread of capitalism.

Furthermore, even though Yugoslavia has collapsed both as a nation and as a system in a horribly tragic way, the idea of workers' management that its economy imperfectly represented persists and may have a new lease on life in the form of workers' ownership. This takes a variety of forms, from the profit-sharing "share economy,"[2] through classic cooperatives, to employee stock ownership plans (ESOPs), all of which exist in the United States and other market capitalist economies and are popular in the privatization efforts of many Eastern European countries.

This systemic turmoil coincides with the intense conflict between the "urge to merge," the push for integration of the world economy and its sub-parts in trade and policy, and the "drive to divide," the push for independence and isolation by increasingly small entities. Also continuing are the deep problems of the less developed countries, many of the poorest of which are in states of outright economic decline as they search for appropriate systems in this changing environment. These difficulties are further exacerbated by a global stagnation of economic growth that aggravates the systemic crises many economies are experiencing.

Thus the study of comparative economics has never been more important. The subject itself is undergoing transformation, just as its objects of study undergo transformation.

Criteria for Classifying Economies

Allocation Mechanisms

All economies must answer the questions of "what, how, and for whom" goods and services are produced. Fundamentally, economies produce and distribute goods and services among members of their societies. Production involves allocating factor inputs between different goods and services and distribution involves allocating produced goods and services among people.

There are three basic kinds of allocation mechanisms: *tradition, market,* and *command.* In a *traditional economy* allocation decisions depend on custom, what has been done in the past. Usually such customs or traditions will be associated with a broader social context defined by a dominant religion. Economic decision making becomes embedded in the broader social context.[3]

An example is the caste system associated with Hinduism in India. Technically illegal since India's independence from Great Britain in 1947, the caste system still dominates both social and economic structures in much of the nation, especially rural areas. The caste system constitutes a system of allocating labor—what one does is what one's parents did, not unlike under European feudalism. Each caste has an economic activity and is self-reproducing in that there is a very strong social inhibition against marrying outside one's caste. At the top are the Brahmins, the priestly caste; at the bottom are the

---

[2]See Martin Weitzman, *The Share Economy* (Cambridge: Harvard University Press, 1984).
[3]Karl Polanyi, *The Great Transformation* (Boston: Beacon Press, 1944).

Untouchables who gather dung for fuel and perform other unpleasant functions. Hinduism justifies this hierarchy through the doctrine of karma and reincarnation. When one dies, the caste into which one will be reborn is determined by one's karma, one's accumulated account of past good and evil behaviors. Thus everyone is where they deserve to be.

In a *market economy* allocation decisions are made by individuals or firms on the basis of price signals emanating from the interaction of supply and demand. These signals generally reveal themselves as individuals or firms engage in exchanging money for factor inputs or goods or services. That such a system can be very efficient is eloquently argued by Adam Smith in his 1776 *Wealth of Nations.* Every economy ever observed has at least some exchange activity, including tightly controlled command economies such as North Korea and very simple traditional economies such as that of the hunter-gatherer Khoi-San of the Kalahari desert in southern Africa. What marks a market economy is that a *majority* of economic decisions are made according to market forces rather than tradition or command.

In a *command economy* the most important allocation decisions are made by government authorities and are imposed by law or by force. Command economies were the last of the three forms to emerge historically—they rose with ancient empires such as Sumer and Egypt, which were the first strong and extended states wielding absolute power over crucial economic decision making. There is good reason to believe that the other two forms long predated the command economies of these empires, which date back a mere 5,000 years.

Forms of Ownership

Karl Marx and Friedrich Engels in the 1848 *Communist Manifesto* argue that the key to understanding an economy is to know who owns the means of production. Ownership determines the distinction between *capitalism* and *socialism,* defined in strictly economic terms. In capitalist economies land and produced means of production (the capital stock) are owned by private individuals or groups of private individuals organized as firms. In socialist economies the state owns the land and the capital stock.

This explanation is overly simplistic. There are a variety of intermediate forms and cases such as cooperatives or worker ownership. Generally such forms are viewed as still being capitalism although some argue that they constitute "true socialism."

It makes a big difference under socialism if ownership is predominantly by the central government or by local governments. The former is more likely to be associated with command decision making, whereas the latter may coincide with market-based decision making. An example of the latter is China where there has been a tremendous expansion of firms owned by local units of government that operate in the market economy independently of central authority in Beijing.

A third possibility is ownership by organized religious groups. In parts of Western Europe between 1000 and 1500 nearly one third of the land was owned by the Roman Catholic Church, with major technical innovations being made in abbeys, economically self-sufficient religious communities. In Iran after 1979 under the Islamic Republic, formerly privately owned businesses were seized by religious authorities and remain under their control, if not their formal ''ownership.''

Generally the concepts of ''property'' and ''ownership'' vary enormously from society to society. These distinctions arise not only from local traditions and practices but from legal rules and definitions as argued by institutionalist economists.[4]

Considering the division between capitalism and socialism raises the question of the ownership system's relationship to allocative mechanisms. We often see economies that are largely capitalist, like the one in the United States, also being largely market-oriented. We have also seen the most prominent examples of socialism, notably the USSR, also being command-oriented. This leads us to describe two extreme categories: *market capitalism* and *command socialism.*

But this simple dichotomization raises the possibility of ''cross forms,'' namely *market socialism* and *command capitalism.* Although less common than the previous two, both have existed.

The classic example of *market socialism*[5] was Yugoslavia. The state owned the capital stock (land was privately owned) but allocative decisions were made by worker-managed firms within a market framework. The collapse of Yugoslavia has raised questions regarding the long-run viability of this particular hybrid, although China is doing well with its peculiar form of market socialism.

Yugoslavia's collapse and the rush towards market capitalism by most of Eastern Europe can be argued to confirm the argument of the Austrian economist, Ludwig von Mises,[6] that rational market calculation is only possible with capitalism because of the need for the profit motive to drive private property-owning decision makers to optimize and generate efficient price signals. However Yugoslavia's collapse may be due to regional and religious conflicts rather than economic failure.

The classic example of *command capitalism* was Nazi Germany. Although the proper name of the Nazi party was the National Socialist Party, Adolf

---

[4]John R. Commons, *The Legal Foundations of Capitalism* (Madison: University of Wisconsin Press, 1931).

[5]Variations on this term include *socialist market economy* used by the Chinese to describe their system of market socialism and *social market economy* used by the Germans to describe their essentially market capitalist economy marked by extensive income redistribution and welfare programs.

[6]Ludwig von Mises, ''Economic Calculation in Socialism,'' in *Comparative Economic Systems: Models and Cases,* 7th ed., ed. M. Bornstein (Burr Ridge: Irwin, pp. 273–79), originally published in expanded form in 1922.

Hitler avoided nationalizing such privately owned corporations as Krupp and I.G. Farben. Nevertheless these industries produced what his economic planners commanded. Similar systems appear temporarily in wartime in market capitalist economies, as in the United States during World War II when no private cars were produced in response to government orders, although the automobile industry remained privately owned.

An important point to understand is that there are no pure examples of any type of system. *All* real economies are mixed economies exhibiting elements of various allocation and ownership systems, even if they can be categorized one way or another.

The Role of Planning

Many comparative economists emphasize the contrast of ''market versus plan'' as a central defining characteristic of economic systems rather than our choice of tradition versus market versus command. Planning deals with *coordination* in an economy. In a centrally planned economy, *planners' preferences* dominate allocative decision making, whereas in a market economy *consumers' sovereignty* dominates allocative decision making.

There is a strong correlation between allocation decisions following a central plan and the general presence of command socialism, as in the USSR and most of its empire. But this correlation misses the crucial point, that planners' preferences determine allocative decision making *only* within a command framework. It is command that rules out consumers' sovereignty.

It is possible to have command without planning. An example is Soviet Russia during the period of War Communism (1917–1921) immediately after the Bolshevik Revolution, when civil war was compounded by invasion by foreign troops. Production followed commands from the center, but in a ''shock'' pattern whereby commands for production of certain goods were made when goods viewed as critical to the war effort became in short supply. A pattern resulted of higgledy-piggledy dashing from producing one ''deficit'' good to another with little effort to consider the impact of each decision or to coordinate such decisions. There was no time to plan or to even set up a planning mechanism.[7]

It is possible to have central planning coincide with market capitalism, the ''planned market economy.'' Such planning is known as *indicative planning* because it lacks the command element. Examples of indicative planning have been France and Japan, although such planning is less influential than in the past.

Even in thoroughly market capitalist economies there is planning by specific government agencies involved in infrastructure investment such as transportation networks, functions that in most economies seem to be in the public

---

[7]The process of ''planning how to plan'' has been labeled *planification* by French planners and economists.

sector. For such cases even the very pro-market capitalist magazine *The Economist*[8] argues in a lead editorial that there is a strong case for planning if carried out intelligently and if accompanied by the use of market mechanisms such as congestion tolls on highways to ensure efficient use of the resulting infrastructure.

Types of Incentives

Economies vary according to the incentive schemes that motivate people to work and produce. The most common incentive scheme is *material,* paying people according to their productivity. In market capitalism this involves paying them their marginal product which maximizes profits for competitive firms hiring labor in such a system.

Material incentives under market capitalism also take the form of rewards for entrepreneurship and capital investment as economic profits and for savings as interest. In theory socialism rejects the former while, also in theory, Islam rejects the latter. Both socialism and Islam generally see material incentives as significant in motivating labor.[9]

An alternative that has been sometimes advocated and less frequently tried is *moral incentives,* trying to motivate work effort by appealing to some higher collective goal. Efforts to implement moral incentives occurred in China under Mao during the Great Proletarian Cultural Revolution from 1966 to 1976 and during certain periods in Cuba under Castro. The Chinese effort followed the slogan ''serve the people.'' The record from both China and Cuba is that these periods generated serious stagnation of output.

But before dismissing moral incentives, note that they have been used temporarily when market capitalist economies have gone into a command mode during wartime. Thus production surged in the United States during World War II despite the imposition of wage and price controls limiting the material gains from hard work. Part of the motivation to work came from the wartime appeal to patriotic national sacrifice.

Also the new traditional economy depends partly on appealing to moral incentives. Islam and most great world religions do not completely deny the pay-for-work principle that undergirds material incentives. But they also see limits to this principle, both from the need for charity to the poor and from the general argument that excessive concentration on material goods is distracting from spiritual matters.

Income Redistribution and Social Safety Nets

Economies vary based on the extent to which and the methods by which governments intervene to redistribute income. This partly depends on how unequal income is to begin with before any redistributive policies are implemented.

---

[8]*The Economist,* ''The Case for Central Planning,'' September 12, 1992.

[9]That socialism has not always successfully implemented material incentives for workers is shown by the old Soviet joke that ''they pretend to pay us and we pretend to work.''

Thus the Japanese government does much less redistributing than those of many other capitalist countries because Japan has a more equal distribution of wages than most other capitalist countries. Command socialist economies also have had less income redistribution because governments initially control the distribution of income through setting wages and forbidding capital or land income.

People differ greatly about the appropriate goal of income redistribution, much less the method. The Austrian economist and follower of von Mises, Friedrich A. Hayek, argues that the only just income distribution reflects a free market outcome in a context of well-defined property rights and complete equality of opportunity for all individuals. This suggests an ideal in which no government income redistribution results in generally greater inequality than is observed in most economies.

Sharply contrasting is the view of John Rawls[10] that the justness of a society is to be judged by how well off its worst-off individual is, the *maximin criterion.* He argues that selfish and rational individuals would support such a criterion if they fully understood the uncertainty of the future and that there is always the possibility that "there but for the grace of God go I." This suggests substantial redistribution towards absolute equality, limited only by disincentive effects becoming so great that the worst-off individual's income drops.

Rawls's view echoes that of many traditional religions. None insist on absolute equality of income, but most place an emphasis on charity and taking care of the poor. Although organized religions may court the wealthy for their possible financial support, there is a vein of contempt towards wealth as exemplified by the remark of Jesus that "It is easier for a camel to pass through the eye of a needle than it is for a rich man to enter heaven."

In his *Critique of the Gotha Program,* Karl Marx enunciated the ideal goal of *pure communism* as being "from each according to his ability, to each according to his need." This does not imply complete equality of income as people have different needs, for example due to different family sizes or health problems. Marx contrasted this goal with that of socialism, which would be "from each according to his ability, to each according to his work."

Clouding this entire discussion is the *equity-efficiency tradeoff,*[11] which states that greater efforts to make income more equal will result in less efficiency, meaning less growth. The argument is that material incentives are what draw forth productive and entrepreneurial effort. Thus vigorous efforts to redistribute income reduce the rewards for work and entrepreneurship and thus reduce the rate of economic growth. Such arguments are influential in many countries towards scaling back redistributive programs. This view has its most vigorous advocates among "supply-side" economists associated with the "Reagan Revolution" in the United States.

---

[10]John Rawls, *A Theory of Justice* (Oxford: Clarendon, 1972).

[11]Arthur M. Okun, "Rewards in a Market Economy," in *Comparative Economic Systems: Models and Cases,* 7th ed., ed. M. Bornstein (Burr Ridge: Irwin, 1994), pp. 71–77.

Most societies struggle with intermediate approaches of one sort or another, although very poor countries generally cannot afford to do much redistributing as there is not much to redistribute. Most carry out some redistribution through their tax codes and through some sort of *social safety net* for certain categories of people: the aged, the unemployed, single mothers with children, the sick, and sometimes others as well. In advanced capitalist countries aging populations and medical care costs that are rising faster than the rate of inflation are putting tremendous fiscal pressure on social safety nets.

Generally in the command socialist economies a wider array of activities and people have been protected by social safety nets, although sometimes the quality of that protection has been questionable as in the case of Soviet medical care. A major problem of the current transition period with substantial economic declines occurring in the former Soviet bloc has been the partial dismantling and weakening of these safety nets.

A final point regarding the equity-efficiency trade-off is that *it is frequently false*. Some of the most rapidly growing economies in the world have reasonably equal distributions of income, such as the East Asian Newly Industrializing Countries (NICs), whereas some of the countries with very unequal income distributions have had poor growth records, such as El Salvador. It is crucial that income and wealth inequalities arise from differences in productivity and entrepreneurship rather than from corruption or inheritance. If inequality is perceived as unfair then the result may well be strikes, guerrilla war, or revolution, none of which are conducive to economic growth.[12]

The Role of Politics and Ideology

The relationship between politics and economics is subject to deep debate. Until nearly 100 years ago no distinction was made between the two disciplines, there being only *political economy*. Many still think that is how the subjects should be analyzed and that they cannot be realistically separated. At the heart of the linkage is ideology, in which certain political and economic systems are linked in distinct packages and given labels such as *communism* and *liberal democracy*.[13]

A central controversy has been whether or not political democracy is indissolubly linked with market capitalism and command socialism with dictatorship. Friedrich Hayek forcefully argues this position in his 1944 *The Road*

---

[12]This problem plagues the former Soviet bloc economies in their transition efforts in that many new entrepreneurs are either former Communist Party officials with special privileges or former black marketeers whose sources of initial finance are viewed as illegitimate by most people.

[13]This use of *liberal* is the classical or European usage, meaning individual freedom and minimal government. The modern American usage, meaning support for government intervention in the economy, arose in the 20th century from the evolution of the British Liberal party towards such a position from its earlier classical position.

to Serfdom, in which he claims that welfare state redistribution inevitably leads to command socialist dictatorship. Milton Friedman supports this view in his *Capitalism and Freedom.* Friedman argues that even if expanded government activity does not lead to full-blown dictatorship, it constitutes a reduction in the freedom of the individual to choose what to do with his or her income because of higher taxes. Such views are labeled *libertarian* and have deep roots in American and British thought. The view that there should be minimal government economic intervention is called *laissez-faire,* a French term from the mid-1700s literally meaning ''let them do it,'' *them* being businesspeople.

Both Hayek and Friedman associate socialism with dictatorship and lack of individual freedom. Complete socialism reduces economic freedom insofar as private ownership of capital and land is forbidden. The old Soviet bloc was characterized by both economic socialism and political dictatorship. These countries are now generally moving towards both market capitalism and democracy.

But in Western Europe Social Democratic political parties exist that call themselves ''socialist''[14] but that support neither extensive nationalization of the means of production nor political dictatorship. They support income redistribution and extensive social safety nets, although even in their heartland in northwestern Europe such approaches are under retreat. Nevertheless we have seen over 60 years of such social democracy in Sweden without the Hayekian prediction of political dictatorship coming true.

The split in Europe between socialist and communist political movements occurred after the 1917 Bolshevik Revolution in Russia when Lenin imposed a *dictatorship of the proletariat* under the leadership of a ''vanguard party,'' later combined with a command socialist economy by Joseph Stalin. Although many Western European socialist parties continued to support nationalization and central planning for a long time, they opposed dictatorship.

Ironically, the ideological father of communism, Karl Marx, claimed that communism entailed the *withering away of the state.* The dictatorship of the proletariat was to be a strictly temporary phenomenon. Well aware of this, the Soviet Communists never claimed to have achieved communism, always labeling their own system *socialist* rather than *communist.*

The key libertarian claim that full-blown economic socialism has never coexisted with political democracy is true. But in some Western European countries democratic governments have carried out substantial nationalizations without going to dictatorship. Although absolutely forbidding private enterprise is incompatible with political democracy and personal freedom, having a great portion of the economy nationalized is not.

A further complication is that market capitalism has coexisted with authoritarian political regimes in parts of East Asia and Latin America. Many of

---

[14]A recent development has been some of the former Communist parties of Eastern Europe taking this name. Thus in Germany there is the old Social Democratic Party, while the former Communists are now the ''Party of Democratic Socialism.''

these countries have recently experienced a trend towards democracy. Nevertheless market capitalism is no guarantee of political democracy even if it is historically correlated with it.

Another competing ideology is new traditionalism, especially Islamic fundamentalism. The focus in Islamic fundamentalism is less on either politics or economics as an end, but on religion and its rules. The basic demand of the Islamic fundamentalists is the imposition of an Islamic law code, a Shari'a.[15] These codes address many issues from social matters such as restrictions on women's behavior to economic matters such as forbidding the charging of interest. But there is no definitive position on capitalism versus socialism. Nor is there a political theory of Islam other than the basic demand that a Shari'a be implemented and obeyed. It does not matter whether the enforcer of the law is a king, a mullah, a military dictator, or a democratically elected president. Indeed the current Islamic Republic of Iran is a functioning parliamentary democracy. But it is not a *liberal* democracy because individual rights and freedoms are subordinated to a Shari'a and the will of religious authorities.

Thus every generalization seems subject to exceptions rendering it almost unusable. But, although liberal democracies have adopted the command mode of allocative decision making on a temporary basis during wartime, none has done so on a permanent basis during peacetime. Here is a more definitive hypothesis: Permanent command control of an economy implies unequivocal loss of personal freedom because none can be allowed to challenge the system of such control. Thus it is permanent command that is incompatible with liberal democracy, not economic socialism.

Criteria for Evaluating Economies

Morris Bornstein[16] presents nine criteria by which the relative performance of economic systems can be compared.

First is the level of output. This figure should be corrected for population and the price level, giving us real per capita output as the measure which equals real per capita income. Despite difficulties in making cross-country comparisons because of differences in data gathering this is probably the best measure of the material standard of living in a society available to us. The highest levels of real per capita income exist in market capitalist economies.

Second is the growth rate of output. This figure must be corrected for population growth. It is often easier for middle to low income countries to grow faster than either the very poorest or the very richest. The very poorest often are caught in "low level equilibrium traps" where no investment can

---

[15]There is more than one such code. See Chapter 5.

[16]"The Comparison of Economic Systems: An Integration," in *Comparative Economic Systems: Models and Cases,* 7th ed., ed. M. Bornstein (Burr Ridge: Irwin, 1994).

occur because all output is absorbed by consumption in an effort merely to stay alive. The middle to low income countries that have escaped from such traps can borrow technology from the most advanced countries and play "catch-up" according to the *relative backwardness hypothesis*.[17] Such borrowing can bring dramatic productivity improvements in an economy that is more "relatively backward" compared to the world's leading economies. The growth of the richest countries is limited by the general advance of technology at the frontier of knowledge. Command socialist economies have sometimes grown quite rapidly for extended periods of time, but they suffer from a tendency towards serious stagnation in the longer run.

Third is the composition of output. The most notable variables of composition are the breakdown between consumption and investment, the share of military output, and public versus private goods. Command socialist economies generally have higher shares going to investment, although the East Asian market economies, such as Japan, also have high rates of investment.

Fourth is static efficiency. Formally this means Pareto optimality, that no one in society can be made better off without making someone else worse off. In this situation resources are being fully utilized to their best potential given the existing technology and as much is being produced as can be produced. Static efficiency implies that the labor force is fully employed and that the composition of goods being produced is what people want. It is widely argued that market economies are more successful in this area, although relative success is rather difficult to measure, and market economies tend to have worse unemployment than command economies.

Fifth is intertemporal or dynamic efficiency, which involves the allocation of resources over time to maximize long-run sustainable growth. An example of nonsustainable output maximization was the effort by the USSR to pump large amounts of oil in short periods of time. This push led to depletion of pressure in the wells, making it difficult to impossible to get out remaining oil later that could have been accessible. Long-run sustainability of growth ultimately depends on maintaining a viable environment, and it is now seen that failure to do so was an important factor in bringing about the fall of the Soviet bloc command socialisms.

Sixth is macroeconomic stability, the lack of large oscillations of output, employment, or the overall price level. It is usually argued that strict command economies achieve greater short-run macroeconomic stability, although there have been some spectacular exceptions.

Seventh is economic security of the individual in terms of income, employment, and related matters such as health care. This criterion is partially related to the previous one, but it also depends on the broader social safety nets of an economy.

---

[17]Alexander Gerschenkron, *Economic Backwardness in Historical Perspective* (Cambridge: Harvard University Press, 1962).

Eighth is the degree of equity of the income and wealth distributions. Generally the socialist and social market economies have more equal distributions than the strictly market capitalist economies.

Ninth is the degree of freedom available to the individual in terms of work, consumption, property, investment, and more broadly in the civil and political realms. This last variable is difficult to quantify, but market economies are well ahead of command economies in this area.

Indeed, many of the items listed above are difficult to quantify. Nevertheless a summary of indexes of some of these criteria is presented in the tables below. Table 1–1 focuses on overall indicators, including per capita GNP, an index of real per capita GNP, annual growth rate of real per capita GNP, annual rate of inflation, share of gross private investment in GNP, the quintile ratio (the ratio of the share of national income going to the top fifth of the population to that of the bottom fifth of the population), and life expectancy at birth. Table 1–2 focuses on the role of government, including the shares of GNP going to central government consumption; defense spending; spending on health; and spending on housing, welfare, and social security (aggregated). It also covers the share of national income collected in taxes.

Data for many countries are extremely unreliable. This is true throughout the less developed countries, which do not have enough money for gathering data. For most of the former and current socialist countries the unreliability of data is notorious due to past propagandistic lying as well as corruption, although some problems with data arose from bureaucratic tendencies to excessive secrecy. Even officials in these countries could not get accurate data.[18] We have seen massive revisions of data for many of these countries recently.

Figure 1–1 presents a depiction of income distributions in several countries using Lorenz curves. These curves are constructed by assuming that a country's population is ranked according to income and distributed along the horizontal axis. The vertical axis then indicates the percentage of total national income going to a group of the population. The degree of inequality is indicated by the degree of curvature with more equal income distributions generating Lorenz curves closer to the 45 degree line. The ranking of the countries shown corresponds to their ranking according to quintile ratios as listed above.

The Lorenz curve can be used to generate another measure of income distribution which will be used frequently throughout this book. This measure is the Gini coefficient. It is the area between the Lorenz curve and the 45 degree line divided by the area below the 45 degree line. Thus Gini coefficients can range from zero to one with higher ones indicating a greater degree of inequality.

---

[18]Many top think tanks of the USSR used data on their own economy estimated by the U.S. Central Intelligence Agency (CIA) in the belief that it was the best available, although after the collapse of the USSR there was criticism in the U.S. Congress of the accuracy of those estimates.

TABLE 1-1   General Condition/Performance of Various Economies

Country	Per Capita GNP ($)	Real Index	Growth Rate	Inflation Rate	Investment Share	Quintile Ratio	Life Expectancy
Market Capitalist							
Switzerland (a)	36,080	95.6	1.4	3.8	24	8.6	78
United States (a)	23,240	100.0	1.7	3.9	16	8.9	77
Australia (a)	17,260	75.0	1.6	6.4	20	9.6	77
Botswana* (a)	2,790	22.4	6.1	12.6	42	16.3	68
Colombia (a)	1,330	24.9	1.4	25.0	18	15.5	69
Indonesia (a)	670	12.8	4.0	8.4	35	4.9	60
Niger (a)	280	3.2	−4.3	1.7	5	n.a.	46
Planned Market Capitalist							
Japan (a)	28,190	87.2	3.6	1.5	31	4.3	79
France (a)	22,260	83.0	1.7	5.4	20	7.4	77
S. Korea (a)	6,790	38.7	8.5	5.9	37	5.7	71
India (a)	310	5.2	3.1	8.5	23	4.7	61
Social Market Capitalist							
Sweden (a)	27,010	76.2	1.5	7.2	17	4.6	78
W. Germany (a)	23,030	89.1	2.4	2.7	21	5.8	76
Netherlands (a)	20,480	76.0	1.7	1.7	21	4.5	77
Costa Rica (a)	1,960	24.0	0.8	22.5	28	12.7	76
Sri Lanka (a)	540	12.2	2.6	11.0	23	4.4	72
Market Socialist							
Yugoslavia (b)	3,060	23.8	2.9	122.9	21	7.0	72
Hungary (a)	2,970	24.8	0.2	11.7	19	3.2	69
Egypt (a)	640	15.9	1.8	13.2	18	n.a.	62
China (a)	470	9.1	7.6	6.5	39	6.5	69
Command Socialist							
USSR (c)	2,540	26.9	0.9	2.1	37	4.1	69
Romania (a)	1,130	11.9	−1.1	13.1	31	n.a.	70
Laos (a)	250	8.3	n.a.	n.a.	12	n.a.	51
Ethiopia (a)	110	1.5	−1.9	2.8	9	4.8	49
New Traditional							
Iran (a)	2,200	22.8	−1.4	16.2	33	n.a.	65
Pakistan (a)	420	9.2	3.1	7.1	21	4.7	59

*Botswana has a substantial state-owned sector, to the point that it can be viewed as borderline market socialist. See Box 19.1. Investment share figure for Botswana is for 1970.

Note: For countries labeled *a* all data is from *World Development Report* of the World Bank, New York: Oxford, 1994. Per capita GNP figures are in 1992 U.S. dollars for 1992. The real per capita income indexes are for 1992 from the United Nations International Comparison Program (ICP), which accounts for differences in costs of living across countries as well as for exchange rates and are percents of the U.S. figure. GNP growth rates reflect the first column measure and are annual averages for 1980–92. Inflation rates are annual averages for 1980–92 of GDP deflators. Investment shares in GDP are for 1992, except for South Korea, China, and Laos for which they are for 1990 from the 1992 *World Development Report*.

Quintile ratios are derived from data from numerous sources, the Report noting the especial unreliability of these data. The years and data are: Switzerland, 1982 household income; United States, 1985 household income; Great Britain, 1988 household income; Botswana, 1985–86 household expenditures; Colombia, 1991 per capita income; Indonesia, 1987 per capita expenditures; Japan, 1979 household income; France, 1979 household income; South Korea, 1988 household income; India, 1989–90 per capita expenditures; Sweden, 1981 household income; West Germany, 1988 household income; Costa Rica, 1989 per capita income; Sri Lanka, 1990 per capita expenditures; Hungary, 1989 per capita income; Pakistan, 1991 per capita expenditures. Life expectancy is at birth for 1992.

For Yugoslavia, labeled *b*, all data are from the 1992 version of the source for *a* and are for the former Yugoslavia prior to its dissolution in 1991, and are for the year 1990 except that GNP per capita growth rate is for 1965–90, the inflation rate is for 1980–90, the quintile ratio is for 1987 for per capita income, and life expectancy is for 1990.

For the USSR, labeled *c*, per capita GNP and the per capita income quintile ratio are derived from ruble estimates for 1989 from Anthony B. Atkinson and John Micklewright. *Economic Transformation in Eastern Europe and the Distribution of Income* (New York: Cambridge University Press, 1992). The growth rate of per capita GNP and the CPI inflation rate are for 1980–85 after adjustment for population growth and the investment share in GNP is adjusted for population growth and the investment share in GNP is for 1988 from the United States CIA *Handbook of Economic Statistics* (Washington: USGPO, 1989). PPP-adjusted real index and life expectancy are from the 1994 *World Development Report* for 1992 for the Russian Federation (PPP figure for 1987 was 38.7). All other figures are for the USSR prior to its 1991 dissolution.

TABLE 1–2 Role of Government in Various Economies

Country	% Government Expenditure	% Defense	% Health	% Housing Welfare Social Security	% Taxes
Market Capitalist					
Switzerland (b)	19.5	2.0	2.3	9.6	17.5
United States (a)	24.3	5.0	3.9	7.6	17.8
Australia (a)	27.4	2.4	3.5	8.5	24.9
Botswana (a)	40.4	5.4	1.9	5.6	30.6
Colombia (b)	13.5	0.9	0.5	2.9	10.4
Indonesia (a)	19.2	1.3	0.5	0.4	18.1
Niger (b)	18.7	0.7	0.8	0.7	12.4
Planned Market Capitalist					
Japan (c)	15.8	1.1	n.a.	3.0	13.7
France (a)	45.0	2.9	7.2	20.3	38.0
S. Korea (a)	17.6	3.9	0.2	2.2	16.4
India (a)	16.8	2.5	0.3	1.0	11.1
Social Market Capitalist					
Sweden (a)	47.5	2.6	0.4	26.7	37.8
W. Germany (b)	30.3	2.8	5.8	15.0	27.6
Netherlands (a)	52.8	2.4	7.3	21.6	45.3
Costa Rica (a)	25.5	0.0	8.2	3.4	20.8
Sri Lanka (a)	28.2	2.4	1.4	4.5	18.1
Market Socialist					
Yugoslavia (d)	5.2	2.8	n.a.	0.3	5.4
Hungary (a)	54.7	2.0	4.3	19.3	47.0
Egypt (b)	53.7	6.1	1.3	7.0	30.8
China	n.a.	n.a.	n.a.	n.a.	n.a.
Command Socialist					
USSR	n.a.	n.a.	n.a.	n.a.	n.a.
Romania (a)	41.7	4.3	3.8	11.1	20.9
Laos	n.a.	n.a.	n.a.	n.a.	n.a.
Ethiopia (b)	23.4	2.2	0.9	1.3	15.8
New Traditional					
Iran (a)	19.7	2.0	1.5	3.9	7.7
Pakistan (a)	21.7	6.0	0.2	0.7	12.2

Note: Caveats regarding these figures include that only central government spending and taxes are reported, which understates the role of government in such strong local government countries as Switzerland and Yugoslavia; that military spending numbers are especially unreliable; and that some countries, especially Botswana and Iran, have major nontax government revenue sources.

Source: Data for countries labeled a are for 1992 and are derived from the 1994 World Bank *World Development Report,* except for countries labeled b for which data are for 1980. For Japan, c, sectoral breakdowns of spending are for 1988 from Takatoshi Ito, *The Japanese Economy* (Cambridge: MIT Press, 1992). Yugoslav, d, data are for 1990 from the 1992 *World Development Report* for the former Yugoslavia prior to its 1991 dissolution.

FIGURE 1–1   Lorenz Curves

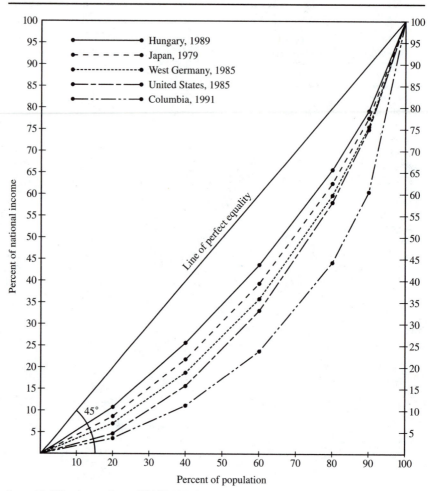

Source: *World Development Report 1994,* World Bank, Table 30.

The numbers presented in Tables 1–1 and 1–2 are broadly consistent with the generalizations made earlier despite various anomalies and odd cases. Some of these may be due to data imperfections, but certainly not all of them. A close examination of these numbers should emphasize the uniqueness of each economy and the difficulty of attempting to classify economies into neatly defined categories. There is ultimately a degree of arbitrariness to such a procedure.

Summary and Conclusions

Fukuyama argues that the world economy is converging on American-style market capitalism. But this is a very complex process in a troubled and transforming world economy. In comparing economies central issues are the allocation system-tradition, market, or command—and the ownership system—capitalist or socialist. Economies vary in their income redistribution approaches, as well as their political systems and ideologies. Bornstein presents nine criteria for evaluating outcomes of economies and we provide data related to these criteria for 26 countries—both for general performance indicators and for the role of government in their economies.

Although many of the data are consistent with our expectations for the economic systems identified for the respective economies, numerous anomalies exist. Thus there are many other elements besides those listed in this chapter that are important to the functioning of an economy and its essential nature. A short list includes the nature of its openness to international trade and investment, its industrial organization, its policies with respect to the environment, the sectoral breakdown of its industries, its degrees of literacy and urbanization, its population density, and the broader cultural attitudes of its people, among others. Many of these will be discussed later in the individual country studies.

Questions for Discussion

1. Why does Fukuyama think that we are at "the end of history" and how is his idea relevant to comparative economics?

2. Are market economies necessarily "capitalist" and are command economies necessarily "socialist"? Why or why not?

3. Even though the U.S. economy is probably the most modern and market capitalist–oriented economy in the world, it has elements of a traditional economy within it. What are some examples?

4. Is market capitalism necessary for freedom? Why or why not?

5. Distinguish between the Hayekian, Rawlsian, socialist, and pure communist views of how income should be distributed.

6. Considering Tables 1–1 and 1–2, what are some countries that exhibit characteristics or performances not in accord with the generalizations made in this chapter with regard to the systemic category into which they are placed? What are those characteristics or performances and how are they anomalous?

Suggested Further Readings

Bornstein, Morris. "The Comparison of Economic Systems: An Integration," in *Comparative Economic Systems: Models and Cases,* 7th ed. ed. Morris Bornstein. Homewood, IL: Irwin, 1994, pp. 3–19.

Friedman, Milton. *Capitalism and Freedom.* Chicago: University of Chicago Press, 1962.

Fukuyama, Francis. *The End of History and the Last Man.* New York: The Free Press, 1992.

Hayek, Friedrich A. *New Studies in Philosophy, Politics, Economics, and the History of Ideas.* Chicago: University of Chicago Press, 1978.

Neuberger, Egon. "Comparing Economic Systems," in *Comparative Economic Systems: Models and Cases,* 7th ed. ed. Morris Bornstein. Homewood, IL: Irwin, 1994, pp. 20–48.

Okun, Arthur M. "Rewards in a Market Economy," in *Comparative Economic Systems: Models and Cases,* 7th ed. ed. Morris Bornstein. Homewood, IL: Irwin, 1994, pp. 71–77.

Polanyi, Karl. *The Great Transformation.* Boston: Beacon Press, 1944.

Rawls, John. *A Theory of Justice.* Oxford: Clarendon Press, 1972.

2

THE THEORY AND PRACTICE OF MARKET CAPITALISM

All the bad things you hear about markets are true: unemployment, inflation, inequalities of income and wealth, monopoly power, negative externalities, and insufficiently supplied public goods. You know, there is only one thing that is worse than the market, and that is no market.

Csaba Csaki, Rector of Economics, University of Budapest (formerly Karl Marx University), August 1990.

Introduction

The vast changes sweeping through the world economy have focused attention upon the nature of the market capitalist economic system, the system that is the goal of many reformers in power in the former communist countries. Even many predominantly market capitalist economies are making efforts to move in the direction of a purer version of this system. It seems, as Fukuyama argues, to be the victorious universal ideology of the world.

We have never seen a pure version of the system anywhere in history, nor are we likely to. Probably the closest to pure market capitalism ever seen were the U.S. and British economies in the middle to late 19th century. They represented the culmination of a historical line of development that, originating in the murky mists of time, formed a coherent system in the 1200s in northern Italy and Flanders with the invention of modern accounting and mass urbanization, and transformed itself into a dominating structure with the Industrial Revolution in Great Britain in the late 18th century. But even at its apogee in the 19th century, governments intervened in many ways, from trade protectionism to subsidizing the building of transportation infrastructure to maintaining military forces.

Those economies exhibited both the virtues and difficulties of unfettered market capitalism. They experienced enormous technological advances and growth as they underwent the Industrial Revolution. Even those critics of market capitalism, Karl Marx and Friedrich Engels, recognized the enormous ability of the system to "revolutionize the means of production" in ways unprecedented in world history.

However, both economies experienced large macroeconomic fluctuations with serious downturns in the 1870s and 1890s and increasingly unequal distributions of income associated with increasing concentrations of industrial monopoly power. After 1900 these problems triggered substantial movements towards greater government involvement in both economies, in the United States especially after the 1930s Great Depression.

Today the economies that come the closest to the ideal of pure, laissez-faire, market capitalism may be Hong Kong and Switzerland. Both have successful records in many ways. In recent decades Hong Kong has enjoyed one of the highest growth rates in the world along with very low unemployment. We shall consider the case of Hong Kong in Chapter 15, but note that, much like in Japan, Hong Kong authorities have used indicative planning. Also Hong Kong is not an independent country but a Crown Colony of Great Britain and is scheduled to revert to the control of the People's Republic of China in 1997. Hong Kong may become less laissez-faire after that.

Switzerland has one of the highest real per capita incomes of any country in the world. Like Hong Kong it also has had very low unemployment rates. It clearly is a success story of market capitalism. Switzerland has an especially weak central government, although the central bank is famous for its strict monetarist policy controlling inflation. Most of the power and fiscal authority lies in the hands of the cantons, local units based on the ethnic divisions of the country. These cantons engage in quite a bit of social welfare spending and market regulation that is similar to, though less than that practiced by the social market economies of northwestern Europe.

The relatively harmonious relations among the Swiss cantons have made them a model for other nations with much ethnic diversity, such as Lebanon and Yugoslavia. Switzerland has had a long record of neutrality and independence from international organizations, exemplified by a recent vote to stay outside of the European Union.

Some very poor less developed countries have smaller state sectors relative to GDP than Hong Kong or Switzerland, for example, Malawi.[1] But most of these also have poorly developed markets and little modern industrial capitalism. Probably the developed economy most oriented to market capitalism after Hong Kong and Switzerland is the United States, despite its substantial increase in government intervention since the 1930s. In considering the practice of market capitalism in this chapter we shall draw heavily from the U.S. example.

---

[1]An argument known as *Wagner's Law* asserts that as an economy's income rises the relative size of its state sector expands.

The dynamic efficiency or technological dynamism of market capitalism is its greatest appeal to countries seeking to emulate its successes. But this dynamism has come through the macroeconomically destabilizing process of *creative destruction* as described by Joseph Schumpeter.[2] It is with respect to static efficiency that most economists see market capitalism as possessing significant advantages, although Adam Smith strongly argued for both market capitalism's dynamic and static advantages.

The Theoretical Efficiency of Market Capitalism

Why have the countries with the highest real per capita incomes in the world also had market capitalist economies, notably Switzerland and the United States? Probably the strongest reason is the general ability of markets to *efficiently* allocate goods and resources through the law of supply and demand. This general ability is summarized in the following theorem: *A complete, competitive, full-information general equilibrium is efficient.*

To understand this theorem, its implications, and its limitations, it is necessary to know what the terms in it mean. *Complete* means that for any good or service that affects someone's utility, there is a market. *Competitive* means that there are many buyers and sellers with free entry and exit, that there are well-defined homogeneous goods and services, and that no individual supplier has any control over the price in the market. *Full information* means that all actors in the economy know everything about consumer preferences, production technologies, prices, or anything else they might need to know for deciding how to act. *General equilibrium* means that every single market is in equilibrium in the sense of the quantity supplied equaling the quantity demanded of the good or service in question. If only one market is in equilibrium this is *partial equilibrium*. *Efficiency* means Pareto optimality, after the Italian economist Vilfredo Pareto. No one in the economy can be made better off without making someone else worse off. If someone can be made better off without making someone else worse off, then the economy is not producing as much as possible. But if Pareto optimality holds, no more can be produced; all that can be done is to reshuffle existing goods and services between people.

Thus the economy is on its production possibilities frontier (ppf), defined as the set of maximum possible output combinations the economy can produce given its resources and technology. But not all points on the ppf are efficient because they may be combinations of goods and services people do not want. The Soviet economy may have been on its ppf, but it was thought to produce too much military and not enough civilian consumer goods.

An efficient economy must be a fully employed economy. Otherwise it would be inside the ppf because the unemployed could presumably produce

---

[2]Joseph Schumpeter, *The Theory of Economic Development* (Cambridge: Harvard University Press, 1934).

FIGURE 2–1   Production Possibilities Frontier

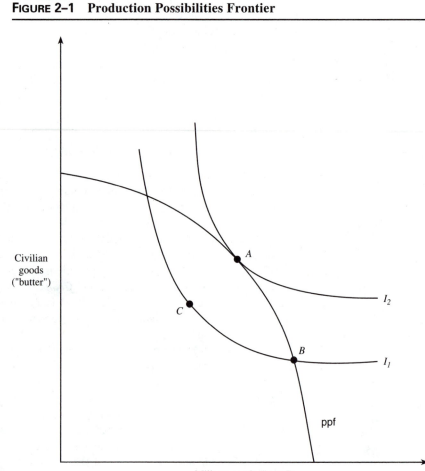

at least more of one good without reducing the output of another. Thus microeconomic efficiency implies macroeconomic full employment.

Figure 2–1 shows a ppf with point *A* being Pareto optimal at the tangency between the social indifference curve[3] and the ppf, *B* at a lower level of utility on the ppf, and *C* representing a point of unemployed factors located inside the ppf.

---

[3]To draw such curves implies everyone has identical preferences, a strong simplifying assumption. For a discussion of the difficulty in forming a social welfare function democratically when peoples' preferences differ, see Kenneth J. Arrow, *Social Choice and Individual Values,* 2d ed. (New York: Wiley, 1963).

This concept of efficiency says nothing about income distribution. An economy might be efficient in Pareto's sense that has a completely equal distribution of income or that has one person with everything and everyone else starving to death, just as long no one can be made better off without making someone else worse off. There might be an "equity-efficiency" trade-off. But that argument involves a different concept of efficiency than Pareto optimality, namely maximum economic growth over time.

The tendency to unequal wealth and incomes under market capitalism has been one of the major arguments against it raised by socialist critics. But this is a criticism distinct from the issue of economic efficiency. The existence of a general equilibrium presupposes a prior distribution of wealth with the income distribution arising from the general equilibrium itself.

Returning to the main argument, why is a complete, competitive, full-information, general equilibrium efficient? The underlying intuition of this argument dates to Adam Smith's invocation of the "invisible hand" of the market working across all sectors to allocate goods in a way that maximizes the "wealth of nations," although Smith had no formal concept of a general equilibrium, which was defined first by Léon Walras in 1874. Although Pareto argued for the link between general equilibrium and efficiency in 1909, it was Kenneth J. Arrow and Gerard Debreu in 1954 who presented a formal mathematical proof of both the existence and efficiency of competitive general equilibrium.[4]

The efficiency of competitive equilibrium is most easily seen by looking at the partial equilibrium case, the outcome in a single market. Figure 2–2 shows a typical competitive market with an upward-sloping supply curve and a downward-sloping demand curve. The solution for three different prices is shown; P_1 above equilibrium, P^* at equilibrium, and P_2 below equilibrium. Q^* is equilibrium quantity.

At P_1 suppliers produce more than they would at equilibrium but demanders buy less than they would at equilibrium, resulting in a surplus equal to the quantity produced that no one wants to buy. The amount that is both produced and sold is less than occurs at the equilibrium. At P_2 demanders buy more than they would at equilibrium but suppliers produce less than they would at equilibrium, resulting in a shortage equal to the quantity buyers want that has not been produced. Again, the amount that is both produced and sold is less than occurs at the equilibrium.

It is at the equilibrium price that the maximum amount will be both produced and sold and thus actually consumed by the public. This argument extends to all markets in the general equilibrium case. Thus to maximize the amount of all goods available for consumption, every market should be in equilibrium.

---

[4]For a discussion of this history and these arguments, see Kenneth J. Arrow and Frank Hahn, *General Competitive Analysis* (San Francisco: Holden-Day, 1971), Chapter 1.

FIGURE 2–2   Equilibrium of Competitive Supply and Demand

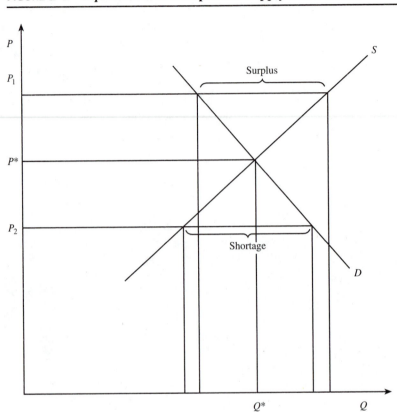

Limits to the Efficiency of Laissez-Faire Market Capitalism

Monopoly Power

No one should underestimate the power and significance of the efficiency theorem. However, no one should be fooled into thinking that absolute laissez-faire market capitalism fulfills the conditions of the theorem and is therefore efficient. In general, laissez-faire market capitalism will not be efficient, which is called the problem of *market failure*.

One condition of efficient equilibrium is that it is competitive. Monopoly power is a source of inefficiency and can arise in a laissez-faire economy. An example is the merger wave that occurred in the United States at the end of the 1890s, culminating in the greatest concentration of monopoly power in U.S. history. This concentration was attacked by President Theodore Roosevelt, the "Trust Buster," after 1901.

FIGURE 2–3   Monopoly and Perfect Competition Compared

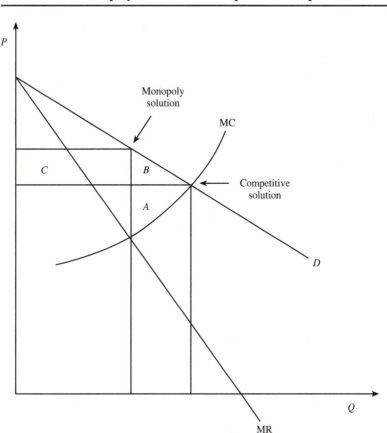

Figure 2–3 compares a pure monopoly outcome with a perfectly competitive solution. The monopolist will maximize profits by setting marginal cost (MC) equal to marginal revenue (MR) whereas if the industry is perfectly competitive the equilibrium will be at $P = MC$, where MC intersects the demand curve. The monopolist will produce less and charge a higher price than would the competitive industry. Triangle *A* shows lost income for the producer and triangle *B* shows lost consumer's surplus (net utility) due to the reduced production. Despite the loss of triangle *A,* the producer has a net gain because he obtains the larger rectangle *C* from the consumer because of the higher price.[5]

---

[5]Probably the basis for political support for antitrust policy in the United States is this "rectangle of redistribution" rather than the missing "triangles of inefficiency." Consumers get angry when "ripped off" by a monopolist whose increased income may be quite visible. The missing triangles are invisible because they do not exist, and according to some estimates are only on the order of 1 percent of GDP anyway.

Despite this apparently cut-and-dried case, caveats are in order. The first is that natural monopolies, industries with economies of scale (declining long-run average costs) even at a level of output equal to total market demand, exist. One firm can produce the total market demand at a lower cost than more than one firm can. Such a case is the electric utility industry. Societies like to take advantage of the efficiencies of large-scale production of electricity.

The existence of natural monopoly presents an inevitable trilemma. Laissez-faire can be followed, in which case consumers will get ripped off. Or the government can regulate the monopoly as state governments do in the United States with electric utilities. Regulation often leads to distortions such as overinvestment in capital stock when firms are guaranteed a particular rate of return on invested capital. Or the natural monopoly can be run by some level of government, which is socialism with all its tendencies to bureaucratic inefficiency, the solution followed in most of Western Europe for electric utilities.

Another caveat involves technological dynamism. It is argued that more competitive industries will be more technologically dynamic because of the pressure of competition. But if research and development (R and D) involve economies of scale, then a large monopolist with large monopoly profits may generate more R and D if it can be sufficiently motivated, an argument made by Joseph Schumpeter in his *Capitalism, Socialism and Democracy*. A possible example of such a "technologically progressive monopoly" in the United States may well have been AT&T with its Bell Laboratories prior to its breakup in 1982, although it can be argued that AT&T was so innovative because it perceived the threat of potential competition that eventually arrived.

Intermediate forms, notably *monopolistic competition* and *oligopoly,* lie between pure monopoly (one firm) and perfect competition (many firms, none with any control over price). Monopolistic competition involves many firms, each having some price-setting power from product differentiation. Some customers will stick with the firm when it raises price because of perceived uniqueness of its product. In the long run such firms produce at a lower level of output than they would if their average costs were minimized, the "excess capacity theorem." However, there is little that any government can do about this and none have tried.

Oligopoly, with a small number of firms in the industry, is a more complicated matter. There are many different models of oligopoly behavior because the optimal behavior of an oligopolist depends on how its fellow oligopolists react to any action it takes. Different reactions imply different outcomes.

Generally, oligopolistic industries range from very monopolistic to very competitive. At the monopolistic extreme is *perfect collusion,* the joint profit-maximizing cartel. Cartels tend to be unstable because a cartel member can make extraordinary profits by "cheating" through price cutting. The oil cartel, OPEC (Organization of Petroleum Exporting Countries), raised oil prices in 1973 and 1979, but in 1986 lost control of the world price as Saudi Arabia increased production to punish Iran and Iraq for cheating on their production quotas. Probably the longest surviving cartel in the world is the diamond cartel, based in South Africa. In the United States most cartels are illegal.

At the other extreme some oligopolistic industries behave like perfectly competitive ones, charging prices equal to marginal costs. These are known as *contestable markets* and are most likely where there are few barriers to entry and exit and the threat of potential, if not actual, competition is ever present. Firms behave competitively to forestall potential entrants. The U.S. airline industry might have been an example. The existence of contestable markets suggests taking a laissez-faire attitude with respect to oligopolies because they may be efficient and competitive, constantly innovating and investing to keep one step ahead of potential competitors.

Among all market economies, the United States has had the most vigorous antitrust policy over time. The beginning of its policy, and still its most used instrument, was the Sherman Act of 1890, which forbids "combinations in restraint of trade" and "efforts to monopolize interstate trade." The Sherman Act was supplemented by the Clayton Act of 1914, which forbids monopolistic stock mergers, interlocking directorates, tying contracts, and price discrimination; the Federal Trade Commission (FTC) Act of 1914, which forbids false advertising; and several later laws. The FTC and the Antitrust Division of the Department of Justice have been the main antitrust enforcement bodies of the U.S. government.

Since 1890 U.S. enforcement of antitrust policies has oscillated back and forth. From 1901 to 1920 enforcement was quite vigorous, from 1920 to 1945 enforcement was more relaxed, and from 1945 to 1982 enforcement was more vigorous. Since 1982 enforcement has been more relaxed, largely because increased competition from foreign imports, especially from Japan, has reduced the need for enforcement.

Controversy exists regarding the actual time path of industrial concentration in the United States. Market share and ownership of assets by the very largest firms have increased some. But taking into account foreign competition, competitiveness has probably increased.

Generally the United States has a more competitive and less concentrated economy than others. This is because of its sheer size—it can support more firms in most industries than can many smaller economies. But this also reflects the stronger tradition of U.S. antitrust enforcement. A limited cross-country comparison is shown in Table 2–1.

The major anomaly in this table is the apparently lower degree of concentration in Japan than in the United States. In Japan, many firms that are officially independent have very close relationships with other firms through the "family of companies" groupings known as *keiretsu*.[6] South Korea has

---

[6]See Chapter 6.

TABLE 2.1   Industrial Concentration Compared

Country Top Ten Firms	Average Size Top Ten Firms	Percent Employment Concentration Ratio	Average Three-Firm
United States	310,554	13.1	41
Japan	107,106	7.3	n.a.
W. Germany	177,173	20.1	56
United Kingdom	141,156	23.1	60
France	116,049	23.2	66
S. Korea	54,416	14.9	n.a.
Canada	36,990	15.3	71
Switzerland	60,039	49.4	n.a.
Sweden	48,538	49.4	83

Source: The first column shows the average number of employees in 1985 in the 10 largest firms and the second column is the percent of industrial employment in those firms in 1985, both figures from Frederic M. Scherer and David Ross, *Industrial Market Structure and Economic Performance* (Boston: Houghton Mifflin, 1990), p. 63. The third column shows simple average of market share held by the three largest firms in 12 industries in 1970 and is from Frederic M. Scherer, M. Alan Beckenstein, Erich Kaufer, and R. D. Murphy, *The Economics of Multi-Plant Operations: An International Comparisons Study* (Cambridge: Harvard University Press, 1975), pp. 218–19 and 426–28.

similar groupings known as *chaebol*.[7] Both Japan and South Korea have higher degrees of concentration relative to the United States than Table 2–1 indicates.

A final remark on monopoly involves its role in the transformation of the former command socialist economies into market capitalist ones. Many industries in the former command socialist economies are state-owned monopolies. Eliminating central planning and controls on prices has allowed these firms to behave monopolistically with resulting aggravation of inflationary tendencies, unresponsive output, and rising resentment by consumers. Furthermore many of these firms are so big that shutting them down threatens social upheavals from high unemployment. Thus the problem of monopoly power is serious for economies making market transitions.

Externalities

Another source of inefficiency in a laissez-faire equilibrium is externalities. These are either costs or benefits that are borne by or accrue to someone other than the person or entity generating them. External costs are called *negative externalities,* the most controversial being environmental pollution. External benefits are called *positive externalities,* one example being technological invention when there is no patent protection for inventors.

A firm generates pollution damaging another industry but does not minimize that damage if it does not have to pay for it. Private marginal cost to the firm does not equal social marginal cost and too much pollution is produced, resulting in inefficiency. If an inventor has no patent protection, then

---

[7]See Chapter 18.

FIGURE 2–4   Negative Externality

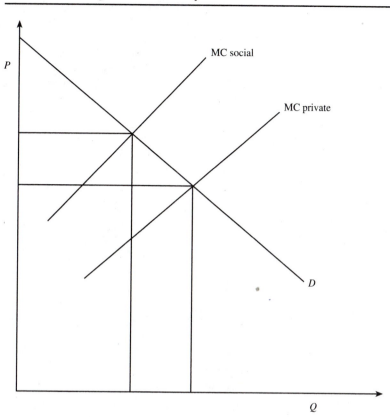

other firms can steal his invention, and he may make no money even if his invention generates great social benefits. Private marginal benefit to the inventor does not equal marginal social benefit of the invention and too little inventing will occur, resulting in inefficiency. The case of a negative externality is depicted in Figure 2–4.

For the efficiency theorem the problem raised by the existence of externalities, either positive or negative, is an *incompleteness of markets.* For unaccounted-for pollution there is no market for environmental quality even though environmental quality is something people desire and that provides utility for them. It has long been argued that the solution to pollution, or externalities in general, is to "internalize" them, to make sure that those generating the externalities either bear the costs or receive the benefits they generate.

Four broad approaches to resolving the problem of externalities have been proposed within market economies. The earliest one was that of A. C. Pigou,[8]

[8]A. C. Pigou, *The Economics of Welfare* (London: Macmillan, 1922).

who suggested taxation of negative externalities and subsidies of positive externalities. For pollution, the tax would equal the difference between the marginal private cost and the marginal social cost, as shown in Figure 2–4. The commodity whose production generates the pollution would be priced higher, and its production would be reduced. The people who consume the polluting commodity ultimately would bear the cost.

This taxation strategy seldom has been tried in the United States. Countries using it include France and West Germany, where the thrust of policies is not to raise the cost so high as to discourage polluters from polluting, but to raise money for subsidy programs that pay polluters to clean up.

A second policy, widely used in the United States, is command and control quantitative or technological restrictions. In terms of Figure 2–4 an efficient strategy moves the equilibrium from the private one to the social one. The optimal size of such a move will vary from industry to industry and from region to region. The social costs of pollution are higher in New Jersey than in North Dakota because of the greater number of people affected by pollution in New Jersey. Nevertheless the tendency until recently has been to apply the same emissions or technology standards for a given industry everywhere. Such an approach is inefficient, although it might be justified on grounds of minimizing administrative costs.

A third approach takes a more laissez-faire attitude and emphasizes the clear definition and enforcement of property rights. This approach derives from the Coase Theorem, which states that if property rights are well defined and negotiation costs are negligible, then externalities will be internalized automatically by a market capitalist economy.[9] Coase presents the example of a railroad whose trains generate sparks that start fires on property adjacent to the railroad's tracks. By mutual negotiation a solution is worked out, such as the railroad compensating the property owners or buying their property. Coase argues that it is irrelevant whether the polluter pays the pollutee for damages or the pollutee pays the polluter not to pollute, although all current law and international agreements contain ''polluter must pay'' clauses.

When property rights are poorly defined and a natural resource is an open access, common property resource, such as fisheries in international waters, there is a tendency for the resource to be overexploited. No one accounts for the effects of his behavior on others using the resource, so a gap between private and social costs emerges. For fisheries such overexploitation leads to the collapse of fish populations as has happened to many species. The essential issue is that of open access rather than common property. Thus the USSR managed the Caspian caviar fisheries well by controlling access, but after its dissolution there was drastic overfishing and a collapse of caviar production as newly independent republics bordering on the Caspian Sea all wanted access.

---

[9]Ronald H. Coase, ''The Problem of Social Cost,'' *Journal of Law and Economics* 3, (1961), pp. 1–44.

Box 2–1

Trading in Offsets in the U.S.

The U.S. Environmental Protection Agency has set upper limits on the emissions of particular pollutants within certain regions. Thus if a region is at its limit and a new business wishes to open that would put the region over the limit, it must negotiate a deal with an existing business to reduce emissions by the requisite amount. Such a deal is known as an "offset" and has been increasingly used to maintain air quality without hampering economic growth. Examples include the following:

1. A cement company in Texas that entered into an agreement with another local company in which it paid the other company for dust-collecting equipment that the other company agreed to install and maintain, the latter a negligible cost.

2. A city-owned refuse-burning power plant in Columbus, Ohio, paid for the installation of pollution controls at two privately owned asphalt plants and for increasing the height of the smokestack at a third plant.

3. A company in Contra Costa County, California, built an oil terminal after paying $250,000 for a permit for an offset created when a local chemical company shut down.

4. The state of Pennsylvania created an offset by altering its road-paving practices to reduce hydrocarbon emissions and used this offset to help attract Volkswagen Corporation to locate a plant in the state.

Source: Tom Tietenberg, *Environmental and Natural Resource Economics,* 3rd ed. (New York: Harper Collins, 1992).

The Coase Theorem implies serious limits: Property rights may be impossible to define and negotiation costs may be very high. These conditions are likely to coincide when the externality involves an inherently collective good "owned" by large numbers of people such as global air quality and global climate in the discussions of global warming and ozone depletion. Everyone in the world is involved both as a source of pollution and as an "owner" of the global climate affected by everyone else's actions. As the difficulties surrounding the global negotiations at the 1992 Rio Conference on the Environment show, these disputes are far from costlessly resolved.

Nevertheless awareness of the Coase Theorem has stimulated the search for the use of market mechanisms where possible to resolve pollution problems. An innovation that has spread rapidly in the United States has been using tradable emissions permits, which involve government setting some overall quantitative limit for the emission of a particular pollutant for a particular area.

The government then issues permits for emissions adding up to that total that firms may buy and sell from each other, thereby creating an artificial market for pollution cleanup. The U.S. Clean Air Act of 1990 relies on this approach.

Marketable emissions permits directly attack the problem of "incomplete markets" underlying the inefficiency of unresolved externalities. As long as there are enough parties to make such a market reasonably competitive, it will achieve the lowest cost solution to cleaning up the given amount. Those firms that can clean up cheaply do so and sell their "permits to pollute" to those who cannot. One form of this program involves offsets as described in Box 2–1.

Active efforts to deal with environmental problems originated in the highest income countries first and generally in the market capitalist countries before the command socialist countries despite the theoretical ability of the latter to plan for avoiding pollution. This pattern may be due more to the greater democracy of the advanced market capitalist economies than due to the inherent nature of their economic systems.

The level of development of an economy and its amounts and kinds of pollution seem to be strongly related. Poorer countries seem to have worse water pollution and more particulate matter in the air. Richer countries tend to emit more greenhouse gases, especially carbon dioxide from fossil fuel burning. Middle-income countries tend to emit the most sulfur dioxides responsible for acid rain, largely a result of burning high-sulfur coal.

Data on different air pollutants in different countries are shown in Table 2–2. Carbon dioxide (CO_2) per capita shows strong correlation with income levels—it reaches a peak in some oil-rich Persian Gulf states, although the United States is not too far behind. Nitrogen oxides (NOX), which come largely from automobiles, also increase in market capitalist economies with more cars, and the United States is at the top of the list of per capita output. Sulfur dioxide (SO_2) comes from burning dirty coal and oil, and per capita emissions are the highest in heavily industrialized command socialist countries, although the United States has the highest levels among the market capitalist countries.

Collective Consumption Goods

Another source of inefficiency for laissez-faire equilibrium is collective consumption goods, also known as *public goods*. The latter name is circular because such goods frequently are provided by the public sector even in strongly market capitalist economies. Why? Calling them "public goods" does not answer the question, but identifying them as "collective consumption goods" emphasizes why the public sector provides them.

The source of the efficiency problem with such goods is incomplete markets. Because of the nature of collective consumption goods it is difficult for private markets to organize themselves to provide them in optimal quantities. Thus it falls to the public sector to do so, although such provision is afflicted with the usual difficulties and inefficiencies associated with the public sector.

TABLE 2–2   Pollution Emissions in Various Countries

Country	CO_2 Per Capita	NOX Per Capita	SO_2 Per Capita
Niger	0.15	n.a.	n.a.
Egypt	1.54	n.a.	n.a.
Mexico	3.70	n.a.	n.a.
China	2.16	n.a.	n.a.
India	0.77	n.a.	n.a.
Laos	0.07	n.a.	n.a.
S. Korea	5.20	n.a.	n.a.
Japan	8.46	n.a.	n.a.
Iran	3.11	n.a.	n.a.
Qatar	37.59	n.a.	n.a.
Albania	3.06	2.8	15.6
Bulgaria	11.87	16.7	114.6
Czechoslovakia	14.47	60.7	178.9
Hungary	6.05	24.5	115.2
Poland	11.54	39.1	103.3
Romania	9.16	16.8	8.6
Yugoslavia	5.61	8.0	69.6
USSR	13.26	14.6	32.4
E. Germany	10.48	42.6	313.3
W. Germany	10.48*	48.4	24.2
France	6.38	30.1	27.1
Sweden	7.00	35.4	25.9
United Kingdom	9.89	43.9	62.1
United States	19.68	79.6	83.2

*The CO_2 figures are averaged across all of Germany.

Source: All figures are for 1989 and are from World Resources Institute, *World Resources, 1992–93* (Oxford: Oxford University Press, 1992), pp. 64–65 for NOX and SO_2 (which are in kilograms) and pp. 346–47 for CO_2 (which is in metric tons).

National defense is an archetypal such good and the cost overruns of the U.S. defense establishment are legion.

The characteristics of a pure public good are *nonexcludability of consumption* and *nondepletability of consumption,* of which the former is more crucial. These two characteristics together imply that the very essence of the good is collective. Everyone consumes it simultaneously and no individual's consumption of it takes away from any other individual's consumption of it. National defense is a classic example and is almost universally provided publicly, even in strongly market capitalist economies. If one individual is defended from foreign invasion then all individuals are so defended, irrespective of whether or not they paid for it.

The essential problem for market provision of true collective consumption goods is the *free rider problem.* The collective nature of the good breaks the link between paying for it and consuming it. If it exists, everyone consumes it whether or not they paid for it. Thus if the private sector were to attempt to provide the good it would have a great deal of trouble selling the good. Many individuals who actually want the good to be provided will not pay for its provision because they can free ride and consume it for free. Even though people want the good they will not pay enough for it to be provided to the Pareto optimal level. The government must use taxation to bring about adequate provision of the good.

One criticism of this view comes from the philosophical perspective known as *methodological individualism,* associated with the pro–laissez-faire Austrian School. An even more extreme version of this view is associated with the objectivist philosophy of the novelist Ayn Rand, which argues that there is no such thing as a human collectivity; ultimate reality is individual people. All apparent collectivities are illusions created to subject individuals to arbitrary tyrannies. However the Austrian School, at least Friedrich Hayek, recognizes the existence of some minimal public goods, notably the constitutional maintenance of basic law and order for the protection of property rights and the functioning of free markets.

Between the extremes of pure private goods such as food and pure public goods such as basic law and order there is a wide spectrum of intermediate goods that have both private and collective aspects. One example is education, which is provided by a mix of public and private sources in the United States, with public sources more prominent at lower grade levels and private sources gaining in significance at higher educational levels. Widespread literacy and elementary education of the populace has a significant collective component because it teaches people how to behave as citizens within the society at the most basic level. At higher levels of education individuals are more able to appropriate for themselves the benefits of their education, although there are still arguably broader spillovers.

This broad spectrum allows much room for variation across societies, even among largely market capitalist economies, regarding the public versus private provision of such intermediate goods. The recent movement in many countries to privatize previously public activities highlights this debate with no clear boundaries or criteria regarding what should be done by whom.

Compared to most other market economies the United States provides more of these intermediate activities privately. Nevertheless the U.S. economy has a substantial public sector, the most rapidly growing part of which has been at the state and local levels. At the federal level there has always been substantial government ownership of land, especially in the West. Overall public ownership of land and structures is on the order of 15 percent of the respective totals. These figures represent moderate declines from 1939, when a period of increasing government ownership ended. Areas with significant public participation in the United States include law and order, national defense, the National Forest Service and National Park Service, major dams, the space program, the Tennessee Valley Authority,[10] and numerous local public services such as education, fire protection, local transportation, airports, harbors, highways, garbage collection, water, sewage disposal, libraries, and even some locally owned utilities. All of these are subject to debate about whether or not they should be privatized.[11]

Finally the *public choice school*[12] of thought observes that decisions regarding private versus public ownership are made by legislative bodies at whatever level of government. These bodies are subject to all the complexities of majority rule, logrolling, special interest groups, and sheer inertia, suggesting that they are ill-suited to efficient decision making regarding the proper balance between the private and public sectors. Even though there is a case for public provision of collective consumption goods, the public choice school sees the public sector as so inefficient and corrupt that generally privatization will be the preferred solution.

Imperfect Information

Of all the assumptions needed for efficiency of an equilibrium outcome, that of perfect information is the most unrealistic. There is no perfect information anywhere about anything.

This problem of imperfect information has spawned a new field, the ''economics of information.'' A major breakthrough came with George Akerlof's analysis of the used-car market in which there is asymmetry of information between the owner of the used car who knows its flaws and the potential customer who does not.[13] But the potential customer understands this and therefore is suspicious of all used cars, suspecting them to be lemons their owners wish to dispose of. The victims of the resulting inefficiency will be anyone who seeks to sell a used car that is *not* a lemon at a decent price. Potential sellers who recognize the problem reinforce it: Those with good cars who do not *have* to sell won't.

Such asymmetries are rife in market economies. In contractual relationships they lead to *principal-agent* problems where someone is hired who does not do what is best for the employer because of his ability to mislead the ignorant employer. Such asymmetries can lead to suboptimizing behavior because of *moral hazard,* especially in the insurance industry. Those most needing insurance will seek it out and will conceal their need from the insurers,

---

[10]As the only federally owned utility in the country, established during the New Deal of the 1930s, the TVA has had a controversial and mixed record.

[11]In some cases partial privatization is what has happened, as with the Federal National Mortgage Association (''Fannie Mae'').

[12]Also known as the ''Virginia School,'' its founders were James Buchanan and Gordon Tullock.

[13]George Akerlof, ''The Market for Lemons,'' *Quarterly Journal of Economics* 84 (1970), pp. 488–500.

thereby raising rates for those who need insurance less. Those who are insured then may behave in ways they would not if they were uninsured. Such moral hazard has been adduced as a cause of the U.S. Savings and Loan crisis. Financial institutions engaged in reckless lending practices because depositors were not scrutinizing the institutions' behavior because their deposits were insured by the government.

There is no easy way out of the dilemmas posed by imperfect information and asymmetries of information. However a possible melioration available to government is simply increasing the amount of relevant information generally available. This constitutes an economic efficiency justification for government data-gathering agencies such as the Bureau of Labor Statistics and the Census Bureau. A trial balloon to privatize information gathering and disseminating by the U.S. National Weather Service that was floated during the Reagan Administration created a storm.

Another perspective is that the very essence of markets is information transmission. Hayek argues that a central planner can never possess adequate information for carrying out optimal or even remotely intelligent planning. Free capitalist markets may suffer from imperfect information, but they beat command socialist planning in this area, according to this view.

In the Hayekian vision it is prices themselves that serve as the transmitters of information regarding relative scarcities. Decentralized and profit-motivated market capitalists respond to price signals in ways that move the economy along optimally even though the individual actors only possess limited knowledge.[14] This emphasis on prices as information signals, even in a world of asymmetries and imperfection, has been much emphasized in the more recent economics of information. But ultimately the problem of imperfect information remains unresolved for all economic systems.

Some Other Problems Regarding Laissez-Faire

Merit Goods and Orphan Goods.   The preceding discussion cites the main reasons why laissez-faire equilibria may not be efficient. Several other arguments against laissez-faire have been put forward, sometimes carrying the inefficiency label. But these arguments have little to do with efficiency or they can be subsumed as special cases of one of the above categories of laissez-faire inefficiency.

One of these special cases is *merit goods*. These are goods that society approves of and seeks to encourage the consumption of, especially in comparison with some other presumably less than merit goods. This is not an efficiency argument but one of value judgment and officiousness by those in

---

[14]Prices may not always accurately transmit information as with speculative bubbles, in which prices rise because agents are busy expecting them to rise.

authority with regard to those not in authority. For example, societies ban the consumption of ''sin'' goods such as certain kinds of drugs, prostitution, gambling, or pornography, among other not-so-good goods. Conceivably there are potential externality issues involved, as for example if drug addicts commit crimes to support their habits or prostitutes spread venereal diseases.

A variation of merit goods involves income redistribution programs. Standard economic arguments suggest that efficient redistribution schemes should be as cash. But in the United States much redistribution takes in-kind forms such as food stamps, public housing, and Medicaid. The reason is that these are considered merit goods that the poor *should* be consuming. Society doesn't give them cash because who knows what they might spend it on!

A related but different argument involves *orphan goods*. These are considered to be especially meritorious, but for lack of a sufficient market under laissez-faire they do not get produced. The classic example is expensive-to-produce medicines for very rare but deadly illnesses. Under laissez-faire the markets may be too small to support production of these medicines, but people feel on moral grounds that they should be provided, with some level of government being the obvious provider of the necessary subsidies. This is currently being done in the United States by the federal government.

Providing such orphan goods may well be a legitimate function of government, but it does not involve correcting an inefficiency. The economy may already be Pareto optimal, and the taxes for these subsidies reduce someone else's utility. The real problem is one of income distribution rather than inefficiency. If those with the rare illnesses in question had sufficiently high incomes they could pay enough to support production of the necessary medicines. Subsidization of the production of these orphan drugs is indirectly a way of redistributing income to those with the rare illnesses.

Capital Market Myopia.   Another possible source of inefficiency is that laissez-faire financial markets generate real interest rates that may be inefficiently high. If so then those markets are overvaluing the present and undervaluing the future, myopia or shortsightedness. Thus, perhaps, government should intervene either to push down interest rates or to use lower-than-market interest rates for calculating benefits and costs of public investment projects.

There is reason to take this argument seriously. However it reflects applications of two of our previously given reasons for possible laissez-faire inefficiency. Most important is externality, particularly an ''intertemporal externality'' with respect to future generations who have not yet been born. To the extent that we are selfish those generations have no voice in today's capital markets and decisions may be made that will adversely affect them because of our high interest rate–induced shortsightedness. The other element is imperfect information. The distant future is fundamentally unknown; we do not know future technologies and resource availabilities, much less the preferences of unborn generations.

It may be that this imperfect information provides a rationale for government intervention, presumably through macroeconomic policy to push down real interest rates in order to value the interests of the future somewhat more. But there is no way to know the right amount.

Regarding the question of applying a different rate to public investment projects than that in the private sector, another problem is that such a policy would suck funds out of private capital investment and into public capital investment, in other words, ''crowding out.'' With no reason to believe that public investment is more productive than private capital investment, such a policy risks introducing inefficiency.

The Role of Labor Unions.   Another issue arising in market capitalist economies is the organization of labor into unions. If labor markets are perfectly competitive and lacking in discrimination on grounds of characteristics irrelevant to productivity, it can be argued that unions do not contribute to economic efficiency. They are vehicles for redistributing income to their members; dealing with safety, job security, benefits, and social functions; and lobbying politically for broader social outcomes. If unions do not offset monopsonistic power of big firms doing the hiring, their potential for exercising monopolistic power in the supply of labor may result in inefficiency.[15]

Although craft unions resemble the medieval guilds of Europe, modern labor unions arose from the revolutionary socialist movements in the 19th century, even though independent labor unions were snuffed out by command socialist regimes once in power. The Grand Consolidated Trade Union of Britain in the 1830s and the Knights of Labor in the United States in the 1870s were such unions, devoted at least as much to the idea of a general working class revolution as to negotiating bread and butter issues. Given these historical roots, labor unions have tended to be weakest in the most relentlessly market capitalist countries such as the United States.

As the harshness of 19th century capitalism moderated in the 20th century, labor unions both became more legally accepted and moderated their approaches to negotiation and political activism. In the United States the American Federation of Labor (AFL) was founded in 1881 by Samuel Gompers, and it eschewed radicalism for *business unionism.* This group consists of unions of workers in craft unions, organized like guilds along lines of skill categories (carpenters, plumbers, etc.). Although in Europe acceptance of unions came earlier, the environment in the United States remained fundamentally hostile until the New Deal of Franklin D. Roosevelt passed the Wagner Act of 1935, which established the modern U.S. system of collective bargaining.

The Wagner Act triggered a period of intense organizing and a conflict between the AFL and the newly formed Congress of Industrial Organizations (CIO). The CIO included industrial unions such as the United Auto Workers

---

[15]The original applications of the Sherman Antitrust Act in the United States in the 1890s were against labor unions, although they were very weak at the time. The Clayton Act of 1914 exempted unions from antitrust law.

and the United Steel Workers that were more radical and had less skilled workers. In 1947 a reaction set in with the Taft-Hartley Act, which put restrictions on union activities. By 1955 the percentage of U.S. workers in unions had peaked and the two federations united as the AFL-CIO. Their base in heavy industries means that their membership and influence have declined in the United States as its economy has evolved towards a postindustrial service pattern.

In contrast, labor unions in Western Europe have a larger proportion of the labor force as members, are more centrally organized, are more accepted by the political establishment, and are more influential in pushing towards greater government intervention in their economies. They serve as the main political-economic base for Western European "social democracy."

Countries vary considerably. In some countries labor-management relations have been cooperative, as in Sweden and Germany, whereas in others they have been contentious, as in France and Great Britain. In Japan, union membership is higher than in the United States, but labor-management relations have been more cooperative. When labor-management cooperation involves economywide negotiating under government encouragement for macroeconomic stabilization, this is known as *corporatism*.[16]

Table 2–3 shows percentages of labor forces belonging to unions for 1955 and 1975 for 13 countries. The U.S. percentage has continued to decline and is now less than 15 percent. The Japanese percentage declined to 28 percent. There is no relation between the degree of unionization and the degree of radicalism of unions. The two least unionized countries in Table 2–3 are the United States and France. In political terms the former has the most moderate unions on the list whereas in the latter many unions have deep links to the still-orthodox Communist Party of France.

Table 2–4 shows days lost to strikes per thousand nonagricultural wage earners and salaried employees for 1955, 1965, 1975, and 1985 for 15 countries. Generally disputes have declined markedly except in the United Kingdom, Sweden, New Zealand, and especially Denmark. The most disputatious countries were Italy and Canada, and the least, Switzerland.

The impact of unionization on an economy depends on many factors. In the United States unionized workers are paid more than nonunionized workers, which may have contributed to the weakening of unions as high wages led to unemployment in the auto and steel industries. If unions cooperate with management and support flexibility in labor policies high unionization may coexist with low unemployment, as in Sweden until recently. Unions may lead to productivity improvements through giving workers a voice. But if unions insist on restrictive laws, such as ones limiting the ability of firms to fire workers (which discourages firms from hiring workers in the first place), then high unionization may lead to high chronic unemployment, as in Belgium.

---

[16]Originally corporatism was an authoritarian system promoted by fascists, but now is more of a voluntary system found largely in social democracies.

TABLE 2–3   Percentages of Labor Force Belonging to Unions

Country	1955	1975
United States	24.7	21.7
Japan	n.a.	34.0
Austria	63.0	59.0
Belgium	53.0	66.0
Denmark	59.0	67.0
Finland	31.0	75.0
France	25.0	25.0
West Germany	34.0	33.0
Italy	n.a.	47.0
Netherlands	38.0	40.0
Norway	54.0	61.0
Sweden	68.0	82.0
United Kingdom	44.0	51.0

Source: Data for the United States are from *Economic Report of the President* (Washington: USGPO, 1990). Japanese figures are from Richard B. Freeman and M. E. Redick, "Crumbling Pillar? Declining Union Density in Japan," *Journal of Japanese and International Economies* 3, 1989, pp. 578–601. European figures are from Jan-Erik Lane and Svante Ersson, *Comparative Political Economy* (London: Pinter, 1990), p. 164.

TABLE 2–4   Days Lost to Labor Disputes per Thousand Workers

Country	1955	1965	1975	1985
United States	429	252	303	74
Australia	361	219	717	230
Belgium	408	29	197	35
Canada	466	416	1,324	319
Denmark	8	153	54	1,087
France	277	71	48	2
West Germany	52	2	3	2
Italy	439	567	1,646	234
Japan	203	201	222	6
Netherlands	46	15	<1	9
New Zealand	81	26	207	703
Norway	116	8	8	39
Sweden	65	1	12	129
Switzerland	1	<1	<1	<1
United Kingdom	180	130	269	303

Source: These figures were provided to us by Robert Horn based on unpublished data gathered by the U.S. Bureau of Labor Statistics, Office of Productivity and Technology, 1988.

TABLE 2–5   Percent of Labor Force Unemployed

Country	1921	1931	1951	1961	1971	1979	1993
Australia	5.9	17.9	1.3	2.3	1.8	6.1	10.7
Austria	n.a.	9.7	3.5	1.8	1.2	1.7	5.7
Belgium	6.1	6.8	4.4	2.5	1.7	7.1	13.5
Canada	5.8	11.6	2.4	7.0	6.1	7.4	11.6
Denmark	3.0	9.0	4.6	1.9	1.1	5.2	12.3
Finland	1.8	4.6	0.3	1.2	2.2	6.0	n.a.
France	2.7	2.2	2.1	1.5	2.6	5.9	11.7
Germany	1.2	13.9	7.3	0.7	0.7	3.3	7.5
Italy	n.a.	4.3	7.3	3.4	4.9	7.1	11.3
Japan	n.a.	n.a.	1.7	1.4	1.2	2.1	2.5
Netherlands	1.7	4.3	3.2	0.9	2.3	6.6	6.2
Norway	n.a.	10.2	1.5	1.8	1.5	2.0	n.a.
Sweden	1.3	4.8	1.6	1.5	2.5	2.1	9.0
Switzerland	n.a.	1.2	0.0	0.0	0.0	0.3	4.6
United Kingdom	11.0	14.8	2.2	2.0	3.8	5.1	10.4
United States	11.4	15.2	3.2	6.5	5.9	5.8	6.8

All data are from Angus Maddison, *Phases of Capitalist Development* (Oxford: Oxford University Press, 1982), pp. 206–208, except for 1993, which are from *The Economist* (August 20–26, 1994), p. 80.

Macroeconomic Instability of Market Capitalism

The General Picture

Although involuntary unemployment of labor due to macroeconomic fluctuations implies that inefficiency exists, the significance of macroeconomic fluctuations goes beyond this to constitute a central and distinct issue for market capitalism as a system. It is no accident that the high-water mark of popularity of the U.S. Communist Party was in the Great Depression. Mass unemployment and unequal distributions of income and wealth, rather than inefficiency, have provided the most pungent propaganda for socialist critics of market capitalism.

That the major market capitalist economies have been less than perfectly stable over time is shown in Table 2–5 and Figure 2–5. The former shows unemployment rates[17] for a variety of countries for a variety of years. Unemployment rates have generally increased since the early 1970s associated with the general stagnation of world economic growth.

Figure 2–5 shows the maximum peak-to-trough decline of GDP over a business cycle for various countries for various periods, a crude measure of instability. There was more such variability before World War II than since.

---

[17]Some variation across countries and over time is attributable to variations in labor force participation rates.

FIGURE 2–5   Maximum Peak-to-Trough GDP Decline over Cycle

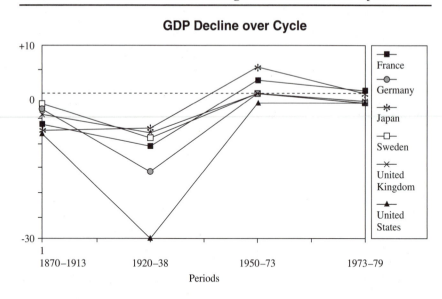

Examination of the components of GDP indicates the most variable element is capital investment, sometimes characterized as a "flighty bird." That capital investment varies considerably can be explained on grounds from exogenous fluctuations in new technologies that can serve as the basis for investment to fluctuations in government monetary policies affecting interest rates to psychological fluctuations of the "animal spirits" of those making investments. The serious question is why these factors lead to fluctuations in the unemployment rate given that in a perfectly competitive labor market wage rates should fall when the demand for labor falls thereby preventing the emergence of any involuntary unemployment. Two broad schools of thought, the *Keynesian* and the *classical* have different answers to this.[18]

The former, deriving its views largely from the British economist J. Maynard Keynes and his *General Theory of Employment, Interest and Money,* argues that rigidities of various sorts exist in labor markets and that capital investment can collapse and stay down for extended periods of time, as in the Great Depression. The implication is that government intervention through fiscal or monetary policies may be advisable to stimulate the economy and to stabilize and smooth out business cycles.

---

[18]These two schools have various subcategories including old and new classicals and Keynesians, post Keynesians, and supply-siders. To the left and right of this broad division stand the pro–command socialist Marxists and their ideological opposites, the very pro–laissez-faire Austrians.

FIGURE 2–6   Alternative Views of Macroeconomic Equilibrium

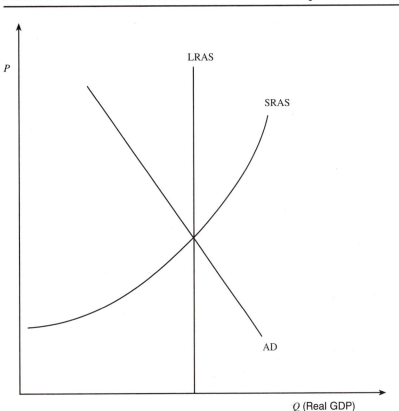

The latter, deriving from 19th century classical political economists such as David Ricardo, argues that market capitalist economies have a powerful self-correcting mechanism. Conscious government intervention tends to generate inflation and to aggravate any fluctuations. To minimize unemployment, unions should be broken up and a stable fiscal and monetary environment should be maintained within a laissez-faire environment.

Figure 2–6 depicts alternative views of macroeconomic equilibrium. *P* now represents the overall price level of the economy and *Q* represents the aggregate level of real output. Aggregate demand (AD) is downward-sloping. However SRAS represents an upward-sloping, short-run aggregate supply curve as conceptualized by Keynesians. Its shape implies that a decline in aggregate demand will cause a decline in real output and a decline in employment. LRAS represents a long-run aggregate supply curve as conceptualized by classicals. Most classical economists recognize that output can decline in the short run for a variety of reasons, but argue that *very quickly* a laissez-faire economy will return to behavior depicted by the LRAS. Declines in aggregate demand will lead to declines in the price level rather than in real output or employment.

Tools of Macroeconomic Policy

Two main macroeconomic policy tools are fiscal and monetary policy. Fiscal policy is a nation's budget, its package of spending and tax rates. Generally the higher spending and the lower tax rates, the higher will be the stimulus to aggregate demand. Monetary policy is the expansion or contraction of a nation's money supply and the lowering or raising of interest rates in its economy, each of the first stimulating aggregate demand and each of the second contracting it.

In parliamentary democracies where the executive leaders are the legislative leaders, responsibility for fiscal policy is well defined. In the United States the separation of the executive and legislative branches of government makes for a messier situation. Executive agencies propose spending packages that are filtered through the Office of Management and Budget (OMB), which generally acts as the president's executive arm on spending proposals. The Treasury makes tax proposals. These are combined and submitted to Congress, which chops them up and sends them through a plethora of committees and subcommittees, rarely succeeding in actually passing a complete budget in time for when it is supposed to take effect. Disagreements between Congress and the president then are worked out through negotiation or, in cases with more conflict, through the veto process. What finally emerges and is actually implemented by the executive agencies may not resemble the desired plans of anybody involved.

In all modern market capitalist economies monetary policy is carried out by a central bank that controls the domestic money supply and at least short-term interest rates. The concentration of decision making in one body generally allows a greater degree of purposiveness and control of monetary policy than exists for fiscal policy. It has been argued that the third most powerful person in the world is the Chairman of the Board of Governors of the U.S. Federal Reserve System, the U.S. central bank (the "Fed").

Nations vary considerably in how their respective central banks relate to entities in charge of fiscal policy. Some central banks have considerable autonomy and independence, notably the Bundesbank of Germany. Others are subordinated to fiscal policy makers, notably the Bank of England, which is administratively under the control of the budget-proposing Chancellor of the Exchequer. The U.S. Fed is somewhere in between—it was created by and is subject to rules established by Congress, and its Board of Governors is appointed by the president for 14-year terms. It is widely argued that the more independent central banks have had better records at controlling inflation.

A Recapitulation of the Strong Case for Laissez-Faire

A major theme of recent world political economy has been a strong shift towards supporting more laissez-faire. The enormous changes in Eastern Europe have had much to do with this, but so have changes in the market capitalist economies. In the former communist world, disillusionment with the old ideology of command socialism has led to great fascination with its extreme opposite, laissez-faire market capitalism. Even the backlash to this— former communists have won elections in some countries—has been marked by support for market-oriented reforms of one sort or another, if only as promises to take a more gradualistic approach.

There is tension between asserting the efficiency of competitive equilibria and recognizing the limits of the applicability of that theorem. While recognizing these limits the stronger advocates of laissez-faire argue against their significance or relevance.

The most straightforward case is made by the *Chicago School,* whose most prominent and comprehensive spokesman is Milton Friedman.[19] The Chicago School argument draws directly from the efficiency theorem and follows by asserting the irrelevance or unimportance of the various exceptions and limits. It claims that markets are almost always efficient and so government should keep its hands off.

Monopolistic or oligopolistic market structures reflect efficient and competitive behavior by the firms involved, unless they are enforced because of some government restriction on entry. Friedman's opposition to government restrictions on entry leads him to oppose the licensing of doctors by government. Most government-initiated antitrust suits are just a waste of time, distracting firms from their market-appointed task of efficiently providing goods and services to consumers.

Most externalities will be resolved by private markets if property rights are properly defined and enforced, as suggested by the Coase Theorem. If they are not, they are probably not very significant and the benefits to be obtained from any possible government intervention will be more than offset by the inefficiencies and waste associated with government activity it is argued.

Many of the goods provided by the public sector are not really collective consumption goods and could be more efficiently provided privately it is claimed. Thus privatization of public goods provision should be vigorously pursued.

Information costs are inevitable and cannot be avoided. Again, inefficient governments are supposedly unlikely to be very helpful in improving matters in this area.

---

[19]A sign of Friedman's special prominence occurred when former Soviet leader Mikhail Gorbachev visited the Hoover Institution at Stanford University, where Friedman was then located. Gorbachev made a special point of seeking him out for praise and a handshake.

In macroeconomics the Chicago School supports the classical approach. Friedman in particular is the most prominent advocate of *monetarism* in the United States and is the father of the proposal that the money supply should grow at a constant rate per year. Beyond that, fiscal policy should involve low-to-no deficits and should not be actively used for stabilization efforts.

With respect to the distribution of income, people should be allowed to keep what they earn from the free market. Inequalities are the necessary outcome of providing sufficient incentives for production, investment, and growth. The equity-efficiency trade-off is real and efficiency should be favored. So government should not redistribute income it is argued.

A more general criticism of government intervention is made by public choice theory, which argues that the government agencies designated to carry out the market-correcting activities are self-interested entities that become captured by special interests operating through their legislative connections.

This analysis became more focused after the discovery of the concept of *rent-seeking* by Anne Krueger, *rent* defined as the return to a factor fixed in supply, such as land or a unique individual. Government agencies can through regulatory actions create artificial scarcities, such as a limited number of import licenses in a less-developed country. Doing so then artificially creates rents that can be captured by special interests or even by the bureaucrats in charge of allocating these scarce items by means of bribery. Large amounts of economic resources become devoted to the creation and capture of these rents, often involving corruption.

Summary and Conclusions

Modern market capitalism evolved out of the merchant capitalism of Northern Italy and Flanders in the late medieval period to reach its closest approach to laissez-faire in the emergence of the industrial revolution in Britain and the United States in the 19th century. These economies have seen increased government intervention in the 20th century, leaving Switzerland and Hong Kong as the most laissez-faire advanced economies in the world today.

A complete, competitive, full-information general equilibrium, in which supply equals demand in all markets, is efficient in the Pareto sense. Thus no individual can be made better off without making some other individual worse off. This theorem does not address the question of income distribution, and critics of market capitalism emphasize its tendency to inequalities of income and wealth, which seem to be worsening over time. Supporters of market capitalism, however, argue that such inequalities are necessary for bringing about economic growth because they provide incentives for work effort and investment.

Box 2–2

Does Rent-Seeking Explain National Destinies?

The rent-seeking theory has been broadly applied by Mancur Olson in his *The Rise and Decline of Nations*. He revives the Jeffersonian notion that every society needs a revolutionary shake-up from time to time in order to maintain its dynamism. Without such occasional shake-ups, often brought about by defeat or conquest by a foreign power, interest groups accumulate power and influence and are able to expand their rent-seeking activities to the point that the economy loses all ability to change or grow as it becomes encrusted with more and more regulations and restrictions designed to protect the increasingly bloated rents of the outdated special interests. He presents the stagnation of never-conquered-since-1066 Great Britain and its ossified class system as a leading negative example and the postwar economic dynamism of defeated Germany and Japan as positive examples. The Olson theory suggests that Russia and her former allies may have bright futures if they can get through their difficult transitions.

The efficiency theorem suggests that a minimal government, laissez-faire economy might be inefficient because of monopoly power, externalities, insufficient public goods, imperfect information, and possible macroeconomic instability. During the 20th century the U.S. economy has developed mechanisms for dealing with these problems, many of which involve some sort of government activity or intervention although much of this has been questioned in the United States since the 1994 election.

Despite this evolution, controversy and debate continue regarding the appropriate scope of government involvement in mixed market capitalist economies. Strong supporters of laissez-faire critique proposed and actual ways in which governments seek to correct the inefficiencies of unfettered markets. This suggests that as the former socialist countries continue to move towards market capitalism they will increasingly encounter serious questions regarding the ultimate balance between the public and private sectors within their economies.

Although the United States is much closer to laissez-faire than most market capitalist economies, its government actively intervenes in a variety of ways to deal with the above problems. A recent trend has been towards policies that may involve establishing a market where none existed before, for example for tradeable pollution permits. Compared with other market capitalist economies, the United States has a very high real income, high level of competitiveness, greater income inequality, weaker unions, more per capita air pollution, a smaller public sector, and historically somewhat greater volatility of its GDP. Thus it shows both the dynamism but also the difficulties of market capitalism as a system.

Questions for Discussion

1. ''Income inequality is necessary for Pareto optimality so that people will work as hard as they can.'' ''If income is distributed equally then there must be Pareto optimality because you can't make one person better off without making someone else worse off.'' Are these statements true or false? Why or why not?

2. How does the U.S. economy compare with other market capitalist economies with respect to its degree of industrial concentration and the nature of its antitrust policies?

3. Socialist critics of market capitalism argue that businesspeople will not care about the environment because they are only concerned about profits whereas socialist planning will be able to take care of the environment. Why then have environmental conditions generally been better in the industrialized market capitalist economies than in the industrialized command socialist ones?

4. What are some goods that are publicly provided in the United States that could be efficiently provided privately instead? Why are they not so provided?

5. Looking at the tables in this chapter, can you find any evidence that the influence of Keynes might have contributed to improved macroeconomic performance among market capitalist economies? How might his influence have failed to improve their performance?

6. How might you critique the ''strong case for laissez-faire'' presented at the end of the chapter?

Suggested Further Readings

Buchanan, James, and Gordon Tullock. *The Calculus of Consent.* Ann Arbor: University of Michigan Press, 1962.

Freeman, Richard B., and James L. Medoff. *What Do Unions Do?* New York: Basic Books, 1984.

Frey, Bruno S. ''Decision Making via the Price System.'' In *Comparative Economic Systems: Models and Cases.* 7th ed. ed. Morris Bornstein. Homewood, IL: Irwin, 1994. pp. 92–114.

Hayek, Friedrich A. ''The Price System as a Mechanism for Using Knowledge,'' *American Economic Review* 35 (1945), pp. 519–30.

Keynes, John Maynard. *The General Theory of Employment, Interest and Money.* London: Harcourt Brace, 1936.

Krueger, Anne O. ''Economists' Changing Perceptions of Government.'' In *Comparative Economic Systems: Models and Cases.* 7th ed. ed. Morris Bornstein. Homewood: Irwin, 1994. pp. 78–91.

Maddison, Angus. *Phases of Capitalist Development.* Oxford: Oxford University Press, 1982.

Olson, Mancur. *The Rise and Decline of Nations.* New Haven: Yale University Press, 1982.

Scherer, Frederic M., and David Ross. *Industrial Market Structure and Performance.* Boston: Houghton Mifflin, 1990.

Smith, Adam. *An Inquiry into the Nature and Causes of the Wealth of Nations.* London: Strahan and Cadell, 1776.

Tietenberg, Tom. *Environmental and Natural Resource Economics.* 3rd ed. New York: Harper Collins, 1992.

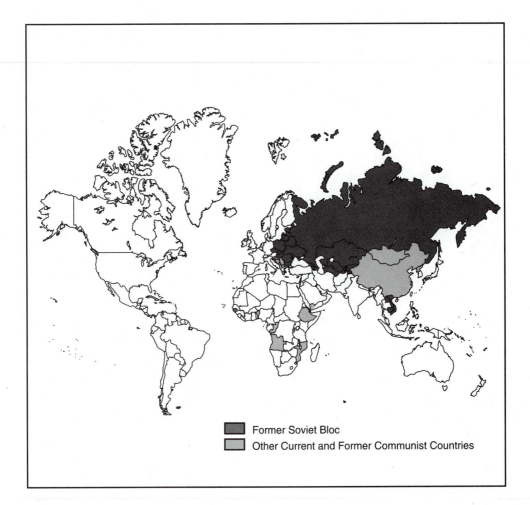

Former Soviet Bloc

Other Current and Former Communist Countries

THE THEORY AND HISTORY OF MARXISM AND SOCIALISM

What is the difference between capitalism and socialism? Under capitalism man exploits man, but under socialism it is just the opposite.
Old Soviet Joke

What is socialism? It is the longest road from capitalism to capitalism.
More recent Soviet joke

Introduction

Socialism is an economic system characterized by state or collective owner-ship of the means of production, land and capital. With the possible exception of state-dominated ancient empires such as Babylonia and Egypt, socialism did not actually exist as a system until the 20th century. Its emergence reflected a long theoretical, ideological, and political development based on criticism of feudal and capitalist systems that existed prior to its modern appearance. This criticism originated from religious perspectives favoring egalitarian income distributions and collective sharing and evolved into a secular theory of history and society in the writings of Karl Marx and his followers.

At the current time, with very few exceptions, countries that have iden-tified themselves as socialist are either attempting to move towards full-blown market capitalism or else in that direction to some intermediate form. Nevertheless there are still reasons to examine the socialist form and its ori-gins. One is that despite the efforts to change such economies, many are still essentially socialist in actual practice. Another reason is that frustrations with these efforts may lead to a revival of socialist ideology in some of these coun-tries, as the scattered electoral success of reformed successors-to-Communist parties indicates. Finally, the difficulties experienced in the market capitalist world have stimulated reconsideration of at least limited elements of the socialist model as reformist devices. Entirely new forms may yet emerge out of the current changes sweeping the world economy.

The Development of Socialist Ideology

Religious and Philosophical Precursors

Socialist ideology originated in religious and philosophical criticism of inequalities in existing societies and the formulation of ideal alternatives in which collective sharing and equality reign supreme. The prophet Amos in the Old Testament railed against the rich, and in the New Testament Jesus expressed sympathy for the poor. The Greek philosopher, Plato, described an ideal society in his *Republic,* although it included nonsocialist elements such as slavery.

In Europe, Christianity provided fertile ground for germinating socialist ideology. Marx and Engels in the *Communist Manifesto* note that, "Nothing is easier than to give Christian asceticism a socialist tinge." Fundamental was the *millennarian* tradition of expecting the arrival of the Second Coming of Christ when all would be judged and there would be heaven on earth for the saved, the Millennium. Outbreaks of millennarian expectations often brought a desire to purge society of all inequalities, especially among the more radical elements of the Protestant Reformation after 1500.

The discovery by Columbus of naked people in America who owned no property and seemed to live in a paradisiacal state influenced Thomas More in 1516 to write his *Utopia,* which described an island where everyone shared and was equal. A group of Anabaptists led by Thomas Munzer followed the millennarian impulse in the 1525 uprising at Mulhausen where collective sharing was instituted in expectation of the imminence of the End of the World. This was suppressed by the Lutherans.

During the Enlightenment of the 1700s this egalitarian impulse became secular in French philosophy, especially with Jean-Jacques Rousseau, leading up to the French Revolution. Despite emergency economic controls during the dictatorship of the Committee of Public Safety under Robespierre, the French Revolution was predominantly a democratic and procapitalist revolution against the feudal aristocracy. But a radical egalitarian fringe emerged that was suppressed. In 1796, François "Gracchus" Babeuf, often identified as the founder of modern communism,[1] led an unsuccessful revolt by the "Conspiracy of Equals" who called for the abolition of private property and the holding in common of land.

---

[1]The term *communism* initially appeared in France around 1840 among those inspired by Babeuf. Local units of government in France were and are called *communes*. The term *socialism* originated in the early 1830s with the utopian socialist, Robert Owen, the "utopian" label derisively appended by Marx and Engels.

Utopian Socialism

What came to be known as utopian socialism was the first movement to label itself *socialist*. The views of its founders, Henri de Saint-Simon, Charles Fourier, and Robert Owen, were diverse. Indeed the label best applies to the latter two, whereas Saint-Simon is actually the father of command central planning.

The heyday of utopian socialism was the 1830s, but Saint-Simon's ideas first appeared in his 1803 *Letters from an Inhabitant of Geneva to his Contemporaries* and he died in 1825. In his final work, *The Fatal Conceit: The Errors of Socialism,* Hayek fingers Saint-Simon as the ultimate father of the ''fatal conceit,'' which he labels ''constructivism,'' the idea that a rational order of society can be planned and constructed from scratch from the top down. This concept reflects Saint-Simon's background in science and engineering, which led him to support ''social engineering,'' a rational central plan ordering society for the benefit of those least well off.[2]

Also French, Charles Fourier probably came the closest to fitting the label of utopian socialist. In the 1830s he criticized industrialization and urbanization and called for creating small communities of about 1,600 people in rural areas called *phalansteries.* Everyone would share all things, including each other sexually, and would do many different kinds of work. He argued that ''mutual attraction'' was the driving force of the universe and that it could be used to order production and all relations within the phalanstery in which all would live in harmony with each other and with nature.

Fourier made no serious effort to establish phalansteries prior to his death in 1837. But after then various efforts were made, most famously Brook Farm in the United States in the 1850s, organized by New England transcendentalists such as Margaret Fuller and Ralph Waldo Emerson. The most successful such efforts were those founded by religious groups. One such was the Amana Farms of Iowa, now a subsidiary of a major multinational corporation.[3]

The British Robert Owen was the practical utopian who actually carried out his schemes. Coming from a working-class background, Owen became a successful capitalist at an early age. From 1800 to 1824 he owned and managed a successful textile company in New Lanark, Scotland, where he introduced numerous reforms, including higher wages, restrictions on child labor, and education for the workers. Although his fellow capitalists scoffed at his concern for his workers, Owen made money. From 1824 to 1829 he attempted to start a utopian community in New Harmony, Indiana, a project that failed. He became leader of the first national labor union in Britain, the Grand National Consolidated Trades Union, which was suppressed in 1834.

---

[2]Through such followers as Auguste Comte, founder of ''social science'' and ''positivism,'' his influence continues in France today in its indicative planning and technocratic tendencies.

[3]It seems to be the fate of successful utopian communities to be absorbed by the larger economy as the idealistic founding generation dies out and its children desire to become ''just regular folks.'' Something along these lines is apparently happening in many Israeli kibbutzes today.

In the *Communist Manifesto* of 1848, Marx and Engels sneer at these figures, assigning them the epithet *utopian.* They do so on the grounds that the utopian socialists spend most of their time concocting ideal societies and engaging in vague moralizing rather than ''scientifically'' analyzing actual historical dynamics and working to change entire existing societies.

But some utopian ideas crept into the work of Marx and Engels, through them into modern socialism, and beyond into modern societies more generally. One example is the utopian plank in the *Communist Manifesto* calling for the ''gradual abolition of the distinction between town and country.'' This idea has been admired by modern urban planners both socialist and non-socialist. Capitalist-but-planned ''New Towns,'' such as Reston, Virginia, have been founded on its inspiration.

The Marxian[4] World View

Some General Observations.   Karl Marx (1818–1883) was born in Trier in the Rhineland of Germany, studied philosophy and jurisprudence in Berlin in the early 1840s, became a radical journalist who participated in the uprisings of 1848 in the Rhineland, and spent most of the rest of his life in penurious exile in London, financially supported by his collaborator, Friedrich Engels, who owned a textile mill. Together they developed the Marxian world view in writings that profoundly influenced socialist thought.

One reason for Marx's enormous influence is that his world view constitutes a *holistic system*—it seeks to explain virtually everything in a unified whole. This allows it to function as a quasi-religion, with people ''converting'' to it and following it with great intensity. The essence of Marx's holism is that he integrated three major strands of 19th-century European thought: German political philosophy, French political sociology, and British political economy.

The Hegelian Dialectic.   The dominating figure of German philosophy in the first half of the 19th century was Georg W. F. Hegel, the first great intellectual influence on Marx. He developed the idea of the *dialectic,* that all phenomena reflect a conflict between pairs of unified opposites whose mutual opposition evolves over time to critical breakpoints where reality qualitatively changes. These opposites were labeled the *thesis* and its *antithesis.* At the critical breakpoint their opposition generates something brand new, the *synthesis* which in turn can generate its own antithesis.

The ultimate Hegelian thesis is the Universal Idea—God; the antithesis is the individual person. The synthesis is the State, in particular in the context of a disunited Germany, the idea of an emergent powerful and nationalistic

---

[4]The term *Marxian* refers to the actual writings and views of Marx himself whereas the term *Marxist* refers to any view or idea strongly influenced by Marx.

German state. Such ideas became popular as the movement for German unification accelerated towards its culmination under Bismarck in 1871 and were influential in the 20th century in the ultranationalist Nazi movement.

In the 1840s when Marx was studying Hegel in Berlin a major split occurred among Hegel's followers. Hegel declared that ''the real is rational and the rational is real.'' The Old or Right Hegelians emphasized the first part: Existing reality and state structures are rational and therefore should be accepted. The Young or Left Hegelians emphasized the second part: Rational ideals are the ultimate reality and actual reality should be changed to conform to them if it does not, by revolutionary means if necessary. Marx identified with this second group.

Historical Materialism.   A central aspect of Hegel's philosophy was that it was idealistic: Hegel said ultimate reality is spiritual rather than material; God is the Universal Idea driving all history. Many Left Hegelians agreed. But Ludwig Feuerbach challenged Hegel's idealism in his *The Essence of Christianity,* denouncing religion because ruling elites used it to delude and control people. He asserted that reality is ultimately material: ''You are what you eat.'' Marx saw Feuerbach as ''standing Hegel on his head'' and agreed.

Marx ''materialized'' Hegel's dialectic by using the French idea that the French Revolution was a conflict between socioeconomic classes. After a major strike in Lyons in 1831, followers of Babeuf such as Auguste Blanqui and Pierre Proudhon identified the central class conflict of the emerging industrial society to be between *bourgeoisie* (capitalists) and *proletariat* (workers). Here Marx found the key to *historical materialism,* the idea that the driving force of history is the dialectic between conflicting socioeconomic classes.[5] He crystallized the idea in the line that opens the main body of the *Communist Manifesto:* ''The history of all hitherto existing society has been the history of class struggles.''

The basis of class struggle is ownership and control of the means of production: One class controls and thus exploits the other class that does not. The technology of a society (*forces of production*) combines with the structure of classes (*relations of production*) to determine the *mode of production.* This is the substructure or base of a society that determines everything else, the superstructure—that is religion, politics, culture, and so forth.

As the dialectic of class struggle proceeds, the mode of production becomes qualitatively transformed into something different. The mode of production of ancient Greece and Rome was slavery, characterized by the struggle

---

[5]In orthodox Soviet dogma Marx's philosophy was labeled *dialectical materialism,* which implied extending a similar methodology to all of science and culture. Although the idea was broached by Engels after Marx's death, the term itself was never used by either Marx or Engels. It was introduced by Lenin's initial mentor, Georgi Plekhanov, and justified Joseph Stalin's ideological control of cultural and scientific activities, such as his foolish suppression of genetic research.

between master and slave. The fall of the Roman Empire thus arose from this contradiction, and the mode of production was transformed from slavery to feudalism. The latter in turn was driven by the struggle between lord and serf and was transformed into capitalism with its struggle between capitalist and worker.

As this struggle reached an apex in the most advanced capitalist countries such as England and Germany, a revolutionary transformation into socialism would occur. Socialism would be marked by exhibiting state ownership of the means of production, direction of production by a common plan, income inequalities and wage payments, and control by a "dictatorship of the proletariat."[6] Eventually communism would develop in which all classes and property ownership would disappear and the state would wither away.

The Labor Theory of Value and the Breakdown of Capitalism.   After the revolutions of 1848 were crushed, Marx fled to London and immersed himself in studying classical British political economy to understand more fully the dynamics of capitalism. There he found David Ricardo's labor theory of value, which argues that the value of a commodity is determined by the amount of labor-time it takes to produce it. This idea contradicts the neoclassical theory that value is codetermined by supply and demand with capital and land contributing to the supply side of the equation.

Marx saw land and capital as productive but not as contributing to value. Following Ricardo he argued that land rent was due only to differences in the productivity of different land locations and that marginal land earns zero rent, the true "return to pure land." Also following Ricardo he saw capital goods as being the product of past labor, simply "indirect labor." But he went beyond Ricardo in asserting that the true reality of capital is not the capital-good itself but the social relation of exploitation between the capitalist and the worker. This assertion is the core of the Marxian doctrine.

The value of a commodity, W, consists of three components, constant capital, c, variable capital, v, and surplus value, s. The first, c, roughly corresponds to fixed capital stock as measured in labor time required to produce it.

The second, v, represents the value of labor power used in production. Applying the labor theory of value to labor itself, v is the amount of labor time it takes to reproduce labor, equal to a subsistence wage.

The third, s, is Marx's modification of the labor theory of value, *surplus value*, that value created by the worker but taken by the capitalist, leading to *exploitation* and *alienation* at the heart of capitalism. According to Marx it is out of surplus value that the capitalist obtains profit.

$$W = c + v + s. \tag{3.1}$$

---

[6]In numerous places in his writings Marx states support for democracy. Based on his forecast that a majority of the population of advanced capitalist countries would be workers, this dictatorship of the proletariat might be democratic. But there are places in his writings where Marx sneers at "bourgeois freedom and individuality," an attitude emphasized by Lenin in his contempt for democracy.

He then defines the *organic composition of capital* as

$$q = c/(c + v), \qquad (3.2)$$

the *rate of exploitation* as

$$s' = s/v, \qquad (3.3)$$

and the *rate of profit* as

$$p' = s/(c + v). \qquad (3.4)$$

Then he argues that capitalists are inevitably driven to engage in capital investment, thereby raising the organic composition of capital. "Accumulate, accumulate! That is Moses and the prophets!" It is easy to see that if c rises while s and v are constant then the rate of profit will decline, which Marx argues is the fundamental tendency of capitalism.[7]

The dialectic leads capitalists to try to raise the rate of exploitation, s/v, either by lowering wages and thereby immiserating the workers, or by working them longer and harder. These efforts heighten the intensity of the class struggle and produce increasingly severe "commercial crises" in which "One capitalist always kills many." This leads to an increasing concentration of capital in fewer and fewer hands while the proletariat expands and becomes more miserable and more conscious of its condition. Eventually the contradiction between the forces of production and the relations of production becomes so intense that the system is overthrown by the revolutionary working class. In Marx's words:[8]

> Centralization of the means of the production and socialization of labor at last reach a point where they become incompatible with their capitalist integument. The integument is burst asunder. The knell of capitalist private property sounds. The expropriators are expropriated.

Controversies in Socialism up to the Bolshevik Revolution

Orthodoxy and Revisionism.   By the death of Engels in 1895 difficulties had arisen for the Marxists of the German Social Democratic Party. Not only had capitalism not collapsed but also real wages were rising, thus undermining the expectation of the imminent arrival of revolution. The first Marxist to point this out was Eduard Bernstein, in his 1899 book, *Evolutionary Socialism*. He argued that since conditions were improving, a reformist and gradualist approach through parliamentary democracy should be used to achieve gains for

---

[7]Ricardo saw a tendency to a falling rate of profit due to rising population leading to rising food prices with land rent squeezing out profit, a Malthusian scenario.

Among modern Marxists debate focuses on what happens when there is technical change. Some claim to have found empirical evidence of a tendency to a falling rate of profit in the U.S. economy (Fred Moseley, *The Falling Rate of Profit in the Postwar US Economy* [New York: Macmillan, 1991]).

[8]Karl Marx, *Capital,* vol. 1, (Hamburg: Verlag von Otto Meissner, 1867) chap. 32.

Box 3–1

Marxism as a Quasi-Religion

Bertrand Russell made a comparison between the Marxist system and Christianity that illuminates how Marxism came to acquire a quasi-religious status among many of its adherents. Russell's comparison illustrates the equivalence of concepts as follows:

Yahweh (God) = Dialectical Materialism

Messiah = Karl Marx

The Second Coming = The Revolution

The Saved = The Proletariat

The Church = The Communist Party

Damnation to Hell = The Expropriation of the Capitalists

The Millennium = The Socialist Commonwealth.

---

the working class. This eventually became the policy of the German Social Democratic Party that exists today, and more generally of modern Western European social democracy.

This view was labeled *revisionism.*[9] Bernstein's arguments provoked a counterattack by the orthodox Marxist, Karl Kautsky, who argued that commercial crises were becoming ever more severe and that eventually there would be a chronic depression. But Kautsky, as a leader of the German Social Democratic Party, practiced revisionism as a policy while waiting for the expected revolutionary upheaval. When the Bolsheviks seized power in Russia, Kautsky criticized them and openly supported revisionism. Besides influencing social democracy, revisionism influenced market socialist reformers later in Eastern Europe.

The Theory of Imperialism and Marxism-Leninism.   Another explanation for the failure of capitalism to collapse, proposed in 1902 by John Hobson, was the theory of imperialism. The advanced capitalist countries had relieved their internal contradictions by engaging in the conquest of less-developed countries, especially in the "scramble for Africa" by the major European powers in the late 19th century. There they could create captive markets and supply themselves inexpensively with raw materials. This theory gained followers among the left wing of the German Social Democrats led by Rosa Luxemburg and the Bolsheviks in Russia led by Lenin. Supporters of this view

---

[9]*Revisionism* entered standard Marxist lexicon as a term of opprobrium. Thus after Nikita Khrushchev denounced Joseph Stalin in 1956, defenders of Stalinist orthodoxy such as Mao Ze-dong in China denounced Khrushchev for revisionism.

opposed entry by their countries into World War I. But Luxemburg supported democracy whereas Lenin did not.

Vladimir Illich Ulyanov, known as Lenin, further developed the imperialism thesis in his 1916 *Imperialism: The Highest Stage of Capitalism,* written during World War I, which prepared the stage for withdrawing Russia from the anti-German war effort after his seizure of power in 1917.[10] He saw Marx's increasing concentration of capital dominated by bankers who paid off the "labor aristocracy" of workers in the advanced capitalist countries with surplus value exploited from the colonialized periphery. Revolution would come in capitalism's "weakest link," which he saw as Russia since it had industrialized too late to participate in the carving up of Africa and was dominated by foreign investment from the leading capitalist powers.

Refocusing revolutionary expectations upon less developed countries became *Marxism-Leninism,* official Soviet doctrine after 1917 and guide of Marxist revolutions in the 20th century in less developed countries from China to Cuba to Vietnam. Marxism-Leninism included the idea that the dictatorship of the proletariat would be led by a vanguard elite within the revolutionary party, since the workers left to themselves would follow "opportunistic" (revisionist) paths. Lenin originally enunciated this idea in his 1902 work, *What is to be Done?.*[11] This view was adopted by the *Bolsheviks* (majority) of the Russian Social Democratic Labor Party in 1903 against the prodemocratic *Mensheviks* (minority).

In August and September 1917, during the brief rule of the post-tsarist Provisional Government led by Alexander Kerensky, Lenin authored his influential *The State and Revolution.* Following the views of Marx and Engels regarding the failed Paris Commune uprising of 1871, he argued that the idea of the "withering away of the state" implied an initial smashing of former state power and then establishment of a state ruled by the vanguard of the proletariat that would crush the remnants of the former ruling class. Only after this was accomplished would the state wither away. This argument provided solid grist for the later assertion of state power in purging political opponents and imposing a strong command economy by Joseph Stalin.

Anarchism and Syndicalism.   Yet another strand of radical thought and activity during this period was that of anarchism and its close relative, syndicalism, both of which argued that the state should be abolished outright. In the case of the anarchists this idea often led to conspiratorial violence directed

---

[10]Lenin spent most of the war years in Zurich, Switzerland. Aware of his views, the German government transported him in a sealed train to Russia after the fall of Tsar Nicholas II in early 1917, hoping he would take power and withdraw Russia from the war. Their hopes were rewarded.

[11]This title was identical to that of an earlier book by the populist (Narodnik) Tchernishevsky who saw the possibility of a Russian revolution based on the communal traditions of the rural peasantry. In a parliamentary election held in December 1917, immediately after the Bolshevik takeover, the party winning the most votes and seats was the pro-Narodnik Social Revolutionary Party. Lenin responded by abolishing the parliament (Duma) and later outlawing all parties except the Communist Party.

at assassinating heads of state. Successful efforts included the 1881 assassination of the "liberal tsar," Alexander II, who emancipated the Russian serfs, and the assassination of U.S. President William McKinley in 1901.[12] Such a philosophy fundamentally disagrees with standard socialism, which supports ownership and control of the means of production by the state.

Anarchism was founded in 1793 by William Godwin of Britain, whose wife, Mary Wollstonecraft, is regarded as the founder of feminism. Influenced by Rousseau, Godwin argued that without government people will peacefully organize themselves into a harmonious and nonoppressive order. This view has links both with utopian socialism and with modern libertarianism.

In 1840 Proudhon linked anarchism with communism and the revolutionary working-class movement in his *What is Property?* (Proudhon's blunt answer: "Property is theft!"). In the 1860s he became the spiritual father of the French trade union movement, which was anarchist for a long time. Marx viewed this position as fuzzy-minded and unscientific.

Marxism and anarchism competed in the 1860s after Marx founded the First International. His main rival was the Russian anarchist, Prince Mikhail Bakunin, who supported conspiratorial and violent revolution and ridiculed Marx for his "statist" tendencies. Bakunin had strong support among the workers' movements in Spain, Italy, Switzerland, and France and in 1872 appeared on the verge of taking control of the First International, leading Marx to dissolve the organization.

In the 1890s proanarchist trade unions in the above countries argued that after the state is abolished, society should be run by the trade unions themselves, and production should be controlled directly by the workers in the production site. This philosophy is *syndicalism.*

In Russia syndicalist influence showed up in the Bolshevik revolutionary slogan, "All power to the Soviets!" which in 1917 were workplace advisory bodies based on local unions supporting the Bolsheviks.[13] In 1921 Lenin crushed a syndicalist uprising at the Kronstadt shipyard near Petrograd,[14] thereby asserting the supremacy of state power in the new regime.

Although anarcho-syndicalism faded after the 1930s it continues to have an important influence on modern thought through the ideas of workers' management and workers' ownership as well as in some environmentalist movements. Anarchism also continues as a right-wing movement in the form of radical individualistic libertarianism.

---

[12]Not all anarchists supported violence as is shown by the example of Russian Prince Peter Kropotkin whose ideas were similar to those of the utopian socialists.

[13]The Russian word *soviet* comes from the verb meaning *to advise.* Until very recently a soviet was a local unit of government. Mossoviet was the city government of Moscow.

[14]From 1703 to 1914 and since 1991 this city has been named Saint Petersburg. It was Petrograd from 1914 to 1924 and Leningrad from 1924 to 1991.

Some Divisions of Socialism Since 1917

General Remarks.   The taking of power by the Bolsheviks in Russia in 1917 transformed Marxist and socialist ideology. Henceforth all movements had to define themselves in relation to the Marxist-Leninist movement emanating from Moscow.

Thus most newer movements developed out of splits within the world movement that had its main base initially in the Communist Party of the Soviet Union (CPSU). Each of these movements sought to distinguish itself from Soviet orthodoxy. We discuss three of these movements.

Trotskyism.   Leon Trotsky, a former Menshevik and founder of the Red Army in the Soviet Union, was Joseph Stalin's chief rival for power after Lenin's death in the 1920s. Exiled in 1927, Trotsky founded the Fourth International, which fragmented into factions after his assassination by a Stalinist agent in 1940 in Cuernavaca, Mexico.

He and Stalin agreed about the need for rapid industrialization. But they disagreed about whether this should be done in isolation or in an international context. Trotsky supported the idea of a ''permanent'' international revolution, that true socialism could not be achieved in the USSR without an international revolution. He criticized Stalin for his dictatorial and bureaucratic tendencies.

Trotskyites have never achieved power anywhere, perhaps because this is a movement that tends to appeal mostly to intellectuals. Modern Trotskyites, such as the Belgian economist Ernest Mandel,[15] argue that the class struggle is an international phenomenon that has spread to include white collar workers as well as the industrial blue collar working class. Trotskyite views have been influential with the New Left in Western Europe and the United States.

Titoism.   Titoism developed as a practice before it became an ideology. Josip Broz, known as Marshall Tito, led communist partisans in throwing the Nazis out of Yugoslavia during World War II with little assistance from the Soviet Red Army.

Initially a strong Stalinist, Tito broke with Stalin in 1948 and declared the political independence of Yugoslavia from Soviet influence. This break led to an effort to develop a distinctive economic system for Yugoslavia that would reinforce the separate path Tito had chosen. The system adopted was worker-managed market socialism, described by some as ''quasi-syndicalist.'' In Tito's Yugoslavia it consisted of state-owned enterprises in a one-party state, operating with little central planning according to market forces, and with managements appointed by worker-selected boards.

After Tito's death in 1981, the system deteriorated in Yugoslavia, eventually culminating in the complete disintegration of the country, to be

---

[15]Ernest Mandel, *Marxist Economic Theory* (New York: Monthly Review Press, 1969).

discussed in more detail in Chapter 14. Ideas similar to Titoism continue to be influential, even in capitalist economies, with the major differences that current versions advocate workers' ownership rather than state ownership and multiparty democracy rather than a one-party state.

Maoism.   In 1949 a Communist insurgency led by Mao Ze-dong took power in mainland China. The Maoist road to power was characterized by reliance on a rural guerrilla movement encouraging egalitarian economic development in zones of revolutionary control.

Immediately after 1949 China was quite friendly with the USSR and imitated the centrally planned command industrialization model of Stalin's USSR. However, China placed more emphasis upon rural agricultural development, egalitarianism, and the use of "moral incentives." After the 1956 denunciation of Stalin by Khrushchev in the USSR, Mao defended Stalin against the "revisionism" of Khrushchev. But in the Great Leap Forward of 1957–1959 and again in the Great Proletarian Cultural Revolution at its height from 1966 to 1969, Mao emphasized decentralization of industry to the countryside, complete communalization of agriculture, total egalitarianism and moral incentives, and complete obliteration of all vestiges of previous culture, as discussed in more detail in Chapter 15.

This rival to the Soviet approach generated many subsidiary movements around the world.[16] In many Third World countries powerful rural guerrilla movements opposed both capitalism and Soviet-supported leftist groups, notably in Angola, Cambodia, and Peru.

Two years after Mao's death in 1976, his philosophy was repudiated in China as discussed in Chapter 15. A decline of support for Maoism followed among its movements, although many of these continue following the rural guerrilla strategy recommended by Mao.

In Cambodia the officially Maoist Khmer Rouge ruled from 1975 to 1979 under the brutal Pol Pot. Cities were emptied and mass slaughter of anyone educated or connected with the former regime was carried out, a plan more of urban destruction than of rural development. In 1979 the Soviet-backed Vietnamese successfully invaded and installed a puppet regime. The Khmer Rouge retreated to the countryside to fight, backed for a long time by the Chinese. Like the Chinese, the Khmer Rouge are no longer officially Maoist, but most observers fear that their basic policy orientation has not changed and they still fight.

---

[16]One government siding with China was Albania in 1961 under Enver Hoxha. After China's opening to the United States and its shift away from Maoism under Deng Xiaoping, Albania went into a Stalinist isolationism against the "imperialism" of the United States, the "social hegemonism" of the USSR, and the "revisionism" of China. In 1990 communism collapsed in Albania, the poorest nation in Europe.

Box 3–2

A New Type of Marxism?

The purest active Maoist group, and arguably the latest development in Marxist ideology, is the Communist Party of Peru, known as *Sendero Luminoso* (Shining Path) since becoming an active guerrilla movement in 1980. In 1964 the party split between a pro-Soviet and a pro-Chinese faction. The latter has been led by a former philosophy professor named Abimael Guzman, known as Chairman Gonzalo. After spending time in China, he led the party to declare itself in 1969 to be a ''Marxist-Leninist-Maoist party of a new type.'' His followers proclaim him to represent the ''fourth stage'' of Marxism, ''Marxist-Leninist-Maoist-Gonzalo'' thought.

After 1980 Sendero Luminoso gained control of much of Peru, drawing on a base among poverty-stricken Quechua and Aymara–speaking Indians in the Andes mountains, descendants of the proud but humbled Inca Empire. In 1992 Gonzalo was arrested, but his movement continues although considerably weakened, with him now an imprisoned martyr. His thought is shown by the following quotation:

> If you're talking about exploitation and oppression, you're talking about the state; if you're talking about the state, you're talking about classes; if you're talking about classes you're talking about class struggle; if you're talking about class struggle, you're talking about mass struggle; and, as time has shown over and over again, if you're talking about mass struggle you're talking about rebellion, armed struggle, guerrilla warfare—as our own situation proves today. Our people, like all the peoples of the world, have their own proud history of struggle etched in their blood and heroism.[17]

The Theory of Economic Socialism

The Socialist Planning Controversy

Pre-1917 discussions of the functioning of socialism tended to be either vague or unrealistic.[18] Lenin in *The State and Revolution* naively suggests that all society would need would be ''the functions of 'foremen and accountants,' functions which are already fully within the ability of the average town dweller and can well be performed for 'workman's wages.' '' Thus the first serious analysis of socialist planning followed neoclassical theory rather than Marxist theory.

---

[17]Central Committee of the Communist Party of Peru, ''Develop Guerilla Warfare,'' English translation (Berkeley: Committee to Support the Revolution in Peru, 1985), p. 17.

[18]Marx and Engels avoided such discussions because they did not want to be ''utopian.''

The socialist planning controversy began in 1908 with Enrico Barone's "The Ministry of Production in the Collectivist State."[19] He applies Pareto's efficiency analysis to the Walrasian general equilibrium model, positing a system with no money in which the state determines "equivalences" (relative prices) between goods and distributes them through state stores in exchange for goods brought by people. The Ministry of Production would have to know all costs of production, all demand functions, and all capital stocks. From this a general equilibrium could be solved for a "collective maximum" that would correspond to an efficient competitive equilibrium in that cost of production would be minimized and price would equal the cost of production.

Barone foresaw most of the points elaborated by participants in the later controversy. He recognized that actually solving the planning equilibrium would be very difficult: "But it is frankly *inconceivable* that the *economic* determination of the technical coefficients [prices] can be made a priori." Anticipating the arguments of later authors he proposed this determination be carried out "in an *experimental* way," that is, by varying prices and seeing what happens in the markets. He anticipated critics by noting the bureaucratic implications: "Account must be taken of the necessary remuneration of the army of officials whose services would be devoted not to production but to the laborious and colossal centralization work of the Ministry (assuming the practical possibility of such a system)."

In 1922 Ludwig von Mises critiqued the practicality of this proposal in his "Economic Calculation in Socialism."[20] Money is necessary to calculate prices.[21] The "artificial market" of the experimenting socialist central planner can never generate "rational" prices because of insufficient incentives. The profit motive based on the private ownership of capital is the fundamental driving force in this Austrian view. Von Mises said, "It is only the prospect of profit that directs production into those channels in which the demands of the consumer are best satisfied at the least cost. If the prospect of profit disappears, the mechanism of the market loses its mainspring."

Two responses to this argument emerged. One followed Barone by proposing a form of market socialism with some planning. The other arose in the Soviet Union during the debates over command versus market in the mid-to-late 1920s and denied the relevance of the static efficiency criterion. It criticized market socialism as well as market capitalism.

---

[19]English translation in F. A. Hayek, ed., *Collectivist Economic Planning* (London: Routledge & Kegan Paul, 1935), pp. 247–90. Original version was in Italian.

[20]See Ludwig von Mises, "Economic Calculation in Socialism," in *Comparative Economic Systems: Models and Cases,* 7th ed., Morris Bornstein, ed. (Homewood, IL: Irwin, 1994), pp. 273–79. Original version was in German.

[21]At the time von Mises wrote, the new Soviet regime was allowing money to disappear through hyperinflation. But after a short time it reintroduced money and never again seriously discussed its abolition.

In 1936 Oskar Lange defended market socialism in "On the Economic Theory of Socialism."[22] He proposed a Central Planning Board (CPB) that sets producer goods prices, determines the level of overall investment, and distributes the "social dividend." Consumer goods prices are set by free market forces and supply comes from state-owned firms that set price equal to marginal cost as in perfectly competitive markets. Setting of producer goods prices proceeds along the trial-and-error lines proposed by Barone.

Lange runs through the list of sources of "market failure" discussed in the previous chapter and argues that in all cases this system resolves the problem and leads to an efficient outcome that is equitable and macroeconomically stable. Monopolists are eliminated so competitive prices are set. Planners account for externalities. Public goods are adequately supplied. Distribution of the "social dividend" ensures reasonable income equality. Central control of investment eliminates macroeconomic fluctuations.

A follower of von Mises, Hayek, counterattacked in 1940.[23] He argued that Lange fails to answer von Mises' argument regarding motivation; without private ownership and the profit motive firm managers will lack the incentive to search out minimum cost or fulfill consumer demand. Secondly he echoed Barone in noting the extreme difficulty in gathering information to carry out the necessary calculations. The decentralized capitalist market is the best information transmission system available. Also because there are no entrepreneurs in such a system technological stagnation results.

In a further twist the Hungarian economist János Kornai argues that the decentralized market socialism in Hungary after the introduction of the post-1968 New Economic Mechanism (NEM) led to state-owned firms operating under a *soft budget constraint* because the government does not want to shut them down.[24] The managers of the firms know they do not have to be efficient; if they lose money they will get bailed out. In principle governments can impose hard budget constraints on firms they own, but such cases seem to be rare.[25]

One response to Kornai's critique is an economy exactly like the one in the United States but with ownership by a "Bureau of Public Ownership" that enforces hard budget constraints and distributes profits as a "social dividend" as a proportion of wages, "pragmatic market socialism."[26] Another involves imitating the Japanese *keiretsu* system, in which groups of

---

[22]See Morris Bornstein, *Comparative Economic Systems,* pp. 280–88.

[23]Friedrich A. Hayek, "Socialist Calculation: The 'Competitive' Solution," *Economica* (May 1940), pp. 130–31.

[24]See János Kornai, *The Economics of Shortage* (Amsterdam: North-Holland, 1980).

[25]One exception has been the Renault automobile company of France. It was "hostilely" nationalized after World War II because its owner had been a Nazi collaborator. The French government did not wish to do the company any favors and for long treated it harshly, imposing a hard budget constraint on it. It is now being privatized gradually.

[26]See James A. Yunker, *Socialism Revised and Modernized: The Case for Pragmatic Market Socialism* (New York: Praeger, 1992).

corporations are centered on major banks that own large amounts of the industries' stock and monitor their performance, imposing hard budget constraints, but with the banks state owned and the social dividend distributed by democratic political processes.[27]

Yet another possibility is the *socialist market economy* of China with its rapidly expanding *town and village enterprises* (TVEs). TVEs operate vigorously in free markets with hard budget constraints, but they are owned by local units of government.

The command planning critique came from E.V. Preobrazhensky in 1926 in the USSR and from Maurice Dobb in 1939 in Britain. Preobrazhensky argued for maximizing capital accumulation in the mixed market socialist economy of the New Economic Policy (NEP) of the USSR in the mid-1920's. He argues for command central planning to extract resources from the economy to engage in rapid capital accumulation to maximize the rate of industrial growth, the policy adopted by Stalin in 1928.

Dobb critiqued Lange by noting that the CPB fixes investment by fixing interest rates, which will be insufficient to guarantee stable investment if output prices can vary. Command planning not only can stabilize investment but also raise it to a higher level, thus ensuring a higher rate of economic growth. Dobb argues that this higher rate of growth more than offsets any microeconomic inefficiencies that might arise, although the long-run performance of the Soviet economy belies his argument.

The Theory of Command Socialist Central Planning

Practice preceded theory in the development of command socialist central planning. Central planning first appeared in Soviet Russia with the 1920 electrification plan (Lenin sloganeered that, ''Communism equals authority of the Soviets plus electrification.''). With the de facto market socialist NEP in 1921, indicative planning under state ownership was instituted for several heavy industrial sectors, such as electricity, steel, and cement. Planning was carried out using the *material balance method,* which became the main planning method used by the Soviet central planning authority, Gosplan, after the introduction of comprehensive command planning in 1928.

Discussed in Chapter 10, the basic outline of Soviet central planning is as follows. Long-term planning was on a five-year time horizon. Five-year plans were broken down into one-year plans from which monthly quotas for individual firms were derived. Each firm had a *techpromfinplan,* or ''technical-production-financial plan.'' It specified output quantities and prices, input quantities and prices, including wages, and levels and kinds of capital investment for the firm, presumably consistent with those for other firms.

---

[27]See Pranab Bardhan and John E. Roemer, ''Market Socialism: The Case for Rejuvenation.'' *Journal of Economic Perspectives* 6 (1992), pp. 101–16.

In practice one year's overall plan generally involved minor modifications of the previous year's plan, based on the outcome of that plan.[28] For the first five-year plan the material balances were drawn up based on the inherited structure of production.

Determining the first five-year plan involved figuring out how much of which final goods were to be produced. Then the amounts of all the inputs required to produce those outputs were estimated and the inputs to produce those inputs and so forth. If production of more tanks is desired more steel is required, which requires more coal and more iron ore as well as more steel to produce the machinery used in mining coal and iron ore and so forth. Sources of inputs can be production, imports, or previously existing stocks.

If a commodity is in "deficit," then either production can be increased, imports can be increased, stocks can be drawn down, or greater efficiency in production must be induced, or demand must be cut back. Ultimately material inputs must be in balance to produce the planned outputs. If the plan represents a set of demands, then material balance implies that supply equals demand in all sectors; the plan should be a general equilibrium.

In the 1930s mathematical approaches to implementing planning began to be promulgated although never used in Soviet central planning. These approaches were developed outside the USSR or their creators didn't promote them because of a Stalinist ideological campaign against "bourgeois mathematical formalism" in economics that was not ended until Khrushchev's de-Stalinization speech in 1956.

The first of these mathematical approaches was *input-output analysis,* developed by Wassily Leontief, who had studied at Leningrad University in the 1920s but had subsequently emigrated to the United States. Input-output analysis is a precise analogue of the material balance method. It depicts the production structure of an economy using a rectangular input-output matrix, whose rows represent inputs and whose columns represent outputs. Some inputs may be primary in that they are not outputs, some outputs may be final in that they are not inputs, and other goods are intermediate being both inputs and outputs, such as steel. An entry in the *i* row and the *j* column depicts how much of *i* is being directly used to produce *j*. Such a matrix is shown in Table 3–1, with the entries representing physically defined flows per common unit of time. Coal, steel, and corn are intermediate goods; labor, capital, and imports are primary goods; and consumption, investment, and exports are final goods.

This can be transformed into a technical matrix, *A,* where each entry tells how much of the *i*th input is required to produce *one unit* of the *j*th output.

---

[28]This leads to the perverse incentive known as the "ratchet effect" whereby firms do not wish to exceed their production quotas because then next year's quota will be raised more. Also firms tend to hoard inputs "for a rainy day," and "storming" occurs, that is, a mad dash to meet the quota at the end of the month as inputs become available, often requiring the services of a "fixer" who purchases them on the black market. Such people have often become entrepreneurs in the transitional market economies.

TABLE 3–1

	Coal	Steel	Corn	Consumption	Investment	Exports
Coal	3	50	1	10	12	8
Steel	10	15	8	0	25	12
Corn	0	0	5	20	45	0
Labor	50	150	85	1150	375	185
Capital	12	45	18	120	60	38
Imports	0	0	11	55	24	6

Letting C be final goods outputs, and X be all outputs, then a materially balanced economy will exhibit

$$AX + C = X. \tag{3.5}$$

AX is simply the intermediate goods used up in producing themselves as well as the final goods, C.

   If C is what is set by the planner then the required levels of all outputs, X, can be determined by a simple rearranging of this equation to obtain

$$X = (I - A)^{-1} C, \tag{3.6}$$

where I is a square matrix with ones on the diagonal and zeros everywhere else. This simple equation tells us that the required levels of outputs are the desired final goods levels, C, plus all the intermediate goods directly required to produce them, both directly and indirectly.

   Solving this problem requires solving a polynomial equation of order equal to the dimension of the A matrix, suggesting a trade-off between detail and solvability. The more detailed, the more useful; but computability is more difficult and gathering accurate data is even more difficult. Soviet economists estimated input-output matrices, but they *never* succeeded in estimating one at a level of detail sufficient to match the level of detail at which planning was actually carried out, perhaps indicating the seriousness of Hayekian information problems.

   Further limitations of this technique are that it assumes constant returns to scale, no technical change, and no substitutability between factors of production. These are all necessary to ensure constancy of the technical coefficients in the A matrix. Thus this method is most applicable at points in time rather than over time. However it brings out the reality of "everything being connected to everything else." Thus it has been used for studying ecological-economic systems.[29]

---

[29]See Walter Isard, *Ecologic-Economic Analysis for Regional Development* (Glencoe: Free Press, 1971).

Optimization can be achieved by using a generalized version of input-output analysis known as *linear programming,* presuming the planner can establish some kind of value weighting of the final desired goods so that they can be added up in a planner's objective function.

The only Soviet economist to win the Nobel Prize in economics, Leonid V. Kantorovich, discovered linear programming. A professional mathematician and engineer, he was approached in 1939 by the Central Plywood Institute to figure out how to match cutting machines and logs in plywood factories. He discovered linear programming as a result but made little of it at first given Stalin's "anti-formalism" campaign, only arguing its full implications for planning in 1959.

Kantorovich was careful to couch his formulation as consistent with the labor theory of value, since labor can be viewed as the only primary input with all outputs being produced by direct and indirect amounts of it in such a system. But an obvious interpretation of linear programming suggests the neoclassical model in which the value of a primary input depends on its marginal productivity and on its scarcity, not on how much direct and indirect labor it took to produce it.

Let V be the planner's objective function (interpretable as aggregate net social value), X be the outputs, P be the weights for the goods (prices), A be the technical input-output matrix of the economy, and B be the primary inputs that are fixed in supply thus serving as constraints upon the economy. Then the *primal* linear programming problem is to maximize

$$V = PX, \qquad (3.6)$$

subject to

$$AX < B, X > 0, \text{ and } B > 0. \qquad (3.8)$$

The solution will consist of a set of levels of outputs.[30]

Ideologically interesting is that the solution will also generate W values associated with each of the constraint variables, indicating the significance of each constraint for the solution. For a given constraint, b, its w indicates the increase in the value of the objective function for an increase in b, in short its marginal productivity. These ws are known as *shadow prices* and the mathematical planners argue that they represent the optimal prices for the primary inputs. For such inputs as land and capital this is tantamount to imputing value based on scarcity and marginal productivity to these factors and thus denying the labor theory of value, unless price and value can differ.

Linear programming, along with nonlinear and dynamic programming, is a common tool used by individual firms and government agencies in market capitalist economies. It also enjoyed some usage at firm levels in some socialist

---

[30]There is also a *dual* problem of cost minimization with a solution consisting of the levels of the primary inputs in the primal problem and the original set of output prices as shadow prices.

economies. But it has never been operationally used for overall central planning in any command socialist economy. Probably the closest any economy-wide planners have come to using it has been in the indicative planning exercises carried out in France.

The Participatory or Cooperative Alternative

Finally we consider the theory of the participatory or cooperative economy, also known as the *labor-managed economy*. Because of the example of Yugoslavia, to be discussed in Chapter 14, most of this discussion has dealt with a market socialist context where the state owns the means of production. But such an economy may be characterized by workers' ownership as well as workers' management. Some of the criticisms of a labor-managed economy might be alleviated under this combination of workers' ownership and management.

The fundamental argument in favor of this combined form is that it may eliminate worker alienation and the struggle between labor and management, thereby increasing worker motivation and productivity. It also may provide a fairer distribution of income. When Tito first introduced this system into Yugoslavia it was argued that it represented the true culmination of Marx's historical dialectic.

Jaroslav Vanek proposes five characteristics distinguishing the participatory economy:[31]

1. Workers will manage the firms. In practice this has usually involved management by professional managers hired by worker-controlled boards.

2. There will be income sharing, often thought by many theorists to be the same as wages equaling the average product of labor, although Vanek argues that it means a "democratic" determination of remuneration levels for specific types of jobs. In practice such firms generally exhibit internal variations in wages.

3. Productive resources are not owned by the workers and therefore must be paid for by rentals, although workers enjoy *usufruct* rights to the fruits of the operation. Firms following one of the capitalist variants of this form do not obey this aspect, as they may own the productive resources.

4. It will be a market economy. Any central planning will be strictly of the indicative rather than of the command sort.

5. Workers can freely choose where to work.

In short the labor-managed market socialist economy supposedly combines the best aspects of capitalism and socialism, constituting a virtuous "third way" between the two. Market efficiency abounds, but the alienating class struggle of standard capitalism is eliminated. Supporters of the capitalist

---

[31]See Jaroslav Vanek, *The Participatory Economy* (Ithaca: Cornell University Press, 1971).

FIGURE 3–1   Labor Supply in Cooperative and Competitive Firms

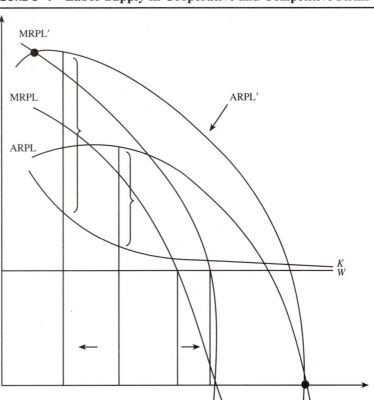

workers' ownership type argue that in their version there will be no Kornai-type soft budget constraint as there might be in the socialist version. Worker-owners will be responsible and efficient worker-managers.

Criticism of this vision originally came from Benjamin Ward[32] who argues that in cooperatively managed firms there will be a tendency for less labor to be hired as workers strive to maximize net income per head of existing workers. This tendency can result in a backward-bending supply curve by the firm when a standard market capitalist firm would have an upward sloping supply curve. Rather than encouraging efficiency, workers' management may do just the opposite.

Figure 3–1 depicts how the case described above can occur in both the socialist and capitalist versions of the cooperative economy. The cooperative firm maximizes net residual income per worker, which equals the average revenue product of labor (ARPL) minus the wage (W) and the capital cost per worker (K), the latter a declining function of the quantity of labor (L). ARPL

---

[32]Benjamin Ward, "The Firm in Illyria," *American Economic Review* 48 (1958), pp. 566–89.

= *PQ/L*, price times output per worker. The standard competitive market capitalist firm hires labor to the point where the marginal revenue product of labor (MRPL) equals the wage, *W*. MRPL equals the price of output times the marginal physical product of labor, which in turn is the addition to output of an additional unit of labor.

Lc is the competitive market capitalist quantity of labor hired where *w* = MRPL. *Lw* is the worker-managed quantity of labor hired where the gap between ARPL and *K* is at its greatest. Ward argues that *Lw* < *Lc*.

Figure 3–1 also shows the backward-bending supply curve case. An increase in *P* results in upward shifts of MRPL and ARPL respectively to MRPL' and ARPL'. This does not shift the locations of either of their respective intersections with the horizontal axis. For the competitive firm its new *Lc'* will be greater than the original *Lc*. But this is not necessarily so for the cooperative economy. As ARPL' becomes steeper with its upward shift the point where the gap between it and *K* is at a maximum may *shift to the left* thereby resulting in a *Lw'* that is *lower* than in the original case. Thus an increase in the price of output might lead to a reduction of employment and output.

Other criticisms include that worker-managed firms may tend to monopolization and may disregard externalities like pollution. Rather than getting the best of both worlds, the cooperative economy may actually combine the worst resulting in a stagflationary economy as happened in Yugoslavia in the 1980s.

A final critique is that such an economy may underinvest in capital in the long run because workers will drain firms of extra income in the short run, especially in the socialist version where workers' lack of property rights in firm assets reduces their incentive for supporting long horizon investment. Workers will take funds out and put them in savings accounts to earn interest.[33]

Vanek responds to Ward's argument and also the monopolization argument by suggesting that entry by new firms will solve these problems. In Yugoslavia such free entry was discouraged, although there has never been any evidence of backward-bending supply curves there despite apparently very low labor mobility. Vanek argues that workers will not want to pollute their own work or living places[34] and will recognize in a competitive environment that their own jobs ultimately depend on the firm making timely and productive investments.

---

[33]See Erik Furobotn and Svetozar Pejovich, ''Property Rights, Economic Decentralization and the Evolution of the Yugoslav Firm, 1965–72.'' *Journal of Law and Economics* 16 (1973), pp. 275–302.

[34]If pollution is truly external, the workers may not care. Table 2–2 shows Yugoslavia to have had a better environmental record than most of its command or capitalist peers.

Despite the collapse of Yugoslavia, the capitalist version of the cooperative economy seems to be enjoying renewed attention. Its form ranges from straight workers' ownership in cooperatives, through employee stock ownership plans (ESOPs) in which workers' ownership operates through a trust fund usually based on pension benefits, to the weakest version involving merely profit sharing. Successful examples of each in the United States include plywood producers in the Northwest for cooperatives, the Weirton Steel Company of West Virginia for ESOPs, and Delta Airlines for profit-sharing. Cooperatives and ESOPs sometimes arise when a plant is threatened with closure and the workers buy it out, although between 1974 and 1986 ESOPs enjoyed special tax breaks and some were formed to allow previous owners to escape pension liabilities while getting the tax break.[35]

Craig and Pencavel[36] compare the Northwest Pacific plywood cooperatives with conventional plywood producers to examine the debate over the cooperative economy. In the cooperatives employment tends to be more stable as workers adjust to demand shocks by adjusting wages, an argument with macroeconomic implications as argued by Weitzman in his *The Share Economy*. Supply elasticity is less than for conventional firms but there are no backward-bending supply curves. They exhibit high productivity and profitability, at least partly through the need for fewer foremen and supervisors as the workers "monitor each other." However they exhibit lower share prices relative to earnings, making it hard for them to raise capital and thus raising the long-run growth issue.[37] Craig and Pencavel hypothesize that this is due to the workers' bearing of extra risk to their wage income.

Thus the future of workable socialist forms that fulfill the goals of Karl Marx may be found in models emerging out of existing market capitalist economies in the form of worker-owned cooperatives. The ideological appeal of such a solution plays a role in the strong support for such ownership in the privatization programs in much of the former Soviet bloc.

Summary and Conclusions

From socialism's origins in ancient religious and philosophical ideas, it emerged in the Renaissance in Europe as a millennarian movement and

---

[35]The first U.S. ESOP founded under the 1974 tax law was ComSonics, an electronics firm in Harrisonburg, Virginia, begun by Warren L. Braun. A cofounder of the U.S. ESOP Association, Braun has since been involved in the establishment of groups advocating the "ESOPization" of the former Soviet economy.

[36]Ben Craig and John Pencavel, "The Behavior of Worker Cooperatives: The Plywood Companies of the Pacific Northwest," *American Economic Review* 82 (1992), pp. 1083–1105.

[37]Some of the most successful have been bought out by large conventional firms like Georgia-Pacific. In some cases the result has been increased hiring of supervisors.

became secularized as class struggle in the French Revolution. The 19th century utopian socialists constructed scenarios for ideal societies.

Karl Marx codified a holistic socialist viewpoint by combining German dialectical philosophy with French political polemics on class struggle and the British labor theory of value to provide a vision of historical motion. He foresaw the development and eventual collapse of market capitalism from its internal class contradictions and its replacement by socialism and eventually communism.

The failure of capitalism to collapse by the end of the 19th century led to divisions within the socialist movement: Revisionists advocated gradualistic reforms, Lenin explained the noncollapse of capitalism by the emergence of imperialism, and the anarcho-syndicalists called for the abolition of all states. Lenin called for revolutionary upheaval in poorer countries and he led a socialist revolution in Russia.

More recent socialist developments include Trotskyism, which developed in the USSR out of the power struggle after Lenin's death; Titoism, which developed in Yugoslavia after World War II and promulgates a worker-managed market socialism; Maoism in China, which advocates rural-based guerrilla movements and radical egalitarianism.

The theory of socialist planning derives initially from neoclassical origins in the form of Barone's work based on the general equilibrium model of Walras and the efficiency analysis of Pareto. The Austrians, von Mises and Hayek, deny the feasibility of planning on the grounds of incentive problems in the absence of the private ownership of capital and the accompanying profit motive as well as inevitable information difficulties for the central planning bureaucracy. Kornai emphasizes that the soft budget constraint arising from a government's unwillingness to shut down firms it owns removes any incentive for efficiency by state-owned firms, even in a market socialist context.

Lange responds by proposing a market-oriented socialist planning that uses trial-and-error techniques to find equilibrium prices. Such a scheme would cure the inefficiencies, inequities, and instabilities of market capitalism. This position is criticized by advocates of command central planning such as Dobb who argue that only it can stabilize the economy and provide a high rate of investment and growth. High growth renders efficiency issues irrelevant. This was the path taken by the USSR under Stalin—growth eventually bogged down under technological stagnation.

As Soviet central planners developed the material balance method in practice, theories of planning developed. Leontief developed input-output analysis, which depicts the material balance problem in a mathematical model. Kantorovich developed linear programming, which allows use of input-output matrices for optimal planning. That optimal shadow prices on primary inputs like natural resources can be interpreted as reflecting their scarcity-related marginal productivities generated a great debate within the USSR over the use of such techniques for socialist central planning.

Advocates of the cooperative or labor-managed economy, associated with Yugoslavia, argue that it reduces alienation and improves productivity, whereas critics argue that it generates monopolization, unemployment, and inflation. Current advocates point to capitalist versions that combine workers' ownership with workers' management as in a number of companies in the United States.

The difficulties of achieving successful transitions to market capitalism in much of the former Soviet bloc has triggered backlashes and backpedalings in a number of countries. Furthermore, the most rapidly growing economy in the world is the socialist market economy of China with its locally but publicly owned town and village enterprises as its most dynamic sector. If socialism is to have a future as well as a past, other than as "the longest road from capitalism to capitalism," then it will probably be in some new form, perhaps combining local workers' ownership with market structures in a pattern as yet unforeseen.

Questions for Discussion

1. Marx and Engels claimed that they advocated "scientific socialism" in contrast to "utopian socialism." What was the basis of their criticism of the latter? Was it justified?

2. According to the Marxian labor theory of value, what is the value of a piece of capital equipment?

3. Is there any relationship between the debate over orthodox Marxism and revisionism and the current debate over gradualism versus sudden "shock therapy" in the transitions from command socialism to market capitalism?

4. Maoists claim to be the true heirs of Marxism-Leninism. Evaluate.

5. How did Hayek respond to Lange's defense of market socialism?

6. Thoroughly evaluate the arguments for and against the possibility of "rational economic calculation under socialism."

7. How can linear programming be viewed as both consistent with and inconsistent with orthodox Marxism?

8. Critics of the "cooperative economy" suggest that it can lead to stagflation. Evaluate the pros and cons of this argument.

Recommended Further Readings

Bonin, John P., Derek C. Jones, and Louis Putterman. "Theoretical and Empirical Studies of Producer Cooperatives: Will the Twain Ever Meet?" *Journal of Economic Literature* 31 (1993), pp. 1290–1320.

Brown, Alan A., and Egon Neuberger. "The Traditional Centrally Planned Economy and Its Reform." In *Comparative Economic Systems: Models and Cases,* 7th ed. ed. Morris Bornstein. Homewood: Irwin, 1994, pp. 357–83.

Dobb, Maurice. ''A Note on Saving and Investment in a Socialist Economy.'' In *On Economic Theory and Socialism,* ed. Benjamin Lippincott. London: Routledge & Kegan Paul, 1939, pp. 41–55.

Hayek, Friedrich A. *The Fatal Conceit: The Errors of Socialism.* Stanford: Hoover Institution, 1988.

Horvat, Branko. *The Political Economy of Socialism.* Armonk, NY: M.E. Sharpe, 1982.

Kornai, János. *The Socialist System: The Political Economy of Communism.* Princeton: Princeton University Press, 1992.

Lavoie, Don. *Rivalry and Central Planning: The Socialistic Calculation Debate Reconsidered.* New York: Cambridge University Press, 1985.

Lenin, Vladimir I. *The State and Revolution.* In *Selected Works.* Moscow: Progress Publishers, 1968, pp. 263–348.

Marx, Karl. *Capital,* vols I–III. Hamburg: Verlag von Otto Meissner, 1867, 1893, 1894.

———— and Friedrich Engels. *Manifest of the Communist Party.* London: J.C. Burghard, 1848.

Vanek, Jaroslav. ''The Participatory Economy.'' In *Comparative Economic Systems: Models and Cases,* 7th ed., ed. Morris Bornstein. Burr Ridge: Irwin, 1994, pp. 289–99.

CHAPTER

4

THE OLD
TRADITIONAL
ECONOMY AND ITS
VARIATIONS

You are lost if you forget that the earth belongs to no one, and that its fruits are for all!

Jean-Jacques Rousseau, *Discourse on the Origin of Inequality Among Men*, 1755

The Origins of the Economy and the Origins of Humanity

There has long been controversy about the nature of the original economy of humanity, reflecting the even longer controversy about the origins of humanity. We see our true nature as being contained in our original state—are we ultimately good or evil? Is what we are today a profound improvement upon and escape from a savage and barbaric past or a fall from an original state of purity and grace into degradation and corruption?

In contrast to ideas of past paradises from ancient philosophers and traditional religions, the 17th-century British political philosopher Thomas Hobbes argued that the life of early peoples was ''brutal, nasty, and short.'' The encounter between European colonizers and the indigenous peoples of the Americas stimulated such ideas as Christian missionaries strove to ''civilize'' the ''savages,'' some of whom practiced mass human sacrifice and cannibalism.

The 18th-century French philosopher Jean-Jacques Rousseau revived the idea of an original paradise before the formation of states when complete equality and harmony reigned in the state of nature. His influence led French thinkers to describe the Native American Indians as Noble Savages, an attitude that has tended to persist in France to the present.[1] The 19th-century American anthropologist Lewis Henry Morgan presented such a view of the Iroquois

---

[1]This view cuts across ideological lines in France. Leftist revolutionary followers of Rousseau accepted it, as do some modern structural Marxists, as well as reactionary royalist romantics such as Chateaubriand whose 19th-century novels widely spread the image of the Noble Savage of North America.

peoples of the Northeast United States, a view that led Friedrich Engels to argue that the original condition of humanity was *primitive communism.*

Such ideas have experienced a revival in modern society in such films as "The Gods Must Be Crazy." This movie presents an idealized image of the Khoi-San (!Kung Bushmen) of Southern Africa who are without property and happily share everything in a state of harmony with nature until a Coca-Cola bottle is accidentally dropped into their midst from a passing airplane. As soon as they discover various uses for this primordial piece of capital equipment disputes erupt over possession of the object. The Khoi-San decide that the "gods must be crazy" to have dropped this "evil" object on them so one of their number takes it to throw it off the "edge of the world."

Does this view of primitive society represent reality or is it just a myth? The origins of the traditional economy and its later development hold the key. Comparative economic anthropologists have analyzed the traditional economy in fundamentally different ways which imply thinking about different economic systems and the nature of *homo oeconomicus,* or economic man in different ways.

A Traditional View of the Traditional Economy

In his *The Great Transformation,* Karl Polanyi argues that the essence of nonmarket and noncommand economies is that they are embedded within larger social and cultural contexts. Whereas in modern market and command economies production and distribution decisions are made largely on economic grounds with sociocultural factors subordinated to the economic ones, people in traditional economies make decisions according to past practices that have evolved slowly along with the religious and family structures of their societies.

Household Economy

Among "precapitalist" economies Polanyi initially recognized three types. One is the essentially self-sufficient *household* economy, also labeled the "domestic mode of production" and the "moral economy." This is the world of the idealized Khoi-San as depicted in "The Gods Must Be Crazy," with essentially complete sharing and equality existing within closely knit family groups.[2] Such societies are very rare and very "primitive" in a technological sense.[3] This is the purest version of the traditional economy.

---

[2]In the real world the Khoi-San do share within their immediate family group according to patterns based on age and gender. But they engage in reciprocal exchanges with other Khoi-San groups and in actual market exchanges with ethnic outsiders such as the Bantu.

[3]In the 19th century preagricultural groups were labeled as *savage* and immediately postagricultural groups as *barbaric.* In the early 20th century *savage* gave way to *primitive* and *barbaric* gave way to *archaic.* Although such people may not use modern machinery or science their cultures may be very complex and their knowledge of things and systems in their environment may be very sophisticated and superior to that of "advanced" outsiders. Other terms that have been used include *nonliterate* and *prehistorical.* However neither of these is satisfactory in that even much more developed societies may have high rates of nonliteracy and some of these prehistorical societies have survived into historical times.

A significant amount of production for nonmarketed family use occurs even in advanced economies, possibly as high as 25 percent of GDP in the United States. The emphasis on treating broader economic institutions *as if* they are family units is an important mechanism by which traditional elements enter into modern highly developed economies such as Japan's.

Reciprocal Economy

A second type is the *reciprocal* economy. In such an economy exchanges take the form of gifts, either of goods or of labor services, that are later reciprocated, usually on the principle of symmetry between the groups making reciprocal exchanges. Although usually the initial recipient reciprocates, sometimes reciprocation can be carried out by another party through a complex chain of established relationships.

The most famous reciprocal economy is that of the Trobriand Islanders just east of New Guinea, studied by Bronisław Malinowski in the early 1920s. There a man provides significant labor services to the family of his wife's brother. The brother-in-law does not typically respond in kind. The original man must count on the labor services of his sister's husband, raising the possibility that reciprocity may not be fully balanced.

The most discussed aspect of the Trobriand Islands economy is the *kula trade,* a ceremonial exercise in which villagers from one island visit another island and present gifts to ''partners'' with whom they have well-established relationships. It is expected that at a later time the recipients will return the visit and bring equivalent gifts. The islands involved form a large circle and the gifts go round and round the circle. Armshells move in one direction and necklace chains move in the opposite direction as part of a ritual social process. Nobody wears these objects and nobody keeps them. Malinowski compares them to crown jewels, much admired but never worn. He also argues that the Trobriand Islanders clearly distinguish the kula trade from regular barter (market) trade, identifying the latter by a separate term, *gimwali.*

Although many observers romanticize reciprocal economies, they can have quite negative aspects. The French theorist Marcel Mauss argued in *The Gift* that there are three overwhelming obligations in a reciprocal society: to give, to receive, and to reciprocate. To fail to do any of the three is to suffer a loss of face, possible serious social ostracism, or worse. Thus Elizabeth Colson[4] observed a woman among the Gwembe Tonga of Zaire giving grain to a visiting distant relative and learning later that the donor feared being a victim of witchcraft if she did not do so.

The threat of loss of face can lead to intense and destructive gift giving of a competitive nature, as in the late 1800s among the Kwakiutl Indians of Vancouver Island who held *potlatches* during which they gave each other large quantities of gifts. Those who gave the most became dominant socially.

---

[4]Elizabeth Colson, *Tradition and Contract: The Problem of Order* (Chicago: Aldine, 1974), pp. 47–49.

Eventually the potlatches involved the destruction of goods and even warfare with other tribes in order to obtain goods to give as gifts. Virtually all economic activity involved accumulating goods to give away in potlatches so as to humiliate one's compatriots. This extreme behavior may have emerged only after contact with Europeans; prior to that the potlatch performed a redistributive function to help those in need.

At least three types of reciprocity may exist. First is *general reciprocity,* corresponding to sharing in a household economy among close kin, not necessarily with any balance. Those better off take care of those worse off, possibly on a permanent basis. The second type is *balanced reciprocity,* which would be like the kula trade of the Trobriand Islanders. Giving implies that one will receive an equivalent gift back.[5] Those involved are not the closest of kin, but they have established and friendly relations. The third is *negative reciprocity* and implies hostility between the parties who are trying to get the best of each other. Extreme forms include such things as theft or wartime pillage implying great social distance.

Redistributive Economy

The third of Polanyi's types of traditional economies is *redistributive.* This type depends on the principle of *centricity,* the existence of an individual or organization that receives transfers of goods from others and redistributes them in some manner. Polanyi argues that such systems are more likely in more developed economies than those in which we see reciprocity or simple householding. He distinguishes "primitive" from "archaic" economies, the latter practicing sedentary agriculture and more likely to be redistributive.

In their simplest form such systems depend on a chief or *Big Man* who does the redistributing. Such a system may depend on producing a foodstuff that can be stored for redistribution, such as grains, rather than one that rots, such as yams. Initially the transfers to the chief are voluntary and the redistributions benefit those less fortunate, as among the ancient Celts. But as the economy becomes more developed the voluntary nature of the transfers to the center decreases and more of what is transferred is kept for the use and aggrandizement of the Big Man. From a device to ensure equality, it becomes the basis for inequality. This process can lead to the emergence of actual states, formal taxation, and distinct socioeconomic classes.

Thus these original states represent the nascent emergence of the command economic system. Imperial China and Pharaonic Egypt were characterized by significant elements of outright command as well as of socialism. The pharaoh

---

[5]Sometimes groups believe that they practice balanced reciprocity when in fact a careful accounting of their gift giving shows that they do not; some individuals are permanent net givers and some are permanent net takers. This may be more likely to happen when the group *believes* that they have balanced reciprocity. Their belief leads them not to account too closely their mutual balances whereas in a hostile trade situation people will be counting very carefully, thus ironically leading to a more balanced outcome.

owned the public works infrastructure of dams and irrigation that underlay agricultural production in Egypt. Economies characterized by a king or emperor overseeing a large-scale infrastructure that controls the flooding and irrigation of a major river system or systems have been labeled *hydraulic despotisms* by Karl Wittfogel.

Marx labeled such systems the *Asiatic mode of production* and viewed them as standing separate from the unilineal path of history. Rather than progressing from slavery through feudalism to capitalism they could stagnate because the state bureaucracy could suppress the class struggle and the dialectic of history. Later under Stalin discussion of such ideas was banned in the Soviet Union, a fact Wittfogel attributed to Stalin realizing that his policies of strong command socialism constituted an ''Asiatic restoration'' in Russia.

Whether such economies are traditional or not depends on the degree to which the despot makes autonomous decisions or is constrained by sociocultural traditions, perhaps maintained by a religious priesthood. Thus even a supposedly divine pharaoh can be overthrown if he threatens established religious traditions too seriously, as happened to Akhenaton who first supported monotheism against the established polytheism of Egypt. An absolute ruler who attacks the traditional base of his power can find himself out of power.

Can a Traditional Economy Also Be a Market Economy?

In a later work[6] Polanyi presented as the three major economic forms, *reciprocity* (now including household sharing), *redistribution,* and *market.* These correspond to our three basic categories, with reciprocity now standing for tradition. Polanyi argued that the world never saw a true market economy until the 19th century when modern market capitalism displaced feudalism in Europe. Prior to then market forces and market exchange existed but never dominated any economy. Such exchanges operated peripherally to the society as a whole as in the trade between the Khoi-San and the Bantu or the ''gimwali'' barter trade of the Trobriand Islanders.

Thus a traditional economy can coexist with elements of market exchange as long as those elements do not dominate the traditional elements. Polanyi argued that a minimal number of economies of the past were actually market economies and thus must be analyzed according to an institutional approach[7] that downplays market forces for other factors. This view was labeled *substantivism* and triggered a great debate about how comparative economic anthropology should be carried out. Ultimately this debate is about the essential nature of economic man.

---

[6]Karl Polanyi, ''The Economy as an Instituted Process,'' in *Trade and Market in the Early Empires,* eds. K. Polanyi, C. W. Arensberg, and H. W. Pearson (New York: Free Press, 1957), pp. 243–70.

[7]There is a deep link between the substantivist view and the old institutionalist approach developed by Thorstein Veblen, John R. Commons, and Clarence Ayres.

Box 4–1

A Primitive but Radically Market Capitalist Economy: The Kapauku of New Guinea

Although primitiveness of production technology is correlated with dominance by traditional economic forms, a dramatic counterexample is that of the Kapauku peoples of Papua New Guinea. Arguably they live in the most market capitalist–oriented society ever known.

The Kapauku use a commodity money, cowrie shells (see Box 4–2, "Primitive Monies") for most transactions. Until recently they used a stone-age agricultural technology producing various crops and animal products. Markets exist for these products as well as for salt and a variety of artifacts. Labor is hired to work in gardens and labor services for magic also are hired. Land is individually owned, bought and sold, and leased, although customary prices handed down from the past tend to dominate in the land market unlike in other markets. Borrowing and lending with interest is widely practiced.

Marriage is determined by market purchase as are friendship, legal and political authority, social prestige, grieving services at funerals, and damages for contractual or criminal violations. There is almost no gift giving or reciprocal or even barter exchange, although food is expected to be given away upon the birth of a child.

Those without money are called *daba* and are viewed as being lazy tramps unworthy of any respect. Those who are poor can become undernourished. But the rich lend lavishly, albeit still with interest, and do not exhibit tendencies to conspicuous consumption as in more developed market economies.

There is no concept of common ownership at all. Irrigation ditches serving many farms are viewed as subdivided into individually owned parts. The only individually unrecompensed common activities are war, building festival facilities, and dragging canoes. Co-wives subdivide family fields and retain their personal production. Children are viewed as autonomous property owners from the age of 10 up.

Leopold Pospisil* saw an 11-year-old boy beating his father for nonpayment of a two-cowrie-shell debt, the father yelling and wailing throughout. The father later told Pospisil that the boy would become a good businessman who would trust nobody. Furthermore the father viewed himself as having gotten a good deal as the punishment administered by his son was not very painful so he got two cowrie shells cheaply.

---

*Leopold Pospisil, *Kapauku Papuan Economy* (New Haven: Yale University Press, 1963).

Schools of Comparative Economic Anthropology

Formalism versus Substantivism

The formalist school of thought argues that all societies and economies can be viewed as market economies, irrespective of how they may view the nature of transactions within their own society. This is probably the original view of behavior in primitive economies by economists prior to the development of anthropology as a discipline. It is exemplified by the famous assertion of Adam Smith:[8]

> The division of labor . . . is not originally the effect of any human wisdom . . . It is the necessary, though very slow and gradual, consequence of a certain propensity in human nature, which has in view no such extensive utility: the propensity to truck, barter, and exchange one thing for another.

Lionel Robbins in 1932 described economics as the study of the universal problem of ''human behavior as a relationship between ends and scarce means which have alternative uses.'' Thus it is argued that scarcity is a universal phenomenon and that all societies must make hard choices between competing ends, however they mask the mechanism of such decision making. In essence formalism is the application of the neoclassical method of economic analysis to all societies.

Within economic anthropology more specific formalist arguments note the many primitive societies such as the Kapauku (see Box 4–1) who engage in strong market practices. Formalists also argue that such apparently reciprocal exchange practices as the kula trade of the Trobriand Islanders simply involve a delayed form of barter exchange. Finally a more sophisticated argument is that even where practices seem to be driven by some cultural or religious rule or structure rather than obvious market forces per se, the individuals involved are still maximizing utility subject to budget constraints because the cultural practices themselves clearly provide utility. Furthermore, those very practices may have developed in response to underlying economic forces.

The substantivist response to these arguments has been to emphasize the argument that what matters is what decision-making process and institutional system determines the majority of production and distribution behavior. Substantivists fundamentally argue that reciprocal exchange is not the same as market behavior, just as the Trobriand Islanders distinguish between the reciprocal kula trade and the market-oriented gimwali trade.

The most extreme form of this argument follows from a school of thought in field anthropology known as *particularism*. This school argues that every

---

[8]Adam Smith, *Wealth of Nations* (London: Strahan and Cadell, 1776), book 1, chap. II, paragraph 1.

society and economy is unique and must be studied on the basis of its own history and institutions without reference to any presumed general tendencies or universal laws.

The formalists argue that substantivist observers of such societies wear a set of blinders based on their desire to see the unusual and the exotic and thus fail to see the usual and the nonexotic. The substantivists respond that the formalists are wearing a set of blinders based on their desire to use neoclassical analysis on all economic behavior, thus oversimplifying the reality of the nature of *homo oeconomicus*. Thus different analysts look at the same facts and see different realities.

A number of other approaches have emerged that combine elements of these two fundamentally competing schools.

Evolutionism

In the view of 19th-century followers of the Darwinian theory of evolution, a single path of evolution leads from primitive society to the most advanced of modern societies, which they viewed as Victorian Britain. This idea of a *uni-lineal* path of evolution became very influential. It was adopted by Lewis Henry Morgan in his study of the Iroquois peoples[9] and under the influence of Morgan was adopted by Friedrich Engels[10] also. This idea led to the formulation of various "stages of history" that all peoples were posited as having to go through on the evolutionary path. The evolutionary approach to distributional systems has sometimes argued that household sharing is the earliest stage (generalized reciprocity), gift giving (balanced reciprocity) is the next stage, out of which barter transactions evolve, and eventually full-blown market exchange using money.

More modern analysts have largely discredited this unilineal view because ethnographic studies demonstrate too great a variety of societal forms and historical paths for it to be credible. Nevertheless the evolutionary perspective remains influential in the more general *multilineal* form, which posits more than one evolutionary path. Evolution still operates in that societies change over time in accordance with the pressure to adapt to new circumstances technologically, environmentally, culturally, and in other dimensions. Furthermore it is widely believed that traditional forms such as reciprocity are more common among less developed economies.

Evolutionism can be viewed as consistent with either formalism or substantivism. "Survival of the fittest" Darwinianism can be argued to mean that those responding best to market forces will be evolutionarily superior. On the other hand the substantivist position argues that social and cultural traditions can evolve independently of purely economic forces.

---

[9]Lewis Henry Morgan, *Ancient Society* (New York: Hold, Rinehart, and Winston, 1877).

[10]Friedrich Engels, *Origin of the Family, Private Property, and the State* (New York: International Publishers, 1942).

Marxism

Marxists view the least developed traditional economies as being ''primitive communisms.'' In the unilineal view that Marx and Engels followed much of the time these primitive communisms were succeeded historically by ancient slavery. At other times Marx and Engels admitted the alternate possibility of the static Asiatic mode of production. At the end of their lives they fell under the spell of Morgan and adopted his evolutionist schema.

More modern Marxist theorists have emphasized the idea of dependency theory in which the encounter between modern capitalism and traditional economic systems leads to the subjection of the latter by the former in an imperialistic relationship.[11] A dualistic economy is established in which both systems coexist, but with the traditional one inferior and eventually destroyed.[12]

In the French tradition dating from Rousseau, the Marxist analysis of the imperialistic relationship merged with structuralist anthropology in a school called *structural Marxism*.[13] The structuralist approach, due to Claude Lévi-Strauss, explains patterns of exchange as relationships between ''self'' and ''other.''[14] Thus the dependency relationship is seen as manifesting itself in a set of deep structural patterns in society and culture. These structures tend to take a dialectical form in which class conflicts predominate in determining the structural form of the relationships between self and other.

Marxism can be seen as consistent with both formalism and substantivism. The formalist element is apparent in its assertion of the primacy of economic forces over others in the functioning of a society. But in its more recent versions such as structural Marxism, the impact of social structures and traditions on economic behavior also are granted their place.

Cultural Ecology

The most recent development in the analysis of traditional economies has been the cultural ecology approach, also labeled *cultural materialism* by Marvin

---

[11]Many revolutionary Marxist movements have actually had their base in traditional rural communal settings that were under assault from external market pressures as with the peasant *mir* in Russia (see Chapter 10) and the collective *ejidos* in Mexico (see Chapter 17).

Many modern ecological economists look to such traditional commons systems as possibly offering solutions to modern problems of overexploitation of resources. Thus even in the modern market capitalist economy of Switzerland, grazing commons exist in high alpine regions, governed by rules restricting access dating from the 1200s.

[12]The dualistic model has been used in standard economic development theory. The traditional sector pays wages equal to the average product of labor according to a principle of intrafamily sharing. The competing market sector pays wages equal to the marginal product of labor according to profit maximization.

[13]See Maurice Godelier, *Rationality and Irrationality in Economics* (Paris: Maspero, 1966).

[14]This approach stresses the alienation of the individual from the organic solidarity of society. Structuralism has been influential in the more recent movements of semiotics and postmodernism.

Harris. This school claims to transcend the old split between formalism and substantivism, although it probably tilts in the direction of formalism. Cultural materialists follow formalism by arguing that culture is driven by economic realities that ultimately reflect the underlying ecological conditions in which the society resides. But they give substantivism its due in that a culture can persist historically into a different environment than the one in which it originated as an autonomous force upon the behavioral rules of the economic system.

Cultural ecology in the form of cultural materialism can be contrasted with Marxism (historical or dialectical materialism). Both see culture as derived from the material base of society. But whereas Marxism sees the material base depending on class relations arising from the mode of production in a dialectical manner, the cultural ecologists eschew dialectics and emphasize the Malthusian pressure of population upon food supplies as determining material base. The source of food depends upon the ecological system that is the material base.

A classic example is Harris's explanation of why Jews and Muslims forbid the eating of pork whereas Christians do not. The Biblical and Qur'anic injunctions against eating pork are framed in terms of the alleged ''uncleanliness'' of pigs. But pigs are clean animals when they are not penned up. The Jewish Talmudist Maimonides argued in the 11th century that it was a health-based argument, derived from the propensity of pigs to carry trichinosis. But cattle carry the more dangerous anthrax and chickens carry salmonella. Furthermore the injunction is in Leviticus, a section of the Bible that many Christian fundamentalists follow. Why do they ignore this particular injunction[15] while it is taken seriously in Orthodox Judaism and in Islam?

Harris[16] argues that the injunction against pork has to do with the desert ecology of the Middle East in which Judaism and Islam initially developed and prospered. Christianity certainly originated there also but came to prosper in Europe rather than the Middle East. The natural food of pigs is nuts from trees. Forests of trees only exist where precipitation (rainfall and snowfall) exceeds transpiration (evaporation), that is, in relatively wet climates. To raise a pig in a desert one would have to feed it grain, precious because it is hard to grow at all. But cattle, sheep, camels, and goats can all graze on grasses in desert areas that grow where crops cannot be grown. Thus pigs are ecologically inefficient in deserts,[17] and they tend to be produced and consumed in wetter

---

[15]Some Christian sects ban all meat consumption, for example, the Seventh Day Adventists. The Ethiopian Orthodox Church bans just pork, as do other officially Christian sects that attempt to adhere to specifically Jewish practices. In Russia it is popular among the Russian Orthodox to avoid consuming pork during Lent.

[16]See Marvin Harris, *Cows, Pigs, Wars and Witches* (New York: Random House, 1974).

[17]Feeding crops potentially consumable by humans to any animal involves a certain ecological inefficiency in that the majority of the calories and proteins in the crop do not become fixed in the meat of the animal but are dissipated from it during its lifetime. This argument is irrelevant to animals that graze where crops cannot be grown.

environments such as Europe and China. This argument has generated much controversy.[18]

The cultural ecological approach accepts part of the formalist view by assuming that in the face of Malthusian pressures on food supplies societies attempt to optimize. Major evolutionary changes in the human economy arise from crises in food production. Thus the rise of sedentary agriculture came after the extinction of giant animals (mammoth, etc.) due to overhunting.[19] Key to this argument is the claim that hunter-gatherers understood how plants grow but felt no pressure to control their growth until the overhunting crisis happened. The widespread reciprocity and egalitarianism of hunter-gatherers reflects the advantages to hunting of fairly small wandering family groups who share in the hunt.

The hydraulic despotism theory of Wittfogel explains the emergence of states in river valleys subject to monsoon rains as due to the need for a centralized authority to build and maintain the hydraulic infrastructure (dams, irrigation ditches) that allow for greater agricultural production. The economy in these states is completely dominated by the hydraulic system as in Pharoanic Egypt. In nonhydraulic economies the infrastructure is relatively insignificant, and independent rain-fed farmers resisted centralizing authority in Northern Europe. Russian despotism was imported from China by the Mongol invasions according to Wittfogel.

More broadly the cultural ecological approach attempts to explain all kinds of things in societies from kinship patterns to attitudes towards warfare. Its greatest critics have tended to come from the ranks of the substantivists who argue that cultural ecology is overly simplistic and proposes unicausal explanations. This criticism is almost certainly right. On the other hand, cultural ecology has had an impressive record of explaining quite a few phenomena that had defied attempts to explain them in the past.

Empirical Data on Old Traditional Economies

There are few systematic data comparing old traditional economies or making generalizations across them, precisely because of their nature as societies lacking modern data-gathering institutions. However Frederic Pryor[20] made a study based on summaries of studies of 60 different traditional economies over a range of geographical areas and historical periods. Recognizing the limits

---

[18]See Paul Diener and Eugene E. Robkin, ''Ecology, Evolution, and the Search for Cultural Origins: The Question of Islamic Pig Production,'' *Current Anthropology* 19 (1978), pp. 493–540.

[19]See Mark N. Cohen, *The Food Crisis in Prehistory: Overpopulation and the Origins of Agriculture* (New Haven: Yale University Press, 1977).

[20]Frederic Pryor, *The Origins of the Economy: A Comparative Study of Distribution in Primitive and Peasant Economies* (New York: Academic Press, 1977).

Box 4–2

Primitive Monies in Traditional Economies

Money is anything that functions as a medium of exchange, a standard of value, and a store of wealth. Hundreds of objects have served as money in one society or another,* most emerging spontaneously within their societies as "commodity monies." Only later did governments consciously establish a money, "fiat money," the first being paper money in Han China 2,000 years ago.

The variety of objects that have served as money is breathtaking. Among the most exotic are red-headed woodpecker scalps among the Karok Indians of Oregon, rats on Easter Island, large stone rings on Yap Island in the Pacific, tobacco in Colonial Virginia, flying fox jaws on Fiji, salt in Ethiopia, copper axe-heads in Peru, squirrel skins in Mongolia, banana seeds in Uganda, cloth mats in Nigeria, sugar in the Caribbean, smoking pipes among the Cree Indians of Quebec, human skulls in New Guinea, knives in China, tin hats in Malaya, rum in Australia, neck rings among the ancient Slavs, and slaves and wives in various cultures, the latter two not generally serving as general media of exchange. This is a very incomplete list. More recently in hyperinflationary situations, vodka in Russia and Kent cigarettes in Romania have unofficially served as money.

Two primitive monies stick out as especially widespread—cattle and cowrie shells. The former did not serve as a general medium of exchange because of indivisibility and high value. But cattle were a nearly universal standard of value and store of wealth across Eurasia and North Africa for thousands of years and were used in high-value transactions. Their role as a primordial money is remembered in the English language in that the word *capital* comes from a Latin word for a head of cattle, *pecuniary* comes from *pecus,* Latin for a single cow, and *fee* comes from *faihu,* an old German word for cattle.

Cowrie shells (*Cypraea moneta*) were used by groups ranging from West Africa to Hawaii and even to some North American Indian tribes.† These small but very hard shells come from the Maldive Islands in the Indian Ocean and were originally used as fertility talismans, being thought to resemble female sexual organs. Their use as money dates from the eighth century, B.C., in China and India. They originally entered West Africa carried across the Sahara to Timbuktu by Muslim traders around the 800s, and were thoroughly entrenched as money by the 1200s. They were brought by ship by the Portuguese after the 1400s to purchase slaves. The slave-trading kings of Dahomey controlled their importation, an early form of monetary policy, and distributed them in annual festivals.

---

*See Paul Einzig, *Primitive Money* (London: Eyre and Spottiswoode, 1949), and Alison Hingston Quiggen, *A Survey of Primitive Money* (London: Methuen, 1949) for reviews of this subject.

†See Jan Hagendorn and Marion Johnson, *The Shell Money of the Slave Trade* (Cambridge, UK: Cambridge University Press, 1986).

Box 4–2 continued

In traditional economies sometimes a commodity is in the process of be-coming money but has not fully done so, being used for some transactions but not others. In such situations we see the ultimate origins of money. Payments for political power, for religious sacrifices, and most frequently for marriage contracts, are the most common such original monetary transactions. Given that for something to function as money people must have faith that others believe it is money, it is not surprising that a fertility cult symbol should have become the most widely used of all primitive monies.

---

of the ability to glean anything from such data, nevertheless Pryor did come to some conclusions.

Support can be found for several of the approaches discussed above. Support for formalism can be seen in that all but 17 of the observed economies had significant market relations. Support for substantivism is found in that a social variable, the presence of polygyny (multiple wives) tended to reduce the degree of market relations, presumably because of the greater ability of larger family units to be self-sufficient. Support for evolutionism is found in that the degree of development of a society was related to the presence of market or command relations rather than reciprocity. Support for cultural ecology can be seen in that the mode of production was a significant variable, notably in that herding economies had more hiring of labor. Support for Marxism is found in the importance of both evolution and the nature of the mode of production.

The importance of economic development in moving economies away from traditional reciprocity and towards market or command systems accords with the standard view that the old traditional economy is a dying phenomenon in our rapidly changing world. This is certainly true. What complicates this story is the emergence of movements based on reviving elements of the tra-ditional economy today within more technologically advanced economies. This is the *new traditional economy.*

Summary and Conclusions

Primitive traditional economies exercise a fascination for modern societies because of our sense that they reveal our true natures. In fact they reveal a wide variety of forms and patterns. There is a tendency for household sharing and reciprocal exchanges to occur among such societies.

We define old traditional economies as those in which the largest share of production and distribution occurs within the household sector and without a modern technology. A variety of such forms can be observed including reciprocity, in which gifts of goods or labor are given that are generally reciprocated later either directly or indirectly; markets either of a barter or monetary kind; and redistributional transfers towards a center, possibly of an involuntary sort such as taxation or slavery.

Approaches to analyzing old traditional economies are sharply split between the formalist approach, which sees all behavior as choices in the face of scarcity, and the substantivist approach, which sees many societies embedding economic decision making within broader sociocultural contexts. Evolutionism, Marxism, and cultural ecology are approaches that combine elements of these two competing schools. Empirical evidence suggests some support for each of these approaches.

We conclude by reminding the reader of the element of truth in the particularist critique. The difficulty of outside observers in truly understanding these societies as well as the vast differences between them compared to the relative homogenization of the modern world economy should make us cautious about making any generalizations too vigorously regarding them. Ultimately they retain their air of mystery.

Questions for Discussion

1. Are reciprocal exchanges just a variation on market exchanges?
2. Why might negative reciprocity lead to pure market relations?
3. How has the U.S. economy reduced substantially its remaining traditional elements within recent decades?
4. In the spectrum between the formalist and substantivist approaches, where would you place the evolutionist, Marxist, and cultural ecology approaches?
5. What might be some limits to the cultural ecology approach?
6. What are some ways that traditional economic elements survive in technologically advanced economies?

Suggested Further Readings

Dalton, George. "Traditional Production in Primitive African Economies." *Quarterly Journal of Economics* 76 (1962), pp. 360–78.

Harris, Marvin. *Cultural Materialism: The Struggle for a Science of Culture.* New York: Random House, 1979.

LeClair, Edward E., Jr., and Harold K. Schneider, eds. *Economic Anthropology: Readings in Theory and Analysis.* New York: Holt, Rinehart, and Winston, 1974.

Malinowski, Bronisław. *Argonauts of the Western Pacific.* London: Routledge, 1922.

Pryor, Frederic L. *The Origins of the Economy: A Comparative Study of Distribution in Primitive and Peasant Economies.* New York: Academic Press, 1977.

Sahlins, Marshall D. *Stone Age Economics.* Chicago: Aldine, 1972.

Wittfogel, Karl A. *Oriental Despotism: A Comparative Study of Total Power.* New Haven: Yale University Press, 1957.

Majority Muslim Population

5   ISLAMIC ECONOMICS AND THE ECONOMICS OF OTHER RELIGIONS

You shall not covet your neighbor's house; you shall not covet your neighbor's wife, or his manservant, or his maidservant, or his ox, or his ass, or anything that is your neighbor's.
—Exodus 20:17, *Holy Bible*

Now the company of those who believed were of one heart and soul, and no one said that any of the things which he possessed was his own, but they had everything in common.
—Acts of the Apostles 4:32, *Holy Bible*

It is evident that, unlike both capitalism and socialism, the goals of Islam are absolute and a logical outcome of its underlying philosophy.
—M. Umer Chapra, *Islam and the Economic Challenge*

Introduction: The Appeal of the New Traditional Economy

The new traditional economy seeks to be the best of all possible worlds, combining old with new, individual with collective, ethical with practical. It is supposed to be the true third way between capitalism and socialism, drawing upon the virtues of each while eliminating the sins of each.

On the one hand, new traditional economies nostalgically look backward to the lost world of the old traditional economy through a misty haze of myth and memorialization. On the other, they seek to function in the modern world with modern technology, indeed to use such technology to further the spread of their religion[1] in the search for a humane socioeconomic order. The harmony of the family and the group will be preserved or renewed in the face of

---

[1]One such example is the phenomenon of televangelism in the United States among Protestant fundamentalists. Another is the use of remote computer terminals for women students to access library materials in Saudi Arabian universities without having to come into contact with any men in the libraries themselves.

modern tendencies to alienation, angst, crime, marital breakdown, and general social disintegration.

Movements reflecting such ideas have sprung up among most major religions of the world. The one most clearly projecting a well-defined view of economics is Islam. This partly reflects that its founder, the Prophet Muhammed, was actually a merchant more knowledgeable about such matters than most other founders of world religions. Nevertheless other religions also reflect certain views regarding appropriate economic conduct or structures. Fundamentalist variants urge their adoption as part of broader campaigns of moral and social transformation.

A Whirlwind Tour of Religions and Economics

Buddhist Economics

In a famous essay,[2] E. F. Schumacher extols the virtues of "Buddhist economics," arguing that the goal of humanity should be spiritual liberation and that Buddhist economics offers a means to this end. He invokes a vision of a balanced attitude towards work, directed at achieving a level of consumption that is satisfying but not saturating. He exalts the harmony of humanity and nature, that trees should be worshipped, that nonrenewable resources should not be wasted, and that local production should be favored over long-distance trade in order to reduce wasteful transportation activities and to encourage self-sufficiency. Unsurprisingly this essay has become popular with the environmental movement.

Is there such a thing as "Buddhist economics" and does it correspond with the idealized image presented by Schumacher? The answer is not simple. In much of the Buddhist world, such as in China and Japan, the religion has played a relatively passive role, supporting market or traditional forms often more deeply based on other religious traditions such as Confucianism. As a dominant ideology Buddhism has been confined to South and Southeast Asian countries where it is practiced in its southern form known as Hinayana ("Lesser Vehicle") or Theravada ("Way of the Elders").[3]

Nations where this form of Buddhism has flourished are Sri Lanka (the former Ceylon), Burma (also known as Myanmar), Thailand, Laos, and Cambodia (also known as Kampuchea). The former two were part of British India prior to the late 1940s and the latter two were part of French Indochina. Also

---

[2]See E. F. Schumacher, *Small is Beautiful* (New York: Harper and Row, 1973), chap. 4.

[3]One exception is Tibetan Buddhism, although since the exile of the Dalai Lama in 1959, Chinese Communism has dominated Tibet rather than Tibetan Buddhism, which has become an internationally influential religion with many Western followers, although it remains dominant in tiny Bhutan. Like Schumacher, the Dalai Lama has prominently supported the world environmental movement.

part of French Indochina was Vietnam prior to 1954, where Mahayana ("Greater Vehicle") Buddhism was practiced. Thailand, known as Siam before World War II, was a buffer between these two colonial entities and maintained its independence.

In Laos and Cambodia no such Buddhist movement exists openly because the official ideology is orthodox Marxism-Leninism, now beginning to undergo transformation to something else. But some observers[4] see Buddhist influences in local forms of that ideology.

Buddhism in Thailand evolved during the 19th century under powerful kings who emphasized a rationalistic and individualistic form of the religion, each individual responsible for his or her own enlightenment. This attitude coincides well with market capitalism and today, Thailand is a rapidly growing example of such an economy, despite the recent emergence of dissident anti-materialist Buddhist movements such as the Santi Asoke sect.

In Sri Lanka and Burma, Buddhism became identified with nationalist and anticolonialist movements and developed a militant form[5] associated with socialist views of economics, labeled "Buddhist socialism" in Burma. The developer of this ideology was U Ba Swe who in the late 1930s referred to Stalin as "builder of Lokka Nibban" or Buddhist heaven on earth. He influenced Burma's first prime minister, U Nu, and was a minister in government from 1948 to 1958. Their ideal was *pyidawatha,* or a welfare state in which each individual could pursue salvation. That government was overthrown in 1962 by General Ne Win who established a brutal and xenophobic military dictatorship still in power. Although this regime proclaims itself Buddhist, monks are among its most serious opponents.

Schumacher emphasizes detachment from materialism and a deemphasis on mindless economic growth. Burma has had a very low economic growth rate since its independence, but the Burmese leadership no longer views this as a good thing. Part of this low growth is due to removal from international trade and bungled socialist central planning under Ne Win. But part is due to elements of Buddhism as expressed in Burmese practices.[6]

A major focus of Burmese Buddhism has been the achievement of individual merit through sponsoring the building of temples. This focus leads to contradictory impulses. On the one hand, this ideal serves as a Protestant ethic type of motivation for accumulating wealth. On the other, it leads to dissipating that wealth in building temples rather than real capital investment and long-run economic growth of society. Along with building temples has gone substantial economic support for the Buddhist priesthood.

---

[4]See Charles F. Keyes, "Buddhism and Revolution in Cambodia," *Cultural Survival Quarterly* 14 (1990), pp. 6–63.

[5]In Sri Lanka this militance has led to serious military conflict between the Buddhist/Sinhalese majority and the Hindu/Tamil minority.

[6]See Melford E. Spiro, *Buddhism and Society: A Great Tradition and Its Burmese Vicissitudes* (New York: Harper and Row, 1970).

Confucian Economics

Arguably Confucianism should not be included in this discussion. It is more a philosophy and cultural influence than a religion. Its current influence does not take the form of religious leaders advocating some fundamentalist adherence to holy scriptures or priestly hierarchies. Nevertheless among East Asian countries under Chinese cultural influence,[7] elements of Confucian influence have an impact on the nature of the economic systems. In such countries as Singapore and Taiwan, as well as more recently in the communist Peoples' Republic of China (PRC), advocacy of Confucian values has been actively encouraged by government leaders, often explicitly as a counterweight to liberal Western influences.

Confucius was a scholar/adviser to political leaders who wrote his ideas in the *Analects,* with many later discussions and additions by other Confucian scholars. The five central concepts of Confucianism are *jen* (benevolence), *i* (righteousness), *li* (propriety), *zhi* (wisdom), and *xin* (faithfulness), the first of these the most important. Confucianism implies a hierarchy in which benevolent elites (the emperor in China and his scholarly Mandarin bureaucrats) rule subjects who in return are loyally obedient to those elites, as long as they truly practice jen. This idea extends to the family, where the son obeys the father and the wife obeys the husband. Thus there is a strong emphasis upon order, hierarchy, education, and benevolence, all considered to be crucial elements of Confucian societies and their economies.

Attitudes towards market forces have been mixed within Confucianism. Passages in the *Analects* support a laissez-faire approach as long as the emperor is properly benevolent and reverent and celestial harmony is maintained. But during the 1100s a form of neo-Confucianism developed that eventually became strongly opposed to commerce, industrialization, and foreign trade. Generally the current Confucian revival in East Asia tends to support reliance on market forces, although with authoritarian state structures and elements of state planning and control. This is true in both very capitalist Singapore as well as in the still-socialist PRC.

Hindu Economics

Hinduism is the predominant religion of India, the world's second most populous nation. The second largest political party in India is the Bharatiya Janata Party (BJP), a Hindu fundamentalist party that supports destroying Muslim mosques on sacred Hindu sites and replacing the official secularism of India with radical Hinduism. Although somewhat vague and contradictory about economics, the BJP supports several economic ideas.

Central to the Hindu socioeconomic worldview is the caste system, the archetype of an old traditional economic system. The caste system, justified

---

[7]Besides countries with largely ethnic Chinese populations this group would certainly include Japan, Korea, and Vietnam.

by the karmic doctrine of reincarnation, persists in the *jajmani* system of fairly self-sufficient groups of local villages trading with each other through the well-defined division of labor provided by the hereditary caste system. Over past centuries various outside rulers, such as Muslim Moguls and Christian British, tried to penetrate and break this system. But it survived, partly due to the Hindu village tradition of paying a share of output to the current ruler without question.

The foundation of Hindu economics was laid down by the father of Indian independence, Mahatma (Mohandas) Gandhi, in his 1909 *Hind Swaraj. Swaraj* means self-rule and self-sufficiency, both nationally and at the village level, in a revitalized caste system purged of evil elements such as suppression of the Untouchables, the lowest caste that Gandhi renamed ''Harijan'' (children of God). The emphasis on economic nationalism and self-sufficiency continues in the BJP today.

Despite his desire to reform the Hindu caste system, Gandhi was essentially an old traditionalist in his economic views, strongly opposing modern industrialization, railroads, and urbanization. He idealized homespun cloth and made the village spinning wheel the symbol of his movement, calling indigenous technology *swadeshi*. Gandhi also opposed excessive consumption, parallelling the views of the Buddhists. He was assassinated by a Hindu extremist for his tolerance of other religions.

Deendayal Upadhyaya transformed this Gandhian inheritance into a new traditional view for the BJP in his 1965 *Integral Humanism.* Largely he reiterates Gandhi's views, although with less emphasis on uplifting the Untouchables and more emphasis on adapting to modern technology. He advocates swadeshi, but interprets it in the sense of ''appropriate technology'' as described by development economists. He still supports a decentralized system of self-sufficient villages with caste systems, but calls for more modern and productive small-scale technologies.

In practice the BJP has been somewhat incoherent about its economic positions. At times it has supported market capitalism against the half-baked, planned socialism of the government. At others it has supported a redistributionist populism found in the works of Gandhi and Upadhyaya. The most consistent policies have been strong opposition to foreign investment, support for the caste system and the rights of the Brahmin (upper) caste, and support for prohibiting the killing or consumption of cows, viewed as sacred by Hindus. Besides greater harassment of religious minorities such as Muslims, laws prohibiting the consumption of beef are the most obvious attribute of states in India where the BJP is in power.

Judaic Economics

The Torah, especially Exodus, Leviticus, and Deuteronomy, contains a long list of very specific rules and injunctions regarding economic behavior. Many are consistent with markets and private property, as exemplified by the Ninth Commandment quoted at the beginning of this chapter. However, many of these are irrelevant in the modern world, such as rules about the selling or treatment of slaves.[8] Some of these economic rules have drawn the attention of some Orthodox Jews as perhaps being appropriate for Israeli society.[9] Among these are the use of tithes for redistributing income and the prohibition of interest among Jews, although not with outsiders.[10]

A dramatic element of the Torah's economic injunctions is the concept of the Jubilee Year, put forward in Leviticus 25. It is a generalization of the prohibition against working on the Sabbath, a rule that has generated the most heated specific demands by fundamentalist groups in Israel, such as forbidding flights on the Sabbath by the national airline, El Al. The generalized version of the Sabbath argues for fallowing land every seventh year. After seven groups of seven years (49) will come a jubilee year. Property will be remitted to its original owner, recently acquired slaves will be freed, the poor sojourner will be cared for, and so forth. At the beginning of the 20th century, the Chief Rabbi of Jaffa, Abraham Kook, argued that this implied the preemptive sale of Jewish lands to the earlier Muslim owners. This advice conflicted with the Zionist movement to build an Israeli nation and was not followed.

In modern Israel the emphasis has been upon building a functioning economy within a hostile environment. Some of the most distinctive institutions of the Israeli economy have not come from religious sources, notably the kibbutz which was inspired by secular European utopian socialism. Indeed the Israeli economy exhibits a fairly high level of state ownership reflecting the socialist nature of the founding Labor Party. Although the fundamentalist movements are very strong in Israel, economic proposals that are perceived to be counter to national survival are strongly resisted.[11]

Christian Economics

In the Roman Catholic Church an important figure in developing economic doctrines was the 13th-century St. Thomas Aquinas, who reconciled Aristotelian philosophy with Christian theology. Among Aristotle's ideas he imported into Catholicism were the idea of the "just price" and an abhorrence of charging interest.[12] Aquinas can be considered an ideologue of the old traditional economy in its feudal European form.

---

[8]Jacob Neusner in *The Economics of the Mishnah* (Chicago: University of Chicago Press, 1990) argues that earlier laws and interpretations tend to reflect a traditional premarket economy whereas later ones reflect more of a market capitalist one.

[9]See Meir Tamari, *"With All Your Possessions": Jewish Ethics and Economic Life* (New York: Free Press, 1987) for a presentation of these rules as a full economic system.

[10]This differentiation between insiders and outsiders with respect to charging interest led to Jews serving a significant role as financiers in medieval Islamic and Christian societies, where the latter two forbade charging interest among their followers.

[11]Besides some of the Sabbath issues one other economic area where the fundamentalists have gotten their way is in forbidding the consumption of pork. The most extreme of the Jewish fundamentalist movements are explicitly anti-Zionist, arguing that a state of Israel can only be reestablished by the Messiah who has not yet arrived.

[12]Actually, forbidding interest as usury dates in Catholicism to the fourth and fifth centuries. The prohibition of interest was made absolute and total in 1311 by Pope Clement V but was relaxed to limit only "excessive" interest after 1600.

This linkage between feudalism and Roman Catholicism led to a lack of enthusiasm for modern capitalism. However, despite the presence of certain Marxist-oriented ''liberation theologists'' among Latin American Catholic clergy, the Church has generally been antisocialist, especially under Pope John Paul II of Poland. He supports market capitalist economics more than any previous Pope, but is still critical regarding its excessive materialism and lack of compassion for the poor. In Italy and Germany the Catholic Church–based political parties have been the Christian Democrats. More conservative than the Social Democrats in Germany or the former Communists and Socialists in Italy, these parties have supported fairly extensive social welfare programs and considerable state economic intervention in both countries.

In contrast, Christian Protestantism has been more closely linked to market capitalism socially and ideologically. Max Weber argued that ''the Protestant ethic is the spirit of capitalism.'' Certainly the Protestant Reformation occurred in countries where and at times when modern market capitalism was rapidly developing, the most supportive attitude coming from Calvinist churches. Nevertheless, among the most radical of the Anabaptists, communal attitudes and approaches emerged, based on the scripture from Acts quoted at the beginning of this chapter. Some of these sects founded communities in the United States during the period of utopian socialist experimentation. But they were a small minority in generally pro–market capitalist Protestantism.

This fervor for market capitalism has exhibited itself prominently in the modern American Protestant fundamentalist movement that now attempts to formulate economic doctrines. However this group is very diverse in its views.

Who speaks for the masses of United States fundamentalists is uncertain. The pro–laissez-faire New Christian Right has been noisy and has formed a successful alliance with the leaders of the New Christian Right social movements, especially the antiabortion movement. Nevertheless survey evidence suggests that many fundamentalists support income redistribution programs by the government, probably reflecting the tendency for such people to be poorer than the average American.[13] This finding also reflects the populist tradition of American fundamentalism from the late 19th century.

Given the differing views among fundamentalist Protestants, mainstream Protestants, and Roman Catholics, the true nature of Christian economics remains unclear.[14]

---

[13]Laurence R. Iannacone, ''Heirs to the Protestant Ethic? The Economics of American Fundamentalists,'' in *Fundamentalisms and the State: Remaking Polities, Economies, and Militance,* eds. M. E. Marty and R. S. Appleby (Chicago: University of Chicago Press, 1993), pp. 342–66.

[14]The position of Eastern Orthodoxy is especially unclear. Traditionally in Russia at least, the Church was even more anticapitalist than Roman Catholicism, although not necessarily antimarket. But the experience of Communist rule in Russia has made the Church more open to market capitalism now.

Box 5–1

Varieties of U.S. Protestant Fundamentalist Economic Views

At one extreme are the strict fundamentalists who abjure discussions of economics or politics entirely, considering such to be a sinful distraction from the focus upon personal salvation. Although very anticommunist, they view the market as ultimately a sinkhole of sin and corruption and denounce their fundamentalist brethren who are involved in political and economic activities.

Somewhat more moderate, but also adhering to the doctrine of Biblical "inerrancy," are the New Christian Right fundamentalists who have been very active in politics with definite views on economics. Closely linked to former presidential candidate Pat Robertson, Jerry Falwell, and the Southern Baptist Convention, this group has been avidly pro–market capitalist. Economists at Jerry Falwell's Liberty University in Lynchburg, Virginia, strongly advocate Milton Friedman's Chicago School approach, albeit with a strong underpinning of Judeo-Christian morality.

More moderate theologically, but more radical in their libertarian economics are the "Christian Reconstructionists" of the Calvinist Dutch Reformed Church. They believe that heaven must be created on earth before Christ will come again, an Austrian economics heaven based on biblical quotations.* Thus the biblical tithe is cited as supporting a flat tax. God's ultimate authority rules out central planning, the latter being a form of idolatry. The Eighth Commandment ("Thou shalt not steal") is seen as forbidding any income redistribution by government. The use of metallic currencies in the Old Testament is seen as support for the gold standard, contrasting with the position of 1890s populist/fundamentalists such as William Jennings Bryan with his anti–Big Business "Cross of Gold" speech.

Despite this trend of U.S. fundamentalists being strongly pro–laissez faire in economics, some are not. The evangelical left includes believers in biblical inerrancy who cite the already noted quotation from Acts and the Leviticus jubilee laws, as well as Jesus' concern for the poor. They† support major government income redistribution, a national food policy, "just" international trade, and guaranteed wages. Further to the left is "radical evangelicalism," advocating full-blown socialism.

---

*See Gary North, *Inherit the Earth: Biblical Principles for Economics,* 1987, Fort Worth: Dominion Press.
†See Ronald Sider, *Rich Christians in an Age of Hunger* (Downer's Grove: Intervarsity Press, 1977).

A Brief History of Islam

The Prophet Muhammed and the Early Years

Islam was founded by the Prophet Muhammed (570–632 A.D.), a successful merchant in the west-central Arabian city of Mecca. Mecca lay at the intersection of major north-south and east-west trade routes and contained a shrine known as the Ka'bah that was the destination of annual pilgrimages by many Arabian tribes. Thirty-two different gods were worshipped there and idols were set up for the benefit of the pilgrims. Muhammed belonged to the Hashemite clan; but Mecca was dominated by the Quraysh clan, which controlled the earnings obtained from pilgrims coming to worship at the Ka'bah.

Around 610 Muhammed began to receive revelations from Allah through the angel Gabriel. These revelations continued until his death and constitute the body of the *Qur'an*,[15] which was not codified into suras (chapters) until after his death. He also made many pronouncements separate from the *Qur'an* which are collectively known as the *Hadith*. These two sources are the foundation of the Islamic law code, the *Shari'a*.[16]

Many early revelations deal with predictions of a Day of Judgment and the End of the World, not unlike the predictions in the Book of Revelations in the New Testament. These suras reflect a wrath against the arrogant attitudes of the wealthy Quraysh and their lack of charity towards the poor. All persons are equal in the eyes of Allah.

A fundamental point of the Shari'a is an absolute and uncompromising monotheism. There is no god but Allah, who is all powerful and utterly transcendent. The central concept of Islam is for the believer to submit to the will of Allah; indeed the word *Islam* means exactly that.

This assertion of monotheism threatened the livelihood of the Quraysh who profited from the pilgrims worshipping the 32 gods of the Ka'bah. In 613 Muhammed went public and preached openly, drawing the strong opposition of the ruling Quraysh. But Muhammed attracted a core of dedicated followers, especially from the poor and dispossessed.

In 622 the *hijra* occurred, or migration by Muhammed and his followers to Medina ("City of the Prophet"), an agricultural city north of Mecca to which he was invited by conflicting tribes desiring a mediator.[17] This was

---

[15]Also spelled *Koran* in much English language mass media.

[16]The word *shari'a* in Arabic originally meant path or way, especially the path to a water hole. Some argue that *Shari'a* refers to a general philosophy of behavior rather than a set of specific injunctions and rules. This argument has been popular with more liberal Muslims opposed to fundamentalist movements.

[17]Some of these tribes were Jewish and Muhammed initially made Islam very similar to Judaism. He always declared Allah to be the one God of the Jews and the Christians. Eventually a conflict broke out and he expelled the Jews, seized their property, and more sharply differentiated Islam from Judaism.

Year 1 of the Islamic calendar and is viewed as the beginning of the world Islamic community, the *umma*.[18] The umma is a religious/political/economic entity in which unity or *tawhid* is paramount. All things are unified in the Islamic religion.

Thus, Muhammed became a political leader as well as a religious prophet. The Qur'anic suras of this time establish rules for marriage, inheritance, and many other issues that arise in the actual functioning of a society. It is these suras, along with the Hadith, that form the base of the Shari'a. During these 10 years, Muhammed succeeded in converting most of the tribes of the Arabian peninsula into the umma, including the Quraysh in Mecca.[19]

After Muhammed's death in 632 the inner circle of his companions selected a successor to him known as *caliph,* who would lead the umma but would not be a prophet. Struggles over the caliphate would eventually divide Islam.

By 644 the caliphs had successfully conquered Syria, Palestine, Egypt, Iraq, Iran, and portions of Central Asia. Over the next 75 years North Africa and Spain would be conquered, culminating 100 years after Muhammed's death with a thrust into central France, thwarted at Tours.

Over this suddenly vast empire the caliphs imposed a reasonably benevolent rule, leaving intact local political and social structures. Believers in monotheism, Jews, Christians, and Zoroastrians, were allowed to practice their religion as long as they paid a special tax.

The fourth caliph was Muhammed's son-in-law, Ali, whose caliphate was contested by Mu'awiya of the Quraysh clan. Ali's supporters came to be known as *Shi'is*[20] while Mu'awiya's supporters came to be known as *Sunnis*. This is the main split within Islam.

In 680 Mu'awiya's son, Yazid I, defeated and killed Ali's son, Husayn, and his Shi'i followers at the battle of Karbala in Iraq, a martyrdom annually mourned by Shi'is on its anniversary. Yazid's victory signaled the general dominance of Sunnis, who constitute about 85 percent of the world's Muslims. Shi'is are dominant in Iran. They are a majority and a plurality respectively in Iraq and Lebanon, but Sunnis dominate both countries politically, socially, and economically. Small Shi'i sects politically dominate in Yemen and Syria.[21]

---

[18]The familial/traditional aspect of this concept is highlighted by the fact that *umma* comes from *umm,* which is the Arabic word for *mother.*

[19]After smashing the 32 idols in 630, Muhammed established the principle of *hajj,* or Islamic pilgrimage to Mecca.

[20]The term *Shi'ite* is frequently used in journalism.

[21]In Yemen the Zaydis are numerically dominant and are often viewed as being the closest to the Sunnis of all the Shi'i groups. In Syria the leader, Hafez El-Assad, and his family are all from the Awalite sect of Shi'ism, which constitutes about 10 percent of Syria's population. The French favored them for positions in the officer corps during colonial rule, which allowed them to seize power later in a military coup. Officially Syria has a secular, Arab socialist (Ba'athist) regime.

East of Iran, Shi'is are frequently of the urban middle class, but generally they are a small minority.[22]

The Rise and Fall of Islamic Civilization

The apogee of Islamic civilization came during the Abbasid caliphate, based in Baghdad after 750. An especially high point was the rule of Harun al-Rashid (786–809). Baghdad was the world's largest city outside of China, and China was Baghdad's only rival in science and the arts. Islamic scholars studied the Greek philosophers, banned in Christian Europe, and expanded upon their knowledge to produce such intellectual achievements as the development of algebra and Arabic numerals. Under Abbasid rule Islam became a truly multinational religion, transcending its Arabic origins even as Arabic became the lingua franca of the empire.

During this period the Sunni Shari'a underwent considerable development and broke into competing versions under the pressure of absorbing peoples with different cultures and traditions into the empire.[23] The foundation of the Shari'a was the *Qur'an* and the Hadith. But these were not definitive because much of the *Qur'an* is in a highly poetic language subject to many possible interpretations and debate arose regarding the validity of certain Hadith—were they actually said by Muhammed or were they made up by someone later to justify a non-Islamic practice?

After the death of Harun al-Rashid the caliphate began a long decline, breaking up into many small successor states by the mid-900s. Despite this the period 900–1700 actually saw the greatest expansion of Islam in terms of numbers of converts. In some areas local populations adopted the long-established religion of the rulers, as in the Middle East. In others, conquest by Muslim successor states was crucial as in Central and South Asia. Finally, in many areas the conversion was led by merchants and missionaries as in Subsaharan Africa, Malaysia, and Indonesia. After 1700 the global expansion of Islam slowed as it encountered the expanding power of industrializing Christian Europe.

The early 20th century brought a low point for Islam as most Muslim states became colonies of Christian European powers—only Turkey, Saudi Arabia, Iran, and Afghanistan maintained formal independence throughout. The modern revival of Islam arose in the context of nationalist and anticolonialist struggles against this domination.

---

[22]This is where the largest numbers of Muslims are. The four countries with the largest Muslim populations are, in descending order, Indonesia, Bangladesh, India, and Pakistan.

[23]For a more detailed account of the development of the Sunni Shari'a see Joseph Schact, *An Introduction to Islamic Law* (Oxford: Oxford University Press, 1964). The four Sunni Shari'as are the Hanifi, the most liberal; the Maliki, popular in North Africa; the Shafi, popular in Southeast Asia; and the Hanbali, the strictest, enforced in Qatar and Saudi Arabia where it has spread as the Wah'habist ideology of the Saudi royal family since 1740. The Shi'is also have Shari'as but allow current leaders more leeway in interpreting them.

The New Traditional Islamic Revival

Islam is surging as a movement, strongly reviving throughout its traditional base as well as rapidly spreading in areas outside its core zone. This surge is mostly due to very high birth rates[24] in many Islamic countries and a migration from them into other areas, including European countries such as France where the Islamic influx has stimulated ultranationalist and antiforeigner political movements. But proselytization is occurring in many parts of the world as well.

In core zone countries either a self-styled Islamic fundamentalist government is in power, or Islamic fundamentalism is the most significant opposition movement. A universal demand of these movements is for imposing and enforcing a Shari'a law code. Because there are several different Shari'as, disputes can arise once implementation is actually attempted,[25] although in many countries one Shari'a is clearly preferred. This demand for the imposition of a Shari'a has extended to countries with significant non-Muslim populations such as Nigeria and Sudan, in the latter aggravating a long-running civil war.

The list of countries that have adopted a Shari'a code includes Sudan, Saudi Arabia, Qatar, Iran, and Pakistan. Afghanistan is in the process of doing so since the defeat of the Soviet-backed Communists. In Algeria an Islamic fundamentalist party that promised to adopt a Shari'a won an election but was prevented from assuming power by the military, resulting in a civil war. Countries moving towards partial adoption include Nigeria, Egypt, and Malaysia. In Jordan and Morocco the monarchs stress their direct descent from the Prophet Muhammed and lavishly fund the *ulama* (Islamic clergy) and the mosques. In the Central Asian republics of the Former Soviet Union Islam is on the rise, and Islamic fundamentalists have been involved in a war with the government in Tajikistan. In some, such as Iraq and Syria, the fundamentalists have been violently suppressed, but in very few Islamic countries is the movement declining.

What lies behind this sweeping upheaval? Most of the Muslim world was subjected to colonial domination by European powers sometime during the last century. Even those nations that retained formal independence were sometimes subjected to powerful outside influence, as for example when the U.S.

---

[24]Perhaps the most controversial element of Islamic fundamentalism is its view of the role of women. Without question the *Qur'an* puts women in a lower status than men economically through unequal inheritance laws, the right of men but not women to multiple spouses, and the greater ease of divorce for men. However, women are allowed to own property, and except for prostitution there are no restrictions on labor market entry. In many Islamic countries women participate in skilled professions, although generally they have substantially lower educational levels than men. Muhammed respected women and some demands by Islamic fundamentalists, such as requiring the wearing of the veil, are not to be found in the *Qur'an* or the Hadith.

[25]One example is that since the official adoption of the Shari'a in Pakistan no thief has had his hand chopped off yet because of a disagreement between different codes as to whether the hand should be chopped at the wrist or at the base of the thumb and fingers. Also it must be proven that a thief did not steal out of need.

CIA organized the overthrow of the Iranian nationalist leader, Mohammed Mossadegh, in 1954, or when the Soviet military installed a puppet leader in Afghanistan in 1979. These experiences established the possibility of Islam becoming identified with national identity in the anticolonialist struggle.

But generally Islam was not the vehicle of the anticolonialist movements that achieved national independence. Many of these were socialist, as in Algeria and South Yemen. In the Arab world many were Arab nationalist, as in Egypt, seeking a transnational unity that never came to pass.[26] But a profound disillusionment has set in with these initial postindependence solutions. The general difficulties of world socialism have shown up in many of these countries. Nevertheless there remains fear of adopting Western-style market capitalism because it might lead to a renewed loss of national sovereignty. Hence Islam's appeal as a Third Way in the economic sphere becomes important.

In most of these countries independence raised national identity issues because their borders were artifacts drawn by the colonial powers with little logic. This is true as well of the newly independent Central Asian republics whose borders were drawn by Stalin. This lack of solid national identity has led to the search for something else and Islam has emerged as that something else.

Another factor has been the success of the Organization of Petroleum Exporting Countries (OPEC) in the 1970s at raising oil prices and the enormous wealth this generated for its member states. OPEC's success showed the possibility of Islamic countries economically asserting themselves against the former colonial powers. The first oil price shock of 1973 was enforced by the oil export embargo put in place by fundamentalist Saudi Arabia, OPEC's biggest oil exporter, to protest U.S. support for Israel during the Yom Kippur War.

Oil price increases triggered a surge of pride in the Islamic world, even as they triggered envy of the wealthy Gulf states. The inequalities of wealth have become a problem and played a role in the rise to power by Shi'i fundamentalists in OPEC's second most powerful member, Iran. However, both Saudi Arabia and Iran have used their wealth to fund and encourage Islamic fundamentalist movements around the world.

Finally there is the nostalgic appeal of Islam's glorious past. It offers an identity that has an international character, in which people can feel both independent and yet part of something greater and more glorious than themselves. The Saudi Arabians in particular have propagandized for the idea of Islamic economics as part of adopting a Shari'a.[27] One's country can be

---

[26]A similar case has been the displacement of the Arab nationalist Palestine Liberation Organization (PLO) by the Islamic fundamentalist Hamas as the leading anti-Israeli movement among Palestinians.

[27]The importance of Saudi Arabia's role has been enhanced because Mecca and Medina are located there. Every year over a million pilgrims from all over the Islamic world come to Saudi Arabia on the hajj to visit those cities and are thus exposed to Saudi influence.

modern, rich, powerful, and yet spiritually superior and in tune with an ancient and noble identity. The appeal of fundamentalist Islam is the appeal of the New Traditionalism.

The Principles of Islamic Economics

Fundamental Concepts

The principles of Islamic economics are derived from the Shari'as, of which there is more than one. Furthermore, even within the accepted foundation of the *Qur'an* and the core Hadith there are varying interpretations of key passages regarding economic matters, even within particular Shari'a schools. As Islamic fundamentalism has increased in influence and become a serious contender for coming to power in many societies, increasingly acrimonious debates have erupted among Islamic economists over these differences of interpretation and thus over what truly constitutes Islamic economics.

Three ideas underpin the Islamic economic system as a whole. The first is *tawhid,* or divine unity, the idea that all economic activity must be in accord with divine commands. The second is *khilafah,* or vice-regency, the idea that humans are the partners of Allah in managing the world and its resources. This implies universal brotherhood, a concept stressed frequently in the *Qur'an* and the Hadith on its own. Finally there is *adalah,* or justice, which implies concern for the welfare of others and cooperation as the basic principle of economic organization. Umer Chapra argues that ESOPs are a method whereby such cooperation can be achieved within an Islamic context.[28]

Zakat, or Almsgiving

Beyond these broad principles lie more specific injunctions, some positive commands, others negative prohibitions. The most important of the positive injunctions is *zakat,* or almsgiving. In theory almsgiving is supposed to be a voluntary activity by the devout, but in practice it became a religious tax used for income redistributional purposes by Islamic governments. In its original formulation zakat is a 2.5 percent tax on most forms of wealth above a minimum necessity level, although higher rates, called the tithe (*'ushr*), are due for agricultural produce. The tithe looks more like an income tax than a wealth tax.

As with tax accounting in most economies these simple rules have generated enormous discussion and the elaboration of numerous special cases and exceptions, with considerable differences between the different Shari'a codes

---

[28]M. Umer Chapra, *Islam and the Economic Challenge* (Leicester: Islamic Foundation, 1992), chap. 5.

that do not seem to follow any clear pattern.[29] Muhammed Siddiqi[30] presents debates of modern Islamic economists who have argued about whether or not higher rates can be charged for newer forms of wealth not specifically mentioned in the *Qur'an* or Hadith. Those specifically covered and thus subject to the Qur'anic fixed rates are flocks and herds, gold and silver, articles of trade, and agricultural produce, which pays the higher rate tithe.

Countries that have introduced state-collected zakat include Pakistan, Saudi Arabia, Malaysia, and Sudan. A study of whether the state-run zakat system introduced in Pakistan in 1980 will be able to eradicate poverty found in the negative.[31] It has been reported that in Sudan zakat distribution to the poor may be having some real impact, at least in local political perceptions.[32]

It can be argued that zakat is merely the basic ingredient of the fiscal policy of an Islamic state. Other kinds of taxes can be raised to cover state expenses, such as income taxes. Furthermore the Shari'a codes allow for taxing non-Muslims at higher rates. In the early caliphates such practices played a role in pushing large masses of people towards conversion.

Hard Work and Fair Dealing

Another positive injunction involves working hard and dealing fairly with others. One should use fair weights and measures. One should work hard at one's chosen profession, presuming it is an honorable one, and enjoy the fruits of one's labors. Rightly acquired wealth is approved of. However one should be modest in the enjoyment of it. Furthermore, one should pay one's workers a just wage and one should charge just prices for one's output. One should be efficient and not wasteful (''Allah does not love people who waste what they have'' *Qur'an* 6: 141). In short, Islam would not disapprove of the Better Business Bureau.

---

[29]In a classic account of economic laws in Shari'a codes, Aghnides spends nearly 150 pages describing these variations. See Nicholas P. Aghnides, *Mohammedan Theories of Finance* (New York: Columbia University Press, 1916), pp.199–347.

[30]Muhammed Nejatullah Siddiqi, ''Muslim Economic Thinking: A Survey of Contemporary Literature,'' in *Studies in Islamic Economics,* ed. K. Ahmad (Leicester: Islamic Foundation, 1980), pp. 191–315.

[31]Faiz Mohammed, ''Prospects of Poverty Eradication Through the Existing Zakat System in Pakistan,'' *Pakistan Development Review,* 30 (1991), pp. 1119–29.

A disproportionate number of Islamic economists have been from Pakistan, reflecting a combination of the British colonial educational system with Pakistan's creation as the first modern Islamic state in 1947. The first self-declared work presenting Islamic economics was by a Pakistani economist writing in Urdu (Sayyid Abdul A'la Mawdudi, *The Economic Problem of Man and Its Islamic Solution* [Lahore: Islamic Publications, 1947, translated to English, 1975]).

[32]''Sudan's Islamic Rulers Split on Links with West,'' *Washington Post,* February 27, 1993, p. A18.

Proper Consumption

Pork, nonritually slaughtered animals, and alcoholic beverages are not to be consumed. Prostitution is forbidden. Gambling is forbidden.

Gharar, or the Avoidance of Chance

The prohibition against gambling led to a more general prohibition against *gharar*, translated variously as chance or uncertainty. One is not to engage in contracts where the outcome cannot be predicted. Thus speculation, forward markets, and lotteries are all forbidden. This prohibition developed later and is not to be found in the *Qur'an*. Its basis is the specific forbidding of a particular game of chance in the *Qur'an*.

The forbidding of contracts involving gharar has led to controversy regarding two specific areas. One is insurance, which has generated three schools of thought. One is that insurance is acceptable because it involves reducing risk for a group using the law of large numbers and is thus different from gambling, which involves an individual choosing to create additional risk for himself. Another group says that insurance is gharar and therefore is unacceptable. A third group objects only to life insurance but not to other forms of insurance. A general outcome of this controversy has been suspicion of private provision of insurance and support for its provision by the public sector.

The other area of controversy involves sharecropping rents, which some Islamic economists disapprove of because of the gharar element involved although they approve of fixed rents. However the discussion of land rent is generally somewhat complicated. Some approve of land rent in all forms. Some disapprove of rent in all forms. Others disapprove of fixed rents while approving of sharecropping (which happens to be the most widespread form of rent in the Middle East). This last viewpoint arises from considering fixed rent to be a form of *riba*, or interest, and sharecropping to be a form of *qirad*, or profit sharing. The former is strictly forbidden whereas the latter is approved of. Those disapproving of all land rent say fixed rents are riba and sharecropping is gharar.

Qirad or Profit Sharing

A deep issue for Islamic economics that remains unresolved is the line between disapproved-of chance taking (gharar) and approved-of sharing risk through profit sharing, known as *qirad*. The line may be that approved profit sharing involves no additionally sought-out risk and that profit-sharing agreements be clearly spelled out so as to minimize uncertainty over the details of risk sharing.

The basis for accepting profit sharing comes from a tradition that the Companions of the Prophet practiced it, as did Muhammed himself in his early business activities. Nothing is specifically said of it in the *Qur'an* and it is only discussed slightly in the Hadith. The different Shari'as display variations regarding what are accepted forms and structures.

A wide variety of specific arrangements have been allowed in the various codes.[33] A universally accepted one that has received much attention from current Islamic economists is called *mudarabah.* This is an Islamic form of venture capitalism in that it includes a financial backer, who might be an Islamic bank, and an entrepreneur-manager. The backer provides an agreed sum of metallic money, or possibly goods.[34] The first party then receives an agreed-upon share of subsequent net profits. A portion of the funds go to the second party as payment for services. If the enterprise fails the first party loses all of the invested funds. The second party loses invested labor time.

In practice such arrangements have been undermined by fraud and dishonesty by entrepreneurs in reporting profits to investors. Thus, although such deals are supposed to be the ideal asset of a truly interest-free bank, during the late 1980s the share of Islamic bank assets that took this form in Iran and Pakistan respectively were only 38 percent and 14 percent,[35] although in Malaysia they accounted for 74 percent of all deals in 1989.[36] Such arrangements reflect the ideal cooperative spirit of Islam. But the failure of many practitioners to fulfill the ideal and to cheat on their partners has been denounced by Islamic economists.

Riba, or the Forbidding of Interest

The core demand of Islamic economists is that interest be forbidden. This demand arises from condemnations in the *Qur'an* and the Hadith of *riba,* which literally means ''increase or addition,'' but which is accepted as meaning interest in some form or other. Some argue that it only refers to increase beyond some level, but this is a minority opinion among current Islamic economists who argue that all interest should be forbidden. It is forbidden both on loaned money over time and within barter transactions where goods are only to be traded for themselves at an equal rate.

Although there are several relevant passages, perhaps the most famous, which also indicates a view of trade, is *Qur'an* (2: 275):

> Those who benefit from interest shall be raised like those who have been driven to madness by the touch of the devil; this is because they say: ''Trade is like interest'' while God has permitted trade and forbidden interest. Hence those who have received the admonition from their Lord and desist, may have what has

---

[33]See Muhammed Anwar, *Modelling Interest-Free Economy: A Study in Macro-economics and Development* (Herndon: International Institute of Islamic Thought, 1987), for a discussion of these varieties.

[34]The fixation on gold and silver as the only true forms of money has led the Saudi Arabians to put silver threads in their paper money.

[35]Mohsin S. Khan and Abbas Mirakhor, ''Islamic Banking: Experiences in the Islamic Republic of Iran and Pakistan,'' *Economic Development and Cultural Change* 38 (1990), pp. 353–74.

[36]Muhammed Anwar, ''The Role of Islamic Financial Institutions in the Socio-economic Development in Malaysia,'' *Pakistan Development Review* 30 (1991), pp. 1131–42.

A possible explanation for this difference might be that all banks in Iran and Pakistan must follow Islamic principles whereas in Malaysia doing so is voluntary. Therefore the latter might be more inclined to a more enthusiastic commitment to stricter Islamic principles.

already passed, their case being entrusted to God; but those who revert shall be the inhabitants of the fire and reside therein forever.

It can be argued that interest violates the fundamental Islamic requirements of brotherhood and justice because it is oppression and exploitation by the rich of the poor, especially when consumption loans for people in desperate circumstances are involved. The rich should take care of the needy, but interest income flows from the poor to the rich. Furthermore this tends to make the interest-receiving rich idle and unproductive, a parasite class. Similar arguments played roles in discussions by Greek philosophers like Aristotle and influenced discussions in the Catholic church.

It can also be argued that the redistribution of income leads to economic stagnation, that consumption is reduced because of the lower average propensity to consume of the rich who invest the income in expanded production, which leads to a surplus as the market has diminished. This is aggravated as interest costs are passed on to consumers as higher prices. Mawdudi saw this stagnation as leading to depression, monopoly, and imperialism.[37] Focusing on profit sharing rather than interest shifts the focus to the entrepreneur and thus stimulates genuine economic growth while removing a source of cyclical fluctuation.

Furthermore, forbidding interest eliminates the ''Hayekian monetary trade cycle'' of excessive investment responses to interest rate changes, leads to a closer link between savings and investment, and reduces destabilizing speculation. In this view, forbidding interest reduces inflation because there will be less overexpansion of credit, fewer people trying to live beyond their means, and lower cost pressures as producers can make profits at lower price levels, with the result that anticipated inflation will not affect investment.

The most serious criticism of these arguments has been that forbidding interest will lead to an insufficiency of savings and hence an insufficiency of real investment and long-run economic growth. Some have responded that zero interest rates mean that future generations will not have their interests discounted and that there will be a greater orientation to the future. Also, zakat may serve as a motive for savings by devout Muslims.

Another problem is how to allocate capital if there is no price for it. Socialist-oriented Islamic economists[38] argue this can be done through central planners using shadow prices generated from mathematical programming techniques, although we have seen that this is easier to advocate than to implement. The nonsocialist Naqvi[39] has suggested setting the zakat rate equal to the opportunity cost of capital, which connects with the above theory about the motive for Islamic savings.

---

[37]Sayyid Abdul A'la Mawdudi, *Interest* (Lahore: Islamic Publications, 1961) (in Urdu). Marx saw interest as arising from exploitative surplus value and thus thought it could lead to imperialism.

[38]See Ausaf Ali, *Studies toward an Understanding of the Developmental Perspective* (Karachi: Royal Book, 1979).

[39]Syed Nawab Haider Naqvi, *Ethics and Economics: An Islamic Synthesis* (London: Islamic Foundation, 1981).

The Practice of Islamic Banking

If proper Islamic banks are not allowed to charge interest, how can they make money? The answer is to finance and support the various allowed qirad or profit-sharing arrangements, such as mudarabah described above. Such an approach effectively makes Islamic banks into the equivalent of non-Islamic mutual funds. Someone depositing money in an Islamic bank de facto becomes part owner of the various enterprises to which the bank has loaned money.

This is the idealistic view. However there are many different allowable arrangements, some of which can be made to function almost exactly like standard interest. Probably the most widely used such arrangement in most Islamic banks is *murabaha.* This involves the financier purchasing goods for the producer and then selling them to him at an agreed-upon inflated price, which is to be paid back to the financier at an agreed-upon later date. Murabaha is viewed as legitimate by most Islamic economists because the financier bears risk during the period he owns the goods.

But this period can be reduced to an ''infinitesimal'' time span and most practicing Islamic banks do keep such periods very short, thereby sharply reducing their own risk. Islamic banks increasingly want to do this as they face frustrations getting their partners to report properly to them on net profits. That this approach can make a mockery of the whole business has been recognized by some Islamic economists, who argue that this method and similar ones should not be used widely.

In any case self-identified Islamic banking is a dramatically growing phenomenon. The first successful such institution was a savings bank founded in 1963 in the Egyptian town of Mit Ghamr. It was shut down by the government in 1968 during a socialist binge, but a full-service Islamic bank was opened in 1972 as the Nasser Social Bank. In 1975 a full-service Islamic bank was opened in Dubai. At the same time the oldest son of then–King Faisal of Saudi Arabia, Mohammed, founded the Islamic Development Bank (IDB), based in Jeddah, Saudi Arabia. This has been a major spearhead of the international movement towards Islamic banking and has been involved in much international trade and development lending. Islamic banks are now operating in over 50 countries. Iran, Pakistan, and Sudan allow only Islamic banks, although in the first two of these countries the interest-like murabaha form has been the most widely used.

Many of the complexities and issues surrounding Islamic banking have come to a head in Saudi Arabia, in many ways the most fundamentalist of all regimes. Despite this tradition, Western-style banking is allowed in Saudi Arabia, having developed from local money-changing operations, but is subject to severe restrictions regarding interest.[40]

---

[40]See Peter W. Wilson, *A Question of Interest: The Paralysis of Saudi Banking* (Boulder: Westview Press, 1991), chap. 2.

But this existing system faces two major challenges. One is the demand by many ulama and some economists such as Umer Chapra,[41] who works for the Saudi Arabian Monetary Agency (SAMA), for the outright prohibition of interest and therefore of non-Islamic banks. This position has strong support from some factions within the royal family, such as those allied to Prince Mohammed ibn Faisal, founder and head of the Islamic Development Bank.

The other major challenge is that Saudi Arabia formally follows the very strict Hanbali Shari'a law code, which means that there is no legal support for the right to collect interest at all, despite standard banking being technically allowed. As the economy's growth slowed following the post-1981 decline in oil prices, many bank loans became ''nonperforming'' and debtors began to go to the religious courts to have their debts declared invalid. The religious courts have responded sympathetically to such appeals.

By 1987 a crisis was declared and SAMA formed a committee to resolve the situation. But its efforts failed as it ran again into the entrenched position of the religious courts, with the result that many Western banks are now pulling out of the country. Kuwait and the United Arab Emirates are also experiencing similar complications. In Saudi Arabia, the ulama have even opposed the issuance of Saudi development bonds to finance the budget deficit that now exists.

Although a likely outcome of all this is to go the full-blown Islamic banking route, that outcome has other difficulties as well. In particular there seem to have been problems regarding their profitability recently. Some of this is due to having made overeager loans during the oil-boom 1970s that have now gone bad. Some may be due to lack of knowledge or experience on the part of the nouveau Islamic bankers. Some may be due to the fraud and misreporting of profits mentioned above.

The upshot of this has been increased caution on the part of Islamic banks and an increased trend towards the more interest-like lending arrangements such as murabaha rather than those that are more like profit sharing, such as mudarabah. Symbolic of this has been the changing composition of the Islamic Development Bank's portfolio between 1975 and 1986, with the former increasing from nil to over 80 percent whereas the latter decreased from 55 percent to 1 percent.[42]

Summary and Conclusions

The new traditional economy presents itself as an ideal that combines the efficiency of markets with the humaneness of socialism. Alienation is to be

---

[41] See M. Umer Chapra, *Towards a Just Monetary System: A Discussion of Money, Banking and Monetary Policy in the Light of Islamic Teachings* (Leicester: Islamic Foundation, 1985).

[42] Timur Kuran, ''The Economic Impact of Islamic Fundamentalism,'' in *Fundamentalisms and the State: Remaking Polities, Economies, and Militance*, eds. M. E. Marty and E. S. Appleby (Chicago: University of Chicago Press, 1993) p. 311.

Box 5–2

Is Islam a Third Way between Capitalism and Socialism?

Does Islam approve of private ownership of the means of production, in short, of capitalism? Aside from approving of trade and profit, the *Qur'an* clearly approves of private property. Some of its most detailed legal discussions regard rules of inheritance, although these rules tend to favor the division of fortunes among many persons.* Thus Islam is at least compatible with a moderate version of market capitalism appropriately modified to be consistent with Shari'a laws.

However, despite the decline of world socialism, a number of modern Islamic economists have argued for a socialist thrust or potential in the religion. This has been the case in Iran where a wave of nationalizations occurred after the taking of power by fundamentalists in 1979. In Libya, the semisocialist regime of Qaddafi incorporates some Islamic ideas into its system.

The quasi-socialist tradition within Islamic economic thought was founded by Abu Dharr al-Ghifari, a Companion of the Prophet. He advocated spending all wealth above a minimum subsistence to be redistributed to the poor. For his troubles he is said to have been banished from Medina. The Ismaili sect of Shi'ism has a strong "tax the rich and redistribute" orientation, although its leader, the Aga Khan, is very wealthy. A subgroup of Ismailis, the Qarmatians, established a regime in Bahrain and Eastern Arabia in the 900s that practiced cooperation among free men (they owned slaves) and had very heavy taxes on the rich for redistribution to the poor.

But this is not state ownership of the means of production. To defend that modern Islamic economists have reinterpreted portions of the *Qur'an.* A point emphasized by the Islamic socialists is that the ultimate owner of everything is Allah. Thus it can be argued that His devout followers, perhaps a state-affiliated ulama such as in Iran, should be in charge of managing His property.

There are competing translations of *Qur'an* 51: 10. Mannon† translates it as follows:

> He [God] set on the earth mountains standing firm, high above it, and bestowed bless-
> ings on the earth, and determined its resources, in four Days, to be equally shared by
> all the needy persons.

However other translations suggest that such equal sharing occurred early in historical time or make no reference at all to it. This is one of those areas where the highly poetic nature of the *Qur'an* leaves it open to a variety of interpretations.

---

*One loophole is the establishment of a charitable religious trust, or *waqf,* which can pass on without division.
†Mohammed Abdul Mannon, *Islamic Economics: Theory and Practice* (Lahore: Muhammed Ashraf, 1970), p. 104.

eliminated as economic motives are subordinated to religious ones in a higher moral universe. In the new traditional economy, all people will live in harmony with each other and with nature, or so its advocates argue.

Buddhist economics has produced a low-growth socialism in Burma and a fairly straightforward market capitalism in Thailand, although modern ecological economists have taken to supporting a variation of the Burmese version. Confucian economics emphasizes order and hierarchy in a system overseen by educated elites but open to market forces. Hindu economics derives from the writings of Gandhi and includes an emphasis on self-sufficient sets of villages, using simple technologies and operating within a reformed caste system.

Judaic economics is largely promarket, although subordinated to the pressure to build up and maintain the Israeli state. Some Judaic theorists have focused on some Biblical rules about tithes as well as the redistribution called for in the Jubilee year as the basis for a new Judaic economics. Christian economics has ranged widely from profeudal, medieval Roman Catholicism to the ultra–pro–market capitalism of the fundamentalist Protestant, New Christian Right in the United States today. Despite the latter, leftist Protestant fundamentalists in the United States focus on different Biblical passages or interpret those cited by the New Christian Right very differently.

The history of Islam ranges from its founding by Muhammed, through the early caliphates, the development of the various law codes (Shari'a), the decline of Islam as European power expanded, and the recent Islamic revival.

The principles of Islamic economics include the zakat tax for redistributing income to the poor; the approval of hard work and fair dealing; the forbidding of the consumption of pork, alcohol, and certain other items; the forbidding of dealing in chance (gharar); the approval of profit sharing (qirad); and the forbidding of interest (riba). The latter led to a discussion of the theory and operations of Islamic banks that do not charge interest. One conclusion is that there is a strong tendency in actual practice to use approved-of financing mechanisms that closely resemble interest.

Islamic attitudes towards property, capitalism, and socialism have involved much debate. Although the *Qur'an* approves of both markets and property, a distinct tradition within Islamic economics has stressed more radical income redistribution and severe limits on private property, leading some Islamic economists to declare it a third way between capitalism and socialism.

Which raises a final question: Can Islamic economies really function and can they achieve their goals? At one level the answer is trivial in that Saudi Arabia has never stopped being an Islamic economy and it is doing quite well, although prior to the discovery of oil there, it was isolated and poor, thus not proving the case one way or the other. Other would-be Islamic economies have been in power too short a time to give a definitive answer, although the example of Iran will be considered more closely in Chapter 16.

Let us conclude by citing two different authorities with strongly divergent viewpoints about Islamic economies. For the positive we have Umer Chapra:[43]

> The institutions of zakat, inheritance, and the abolition of interest are not just values that every Muslim has to comply with faithfully for his personal well-being in this world and the Hereafter, they also have an important role to play in economic restructuring . . . However, all these are parts of a total socioeconomic reorganization and their full potential cannot be realized if applied in an isolated manner. The Islamic program has to be accepted and enforced as a whole, and not just in parts, for total effectiveness.

For the negative we have Timur Kuran[44] who after forecasting takeovers by Islamic fundamentalists in many places declares

> Failures along the way could easily be taken to mean educational efforts need to be redoubled and non-Islamic influences curbed further. In this vain search for the Islamic utopia the political establishment would become increasingly repressive, making it treacherous to suggest that Islam does not offer clear and definitive answers to all economic problems. Meanwhile, the discipline of Islamic economics could feed on itself for decades, mistaking apologetics for serious reflection and cosmetics for genuine reform. The twenty-first century could thus become for Islam what the twentieth was for socialism: a period of infinite hope and promise, followed by disappointment, repression, disillusionment, and despair.

We shall not attempt to adjudicate between the shining optimism of Chapra and the dark pessimism of Kuran. However, we share with them the forecast that over the near future we shall see an increasing number of countries attempting the experiment of Islamic economics.

Questions for Discussion

1. In what sense can Buddhist and Hindu economics be said to be supportive of modern ''Green'' movements?

2. Compare and contrast Buddhist, Confucian, and Hindu views of the role of the state in the economy.

3. Compare and contrast Judaic, Catholic, Protestant, and Islamic views of market capitalism.

4. Why does Islam seem to have a more fully developed economic system than other major world religions?

---

[43]M. Umer Chapra, *Islam and the Economic Challenge* (Leicester: Islamic Foundation, 1992), p. 226.

[44]Timur Kuran, ''The Economic Impact of Islamic Fundamentalism,'' in *Fundamentalisms and the State: Remaking Polities, Economies, and Militance,* M. E. Marty and R. S. Appleby, eds. (Chicago: University of Chicago Press, 1993), p. 332.

5. Why in most modern economies is zakat unlikely to be able to resolve major income inequalities?

6. Distinguish four different attitudes to land rent among Islamic economists.

7. What are some economic arguments for and against the Islamic forbidding of riba?

8. Why do we see a trend in modern Islamic banks towards more interest-like kinds of loan arrangements?

Suggested Further Readings

Ahmad, Khurshid, ed. *Studies in Islamic Economics.* Leicester: Islamic Foundation, 1980.

Chapra, M. Umer. *Islam and the Economic Challenge.* Leicester: Islamic Foundation, 1992.

Lapidus, Ira M. *A History of Islamic Societies.* Cambridge, UK: University of Cambridge Press, 1988.

Marty, Martin E., and R. Scott Appleby, eds. *Fundamentalisms and the State: Remaking Polities, Economies, and Militance.* Chicago: University of Chicago Press, 1993.

Pryor, Frederic L. ''The Islamic Economic System.'' *Journal of Comparative Economics* 9 (1985), pp. 197–223.

Richards, Alan, and John Waterbury, *A Political Economy of the Middle East: State, Class, and Economic Development.* Boulder: Westview Press, 1990.

Rodinson, Maxime. *Islam and Capitalism.* Translated by Brian Pearce. New York: Pantheon, 1973.

VARIETIES OF ADVANCED MARKET CAPITALISM

Part II contains the first set of country case studies, representing the varieties of advanced market capitalism. These cases must be compared with the archetypal case of the United States, presented in Chapter 2 as the example in the theoretical discussion of market capitalism as a system.

Chapter 6 discusses the world's second largest economy, that of Japan. Japan's is one of the hardest economies in the world to understand and to classify because much controversy exists about its true nature. Clearly it is market capitalist and very advanced. But it also combines significant elements of neo-Confucian tradition, making it somewhat of a new traditional economy, and also important elements of planning and bureaucratic coordination, even though the direct share of government in the economy is quite small. It serves as a role model for many of the other East Asian economies.

Chapter 7 presents the case of France, notable as the advanced market capitalist economy that has most seriously used indicative planning. This chapter also contains extensive discussion of the nature and prospects of the European Union.

Chapter 8 covers the Swedish economy, which has had the most extensive income redistribution of any market capitalist economy. Despite its ''socialist'' label, it has no central planning and little state ownership of firms. But it has government-run active labor programs to retrain labor and reduce unemployment as well as a corporatist centralized wage bargaining process that long encouraged macroeconomic stability.

Chapter 9 looks at the social market economy of Germany. It is dominated by the problem of unifying two distinct economic systems into one national economy. Germany is a symbol of the larger problem of the world economy, of integrating distinct economic systems into a functioning world economy.

With some exceptions, most of the country case studies have approximately parallel structures. After some general discussion they begin by examining the historical and cultural foundations of the society and nation to see the tendencies that manifest themselves in its economic system. Then we study the microeconomic functioning of the system to see the essential nature of its decision-making processes. Next we move to macroeconomic performance and more broad areas of performance such as living standards, distribution of income, and environmental problems. Finally we consider the economy's relationship with the rest of the world economy.

CHINA

RUSSIA

NORTH
KOREA

SOUTH
KOREA

TAIWAN

CHAPTER 6

JAPAN: TRADITIONAL ELEMENTS IN A PLANNED MARKET ECONOMY

But to expect Americans, who are accustomed to thinking of their nation as number one, to acknowledge that in many areas its supremacy has been lost to an Asian nation and to learn from that nation is to ask a good deal. Americans are peculiarly receptive to any explanation of Japan's economic performance which avoids acknowledging Japan's superior competitiveness.
—Ezra F. Vogel, *Japan As Number One*, 1979, p. 225

The modern myth of Japan is assuredly the biggest hoax of the present age . . . The economy has obviously slowed down, income distribution has become skewed, while landowners have become rich ordinary families can no longer afford their own home. There are now poor people as well as many old people who are scared about what will become of them.
—Jon Woronoff, *Japan as-Anything but-Number One*, 1991, pp. 7–8

The industrialized capitalist countries are engaged in severe economic competition. Private companies square off toe to toe. Sometimes, in the heat of the contest, their cheering sections—government officials and politicians—vilify opponents, yell ''unfair,'' and demand new rules. Japan has quietly endured this rhetorical crescendo from the United States for years. We cannot remain silent forever. It is time to speak out.
—Shintaro Ishihara, *The Japan That Can Say No*, 1989, pp. 40–41

Introduction: Japan as a New Traditional Economy?

From the ashes of defeat and poverty at the end of World War II Japan experienced the most rapid rate of sustained economic growth in the world to become its second largest economy. It achieved this while maintaining fairly low unemployment and inflation rates and a greater degree of income equality than most capitalist economies. Its people have the world's longest life expectancy. It leads in many areas of technology. It has large trade surpluses

127

that do not decline. It has become the world's largest creditor and possibly its leading financial power. Despite recent difficulties many think that it is "Number One."

These achievements inspire admiration and envy from other nations. Conflicts with other nations over trade issues threaten to plunge the world economy into a trade war and depression. Japan's very success makes its every action important for the whole world economy.

There is little agreement about the nature of Japan's success, and some questioning about whether it is successful. A profound truth about Japan is that every supposed fact about it abounds in paradox and multiple interpretations.[1] For every interpretation by an admiring "Japanologist" there is a counter interpretation by a critical "revisionist."

Where admirers see effective Japanese management bringing about harmonious labor-management relations, critics see oppression of labor movements by triumphant management. Where admirers see highly educated and technically innovative workers, critics see robotized rote learners who only know how to imitate but not to create. Where admirers see ever-rising living standards, critics see "workaholics in rabbit hutches." Where admirers see innovative government-business relations, critics see a corrupt "Japan, Incorporated." Where admirers see an open and cosmopolitan nation with lower tariffs and quotas than its trading partners, critics see an insular and arrogant nation cheating its trading partners through devious methods. Where admirers see a democratic and pacifistic nation, critics see a nation where dictatorial structures from its dark past persist and a potentially militaristic nationalism is rising.[2]

Even among admirers there are debates about the basis of Japanese success. Advocates of different schools of economic thought and ideology seek to "take credit" for Japanese success by attempting to fit it Rashomonlike into the straitjackets of their favored approaches. Thus advocates of government economic intervention argue that bureaucratic guidance through indicative planning and industrial policy has been key to Japanese success. Advocates of laissez-faire argue that these have been more of a hindrance than a help, with the most dynamic sectors ignoring the government bureaucrats.

The Japanese economic system is a subtle mixture of structures and systems unique in the world, despite attempts by others at imitation. Undoubtedly it is a market capitalist economy. Nevertheless government does engage in indicative planning and has significant influence. Japan was the first society

---

[1]This is a deep characteristic of Japanese culture, as illustrated by the Japanese film, Akira Kurosawa's *Rashomon,* in which an incident is recounted afterwards differently by different participants. The Japanese distinguish between *tatemae,* a surface illusion, which is initially presented in a discussion or negotiation, and *honne,* which reflects the underlying reality.

[2]This last paradox is an old one in Japanese culture. As described in the world's first novel, *The Tale of Genji,* by the 11th-century Lady Murasaki, *samurai* were supposed to be both sensitive poets and fierce warriors. This paradox is captured in the title of Ruth Benedict's 1946 classic of Japanology, *The Chrysanthemum and the Sword.*

of non-European origin to carry out industrialization and modern economic growth. It succeeded in adopting foreign technologies and practices without giving up its indigenous culture, symbolized by the late 19th-century slogan, ''Japanese spirit and Western ability.''

Japan may actually be the most successful example of a new traditional economy in the world. Many argue that the key to Japan's success is the ''familistic groupism'' of Japanese society, often labeled a ''feudalistic hold-over,'' that supposedly is responsible for both its harmonious labor-management relations and its harmonious government-business relations.

In Chapter 4 it was argued that the household economy is the essence of the traditional economy. Japanese society is not dominated by a fundamentalist religious movement, but it is permeated by the idea that companies, groups of companies, bureaucracies, and society as a whole are families or households.[3] Thus the Japanese economy combines a traditional household orientation with advanced modern technologies and approaches. But given the dominance of market capitalism and the role of government guidance, a more accurate description is ''planned market capitalism with traditional elements.''

Historical and Cultural Background of the Japanese Economy

The Absorption of Chinese Culture

The ability of the Japanese to absorb foreign influences and technologies while maintaining their cultural core arose from having a strong sense of identity. That came from their high degree of homogeneity stemming from their long isolation. Like Britain Japan is an island nation, but 100 miles off the nearest continent rather than just 20.

The original religion was Shinto, emphasizing worship of ancestral and nature spirits and of the emperor because of his claimed descent from Amaterasu, goddess of the rising sun, a status disavowed by Emperor Hirohito at Japan's surrender in 1945.

The model for Japan's integrating foreign influences into its society was its absorption of Chinese culture in the sixth and seventh centuries. Chinese writing was adopted but modified.[4] Buddhism and Confucianism were introduced but also were modified, without displacing native Shintoism. Whereas in most societies an individual will be one religion to the exclusion of others, most Japanese view themselves as simultaneously following all three, an example of their ability to deal with multiple realities. Shintoism is followed for marriages, Buddhism for funerals, and Confucianism for civil and political behavior.

---

[3]In Japanese before the modern era the word for house, *ie*, meant both family and business enterprise. Many Japanese argue that the *ie* is the foundation of Japanese civilization.

[4]Linguistically Japanese is related to Korean, but very distinct from any variety of Chinese.

Shintoism and Buddhism[5] do not have much influence on Japanese economic thought or behavior, but the Japanese form of Confucianism does.[6] After 1600 Confucian values became deeply entrenched in the educational system, emphasizing especially loyalty to one's immediate superiors and respect for state authority. After 1868, influential businessmen emphasized Confucian values and the transfer of the *bushido* code of the samurai warriors to business management practices, symbolized by the modern phrase ''from samurai to sarariman'' (salaryman). The most important Confucian value in Japan is *wa* (harmony), which, along with loyalty, cements the familistic groupism that dominates the Japanese economy.

The Tokugawa Shogunate and the Meiji Restoration

After 1185 rule was in the hands of military commanders known as shoguns, appointed by the emperor to whom they were nominally subject.[7] During the 1500s Portuguese traders and Jesuit priests penetrated Japan and almost dominated the country, but they were expelled in 1603 after which the nation closed up under the Tokugawa shogunate. During this isolation, Japan had considerable development of business,[8] transportation infrastructure, and literacy, laying a foundation for later economic takeoff.

After being forcibly opened to outsiders in 1853 by the arrival of Commodore Perry's ''black ships'' from the United States, Tokugawa society fell into crisis. Humiliated by military defeats, landless samurai under the slogan ''revere the emperor, expel the barbarians'' overthrew the Tokugawa shogun in 1868. This was the Meiji Restoration, named for the emperor of the time.

Those who came to power both opened the country dramatically to foreign influences and technologies and removed all rights and powers of the samurai, thereby ending feudalism. The samurai were paid off with bonds in 1873 with which many of them started businesses. Farmers were given the land. Students were sent abroad to study, especially to the United States and Germany.

---

[5]The best known form of Japanese Buddhism is Zen, very popular with the samurai from the 1200s onwards. Some argue that Zen increases the ability of Japanese managers to deal with indirection and vagueness and that it enhances creativity in research and development (see Box 6–1).

[6]A main difference between Chinese and Japanese Confucianism is that the former emphasizes benevolence as the supreme virtue whereas the latter emphasizes loyalty. This combined with state Shinto emperor worship to support Japanese militaristic nationalism in World War II. It also helps maintain status hierarchies in Japanese companies and bureaucracies. See Michio Morishima, *Why Has Japan 'Succeeded'? Western Technology and the Japanese Ethos* (Cambridge: Cambridge University Press, 1982), and Tessa Morris-Suzuki, *A History of Japanese Economic Thought* (London: Routledge, 1989).

[7]Usually the real ruler would be a prime minister or an adviser to a prime minister to the shogun. This tradition of indirect rule persists today, with the greatest power being in the hands of party politicians with no official positions. This has led some foreigners to complain that ''no one rules'' and that negotiations with prime ministers or other officials about trade or other issues are pointless.

[8]The ancestors of two of the six dominant modern *keiretsu,* Mitsui and Sumitomo, were founded in this period, the former as a dry goods business, the latter as a copper miner and smelter.

The state started many industrial enterprises, pushing industrial development under the slogan ''rich country, strong military,'' only to privatize them after a fiscal crisis in 1883. Industrial growth took off—cotton spinning became the first internationally competitive industry by 1900, and iron and steel, railroads, mining, and machinery also expanded rapidly, initially supported by ''infant industry'' tariffs.

Japan also imitated the European penchant for imperializing neighbors.[9] In 1895 Taiwan was conquered after a war with China. Next came the 1905 Russo-Japanese War, culminating in the first victory of an Asian power over a European one in modern times,[10] and Japan took control of Korea. By the 1920s, the economy was dominated by four leading *zaibatsus:* Mitsui, Mitsubishi, Sumitomo, and Yasuda, conglomerates that each had a dominating bank of the same name.

In 1931 the Japanese army seized the Chinese province of Manchuria and established the puppet state of Manchuko. Economic central planning elements were tested there that were used later. In 1937 Japan invaded China, later allying with Germany and Italy. Its 1941 bombing of Pearl Harbor brought the United States into World War II. On August 16, 1945, Japan surrendered after the United States dropped atomic bombs on Hiroshima and Nagasaki.

The American Occupation and Its Aftermath

On September 2, 1945, General Douglas MacArthur arrived to become the Supreme Commander of the Allied Powers and the virtual ruler of Japan until the Occupation ended in 1952, the first time in Japanese history that a foreign power ruled. After an initial period of radical purgings and reforms up to 1947, MacArthur encouraged continuity of rule by traditional elites[11] as Japan was increasingly seen as a Cold War ally.

The United States imposed a constitution that formally demilitarized Japan. Much of the bureaucracy survived unscathed, except for a few name changes. Labor unions were legalized, as were the Communist and Socialist parties. The zaibatsus were broken up. Land was redistributed. Again the Japanese integrated foreign influences into their society and culture, this time from the United States.

Until around 1960 labor militancy was considerable before ''harmonious'' relations with management finally emerged. In 1955 the two leading

---

[9]Japan denied that it practiced imperialism, arguing that it was fighting against the racist imperialism of Europe and the United States, a view still held by some in Japan. During World War II Japan claimed to be establishing the ''Greater East Asia Co-Prosperity Sphere.'' Japanese soldiers were surprised when they were not welcomed in such European colonies as Vietnam and Malaya. Some argue a Japanese-dominated Co-Prosperity Sphere, wherein Japanese investment ties economies closely to buying Japanese goods, has been established de facto.

[10]Russia and Japan have an ongoing dispute over islands taken by the Soviet Union at the end of World War II.

[11]A supreme symbol of that continuity was MacArthur's lack of a demand for Emperor Hirohito to step down. Hirohito reigned from 1926 until his death in 1989.

conservative parties united to form the Liberal Democratic Party (LDP), which ruled Japan until 1993.[12] From the mid-1950s to the 1970s the old zaibatsus re-formed as loosely organized *keiretsu,* each centered on a bank and a trading company. Mitsui, Mitsubishi, and Sumitomo kept their names, but Yasuda became Fuyo and two other leading keiretsu emerged, Sanwa and Ikkan.

By 1955 real per capita income reached its highest prewar levels. By the late 1960s large and persistent trade surpluses emerged. By the mid-1970s per capita income equaled that in many advanced economies and continued to grow more rapidly than in any of them, despite decelerating. In 1975, Japan became one of the G-7 countries[13] whose leaders meet in economic summits each June. Japan had arrived as a world economic leader.

The Microeconomic Foundations of the Japanese Economy

The "Three Sacred Treasures" of Labor-Management Relations

At the foundation of the Japanese economy is its highly educated and well-motivated labor force. The country has few natural resources and at the end of World War II much of its capital stock was destroyed. Many Japanese innovations that improve quality and productivity have been suggested by workers on site, often through *quality circles.* Such loyalty and commitment to the firms they work for is something that many other countries have sought to emulate.[14]

Basic to Japanese labor are the "three sacred treasures":[15] lifetime employment, seniority-based wages, and enterprise unions. More conventional wisdom about Japanese industry is that it offers frequent intraenterprise job rotation by multifunctional workers, much on-the-job firm-specific training, widespread bonus payments and flexible compensation schemes, contracts negotiated annually in a synchronized manner, stable employment, and large severance payments at retirement but few pensions. This conventional wisdom has been questioned, notably because of the *dual economy.* Portions of the conventional wisdom do not apply to the 50 percent of the labor force in small firms or to most women workers in large firms.[16]

---

[12]It is an old wisecrack that the LDP is neither liberal, democratic, nor even a party.

[13]The other six are the United States, Canada, the Federal Republic of Germany, France, the United Kingdom, and Italy. Japan is also in the smaller G-5 that omits Canada and Italy and the even smaller G-3 that further omits the United Kingdom and France.

[14]Jon Woronoff (*Japan-As-Anything But-Number-One* [Armonk: M. E. Sharpe, 1990], chap. 2) claims that this loyalty is a false *tatemae* phenomenon. Workers are forced to join quality circles and are pressured into exhibiting apparent loyalty to their firms while the real *honne* is that they hate their bosses and their jobs just like workers everywhere.

[15]This term was invented by an American, James Abegglen, *The Japanese Factory* (Glencoe: The Free Press, 1958).

[16]Women are strongly discouraged from working if they get married and have children, although this attitude is changing.

Lifetime Employment.   Lifetime employment is seen as key to engendering loyalty and drawing forth innovative suggestions to improve productivity. Critics suggest lifetime employment is limited to about 30 percent of the labor force, mostly educated males in large firms who must retire at age 55 with large severance payments, although often with assistance in getting other jobs in smaller firms. However comparisons of tenure patterns between Japan and the United States find Japanese workers more likely to stay with a single firm for a longer time, even in small firms.[17]

This system depends on stability of employment, which has been aided by rapid growth of the economy. It is eased by the synchronized annual negotiating system and by the relatively docile enterprise unions. Also the bonus system, amounting to up to 30 percent of compensation in some cases, may amount to a form of profit sharing that stabilizes the economy as in the "share economy" theory, although this has been questioned.[18] If the recent slowdown of the Japanese economy leads to permanently increased unemployment we could see pressure on the system of stable employment.

One element of long-term employment is the development of firm-specific human capital by rotating workers from job to job within the firm. Workers know all about the firm, but lack skills transferrable to other firms. This on-the-job training of blue collar workers leads to their "white collarization" in larger firms and thus their greater loyalty to the firm. But loyalty is a two-way street. Firms are more willing to engage in firm-specific training if they believe workers will stick around for a long time.

Although some argue that lifetime employment reflects a deep Confucian code, it and many other distinctively Japanese practices are probably more recent developments. The real beginning of these practices may have been during World War II when the government became concerned about worker morale issues for maintaining military production.[19]

Seniority Wages.   Seniority wages, with lifetime employment, are viewed as part of the general package that produces loyalty to the firm and also as consistent with the Confucian view of respect for elders. If one sticks with the firm one moves up in salary.

In Japan there is a steeper age-wage profile for blue collar workers than in other countries, reflecting the white collarization of Japanese blue collar workers, along with an across the board greater tendency for seniority wages in Japan than in the United States.[20] Nevertheless there is a trend towards more emphasis on merit rather than seniority in wage setting, with strong

---

[17]See Masanori Hashimoto and John Raisian, "Employment Tenure and Earnings Profiles in Japan and the United States," *American Economic Review* 75 (1985), pp. 721–35.

[18]See Merton J. Peck, "Is Japan Really a Share Economy?" *Journal of Comparative Economics* 10 (1986), pp. 427–32.

[19]See Tetsuji Okazaki, "The Japanese Firm Under the Wartime Planned Economy," Research Institute for the Japanese Economy Discussion Paper 92–F–4, University of Tokyo.

[20]See Masanori Hashimoto and John Raisian, "Employment Tenure and Earnings Profiles."

expectations among both management and labor in Japan that the system will move in the direction of performance-based pay.[21]

Enterprise Unions. Enterprise unions (to be contrasted with industrial or craft unions prevalent in the United States) go along with the above package. If one is committed for life to a specific company and one has been working in several different jobs with the company, thus not being tied to a particular skill or craft, then it is logical to belong to a union that negotiates directly with that company and only that company. Stability of labor-management relations leads to the "happy family of the firm." Such unions contain both white and blue collar workers and partly account for the smaller wage differentials between them. Enterprise unions are the pattern in Japan and they are strongly supported by both management and labor. Nevertheless some critics consider them to be ineffective "patsies" for management interests.

Like the United States, Japan has had a steadily declining rate of unionization, from a peak of 55.8 percent of the labor force in 1949 to 29.1 percent in 1984.[22] This decline may reflect docility of the unions, which did not always hold. In the 1940s and the 1950s Japan had a higher strike rate than in Britain or France, and the unions were linked to radical left-wing politics, including some with Japan's Communist Party. The turning point towards moderation came with the breaking of a long steel strike in 1959 and a more bitter mining dispute in 1960.

The change in leadership of the steel unions after 1959 led to the synchronized system of spring negotiations. This avoids staggered wage contracts, minimizing inflationary momentum that can arise as one union imitates another, thus improving inflation-unemployment trade-offs and stabilizing employment. After the first oil price shock in 1973 the unions asked for high wage increases that triggered increases in both unemployment and inflation. After the second oil price shock in 1979 they avoided high demands, thereby maintaining greater macroeconomic stability.

The Japanese Firm and the Japanese Manager

The Keiretsu System. The most distinctive element of Japanese industrial organization is the existence of interlocked associations of firms known as keiretsu, which are either *horizontal keiretsu* or *vertical keiretsu*. Horizontal keiretsu are essentially revivals of the prewar zaibatsus,[23] firms in different industries all linked to a common bank and trading company. Vertical keiretsu

---

[21]See Ken Sakuma, "Changes in Japanese-Style Labor-Management Relations," *Japanese Economic Studies* 16 (1988), pp. 3–48.

[22]Ken Sakuma, "Changes in Japanese-Style Labor-Management Relations."

[23]The difference is that zaibatsus were single holding companies whereas the firms in keiretsus maintain their formal independence.

TABLE 6–1   Intrakeiretsu Relations

Keiretsu	Number of Firms	Interlocking Shares	Intragroup Loans
Mitsui	24	17.10%	21.94%
Mitsubishi	29	27.80	20.17
Sumitomo	20	24.22	24.53
Fuyo	29	15.61	18.20
Sanwa	44	16.47	18.51
Ikkan	47	12.49	11.18

Source: Takatoshi Ito, *The Japanese Economy* (Cambridge, MA: MIT Press, 1992), p. 181.

are a set of suppliers and distributors linked to a major industrial producer by long-term contracts. U.S. trade negotiators charge that vertical keiretsu are anticompetitive and keep out U.S. suppliers. A keiretsu is yet another familistic grouping typical of the Japanese economy.

The two kinds of keiretsu coexist. Thus Toshiba Corporation, which makes computers, consumer electronics, semiconductors, and heavy machinery, is at the center of a vertical keiretsu that includes 11,000 franchised distributors, about 200 direct suppliers, and about 600 suppliers of the direct suppliers. At the same time Toshiba is a member in good standing of the Mitsui horizontal keiretsu. But some vertical keiretsu stand alone, such as those associated with Honda and Sony, both very independent companies. Members of horizontal keiretsu tend to be large companies that practice the three sacred treasures of labor-management relations whereas peripheral firms of vertical keiretsu tend not to.

All keiretsu have much cross-holding of stocks. Horizontal keiretsu have much bank ownership and a large proportion of loans from the bank. In some horizontal keiretsu the CEOs of firms meet on a weekly basis to coordinate strategies and behaviors. These relations extend to their workers who tend to buy from companies in their company's keiretsu.

Table 6–1 shows the number of firms, the average percentage of interlocking shares, and the average percent of intragroup loans for the six largest horizontal keiretsu in 1987. These Big Six together had 4.14 percent of employees, 12.96 percent of assets, 15 percent of capital, 14.35 percent of sales, and 11.7 percent of gross profits in the Japanese economy.[24]

Table 6–2 shows some major companies in some leading sectors associated with two of the Big Six horizontal keiretsu, one from the more tightly controlled group (Mitsui) and one from the less tightly controlled group (Ikkan).

Some keiretsu have more than one firm per sector and some firms belong to more than one keiretsu, notably Hitachi which belongs to Fuyo, Sanwa, and

---

[24]Takatoshi Ito, *The Japanese Economy* (Cambridge, MA: MIT Press, 1992), p. 188.

TABLE 6–2   Selected Keiretsu Members

Sector	Mitsui	Ikkan
Banking	Mitsui Bank	Dai-Ichi Kangyo Bank
Life insurance	Mitsui Life	Asahi Life
		Fukoku Life
Trading	Mitsui Bussan	C. Itoh
		Kanematsu Gosho
Construction	Mitsui Construction	Shimizu Construction
	Sanki Kogyo	
Food & drink	Nihon Mills	
Textiles	Tohre	Asahi Kasei Kogyo
Cement	Onoda Cement	Chichibu cement
Steel	Nihon Seikojo	Kawasaki Steel
		Kobe Seiko
		Nihon Heavy Industries
Electronics	Toshiba	Hitachi
		Fujitsu
		Yasukawa Electronics
		Nihon Columbia
Automobiles	Toyota	Isuzu
Shipbuilding	Mitsui Shipbuilding	Ishikawajima harima
		Kawasaki Heavy Industries
Optics		Asahi Kagaku
Department stores	Mitsukoshi	Seibu Department Store

Source: Takatoshi Ito, *The Japanese Economy* (Cambridge, MA: MIT Press, 1992), pp. 185–87.

Ikkan simultaneously. These are the three less loosely interconnected, hence less zaibatsu-like, of the Big Six horizontal keiretsu. Many of these firms remain predominantly owned and controlled by the family of the founder-entrepreneur, Toyota being a prominent example.

It has been argued that these entities are able to enjoy network externalities of one sort or another. But there is evidence that group membership may have a negative impact on profitability relative to independents run by founder-entrepreneurs such as the late Akio Morita of Sony.[25] These firms make higher interest payments to their coordinating banks, which seem to be the big gainers in terms of profits, although the firms may gain security of financing.

Broadly there has been a trend towards banks and companies owning each other's stock beyond keiretsu relationships, with the share of Japanese stocks held outside of keiretsu relationships rising from 32.7 percent in 1955 to 67.1

---

[25]Richard Caves and Masu Uekasa, *Industrial Concentration in Japan* (Washington: Brookings Institution, 1976), pp. 72–83.

percent in 1989. In contrast the proportion of banks and companies that own each other's stock for the United States in 1988 was 35.4 percent.[26] This has led some to wisecrack that Japan is a "capitalism without capitalists."

This pattern arose after Japan joined the Organization for Economic Co-operation and Development (OECD) in the 1960s and was pressured to open its stock market to foreign investors. This high level of cross-holdings prevents foreigners from taking over companies, and in 1989 foreigners owned only 3.9 percent of Japanese stocks.[27]

Vertical keiretsu may achieve efficiencies because their stable long-term contracts allow for "just-in-time" delivery (*kanban*) systems that minimize inventory costs and encourage superior quality controls. A large firm will generally have more than one supplier for a part, thus maintaining a degree of competitiveness that does not exist when parts suppliers are merely subsidiaries of the major firm, as is often the case among U.S. automobile producers. Often the major firms help the smaller firms with investment and marketing. But the smaller firms generally bear the brunt of unemployment in a slow-down, providing a buffer for the major firms that helps them maintain their lifetime employment systems.

Managerial Decision Making.   For some time there has been a fad in the United States and, to a lesser extent in Europe, to imitate aspects of Japanese management practices. For example, the Saturn subsidiary of General Motors was consciously set up along Japanese lines in contrast to the rest of GM, and recently it became more successful than the rest of GM. Although some argue that managerial practices cannot be exported from Japan because of cultural uniqueness, the success of Japanese automobile subsidiaries in the United States relative to U.S. producers suggests otherwise.[28]

Masahiko Aoki[29] argues that Japanese firms reflect a *J-mode* type of organization in contrast with an *H-mode* found in most U.S. and European corporations. The J-mode is characterized by "horizontal coordination among operating units based on the sharing of ex post on-site information (learned results)." This contrasts with the H-mode characterized by "hierarchical separation between planning and implemental operation and the emphasis on the economies of specialization." The J-mode depends upon both long-term relationships between workers and firms and long-term relationships between banks and firms, which tend to hold for keiretsu members with lifetime employment systems.

---

[26]*OECD Economic Surveys: Japan, 1991/1992* (Paris: Organization for Economic Cooperation and Development, 1992), p. 75.

[27]*OECD Economic Surveys.*

[28]However some U.S. companies touted as following Japanese practices such as lifetime employment have fallen on hard times, for example, IBM.

[29]Masahiko Aoki, "Toward an Economic Model of the Japanese Firm," *Journal of Economic Literature* 28 (1990), pp. 1–27.

Small pay differentials between workers and top managers in Japanese firms and the fact that usually top managers have risen from within the firm increase the loyalty and links between the two, making management essentially the representative of the employees. Thus Japanese firms resemble labor-managed firms although rank hierarchies are strongly maintained. Aoki maintains that horizontal coordination only works because of the existence of a rank incentive structure.

Horizontal coordination is carried out through elaborate processes of consensual decision making (*nemawashi*), which involves discussion of a decision with virtually everyone involved. Westerners sometimes complain that Japanese decision makers have too many meetings and are slow to come to decisions. But advocates of the system note that once a decision is reached, everyone is "on board" and knows what is involved. Thus the decision is more likely to be carried out effectively than a typical H-mode, purely top-down decision.

Not only do Japanese firms coordinate across equal levels, but also they encourage input from the bottom up. This leads to *ringi-sho,* or the writing of memos by underlings that are channeled upwards to superiors. Ringi-sho connects with the widespread use of quality circles and the dependence upon workers for suggestions for improving the firm's performance.[30] Maintenance of strict seniority-based rank hierarchies allows superiors to defer to underlings for their expertise when it is superior. Intracorporate solidarity and information sharing are further encouraged by such leveling devices as having only one cafeteria and parking lot for all employees rather than segregating top management in an overpaid ghetto of ineffective decision making.

Given the long-term nature of employee-firm relations and of bank-firm relations, Japanese managers use longer time horizons for strategic planning. A manifestation of long-term planning is a greater emphasis upon maximizing market share subject to a minimum profit constraint rather than maximizing short-run profits.

Long-term bank financing allows Japanese firms to resist pressures that come from stock markets for short-run profits through threats of takeover raids. Firms are further insulated against such pressures by the high level of cross-holdings of stocks between firms and between banks and firms. This willingness of banks to take a long-term view depends on the high Japanese savings rate, which allows for low interest rates that stimulate both capital investment and a longer time horizon for that investment. This low cost of capital may be ending in Japan with the emergence of bank debt problems.

An example of the long-term view of Japanese managers versus the short-term view of U.S. ones is the development of the VCR, invented in the United

---

[30]Another element is widespread use of statistical quality control methods, introduced after World War II by the U.S. quality control expert, W. Edwards Deming, and ignored at the time in the United States. The Japanese established a prize for quality control in his name.

States and initially produced there. Unlike some other products where the United States lost out due to intensive Japanese competition (e.g., TVs), U.S. producers such as Westinghouse voluntarily gave up producing VCRs because of the initial slow growth of the market and the resulting low rates of return on investment. This occurred prior to Japanese entry into the market. During the 1980s VCRs were the most rapidly growing consumer market in the United States, but no U.S. firms participated.

Industrial Policy by Government

A controversial aspect of the Japanese economy is the role of government, famous for cooperative government-business relations labeled "industrial policy." The controversy arises over how much such cooperation actually goes on; if it goes on, how effective it is; and if it goes on and is effective, whether it is to be admired or condemned.

These disputes focus on the role of the Ministry of International Trade and Industry (MITI), main implementor of industrial policy. A lesser role is played by the Ministry of Finance (MOF) through its control over tax subsidies and the banking system, although the Ministry of Agriculture also attracts attention because of its protectionist policies, somewhat relaxed recently.

Those who argue that the state is the driving force of the Japanese economy point to the apparent supremacy of government bureaucrats. A sign of this is that after retirement from government, high-level bureaucrats "descend from heaven" (*amakudari*) to high-level employment in top firms. Chalmers Johnson[31] identifies the 15 MITI Vice Ministers (top internal officials) from 1949 to 1978 and their amakudari positions. These include President and Chairman of Toshiba, President of New Japan Steel, Chairman of Nippon Kokan Steel, President of Japan Petrochemical Corporation, Managing Director of Mitsui Trading Company, Executive Director of Toyota, and President of Sumitomo Metals Corporation, among other equally impressive positions.

All of these men served in MITI and its predecessor ministries from before or during World War II.[32] Thus Johnson sees substantial continuity between wartime planning practices carried out by the Ministry of Munitions and its postwar successor, MITI. These policies include sectoral financial targeting, encouragement of bank rather than equity financing, encouragement of better labor relations, and the use of selective cartelization.

---

[31]Chalmers Johnson, *MITI and the Japanese Miracle: The Growth of Industrial Policy, 1925–1975* (Stanford: Stanford University Press, 1982), p. 72.

[32]Many of them were part of the promilitary "reform bureaucrat" movement of the 1930s who first experimented with economic planning in Manchuria. Some were initially influenced by the Soviet model of five-year plans for industrialization, but later followed the "corporate state" approach of Nazi Germany.

The basic pattern of MITI intervention in markets relates to product cycles. MITI gets in at the early stage and at the end stage, but gets out during the middle stage. In the beginning stage of an industry targeted for growth, favored policies include infant industry tariffs,[33] subsidies for special capital investments (often coordinated with the MOF), and *rationalization cartels* that seek to take advantage of economies of scale or carry out MITI-financed R&D projects. Rationalization cartels were used in the early 1950s for steel, coal, shipbuilding, electric power, synthetic fibers, and chemical fertilizers, and in the late 1950s for petrochemicals, machine tools, and electronics. Currently they focus upon computers, high definition TV, superconductivity, and biotechnology.

At the end of the product cycle, MITI eases the closeout using *depression cartels.* These were used in both coal and shipbuilding in the 1970s. However both of these kinds of cartels have been less used lately because of increased antitrust enforcement in response to international pressure. The use of cartels for R&D has continued and has recently been imitated in the United States. Also more recently MITI has shifted to aiding adjustment for reducing environmental pollution and aiding adjustment to results of trade disputes.

Those applauding the use of industrial policy in Japan point to the overall rapid growth of the Japanese economy and the export success of such favorably targeted industries as shipbuilding, steel, and computers. Those questioning the effectiveness of MITI's policies note that several of the most effective export sectors were not targeted, including sewing machines, cameras, bicycles, motorcycles, pianos, radios, tape recorders, magnetic tapes, audio components, watches, pocket calculators, machine tools, textile machines, ceramics, and robotics.

MITI failed in the late 1950s to cartelize the automobile industry down to two firms. One firm very resistant to MITI's entreaties was Honda, perhaps the most technically innovative of the Japanese automobile companies and a great export success. Another firm resistant to MITI has been the technically innovative and export-successful Sony, which rejected MITI's advice not to produce transistor radios in the 1950s. Both companies were founded and led by strong-willed entrepreneurs operating outside of the planning and keiretsu systems.

Another criticism of MITI's effectiveness is that many of its subsidized research projects have not worked out as hoped for, a noticeable recent trend. A dramatic example is the failed project for fifth-generation computer development that followed successful earlier projects in the computer area.

Thus Japan is experiencing the pressures to move away from government management of the economy that are felt elsewhere. The heyday of MITI as

---

[33]Import restrictions were lifted on buses and trucks in 1961, on color TVs in 1964, on automobiles in 1965, on color film in 1971, on cash registers in 1973, on large memory integrated circuits in 1974, and on computers in 1975, all industries where Japan is now an export power.

TABLE 6–3   Economic Growth Rates

Years	Japan	France	Germany	United States
1966–73	10.1	5.8	4.3	3.6
1973–80	4.3	2.9	2.6	2.5
1980–85	3.8	1.1	1.4	1.9

Source: From Bela Balassa and Marcus Noland, *Japan in the World Economy* (Washington: Institute for International Economics, 1988), pp. 6–7.

the guiding light of the Japanese economy was in the 1940s, 50s, and 60s, when it was relatively easy to identify a sequence of industries on which the economy could focus in turn as it played a catch-up development game. Now that it has caught up and is competing at the cutting edge of world technology, MITI's effectiveness is reduced.

Will Japan Become Number One?

Macroeconomic Performance

From 1880 to 1940 the average annual rate of growth of real GDP was 3.41 percent, a rate exceeding that of any other country during that period. Since World War II Japan also has had the highest economic growth rate among the major advanced economies, all the while maintaining unemployment in the 1 to 2.5 percent range. This high rate of growth has been driven by a high rate of capital investment backed by a high savings rate.

Table 6–3 shows growth rates of GDP for Japan and France, and of GNP for Germany and the United States during the 1966–1985 period.

That rates of growth in all of these leading economies have declined, a trend that continues, is a simple snapshot of the global growth crisis mentioned in Chapter 1. In only two years since World War II has Japan had a negative growth of GDP, in 1954 and in the first oil shock year of 1974, although it had negative growth in several quarters of zero-growth 1994.

Underlying the high rate of capital investment is a high savings rate. Figure 6–1 shows gross savings rates as a percentage of GNP over time for several major economies.

Since World War II Japan has had a very high savings rate. That this was not so prior to the war undermines the theory that the high savings rate reflects Confucian ideals or practices. Among competing explanations are that saving is caused by high growth rates as consumption increases lag behind income increases, that individuals save to make downpayments on homes that are wildly overpriced, that workers save for old age because of the combination

FIGURE 6–1   Gross Savings as Percent of GNP

Source: From Bela Balassa and Marcus Noland, *Japan in the World Economy* (Washington: Institute for International Economics, 1988), p. 83.

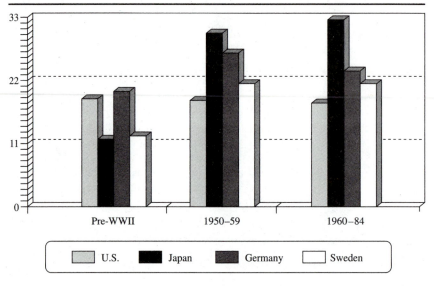

of early retirement with low pensions and low social security payments, that the lumpiness of large biannual bonuses encourages savings, that there is no capital gains tax except on land, and that through most of the postwar period Japan had a relatively young population.

This last point raises serious concerns about the future. One sign of Japan's success is that it now has the longest life expectancy in the world. But this is leading to a rapidly aging population, which when combined with early retirement implies a rising ratio of those not working to those working (dependency ratio) that may well lead to a depressed savings rate. By 2005 Japan's dependency ratio will substantially exceed 60 percent, higher than any other leading industrial country.[34]

Macroeconomic Planning and Policy

Japan has a basically market capitalist economy with elements of tradition as well as significant amounts of indicative planning and guidance. Beyond the sectoral and technological planning carried out by MITI, the Economic Planning Agency (EPA) regularly puts forth macroeconomic plans with associated sets of policy goals.

The indicative nature of these plans means that they are more forecasts than plans. For most of the plans up until the 1970s, the actual growth rate of

---

[34]*OECD Economic Surveys*, p. 64.

the economy exceeded the planned growth rate, with the reverse generally being the case since.

Although the EPA draws up the plans, it is the Ministry of Finance (MOF) that carries them out and implements macroeconomic policy. Not only is it in charge of the budget and fiscal policy, but also of the central bank, the Bank of Japan. This makes Japan like Great Britain in not having an independent central bank. Although inflation has been moderate in Japan, inflation is one macroeconomic variable on which it has not been a world leader in performance until recently.

The structure of fiscal policy has attracted attention because of the relatively low levels of government spending and taxation in Japan. Supply-side economists in the United States emphasize the near nonexistence of capital gains taxes as a possible source of Japanese economic success. But the highest marginal income tax rates are 50 percent, higher than in the United States, as are the corporate income tax rates. It is argued that the relatively low level of social transfer payments encourages savings and hard work. Another element of the low spending is low defense spending, stemming from the U.S.–mandated demilitarization.[35]

Quality of Life

According to the 1993 UN *Human Development Report,* Japan has the highest quality of life of any country in the world and thus in a sense may already be "Number One." The UN's index focuses upon measures of real per capita income adjusted for purchasing power parity, education, and life expectancy. Japan was tops in life expectancy at 78.6 years for 1990 and does very well on the other two measures. However the index for the white population of the United States is still higher than that of Japan. Also a measure accounting for gender discrimination puts Sweden on top and Japan 17th. In Japan women earn only 51 percent of what men do, compared to about 70 percent in the United States and over 85 percent in Sweden, Norway, and France.

Table 6–4 shows some indicators of living standards for various countries in 1990. In nominal terms Japan is well ahead of these countries in per capita income and per capita consumption. But it gets dragged down using the purchasing power parity (PPP) adjustment because of the high cost of food and housing in Japan relative to the others.

Another area in which the quality of life in Japan is high relative to other nations is its low crime rate. Thus the U.S. murder rate is 8.6 per 100,000 and the Japanese is 1.4; the U.S. rape rate is 37.5 per 100,000 and the Japanese is 1.4, and the U.S. armed robbery rate is 225.1 and the Japanese is 1.6.[36] This

---

[35]The Japanese Self Defense Forces were established with U.S. approval in 1954. The 1 percent of GDP spent on defense makes Japanese defense spending among the world's highest, given the large size of the economy. The low level of defense spending relative to the United States has meant that more Japanese engineers have been available for making civilian industry more competitive.

[36]*The Economist,* "Japan Compared" (December 24, 1988), p. 50.

TABLE 6–4   General Living Standards

	France	Germany	Japan	Sweden	United States
Private per capita consumption using current PPPs, U.S. $	9441	9841	10122	8748	14465
Passenger cars per 1,000 inhabitants	494	526	455	462	748
Telephones per 1,000 inhabitants	610	680	555	889	650
Doctors per 1,000 inhabitants	2.6	3.0	4.6	3.1	2.3
Infant mortality per 1,000 live births	7.2	7.5	4.6	5.9	9.2

Source: From *OECD Economic Surveys,* Basic Statistics, 1992.

TABLE 6–5   Selected Gini Coefficients

	Japan	Sweden	W. Germany	United States	OECD average
Before taxes	0.335	0.346	0.396	0.404	0.366
After taxes	0.316	0.302	0.383	0.381	0.350

Source: From Martin Bronfenbrenner and Yasukuchi Yasuba, ''Economic Welfare,'' in *The Political Economy of Japan: The Domestic Transformation,* eds. K. Yamamura and Y. Yasuba (Stanford: Stanford University Press, 1987), p. 111.

comparison reflects cultural values, although policies towards guns in the United States play a role.

Japan has one of the more equal income distributions in the world. This equality is not due to government redistribution but reflects the egalitarian wage structure arising from the labor-management system. Income distribution is seen by looking at before- and after-tax distributions. Before taxes Japan is more equal than Sweden, but it is less so after taxes. Table 6–5 makes the two comparisons for Gini coefficients[37] for selected countries for the mid-1970s.

Some dark sides of the Japanese paradise are captured in the widely repeated phrase about ''workaholics in rabbit hutches.'' The Japanese work much longer hours with fewer vacations than almost anybody anywhere. In large metropolitan areas, especially Tokyo, they spend long times commuting under highly congested conditions.[38] They pay very high prices for cramped living quarters often lacking the sanitary facilities of most developed nations. Housing and congestion questions are addressed in Table 6–6.

---

[37]Gini coefficients are the ratio of the area between a Lorenz curve and the diagonal line to the area under the diagonal line. A Lorenz curve relates percent of rank-ordered population to percent of income. Perfect inequality would generate a Gini coefficient of one, perfect equality a Gini coefficient of zero. See Chapter 1 for further discussion.

[38]Japan is one of the most congested countries in the world. It is slightly smaller than California but has about half the population of the United States. Much of Japan is uninhabitable mountains, further increasing the congestion.

TABLE 6–6 Housing and Infrastructure

	Japan	United States	United Kingdom	France
Floor space per resident				
Square meters	25.0	61.8	35.2	30.7
Year	1988	1987	1988	1984
Urban park space per resident	Tokyo	New York	London	Paris
Square meters	2.5	19.2	30.4	12.2
Year	1988	1976	1976	1984
Sewerage service coverage ratio				
Percentage	45	73	95	64
Year	1991	1986	1982	1983
Expressway extension per 10,000 vehicles				
Kilometers	0.96	4.55	1.16	2.69
Year	1991	1988	1989	1989

Source: *OECD Economic Surveys,* p. 60.

Another problem is environmental pollution, although there has been improvement in this area since the 1960s. In the late 1960s several major disasters occurred that triggered major efforts to clean up, most infamously the Minamata disease caused by mercury pollution in shellfish and the itai itai (ouch ouch) disease caused by cadmium pollution. From 1965 to 1980 sulfur dioxide emissions in parts per million declined from 0.057 to 0.016 and organic water pollutants in parts per million declined from 23.11 in 1970 to 9.20 in 1980.[39] These trends, plus the high life expectancy, suggest that Japan is getting pollution under control.

Finally, Japanese society suffers from serious problems of discrimination. Besides the low wages received by women, discrimination also exists against foreigners (*gai-jin*), the largest such group being Koreans. Most Koreans are descendants of people brought in to work when Japan ruled Korea, but they still are not allowed to become citizens and their professional activities are restricted. Japanese also discriminate against the indigenous Ainu who live in the North and a group known as the Burakumin who are descended from people who held undesirable jobs in the feudal period.

Is the "Economic Miracle" Over?

Although Japan's economic growth rate consistently exceeded that of its rivals for the position of "Number One" during the postwar era, the United States, Germany, and the former Soviet Union, its growth rate has more dramatically decelerated than those of its rivals, except for the FSU. After an enormous

---

[39]Martin Bronfenbrenner and Yasukuchi Yasuba, "Economic Welfare," p. 111.

proliferation of hype regarding Japan's prospects we have more recently been inundated with allegations of the opposite, that Japan has run out of steam and that its economic miracle is over. Whereas in the late 1980s it looked only a matter of a few decades before Japan surpassed the United States in aggregate GDP, this outcome now seems less likely. Several theories have been advanced for this altered situation.

One focus is upon the central savings-investment nexus. Japan is a rapidly aging society that will experience rising dependency ratios, tending to depress the savings rate, a victim of its own success as a society able to support long life. A solution to this problem might be to delay retirement. But doing so would clash with the Confucian value system that emphasizes respect for elders. In a typical large Japanese corporation, when someone is appointed Chief Executive Officer all those who are his age or older retire, reinforcing the tendency to early retirement in Japan.

Another stimulus to Japanese investment has been the low cost of capital, due mostly to the high savings rate. But as Japan's financial system has been opened up, these high savings have been channeled abroad, thereby tending to reduce this international differential.

Another source of the low cost of capital until recently was the high price-earnings ratios in the Japanese stock market relative to other countries. These high price-earnings ratios reflected high expectations regarding future Japanese growth and future earnings of Japanese corporations. But as the growth of the Japanese economy visibly decelerated it became clear that these expectations were exaggerated and the values of Japanese stocks fell sharply ending the ''bubble economy.'' In this respect economic growth is a self-fulfilling prophecy. The expectation of high growth helped generate high growth by lowering the cost of capital. When that expectation disappeared, the cost of capital rose thus making it harder to grow. More generally Japanese banks have damaged portfolios, weakening their financing of long-run growth.

Many now regard the crash of asset values as the watershed event of the Japanese economy that both symbolizes and actualizes its newly realized constraints. It is now widely accepted that the run-up in stock prices in the late 1980s was a speculative bubble that crashed. In the early 1970s price-earnings ratios were about equal in the United States and Japan. By the end of 1989 when the Nikkei index of major stock market prices peaked at over 38,000, Japanese ratios were about four times those in United States. By late 1992 the Nikkei had fallen to around 14,000. It rose for awhile after market interventions by the MOF and an easing of monetary policy, but has declined again in mid-1995 to this general level as GDP growth has failed to restart.

Lying behind the speculative bubble in stocks and also such losing foreign investments as the purchase of Pebble Beach golf course in California was an enormous run-up in land and real estate prices in Japan. Owners of highly priced real estate could use it as collateral to borrow from Japanese banks for buying stocks or making foreign investments. At the peak, residential property in downtown Tokyo was worth 40 times more than equivalent properties in downtown London.[40] This led to wild estimates that the palace grounds of the emperor were worth more than the state of California and that metropolitan Tokyo was worth more than Britain, France, and Germany put together. These prices have declined without turning up during the 1990s, although not by as much as stock prices.

These high real estate prices aggravated the housing shortage problem. Whereas the ratio of housing prices to annual income was about one to one in 1950 in both Tokyo and Japan as a whole, by 1983 it had risen to 7.9 for Tokyo and 6.7 for Japan as a whole.[41] And land prices would nearly double after that before peaking. The land problem fundamentally arises from a combination of low property taxation, especially of agricultural land in cities,[42] but high capital gains taxation on real estate, along with a variety of land use restrictions. These forces lead to a "lock-in" effect that produces a strong disincentive to sell land. But at least half of the peak land prices reflected a speculative bubble that has now ended.

This collapse of asset values has coincided with a broader systemic crisis in Japan. The gains in wealth from the bubble were very unevenly distributed, undermining the groupist solidarity of Japanese society. Scandals erupted regarding the involvement of high politicians in the speculation. The disgust of the Japanese public reached the point that the ruling Liberal Democratic Party split and fell from power in July 1993.

The deceleration of growth could be a self-reinforcing process if it undermines the microeconomic foundations of the economy by causing layoffs in the large corporations and the end of the lifetime employment system. Breaking the loyalty of Japanese workers to their companies could be a fatal blow.

But all of this may be just a course correction, an adjustment to a more realistic path after an overheated episode in the late 1980s. The most fundamental question has to do with technological leadership. Will Japan take it from the United States across the board? If so, it will become the world's unequivocal economic leader. If not, it will at best remain Number Two.

Optimists about Japanese prospects stress how Japan has outcompeted the United States in industry after industry, moving up from low technology industries such as steel to higher ones such as automobiles, cameras, TVs, and a variety of consumer electronics. The role of MITI in industrial policy, including its funding of R&D, is often cited, as is the continuing much higher rate of capital investment. Also the far higher level of education in mathematics and science of the workforce relative to the United States is emphasized, as well as the harmonious intrafirm relations.

---

[40]Yukio Noguchi, "Land Problem in Japan," *Hitotsubashi Journal of Economics* 31 (1990), pp. 73–86.

[41]Takatoshi Ito, *The Japanese Economy,* p. 412.

[42]There are rice farms in Tokyo.

Skeptics abound. Some argue that Japanese companies achieved their greatest successes when they were able to license existing technologies from abroad and then perfect them. But in outright competition to generate new technologies from scratch the United States retains fundamental advantages. These critics cite the ability of leading elements of the U.S. computer and software industries to maintain their leads despite the massive focus of MITI on this sector. Their central argument is that the groupist mentality of the Japanese may be great for imitating, but it does not encourage the sort of individual creativity that underlies frontier research and major technological breakthroughs.

The most basic problem may be at the highest level of academic scientific research where Japan has produced very few Nobel Prize winners compared to the United States. Whereas Japanese high schools may far outcompete U.S. ones for teaching mathematics and science, this learning is largely rote. At the university level rigid seniority-driven vertical hierarchies stifle research and the most creative Japanese researchers end up going abroad. The sources of Japan's success become the sources of its failure.

But this view is not universally accepted. That Japan is not currently the world's scientific leader does not mean it cannot be. The United States was a leader in innovation and new product development in the mid-19th century long before its emergence as the world's basic science leader at the end of World War II. Increasingly Japan is not merely imitating, but is inventing new products, the Sony Walkman being a notable example. Furthermore it is vociferously argued that the "rote imitators" argument is a racist insult that ignores the many creative and innovative Japanese citizens in many different areas such as architecture, clothing design, literature, and film. Box 6–1 examines this creativity in more detail.

The enigma of Japanese creativity is rather like the paradox of Zen Buddhism. It can be viewed as both a source of ultimate creativity or as a source of mindless obeisance to superiors. The "annihilation of the ego" can be either a liberating enlightenment or the submission of the samurai to his master's any command. The most famous Zen koan, "What is sound of one hand clapping?" can be seen as a mystical source of contemplation or as the trigger for a well-known rote response, the devotee swinging one of his hands through the air in a one-handed "clap." And all of the above may be true in an appropriately Japanese, Rashomonlike "multiple reality" manner.

Japan and the World Economy

The question of technological competition between the United States and Japan comes to a head in the area of international trade. Among the most visible signs of Japanese economic success has been its ability to penetrate many export markets and to develop large trade surpluses. But these surpluses, along with the widespread perception that Japanese markets are unfairly protected from imports, has triggered enormous resentment and anti-Japanese sentiments around the world.

Box 6–1

The Cultural Foundations of Japanese Technological Innovation

Sheridan Tatsuno argues that the Zen Buddhist tradition of Japan underpins a cultural tradition of technological innovativeness. He points out connections between Japanese traditional arts and areas in which Japanese have been successful in modern technologies:*

Traditional Art	Aesthetic Principle	Business Application
Wood carving	Miniaturization	Pocket TV
	Animism	Video animation
Bonsai	Miniaturization	Electronic products
	Trained growth	Bioengineering
Flower arrangement	Creative forms	Robot design
	Naturalism	Commercial landscaping
	Asymmetry	Amorphous crystal growth
Rock gardens	Reductionism	Home construction
	Aesthetic asymmetry	Science city design
	Meditative space	Research lab design
Architecture	Multipurpose rooms	Apartment housing
	Open to nature	Office complexes
	Natural materials	Office interiors
Paper folding	Manual dexterity	"Transformer" toys
	Complex 3-D forms	Computer-aided design
Hand-sewn juggling balls	Aesthetic play	Educational toys
Abacus	Manual dexterity	Calculator keyboards
	Visualization	Computer simulation
Chopsticks	Manual dexterity	Robot fingers
Folding fans	Collapsible space	Laptop computer design
	Aesthetic function	Ergonomic furniture
Japanese characters	Visualization	Fifth-generation computers
	Image recognition	Visual scanners
Wrapping cloth	Multipurpose; compact	Folding solar panels

This list may be quite fanciful, but it does emphasize that the image of the mindlessly imitative Japanese is misplaced. The rising generation of highly educated young Japanese is quite likely to be more creative than its predecessors.

---
*Sheridan Tatsuno, *Created in Japan: From Imitators to World-Class Innovators* (New York: Ballinger, 1990), p. 57.

Box 6–2

Does Japan Follow a Long-Term Strategy?

In 1857, Masayoshi Hotta, an adviser to the shogun declared:

> I am therefore convinced that our policy should be to stake everything on the present opportunity, to conclude friendly alliances, to send ships to foreign countries everywhere and conduct trade, to copy the foreigners where they are at their best and so repair our own shortcomings, to foster our national strength and complete our armaments, and so gradually subject the foreigners to our influence until in the end all the countries of the world know the blessings of perfect tranquillity and our hegemony is acknowledged throughout the globe.*

---

*Quoted in Clyde V. Prestowitz, Jr., *Trading Places: How We Allowed Japan to Take the Lead* (New York: Basic Books, 1988), p. 21.

Disputes between the United States and Japan have increased recently and a new atmosphere has emerged. At the heart of the arguments of the U.S. revisionists seems to be a resentment of Japanese trade surpluses. The case has been articulately made by former U.S. trade negotiator Clyde Prestowitz[43] who argues that Japan, viewing things in power terms, always gets the best of the United States in trade negotiations because it has wily MITI bureaucrats who take a long-run view.

Prestowitz has little patience for traditional trade negotiations and demands "results-oriented" agreements such as a deal for 20 percent of the market share for semiconductor chips, rather than agreements that ratify rules, which he claims the Japanese always cheat on. Such views have found sympathy in the Clinton administration, which has had confrontational relations with Japan over trade issues, partly because Japan has its own analysts who are the mirror image of the U.S. revisionists.

An assertive and popular example is Shintaro Ishihara, quoted at the beginning of this chapter, who participated in trade negotiations with the United States as Transport Minister. He charges that United States–Japan trade frictions arise from American racism and hypocrisy and that the United States must accept the "imminent demise" of the "modern era," in which the United States has dominated Japan. The title of his book, *The Japan That Can Say No,* has become a popular slogan in Japan.

Are there any facts that are clear from this controversy? One is that Japan experiences and has experienced for some time significant trade surpluses. In

---

[43]Clyde V. Prestowitz, Jr., *Trading Places: How We Allowed Japan to Take the Lead* (New York: Basic Books, 1988).

1991 its trade surpluses equaled $103 billion, and a substantial portion of that came from the United States.[44] Generally Japan exports manufactured goods and imports raw materials and agricultural goods. Japan feels driven to export because of its extreme dependence on imports.

But why does Japan have such large surpluses? It has the lowest tariffs and quotas of any major industrialized nation, if one does not count agriculture.[45] With respect to the United States, 90 percent of Japan's trade surplus is in four sectors: automobiles, computers, VCRs, and semiconductors. The Japanese position is that the surpluses reflect superior Japanese competitiveness in price and quality. Critics question this assertion, arguing that the Japanese have targeted these high-technology sectors through industrial policy that uses dumping and other unfair techniques to "hollow out" critical U.S. industries, one after another.

Critics claim that Japan uses a variety of informal barriers to imports, including "administrative guidance" by ministries including MITI, overly "fastidious" interpretations of customs procedures, ridiculous safety standards,[46] bureaucratically arbitrary testing and certification procedures, biased public procurement policies, MITI's rationalization and depression cartels and subsidizing of high technology R&D,[47] unfair patent rules, and inefficient retail distribution channels.[48] Furthermore critics charge that the vertical keiretsu system and the high savings rate constitute "structural impediments" to imports. The Japanese respond that their trading partners engage in similar practices.[49]

Despite these many difficulties there are U.S. companies that have succeeded in penetrating the Japanese market. Some successes include IBM, Texas Instruments, Motorola, MacDonald's, Coca-Cola, and Gillette, although executives from some of these companies have complained of the barriers they have faced.

A hope for overcoming these difficulties lies in multilateral negotiations such as the Uruguay Round of General Agreement of Tariffs and Trade (GATT) negotiations, completed in December 1993, which resulted in the formation of the World Trade Organization (WTO). Unfortunately the 1995

---

[44]*OECD Economic Surveys,* p. 27.

[45]*OECD Economic Surveys,* p. 86. Japan had an absolute ban on importing rice until late 1993, leading its citizens to pay six times world prices for rice. But it imports large amounts of corn and soybeans from the United States. The United States protects many agricultural products, with the European Union being even more protectionist with respect to agriculture.

[46]A notorious example of safety standards was the restriction on importing U.S. baseball bats on alleged safety grounds.

[47]The Japanese correctly respond that the United States does this too for computers, aircraft, and biotechnology.

[48]Inefficient channels are found in the secondary sector of the Japanese economy, labor-intensive "mom and pop" operations, and it is hard for a foreign producer to deal with them.

[49]A much touted case was France's routing of all Japanese VCRs through the internal city of Poitiers for customs inspection where they piled up due to a lack of customs inspectors there.

United States–Japan dispute about auto parts trade completely bypassed the WTO. In November 1994, the Asia Pacific Economic Cooperation (APEC) group[50] declared free trade as a goal by 2020. Achieving such a goal requires mutual good will, a commodity currently in short supply between the United States and Japan on this issue.

Summary and Conclusions

The Japanese economy is the most successful new traditional economy in the world. It has combined a family-oriented approach derived from its unique combination of Shintoism, Confucianism, and Buddhism with the successful adoption of modern technology in a planned market capitalist context. After opening to outside trade in the 1850s and the subsequent Meiji Restoration, Japan embarked on an outwardly oriented path of rapid economic expansion that has continued to the present time, except for the disruption associated with World War II. The immediate postwar Occupation by the United States brought changes, but Japan has preserved its national culture and identity while absorbing outside influences and technologies.

Japan's large corporations practice a form of management that emphasizes close relations with workers. They have lifetime employment, seniority wages, and enterprise unions. Japanese managers engage in widespread consultation and horizontal coordination in their decision making, as well as encouraging the input of those below in well-defined hierarchies. Because of long-term financing from banks, managers use longer time horizons in their decision making than occurs in most economies. Most large corporations belong to either horizontal or vertical keiretsus, associated groups of companies that coordinate their activities to some degree.

Government works cooperatively with business through an indicative planning process. Industrial policy targeting rising and declining sectors for assistance is carried out by MITI, which also subsidizes R&D activities. But some of the most successful Japanese corporations have stayed outside of both the keiretsu and the industrial policy structures.

Long-term macroeconomic performance has been very impressive, and Japan now has the second highest aggregate GDP in the world, surpassing the United States in nominal per capita income. Unemployment has remained low and the distribution of income has been fairly equal.

By some measures Japanese citizens may have the highest quality of life in the world. They enjoy the longest life expectancy, high material standards of living, high levels of education, and very low crime rates. However, housing

---

[50]Members are Australia, Brunei, Canada, Chile, China, Hong Kong, Indonesia, Japan, Malaysia, Mexico, New Zealand, Papua New Guinea, the Philippines, Singapore, South Korea, Taiwan, Thailand, and the United States.

shortages persist as well as significant discrimination against women and minority groups.

Despite past success economic growth has substantially slowed down and may not pick up again. The aging of the population bodes ill for its high savings and investment rates, which are also hurt by the crash of the speculative bubbles in stocks and real estate. Japan's ability to generate cutting-edge technology rather than just borrow from others has been seriously questioned, although some analysts are more optimistic. In many areas the Japanese economy is moving to resemble that of the United States.

Japan faces serious questions about its trade relations with the rest of the world, especially the United States, its main rival for being Number One. Ultimately the role Japan plays depends on its willingness and ability to deal successfully with the rest of the world, an effort complicated by recent internal political upheavals. Whatever the outcome, the decisions and directions that Japan takes will be of profound importance for the entire world.

Questions for Discussion

1. In what sense can Japan be viewed as a new traditional economy? In what sense might this claim not be true?

2. How do the "three sacred treasures" of labor reinforce each other? What trends in the Japanese economy may be leading to their disappearance?

3. Distinguish horizontal and vertical keiretsu. How do they both help and hinder the Japanese economy?

4. Distinguish the "J-mode" of management from the "H-mode." What are advantages and disadvantages of each?

5. Why has industrial policy become less effective in Japan recently?

6. What are the arguments for and against the possibility that Japan will surpass the United States in technological leadership?

7. Will real acceptance by Japan of free trade lead to a loss of Japanese economic identity and a convergence on the U.S. model?

Suggested Further Readings

The Economist. "Death of a Role Model." July 9, 1994.

Ito, Takatoshi. *The Japanese Economy.* Cambridge: MIT Press, 1992.

Komiya, Ryutaro. *The Japanese Economy: Trade, Industry, and Government.* Tokyo: University of Tokyo Press, 1990.

Nanto, Dick K. "Japan's Industrial Groups." In *Comparative Economic Systems: Models and Cases,* 7th ed. ed. Morris Bornstein. Burr Ridge: Irwin, 1994, pp. 236–52.

Patrick, Hugh T. "Japanese Industrial Policy." In *Comparative Economic Systems: Models and Cases,* 7th ed. ed. Morris Bornstein. Burr Ridge: Irwin, 1994, pp. 223–35.

Reischauer, Edwin O. *The Japanese Today: Change and Continuity.* Cambridge: The Belknap Press of Harvard University Press, 1988.

Shimada, Haruo. "The Perception and the Reality of Japanese Industrial Relations." In *Comparative Economic Systems: Models and Cases,* 7th ed. ed. Morris Bornstein. Burr Ridge: Irwin, 1994, pp. 253–67.

van Wolferen, Karel. *The Enigma of Japanese Power.* New York: Alfred A. Knopf, 1989.

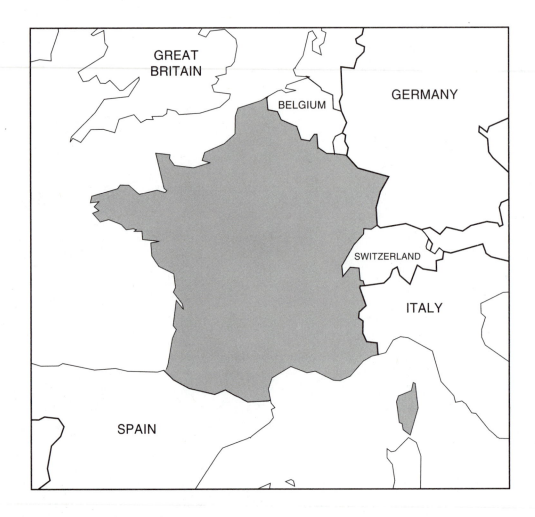

WHITHER INDICATIVE PLANNING? THE CASE OF FRANCE

The French suffer from a deep-seated sickness. They will not understand that the times demand of them a gigantic effort of adaptation . . . They cannot do without the State and yet they detest it, except when there is danger . . . They do not behave like adults.

—Charles de Gaulle, as quoted by Alain Peyrefitte, *The Trouble with France*[1]

It has been and still is France's destiny to live between the contrary pulls of plural and singular: for plural read diversity, as ineradicable as bindweed; for singular read the tendency towards unity, something both spontaneous and consciously willed—but not willed only . . . France should not by rights exist, it has yet to be invented. And yet France has long been in existence, it is no myth, and it did indeed invent itself many years ago.

—Fernand Braudel, *The Identity of France*

Introduction

France is the advanced market capitalist economy that has most publicly and prominently engaged in indicative planning. As in Japan the use of indicative planning has coincided with considerable economic success. But as in Japan France is downgrading indicative planning and allowing greater laissez-faire in policy.

If Japan is a land of paradoxes, France is more so. Lying in the narrowing zone at the western end of the Eurasian land mass, France has received multiple waves of migrations from many directions. Its national unity has been created by force out of a diverse population. There is no natural tendency to harmony; indeed in France we see just the opposite.

---

[1]Translated by William R. Byron (New York: New York University Press, 1981).

The drive to national unity led to a strong centralized state, one that intervenes in or "directs" the economy, a practice known as *dirigisme* in French. Simultaneously there has been vigorous resistance to this dirigiste tradition. The term *political economy* was first introduced in France in 1615 to argue for dirigiste/mercantilist policies of state intervention in the economy. But the term *laissez-faire*[2] was also first introduced in France in 1751 by the Marquis d'Argenson to oppose such entrenched policies.

These contrasting traditions of economic policy and thought have intersected complexly with other sharp conflicts. The Wars of Religion were especially hard fought in France, a fact seen by Peyrefitte as a central source of "the trouble with France." Hyperconservatism and resistance to change is deeply entrenched in France, especially in rural areas.[3] This tradition supports dirigisme as a protectionist device preserving old ways of doing things. Yet, as noted in Chapter 3, France has been a fountainhead of world radicalism with a history of major revolutionary outbursts in 1789, 1830, 1848, 1870, and 1968.[4] Although some of these had laissez-faire orientations, the later ones were strongly socialist and supported dirigisme.

The revolutionary tradition in France also reflects its deeply rooted class conflict. Karl Marx conceived of the class struggle while thinking about France and the French Revolution. The term *communism* is of French origin. Although this split has moderated recently, France's sharp class divisions show up in sharp differences among political parties traceable back to the French Revolution. The French Communist Party is among the most orthodox Marxist in the world and, despite considerable loss of electoral support,[5] remains deeply entrenched in certain neighborhoods of metropolitan Paris (the "Red Belt") and in other major cities. Many of these neighborhoods were strong supporters of the revolution in 1789, and in them are streets named not only for Marx and Lenin but also for Robespierre, father of the Terror in 1793.

Despite these conflicts, French nationalism is a powerful force and source of dirigisme in French policy. Indicative planning was introduced in 1946 after France's national humiliation in World War II with the hope of rebuilding the French economy so that France could return to its glorious past when it was

---

[2]*Laissez-faire* literally means "let [them] do [it]." This imperative appeal is addressed to the government officials. The implicit *them* are businesspeople who are to be allowed to do as they want without government interference.

[3]An example of this hyperconservatism is resistance to introducing the potato. Brought from South America, it was on the king's plate in England in 1619, but not so in France until 1787. French fries were only invented in the 19th century.

[4]Whereas most radical upheavals of the 1960s in advanced countries largely involved students, in France workers were also significantly involved.

[5]Many former Communist voters have switched to the far-right, anti-immigrant National Front. Many immigrants are in working-class neighborhoods and are seen as threats to existing jobholders. Both of these parties oppose European unification and support protectionism in trade relations.

the most powerful nation in the world. This last goal was not achieved, but the postwar economic performance of France has been impressive.

As in Japan, the heyday of indicative planning in France was the 1950s and 1960s when its economy rapidly rebuilt and then moved into high-technology development. Its credibility was permanently damaged by the first oil price shock of 1973, which knocked plans and projections awry. Since then indicative planning has been a politicized football, being taken less seriously when conservative parties are in power and more seriously when the Socialists are in power. With the massive defeat of the Socialists in the Assembly elections in March 1993 and the appointment of a Gaullist[6] to the premiership, indicative planning was downgraded, although then-President Francois Mitterand (1981–1995) was a Socialist.[7] This trend continues with Mitterand's successor, the Gaullist leader, Jacques Chirac, although he has moderated his previous pro–laissez-faire position.

Another reason why indicative planning has lost influence in French policy making has been the drive for European unification and the increasing integration of the French economy in the economy of the European Union (EU). Integration has led to a loss of control over policy by the French government as it has had to coordinate with other countries, especially with Germany, in the European exchange rate mechanism (ERM). Although the French strongly supported unification, presumably to keep Germany under control, fear of loss of their own autonomy led to a near defeat of the referendum on the Maastricht Treaty by the French electorate in September 1992. Some observers see indicative planning as having reemerged at the level of the EU, just as it is becoming increasingly irrelevant for the French national economy.

Historical and Political Background

Before there was France, there was the Roman province of Gaul, conquered by Julius Caesar. Peyrefitte calls France "Caesar's Granddaughter," her mother being the Roman Catholic Church,[8] which baptized and anointed as king in 496 the chieftain of the Germanic Franks, Clovis, conqueror of Paris.

---

[6]De Gaulle himself supported indicative planning. It was in the late 1970s that the Gaullist party shifted to a more pro–laissez-faire stance under Jacques Chirac's leadership, although there remains a dirigiste faction within it.

[7]Since the formation of the Fifth Republic in 1958 France has had a strong president who serves a seven-year term and has the power to appoint the premier and to dissolve the Assembly. Until 1986 the president was of the same party that dominated the Assembly. But in 1986–1988 and in 1993–1995 that was not the case and France experienced "cohabitation." In these situations the premier controls domestic policy, including economic policy, while the president controls defense and foreign policy.

[8]The role of the Roman Catholic Church has long been controversial in France. Although the population is overwhelmingly Catholic, a substantial proportion of France's industrial and financial entrepreneurs came from the Protestant and Jewish minorities.

It took 1,300 years for the nucleus of France in the rich agricultural basin[9] around Paris to expand to its modern limits, approximating the boundaries of ancient Gaul.

Around 1500 France surpassed China as the nation with the world's largest GDP, a position it held until about 1830 when Britain surpassed it. In the late 1600s this economic lead underlay the military and political preeminence of the centralizing regime of Louis XIV, the "Sun King." From 1661 to 1683 his Minister of Finance was Jean-Baptiste Colbert, father of dirigisme, also known as *Colbertisme.*

Colbert pushed industrialization through dirigiste policies. Entrepreneurs in favored firms or industries were given numerous gifts, pensions, interest-free loans, tax breaks, exemption from military obligations, grants of monopoly power, and protection from imports[10] and guilds. Although unusual, state enterprises were established, the most famous being the Gobelins textile producer in 1667, the longest running state-owned enterprise in France. Colbert also instituted detailed industry-specific regulations to improve the quality and international competitiveness of French products.

The physiocrats, notably François Quesnay and the Marquis d'Argenson, criticized Colbertisme. Under their influence, Jacques Turgot, Minister of Finance for Louis XVI, tried to deregulate internal agricultural trade and eliminate internal monopolies and guilds in 1774.[11] But he was forced from office in 1776 after bad harvests and riots.

The French Revolution was the endlessly controversial, watershed event that defined the modern French state, its subdivisions, its currency, and its class conflicts.[12] When asked to assess its significance, the late Chinese Premier Zhou En-lai declared, "It's too soon to tell." In economics the Revolution began on a pro–laissez-faire note but then moved in a dirigiste direction, culminating in Napoleon Bonaparte's military dictatorship and attempted world conquest.

After Napoleon's defeat in 1815, France followed Britain and Belgium as one of the first countries to industrialize. But between 1830 and 1930 it went

---

[9]France is a major agricultural exporter, famous for its cuisine. Its high agriculture subsidies are a source of conflict with many trading partners. It has a relatively high proportion of population in agriculture for a nation so well off, aggravating its hyperconservatism.

[10]Despite his external protectionism, Colbert established a customs union in 1664 in most of the northern half of France, *les cinq grosses fermes* (the five big [tax] farms), which stimulated the economic unification of France. The north-south split in France is the deepest and most persistent, the more Germanic north being wealthier and more urban-industrial with the Mediterranean south being poorer and more rural, except in the Rhône valley and on the Riviera.

[11]A motivation for Turgot's reforms was a budget deficit. This simply got worse during the Revolution as citizens refused to pay taxes. Eventually full-blown hyperinflation developed by 1794.

[12]It also gave us many political categories of the modern world. Thus *left* and *right* originated in the French Assembly in 1789 as designating, respectively, anti- and promonarchists. The term *nationalism* also came from France.

from having the world's largest GDP to being fourth behind the United States, Germany, and Britain.[13]

A leftist regime led by Léon Blum came to power in the depression year of 1936. It fell within a year, but first it nationalized military production and established a Ministry of National Economy that attempted to dominate the conservative Ministry of Finance. The Ministry of National Economy was dismantled after Blum's fall, but it foreshadowed the postwar planning apparatus.

In 1940 Germany easily defeated France. Part of the country was directly occupied and part was ruled by the puppet Vichy regime of Marshall Pétain. This defeat inspired the introduction of indicative planning after the war when the leader of the anti-Nazi Resistance, General Charles de Gaulle, headed the government. The Communist Party was the largest in the country, riding a wave of popularity for its role in the Resistance, and it supported central planning. But the Vichy regime had introduced bureaucratic changes and technocratic planning practices that carried over into the postwar planning system.

The Theory of Indicative Planning

General Arguments

Although French openness to indicative planning came from its dirigiste tradition, indicative planning in its ideal form is not dirigiste. Dirigisme, or direction, implies an element of coercion or strong incentive. Ideal indicative planning is purely voluntary. It is successful because those affected have been involved in its formulation, view it as credible, and act on its projections, thereby making it into a self-fulfilling prophecy.

The fundamental argument for indicative planning involves providing information. This argument was first expressed by Keynes when he argued that "Many of the greatest economic evils of our time are the fruits of risk, uncertainty and ignorance." He argued that "the cure lies outside the operation of the individuals," and called for "the collection and dissemination on a great scale of data relating to the business situation," and for the creation of "some appropriate organ of action" that would "exercise directive intelligence" but would "leave private initiative and enterprise unhindered."[14]

---

[13]Later it would fall behind the Soviet Union and Japan, then regain the fourth slot by moving ahead of Britain and the now-dissolved Soviet Union. Recently, France has fallen behind China.

[14]J. M. Keynes, "The End of Laissez-Faire," in *Essays in Persuasion* (London: Macmillan, 1931), p. 317. Although the idea of indicative planning was of British origin, the one attempt at such planning in the United Kingdom in the mid-1970s was a total failure and was quickly abandoned.

Information Pooling, Concertation, and Coherence

The French planner and theoretician, Pierre Massé, further developed Keynes's argument, drawing on experience with French indicative planning.[15] He introduced the concept of *information pooling.* Planners carry out "generalized market research" allowing a common view of the future. This research involves consulting with leading actors in the economy for their input, a process called *concertation.* After this step the elements of the plan are adjusted to assure *coherence* and to guarantee policy coordination. The goal is *l'économie concertée,* or *concerted economy,* which operates like a symphony, somewhere between the extremes of command planning and laissez-faire.

Massé also stressed the *exhortive* aspect of indicative planning. Not only is information about investment possibilities made available to firms, but firms are encouraged to believe the possibilities are possible and feasible. Thus a higher rate of investment might come about in a self-fulfilling prophetic manner. Exhortive planning may have worked in France in the 1950s after a long period of low growth, when the planners may have broken through the entrenched hyperconservative risk aversion of businesses.

Criticisms of concertation include that planners are no better at predicting surprise exogenous shocks than businesses and that economies need a variety of investment strategies to balance the national portfolio of investments. If everyone is following the plan and the plan is based on incorrect forecasts of external trends, society will be worse off than if some investors are preparing for the true outcome.

The Austrian School argues the impossibility of *any* central planner being able to gather sufficient information in a complex and everchanging environment to formulate a useful plan. If firms face risk, uncertainty, and ignorance, as Keynes argued, governments are even worse off. Firms have localized information and prices are the best information transmitters, as long as markets are allowed to operate freely.

Informational Externalities and Economies of Scale

Responses to the Austrian view include that part of the necessary information set of actors to achieve efficient behavior includes the intended or likely behavior of other actors.[16] In a purely decentralized economy such information is costly to obtain, implying an informational externality problem potentially amenable to concertation. But concertation may work only if there are economies of scale in information gathering. One reason indicative planning may

---

[15]Pierre Massé, "French Methods of Planning," *Journal of Industrial Economics* 11 (1962), pp. 1–17; "French Planning and Economic Theory," *Econometrica* 33 (1965), pp. 265–76.

[16]Roy Radner, "Competitive Equilibrium under Uncertainty," *Econometrica* 36 (1968), pp. 31–58.

have become less influential is because of improved computing and information technology. In the United States, specialized firms perform the forecasting functions of would-be indicative planners.

A related argument is that the efficiency of general equilibrium depends on the existence of complete futures markets, which do not exist. In principle an information pooling process can perform the role of nonexistent futures markets and lead to an efficient equilibrium.[17] Critics of this approach note that participants in such a process, including the government, might have incentives to cheat by misrepresenting information[18] and that participants may be so uncertain about the future they may be unable even to formulate long-term contingencies.

Multiple Equilibria and Coordination Failure

An argument bringing together these strands in one knot is that informational externalities combined with the existence of economies of scale imply multiple equilibria, some of which are more efficient than others.[19] In this view *coordination failure* may occur in the absence of some sort of indicative planning and a suboptimal equilibrium may be selected.[20] Guidance toward a superior equilibrium may involve an exhortive element as well as a strictly informational one.

Nevertheless all these schemes depend upon the planners having high credibility. French planners have suffered from a credibility problem due to inaccurate forecasts since the mid-1960s.

The Practice of French Indicative Planning

The Institutions of French Indicative Planning

Three motives inspired de Gaulle's adoption of indicative planning in January 1946. One was to avoid another humiliating defeat such as the one that occurred in 1940, which was widely attributed to a "decadent" and weak economy. Military strength requires national economic strength.

---

[17]James E. Meade, *The Theory of Indicative Planning* (Manchester: University of Manchester Press, 1970).

[18]It may be possible to institute revelation schemes that punish cheaters, but this would involve moving to coercion and away from ideal indicative planning.

[19]Jeff Frank and Peter Holmes,"A Multiple Equilibrium Model of Indicative Planning," *Journal of Comparative Economics* 14 (1990), pp. 791–806.

[20]The issue of coordination extends to government agencies. Even without private sector cooperation, the public sector may coordinate. Development of an independent public nuclear power capability may be a success story of French planning, although it is now criticized by many environmentalists.

Another motive was to offset the power of the three Communist members of the cabinet. They supported planning of a Stalinist command type and had supported a 1944 attempt to revive Léon Blum's all-powerful Ministry of National Economy. In May 1945, upon the surrender of Germany, de Gaulle sided with the Ministry of Finance and eliminated the Ministry of National Economy. The Commission Général du Plan (CGP, General Commission of Planning) established in 1946, is subordinate to the Ministry of Finance and has no command authority. But it coopted the Communists in their demand for a central planning apparatus.

The third motive was to provide a mechanism for negotiating with the United States over Marshall Plan aid and offered assurance that such aid would be administered intelligently.[21] Indeed the First Plan (1946–1952) had a more dirigiste/command character than later plans because the CGP played an important role in distributing Marshall Plan monies based upon it. The founder of the CGP, its first director, and the developer of the First Plan was Jean Monnet, also father of the European Coal and Steel Community, predecessor of the European Union.

The staff of the CGP was kept small, and following Monnet's ideas it relied on persuasion to achieve influence rather than authoritative control. Many planning activities are actually carried out by related entities. An important institution on the input side is the Institut Nationale Statistique des Études Économiques (INSEE), an arm of the Ministry of Finance that gathers the statistical data used in making forecasts and maintains and develops the econometric models used in making the forecasts.[22] Also on the input side is the Ministry of Industry, though it is not as powerful as its Japanese counterpart, the Ministry of International Trade and Industry (MITI).

The concertation process is carried out by the Economic and Social Council, which has been concerned more recently with social issues such as education, women's rights, and income distribution. Also involved in concertation are the Modernization Commissions. These are both vertical, concerned with specific industries, and horizontal, dealing with issues cutting across the economy and concerned with coherence. Another body involved is the regional planning agency, Délégation à l'Amènagement du Territoire et à l'Action Régionale (DATAR).

The election of the leftist government of Mitterand in 1981 brought further changes in the planning apparatus. A Commission of Planning was established to carry out higher level coordination. More groups were brought in representing women, environmentalists, unions,[23] and foreign entities, especially

---

[21]A measure of ideological change since then is that such a move by a country today seeking aid from the United States would be absurd. Ideology appeared then in the U.S. condition for granting Marshall Plan aid that the Communists be removed from the cabinet. They were.

[22]The Ministry of Finance got rid of the old Ministry of National Economy partly by refusing to give the Ministry of National Economy any data. Truly, knowledge is power.

[23]In principle the unions were always in. But after the First Plan they largely dropped out, especially the largest one, the pro-Communist CGT, charging that business interests were in control of the process. Their position reflected continuation of the deep class conflicts in French society. Unions are more willing to be involved under Socialist governments.

the EU, which now provides forecasts that enter the planning process. Industrial strategy groups were created. The first Mitterand government enacted a major administrative decentralization that allows planning at local levels that must be concerted as well. Concerting parties are pressured to sign contracts agreeing to follow the plan, especially nationalized companies.

Some see a conflict between widening and deepening the planning process. The former brings in more parties, thus making the plan more democratic and more popular. But widening tends to lead to dissipation and a lack of focus.

A complicating institutional issue is the relationship between the CGP and the Ministry of Finance. As in Japan the Ministry of Finance is the supreme bureaucratic body, controlling budgets and jealously guarding its power against the CGP and other entities.[24] Monnet understood this and worked to appease the Ministry and involve it in the planning process so that it would support the outcome.

His successors have had varying success at imitating his approach. An important break came in 1963 when an unexpected immigration wave from Algeria upset plan forecasts. The Ministry of Finance forced a change in the plan because of the resulting budgetary crisis. The Minister of Finance then and over most of the next decade was Valéry Giscard d'Estaing who became increasingly hostile to the CGP. His term as president (1974–1981) marked a low point of planning influence in postwar France.

Another issue is the nature of the French bureaucracy itself. As in Japan the top bureaucrats (*hauts fonctionnaires*) are a supreme elite who come from a small number of top educational institutions[25] and who move easily between top government posts and top business positions, a process equivalent to the Japanese *amakudari*. This unity of bureaucratic and business elites in both countries partly accounts for the relative success of indicative planning in the two economies as it facilitates the consultative process.

The Plans and Their Performance

The nature of the plans, their influence on decision makers, and their conformance with the performance of the French economy has evolved. Plans were more sectorally focused in the 1950s and more influential. Their focus broadened later to macroeconomics at the expense of influence, especially as some of their forecasts failed spectacularly in the wake of exogenous shocks. The plans were ignored in the late 1970s but have been more influential since then. Recently they have focused on preparing the French economy for full integration into the European Union. Given the significance of this issue, planning

---

[24]In early 1994, the central bank, the Bank of France, was made independent of the Ministry of Finance.

[25]In France the top institution is the ENA, l'École National d'Administration, whose graduates are *les énarques,* known for their apolitical technocratic views. ENA was founded in 1945 because the previous top institution, l'École Polytechnique, was tainted by having many of its graduates participate in the Vichy regime.

continues to play a role, even though the defeat of the Socialists in the Assembly elections of March 1993 led to some downgrading.

The goal of the First Plan (1946–1952) was industrial reconstruction from war damage. In May 1944 industrial production was 44 percent of production in 1939.[26] The planning method was simple compared to later efforts, emphasizing investment targets, and it was more dirigiste because of the ability to direct Marshall Plan funds. These funds financed about one-third of investment from 1948 to1950.[27] The plan focused on six basic sectors, coal, electricity, steel, cement, agricultural machinery, and transportation. It included no macroeconomic or social components. The plan came close to being fulfilled, falling slightly short in most sectors.

The Second Plan (1953–1957) introduced concertation and the Modernization Commissions. This plan and the Third Plan (1957–1961) were the most successful of the plans. They introduced macroeconomic forecasting and produced growth close to their high targets. These were the plans that succeeded in the exhortive function of convincing businesspeople that higher growth was possible, thus possibly helping growth to come about. The growth rates in this period were easily the highest ever seen in French history until then as a major move to modernization and internationalization began. But sectoral forecasts were far off, a pattern consistently seen since.

Under the direction of Pierre Massé, the Fourth Plan (1961–1965) included a variety of social goals such as expanded social infrastructure investment and emphasis on regional planning. Six sectors were targeted for particular expansion and the energy sector was to be modernized, beginning the development of the French nuclear power industry. Despite disruption from the 1963 Algerian repatriation, growth exceeded forecasts.

The Fifth Plan (1965–1970) contained detailed microeconomic elements but had a macroeconomic focus, particularly on international competitiveness and controlling inflation. The last goal was not met—inflation averaged 4.4 percent per year against the target of 1.5 percent.[28] Growth exceeded the target for the last time in a French plan, but was disrupted by the 1968 student-worker uprisings that led a year later to adamantly proplanning Charles de Gaulle retiring from the presidency.

The Sixth Plan (1970–1975) largely continued the Fifth in its goals, although it placed more of a ''supply side'' emphasis on rapid industrial expansion. This plan fell miserably short of its goals after the first oil price shock hit in 1973.

---

[26]Henry W. Ehrmann, *Organized Business in France* (Princeton: Princeton University Press, 1957), p. 88.

[27]Stephen S. Cohen, *Modern Capitalist Planning: The French Model* (Cambridge: Harvard University Press, 1969), p. 88.

[28]Saul Estrin and Peter Holmes, *French Planning in Theory and Practice* (London: George Allen & Unwin, 1983), p. 68.

Under antiplanning President Giscard, the Seventh Plan (1975–1980) ignored microeconomic aspects entirely and sought to achieve macroeconomic balance alone. It failed.

The Eighth Plan (1980–1984) had a microeconomic emphasis, pushing for high-technology development. This plan coincided with a wave of nationalizations in 1981 and 1982 early in Mitterand's presidency. His coalition government with the Communists carried out many social policies as well, including major income redistribution[29] and wage increases. These policies led to rising inflation and a falling franc. In 1983 Mitterand tied the franc to the German mark in the Exchange Rate Mechanism (ERM) and adopted an antiinflationary policy.[30] This major policy shift led to a break with the Communists, who left the government. This plan also saw the first use of multiple scenarios.

The Ninth Plan (1984–1988) expanded participation in the concertation process. The major focus continued to be on industrial modernization and high-technology development. It also saw greater emphasis on regional planning because of Mitterand's administrative decentralization, on an effort to prioritize projects out of the plethora planned, and on introducing planning contracts. In its last two years this plan went into abeyance during the cohabitation between the Socialist Mitterand and the Gaullist premier, Jacques Chirac, who seriously contemplated abolishing the CGP.

The Tenth Plan (1989–1992) focused on European integration and preparing France for the complete removal of market barriers in the EU on January 1, 1993. Elements included emphasis on reform and upgrading education,[31] now somewhat decentralized,[32] and achieving full employment. The latter goal was not achieved when recession reemerged in 1991. The Eleventh Plan focuses on accommodation to the Maastricht Treaty of 1991.

Table 7–1 shows plan forecasts of GDP annual growth rates compared with actual performance.

Since 1970 actual growth has fallen below planned growth, thereby undermining the credibility of the planners. Microeconomic forecasts have been even further off. But such outcomes may not disprove planning if the failure was due to unforecastable exogenous shocks. Planners may still forecast better

---

[29]Prior to 1981 France had one of the most unequal distributions of income among advanced economies.

[30]This policy was eventually successful. By 1993 the French inflation rate was lower than the German one.

[31]As of 1989 only 7 percent of the adult French population had a university education compared to 23 percent in the United States, 15 percent in Canada, 13 percent in Japan, 12 percent in Sweden, 11 percent in Norway, 10 percent in Germany, 9 percent in Britain, and 8 percent for Europe as a whole (*OECD Economic Surveys: France* [Paris: Organization for Economic Cooperation and Development, 1992], p. 93).

[32]French education was long among the most centralized in the world. Ministers of Education used to brag that at any hour they knew exactly which page of which book every student of a certain grade would be reading.

TABLE 7–1   **Plan Forecasting Performance**

Plan: Years	Forecast Growth Rate		Actual Growth Rate
Second: 1953–57	4.4		5.2
Third: 1957–1961	4.9		4.5
Interim: 1960–61	4.3		6.3
Fourth: 1961–65	5.5		6.3
Fifth: 1965–70	5.0		5.8
Sixth: 1970–75	5.9		3.8
Seventh: 1975–80	5.2		3.8
Eighth: 1980–84	Favorable 3.2	Unfavorable 2.7	1.2
Ninth: 1984–88	Favorable 2.2	Unfavorable 1.6	1.1

Source: From Saul Estrin and Peter Holmes, "Indicative Planning in Developed Economies," *Journal of Comparative Economics* 14 (1990), p. 542.

than private markets. Evidence that at least private markets do no better than the planners can be found from looking at interest rates as indicators of private market forecasts.[33]

Finally, the process of generating the Cecchini Report[34] for the European Commission, in which participants were asked to forecast the effects of the removal of market barriers in the EU, was classic French-style indicative planning. This very process helped stimulate the investment boom that took off after 1985 in an exhortive anticipatory manner. Something similar may be possible for the Maastricht Treaty stage of the European unification process, permanently moving the locus of indicative planning to the EU as a whole.

Industrial Policy

In comparing French and Japanese industrial policies, the French have more frequently nationalized industries than have the Japanese. Another difference is that French policy has been less consistent than Japanese, probably reflecting the greater power of MITI compared to the French Ministry of Industry.

Some state-owned firms in France date to Colbert in the 1600s, including Sèvres porcelain and Gobelins textiles. But until Léon Blum nationalized parts of the military production industry in 1936, most French enterprises were privately owned by bourgeois *patrons*.[35] Many French firms were small and family owned, even in industries that tend to be large corporations in other countries.

---

[33]Estrin and Holmes, "Indicative Planning in Developed Economies."

[34]P. Cecchini, ed., *1992 The European Challenge* (London: Gower, 1988).

[35]Other state-owned firms as of 1936 were railroads, the postal savings bank, and Crédit Agricole, which lends to farmers.

TABLE 7–2   **Shares of Value Added in State-Owned Enterprises**

Industry	Before 1982	After 1982
Ferrous ores	0	68.3
Semifabricated steel	0	16.8
Basic nonferrous metals	16.3	60.7
Glass	0	34.7
Basic chemicals	11.6	47.8
Pharmaceuticals	6.6	24.3
Industrial equipment	1.7	18.3
Electrical equipment	0	18.7
Household durables	0	8.7
Aerospace	53.8	84.3
Plastics	2.2	10.4

Source: From Henri Aujac, "An Introduction to French Industrial Policy," in *French Industrial Policy,* William James Adams and Christian Stoffäes, eds. (Washington: Brookings Institution, 1986), p. 30.

After World War II a wave of nationalizations occurred, affecting the Bank of France, the four largest commercial banks, the four leading groups of insurance companies, all electric power and gas producers, the coal mining industry, Air France, and the Renault automobile company, the latter specifically because of wartime collaboration with the Nazis by its owner. Until 1981 no other firms were nationalized, although occasionally new public enterprises were created from scratch or the government bought part ownership as it did with Dassault Aircraft in 1978. Until 1986 none of these industries was denationalized.

In early 1982, under the Socialist/Communist government of Mitterand, another major wave of nationalizations occurred, the last such in any major economy in the world. Large enterprises across a wide range of sectors were nationalized, many of them the products of government-encouraged mergers in earlier years, including Honeywell-Bull in computers, Rhône-Poulenc in chemicals, Usinor and Sacilor in steel, Thomson in electronics, and the French telephone subsidiary of ITT. After this, state-owned enterprises (SOEs) constituted 30 percent of the value added in industrial production and 50 percent of R&D spending. Table 7–2 shows shares of 1979 value added in SOEs in selected industries before and after 1982.

After 1986, the Gaullist Chirac government initiated a gradual privatization program involving sales of shares of some of these enterprises to the French public. A few, such as the commercial bank Société Générale, were fully privatized before the Socialists returned to power in 1988 when privatization was halted. But no more nationalizations occurred either.

After defeating the Socialists in March 1993, the Gaullist government began privatizing 21 companies, including some of the largest nationalized in 1982 such as Rhône-Poulenc, Bull, and Thomson, and some dating back to

Box 7–1

Profitable State-Owned Enterprises in France?

Most French SOEs have been profitable, in some cases more profitable than privately owned French firms competing with them, for example, state-owned Renault versus privately owned Peugeot. How could this be? The key is that by and large these companies were not subsidized and were under orders to behave like profit-maximizing, market capitalist firms. They faced ''hard budget constraints'' because they had no guarantee from the government that they would be bailed out if they failed.*

An extreme case was Renault toward which the government actually took a hostile stance because of its owner's wartime collaboration. The company had to make it on its own and it did. Indeed, both Renault and Air France sometimes found themselves at odds with the national plans or other directives of the government and actively fought them. Although the French are now privatizing, they showed how to have a relatively efficient set of state-owned enterprises.

---

*There are exceptions, such as the scandal-ridden bank, Crédit Lyonnais, and in the steel industry where subsidies rose to keep firms afloat. But even there firms have been allowed to fail. Air France has suffered losses recently, but then so have most privately owned airlines.

---

the 1940s such as Air France and Renault. Unlike the 1986–88 program, foreign buyers have been allowed, although the government is retaining part ownership in companies in the defense, health, and security sectors and in Renault. Railways and telecommunications remain nationalized. France has joined the worldwide trend to capitalism.

During 1946–63, industrial policy emphasized reconstruction and modernization through indicative planning. Starting in 1963, President de Gaulle decided to build up the French military, thereby encouraging specific high-technology industries through government purchases, particularly nuclear weapons, computers, aerospace, and conventional military equipment. In aerospace France came to be highly competitive in world markets, but not in computers.

Between 1969 and 1974 under President Georges Pompidou concern about international competition increased. The focus of economic policy was to develop ''national champions,'' and a series of mergers in various sectors was encouraged. Some of the resulting firms became reasonably competitive, such as the Compagnie Générale d'Électricité. Others did not, such as in the steel industry. This was the *Grand Industrial Policy* and many mergers took a conglomerate form across sectoral lines.

Between 1974 and 1978, President Giscard pursued a more laissez-faire policy, although he attempted to save certain declining industries such as footwear and leather goods. From 1978 to 1981 his policy resembled Pompidou's, but without encouraging conglomerate mergers.

From 1981 to 1984 policy focused on SOEs. Since then, the focus has been on preparing for European unification.

The tools of industrial policy have included export subsidies, R&D funding, tax breaks, preferential lending by state-owned banks, and a relaxed antitrust policy. The latter may have especially contributed to inefficiency and reduced productivity improvements in the French economy.

Labor and Management

Governments in France have long sought to bring about harmonious labor-management relations. But in contrast to Japan, harmony has proven to be difficult to achieve because class conflicts run deep in France. It was the striking silk workers of Lyon in the early 1830s who inspired Karl Marx to assign to the industrial proletariat the role of world progressive hero class. The French union movement dates from that period and has been one of the world's most militant and politically revolutionary.[36]

One major effort to suppress the class struggle came during the Vichy regime in the early 1940s. Its official ideology was *corporatism,* based on 1890s Roman Catholic Church ideas of solidarity between the classes.[37] The keystone of the effort was the Labor Charter of 1941, mandating formation of combined labor-management committees that would resolve outstanding issues while forbidding strikes and lockouts. Both employers' associations and unions resisted joining these committees and the effort was generally a failure, although social committees were established that dealt with issues in health care and working conditions, and some of these evolved after the war into bases for labor-management cooperation. But unions have generally been suspicious of cooperation because of its association with the Vichy regime and the view that it merely suppresses the labor movement.

As can be seen from Tables 2–3 and 2–4 in Chapter 2, union membership has not been high, but strike activity has been. However, a sharp drop in union membership occurred in the early and mid-1980s during the first Mitterand government when he ruled in tandem with the Communists. Large wage boosts and other prolabor policies were implemented. Proposals for workers' management, called *autogestion,* also were put forth. These schemes foundered as the Communists left the government after Mitterand pledged to tie the franc into the ERM, thereby restricting further wage boosts. Today relative labor

---

[36]See Edward Shorter and Charles Tilly, *Strikes in France: 1830–1968* (London: Cambridge University Press, 1974).

[37]See Frederic L. Pryor, ''Corporatism as an Economic System: A Review Essay,'' *Journal of Comparative Economics* 12 (1988), pp. 317–44, for a discussion of these ideological roots.

peace is maintained more by double-digit unemployment rates than because of a resolution of the old class conflicts.

Regional Planning

An aspect of French planning not in Japanese planning is an emphasis upon developing less developed regions. This extends the long process of nation building and absorption of peripheral zones that France has undergone. But it also arises from an anti-Paris sentiment outside of the capital, which is way ahead of the rest of the country in per capita income terms.[38]

Starting in 1954 policies were adopted to reduce regional inequalities, although at first these policies were disconnected from the indicative planning run by the CGP. These policies included restrictions on industrial development in Paris,[39] investment grants and other subsidies including tax breaks for firms setting up in a Critical Zone (of which eventually there were two tiers), and the division of the country into 22 planning regions. In 1963 DATAR was established to implement these policies and to coordinate with the CGP in the indicative planning process. Unlike the CGP, DATAR has a budget and some executive authority.

Regional development policies became linked with the Grand Industrial Policy of Pompidou in the early 1970s. The conglomerate mergers encouraged then were to have regional bases so that the resulting national champions could function as *growth poles* and would support many suppliers and small firms within given regions.

Policies also emerged that were designed to halt decline in industrialized regions where industries began to die, especially in the Lille region in the far north and in Lorraine in the northeast where the steel industry was concentrated but declining. Again these policies were linked with industrial policy— as subsidies to the steel industry coincided with subsidies to these regions. More recently under pressure from the EU, these firm subsidies have been reduced and firms have failed.

Under Mitterand there was a move towards decentralizing planning and a variety of administrative functions. The basic regional planning units were the 22 established in 1956, which now gained expanded powers.[40] Decentralization led to a basic contradiction. The original point was to equalize regional

---

[38]In 1980, using the national average as the index of 100, Paris was at 137 whereas no other region was as high as 100 (J.R. Hough, *The French Economy* [New York: Holmes and Meier, 1982], p. 180). The poorest parts of France are in the southwest and in Brittany in the far west.

[39]This contrasts with Japan, which has made no effort to halt the implosion of labor and capital into Tokyo, now tied with Mexico City for being the world's largest metropolitan area.

[40]There is a nostalgic correspondence between these planning regions and the prerevolutionary provinces that were eliminated in favor of departments, the official units of local government.

income differentials. But putting fiscal responsibility in the hands of local rather than national authorities may lead to increased inequalities. Richer regions can afford to support better schools and gain an edge that the highly centralized system did not give them over poorer regions.

There is no consensus regarding the success or failure of this effort. Overall the trend has been towards greater regional equality of income distribution. But such trends are discernible in the United States, which has very little regional planning. Other countries, such as the United Kingdom have seen increasing inequalities in regional income distributions. The United Kingdom has had some regional policies.

Furthermore, the problem of the declining industrial regions is getting worse rather than better. As with the broader planning effort, help for declining areas is moving to the level of the EU, which provides subsidies to less developed regions throughout the EU, including to some areas of France.

France, Europe, and the World Economy

The tradition of Colbertisme included a deep vein of protectionism in its nationalist mercantilism. This tradition lived on strongly in French policy— France was among the most protectionist of major nations until after World War II, with the exception of a free trade interlude from 1860 to 1871. But just as the defeat in 1940 turned France towards indicative planning, so it also turned France towards a more internationalist and free trade stance, especially with regard to Germany. Thus as Luigi Barzini explains,

> Three wars since 1870, all of them fought against Germany, cracked [France's] faith in its invincibility, and this is why France must now keep abreast of the Germans, keep them under surveillance, maintain the most intimate relations with them, and hold them in an embrace as close as a stranglehold. If France cannot dominate Europe alone, it hopes that maybe the two nations together might do so.[41]

To the extent that the desire to end the ancient Franco-German enmity was the political/diplomatic driving force for the creation of the European Union it has been a smashing success. But it has also been a smashing success economically, such that most nonmember nations in Europe now want to join.[42] The principal competing hypothesis to the alleged benefits of indicative planning for successful postwar French economic growth is the benefits of integration into the free-trading EU.

The case for free trade in the EU being the driving force of postwar French economic growth is strong. Exports have grown more rapidly than the

---

[41]Luigi Barzini, *The Europeans* (New York: Simon and Schuster, 1983), p. 154.

[42]A few naysayers are very wealthy Switzerland as well as Iceland and Norway, which are heavily dependent on the fishing industry, which they fear the EU will regulate. Even these three have largely free trade with the EU.

economy as a whole and the composition of exports has increasingly gone to the EU. Exports have always been somewhat more volatile than GDP, but the ratio of exports to GDP rose from 8.9 percent in 1958 to 17.3 percent in 1979[43] and to 25.1 percent by 1990 in 1980 prices.[44]

Trade between France and its future EU partners declined from a 35.5 percent share in 1913 to a mere 17.9 percent share in 1949.[45] Most of that decline was due to a shift to France's colonial empire—its share peaked in 1938 at 46 percent and still exceeded 40 percent in 1952.[46] From 17.9 percent in 1949, the EU's share of French exports soared to 64.8 percent in 1990.[47]

Although impressive this decline does not resolve the issue of free trade because the major lowering of trade barriers occurred at the end of the 1950s and the beginning of the 1960s. Thus it may be that indicative planning was more important in the 1950s when its information and exhortive roles may have shaken up French business leaders. But once the lowering of trade barriers took effect the expansion of exports to the EU probably became more important. Indeed the highest growth rates ever recorded for the French economy came in the 1960s when it also outperformed all other members of the EU, although this throws the ball back a bit into the court of planning.

France's role in the EU has imitated the attitudes of French citizens towards their own government as described by General de Gaulle in the quote at the beginning of this chapter. The French have been among the most enthusiastic supporters of the EU and of European unification, despite barely supporting the Maastricht Treaty in a 1992 referendum. One aspect that has encouraged their support is the perception that they have a lot of influence—the operative language among the "Eurocrats" at the European Commission in Brussels is French,[48] and the European Parliament meets on French soil in Strasburg, albeit on the German border.

However, France has often played the whiny bad boy of the EU, blocking initiatives supported by other countries and asserting its national interests forcibly and frequently. One example was de Gaulle's blocking of Britain's initial application to join in 1961. More serious was his insistence on an expensive Common Agricultural Policy that mainly benefits French farmers. Until late 1993, the Uruguay Round of GATT negotiations was held up by disagreements

[43]Hough, *The French Economy,* p. 200.

[44]*OECD Economic Surveys: France,* p. 145.

[45]J.J. Carré, P. Dubois, and E. Malinvaud, *French Economic Growth,* John P. Hatfield, trans. (Stanford: Stanford University Press, 1975), p. 405.

[46]William James Adams, *Restructuring the French Economy: Government and the Rise of Market Competition since World War II* (Washington: Brookings Institution, 1989), p. 147. Although France gave up most of its formal colonial empire by 1962, it maintains close economic and diplomatic links with a group of former African colonies that tie their currencies to the French franc. Even Socialist governments have militarily intervened to support governments in these countries, as in Chad.

[47]*OECD Economic Surveys: France,* p. 145.

[48]This contributes to British uneasiness about European unification, along with the apparently socialist and bureaucratic tendencies of the Eurocrats, which have upset pro–laissez-faire figures such as Margaret Thatcher. This unease was enhanced in the late 1980s by a French Socialist, Jacques Delors, serving as president of the European Commission.

Box 7–2

The Formation and Development of the European Union

The European Coal and Steel Community (ECSC) was established by the Treaty of Paris in 1951, with the goal of removing tariffs and quotas related to trade in coal, iron ore, and steel among the original six members: France, West Germany, Italy, the Netherlands, Belgium, and Luxemburg. Besides the implicit goal of pacifying the Franco-German frontier, the explicit logic of the ECSC arose from the fact that there was a lot of iron ore in the northeastern French province of Lorraine and a lot of coal in the southwestern German province of Saar, both very near each other but on opposite sides of the international border. For the production of steel, requiring those two inputs, the border was made economically irrelevant by the Treaty of Paris.

In 1957 the same countries signed the Treaty of Rome establishing the European Economic Community (EEC) or Common Market, which would be a customs union possessing a common external tariff and quota boundary, but with substantial reductions between member nations. Adding additional functions later it became the European Community (EC). In 1973, the United Kingdom, Ireland, and Denmark joined, in 1981 Greece joined, and in 1986 Spain and Portugal joined. In 1984 the members agreed to completely eliminate all customs barriers and harmonize most regulations by January 1, 1993, a goal that was achieved.

In 1991 the Maastricht Treaty was signed, establishing the European Union and committing the members to complete currency unification later in the decade, although movement towards achieving this goal has slowed somewhat. In 1995 Austria, Finland, and Sweden joined the EU. The EU's administrative capital is in Brussels, Belgium, and its legislative capital is in Strasburg, France.

This process of formation and development was one of adding layers of agreements to older ones, creating a pattern of nested organizations. Thus there still is the ECSC nested within the EEC, which is nested within the EC, which is nested within the EU, each of these successive entities defined by the new set of agreements associated with it.

over agriculture, and France's opposition to loosening EU agricultural policies was the main culprit in the gridlock.

France continues to carry out protectionist policies by bureaucratic subterfuge and engages in mercantilist export promotion, which is linked to industrial policy[49] through an aggressive export bureaucracy and a system of

---

[49]France has transferred much industrial policy to the EU level. It closed down the nationalized Creusot-Loire steel company in response to EU pressure. Several joint EU ventures, notably Airbus, the Ariane space satellite program, and the CERN nuclear research facility, have had considerable success.

insurance and interest subsidies. This protectionist tendency is directed less at other EU members, except when agriculture is involved, and more at making the EU itself a protectionist fortress against the outside world. Protectionism has led France to prevent the EU from allowing easy entry of Eastern European commodities, much to the dismay of Germany and Britain. Also France argues against allowing other countries into the EU and in favor of more intensive integration among existing members, deepening rather than widening the organization, again in disagreement with Germany and Britain.

Thus France has gone a long way towards surrendering its national sovereignty in the European Union. But part of its willingness is connected with the willingness of the EU to accede to French ways of doing things, from indicative planning through industrial policy to mercantilist protectionism. Colbertisme may have died in Paris only to have moved to Brussels.

The outcome of the relationship between the EU and the rest of the world economy is very important. If France succeeds in blocking an expansion of trade relations between the EU and the rest of the world, especially Eastern Europe, the results could be tragic.

Summary and Conclusions

France has engaged in public and influential indicative planning. In contrast to the indicative planning in Japan, France's concertation has had strong informational and exhortive components. It also has been more macroeconomically oriented, with less stress on industrial policy than in Japan. Also France has had a strong component of regional planning, unlike Japan. Yet another difference with Japan has been that France has had a much larger state-owned sector, one that has functioned fairly efficiently, but that is now being substantially privatized. In both Japan and France indicative planning has declined in influence since the 1960s.

This indicative planning reflects a long tradition of state intervention in the economy going back to the dirigisme practiced by Colbert under King Louis XIV, when France was the world's leading military and economic power. France's decline after that has been attributed by supporters of laissez-faire to dirigiste policies. After World War II the French economy experienced remarkable growth, accompanied by both indicative planning and integration of the French economy into the European economy of the European Union. France has high unemployment that has led to major policy reassessments and the move to privatization.

The major current thrust of the French economy is to further integrate with the EU. But it also seeks to mold the EU in its own image, pushing for indicative planning as well as industrial and protectionist policies aimed at the rest of the world. Thus, whether the European Union opens more to the rest of the world economy or retreats behind a wall of protectionism depends importantly upon France, and the outcome presents serious implications for the whole world economy.

Questions for Discussion

1. How have the dirigiste and laissez-faire traditions conflicted in France?
2. What are the theoretical arguments for and against indicative planning?
3. How do French indicative planning and industrial policies compare with those of Japan?
4. Why have French state-owned enterprises been more efficient than those in most countries?
5. What was the link between France's Grand Industrial Policy and the regional planning effort and how are both changing as France integrates further with the European Union?
6. Why have French labor-management relations been so bad?
7. How has France's attitude towards the European Union resembled that of French citizens towards their own government?

Suggested Further Readings

Adams, William James. *Restructuring the French Economy: Government and the Rise of Market Competition since World War II*. Washington: Brookings Institution, 1989.

———and Christian Stoffäes, eds. *French Industrial Policy*. Washington: Brookings Institution, 1986.

Braudel, Fernand. *The Identity of France, Vol. I: History and Environment*. trans. Sian Reynolds. New York: Harper and Row, 1988.

Cazes, Bernard. ''Indicative Planning in France.'' In *Comparative Economic Systems: Models and Cases,* 7th ed., ed. Morris Bornstein. Burr Ridge: Irwin, 1994, pp. 160–72.

Estrin, Saul, and Peter Holmes. *French Planning in Theory and Practice*. London: George Allen & Unwin, 1983.

Grémion, Catherine. ''Decentralization in France: A Historical Perspective.'' In *The Mitterand Experiment: Continuity and Change in Modern France,* eds. George Ross, Stanley Hoffman, and Sylvia Malzacher. New York: Oxford University Press, 1987, pp. 237–47.

Hayward, Jack. *The State and the Market Economy: Industrial Patriotism and Economic Intervention in France*. New York: New York University Press, 1986.

Wallace, Anthony H. ''The 1992 Single Market Program of the European Community.'' In *Comparative Economic Systems: Models and Cases,* 7th ed., ed. Morris Bornstein. Burr Ridge: Irwin, 1994, pp. 205–22.

CHAPTER 8

SWEDEN: THE CRISIS OF THE CORPORATIST WELFARE STATE

Each time that I have gone back one thing that has impressed me more than anything else is the seeming wholeness of life. It is reflected in a calm, a poise, a certain health rare in our time . . .

It may be merely that the Swedes have made haste slowly, with that deliberate tempo of speech and manner which the world has found a little funny. They have fought shy of the arbitrary advances by which humanity has sought to pull itself up by its bootstraps. Their progress has never been marked by dogma.

—Marquis W. Childs, *Sweden: The Middle Way*

In the seventeenth century, Sweden was at the height of its military power, controlling the major part of Northern Europe. As befitted a major world power, Swedish leaders commissioned the construction of a great warship, known as the Vasaship. Indeed, they sought to create the most heavily armed, technically advanced warship of the time. The planning was meticulous. The execution of design was at the highest technical levels of Swedish craftsmanship. On the day of the ship's launching, everyone from the royal family to the lowly shipbuilders looked on as their majestic creation slipped into the water, the ballast inside its hold shifted, and the great ship sank peacefully beneath the waters of Stockholm harbor.

—Hugh Heclo and Henrik Madsen, *Policy and Politics in Sweden: Principled Pragmatism*

Introduction

The world has watched with a mixture of fascination and dislike the evolution of the Swedish economic system, fascination on the part of those who admire its many virtues and achievements, dislike by advocates of laissez-faire, including many inside Sweden itself. However, as the Swedish economy

179

experienced increasing difficulties recently and a non–Social Democratic government between 1991 and 1994 moved the system towards the mainstream, the shoe shifted to the other foot. Advocates of laissez-faire applauded as Sweden joined the global trend while admirers of its welfare state watched despondently.

Even after the recent changes, Sweden's economy remains different from that in the United States and most of the rest of the market capitalist world. It may, however, be converging on its neighbors in Scandinavia, and less so, on Germany, Austria, Belgium, and the Netherlands.

In Chapter 1 we labeled economies such as Sweden's *social market economies,* a term originally applied to the West German economy in the 1950s. These economies avoid central planning and rely on market forces and private ownership of the means of production[1] while providing relatively high levels of government income redistribution and social welfare spending. Thus they take a *middle way* between laissez-faire market capitalism and command socialism. Also they have been characterized by parliamentary democratic political systems with high levels of personal civil liberties and periods of rule by Social Democratic or Labor Parties since World War II.

Sweden went much further in these directions than the others. While adhering to market forces in product markets, private ownership of land and capital, and a strict fiscal policy until the mid-1970s,[2] Sweden developed the most extensive income redistribution and social support system along with the highest levels of taxation of any nonsocialist economy in the world, often described as a system of ''cradle to grave'' security. It also developed centralized wage bargaining labeled *corporatism,* an equalizing *wage solidarism* approach, and active government intervention in labor markets for retraining.

As late as 1980 the Swedish economy was one of the top three non–oil-exporting nations in the world in real per capita income, but it is no longer in the ranks of the top 10. According to the 1993 UN *Human Development Report,* Swedish women have the best living conditions in the world. Sweden has probably come closer to eliminating poverty than any nation ever, with only about 1 percent of its population belonging to an economic underclass.[3] From the beginning of World War II to 1993 its unemployment rate never exceeded 4 percent and generally was in the 1–2 percent range, coinciding

---

[1]Austria has been an exception in having significant public ownership of the capital stock.

[2]It has been nonsocialist governments that have tended to violate these strictures. Most of the few nationalizations came in the 1890–1920 period under Conservative governments and were designed to prevent foreign takeovers. Another wave occurred to prop up employment under the nonsocialist government of 1976–1982 when the budget deficit soared to 13 percent of GDP.

[3]This group consists largely of jobless youths and some elderly and disabled, despite the extensive social welfare safety net (James Angresano, *Comparative Economics* [Englewood Cliffs: Prentice Hall, 1992] p. 282).

with very high labor force participation rates.[4] Despite high employment, Sweden's inflation rates were in line with those in the rest of Europe until the late 1980s.

Sweden seemed to transcend the equity-efficiency trade-off. It had high real growth with high income equality and considerable macroeconomic stability, all within a highly democratic political structure marked by extensive individual liberties in social and cultural matters. Despite its current problems, this record still leads some to present the Swedish model as an ideal for Eastern European economies in transition.[5]

But the critics are having their day, most vociferously inside Sweden itself. They argue that most of the rapid growth occurred prior to 1950 while its income redistribution and social welfare system was still mostly undeveloped.[6] Whereas in the past the Protestant work ethic of Lutheran Sweden kept people working despite generous social welfare benefits and high taxation levels, a lazy new generation has supposedly appeared that is undermining the system by taking advantage of its benefits, especially generous sick and parental leaves. Since the mid-1970s or even the mid-1960s, the performance of the Swedish model has steadily worsened with seriously decelerating growth and accelerating worker absenteeism. Centralized wage bargaining has broken down and accelerating wage boosts, inflation, and budget and current account deficits have resulted.

Swedish voters replaced the long-ruling Social Democrats in 1991 with a pro–laissez-faire coalition government led by Carl Bildt of the Moderate Party.[7] Supporting Sweden's application to join the European Union, this government made noticeable cutbacks in the social welfare system and accompanying tax cuts. Trying to break the wage-price spiral, this government

---

[4]This contrasts with both Japan and Switzerland, which have had equally low unemployment rates, but which have had lower labor force participation rates because of substantial discrimination against women in their labor markets.

[5]James Angresano, ''A Mixed Economy in Hungary? Lessons from the Swedish Experience,'' *Comparative Economic Studies* 34 (1992), pp. 41–57.

[6]Assar Lindbeck, ''The Swedish Experience,'' Institute for International Economic Studies, Seminar Paper No. 482, Stockholm, 1990. This rapid pre-1950 growth was significantly aided by Sweden's neutrality in both World Wars I and II, during which it exported significant raw materials and industrial goods to Germany. Its only rivals from 1950 through 1980 for the top status in real living standards were Switzerland, which was similarly neutral and exporting to Germany, and the United States, on whose soil no fighting occurred except at Pearl Harbor, and on a few Aleutian Islands in World War II.

[7]Since 1932 the Social Democrats have been the largest party in the Riksdag (parliament). They ruled during 1932–1976, 1982–1991, and since 1994, usually in open or tacit coalitions with other parties. The now pro–laissez-faire Moderates used to be known as Conservatives, dating from a promercantilist party from the 1770s based on the upper aristocracy. Their coalition partners were the Center Party, formerly known as the Agrarian Party, a rural-based party with 19th-century roots that has often been a swing party between Left and Right, and the promarket but prowelfare state Liberal Party, which frequently led governments between 1905 and 1930. Other parties in the Riksdag are the Party of the Left (formerly the Communists), frequently silent backers of the Social Democrats, and the Greens, founded in 1981.

allowed the unemployment rate to soar to nearly 9 percent by the end of 1993. In September 1994, the Social Democrats returned to power under Ingvar Carlson, but they are constrained by a high budget deficit and Sweden's entry into the EU in early 1995 after a positive referendum vote in November 1994. The *Swedish model* will never be the same again, even if it still remains more welfare-state oriented and corporatist than most in the world.

Historical and Cultural Roots of the Swedish Model

Foundational characteristics significant in explaining Swedish history and character include an independent peasantry that was never enserfed, a powerful Protestant state church,[8] a deeply rooted respect for law, ethnic homogeneity of the population, a long history of organized government, a tradition of honesty and effectiveness in the bureaucracy,[9] weakness of the middle class,[10] and an intellectual tradition of rationality and practicality.

If the Swedish middle way depends on a pragmatic balancing of individual and communal, these traits were already present in pre-Christian Viking times (500–1100). A rugged and democratic individualism was enforced by the Vikings' wide-ranging travels and the rigorous climate. Local parliaments, whose laws were respected, elected their kings.[11] But agriculture was in commonly held open fields, reflecting a communalism encouraged by the need to cooperate against the harsh environment.[12]

After adopting Lutheranism in the 1500s, Sweden entered a period of royalist power and national expansion, bringing it to lead the Protestant cause in the Thirty Years War (1618–1648). This period saw the birth of Sweden's

---

[8]This laid a base for the tradition of hard work. But the 19th-century revolt against the church played an important role in the formation of the socialist political and economic movements that can be argued to have displaced it. Thus Heclo and Madsen (*Policy and Politics in Sweden: Principled Pragmatism* [1987], Philadelphia: Temple University Press p. 5) declare, ''An outsider is struck by the churchlike quality of the mammoth labor movement and its concern for proper public action and thinking. The power of this Social Democratic 'church' dominates Sweden's political landscape.''

[9]The modern bureaucracy was founded during the Great Power era of the early 1600s. It was staffed by aristocrats or talented laymen and acted as a brake on royal absolutism. As in France and Japan it is prestigious and has traditionally attracted highly qualified individuals.

[10]This was due to the late development of Sweden's industrial revolution, which occurred only after 1870, associated with a weak tradition of pro–laissez-faire views.

[11]Although democracy was invented in ancient Greece, it has continuously existed for the longest time in Scandinavia. The oldest operating parliament in the world is the Althing of Iceland, and the British parliament came from Viking invaders.

[12]Modern Sweden has many consumer and agricultural cooperatives. A deeply entrenched communalist idea of sharing from the Viking period is *lagom,* from the drinking horn passed amongst Viking villagers, which has come to mean ''just right'' or ''fairness'' in modern times. One was expected to drink just the right amount from the horn, not too little and not too much.

efficient bureaucracy, the establishment of an efficient financial system including Europe's oldest continuously existing bank, and the development of capitalist institutions in iron and copper mining, Sweden's leading export industries.

During the less expansionistic but more liberal 1700s science, technology, and education[13] developed vigorously. The enclosure movement in agriculture began, which ended the traditional open field system by the 1860s and displaced rural workers who would form the base of an urban industrial working class, although many strongly independent farmers arose.

After a related expansion of the iron and timber export industries, the Swedish economy took off in the 1870s with expansion led by railroad investment that saw the world's fastest rate of growth until 1950, exceeding even Japan's.[14] Important in this performance were technical innovations by Swedish entrepreneurs, which became the bases of later industrial empires. These innovations include invention of chemical pulp processing (Svenska Cellulosa is Sweden's 10th largest firm), significant improvements in telephones (L.M. Ericsson is Sweden's sixth largest firm), innovations in steam turbines (Asea is Sweden's largest firm), innovations in self-adjusting ball bearings (SKF is Sweden's ninth largest firm), and the invention of dynamite (Nobel Industries is Sweden's eighth largest firm and funder of the Nobel Prizes).[15]

This rapid industrialization led to the emergence of a working class movement. In 1889 the Social Democratic Party (SAP) was founded by union members and in 1898 the union federation, Landsorganisationen (LO) was founded. Employers formed their own organization, the SAF, in 1902. A period of bitter economic, social, and political conflict ensued with many strikes and a near revolution in 1918, resulting in universal suffrage and absolute parliamentary supremacy. The economy plunged after 1930, leading to electoral victory by the Social Democrats in 1932, who would remain in power until 1976.[16]

---

[13]Sweden has one of the best educated labor forces in the world. See footnote 31 in Chapter 7.

[14]Although British and French investors played a role, the existing Swedish banks were important. The wealthiest family in Sweden, the Wallenbergs, began as the founders of the Enskilda Bank in the 1840s. In 1966 the head of the family, Marcus Wallenberg, served on the boards of directors of 60 companies, and as of 1989 Wallenberg interests still possessed over 25 percent of the voting shares in 6 of Sweden's 10 largest companies. This tight control has led some companies to take a longer time horizon perspective, much like Japanese corporations.

[15]See Assar Lindbeck, *Swedish Economic Policy* (Berkeley: University of California Press, 1974), chap. 1, and ''A Survey of the Swedish Economy,'' *The Economist* (March 3, 1990).

[16]Their hold on power would be solidified by a deal with the Agrarian Party. The Social Democrats supported agricultural price supports in exchange for support of Keynesian-style public works to end unemployment. The ''Stockholm School'' of economics, notably Ernst Wigforss and Gunnar Myrdal, developed theories of aggregate demand management independently from Keynes.

Labor Market Institutions

Corporatism

Most observers argue that key to Sweden's ability to maintain both low un-employment and low inflation for decades was the nature of its labor market. Most important has been the centralized wage bargaining system widely called *corporatism*.

As noted in Chapter 2, corporatism has two versions: authoritarian and liberal. The former involves the state establishing and enforcing centralized wage bargaining as in fascist economies such as Mussolini's Italy, Vichy France, and Nazi Germany, which called themselves *corporate states*.

Liberal corporatism is largely self-organized between labor and management with only a supporting role for government. Leading examples of such systems have been in small, ethnically homogeneous countries with strong traditions of Social Democratic or Labor Party rule. Using a scale of zero to two and subjectively assigning values based on six previous studies, Frederic Pryor finds Norway and Sweden the most corporatist at 2.0 each, followed by Austria at 1.8; the Netherlands at 1.5; Finland, Denmark, and Belgium at 1.3 each; and Switzerland and West Germany at 1.0 each. At the anticorporatist end with zero each are the United States and Canada.[17] Other studies have generated other rankings with different measures, but all agree that Sweden has one of the most corporatist of current economic systems.

The lowest wage rigidity and the lowest changes in unemployment seem to occur at the two extremes, the most corporatist (Sweden, Norway, and Austria) and the least corporatist (United States and Canada).[18] Sweden, Norway, and Austria have all had good unemployment/inflation performances, matched only by Switzerland and Japan since 1945. However some argue that this good performance is unstable over time,[19] a problem relevant to Sweden.

The Rise and Fall of Swedish Corporatism

Sweden's severe labor-management strife ended in 1938 when the *Saltsjö-baden Agreement* between the LO (representing labor) and the SAF (repre-senting management) was signed. This agreement had several parts, the most important institutionalizing a centralized wage bargaining process that con-tinues to the present.[20]

---

[17]Frederic L. Pryor, ''Corporatism as an Economic System: A Review Essay,'' *Journal of Comparative Economics* 12 (1988), p. 326.

[18]See L. Calmfors and J. Driffill, ''Bargaining Structure, Corporatism and Macroeconomic Performance,'' *Economic Policy* 6 (1988), pp. 14–61.

[19]See Matti Pohjola, ''Corporatism and Wage Bargaining,'' in *Social Corporatism: A Superior Economic System?*, eds. J. Pekkarinen, M. Pohjola, and B. Rowthorn (Oxford: Clarendon Press) 1992, pp. 44–81.

[20]The government was not formally a part of this agreement, although it played a role in convincing the LO to go along. The Minister of Finance traditionally participates as a peripheral party to the negotiations.

This agreement and its implementation serves as the basis for labeling Sweden corporatist. But it represents a balance of power between still-conflicting groups, not a cessation of struggle. Hence Sweden may be *conflict corporatist* rather than *consensus corporatist* like Austria, the former type achieving greater gender and other kinds of equality due to the greater assertiveness of labor in such systems.

Nevertheless, considerable consensus operated for a long time within the Swedish bargaining system. During the Swedish economy's golden age of the 1950s and 1960s consensus was based on shared concerns about macroeconomic stability and international competitiveness. Concern with the latter led to a further agreement between the SAF, the LO, and a federation representing white collar workers, the TCO, that resulted in the *EFO model,* named for the economists representing each group, Edgren, Faxén, and Odhner.[21] It stated that productivity improvements in the internationally competing (tradeable) goods sector would set the standard for wage increases in the whole economy.

Another factor in this harmonious consensus was personal—the chief negotiators involved were long in office and maintained regular and friendly communications, as did their staffs. This personal stability included the Minister of Finance, Gunnar Strang, in office from 1955 to 1976, and Prime Minister Tage Erlander, in office from 1946 to 1969.[22] The negotiating environment was also eased by the good economic performance.

But consensus has disappeared and conflict reemerged. Swedish corporatism is in serious trouble, if not dead outright. The causes seem to involve a reversal and unraveling of those factors that made it work initially. These factors have included a heightening of international competitive pressures after the first oil price shock of 1973, a rise in public sector employment, a loss of restraint in wage demands by labor because of a lack of fear of unemployment, and losses of power by the Social Democrats, triggering distrust by the LO of the government. All these factors combined to gradually decentralize wage bargaining, and actual wage settlements exceeded those centrally set, a phenomenon known as *wage drift.*

A basic factor in the disappearance of consensus has been the long-term increase in public sector employment, with twofold results. Public sector workers are in the nontradeable goods sector, and thus their increase implies an increase of that sector relative to the tradeable goods sector. This makes it harder to impose the EFO model in which tradeable goods sector wages determine nontradeable goods sector wages. Furthermore, public sector workers are not restrained by firm profit constraints on their wage demands, resulting in increased militance by public sector workers with soaring wage demands

---

[21]See Gösta Edgren, Karl-Olof Faxén, and Clas-Erik Odhner, *Wage Formation and the Economy* (London: Allen & Unwin, 1973).

[22]He was succeeded by the more ideological and charismatic Olof Palme who was mysteriously assassinated on a Stockholm street in 1986, an event some claim marked Sweden's loss of innocence.

TABLE 8–1   Wage Drift and Unemployment Rates

Year	Negotiated	Wage Drift	Total	Unemployment Rate (%)
1980	7.8	1.7	9.5	1.4
1982	4.6	1.7	6.3	2.5
1984	5.6	2.3	7.9	2.8
1986	6.0	2.6	8.6	2.5
1988	4.2	2.3	6.5	1.7
1990	6.1	3.9	10.0	1.5
1992	2.7	0.8	3.5	4.2

Note: *Negotiated* means percent increase in wages negotiated centrally for all workers. *Wage Drift* is the extra percent locally negotiated beyond that. *Total* is the sum of the two.

Source: From NIER, *The Swedish Economy: Autumn 1992* (Stockholm: National Institute for Economic Research, 1992), pp. 78 and 82, and *OECD Economic Surveys: Sweden 1990/1991* (Paris: Organization for Economic Cooperation and Development, 1990), p. 127.

and settlements disconnected from the LO-SAF centralized bargaining outcomes. More generally the blue-collar LO has come to represent a smaller proportion of the total unionized labor force, falling from 81 percent in 1950 to 58 percent in 1990.[23]

Emergence of the wage drift problem is shown in Table 8–1. It went on through the 1970s and accelerated in the late 1980s. This acceleration coincided with an exceptionally low unemployment rate that encouraged excessive wage demands in the increasingly decentralized bargaining context, although excessive wage demands have now ended with increased unemployment.

Explosive wage increases in the late 1980s exceeded productivity gains and led to labor cost increases substantially in excess of those experienced by Sweden's international trade competitors, running ahead of 11 main competitors by more than 3 percent annually in most of the late 1980s and more than 5 percent annually in 1989 and 1990. The crisis generated by this hit in 1990 as a swelling current account deficit,[24] culminating in the replacement in late 1991 of the Social Democratic government that had ruled since 1982 by a Moderate-led coalition committed to breaking the wage-price spiral. The changed policy stance in 1992 shows up in Table 9–2 and the lower rate of labor cost increase. By 1992, competitors' labor costs were rising more than 3 percent ahead of Swedish.[25] By late 1994 the current account had reached near balance.

---

[23]Christian Nilsson, "The Swedish Model: Labour Market Institutions and Contracts," Trade Union Institute for Economic Research, Working Paper Nr. 109 (Stockholm, 1992), p. 13.

[24]Sweden had a small current account surplus in 1986 (*OECD Economic Surveys,* p. 126); by 1990 this had become a deficit of about 3 percent of the GDP (NIER, *The Swedish Economy,* pp. 9, 54).

[25]NIER, *The Swedish Economy: Autumn 1992* (Stockholm: National Institute for Economic Research, 1992), p. 140.

Wage Solidarism

Whereas corporatist wage bargaining exists in a number of economies, a characteristic of Sweden's labor market that is unique is *solidaristic wage bargaining.* The goal of this type of bargaining is to equalize wages across firms and skill and seniority levels. Solidaristic wage bargaining was the brainchild of the LO economists Gösta Rehn and Rudolph Meidner and was accepted in 1962 by the LO.[26]

Most economists criticize such an approach, arguing that it damages incentives and labor mobility. Rehn and Meidner argued just the opposite regarding labor mobility. They emphasized the need for sectoral restructuring within the Swedish economy to maintain Sweden's international competitiveness and saw the solidaristic wage policy as encouraging restructuring. Such a wage policy would drive weak firms out of business more quickly while providing greater profits for stronger firms to invest more and grow more rapidly. With few wage differences, workers would be able to shift easily from the failing firms to the expanding ones. This approach may have worked as intended in the 1960s.

From the early 1960s to the early 1980s, wage solidarism tended to equalize wages across skill and seniority categories. But the trend has been in the opposite direction since then, with increased decentralization of bargaining and wage drift. This shows in the ratio of the wages of younger workers to those of older workers. For employees with nine years of schooling the ratio of wages of those aged 16–19 to those 20 and older rose from 0.43 in 1968 to 0.71 in 1981.[27]

This solidarism shows up in broader measures of income distribution. The Gini coefficient for wage incomes declined from 0.195 in 1975 to 0.169 in 1982 (approximately the year of greatest equality), but rose to 0.176 by 1987.[28]

Recently undermining the efficiency of wage solidarism has been the very restructuring of the Swedish economy desired by Rehn and Meidner, away from a resource-based heavy industrial economy towards a more information-based high-technology one. In that type of economy, learning by doing on a specific job becomes more important for productivity increases than before. But such learning by doing is responsive to wage differentials that provide the incentives for acquiring the skills. Thus wage solidarism may now be a disincentive to economic growth.

Also, since 1970 workers have become less interested in changing jobs and prefer to stay where they are. This is because migration is often involved in job switches, many of the dying industries being located in the north (especially mining) and many of the growing ones being located in the south.

---

[26]Rudolph Meidner, *Coordination and Solidarity: An Approach to Wages Policy* (Stockholm: Prisma, 1974).

[27]Robert J. Flanagan, ''Efficiency and Equality in Swedish Labor Markets,'' in *The Swedish Economy,* eds. B.P. Bosworth and A.M. Rivlin (Washington: Brookings Institution, 1987), p. 142.

[28]Ministry of Finance of Sweden, *The 1990 Medium Term Survey of the Swedish Economy* (Stockholm, 1990), p. 339.

Thus the LO began to push for job security policies that undermine the efficiency rationale for wage solidarism.

Government Policies and the Labor Market

Active Government Labor Policies

Concern by the LO economists, Rehn and Meidner, with the question of economic restructuring led them in 1951 to formulate the *Rehn-Meidner Plan.* Their plan urged active government programs for retraining and relocating workers from dying sectors to growing ones. Sweden has had the most extensive and successful relocation program in the world. Considerable sectoral restructuring has occurred while keeping unemployment relatively low. Sweden has spent much on these policies, about 2 percent of GDP in 1987, approximately twice the level of Denmark, its nearest rival in this regard.[29]

The Rehn-Meidner Plan's largest active policy is occupational retraining. Other programs include training to avoid being laid off, relief work, youth teams, and recruitment support. The Moderate-led government introduced two new programs in 1992, a youth training scheme and a temporary development scheme for those receiving unemployment compensation. In 1991 1.9 percent of the labor force was involved in these programs, rising to 3.2 percent in 1992 and 5.1 percent in 1993.[30]

The attitude of the LO towards such programs shifted after 1970 to place a greater desire on preserving existing jobs rather than retraining for or moving to new ones. This shift led to legislation in the 1970s that made it harder to lay off workers. The nonsocialist government in power between 1976 and 1982 increased subsidies to businesses to keep them going and nationalized several firms for the same purpose, undermining the tight fiscal policy of the Social Democrats who began to cut back public spending as a percent of GDP after returning to power in 1982.

Another policy favored by LO economists was the *wages fund.* This fund was to be created by a payroll and excess profits tax and would buy up shares of corporations to be owned by the unions. The SAF bitterly opposed this plan. The Social Democratic government instituted it in 1983, but the Moderate-led government abolished it in 1991.

The Welfare State, Taxes, and Labor Supply

Probably the most famous feature of the Swedish economy is the scale of its cradle to grave welfare state programs, unmatched by any other market

---

[29]"A Survey of the Swedish Economy," p. 5.
[30]NIER, *The Swedish Economy,* pp. 79–80.

Box 8–1

Sweden: Feminist, Feminine, or Both?

The UN claims Sweden has the highest quality of life for women in the world. Besides being prime beneficiaries of the numerous social welfare programs such as parental and sick leave, full abortion rights, and an extensive public day care system, they have the highest labor force participation rate of any industrialized market economy and face among the least wage discrimination. They work more, but take more time off. Furthermore they have been highly concentrated in the public sector, which until recently had been expanding rapidly. Thus, they have felt vulnerable to recent cutbacks and were notable among those concerned about Sweden joining the EU, fearing more pressure to weaken existing programs.

Sweden clearly qualifies as feminist, but some argue that it also qualifies as *feminine,* clashing with the macho Viking image but not with the communal sharing legacy of the Viking lagom drinking horn.* This feminism may show up in Swedish management that takes a familistic orientation with reduced hierarchies—and apparent indecisiveness in the eyes of foreigners.† But these structures can be flexible and innovative as shown by the use of work teams engaging in Japanese-style consultation rather than assembly lines at Volvo's newer car factories.‡

---

*G. Hofstede, *Culture's Consequences* (London: Sage, 1980).
†Gunnar Hedlund, "Managing International Business: A Swedish Model," in *Sweden at the Edge: Lessons for American and Swedish Managers,* ed. M. Maccoby (Philadelphia: University of Pennsylvania Press, 1991), pp. 201–20.
‡Berth Jönsson, "Production Philosophy at Volvo," in *Sweden at the Edge,* pp. 109–20.

---

capitalist economy. A rudimentary public health system begun in 1874 became a universal health insurance system in 1955.[31] A public pension system was established in 1914 and made universal in 1959. Holidays with pay were established in 1931 at four days a year and expanded in 1989 to five weeks plus two days. Three-month maternity leave was introduced in 1945 and was gradually expanded to an 18-month general parental leave at 90 percent pay in 1991.

From 1974 the government paid 90 percent of salary for unlimited sick leave. Many observers claim that Swedish workers abuse this policy, taking more sick leave than any others in the world, an average of 26 days per year

---

[31]The biggest current complaint with the Swedish health system is long waiting lists for certain kinds of elective surgery, up to two years for eye cataracts and hip replacements ("A Survey of the Swedish Economy," p. 15).

TABLE 8–2   **Public Sector in Various Countries, 1988***

Country	Spending	Transfers	Taxes	Employment
Sweden	59.9	31.6	55.3	31.8
Denmark	59.8	31.4	52.1	29.8
Norway	55.1	30.4	47.6	25.8
France	50.0	28.3	44.1	22.9
Italy	49.6	29.1	37.0	29.1
Germany	45.2	23.5	37.2	15.5
Canada	43.7	22.7	34.7	20.3
Finland	38.9	15.7	37.9	20.6
United Kingdom	38.4	17.4	37.0	20.7
United States	34.0	14.1	28.9	15.1
Japan	31.8	17.3	31.5	8.3

From *OECD Economic Surveys: Sweden 1990/1991* (Paris: Organization for Economic Cooperation and Development, 1990), pp. 61, 63.

Note: Public sector spending, transfers, and taxes are in percents of GDP, and employment is percent of labor force in public sector. Divergences between this table and Table 1–2 reflect that this table includes all levels of government, not just the national level.

in 1988 up from 18 in 1983.[32] As of 1990 about one-fourth of Swedish workers were absent per day, 10 percent due to illness and 15 percent because of watching children, vacation, or one of the 101 reasons for which workers can be on leave.[33]

These programs cost a lot of money. Sweden has the highest percentage of GDP devoted to government spending, including transfer payments, of any market economy, even though it has been declining from a peak of 67 percent in 1982. Table 8–2 shows public sector spending, transfer payments, taxes as percents of GDP, and public sector employment as a percent of total employment for several economies in 1988.

Not all of the rising trend of transfers was paid for by increased taxes; some was financed by cutbacks in other areas of government spending, notably infrastructure investment. The latter peaked in the late 1960s and has declined by about 20 percent since to about 3 percent of GDP whereas transfers nearly quadrupled during the same period.[34] This led to an actual deterioration of Swedish infrastructure, but the Moderate-led government increased infrastructure investment substantially.

Besides the association between generous sick leave and worker absenteeism, another labor supply issue is the effect of high tax rates, especially

[32]"A Survey of the Swedish Economy," pp. 15–16. Sick leave was cut back in 1992. Employers are now responsible for paying for the first 14 days, the percentage of pay covered has been reduced, and individuals must now make a contribution to the health insurance fund.

[33]"A Survey of the Swedish Economy," p. 15.

[34]Villy Bergstrom, "Aspects of the 'Swedish Model' and Its Breakdown," (Stockholm: Trade Union Institute for Economic Research, 1992), p. 14.

high marginal income tax rates. Prior to 1991 the top rate was 75 percent, which became effective in the 40,000 to 50,000 U.S. dollars per year range, depending on exchange rates.[35] For that level of income the tax rate exceeded that of any other market economy. High tax rates may have reduced labor supply by prime age men and women 6 percent to 10 percent relative to what would be the case with U.S. tax and spending levels.[36]

Such a supply-side effect raises the Laffer Curve issue of tax revenues and tax rates, and Sweden may have had marginal tax rates sufficiently high so that a cut would actually increase revenues.[37] Such high tax rates have triggered considerable tax avoidance and use of the underground economy, with the scale of such activities possibly exceeding 25 percent of official GDP.[38]

The Social Democratic government initiated a tax restructuring in 1991 that reduced the top marginal income tax rate to 50 percent and shifted to greater reliance on the value-added tax (VAT). The nonsocialist government made more adjustments, including reducing payroll charges and giving more control to local governments over finances. These changes, combined with cuts in sick leave and other transfer payments, were designed to increase the supply of labor and to reduce the structural budget deficit. But the latter goal was frustrated by the recession, which caused a shortfall in revenues and a surge of payments for unemployment compensation, leading to a deficit greater than 10 percent of GDP. The fiscal problems of the Swedish government have been aggravated by Swedish banks boycotting government bonds due to the high deficit, thus raising the cost of government borrowing.

Although the current trend in Sweden is to cut back on benefits and reduce the progressivity of the tax system, Sweden has a higher degree of both income and wealth equality than other market economies. Table 8–3 shows the shares of factor incomes and of disposable income (after taxes and transfers) going to the top and bottom quintiles of the population as well as the percentage of wealth held by the top 1 percent of the population for several countries.

The trend in income distribution in Sweden has been toward greater inequality since the early 1980s. The share of wealth held by the top 1 percent remained fairly constant from 1975 to 1987, although the composition of the top group shifted from rural landowners to wealthy urbanites.[39] But for 1978 to 1987 the Gini coefficient of wealth distribution went from 0.783 to 0.841 because many poorer households went into debt.

---

[35]*OECD Economic Surveys*, p. 64.

[36]Gary Burtless, ''Taxes, Transfers, and Swedish Labor Supply,'' in *The Swedish Economy*, p. 241.

[37]Charles E. Stuart, ''Swedish Tax Rates, Labor Supply, and Tax Revenues,'' *Journal of Political Economy* 89 (1981), pp. 1020–38.

[38]Edgar L. Feige, ''The Swedish Payments System and the Underground Economy,'' (Stockholm: Industrial Institute for Economic and Social Research, 1985).

[39]Ministry of Finance, *The 1990 Medium Term Survey*, p. 344. Despite this high degree of wealth equality, a small elite of very wealthy people remain who control the commanding heights of the economy, the Wallenberg family being the leading example.

TABLE 8–3   Income and Wealth Distributions

Country	Factor Income	Disposable Income	Wealth
Sweden	33.2/6.5	24.2/16.4	17
US	38.8/4.2	32.0/9.0	25
UK	36.3/4.0	30.6/12.4	32
Germany	44.7/2.3	36.2/13.1	28
Canada	36.0/5.4	31.4/10.8	19.6
Norway	34.9/4.4	27.2/14.7	
Israel	43.2/4.9	35.0/12.0	
France			19
Belgium			28
Denmark			28

Source: Income distribution figures are from *OECD Economic Surveys:* Sweden 1990/1991 (Paris: Organization for Economic Cooperation and Development, 1990), p. 74; the left figure represents the percent for the top quintile and the right the percent for the lowest quintile for each type of income. Wealth distribution figures are from Lars Bager-Sjögren and Anders Klevmarken, ''The Distribution of Wealth in Sweden: 1984–1986,'' Working Paper No. 91 (Stockholm: Trade Union Institute for Economic Research, 1991), p. 7, and are the percents of wealth owned by the wealthiest 1 percent of the populations.

Sweden and Europe: Can Growth Revive?

Macroeconomic Policy and Performance

It has long been asserted that Sweden's macroeconomic policy has been Keynesian, or even ''ultra-Keynesian.'' Although true to some extent, this categorization is overly simplistic. *Keynesianism* has often been identified with the use of fiscal policy to maintain full employment, especially the willingness to run discretionary budget deficits during recessions. This approach was not part of the policy of the Social Democrats during their long hegemony from 1932 to 1976, budget deficits only noticeably appearing during the 1976–1982 interregnum of nonsocialist rule, although they have been more common since. Strict fiscal policy, including regular surpluses, was long the norm. The goal was to have low interest rates without stimulating inflation.

Swedish policy was Keynesian in its emphasis on maintaining full employment at all times. During the 1930s a public works program supported this goal. But the corporatist wage bargaining system that kept inflationary pressures down from the supply side and thus abetted the generally stimulative monetary policy has been central to Swedish policy. Although corporatism is not usually identified with Keynesianism, Keynes once made statements interpretable as supporting something like it,[40] and many self-identified post-Keynesians support it.[41]

---

[40]J.M. Keynes, *The End of Laissez-Faire* (London: Hogarth, 1927) pp. 41–42.

[41]Philip Arestis, ''Post-Keynesian Economic Policies: The Case of Sweden,'' *Journal of Economic Issues* 20 (1986), pp. 709–23.

But one innovative policy Sweden has long practiced virtually alone in the world is in the spirit of Keynes's view that socialization of investment is "the only means of securing an approximation to full employment."[42] This is an *investment fund* filled by tax-deductible profits contributed by corporations to the Central Bank. The government then releases these funds to the corporations during recessions. This policy works to smooth out investment behavior over time, thus smoothing out business cycles.

As a last resort the Swedish government has resorted to devaluing the krona to stimulate exports, at nearly a third of GDP the driving force of the Swedish economy. A successful devaluation occurred in the early 1930s when Sweden was one of the first countries to disconnect from the moribund gold standard. This devaluation, and the stimulus it gave to exports (especially to Hitler's rearming Germany), probably had more to do with Sweden's shallow depression and rapid recovery than any erstwhile Keynesian fiscal or monetary policy.

Unfortunately, the last resort tool increasingly became the first resort tool with governments devaluing the krona more frequently since the early 1970s. This reinforced the wage-price spiral and workers indulged in wage drift, figuring they could get away with it because the government would simply devalue. But the plunges into current account deficits became more sudden and disconcerting, resulting in disgust on the part of the leading Swedish corporations, which have increasingly turned to investing abroad rather than in Sweden.[43]

Expected membership in the EU led to pegging the krona to the German mark, which removed devaluation as a policy tool and completely altered the macroeconomic policy landscape. Most noticeable was the end of using low interest rates to stimulate investment as monetary policy became focused on defending the krona in the ERM. The most dramatic upshot of this came in September 1992 during the currency crisis that resulted in the United Kingdom and Italy dropping out of the ERM and devaluing their currencies. In order to defend the krona, the Swedish Central Bank temporarily raised overnight interbank interest rates *to 500 percent*!

Swedish macroeconomic performance since 1960 is presented in Figure 8–1. Averages of growth rates of GDP, unemployment rates, and inflation rates are shown for Sweden and for the European members of the Organization for Economic Cooperation and Development (OECD).

---

[42]J.M. Keynes, *The General Theory of Employment, Interest and Money* (London: Harcourt Brace, 1936), p. 378.

[43]In 1981 Swedish investment in the EU was about 4 billion kroner (plural of krona) and EU investment in Sweden was about 1 billion kroner. In 1989 the former was in excess of 30 billion kroner whereas the latter was about 2 billion kroner ("A Survey of the Swedish Economy," p. 21). This trend has led to an employment shift; in 1978 the 17 largest multinational corporations in Sweden had 266,000 employees in Sweden and 261,000 abroad whereas by 1988 they had only 213,000 employees in Sweden and up to 342,000 abroad (Ministry of Finance, *The 1990 Medium Term Survey,* p. 236).

FIGURE 8–1a   Swedish and European Macroeconomic Performance

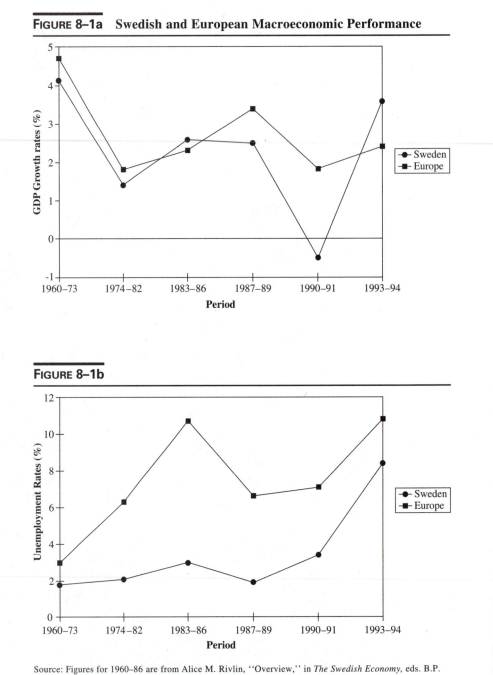

FIGURE 8–1b

Source: Figures for 1960–86 are from Alice M. Rivlin, ''Overview,'' in *The Swedish Economy,* eds. B.P. Bosworth and A.M. Rivlin (Washington: Brookings Institution, 1987), p. 4; for 1987–91 estimated from NIER, *The Swedish Economy: Autumn 1992* (Stockholm: National Institute for Economic Cooperation and Development, 1992), pp. 19, 138, 139; and for 1993–94 from *The Economist,* November 12, 1994, p. 122.

FIGURE 8–1c

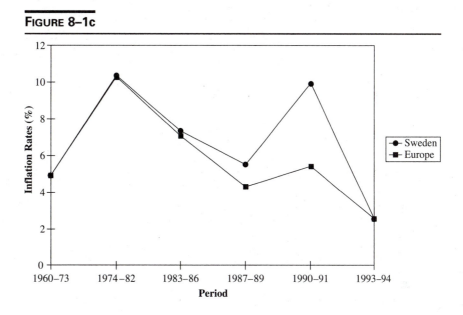

Keeping in mind that Sweden started out ahead of the rest of OECD Europe in per capita income in 1960 and that OECD Europe is Sweden's main trading partner, Figure 8–1 tells a simple story. From 1960 to the mid-1980s Sweden's GDP growth and inflation performances were generally in line with the rest of Europe's while it did substantially better in unemployment. Then Sweden's growth slowed while its inflation rate increased and its unemployment rate moved closer to Europe's while remaining lower. But deep in recession at the end of 1993, Sweden saw its near 9 percent unemployment rate almost converging on the European average, although Sweden has since moved out of recession before the rest of Europe with an inflation rate again at the European average.

Sweden and the European Union

During the summer of 1991 Sweden applied to join the EU, was accepted, voted to join in a referendum in November 1994 by 52 percent to 48 percent, and entered on January 1, 1995, along with Austria and Finland, all officially neutral states.[44] This move on Sweden's part is momentous and probably the death knell of the Swedish model in its pure form. Although like Denmark it may be able to retain a more generous welfare system than other EU members,

---

[44]Previously Ireland was the only neutral state in the EU, all the other members also belonging to NATO. However with the end of the Cold War and the dissolution of the Warsaw Pact, neutrality is not what it used to be.

its macroeconomic policies are already tied to those of Germany and the EU and will certainly become more so if the promise of the Maastricht Treaty to replace national currencies with a common currency (ecu) is fully implemented. Its longstanding low unemployment rate policy has probably permanently ended with the convergence of its unemployment rate on European averages.

The driving force behind the decision to enter the EU was the clear reality that the Swedish economy is becoming increasingly integrated with that of Europe anyway. The surge of investment by Swedish corporations in the EU, noted above, is the clearest sign of this inevitability.[45] This trend was further stimulated by Swedish corporations' frustration with rapidly rising Swedish wage rates. The growth of the Swedish economy from the late 19th century has been driven by its technologically progressive export industries. Joining Europe so that these industries do not totally flee seems to be an important motive. Furthermore, increased competitive pressures should aid Swedish consumers by lowering price-cost margins and should improve overall Swedish growth and efficiency by encouraging large-scale, high-technology exporters, exactly those firms whose investments abroad have been a source of concern.

Within Sweden the opposition to joining the EU resembled that in other countries such as France, a curious alliance of the Right and the Left. On the Right were protected industries that feared competition, notably farmers who have been heavily subsidized ever since the Agrarian (now Center) Party cut a deal with the Social Democrats in 1933. On the Left were the environmentalists of the Green Party[46] and those in the Party of the Left (formerly Communist) and the left wing of the Social Democrats who opposed ending the full employment policy and feared further inroads into the welfare system, especially women.

That fears about the welfare system are not groundless is seen by events in the former East Germany since unification with West Germany. As discussed in the next chapter, West Germany's social policies are much less favorable to women than were those in East Germany or than those currently in Sweden. Unification meant cutting welfare programs in eastern Germany, and women have borne the brunt of rising unemployment there. If Germany will set EU social policies, Swedish women may face further cutbacks, although the Swedish economy is more competitive than that of eastern Germany and should not experience the crash in employment that it has. Also,

---

[45]Several of Sweden's major corporations have merged outright with foreign firms, notably its largest, Asea, with Switzerland's Brown Boveri and its fourth largest, Saab-Scania, with the United States' General Motors, a major presence in the EU. Volvo attempted a merger with France's Renault that did not transpire.

[46]The Center Party also has taken strong proenvironmentalist positions. Sweden has had a very strong environmental policy since the 1970s, generally stricter than in the EU. An example is a stricter standard for automobile emissions. But, Sweden has a *looser* policy in hunting regulations—the EU forbids bear hunting whereas Sweden allows it.

Sweden will retain more autonomy than has no-longer independent eastern Germany.

On the positive side is the hope that joining the EU will enhance efficiency and competitiveness sufficiently so that Sweden will be able to afford at least a reasonable facsimile of its former programs. That it might be able to do so is indicated by Denmark's performance. Although in the EU for some time, Denmark still has social welfare programs nearly as generous as Sweden's. What it has not been able to maintain has been full employment, and given Sweden's weakened centralized wage bargaining system it seems unlikely that Sweden will be able to return to full employment either, although the government has actually expanded the active labor market policies. As in most of the rest of the market capitalist world, competitive wages are likely to be maintained at least partly by the threat of unemployment. That Sweden's voters are torn is shown in that in September 1994 they voted for the Social Democrats who will protect social programs and shortly thereafter for the EU referendum, which threatens those programs.

Is the Swedish Model Dead?

In a much-cited paper,[47] Erik Lundberg presents eight reasons for an alleged fall of the Swedish model. One is the collapse of support for the Social Democrats after 1976.[48] But even the Social Democrats agree on the need for "stiff medicine" because of massive budget deficits, and they supported entry into the EU, despite internal splits on the issue.

Second is the expansion of the concept of full employment that occurred in the late 1960s. This ideal led to reckless macroeconomic and wage-setting policies that ultimately undermined the goal of full employment. Support for this goal has declined more recently, however.

Third is stagnation of the growth rate, which exacerbates all conflicts. Lundberg cites the debate over nuclear power and the alleged laziness of the younger generation as troubling trends. The future of these trends is uncertain.

Fourth is excessive wage solidarism combined with overly high tax rates that reduced work incentives and distorted investment into dying industries in the late 1970s. Increasing wage and tax rates have been a declining phenomenon since the early 1980s.

Fifth is the breakdown of the EFO model of wage setting, largely due to the increased public sector employment, with the resulting explosion of wages beyond productivity increases and the concomitant loss of international competitiveness. This trend may have been reversed.

---

[47]Erik Lundberg, ''The Rise and Fall of the Swedish Model,'' *Journal of Economic Literature* 23 (1985) pp. 1–36.

[48]It is difficult for outsiders to understand the pervasiveness of the SAP as a social institution in Sweden. Its intimate links with the LO have involved it in owning and directly operating cooperatives and many other institutions throughout Sweden.

Box 8–2

The Swedish Energy-Environment Trade-off

A growth conundrum for Sweden involves policies towards energy and the environment. Sweden's policies make it difficult to increase electricity output, resulting in rising electricity prices that have further fueled the exodus of Swedish firms. Some of Sweden's important exporters, such as the pulp and paper industry, are very energy-intensive. Sweden faces a serious energy-environment trade-off.

After the 1973 oil price shock the Social Democratic government accelerated an ongoing push to rely on nuclear power to reduce oil imports. Sweden was a world leader in civilian nuclear technology.* Today it leads in megawatt hours per person of electricity produced by nuclear power and is third behind France and Belgium in the percentage of its electricity provided by nuclear power at just under half.

In 1976, the Center Party defeated the Social Democrats on an anti–nuclear power platform. A referendum on the issue in 1979, the year of the Three Mile Island nuclear accident in the United States, decided not to build any new reactors beyond the existing 12 and to shut them all by 2010. Recent governments have promised to close two by 1996.

Since then Swedish governments, also for environmental reasons, have ruled out building more hydroelectric plants on remaining undammed rivers, the major nonnuclear source of electricity, and unilaterally adopted the goal of not increasing carbon dioxide emissions above 1988 levels. That goal rules out using coal, oil, or natural gas to replace nuclear power. Prospects for such alternatives as solar, wind, or geothermal energy are not good.

Thus, if two nuclear power plants shut down by 1996 and the other restrictions on energy sources remain, the price of electricity may nearly triple from its 1985 level by 1997.† Uncertainty over energy costs has already led one producer (Granges, a metals group) to build a smelter in Iceland rather than in Sweden. The Swedes face a difficult dilemma.

*Prior to 1969, Swedish nuclear development was oriented towards a potential bomb.
†*OECD Economic Surveys: Sweden 1990/1991* (Paris: Organization for Economic Cooperation and Development, 1990), p. 53.

Sixth is misguided policies from 1975–1978 to prop up dying industries with various subsidies. This factor seems to have largely disappeared since then.

Seventh is the increased use of inflationary stabilization policies. This, too, has significantly changed, although large budget deficits have yet to be eliminated.

Eighth is the loss of policy autonomy due to the increasing internationalization of the economy. Joining the EU is the final guarantee of this process.

A ninth reason for the alleged fall of the Swedish model, not in Lundberg, is that although Sweden continues to have a high rate of R&D spending, its spending has remained concentrated in industries tied to Sweden's old natural resource base.[49] Sweden is failing to develop the newer microelectronics industries that are the wave of the future. This failure may be tied to a deeper loss of entrepreneurship resulting from the conformist and cocoonlike welfare state, and resurrecting entrepreneurship may be the ultimate key to reviving Swedish growth in the long run.

Lundberg argues that the model has not really fallen but merely experienced a "break in the trend," and that Sweden will continue to maintain its commitment to full employment and a generous social welfare policy. Now the former commitment appears to have been abandoned, despite the government's expansion of active labor market policies, and the latter is under challenge although still continuing.

Thus the Swedish model is not dead, but it has suffered serious body blows since Lundberg wrote and is struggling desperately to remain alive. If one compares the Swedish model to a ship, it is being buffeted by powerful outside forces and its "ballast has shifted." It remains to be seen whether the recent and current course adjustments will be sufficient to keep it afloat, or whether it will sink "peacefully beneath the waters" as did the mighty Vasaship of yore.[50]

Summary and Conclusions

Sweden has been one of the most successful economies in the world and probably the clearest example of a redistributionist social market economy. It combines a rigorous respect for free markets in output and private ownership of the means of production with the most active intervention in labor markets of any government in the world for the purposes of retraining, informing, and relocating laid-off workers to new jobs. It has practiced a corporatist centralized wage bargaining system since 1938 between the main labor federation (LO) and the main employer federation (SAF). The LO has pursued a solidaristic wage policy, partly with the goal of restructuring the economy. Centralized wage bargains were set based on productivity improvements in the export sector, which has been the economy's growth engine. Income redistribution programs have been more extensive than those in any other market economy. Sweden has had generous sick and parental leave policies, a system often described as providing cradle to grave security.

---

[49]See Charles Edquist and Bengt-Åke Lundvall, "Comparing the Danish and Swedish Systems of Innovation," in *National Innovation Systems: a Comparative Study,* ed. R.R. Nelson. New York: Columbia University Press, 1993.

[50]The Vasaship was discovered largely intact in Stockholm harbor in 1961 and was later raised at great risk to life and limb. It currently occupies a museum on the harbor entirely devoted to it.

These policies have generated great successes over time. From 1870, when industrialization took off, to 1950, Sweden had the highest economic growth rate in the world, putting it into the top three in the world in real per capita income. At the same time it has had greater income and wealth equality than any market capitalist economy, probably coming closer to eliminating poverty than any other society. Until 1992 it maintained low unemployment rates that never exceeded 4 percent while maintaining inflation rates comparable to the rest of Europe. It may have achieved the highest quality of life for women of any nation. At the base of these achievements has been a small group of technically and managerially innovative corporations that have maintained a strong competitive edge in a number of industries.

But the Swedish model has experienced increasing difficulties in recent decades and is now undergoing a process of change and adjustment. High tax rates and generous sick leaves adversely affected labor supply, especially among a less hard-working younger generation. Rising public sector employment broke down the centralized wage bargains with the spread of wage drift. Accelerating wage increases caused accelerating inflation and led to current account deficits and currency devaluations. Because of these problems and rising electricity costs, leading Swedish corporations have increasingly shifted their capital investment outside of Sweden to the rest of the EU. The Swedish economy fell into recession in 1992–93 with unemployment rates unseen since the 1930s.

Recent government policies have included tax cuts, reductions in sick leave benefits and other social welfare policies, and a strictly anti-inflationary macroeconomic policy. The Swedish krona has been pegged to the German mark in the ERM as Sweden joined the European Union.

These policy changes alter the purist version of the Swedish model as it previously existed, moving it more in the direction of other European economies. Certain distinctive characteristics such as the full-employment policy may be permanently lost as Sweden integrates into the EU. Nevertheless, if the current reforms can restore the competitive thrust of the Swedish economy, there is reason to believe that a modified version of its system, one that still includes much income redistribution, an active labor retraining and adjustment policy, and better treatment of women than in most countries, will survive.

Questions for Discussion

1. What are the different types of corporatism and what are the advantages and disadvantages of each? What are the sources of wage drift and how has it affected Sweden's future prospects as a corporatist economy?

2. What are the relationships between the EFO model, the Rehn-Meidner Plan, and wage solidarism? How do they reinforce or undermine each other and what are their economic impacts over time?

3. Many observers argue that Swedish taxes are too high. Evaluate this argument.

4. Is the equity-efficiency trade-off relevant for Sweden?

5. It has been argued that Swedish macroeconomic policy is ultra-Keynesian. Evaluate this argument.

6. What are the implications of Sweden's having joined the European Union for the future of the Swedish model?

7. Evaluate the applicability of the various parts of the Swedish model to various other economies in the world, such as those in Eastern and Western Europe, Japan, and the United States.

Suggested Further Readings

Bosworth, Barry P., and Alice M. Rivlin, eds. *The Swedish Economy.* Washington: Brookings Institution, 1987.

Childs, Marquis. *Sweden: The Middle Way,* 3rd edition. New Haven: Yale University Press, 1947.

Delsen, Lei, and Tom van Veen, ''The Swedish Model: Relevant for Other European Countries?'' In *Comparative Economic Systems: Models and Cases,* 7th ed., ed. Morris Bornstein. Burr Ridge: Irwin, 1994, pp. 137–59.

''A Survey of the Swedish Economy.'' *The Economist* (March 3, 1990).

Freeman, Richard B. ''The Large Welfare State as a System.'' *American Economic Review* 85 (1995), pp. 16–21.

Heclo, Hugh and Henrik Madsen. *Policy and Politics in Sweden: Principled Pragmatism.* Philadelphia: Temple University Press, 1987.

Koblik, Steven, ed. *Sweden's Development from Poverty to Affluence: 1750–1970.* Minneapolis: University of Minnesota Press, 1975.

Lindbeck, Assar, Per Molander, Torsten Peorsson, Oltef Petersson, Angmar Sandmo, Birgitta Swedenborg, Niels Thygesen. *Turning Sweden Around.* Cambridge: MIT Press, 1994.

Lundberg, Erik. ''The Rise and Fall of the Swedish Economic Model.'' *Journal of Economic Literature* 23 (1985) pp. 1–36.

Maccoby, Michael, ed. *Sweden at the Edge: Lessons for American and Swedish Managers.* Philadelphia: University of Pennsylvania Press, 1991.

Pekkarinen, Jukka, Matti Pohjola, and Bob Rowthorn, eds. *Social Corporatism: A Superior Economic System?* Oxford: Clarendon Press, 1992.

Pryor, Frederic L. ''Corporatism as an Economic System: A Review Essay.'' *Journal of Comparative Economics* 12 (1988), pp. 317–44.

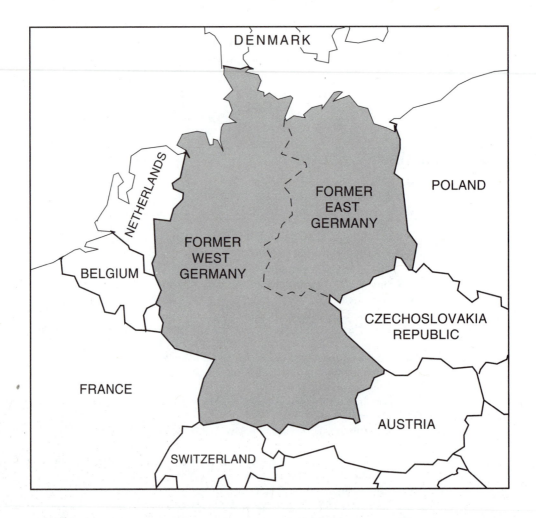

THE UNIFICATION OF GERMANY AND THE UNIFICATION OF EUROPE

The particularism of the stocks, dynasties, and cities, the dualisms of west and east, of Protestants and Catholics, of Lutherans and Reformed, of Prussia and Austria, of imperial patriotism and colonial expansion eastward, of mysticism and scholasticism, of rationalism and faith, of nobility and bourgeoisie, of civilian and military, of bureaucracy and public opinion, of capitalism and labor—all these tensions in German history needed to be resolved. The attempt would be made at first in a provisional way by claim to supremacy put forward as a missionary concept; only after such an effort failed would compromise be tried.

—Veit Valentin, *The German People: Their History and Civilization from the Holy Roman Empire to the Third Reich* (New York, Alfred A. Knopf)

Introduction

The problem of Germany is the problem of Europe: Can unity be created from diversity while respecting diversity? For over a thousand years the much-divided Germans have struggled to create unity, but each time they succeeded they overreached themselves by attempting to absorb their neighbors in a universal empire. The same question haunts Europe: Does the unification of West and East Germany mean that there will be "a European Germany or a German Europe"?

An economic manifestation of this problem is the weakening of the European exchange rate mechanism (ERM),[1] due to high German interest rates

---

[1]Currencies in the ERM stay within a band with respect to each other in value. In September 1992 the United Kingdom and Italy dropped out after experiencing speculative attacks, and the Spanish peseta was devalued while remaining within the system. In August 1993 the band was widened from 2½ percent to 15 percent after speculative attacks against the French franc and the Danish krone. The ERM is the centerpiece of the European monetary system (EMS), which members agreed at Maastricht in 1991 would be a halfway house to a single currency, the European currency unit (ecu).

brought on by high budget deficits arising from the costs of German unification. Despite lowering rates, the German central bankers refuse to bend their monetary policy for European unity and forced devaluations of other currencies in the ERM. The unification of Germany makes it harder to unify Europe and makes it more likely that a unified Europe will be a German Europe rather than a European Germany.

German GDP is the world's fourth largest and one of the highest per capita. Drawing on a highly educated and hardworking population, Germany industrialized rapidly in the late 19th century after its unification in 1871 by the Iron Chancellor, Otto von Bismarck. This fed ambitions underlying Germany's aggressive role in World Wars I and II.

Germany's overwhelming defeat in World War II brought a collapse of its economy and division into the Federal Republic of Germany (FRG) in the West, which adopted a market capitalist economic system, and the German Democratic Republic (GDR) in the East, which adopted a command socialist economic system.[2] These two competed vigorously in the Cold War, both growing more rapidly than most economies of their respective systems. But the FRG's growth outstripped the GDR's. After freeing prices and introducing a new currency in 1948, FRG economic performance was labeled the *economic miracle* (*Wirtschaftswunder*). In 1990 the GDR ceased to exist and joined the FRG as a broken-up set of Länder (provinces).

Today Germany has the archetypal *social market economy,* a term invented in postwar West Germany. It respects private property and market forces, eschewing central planning.[3] But it has an extensive social safety net and income redistribution system. In the 1880s, Bismarck established the world's first government-run health insurance, social security, and workmen's compensation systems.[4]

Comparing the German economy to Sweden's, also a social market economy as described in the previous chapter, Germany's social welfare system is not as extensive, nor are its taxes as high or as progressive. Germany does not use active labor policies, but its apprenticeship system produces a highly skilled blue-collar labor force.[5] It does not have corporatist centralized wage bargaining, but it has *co-determination* (*Mitbestimmung*) in which works

---

[2]There was more division because former German territories in the East were annexed by the USSR and Poland. The FRG only gave up its demand for those territories in 1990 under pressure from the international community to gain acceptance of its unification with the GDR.

[3]Between 1967 and 1972 a half-hearted effort at ''Concerted Action'' occurred—major economic actors discussed trends and policies in an imitation of French concertation with hints of Swedish corporatist bargaining.

[4]The main supporter of such legislation at the time, the German Social Democratic Party, was outlawed. Bismarck co-opted its policies while suppressing it.

[5]In contrast to Sweden's, Germany's apprenticeship system reduces labor mobility by its specialized training. It directly descends from the medieval guild system with its masters, journeymen, and apprentices.

councils advise management and labor leaders sit on supervisory boards of corporations, bringing about considerable labor-management cooperation.

Compared to most countries, including Japan, Germany has a strong banking sector that dominates the economy and owns large portions of stock in major corporations. During the late 19th century the banks encouraged protectionism and cartelization of industry, which lasted until the end of World War II. This bank domination has persisted in the postwar decartelized free trade economy.

Furthermore, the central bank (Bundesbank) is, along with Switzerland's, the most independent from political influence in the world. It executes a rigorous monetarist policy, which gives Germany consistently low inflation.[6] The Germans are suspicious of giving up their strong deutsche mark and sound money policies for a probably weaker ecu and looser "Eurofed,"[7] and thus they have cracked the ERM with their strict policies.

Despite its successes, Germany recently dragged the EU into a serious recession from which both are now emerging. But two other elements with long-term implications lead observers to discuss Germany's "fading miracle."

One is a long-term slowdown of growth greater than the general global slowdown that has occurred. This slowdown has been accompanied by a long-term increase in unemployment and outbreaks of neo-Nazi skinhead violence directed at foreigners. German growth has long been led by exports of technologically advanced engineering products, with Germany at times being the world's top exporter. But now Germany faces increasingly stiff competition, especially from Asian producers, and many wonder if it is losing its edge.

The other problem is that unification with the former GDR is costlier and more difficult than anyone predicted. FRG Chancellor Helmut Kohl had forecast that the outcome would resemble the Wirtschaftswunder in West Germany after 1948. But the 1990 East German economy was further from market capitalism than the 1948 West German one; there was private ownership of the means of production in the 1948 West but there was not in the 1990 East. Also the productivity, quality, and environmental differences between the economies were much greater than had been thought.

Combined with the collapse of the entire European socialist bloc and the sharp contraction of markets for East German goods in the former Council on Mutual Economic Assistance (CMEA)[8] countries was a massive collapse of output in eastern Germany. This led to greater expenditures on unemployment

---

[6]This policy reflects memories of the 1923 German hyperinflation, which undermined the interwar Weimar Rupublic and paved the way for Hitler. Anti-inflationary policy was aided until recently by modest union wage demands.

[7]The European Monetary Institute formally opened in 1994. It provides the institutional nucleus for a future EU central bank.

[8]The CMEA, or COMECON, was the trade organization of the part of the socialist bloc dominated by the former Soviet Union.

compensation and privatization efforts by the FRG government than expected. The resulting budget deficits[9] led the Bundesbank to raise interest rates, bringing about the general European recession and the ERM-cracking currency crises.

The process of privatizing and integrating the former GDR economy has gone far and as of 1994 output was increasing again. But deep differences remain between East and West with rising resentments between *Ossis* (East Germans) and *Wessis* (West Germans), the former complaining of domination by the latter and the latter complaining of excessive expenses to support the allegedly lazy former. Eastern unhappiness is symbolized by the reappearance in the Reichstag (parliament) in 1994 of the former Communists, now the Party of Democratic Socialism.

Historical Background of the German Economy

The Origins of the "German Problem"

The Romans called them *Germani,* although their own identity then was tribal, and there were many tribes.[10] Blocking European unity in 9 A.D. by defeating an invading Roman army, they would conquer that empire four centuries later.

In 800 the Frankish leader Charlemagne attempted to create a universal unified European state, the Holy Roman Empire.[11] For the next thousand years, there would be a Holy Roman Emperor, a German pretending to rule a universal Christian state in Europe.

Here was the "German Problem" for Europe. There really was no Germany—it consisted of tribal entities with ill-defined borders. Germany sought to rule Europe,[12] but its own power was in the hands of local dukes, archbishops, princes, and the like. Only with the 1871 Bismarckian unification would there be a Deutsches Reich (German Kingdom).[13]

Because of being a trade route in Central Europe and a center of innovations symbolized by Gutenberg's invention of the printing press, the German economy experienced substantial growth in the 1400s and 1500s. But it was shattered by a disaster, the Thirty Years War (1618–1648), the ultimate

---

[9]Chancellor Kohl had promised there would be no tax increases.

[10]The most prominent core German tribes were the Saxons, Bavarians, Franks, Allemani (later called Swabians), Thuringians, and Frisians. Several of these provided the names for modern German Länder (Saxony, Bavaria, Thuringia).

[11]In the 1700s Voltaire quipped that it was neither holy, Roman, nor an empire.

[12]This effort involved a conquest movement eastward into Slavic lands, creating Austria and later Prussia, whose militaristic and authoritarian *Junker* aristocracy brutally enserfed the Slavic peasants and would later unify Germany.

[13]Modern Germany is an artificial creation out of still-disparate tribes. There are substantial differences between the German spoken in different regions, and the northern Germans from Hamburg are more physically similar to the southeastern English than to Latinized southern or Slavicized eastern Germans.

European showdown between Protestantism and Catholicism. It left Germany divided religiously, a third of its population killed, and its economy ruined.

The Rise and Fall of Imperial Germany

In 1871 Prussia's Chancellor Bismarck overcame tribal separatism to unify Germany[14] by getting the tribes to join in the successful Franco-Prussian War. Prussia led the unified German Empire partly because it had experienced the most economic growth, including nascent industrialization.

The German economy expanded and industrialized rapidly after 1871. Between then and 1913, just before World War I, exports more than quadrupled and steel production surged past Great Britain's, leading to intense commercial competition with Britain that drove their diplomatic and military rivalry. The British overcame their ancient antipathy towards the French to ally against Germany. Their victory over Germany in World War I led to the replacement of the empire with a republic.

A feature of German growth was its lead in general science and technology prior to industrialization.[15] One area with early economic payoff was the chemical industry, which Germany led after organic chemistry studies of scientifically applying fertilizer in the 1840s. In the 1880s, Otto Benz invented the first true automobile and founded Daimler-Benz, producer of high-quality Mercedes-Benz cars. High-technology export goods remain a key feature of German economic success. This feature is reinforced by the fact that more German managers possess engineering backgrounds than do managers in other countries.

The Weimar Republic and the Nazi Command Capitalist Economy

In November 1918, the Social Democrats took control of the government and established the Weimar Republic. Signing the surrender and the 1919 Versailles Treaty, which took territory from Germany and imposed massive reparations payments, alienated nationalists. They would eventually follow

---

[14]Of the states joining the German Empire, the most reluctant was the Kingdom of Bavaria in southeastern Germany, which harbored serious separatist movements well into the 20th century. It was one of the larger old German states and resented Prussian domination partly for religious reasons as a Catholic state, northeastern Prussia being Protestant. The Bavarians have their own political party, the Christian Social Union, which allies with the Christian Democrats but is more conservative.

The unification did not solve the German Problem because there were many ethnic Germans outside the empire in Switzerland, Austria, and elsewhere, and many non-Germans, especially Poles, within it. These issues stimulated the expansionism of Germany in the two world wars.

[15]Germany lost its scientific leadership to the United States in the 1930s when Hitler's persecution of Jews and other groups caused a migration of top scientists to the United States. The most famous was Albert Einstein, who convinced President Roosevelt in 1938 to authorize the Manhattan Project that built the atomic bomb. Many of the Manhattan Project's participants were also refugees from Germany.

Box 9-1

The German Hyperinflation

Hyperinflation is shown in the following table, which shows the exchange rate of the mark to the U.S. dollar from 1914 until November 1923. Although the economy stabilized after this until the Great Depression struck in 1929, the hyperinflation deeply discredited the Weimar Republic. Many people saw their life savings wiped out in a very short space of time and became open to the idea of searching for a scapegoat. At the end of the hyperinflation, people had to take wheelbarrows full of money just to do their grocery shopping.

Marks per U.S. Dollar, 1914, 1919–1923

Dates	Value
July 1914	4.2
July 1919	14.0
July 1921	76.7
July 1922	493.2
January 1923	17,972.0
July 1923	353,412.0
August 1923	4,620,455.0
September 1923	98,860,000.0
October 1923	25,260,208,000.0
November 15 1923	4,200,000,000,000.0

Note: The figures are monthly averages.
Source: From Gustav Stolper, Karl Häuser, and Knut Borchardt, *The German Economy: 1870 to the Present* (New York: Harcourt, Brace & World, 1967), p. 83.

---

the National Socialist (Nazi) leader, Adolf Hitler, who argued that these acts resulted from an "international Jewish conspiracy."

Besides reducing military spending, removing agricultural tariffs, and introducing Workers' Councils to advise managements in the workplace,[16] the economic policies of the Social Democrats differed little from prewar ones. Its policy making was overwhelmed by the reparations payments announced in 1921. Payment difficulties stimulated hyperinflation, which accelerated until a new currency and reform program were implemented in November 1923, relying upon U.S. loans.

The Great Depression hit Germany harder than any country. At its pit in 1932 the Nazis became the largest party in the Reichstag. In January 1933

---

[16]These councils presaged the modern co-determination system, but they were largely ineffectual.

Hitler was appointed Chancellor. He soon outlawed all other parties, seized absolute power as Fuhrer, and declared the Third Reich. In 1939 his invasion of Poland began World War II in Europe. Hitler oversaw the Holocaust, in which six million Jews and millions of other people were killed. In 1945, faced with German defeat, Hitler committed suicide.

Hitler imposed a command capitalist economic system that achieved economic growth until it was distorted by war.[17] For Hitler, economic ideology and practice were subordinated to his anti-Semitic and militaristic nationalist politics. In the early 1920s the National Socialist German Workers' Party (the Nazi Party's full name) had an anticapitalist bias, opposing interest and land rent and calling for nationalizing many businesses. But Hitler was anti-Communist and appealed to small and big business for support.[18] In 1929 the official party line supported a "corporate state." In practice Hitler did not nationalize industries and purged the socialist wing of the Nazi Party shortly after his seizure of power.

The focus of Hitler's economic program was to build up the military as rapidly as possible and as independently from other nations as possible. He imposed price controls and compulsory cartelization and outlawed independent labor unions. The government controlled foreign trade and foreign exchange transactions, made bilateral deals with countries southeast of Germany, and emphasized self-sufficiency. Economic sectors were organized in "chambers" that followed government orders. Early in Hitler's rule, he emphasized infrastructure investment, such as constructing highways (autobahns).

Prior to the war Hitler's economic policies were quite successful. Germany came out of the Depression rapidly—its GDP doubled between 1932 and 1938, and the unemployment rate fell from 29.9 in 1932 to 0.5 in 1939 when the war began. But the economy had already hit bottom and begun to grow in 1932 prior to Hitler's ascension to power.

A Tale of Two Postwar German Economies

The West German Wirtschafstwunder and Its Fading

The Partition and the Miracle.   Germany surrendered on May 9, 1945, and was partitioned into six zones. Two were annexed respectively by Poland and the Soviet Union and experienced massive out-migrations to western parts of Germany. What is today Germany was split into four zones of occupation by France near its border in the southwest, by the United Kingdom in the north, by the United States in the south, and by the USSR in the east. Berlin was a

---

[17]Although Germany had a 0.5 percent unemployment rate in 1939, between then and 1944 armaments production nearly quadrupled. Slave labor from conquered territories was used.

[18]Hitler's compulsory cartelization policy weakened small businesses. Most big businesses initially supported Hitler unenthusiastically. But, it was a widespread postwar consensus that Hitler was put in power by the big cartels, some of which were then broken up.

special area, which was also subdivided into four zones of occupation. In 1947 the U.S. and U.K. zones were united in ''Bizonia,'' to the initial opposition of the French and Soviets. The deepening Cold War and Marshall Plan aid led the French to let their zone join in the newly declared Federal Republic of Germany (FRG) in 1949, and the Soviet zone became the newly declared German Democratic Republic (GDR) that same year.

The German economy of 1946 had experienced a massive collapse. Compared to 1939 national income was less than half, industrial production less than a quarter, rail freight a third, and food consumption barely above half.[19] This was a horrible situation, but one that offered the possibility of future rapid growth through rebound. But how to achieve rebound? At first there was no interest in achieving it in the Soviet zone, but there was in the American and British zones from 1947.

The capital stock of West Germany was actually higher in 1946 by 16 percent than it was in 1938 and only limited reductions had occurred in the labor force.[20] But, there were three problems: First, destruction of transportation and communications infrastructure created production bottlenecks. Second, huge portions of capital stock had been diverted to military production, which had ceased. Third, economic paralysis resulted from fixed prices, rationing, and monetary overhang[21] left over from Hitler's economic system. The first problem was readily remedied by 1947 through sectorally concentrated capital investment.

In January 1948 Ludwig Erhard became Administrative Director of the Bizonal Economic Administration and sought to resolve the other two problems. He was associated with economists based at Freiburg University known as *Ordo-liberals*. They strongly supported free markets and private property. But they also wanted a state strong enough to break up cartels, which they blamed for the Nazi episode.[22] They also supported government provision of a social safety net, hence the ''social market economy.''

Erhard's first move came in March 1948 when he established a central bank. It was built up out of state banks created in the Länder by the Allies, and its governing board was dominated by the presidents of the Länder banks.[23] This governing board remains the basis of control of the Bundesbank and its policy-making independence.

---

[19]Gustav Stolper, Karl Häuser, and Knut Borchardt, *The German Economy: 1870 to the Present,* trans. T. Stolder (New York: Harcourt, Brace & World, 1967), p. 205.

[20]Holger C. Wolf, ''Postwar Germany in the European Context: Domestic and External Determinants of Growth,'' ED–93–11 (Stern Business School, New York University, 1993) pp. 3–4.

[21]*Monetary overhang* arises in a goods economy when there is much money in circulation but goods are in short supply and prices are fixed.

[22]Some firms were broken up, most prominently the chemical giant, I. G. Farben, which became Bayer, Hoechst, and BASF.

[23]An important characteristic of the FRG was already manifest, its high degree of decentralization with many social and economic policy-making powers in the hands of the Länder. In this way the FRG has achieved its own resolution of the long-running conflict between the tribes and national unity.

On June 20, 1948, without prior notice, a new currency, the deutsche mark, replaced the old Reichsmark at a 1-to-1 ratio for current wages and prices, but at a 1-to-10 ratio for all debts, thereby wiping out monetary overhang at one stroke. A few days later Erhard removed price and rationing controls on all but a few essential foods plus coal, steel, and electric power, while retaining foreign exchange controls that remained in place until 1958. The result was the immediate appearance of previously hoarded goods on shelves and an increase in industrial production of 50 percent in 1948 and of 25 percent in 1949.[24] This began the *Wirtschaftswunder,* the West German economic miracle. Its success made it the model for reform of the East German economy and it is the prime inspiration for all ''Big Bang'' (everything-all-at-once) reform programs throughout Eastern Europe.[25]

After some initial stumbles,[26] the Wirtschaftswunder continued strongly during the 1950s, led by a tripling of exports between 1950 and 1958 and a growth rate of industrial production between 1950 and 1955 greater than any nation in Europe. The FRG's acceptance into various international economic bodies, especially the European Coal and Steel Community, enhanced exports. Although West Germany received $4.5 billion worth of Marshall Plan aid, that figure was a lower percentage relative to the economy than in many other European recipient countries. Possibly the real significance for the FRG of the Marshall Plan was its support for establishing the trading system in Western Europe and for integrating the FRG into that system.

The Fading Miracle.   Because the Wirtschaftswunder was so dramatic, the slowdown of growth later also seemed dramatic. 1955 was the last year the FRG had a double-digit real growth rate (12 percent). It surged to 9 percent in 1960 after the final currency decontrols and hit 8.2 percent in 1969, but it has not come close to such rates since.[27] Annual rates of increase in productivity have steadily declined from a 5.1 percent average over 1951–64, to 4.4 percent over 1964–73, to 2.9 percent over 1973–79, to 1.5 percent over 1979–87.[28] Why has the miracle faded?

One school of thought says the slower growth rate was an unavoidable consequence of combining a generally declining world economic growth rate with the fact that the FRG had ''caught up.'' The latter part is supported by the very strength of the rebound effect in the late 1940s and early 1950s.

---

[24]Stolper, Häuser, and Borchard, *The German Economy,* p. 231.

[25]It played a role in finalizing the split between East and West Germany, formalized in 1949. The Soviets refused to allow such a blatantly market capitalist approach in the East.

[26]Despite current fond memories, the public initially was slow to accept that it was beneficial. Unemployment rates continued to rise through 1950. It was not until 1954 that more West Germans said they perceived an improvement rather than a worsening in living standards (Wolf, ''Postwar Germany in the European Context,'' p. 25).

[27]V.R. Berghahn, *Modern Germany: Society, Economics and Politics in the Twentieth Century* (Cambridge: Cambridge University Press, 1982), p. 262.

[28]W.R. Smyser, *The Economy of United Germany: Colossus at the Crossroads* (New York: St. Martin's Press, 1992), p. 28.

An alternative response is a German variant of *Eurosclerosis,* a theory popular with the Ordo-liberals. All of the EU has slowed down. Since the 1970s the EU has had persistently high unemployment rates compared with the United States and Japan. The Eurosclerosis view argues that this slowdown is due to restrictive labor market practices and other regulations inhibiting the market economy that have grown up over time.

In the FRG unemployment rates averaged 0.9 percent over 1960–64,[29] 1.2 percent over 1965–69, 1.3 percent over 1970–74, 4.4 percent over 1975–79, 7.0 percent over 1980–84, and 8.8 percent over 1985–89. After a brief decline in 1990 and 1991, they rose again as the FRG went into recession, aggravated by the double-digit unemployment rates in eastern Germany, but they are declining again gradually. Whether these high unemployment rates are due to excessively high wages, restrictive firing rules (as charged by the Eurosclerosis group), or the co-determination system, they aggravate the revival of neo-Nazi activities and skinhead attacks on foreigners.

Industrial Relations.   Germany has a unique system of labor-management relations that the Eurosclerosis group blames partly for the ''fading of the miracle.'' *Mitbestimmung,* or co-determination, comes in two parts. The first was introduced in 1952 and mandates the establishment of *works councils* in establishments with more than five employees. Elected by workers at a work site, councils are supposed to advise management on day-to-day operations. They do not set prices or output levels or negotiate wages. They deal with working hours, hiring and firing rules (the complaint of the Eurosclerosis group), and technical aspects of production.

The other aspect of co-determination is election of workers to company supervisory boards, made compulsory in 1976 for firms with more than 500 employees. German corporations have two levels of oversight bodies, the supervisory board being above and appointing the more frequently meeting board of directors or management board. The law mandates that shareholders[30] elect two-thirds of the members of the supervisory board while the remaining one-third is split between workers elected by their colleagues and union representatives. Workers themselves take the works councils more seriously than their representation on the supervisory boards.

Both of these systems were designed to bring about peace between labor and management, reducing output lost to strikes, and to moderate wage demands thus helping to reduce inflation. The former goal was largely met and losses due to strikes declined to about one-tenth of what they were in the interwar period,[31] a substantially lower figure than in most other European countries. But there has been a big increase in strikes since the FRG-GDR

---

[29]This lowest level of unemployment coincided with the cutoff of immigration from the GDR after the building of the Berlin Wall in 1961.

[30]The supervisory boards are stacked with bankers. In 1985 for the 24 largest German firms, the portion of shares held by all banks was 82.67 percent and the portion held by major banks was 45.44 percent (W. R. Smyser, *The Economy of United Germany,* p. 86).

[31]Berghahn, *Modern Germany* pp. 286–7.

unification. Although German labor costs are now the world's highest, inflation had remained low until unification and current account balances had remained in surplus until then as well.

Ordo-liberal critics of these arrangements argue that together they have interfered in the workings of the market. An effort at quasi-corporatist, quasi-indicative planning, "Concerted Action" by the government during the late 1960s and early 1970s symbolized this interference.

Labor unions left Concerted Action after becoming a minority on the supervisory boards, as determined in the 1976 law on co-determination, and they have become increasingly militant. Strike activity increased in 1978, and one strike was directed for the first time at preventing a new technology (in printing) from being adopted, a direct threat to the driving force of German economic growth. More aggressive labor has since pushed such ideas as shorter work weeks, now the shortest in the world. With unification all of these issues have become more intense and labor-management relations have dissolved into general hostility, despite the persistence of the institutions of co-determination.

The Social Safety Net.   Prior to unification social policies were less of an issue, although the share of GDP for social programs increased at about 10 percent per year during Social Democratic rule in the 1970s, a trend reversed after the party was removed from office in 1982. In the early postwar era the major effort was simply to restore the programs that had existed before Hitler wrecked them, many dating from Bismarck's time. Only in the late 1960s was an effort to expand social programs initiated, starting with a direct child allowance. The FRG also made compensatory payments to victims of Nazi oppression. Upward cost pressure has occurred because of a rising percentage of old people receiving social security and because of rising medical costs. Unemployment compensation costs have risen as unemployment has risen.

The German social safety net is highly decentralized, organized either on industrial lines or locally. Medical coverage is provided by bodies funded by combined payroll-employer payments and are self-financing, although that is not true of old age insurance. This decentralization reflects the relatively decentralized nature of the FRG, in which the Länder have considerable power. The issue of the social safety net has become highly controversial since the FRG-GDR unification—costs for such programs have soared in the East and cuts have been made in the West.

The Development of the East German Command Socialist Economy

East Germany, the German Democratic Republic, was one of only two areas in the world (the other being the Czech Republic) that came to have a Marxist-oriented regime after having achieved industrialization. In contrast to Marx's forecast it was an external force, the Soviet military, that imposed the regime on the society after the German surrender in 1945.

The group of men, led by Walter Ulbricht, who led the GDR in its early years came from a minuscule fragment of the pre-Hitler Communist Party of Germany, which was proudly descended from the Spartacus League of 1919 and from Marx and Engels themselves.[32] After Hitler came to power many party members were arrested and executed, others gave up and converted to National Socialism, and others escaped westward, thus becoming considered unreliable. Among those who went to the Soviet Union, many died in the Great Purges of the late 1930s, some allegedly due to Ulbricht's own orders. Thus it was only a remnant that was left to take power after the Soviet army conquered Berlin.

Although the area of the GDR was slightly ahead of that of the FRG in per capita output in 1939, it fell behind immediately in the postwar period. The USSR carted off wholesale entire factories, livestock, timber, machinery and equipment, and railroad rolling stock in large quantities, both as reparations and to help rebuild the Soviet economy. This policy continued until August 1953, when a major uprising by workers protesting their wages and living conditions brought an end to it in the immediate post-Stalin period. Thus after 1947, while the United States was building up West Germany with Marshall Plan aid,[33] the USSR was pushing East Germany down. The huge gap that opened up was never overcome, despite strenuous efforts by the East Germans.

Prior to its absorption by the FRG, the GDR had a reputation for being the most efficient command socialist economy with the highest income, as well as one of the most rigidly and tightly controlled. Only some elements of these generalizations were true. A difficulty in discussing the GDR economy is that statistics were frequently falsified. For example, estimates from different sources of GDR per capita output as a percentage of that in the FRG for the 1980s ranged from below 40 percent to over 100 percent.[34]

After forming in 1949, the GDR only slowly adopted the command socialist system. Up to 1953 the Soviet leadership was uncertain whether it wanted to develop the GDR at all or just to plunder it and keep it down. The ease of getting to the West before construction of the Berlin Wall in 1961 also

---

[32]Although born in Trier in the Rhineland, Marx as a young man studied at the University of Berlin and also at Jena, both in eastern Germany. The Spartacus League sprang from the German Social Democratic Party, and both Marx and Engels encouraged the latter's development. In East Germany the Communist Party and the Social Democrats were forcefully united in 1946 into the Socialist Unity Party, under the domination of the Communists, which would rule the GDR without democracy. The West German Social Democratic Party formally abjured Marxism at a conference in 1959 after a particularly poor electoral performance against the Christian Democrats, after decades of de facto revisionism.

[33]The initial U.S. posture towards Germany was hostile as expressed in the Morgenthau Plan and there were some reparations deliveries. An early sign of the coming split was U.S. General Lucius Clay's order on May 27, 1946, to halt such deliveries, paving the way to differential treatment between East and West.

[34]"A Survey of Germany," *The Economist,* May 23, 1992, p. 7.

operated as a constraint on moving too quickly. Thus, although five-year plans were introduced in 1951, the process of nationalization occurred slowly. The initial wave after the war focused on the property of refugees and war criminals and the very largest firms, especially banks and insurance companies. As late as 1955 over a quarter of output was privately produced and as late as 1959 a majority of agricultural acreage was still privately owned.[35]

By the early 1960s most of the economy was nationalized, some of it in the form of partial state ownership, although a small private sector remained, even after another wave of nationalizations in 1972. In 1963 reforms brought prices in line with costs of production, instituted the use of profits as a principal criterion, and allowed managers some autonomy to retain some profits for discretionary usage. None of this accords with the usual image of the GDR economy.[36]

The GDR integrated into the Soviet bloc, becoming a member in good standing of both the CMEA and the Warsaw Pact, the defense group opposed to NATO. Indeed the GDR generally stood for hard-line positions in both foreign and domestic policies within those organizations and eventually exhibited a certain arrogance based on its alleged lead in productivity, as well as its ideological purity as the home of Marx and Engels. Over time it supplied the CMEA with high-technology goods, such as optical equipment and computer chips, thereby reinforcing its image of economic superiority within the bloc.

In 1979 the GDR introduced the most distinctive feature of its economic system, the *Kombinate*. These were 126 centrally directed combines, employing an average of 25,000 workers in some 20 to 40 enterprises related either vertically or horizontally. These Kombinate were subsequently subject to ''perfected'' steering mechanisms that avoided a focus on gross output, and in the late 1980s they were to carry out technological intensification, the GDR being one of the few command socialist economies to do so.

The Kombinate in a sense revived the sectoral chambers of the Nazi command economy. The two systems differed in their types of ownership, one public, one private. They also differed greatly with respect to income distribution policies, with the GDR having more equal incomes and a well-developed social safety net. Also, the Nazi regime emphasized that women should have children, stay at home, and go to church (*kinder, kuche, kirche*), whereas the GDR had one of the world's highest labor force participation rates by women.

---

[35]Berghahn, *Modern Germany*, p. 277. Agricultural productivity in the FRG exceeded that in the GDR at unification. But because of economies of scale and high soil quality, if they can be successfully integrated into the market economy the collectivized farms of eastern Germany have the potential to be more productive than the small family farms of western Germany, which survive largely because of massive state subsidies.

[36]That image was partly based on the political repressiveness of the regime, dramatically symbolized by its willingness to shoot people escaping over the Berlin Wall.

Shortly before German reunification came a resurgence of local pride regarding the Prussian past, really an admission that the FRG was far ahead economically. But critics charged that the FRG had become an American colony and had lost its "Germanness" in a sea of international capitalist homogeneity. The political split between the two Germanies reflected traditional attitudes in the two, the Prussian East having a long authoritarian past and the West having long been a center of prodemocratic views.

The Two Economies Compared

General Observations.   Comparing the economies of the FRG and the GDR was long a favorite sport of comparative economists because the two Germanies had similar cultural and geographical backgrounds but different economic systems, thus allowing the possibility of some sort of controlled experiment comparison.[37] But there are complications with this idea. The two Germanies had very different immediate postwar experiences—the United States aided the FRG where as the USSR suppressed the GDR economically. Also, being smaller, the GDR suffered more from the disruption of internal German trade than did the FRG. Furthermore, the GDR was integrated into the poorer CMEA trade bloc in contrast with the FRG's integration into the EU trade bloc.[38]

Another problem is seriously distorted GDR data. Immediately after unification in 1990, even at the one-to-one currency exchange rate that was implemented, per capita income in the East was only slightly above one-third of that in the West. Nevertheless almost all studies (prior to unification) found the GDR to have been growing consistently more rapidly than the FRG after the mid-1950s. The CIA[39] found 1981 per capita income in the GDR to be 87.6 percent of that in the FRG. Supposedly the GDR led in growth rates through most of the 1980s.[40]

Despite these difficulties generalizations can be made, most of them consistent with stock stories regarding the differences between market capitalism

---

[37]See Martin Schnitzer, *East and West Germany: A Comparative Analysis* (New York: Praeger, 1972), and Paul Gregory and Gerd Leptin, "Similar Societies under Differing Economic Systems," *Journal of Comparative Economics* 1 (1977), p. 524.

[38]This is partly misleading. Because it never recognized the separateness of the GDR, the FRG allowed imports from it duty free. Thus the GDR had a back door into the EU because its goods could be re-exported from the FRG to the EU duty free. This led some to call the GDR the EU's "13th member." Previous access to the EU reduced the GDR's gains from unification because it gained little new access to previously unavailable export markets.

[39]Central Intelligence Agency, *Handbook of Economic Statistics* (Washington, USGPO, 1986), pp. 26–27.

[40]After 1987 according to official statistics, West German growth exceeded East German as the entire EU experienced a boom, since ended, whereas the entire CMEA bloc went into a stagnationist crisis. The GDR resisted it better than most of its fellow CMEA members, a fact that hardline GDR leader, Erich Honecker, annoyingly pointed out to his proreform Soviet colleague, Mikhail Gorbachev.

TABLE 9–1   Consumer Durables Endowments

Goods	East	West
Percent of population owning		
Private car	54	96
TV set	96	99
Color TV set	57	95
Telephone	17	99
Refrigerator (without freezer)	99	81
Freezer (with or without refrigerator)	43	75
Washing machine	99	97
Proportion of		
Living space built after 1948	35	70
Units with bath/shower	82	96
Living space per capita (*in square meters*)	27.6	35.5

Note: Except for living space per capita all figures are percentages and are for 1989.

Source: From Hans-Werner Sinn, ''Macroeconomic Aspects of German Unification,'' in *Economic Aspects of German Unification: National and International Perspectives,* ed. P.J.J. Welfens (Berlin: Springer Verlag, 1992), p. 126.

and command socialism. In particular, the FRG had greater efficiency, higher general living standards, and broadly superior environmental quality, whereas the GDR had greater macroeconomic stability, including nearly continuous full employment, a greater degree of income equality, and a somewhat more extensive social safety net.

Efficiency.   After unification, when firms in the two Germanies faced each other in direct competition, those in the West boomed while those in the East collapsed. The sudden discovery that per capita incomes were not almost equal but that those in the East were only one-third of those in the West strongly supports the greater efficiency of the FRG economy, certainly dynamic, if not static efficiency.

Part of this superior efficiency in the FRG is related to an element that was very hard to measure prior to unification, but that was fundamental, namely product quality. Quality was simply much higher for most Western goods, which had been subject to consumer preferences and market competition, than for Eastern goods produced in response to planner's preferences for captive markets.

General Living Standards.   With respect to broad living standards see Tables 9–1, 9–2, and 9–3. Although people in the FRG were better off in most categories, people in the GDR were better off in certain collectively provided goods, notably public transportation, housing and electricity (which cost less), and day care. However, no accounting for quality differences is made in these

TABLE 9–2   Cost in Marks of Goods and Services

Goods and Services	East	West
Food		
Potatoes	4.05	5.32
Tomatoes	4.40	2.10
Apples	1.40	2.10
Bananas, 500 kg	18.50	4.10
Bratwurst, kg	11.00	9.90
Herring, 200 g	3.70	1.99
Edam cheese, kg	9.60	9.90
Butter, kg	9.00	8.76
Sugar, kg	1.59	1.72
Clothing		
Men's coat	1,600	259
Women's dress	174.50	69.50
Men's leather shoes	119.20	34.95
Boy's T-shirt	30.80	10.90
Children's shoes	41.20	37.95
Consumer Goods		
Light bulb, 40 watts	1.50	1.90
PKW, Lada Nova, 550 ccm	24,500	10,210
Men's watch, quartz digital	260	25
Child's wagon	420	198
Bedroom furniture	4,728	1,870
Electric range with oven	815.00	389.50
Ladies' bicycle, no attachments	490	289
Rent and Transportation		
Month's rent, 2-room apt., no bath	33	190
Consumer electricity, 75 kwh	7.50	29.30
Local streetcar or bus fare	.20	1.93
Day nursery, monthly rate	7	140
Air fare to Romania, round trip	1,196	926
Women's permanent	9.90	45.00

Source: From Martin Schnitzer, *Comparative Economic Systems,* 5th ed. (Cincinnati: South-Western, 1991), pp. 230–1. Numbers are for 1987.

tables, which tends to favor the FRG. Table 9–1 presents the endowments of various consumer durables in the two states; Table 9–2 shows the costs in marks of various goods and services in the two states, and Table 9–3 shows the time an average person would need to work in order to obtain the good or service.

Price changes facing East Germans during the six months following currency unification with West Germany on July 1, 1990, moved in directions one would expect from the above tables except for rent and energy, which

TABLE 9-3   **Work Time to Purchase Item, Hours and Minutes**

Type of Purchase	East	West
Men's shirt	7.19	1.22
Women's pantyhose	2.40	0.12
Children's shoes	7.21	2.35
Color TV	1,008.56	81.34
Washing machine	491.04	59.09
Rail fare, 15 km	0.27	1.46
Dark bread	0.07	0.12
Milk, liter	0.07	0.05
Pork cutlets, 1 kg	1.47	1.01
Coffee, 250 g	4.20	0.21

Source: From Martin Schnitzer, *Comparative Economic Systems,* 5th ed. (Cincinnati: South-Western, 1991), p. 232, for 1989.

remained constant because still fixed by the government, for an overall price decline of 1 percent.[41]

Environmental Quality

This may be the area that most favors the FRG. Polls taken in 1988 and 1990 comparing levels of satisfaction of East and West Germans with various aspects of their lives showed the greatest disparity in this area, with Wessis about twice as satisfied as Ossis.[42] In 1985 sulfur dioxide emissions per capita were 7½ times as great in the GDR as in the FRG and nitrogen oxide emissions were about 20 percent greater,[43] the former reflecting the use of dirty lignite coal in the East whereas the latter reflects the higher use of cars in the West than the East. Per capita carbon dioxide emissions were almost twice as great in 1986 in the GDR as in the FRG.

It is difficult to get proper numbers about water pollution because some water flowing through the GDR came from Czechoslovakia and was already polluted. But general trends are clear. In the West, pollution levels in the Rhine

---

[41]George Akerlof, Andrew K. Rose, Janet L. Yellen, and Helga Hessenius, "East Germany in from the Cold: The Aftermath of Currency Union," *Brookings Papers on Economic Activity,* no. 1 (1991), p. 10.

[42]Detlef Landua, "The Social Aspects of German Reunification," in *The Economics of German Unification,* eds. A. G. Ghaussy and W. Schäfer (London: Routledge, 1993), p. 202. Other areas where Wessis were more satisfied than Ossis were living standards, housing and income, and public safety. Areas where they were almost equally satisfied were home and family life, health care, and education. In no area were Ossis more satisfied than Wessis.

[43]Günter Streibel, "Environmental Protection: Problems and Prospects in East and West Germany," in *Economic Aspects of German Unification,* p. 201.

were cut to about 10 percent of previous levels for several major pollutants between 1971 and 1986 whereas they increased in the major rivers of the East.[44] Another serious problem in the East is abandoned toxic waste dump sites.

In 1988 per capita expenditures on environmental protection were 388 marks in the FRG and 107 marks in the GDR.[45] Since unification a crash environmental cleanup program in the East has begun, funded by the unified federal government.[46] Its priorities include discovery and cleanup of waste dump sites, major cleanup or restoration of sewage treatment plants and sewer lines, modernization of lignite-burning power and heating plants, and modernization of air pollution control equipment in 6,735 installations.[47]

Macroeconomic Stability

The FRG has one of the better records in this area in the market capitalist world, sharing the best postwar inflation record with Switzerland. Its unemployment has gone up and down. It has avoided the double digit range throughout the postwar era and actually got its unemployment rate below 1 percent during the early 1960s, although it has gone up substantially since then.

But strict control over investment and prices by the central planners in the GDR gave it a superior record in these areas, with almost zero inflation until recently[48] and unemployment rates consistently below 1 percent throughout. As of January 1990 the unemployment rate in the GDR was 0.1 percent. By early 1992 one out of three East German workers had lost their jobs.

Distribution of Income and the Social Safety Net

The distribution of income was more equal in the GDR than in the FRG, although the gap narrowed over time. Thus in 1970 the top and bottom quintile shares of income were 31.1/9.7 in the GDR and 39.9/8.3 in the FRG, whereas in 1983 they were 30.2/10.9 in the GDR and 34.3/9.8 in the FRG, respectively.[49] These figures overstate the degree of actual equality in the GDR because they do not take into account special favors and goods available to the top ruling elite, which were scandalously substantial.

---

[44]Streibel, ''Environmental Protection,'' p. 185.

[45]Streibel, ''Environmental Protection,'' p. 202.

[46]In this regard eastern Germany is lucky because in other East European countries economic difficulties have forced environmental cleanup to take a back seat, despite the prominent role played by environmentalists in the reform movements.

[47]Klaus Zimmermann, ''Ecological Transformation in Eastern Germany,'' in *The Economics of German Unification*, pp. 218–19.

[48]This does not account for the black market, where there certainly was inflation, nor does it account for time spent standing in line for goods, which could be several hours per day.

[49]Schnitzer, *Comparative Economic Systems*, p. 227.

Social safety net policies were surprisingly similar, both having ultimately derived from the old Bismarckian programs. Nevertheless differences can be noted. One was that administration in the East was centralized, there being no Länder. Individuals did not make payroll contributions for health care funds and health care coverage was wider, although the quality was lower and dropping. Doctors were state employees in the East but private in the West, resulting in those in the East leaving for higher incomes in the West. Social security pensions were higher in the West than in the East, an average of 1,018 marks per month versus 427 respectively,[50] one area where Ossis are gaining from unification.

The East was substantially more generous than the West in providing day care. Day care facilities were heavily subsidized in the East and barely subsidized at all in the West, a fact showing up in the relative prices for day care in Table 9–3. This correlated with substantial differences in employment of married women with children in the two states. In 1988 62 percent of married women aged 18–40 with children aged 1–6 worked in the East whereas only 28 percent worked in the West. For married women aged 25–65 with school-aged children aged 7–18, 88 percent worked in the East whereas only 32 percent worked in the West.[51] As the western system has been imposed on the East, women have been more likely to become unemployed than men. Along with increased restrictions on abortion availability, female unemployment has caused anger in the East among women.

The Costs and Prospects of Unification

The Process of Unification and Its General Prospects

The process of unification was modeled on what was done in the West in 1948. The results have been dissimilar so far, but the long-run outcome remains uncertain. Unification began with the fall of the Berlin Wall on November 9, 1989,[52] a date many identify as the effective beginning of the end of the Cold War.[53] In March 1990, elections were held in the East and Chancellor Kohl's

---

[50]Sinn, ''Macroeconomic Aspects of German Unification,'' p. 121.

[51]Landua, ''Social Aspects,'' p. 98.

[52]An unfortunate coincidence is that this was the 51st anniversary of Kristallnacht, a night when fanatic Nazis attacked stores and homes owned by Jews, smashing glass and crystal particularly, and attacking Jews themselves, an outburst heralding an upward ratcheting of the Nazi anti-Jewish campaign.

[53]Soviet leader, Mikhail Gorbachev, played a crucial role in the fall of the Berlin Wall because he signaled an unwillingness to use force to keep the Wall up. He had been unhappy with the hardline GDR leadership. Prior to the fall of the Wall, there had been a surge of East Germans emigrating through Hungary after it opened its border with Austria, a border since closed by the Austrians.

Christian Democrats won a decisive victory, promising rapid and painless absorption into the FRG under its existing constitution. On July 1, 1990, the currencies were unified at a one-to-one rate, although at a schedule of lower rates for Ostmark balances above certain levels, and most price and trade restrictions were removed. On October 3, 1990, came full legal and political unification. On January 1, 1991, the West German tax system was applied in the East.

This was the most rapid of all Big Bang economic transformations of a formerly command socialist economy into a market capitalist economy. It exhibits some of the costs and benefits of such an approach, although some of both probably apply strictly to this case alone. Mostly the costs have been visible. But with an apparent bottoming-out of output in the East and the reappearance of growth there in 1994, the light at the end of the tunnel is visible.

Although some of the aspects facing the former GDR are common to all economies attempting to transform from command socialist to market capitalist, two stick out relative to others, one positive and one negative. The positive is that being absorbed into the existing political, legal, and regulatory framework of the FRG has resolved the institutional problem—the GDR inherits a pre-existing and generally successful set of laws and property rules, functioning stock and bond markets and banking system, and a largely stable and moderate democratic political framework. These factors lead many observers to be extremely optimistic about the area's future prospects.

Furthermore, the former GDR also inherits the credibility of the West German macroeconomic managers, notably the redoubtable Bundesbank and its well-earned anti-inflation reputation. Unfortunately one of the costs of unification has been damage to that credibility due to the difficulties arising from the unification itself, especially the apparent failure of the FRG leadership, particularly Chancellor Kohl, to anticipate the scale of potential problems.[54] The Bundesbank may have so aggressively raised interest rates as budget deficits swelled from 1990 through 1992 because it was concerned about losing that hard-won credibility, although foreign critics charged the Bundesbank with overdoing it.

The great negative of the economic unification was the one-to-one currency unification, now known to constitute a wild overvaluation of the Ostmark (the former GDR currency). Combined with a drive for nominal wage equality between East and West, despite lower productivity in the East, overvaluation significantly contributed to the depth of the collapse of output in the East, which was the source of the unexpected costs triggering budget deficits that raised interest rates.

---

[54]Kohl and the Bundesbank split on this point—the latter opposed the one-to-one currency unification on grounds that have since been confirmed, namely an anticipated collapse of output in the East.

In contrast, Poland, which has also followed Big Bang policies, had a smaller decline in output probably because it allowed a devaluation of the Polish currency (złoty) when it decontrolled prices. Given the political unwillingness in Germany to undo this, pessimists predict that this overvaluation will be a long-run drag on the former GDR economy, discouraging future investment, permanently draining it of its most skilled workers who will move west, and creating a permanently depressed regional economy such as one finds in southern Italy or northern Britain, even though the German economy as a whole may do reasonably well. This scenario is probably exaggerated, although as of 1995 most investment in the East has been concentrated in major cities such as Dresden and Leipzig, with other areas very depressed. Over time the western part will outweigh the eastern part, with a population in 1989 four times as great and an aggregate GDP 10 times as great.

The Output Collapse in the East

The output collapse in the East was one of the most dramatic ever seen. Taking average real 1989 GDP as an index of 100, the index stood at 54 in the second quarter of 1991.[55] In a single year, September 1989 to September 1990, net manufacturing output fell 51.1 percent.[56]

The proximate cause of this collapse was a price-cost squeeze facing firms, driving them to bankruptcy or to output reductions and layoffs. There were six underlying causes, three on the cost (supply) side and three on the price (demand) side.

Most important on the cost side were excessive wages in the East arising from the one-to-one currency unification rate[57] and the drive for equality of nominal wages with the West without equality of productivity.[58] Some western Germans claim that contributing to labor productivity shortfalls is an alleged laziness of eastern workers relative to western ones. If this is true, it reflects 45 years of a "we pretend to work and they pretend to pay us" mentality. Such charges by Wessis aggravate the increasingly bad relations between them and the Ossis.

A second factor was technologically outmoded capital stock, which raised costs directly and implied future higher costs for retooling. The third

---

[55]*1991/1992 OECD Economic Surveys: Germany* (Paris: Organization for Economic Cooperation and Development, 1992), p. 20.

[56]Rolf Hasse, ''German-German Monetary Union: Main Options, Costs and Repercussions,'' in *The Economics of German Unification,* p. 44.

[57]An oddity of the currency unification that damaged existing small private enterprises in the East was that liquid assets were only exchanged at a two-to-one rate whereas debts were exchanged at a one-to-one rate.

[58]It may be that the rate of currency unification was irrelevant and that it was the demand for nominal wage equality that was the problem. It may have been better to impose increased wages at once through the currency rate rather than letting the increase drag on through disruptive strikes with the accompanying uncertainty and social and political disruption.

such cost was the heavy pollution produced by much of the eastern productive plant—no private party wanted to be held responsible for cleanup. The government has assumed responsibility in this area.

The immediate source of the collapse of internal demand resulted from the sudden availability of western goods at reasonably low prices,[59] also a result of the overvaluation of the Ostmark at currency unification. Important factors in the collapse of demand were both sheer novelty and fundamental quality. The first factor was overdone and somewhat temporary with a nostalgic return to eastern goods in certain markets later. But the quality issue was very real and decisive in many areas, such as in ending production of the East German Trabant car.

The second round of the demand collapse was the negative multiplier effect of the first one. The initial decline in demand triggered a series of layoffs and income declines that further suppressed demand, although this second collapse has been mitigated by infusions of assistance from the West.

The third source of demand decline came from the general collapse of the CMEA and the loss of former markets in Eastern Europe by the former GDR. Some of the shining stars of the former GDR economy had been high-technology goods it supplied to the rest of the CMEA, such as optical equipment and microchips. To the extent that the former buyers can still buy, they now have available other producers such as the Japanese who offer higher quality at lower prices. But beyond that these economies have all suffered output declines and have reduced all imports.

The Rise of Unemployment in the East

The output collapse caused a surge of unemployment, with the figure of one out of three workers losing their jobs widely reported. However the official unemployment rate was only 16.5 percent in January 1992. What happened to the other half of the laid-off workers? Some retired early, some (especially women who lost their inexpensive day care) dropped out of the labor force, some became "short time" workers, some went into retraining programs, some migrated to the West or are commuting there for work, and some have found other employment in the East.

A rough measure of this pattern is given in Figure 9–1. Of 4.1 million workers in state firms at the end of 1989, 2.4 million had been removed from that category at the end of 1991 by the *Treuhandstalt* privatization agency. Figure 9–1 shows what those 2.4 million workers were doing. These percentages continued to hold through the end of the Treuhandstalt's activities by the end of 1994.

---

[59]Some of this collapse of demand stimulated the West German economy as it sold goods to the East, and output expanded in the West as it contracted in the East until the end of 1992 when the West went into recession as well. But the surge of imports to the East caused the overall current account balance to go into a rare deficit, thus triggering borrowing from abroad and adding to the pressure for higher interest rates.

FIGURE 9–1a   **Labor Adjustments in Treuhandstalt Firms**

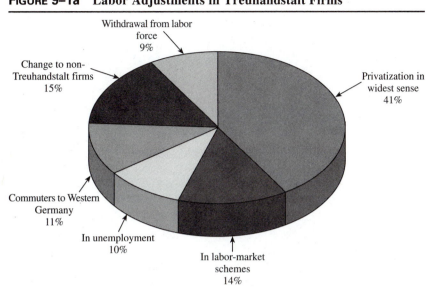

Source: From 1991–1992 *OECD Economic Surveys: Germany* (Paris: Organization for Economic Cooperation and Development, 1992), p. 53.

The Privatization Process

For transforming economies it is easier to reintroduce the market than it is to reintroduce capitalism because a rudimentary market can be introduced by eliminating central planning and decontrolling prices, something accomplished to varying degrees in most of Eastern Europe despite some institutional and legal complexities. But to fully reintroduce capitalism means to privatize the existing set of state-owned assets, which is a complicated and controversial process.

Some countries, notably the Czech Republic and Russia, have rapidly privatized using vouchers to distribute state-owned assets to the population. Others have attempted more gradualistic approaches, usually involving selling an asset to a nonvouchered buyer with some financial capital in the hope that the buyer will make some capital investment for retooling or whatever. Proponents of this gradual approach hope that private ownership in turn will provide a more solid foundation for the future economy. Germany took the gradual approach, although it moved as rapidly as possible within its chosen framework.

The German approach involved establishing the above-mentioned Treuhandstalt agency (THA) to dispose of state-owned firms. The THA established a committee for each firm to be privatized that searched for a core business that could be saved. Rarely did the THA try to sell an entire firm, especially if it was a former Kombinate and thus rather large. Rather firms were usually broken up into pieces that were then sold off by whatever mechanism could be agreed upon.[60]

As of the end of March 1992, 42 percent of THA firms remained to be privatized, 30 percent had been sold to Germans (overwhelmingly from the West), 10 percent had been liquidated (mostly firms that sold goods to dead former CMEA markets such as military goods), 7 percent had been sold to foreigners, 6 percent had been reprivatized (returned to a previous owner or their heirs), and 5 percent had been transferred to municipalities.[61] The disposition of THA firms since then involved a higher rate of liquidations because the firms involved were among the least productive and hardest to sell of all the firms. The THA formally ceased to exist at the end of 1994.

Reprivatizations have caused serious complications. In many cases assets are tied up in disputes over ownership among previous owners, especially over real estate. These disputes now clog the courts and will take years to sort out. The situation is especially complicated because former owners have been granted fairly generous rights and also because several waves of property confiscations led to multiple past ownerships. Jewish-owned properties were seized by Nazis and Nazi-owned properties were redistributed to other individuals after the war but before they were nationalized. As many as 15 different parties are contesting ownership of a single asset.

The Budget Deficit

Chancellor Kohl and his advisers did not expect a budget deficit because they forecast a 1948-style Wirtschaftswunder with quickly soaring output. When the opposite happened government spending soared to cover unemployment compensation, higher old age pensions, environmental cleanup, and loans to the THA. A Unity Fund was established to finance these activities, which quickly grew to over 30 billion deutsche marks. Borrowing by the THA has been on a similar scale. From a surplus of 0.2 percent of GDP in 1989, the budget went into a 3 percent of GDP deficit as of 1992, 4 percent if THA borrowing is included.[62]

This problem is gradually improving as expenditures by the Unity Fund decline and by the THA have ceased. Also the Kohl government belatedly enacted some tax increases and spending cuts in social welfare areas.

---

[60]In some cases the sale price was *negative* after grants, debt cancellations, unemployment payments, environmental cleanup costs, and other payments were counted (OECD, *Economic Surveys,* p. 52).

[61]*OECD Economic Surveys,* pp. 51–54.

[62]*OECD Economic Surveys,* p. 39.

Box 9–2

The "Colonization of East Germany"?

A subtle problem, but perhaps the most dangerous for the long-run prospects for national unity, is the increasingly aggrieved feeling that exists in the East of having been "colonized" by the West.* Given the scale of the unemployment increases, the increased child care burdens on women and restrictions on abortion, and the decline in income, this feeling is understandable. Also now many employers are Wessis; the Wessis are on top and they are on the bottom. Of course the Wessis have their own complaints: that the Ossis are lazy, that the unification is costing too much in taxes, that social spending has been cut back, and that interest rates are higher.

A noneconomic component of this perception is the purge of various institutions in the East. Anyone who was a member of the former ruling Socialist Unity Party or who worked with the Stasi secret police has been automatically fired from any public position. Whole categories of civil servants were fired, including the entire judiciary and whole university departments. A general "political correctness" investigation goes on in the East that is both adding to unemployment and exacerbating Ossi resentments. Many of those who have fallen victim to this campaign include people who were dissidents against the GDR regime and aided in its overthrow. Now they have become dissidents once again.†

The new unity of Germany will probably hold, simply because the West profoundly dominates the East. But if that is the only reason it does so, then it will be an unstable unity, a development Germany's neighbors fear.

---

*See Dorothy Rosenberg, "The Colonization of East Germany," *Monthly Review* 43 (September 1991), pp. 14–33.

†The murkiness of all this is seen in the charges that he was a Stasi informer leveled against 81-year old novelist and former dissident, Stefan Heym, when he entered the Reichstag as a member of the post-communist Party of Democratic Socialism in late 1994.

A "European Germany or a German Europe"?

The unification of Germany generates pressures both towards European unification and away from it. A major pressure for unification comes from fear. Although former President Mitterand of France supported German unification against British doubts, he did so recognizing its inevitability and hoping to keep the outcome under control. This meant pushing through the Maastricht Treaty and pushing the full unification of Europe to rope Germany in and keep it under the control of the higher European entity, thus ensuring a "European Germany."

The Maastricht Treaty was signed in December 1991 and has been approved by all EU member states. But complications have arisen, most importantly involving currencies. At Maastricht, Germany demanded and got major concessions. Not only will the future European central bank be located in Frankfurt where the Bundesbank is, but also any country joining the common currency must meet a stringent set of macroeconomic criteria regarding budget deficits, inflation rates, and so forth, so stringent that as of early 1995 the only EU member eligible to join was Luxemburg. Under current arrangements, Germany and the deutsche mark dominate the EU and the other currencies in an asymmetric relationship, and Germany is reluctant to give that up.

Another major issue is Eastern Europe. Absorbing the former GDR automatically increased Germany's involvement there. Germany had to pay Russia to allow for the unification. It has become Russia's largest creditor, thereby dragging Germany into the complex problems arising from the dissolution of the FSU and the ongoing struggles there over reform.

Also, before World War II Germany had extensive trade relations with the nations to the East, relations artificially disrupted by the division of Europe in the Cold War. Now Germany seeks to revive those trade relations and has been ahead of all other countries outside of Eastern Europe in expanding trade and investment there. As a result, Germany has become the champion of those countries that seek to join the EU, although not of the former republics of the USSR, except for the Baltic ones.[63]

Germany's relationships with Eastern Europe create conflict with France and other EU members not wishing to expand the EU eastward. They would rather intensify the drive to unity among existing members. An underlying fear is that Germany is not just after economic gains, but may be reviving its ancient drive for political domination of the East as well, despite having renounced its claims on territories lost in World War II. Will the emergence of German unity once again lead it to seek to establish a universal empire, however subtly?

A German response is that bringing Eastern European nations into the EU will further dilute its own role as the EU gets bigger. Furthermore, Germany is driven by its own fears, particularly that immigration from these countries might increase if their economies are not developed. It is anti-immigrant sentiment that drives the most extreme neo-Nazi activists in Germany. Germany's opening to the East is an effort to protect both itself and its neighbors from its own historical demons.

---

[63]A further subdivision appeared in a 1994 German study advocating "tiers" within the EU, with an "inner core" of Germany, France, the Netherlands, Belgium, and Luxemburg possessing a unified currency. It sees Poland, the Czech Republic, Slovakia, Hungary, and Slovenia as being ready for EU membership sooner than other East European states. This study, disavowed by the German government, created great controversy.

The unification of Germany means it will be the leader of Europe. Thus the fate of the German economy will determine the fate of the European economy. Will there be a German-led, Europeanwide Wirtschaftswunder, or will ''Eurosclerosis'' take over and drag all down into ethnic and nationalistic conflict?

Whether Germany can match the competition in high technology from Japan and the United States may be important in deciding that question. The signs are troubling for Europe on the high-technology front. Although Germany maintains a level of R&D spending equal to that of Japan and the United States in percent of GDP, its slow GDP growth means that absolute R&D spending has not grown rapidly. Germany maintains a strong position in machine tool and automotive technologies (Siemens and Daimler-Benz were first and second in European R&D spending in 1989), but it has fallen to second behind the United States in biotechnology and is a distant third in computers and information technologies, areas likely to be critical in the future.[64]

An important reason Germany has failed to keep up in R&D has been weak support by the federal government for such expenditures. A deeply entrenched factor is abdication to the Länder of much responsibility for such financing and for encouraging economic development more broadly. Although granting power to the Länder solves the problem of reconciling the separatist tendencies of the German tribes with the existence of a unified nation-state, the inability to grant greater powers to the central German government could doom the entire European enterprise to another German-centered disaster.

Summary and Conclusions

Germany has long struggled to achieve national unity out of diverse elements among its peoples. The struggle for unity has been complicated by uncertainty as to who were its peoples and where were the appropriate boundaries of their domains. Although Germany achieved moments of great unity under the inspiration of universal empires, it has also experienced catastrophes of national disintegration and economic collapse as in the Thirty Years War and at the end of World War II. But the German people always rise again, as they are doing with the unification of East and West Germany.

Germany's economic strength has depended upon the skills, genius for creation, and hard work of its people. A center of advanced education and scientific achievement, the German economy has long been a technological leader of the world economy. As the fourth largest economy in the world, it competes at the high end of technology with the two largest economies, the United States and Japan.

---

[64]Smyser, *The Economy of United Germany,* pp. 108–110.

Germany's industrialization in the late 19th century was very rapid. Although Germany's unifier in 1871, Chancellor Bismarck, ruled despotically, he introduced the first government-funded social security, health insurance, and workmen's compensation systems in the world. This established the tradition known after World War II as the social market economy, a system characterized by market capitalism with an extensive social safety net. This system has been imitated by many nations since.

During the Great Depression the Nazi dictator, Adolf Hitler, established a command capitalist economy. It grew successfully at first, but then Hitler started World War II, which led to a total economic collapse as well as military and political defeat. Germany was divided into East and West by the victorious allies. The East became part of the Soviet bloc and a command socialist economy was established. In the West a social market economy was established, and an economic miracle of rapid growth appeared after price and currency reforms in 1948. West Germany's economy has also been characterized by labor-management co-determination and substantial bank ownership and control of major corporations.

Over the postwar era, the West German economy integrated into the wider European economy through the institution of the European Union. Eventually its success led it to reabsorb what had been independent East Germany in 1990. The process of unification has been more difficult and costly than expected, with consequences complicating further European unification. The great drama today of Germany is first, whether or not it can successfully complete its unification and second, whether or not it can return to leading Europe towards a peaceful and productive balance of unity and diversity on a path to a sustainable and fulfilling future.

Questions for Discussion

1. What is the source of the ''German Problem'' in Europe and how does it affect prospects for European unification?

2. Compare and contrast Hitler's command economy with that of the former East Germany.

3. Compare and contrast the 1948 West German reform policies with those applied in 1990 in eastern Germany during unification with the FRG.

4. What elements of the German economy resemble those of Japan's?

5. Compare and contrast German labor market policies with those of Sweden.

6. How does the German economic system compare with that of the United States?

7. Compare the social safety nets of the former East and West Germanies.

8. Evaluate the claim that West Germany has ''colonized'' the former East Germany.

9. Why has the unification of Germany cost more than expected and what are the implications of this fact?

10. Explain and evaluate the claim that Germany is a ''fading miracle.''

Suggested Further Readings

Akerlof, George A., Andrew K. Rose, Janet L. Yellen, and Helga Hessenius. ''East Germany in from the Cold: The Aftermath of Currency Union.'' *Brookings Papers on Economic Activity* 1 (1991), pp. 1–87.

Berghahn, V.R. *Modern Germany: Society, Economy and Politics in the Twentieth Century.* Cambridge: Cambridge University Press, 1982.

Bryson, Phillip J., and Manfred Melzer. *The End of the East German Economy: From Honecker to Reunification.* New York: St. Martin's Press, 1991.

Dornbusch, Rudiger, and Holger Wolf, ''Economic Transition in Eastern Germany.'' *Brookings Papers on Economic Activity* 1 (1992), pp. 235–72.

The Economist. ''A Survey of Germany.'' May 23, 1992.

Giersch, Herbert, Karl-Heinz Paqué, and Holger Schmieding. *The Fading Miracle: Four Decades of Market Economy in Germany.* Cambridge, UK: Cambridge University Press, 1992.

Ghaussy, A.G., and W. Schäfer, eds. *The Economics of German Unification.* London: Routledge, 1993.

Heath, J., ed. *Revitalizing Socialist Enterprise: A Race Against Time.* London: Routledge, 1994.

Pohl, Gerhard. ''Economic Consequences of German Unification.'' In *Comparative Economic Systems: Models and Cases,* 7th ed., ed. Morris Bornstein. Burr Ridge: Irwin, 1994, pp. 173–204.

Sinn, Gerlinde and Hans-Werner Sinn. *Jumpstart: The Economic Unification of Germany.* Cambridge: MIT Press, 1992.

Smith, Eric Owen. *The German Economy.* London: Routledge, 1994

Smyser, W.R. *The Economy of United Germany: Colossus at the Crossroads.* New York: St. Martin's Press, 1992.

Valentin, Veit. *The German People: Their History and Civilization from the Holy Roman Empire to the Third Reich.* New York: Alfred A. Knopf, 1946.

Welfens, P.J.J., ed. *Economic Aspects of German Unification: National and International Perspectives.* Berlin: Springer Verlag, 1992.

PART

III

VARIANTS OF TRANSITION AMONG FORMER SOCIALIST ECONOMIES

Part III consists of a set of case studies of economies that have been predominantly socialist in the past, again defined by reference to state ownership of the means of production. All these economies are currently engaged in efforts to make a transition by some path in the direction of more markets and capitalism than in the past.

However the title of this section makes no reference to past command or planning practices because some of the cases discussed, notably Hungary and Yugoslavia, have been market socialist for a long time with little to no centrally planned command elements. Also, the title uses the word *former* rather than *post* or *ex* because some of the cases, notably China and some of the former Soviet republics, are still predominantly socialist, despite some transitional movements, and remain officially committed to socialism.

Chapter 10 presents the canonical case of centrally planned command socialism, namely the Soviet Union before its breakup in 1991. The general nature of command socialism is discussed as well as aspects specific to the Soviet Union. Reasons for the system's collapse are elucidated.

Chapter 11 carries the story of Chapter 10 forward to consider the now-independent former republics of the Soviet Union and their alternative situations and scenarios. Besides stressing the historical and cultural factors unique to each former republic, we examine their interrelationships and prospects for continuing economic connections with each other, along with the nature of their respective reform paths.

Chapter 12 presents the case of Poland, prominent as the model of ''shock therapy'' reform. Details of some other Central and East European cases are also presented, especially of the fairly successful Czech Republic. Poland has succeeded in moving towards markets and after a period of severe economic decline has resumed general economic growth led by an exporting entrepreneur-based sector. However, Poland has experienced a political backlash—former communists came to control the government, and the privatization process remains incomplete.

Chapter 13 discusses the case of Hungary, long famous as the most market oriented of the Soviet bloc economies. Partly as a result of already being somewhat marketized, Hungary has followed a more gradualistic program. The result has been a less dramatic collapse of output but a less clear bottoming out and turnaround of macroeconomic performance. Hungary has approached privatization through a "full value" sale of state assets, which has guaranteed full funding of privatized firms.

Chapter 14 considers the tragic case of the now-shattered Yugoslavia, home of worker-managed market socialism. Although it dissolved into ethnic warfare after a period of hyperinflation and worsening regional economic inequality, Yugoslavia remains the most important example of what some still consider the most viable form of a possible socialism. The current success of the former Yugoslav republic of Slovenia, which has the highest per capita income of any former socialist state, suggests that the Yugoslav model was not all a disaster.

Chapter 15 analyzes the case of the Peoples' Republic of China (PRC), recently the world's most rapidly growing economy. Still politically communist and officially committed to a "socialist market economy," China represents yet another pattern of gradualistic reform and transition. Different from the other cases in its Asian/Confucian historical and cultural background, its lower level of economic development and greater rural population, and its sheer size as the world's most populous nation, China presents numerous contrasts aside from its far superior recent economic performance. One peculiarity of the Chinese economy is its decentralized town and village enterprises (TVEs), which can be viewed as a form of local market socialism. We also compare the PRC economy with those of Hong Kong and Taiwan.

Out of this array of cases come few generalizations that hold without exception. Generally more rapidly transforming economies fall faster but recover faster, although gradualistic China has not fallen at all. Generally transitions manifest the ills of market capitalism such as greater income inequality and macroeconomic fluctuations as well as the virtues such as the elimination of lines for consumer goods and improved availability and quality of services. More generally almost every case has led to outcomes that were not predicted by any observers ahead of time, thus providing a caution to all economic analysts.

Arctic Ocean

Moscow

Pacific Ocean

Indian Ocean

THE FORMER SOVIET UNION: THE MYTH AND REALITY OF THE COMMAND ECONOMY

We speak of an economy being ''commanded'' when the state uses the means of authority at its disposal to force the whole of the economy in the direction it desires.

—Adolf Weber, *Marktwirtschaft und Sovjet-wirtschaft*

Command economy is one of the most notorious falsifications of the socialist economic system by anticommunists. It claims that economic decisions under socialism are made on the basis of arbitrary commands from the center bringing about inflexible and overbureaucratized structure. In reality planned organization and management of socialist production is based on principles of democratic centralism, namely a combination of the centralized control and initiatives of workers, the virtual owners of the means of production.

—*The Dictionary of Political Economy*[1]

Introduction

The demise of the Union of Soviet Socialist Republics raises numerous questions about its causes. Western observers point at the crisis of the socialist economic system of the former USSR and its variation, the centrally planned command economy. The dramatic disappearance of the hammer and sickle red banner symbolizing the Soviet Union provoked a theory of the historical inability of Soviets (worker-elected bodies of governance) to perform socioeconomic functions beyond rubber stamping the Communist Party's directives. The secessionist movements and the ultimate disintegration of the *union* of the republics poses as a third possible cause.

---

[1]Ed. M. Volkov (Moscow: Politizdat, 1979).

The demise of the former Soviet Union (FSU) was brought about by the imperative of an open economy and the slowdown in the arms race. The historical inadequacy of the ossified economic structure with regard to volatile international markets was revealed. Initial reforms were devised to prop up the existing socialist system with legalized but controlled markets.

But complementing the socialist centrist structure with a decentralized market-driven microeconomic initiative proved unfeasible. Real decentralization for working markets presumed a switch from state to private property, thus challenging the foundation of the socialist system. The time has come to make the toughest choice: to embrace market capitalism or to create a third way uniquely reflecting the entrenched duality of the Soviet economic system and before that, Russian economic tradition. This dilemma remains unresolved.

Historical Background of the Soviet Economy

The Setting

Until December 25, 1991, the Union of Soviet Socialist Republics (USSR) was the largest country in the world—with one-sixth of the earth's inhabited land it was almost 2.5 times the size of the United States. Its population of about 293 million people, third largest in the world, was composed of 128 ethnic groups. Some 72 percent of the total population were Eastern Slavs, of whom more than 70 percent (just over 50 percent of the total population) were Russians. The remainder of the Eastern Slavs group were Byelorussians and Ukrainians. Other ethnic groups belonged to Turkic, Baltic, Finno-Ugric, Caucasian, Persian, Armenian, Latin, and other linguistic families. The religious profile of the country was prevalently the Russian Orthodox Church along with Islam in Central Asia and Azerbaijan and Tatarstan, Protestantism in Estonia and Latvia, Roman Catholicism in Lithuania and Western Ukraine, Buddhism in Kalmykia and Buryatia, Judaism scattered throughout, and others as well. Due to official communist atheism and the suppression of religious activities, the numbers of actively faithful were around one-third of population.

The history of the *Soviet* state starts in 1917 with the October revolution that empowered the soviets (councils) of workers and peasants to implement communism, mapped by Karl Marx and Vladimir Lenin. Though Marx had reservations about the likelihood of revolution in Russia because of its inadequate capitalist development, the leader of the Russian Social Democratic Party, Lenin, argued that the Russian working class was less corrupted due to the tardiness of Russian imperialism and thus more committed to the goal of the communist revolution.

The *Union* of the Soviet Socialist Republics was formed in December 1922 comprising the Russian Soviet Federal Socialist Republic (RSFSR), the Ukraine, Byelorussia, and the Transcaucasian Federation (Georgia, Armenia, and Azerbaijan).[2] In November 1922 the Far Eastern Republic rejoined the Russian Federation.

The Economy of the Russian Empire before 1917

Prior to 1917 the Russian Empire was an intermediate case between under-developed Asia and industrially developed Western and Central Europe. It represented a duality between traditional agriculture and industrial development driven by militarization. The dual economy produced ambivalent attitudes towards change and reforms, which were viewed as favoring industry at the expense of agriculture. The economic culture of Russia was shaped by this duality and the persistence of traditionalism.

The Peasant Emancipation Act of 1861 abolished serfdom and granted serfs personal freedom. However this freedom was constrained by collective decision making in rural communes (*mir*). The Russian mir with its collective land ownership formed in the late 1400s and survived into the 19th century in central Russia, impeding private farming in most of the Russian Empire (except for the Baltic states and Poland, which only became parts of the Russian Empire in the 18th century).[3] This persistence of communal agrarian practices fed the uniqueness of Russian economic tradition. Russian Populists (*Narodniki*) believed that the agrarian commune could allow Russia to avoid industrial capitalism and leap into agrarian communism, given the Russian peasants' egalitarian and collectivist instincts, foreign to the individualism of the German or French peasantry. Russia's uniqueness is revisited by today's reformers seeking ''the third way.''

Inward-looking Slavophile traditionalists viewed industry as alien to Russian culture. The foundation of heavy industries in the late 1600s under Tsar Peter the Great was associated with his pro-Western policy that sought to break away from ''barbaric traditionalism'' and modernize Russia.[4] Belated industrialization was driven by militarization after the defeat of the Russian Army in the Crimean War with Turkey, Britain, and France in 1854. The majority of industries used serf labor before the emancipation of serfs. Historically industrial spurts were forced upon the economy by the tsar's decisions, thus adding to absolutist paternalism in the economic tradition.

Over 200 years of Tatar-Mongol invasions and rule prior to the centralization and the tsardom of Russia brought elements of oriental traditionalism

---

[2]Prior to that date the Russian Federation had already incorporated on a national autonomy basis the Bashkir (1919), Tatar (1920), Karelian (1920), Chuvash (1920), Kirgiz (later Kazakh) (1920), Udmurt (1920), Mari (1920), Kalmyk (1920), Gorskaya (1920), Daghestan (1921), Komi (1921), Kabardinian (1921), the Crimea (1921), Buryat (1922), Chechen (1922), Yakut (1922), and Cherkess (1922) republics and regions.

[3]The effects of emancipation were far from uniform. The regions of Ural and the Don were settlements of the Cossacks, largely self-governing communities of colonists who owed certain military service obligations to the Crown. In the Baltics serfdom was eliminated much earlier.

[4]Outward-looking Westernizers, enlightened monarchs (Catherine the Great, Alexander II), and aristocracy (Decembrists) opposed the conservative Slavophiles. More recently, outward-looking Gorbachev confronted inward-looking Yeltsin. The ultimate Slavophile revival is associated with novelist Alexander Solzhenitsyn's return to Russia in 1994.

such as subordination and passivity, as well as dislike of taxes, which were regarded as a forced tribute. Russian egalitarian communalism was reasserted after the defeat of the Tatars by Tsar Ivan the Terrible in the mid-1500s. Traditionalism and Russian Orthodox Christianity, merged with tsarist paternalism on the one hand and progressive occidentalism on the other, were the blessing and the curse of the Russian Empire, reinforcing cultural, economic, and political dualism. The economy split along the agrarian vs. industrial divide and later between introverted vs. extroverted economic development. This dualism emerged during the Soviet period as the divide between the official political economy and the informal illegal market economy.

The Formative Years of the Soviet Economy

Except for the brief period of *War Communism* (1918–1921), the ultimate wartime command economy with rationing and no money, the socialist economy in Soviet Russia did not start until the First Five-Year plan in 1928. However, a socialist foundation was laid in 1917 with the decrees nationalizing land and banks and authorizing workers' control.

The start of the socialist economy was delayed in 1921 by the *New Economic Policy* (NEP), which sought to repair a conflict between the peasantry, alienated by wartime requisitioning, and the workers. The NEP was a strategic retreat from the socialist agenda and allowed limited markets. Partial reprivatization of prior nationalized industries and banks took place. As a result the recovery of agriculture surpassed that of industry and was perceived as a threat to the goals of the revolution. The NEP was thus aborted, and the Soviet economy rejected the use of market forces and turned to command central planning.

Command Economy: The Only Choice?

Launching the Model

The centrally planned command economy was introduced in the Soviet Union where five economic subsystems were present:

1. Self-subsistence with no market exchange (commune).
2. Private ownership with no hired labor (individual proprietorships in services and artisanships, family farms).
3. Markets based on private ownership with hired labor (market capitalist economy as privatized corporations, mainly in light industries and trade).
4. Markets based on public ownership (state capitalist market economy in intermediate machinery and foreign trade).
5. Public ownership without markets (socialist direct allocation of resources in heavy industry, raw materials production, transport and communications, and public utilities) based on nationalization decrees in 1917–1918.

This economic pluralism produced political splintering in the ruling Communist Party. Leon Trotsky advocated superindustrialization in the Soviet Union that would lead worldwide permanent communist revolution. The faction of ''peasants-enrich yourselves,'' led by Nikolai Bukharin, called for liberalization of domestic and international markets. Decentralizers such as Nikolai Tomsky proposed a greater role for trade unions in existing state enterprises.

Joseph Stalin supported ''socialism in one separately taken country.'' He outmaneuvered and physically exterminated his opponents and his program won, establishing the cult of Stalin. Stalin played to the uniqueness of Russia and its mission to lead other nations. Assuming paternalism, Stalin reasserted economic traditionalism in the guise of revolutionary socialism.[5]

Implementing ''socialism in one country'' implied speedy industrialization for self-sufficiency, military buildup, and social transformation from above of the agro-industrial economy into an urban industrial one. The concept disallowed market allocation of resources prone to underemployment. The state monopolized foreign relations, closed the economy through restricted foreign trade, and limited trade specialization.

Accelerated industrialization accepted unbalanced economic growth[6] and placed heavy emphasis on producer and military goods at the expense of agriculture. Pressure for superindustrialization was reinforced by the perceived hostility of Britain, Japan, and Poland and by the Nationalists in China turning on the Communists.

The pending war scare favored a big leap instead of gradualism. The debate on industrialization between the *geneticists* and the *teleologists* reflected upon the feasibility of economic engineering. The geneticists argued that planning could guide the market, as with indicative planning (see Chapters 6 and 7). Representatives of this group, such as Nikolai Kondratiev, argued for the objectivity of economic laws and viewed planning as a navigating tool. Teleologists, for example Vladimir Strumilin, leaned towards social engineering with allocation of resources determined by planners and constrained by the physical limits of the economy. Geneticists assumed movement toward a general market equilibrium, whereas teleologists pursued a biased economy with an imposed equilibrium reflecting the preferences of the ruling elite. Teleology sought to eliminate markets that bred capitalism.

Superindustrialization favored the teleologists who asserted long-run plans and opposed market forces. Central comprehensive planning—the First Five-Year plan was inaugurated in 1928—ensured political control over the

---

[5]Russian philosopher Nikolai Berdyaev wrote that Russian revolution was fated to be totalitarian with the Russian mentality of ''all or nothing.'' Nikolai Berdyaev, *Russian Thought in the 19th and 20th Centuries* (Amsterdam: Martinus Nijhoff, 1947).

[6]The idea of unbalanced growth was formulated by Evgeny Preobrazhensky who advocated *primitive socialist accumulation* of capital through savings extracted from agriculture. Bukharin defended the balanced growth model as one that avoided discrimination against peasants and allowed for both state and private property in industry and agriculture respectively. Shanin proposed unbalanced growth focused on agriculture operating in a market environment with investment planned only in the short run.

diverse republics, grouping them into economic regions to meet nationwide production needs and forging their interdependence.

Soviet taut planning prioritized industry over agriculture for sociopolitical reasons, emphasized regional specialization and deemphasized republic-level diversification, and established state monopolies in key industries. This model was to complete the socialist transition in the shortest time and to eliminate the alien-to-socialism patriarchal and entrepreneurial subsystems. To do so Stalin launched collectivization in agriculture, forcing collective ownership upon peasants as a stepping stone to comprehensive public ownership. The success of Stalin's industrialization turned out to be a disaster for agriculture in the Soviet Union, which developed for the most part an overindustrialized and overurbanized economy with an inadequate agricultural sector that was no longer self-sufficient.[7]

Soviet Central Planning: The Beginning

Central to Stalin's command economy was central administrative planning to eliminate the ''frivolity'' and ''waste'' of market forces, thus pushing structural and social reorganization of the economy. Central planners steered individual sectors to assigned targets and instructed every enterprise, industry, and region in what steps to take, when, and how. In every economy the issue of proportionate allocation of resources is crucial. Central planning established these proportions of production and exchange a priori, following the political and social decisions of the ruling party Politburo.

Soviet economists claimed that central socialist planning had superior foresight compared to the alleged myopia of short-run profit maximization under capitalist markets. The structural imbalance of industrialization was to be compensated for in the long run by future increases of production in the deprioritized sectors, consumer and agricultural goods.

The first Soviet plans were pressure plans relying on mass enthusiasm with little use of material incentives. They played a dual role, allocating resources and setting targets for economic growth. This duality was reflected in the debate over whether the First Five-Year Plan would have a forecasting or command nature. The First Five-Year Plan actually conceived the command economy. The preparatory stages (1925–1926) used indicative planning to generate ''control numbers,'' spelling out various economic possibilities. The Five-Year Plan aggregated adjustable annual plans. In general, Five-Year Plans were more of a forecast nature while One-Year Plans were more of a command nature.

The Central Planning Board (*Gosplan*) was responsible for plans feasibility studies and for research on the methodology of balancing nationwide proportions. But the issue of adequate information posed a critical challenge.

---

[7]Adequacy of agriculture in certain individual republics such as Ukraine, was quite good. However, redistributive practices to meet national demand created persistent shortages in them. During collectivization there was massive killing of animals by peasants and a horrible famine, centered on Ukraine, killed millions of peasants, in addition to state-ordered purges.

With limited markets information was incomplete, and thus 100 percent implementation of plans could not be guaranteed. Target planning emphasized specific sectors and forced unbalanced growth—the absolute numbers of output were deemphasized and relative indicators of economic dynamics were elevated. Ultimately a philosophy of using planning as a disciplinary tool prevailed, marking the victory of politics over economics.

The First Five-Year plan stated a goal to catch up with capitalist industrial countries. Optimistic annual rates of industrial growth were put at 21 to 25 percent and pessimistic ones at 17 to 21 percent (based on domestic prices). The average rate of growth during the planned period was claimed to be 21.6 percent.[8] The speed of industrialization was puzzling given that rates of growth were targeted while generally ignoring the resource base. But this performance reinforced planning as a mobilizing device.

The success of the initial industrialization push cannot be solely attributed to central planning. It was accomplished at the tremendous cost of forced collectivization and a major decline in living standards. Siphoning consumer resources into investment dramatically lowered private consumption below historical standards of other economies with the same levels of per capita GDP. From 1928 to 1937 the share of private consumption declined from 64.7 percent to 52.5 percent, a decline that took 40 years in Germany, 50 years in England, 30 years in the United States, and over 50 years in Japan. This decline in private consumption led to the shortage economy characterized by chronic plan underfulfillment in consumer and agricultural goods.

The pressure economy with taut planning mobilized resources for investment: the USSR invested a quarter of GDP, higher than in any other country. Concentrated investment in growth-supporting sectors was based on domestic savings with virtually no borrowing from abroad.[9] Central planning emerged as a political instrument of superindustrialization and was effective in that respect during initial extensive growth.

Industrialization produced an extensive bureaucracy in planning and executive institutions interested in perpetuating its political and economic power. Command industrialization formed the basis for the merger between the party, the planners, and the ministerial and local government bureaucracies, resulting in the formation of a new class, the *nomenklatura*,[10] which presided over this vertical hierarchy.

---

[8]B. V. Zembatova, *Planirovanje: Prostyi i Slozhnyi Istiny,* (Moskva: Nauka, 1990), p. 75. The numbers supplied by Soviet scholars usually exaggerated the growth performance because of elevated industrial prices and generally distorted statistics. According to alternative estimates in the West, Soviet growth performance was still very high, averaging between 4.5 percent and 11.9 percent between 1928 and 1937. Per capita rates of growth in Japan were higher between 1920 and 1930, and Germany matched them during the postwar period.

[9]Purchases of Western machinery and equipment in the early 1930s, financed by agricultural exports, were phased out after 1931, coinciding with the closing of the economy deemed self-sufficient.

[10]The nomenklatura consisted of party members appointed to particular government jobs.

The prewar five-year plans asserted the administrative, command, taut, and priority nature of Soviet planning. Modifications of the planning system commenced with Stalin's death in 1953 and started the cycle of reforms.

Soviet Central Planning and Its Implementation

THE PUZZLE OF THE SOVIET ECONOMY

Here are several contradictions of the Soviet economy:

1. There was no unemployment, however nobody worked.
2. Nobody worked, however the plan was always fulfilled.
3. The plan was always fulfilled, however there were always shortages.
4. There were always shortages, however the country was creating the land of plenty.
5. The country was creating the land of plenty, however there were always lines.
6. Everybody knew the way around queueing, however everybody was unhappy.
7. Everybody was unhappy, however political decisions were approved of unanimously.

—Old Soviet parable

The counterposition of planning and market as allocative mechanisms has a long history in economics. However, planning and market are not perfect allocative substitutes. Their goals are different. Planning is concerned with growth through expanded reproduction and particular investment and deemphasizes consumption. The market seeks to satisfy individual consumer preferences. Soviet planning prioritized investment to catch up with the West industrially and militarily. Therefore planning ignored static efficiency in favor of high rates of economic growth.

Planning was implemented in the Soviet Union through a system of annual, medium-term (5 years), and perspective (15 years or more) plans. The latter two were highly aggregated to enable planners to cope with their task, namely to translate party policy into a developmental strategy. Annual plans were drafted by individual enterprises and disaggregated in order to balance resources with projected product needs. Central planning fostered enterprise *gigantomania* (the building of overly large production facilities). Over time this led to industrial and regional monopolization, later impeding market reforms.

Implementation of plans was complicated by constant informal bargaining by enterprises to lower their quotas due to the infamous *ratchet effect*. This effect arose from an increase in planned assignment if the previous plan achieved its target. Such achievement was viewed as evidence of hidden resources and insufficiently taut targets. This environment made managers bargain to lower output quotas and lie about available resources.

Another practice, *storming,* arose from holding off production followed by strenuous attempts to meet production obligations at the last minute. This practice reflected anticipated shortages in resources due to informal bargaining and plan adjustments with subsequent hoarding of inputs for the final push. In this environment plentiful resources coexisted with constant paranoia about their shortage. Under storming, plan implementation resulted in massive production of substandard goods, further aggravating shortages. Between episodes of storming, officially employed labor did little. The problems of plan implementation in the USSR raise the question of whether the Soviet economy was centrally planned or merely centrally managed.

The retail surface of the Soviet economy used markets in which commodities were bought and sold according to prices using money. The origin and roles of prices, however, were different from those of a market economy because they did not determine production or resource allocation.

Planners used prices to ensure compliance with plans and for continuous control over plan implementation. Although resources were allocated mostly in physical terms, prices permitted comparative valuation. The valuation of physical amounts concerned sales, costs, profits, and tax payments. Soviet domestic prices were distorted because they reflected planners' priorities in distribution and production and not relative scarcities. This feature of Soviet pricing disabled rational decision making by producers.

Wholesale prices were distorted the most; the planners used these prices to balance intersectoral outputs and to provide for comparison of alternative production mixes based on different technologies. In agriculture, government procurement prices for designated quotas promoted specific crops and controlled collective farms. Artificially low procurement prices entrenched farmers' indebtedness and their dependence on state credits.

Retail prices offset the consequences of the socialist principle of distribution, from each according to his ability to each according to his work, that produced inequality in the income distribution. The government sought to diminish this inequality through two policies: free provision of public goods (health care and education) and fixing prices for goods of mass consumption (food, housing, transportation) at low levels while raising prices for luxury goods.[11] Fixed low prices for staples allowed entrepreneurial individuals to engage in arbitrage selling to higher bidders in the shadow economy. Thus retail pricing ultimately aggravated inequality. Furthermore, provision of public goods was segregated by location, social stratum, and workplace, thus violating the principle of equity.

Prices were very sticky. Thus the gap between prices and scarcity values increased over time and lowered the effectiveness of planning. The idea of the planned creation of a socialist market in which efficiency of production rose with diminishing inequality in income distribution failed miserably. But it

---

[11]Individual cars were regarded as violating collectivism and thus were classified as luxury goods, prohibitively priced.

succeeded in producing a second economy in which market forces partially corrected artificial shortages. Prices in second economy markets reflected relative scarcities.

Soviet Agriculture: Peculiarity of the Soviet Model[12]

In times past Russia was the breadbasket of Europe. From 1909 to 1913, Russian grain exports amounted to around 30 percent of world grain exports. But after the revolution agricultural performance dwindled.

Three categories of agricultural producers survived: state, collective, and private farms. This sector had a special history of its own with regard to prices, incentives, planning, and party policies. Stalin's industrialization was contingent on the mass collectivization of peasants and the expropriation of the well-off peasants (*kulaks*).

The collective farm (*kolkhoz*) was a pseudocooperative, with elected[13] management ensuring a supply of agricultural products to the state at minimum cost. This goal was reached by keeping income of peasants at subsistence levels maintained by household plots and individually owned livestock.[14] Collective farms were exploited by low procurement prices and by overcharging for state-owned tractors and machinery. Consumer goods and utilities were sold to kolkhozy at high prices or made unavailable at any price (electrical energy was denied for awhile to collective farmers as a low priority, for example). Until 1966 collective farmers did not have guaranteed wages and were paid in "labor days" calculated from the time estimated to accomplish specific tasks. Labor days payment was calculated arbitrarily and variable depending on regions, seasons, and specific farms. Generally it was in agroproducts and remained uncertain before actual disbursement.

Sovkhozy, or state farms, were set up as "factories in the fields," and were run under more favorable policies. When underpaid in delivery prices, these farms were compensated by subsidies. The farmers were state employees and got a guaranteed wage. They were given access to better inputs at wholesale prices. The asymmetric coexistence of the two forms of property and institutional arrangements in agriculture served the sociopolitical goal of crowding out entrepreneurship in the traditional sector, which tended to persist in the collective farms. Economically it led to a dramatic decline in productivity and in absolute production—in collective farms because of price discrimination and compulsory deliveries, in state farms because of subsidization

---

[12]For a discussion of Soviet agriculture see Chapter 3 in Marshall Goldman, *USSR in Crisis: The Failure of an Economic System* (New York: W. W. Norton, 1983).

[13]Elections were generally perfunctory because nomenklatura candidates ran unopposed.

[14]Urban people came to believe that peasants were better off, living off the land. The city joke went that a peasant came to the city to exchange his money, bringing a bag of it. Upon counting it the bank clerk found that it was one ruble short of 100,000 rubles. "What a pity," says the peasant, "I took the wrong bag. The other one was exactly 100,000."

of farms that operated at a loss. The failure of Soviet agriculture necessitated the first reforms initiated after Stalin's death.

The third category of agricultural producers included the individual farmer and family. Economically individual farmers are generally in the private sector; however in Soviet reality they occupied a unique segment of economic activity. Land in "auxiliary household plots" was not privately owned; it was cultivated only by peasants and state employees in rural and suburban areas. Livestock was privately owned but usually pastured on collective or state land. Individuals worked on these plots for themselves and owned their produce. But they also worked for the collective or state enterprises, creating a tension in dividing time between private and collective. Even though private plots in the USSR occupied at their height in the 1970s a maximum of only 4 percent of arable land, they accounted for 40 percent of its fruits, berries, and eggs; over 60 percent of potatoes; and about 30 percent of its milk, meat, and vegetables.[15]

Individual plots were a legal element of the "second economy," and their products traded for money. Generally second economy activity was a crime.[16] But individual agricultural plots were declared legal economically although they were for personal gain. The difference between lawful and unlawful economic practices in agriculture was murky, allowing for dual use of state or collectively owned property and outright pilfering. *Shadow economy* would be a better characterization for this type of economic activity because it did not circumvent the official economy; rather it alleviated the peasants' underconsumption.

Timofeev maintains that "black market is the art of survival in the circle of restrictions and prohibitions: the state enforces kolkhoz, the peasants sneak in the individual plot . . . the authorities want one meat-free day a week, the people start breeding rabbits in their apartments, the state provides for an incompetent doctor for free, the people bring a hefty gift and see a good doctor and without any wait".[17] The symbiosis between socialized property and individual gain pursuit produced a Soviet economic mentality of disregarding the law that handicaps market reforms. This mentality led to "a pursuit of gain without reckoning the responsibility of a proprietor and the acceptance of kleptocracy."

Agriculture in the classical Soviet command model was deprioritized, resulting in dependence on grain imports. This dependence questioned the ability of the model to maintain itself as a closed economy since it was unable

---

[15]Goldman, *USSR in Crisis,* p. 83. Private plots were spread unevenly among regions. Liberalization in the late 1940s was followed by a crackdown in 1959. Private plots were more common in Transcaucasia and in the Baltics. There, individual plots accounted for almost 50 percent of agricultural output, 43.6 percent in Lithuania specifically (Lev Timofeev, *Cherny Rynok kak Politicheskaya Sistema,* [Vilnius: VIMO, 1993], p. 24).

[16]In 1963 the death penalty was applied to economic crimes.

[17]Timofeev, *Cherny Rynok kak Politicheskaya Sistema,* p. 13.

to feed itself. The increasing role of imports inspired reforms in the export sector and overall.

Closed Economy: Command Trade Isolationism

One reason the Soviet Union lasted as long as it did was that Stalin's initial model was the closed economy, enforced much longer than most features of the system. Its ideological underpinning was Stalin's idea of an autarkic socialist country, encircled by hostile imperialist countries. The anarchy of the world markets could undermine the effectiveness of central planning. Therefore domestic firms were ''protected'' from foreign competition and world prices.[18]

The state assumed authority over foreign trade and foreign currency transactions through state monopolies, respectively the all-union Ministry of Foreign Trade and *Vneshtorgbank* (Bank for Foreign Trade). The state monopoly of foreign trade was as old as the Soviet Union. Even during the NEP liberalization this monopoly was maintained. Moreover this state monopoly restated the overall authority of the all-union Center over dealings abroad by individual republics. If a factory in Minsk (Byelorussia) could not buy from a factory in Kiev (Ukraine) without planners' consent, it could not possibly buy from Warsaw or Lyon either. The policy of self-sufficiency set a minimal role for imports only of goods not procurable domestically.

Imports and exports were determined by planners through balancing domestic inputs with projected outputs, matching potential discrepancies. Export production derived from the need to pay for imports. Producers of exportable goods did not have direct relationships with foreign buyers, but dealt exclusively with foreign trade bureaucracies organized at the industrial level. Domestic producers did not understand export revenues because official statistics showed them in ruble values whereas actual exports were in foreign currencies converted into rubles at the official rate, notorious for its arbitrariness.[19]

Foreign trade relations were mostly bilateral and highly politicized. In 1948 the USSR cut its oil exports to Yugoslavia by 50 percent as the country broke away from the Soviet bloc. China, the largest purchaser of Soviet petroleum from 1955 to 1961, found its imports curtailed sharply during the Sino-Soviet split. Oil shipments to Castro in 1968 were held back when he became too independent. In late 1958 oil deliveries to Finland were halted until the country came up with a president more acceptable to Moscow.[20]

---

[18]The oil shock of 1973–1974 caused world prices to quadruple but had no effect on Soviet domestic prices, which were revised only in 1982.

[19]The USSR was a founding member of the International Monetary Fund as a participant of the 1944 Bretton Woods conference. However it soon withdrew and resorted to the abandoned gold standard in foreign currency transactions.

[20]Goldman, *USSR in Crisis,* p. 138. It has been revealed that Finland's longtime president, Urho Kekkonen, installed due to this crisis, was a KGB agent.

The use of trade for greater integration with the socialist satellites came through the Council of Mutual Economic Assistance (CMEA), known as Comecon, founded in 1949.[21] Briefly after World War II, the East European countries pursued diverse models. But by the end of the 1940s the USSR had asserted its dominance over the region and established Comecon as a multilateral body to coerce these countries to adopt a uniform strategy of communist industrialization in line with the USSR. This strategy incorporated two principle characteristics: (1) extensive development with a priority of capital goods at the expense of consumer goods, (2) autarkic focus on import substitution and minimal dependence on western markets.

Industries in CMEA countries developed dependence on Soviet energy resources and deliveries of raw materials. The idea of a socialist international division of labor suggested intraindustrial rather than interindustrial specialization. This led to a collective isolationism from world markets and a tendency to create a socialist alternative to international capitalist trade.

On the positive side, intra-CMEA specialization acknowledged the benefits of trade for economic development. On the negative side, the international socialist division of labor was shaped through concerted planning rather than markets. Plan coordination sought tighter integration of individual economies and explored supranational plans.[22]

The problems of inefficiency and noncompetitiveness of individual national industries escalated in the mid-1960s, leading to declining intrabloc trade. These problems called for changes in mutual trade and with the West. However for the Soviet Union intra-CMEA trade had become critically important: In 1966–1970 more than half of USSR imports came from East European countries, including 85 percent of ships, boats, and marine equipment; 60 percent of railway equipment; and over 50 percent of machinery for light industries.

Soviet trade with the West was also very politicized and instrumental in systemic confrontation. Liberalization of trade with the West was brought about by technological backwardness in the course of the arms race. In the early 1970s Soviet foreign trade was an alternative to the Cold War and a means of relaxation of tension. The decade of trade promotion ended in 1979 with the Soviet invasion of Afghanistan.

The benefits of trade during that decade made the Soviet Union addicted to readily operational ''turn-key'' plants and consumer goods purchased at the height of oil prices. Adventurist foreign policy in developing countries

---

[21]CMEA membership comprised the USSR, Czechoslovakia, Hungary, Poland, East Germany, Romania, Bulgaria, and Albania (which withdrew in 1961). Mongolia, Cuba, and Vietnam joined later. Yugoslavia was an associate member, and North Korea belonged to many of its subordinate organizations.

[22]Khrushchev proposed to make the CMEA supranational in the early 1960s. In 1971 it adopted a ''Comprehensive Program for the Extension and Improvement of Collaboration and the Development of Socialist Economic Integration of the CMEA Countries,'' which stepped toward Lenin's vision of a single world economy with one plan.

contradicted the economic gains from trade. That divided Soviet pro-Western technocratic cosmopolites, who advocated the economic and technological benefits of further trade, from prosocialist hardliners, who put the politics of global expansionism above the economics of international commerce.

The artificiality of social engineering in the Soviet command economy revealed itself from its very beginning during the planning debate of the late 1920s. Staunch ideology and its political enforcement by all means, including massive purges of dissenters, kept the model alive. However, outward expansion of Stalin's model made the political economy of command socialism vulnerable and ultimately discredited when its inherent dualism came into the open.

Reform Cycle: Can a Command Economy Be Reformed from Within?[23]

Reluctant Reform Thinking

The Soviet command economy epitomized pervasive protectionism and paternalism. Enterprises were shielded against insolvency and bankruptcy through centralized subsidies. The people were protected against economic fluctuations and the possibility of unemployment through coordinated public education and mandatory assignment to guaranteed jobs. The state monopoly of foreign trade protected domestic firms from external shocks and competition with foreign goods. The network of interrepublican commodity flows created a sense of certainty in domestic trade and increasing interdependence. A similar arrangement was fostered in intra-CMEA trade. This economic stability lacked impetus to change.

The terms *reform and reformism* in Soviet parlance were until recently ideologically unacceptable because they connoted dangerous Western imports.[24] Ideological fervor called for perfecting the Soviet ''most advanced model.'' With the death of Stalin rethinking of Soviet economic accomplishments and their costs took place. The process of political destalinization gradually spilled into economics, especially after Khrushchev's 1956 speech to the 20th Party Congress.

The strengths of Stalin's model were the mobilization of resources for industrial catch-up, the development of a military–industrial complex, and the postwar recovery through extensive growth. However its weaknesses became more pronounced in the more complex postwar economy as resources for

---

[23]See Gertrude E. Schroeder, ''Soviet Economic 'Reform' Decrees: More Steps on the Treadmill,'' in *Soviet Economy in a Time of Change,* Joint Economic Committee, Congress of the United States (Washington: USGPO, 1982), pp. 65–89.

[24]Lenin villified Kautsky and Bernstein (Chapter 3) as ''traitors'' and ''renegades'' for their reformist ''revisionism.''

extensive growth approached exhaustion. This arose from the undervaluation of the opportunity costs of planned priorities with absent appropriate criteria to assess economic performance. Ubiquitous protectionism downplayed economic incentives and prevented subordinates from making well-substantiated decisions. The vertical institutional structure compartmentalized responsibilities and ministerial and parochial economic behavior.

As a result a chain reaction followed when a substandard component of one enterprise caused the quality of the finished commodity to go down and no parties bore responsibility. Ministerial compartmentalism[25] also triggered destruction of the resource base due to improper exploitation, collateral damage to agriculture from irrigation and water management projects, and the like.[26]

With greater complexity of the economy goals became more varied, coordination became more challenging, and control over subordinate activities and information verification became more difficult. With greater production possibilities and emerging resources constraints, *efficient* use loomed large as a desideratum.

First Attempts at Reforms

Nikita Khrushchev, Communist Party Secretary during 1953–1964, initiated destalinization in domestic politics and economics. In foreign policy he embraced the idea of peaceful coexistence and competition between socialism and capitalism. This policy revoked Stalin's idea of a bipolar world of two irreconcilable hostile camps and introduced ''limited sovereignty of socialist states,'' recognizing possible separate roads in Eastern Europe.

These new concepts imposed increased standards of well-being and consumption without cutting back on the military, which maintained control over the Soviet bloc. The Soviet economy was to deliver increasing amounts of guns and butter.[27] The USSR also was to serve as a model for the Third World experiencing decolonization. These circumstances prompted the first round of reforms in three areas: agriculture, which failed to recover from the losses of the war as fast as industry; administrative decentralization through delegating authority for decision making to regions and away from ministries, and an aggressive use of foreign trade and military and industrial assistance to aid regimes sympathetic to the USSR.

---

[25]Executive power was exercised by industry-based ministries overseeing production of a specific industry nationwide. Organizationally these ministries were vertically subordinate to Gosplan and the Council of Ministers and ultimately to the Central Committee of the Communist Party and its ruling Politburo.

[26]Massive marsh drainage projects in Byelorussia (now Belarus) increased the acreage of arable land, but caused bad floods due to the elevation of underground waters. The greatest such disaster was the shrinkage of the Aral Sea in Central Asia due to diverting water for cotton production.

[27]Riots in Poland in 1956 were suppressed with the threat of using Soviet troops. Soviet armed forces were used the same year in Hungary where an uprising got out of control.

This first round of reforms demonstrated the inherent flaws typical of the reform cycle prior to the Soviet collapse, namely attempting to change the systemic mechanism without altering its principle.

Khrushchev sought to raise his political stature in the political succession after Stalin's death through agricultural reforms,[28] including switching from levies in kind on privately owned cattle and other animals to reduced monetary taxes, with the state raising procurement prices and canceling old debts. These moves promoted marketization of agricultural products and increased economic incentives. As a result the income of the average peasant family rose almost 400 percent between 1953 and 1954.[29] Simultaneously Khrushchev initiated the *virgin lands* campaign in the classic Stalinist style of extensive growth, bringing 2.3 million hectares in Kazakhstan under the plow, arbitrarily sowing it to wheat and corn in disregard of climate and soil conditions.[30] Khrushchev's penchant for favoring agricultural spending was disliked by the heavy industrial and military complexes.

To alleviate the burden of comprehensive control by central bureaucratic authorities Khrushchev replaced nearly all central ministries (except defense and nuclear power) in 1957 with regional economic councils (*sovnarkhozy*) that gave those regions and individual republics their first taste of partial economic autonomy. This decentralization was undertaken without challenging the authority of central planning. On the contrary, decentralized management was to be coupled with new emphasis on central planning and continuing discouragement of horizontal relations among regions. In 1961, 105 initially created regional councils were reorganized into 17, attesting to creeping recentralization. The 1963 creation of the Supreme Council of National Economy as supercoordinator of regional councils under Gosplan aegis was another indication.

After the failure of administrative decentralization and with the country facing declining productivity, a marginal move towards economic decentralization began through an *experimental* use of the profit motive. In 1962 the Communist Party newspaper *Pravda* carried an article by Evsei Liberman proposing to make individual enterprises efficient, giving labor and management a share in profits, and requiring self-accounting and awareness of costs. Readiness to experiment was forced by budgetary problems and the resulting threat of hidden inflation coming into the open.[31]

---

[28]Khrushchev faced opposition after Stalin's death from Lavrenti Beria, Georgi Malenkov, and Lazar Kaganovich and needed quick economic success.

[29]Woodford McClellan, *Russia: A History of the Soviet Period* (Englewood Cliffs: Prentice Hall, 1986), p. 234.

[30]The plowing of vast territories unprotected by forests led to loss of fertile topsoil due to windstorms and subsequently to major declines in crops in 1961 and 1963, undermining Khrushchev's support. He was later labeled a "hare-brained schemer."

[31]Monetary reform in 1961 exchanged 10 old rubles for one new one, disguising an up to 50 percent price hike on consumer goods and food in particular that produced serious unrest in a number of industrial cities, with open violence in Novocherkassk.

Use of profit incentives was to improve planning instead of causing the state to abandon it, raising its scientific level and optimizing plans implementation. The principle of planning was to remain with implementation to be monitored and controlled through monetary levers such as profits, credits, and bonuses with planned prices. This reform considered the monetary valuation of economic performance instead of using physical amounts of output as a measure, and allowed possible feedback from sales to output decisions. Enterprises experienced greater freedom in day-to-day operations. But these reforms were undermined by the rigidity of state-determined prices and the inflexibility of wages still tied to output per worker or gross output.

Reforms and Economic Stagnation

Following the fall of Khrushchev, regional decentralization was abandoned and in 1965[32] the reconversion to the branch principle of industrial management took place during the early years of Leonid Brezhnev's tenure (1964–1982). Newly created bureaucracies exercised tutelage over enterprises, trimming enterprise management leeway. Officials claimed that economic methods of management should not decrease the role of administrative methods. To reassert administrative authority a larger role for five-year and long-range plans targeting new scientific technologies was imposed.

Accelerating reform in Hungary and Czechoslovakia in the late 1960s tested the limits of Soviet reform tolerance. Putting down the ''Prague Spring'' movement in Czechoslovakia in 1968 reemphasized the limited sovereignty of Soviet East European satellites. Under the threat of radical deviations from the Soviet model, including withdrawals from the Warsaw Pact, the USSR reinforced socialist internationalism and socialist economic integration through more extensive coordination of national plans. That reversed the reform movement and during the 1970s led to recentralized amalgamation of enterprises into large associations to facilitate central control.

The ambivalence of reform practices led to entrenchment of the traditional features of the Soviet model and grass roots distrust of reform proposals. The monopoly of the Communist Party over political and economic decisions and state ownership were systemic obstacles to reforms. Reform initiatives remained in the hands of the party and government leaders, making them more politically than economically driven.

Gorbachev's ''Revolution''

When Mikhail Gorbachev took over the Communist Party and the Soviet state in 1985 after a brief interregnum of inept successors to Brezhnev, many people inside and outside the USSR pictured him as a radical reformer, even as a

---

[32]The Alexei Kosygin reforms of 1965 recentralized economic bureaucracy and reorganized industry into superassociations of enterprises and research institutes for scientific planning even while temporarily instituting some of the enterprise-level profit accounting practices proposed by Liberman.

revolutionary. But initially after assuming power Gorbachev demonstrated continuity with his predecessors on all but a few issues.[33] The Soviet growth rate had been declining steadily. Soviet official statistics reported annual growth rates of 10.3 percent during the 1950s, declining to 4.2 percent during the 1960s, further decreasing to 2.1 percent in the 1970s, with a 0.6 percent rate of growth in the 1980s.[34]

With plummeting Soviet economic performance and a widening technological gap with the West, Gorbachev's initial strategy was to forge greater political and economic unity with Warsaw Pact countries and proceed with concerted reforms. To secure controlled progress Gorbachev made new overtures to the West to relax tension and achieve a new détente. To justify these moves the "new thinking" was developed, emphasizing interdependence of nations and the challenge of global problems such as the burden of the arms race, environmental problems, and issues of the less developed countries. However this new thinking did not affect Soviet ideology, which adhered to the fashionable idea of "socialism with a human face." Gorbachev's promotion of East European reform nevertheless demonstrated a foreign policy in which economics outweighed politics. He foresaw reducing costs for the USSR to support loyal regimes and refocusing on urgent internal needs of economic restructuring (*perestroika*).

During Gorbachev's first years came innovations that foreshadowed the radical reforms of the 1990s. First, he raised the issue of *real* socialism contrary to the *ideal* pictured by official social sciences and statistics. He demystified the Soviet economy and opened debate over the divergence between existing practices and theoretical socialism in his policy of openness (*glasnost*). Secondly, he opened up the economy, hoping that international competition would provide incentives to change. He eliminated the state monopoly of foreign trade to end the insulation of Soviet enterprises from international trade, understanding the success of gradual opening in China where trade spurred growth.

Greater openness about debilities of the Soviet economy was forced upon Gorbachev by the 1986 Chernobyl disaster, which demonstrated the failure of the Soviet model to provide energy without jeopardizing the environment and human lives. The initial reaction of the leadership to the nuclear plant explosion was to keep it secret and to pronounce all attempts to publicize it "an imperialist plot to discredit the Soviet Union."[35] The international externalities of the disaster and public uproar led the leadership to admit the magnitude of the accident and to invite foreign specialists to aid with its containment and

---

[33]Schroeder, "Soviet Economic 'Reform' Decrees," pp. 219–41.

[34]Daniel Gros and Alfred Steinherr, *Economic Reform in the Soviet Union: Pas de Deux between Disintegration and Macroeconomic Destabilization,* Princeton Studies in International Finance, No. 71 (Princeton: Princeton University, 1991) p. 1.

[35]The most ridiculous explanation given post factum to justify silencing the accident was "not to spoil May Day celebration for the Soviet people."

implications. The following investigation resulted in massive exposure of numerous other environmental disasters and economic mismanagement incidents, leading to questions about the ability of the system to provide economic development without ecocide.[36]

Radicalization of reform accelerated with popular realization of the debilities of the Soviet system, which varied in different republics due to different economic experiences prior to imposition of the Soviet model. The Baltic republics led with their painful secession in 1989, marking a turning point in the historical integrity of the Soviet Union.

Radical reform started in 1990 with open debate over transition to a market economy through dismantling planning and introducing different kinds of property relations to promote individual entrepreneurship. The thrust was to replace the vertical hierarchy of planning by horizontal market linkages through direct interaction between demand and supply, thus implementing economic decentralization. With the fall of central authority and the increasing alienation of the Communist Party from economic matters a multitude of plans for introducing markets appeared, echoing the debate of the 1920s. Inside reformers proposed scenarios: partial destatization of industrial property, or forceful emphasis on privatization first, or decontrol of prices and self-adjusting institutional reconfiguration to transform monopolistic firms into self-accounting and autonomous competitive decision makers. Some proposals (Shatalin's Plan of transformation in "500 days," for example) reflected fear of the frustration of previous gradual reforms and called for freeing markets in one sweeping move.

The decentralization of economic decision making stimulated individual republics' governments and the centrifugal trends in the CMEA, bringing its ultimate demise. The disintegration of the Soviet Union in 1991 and the dissolution of Comecon the year before triggered fragmentation of the reform movement and the rise of economic nationalism, again diverting the reform process into political realms.

Away from the Centrally Planned Economy: To Where?

The Soviet economic system was based on the following principles:

- State planning for state-owned industries, demand structuring by the state budget and state-determined monetary policy with a one-tier banking system.
- Production in a state-run system of mostly monopolistic firms, producing a narrow range of goods at state-administered prices, and facing monopolistic suppliers.

---

[36]Murray Feshbach and Alfred Friendly, Jr., *Ecocide in the USSR: Health and Nature under Siege* (New York: Basic Books, 1992).

- Risk-averse managers/administrators reluctant to innovate or introduce quality improvements who aimed at hoarding material factor inputs to easily fulfill quantitatively specified state plans.
- A full employment guarantee and as a consequence the systemic impossibility of firms going bankrupt— a ''soft budget constraint'' policy.
- A state monopoly in foreign trade with administered prices and exchange rates reflecting the inconvertibility of the domestic currency.
- Fiscal revenues generated mainly by turnover taxes and mandatory transfers of profits used to subsidize insolvent firms and prices for mass staple goods and for providing public goods.[37]

Command central planning was justified by its alleged ability to accomplish sustained rates of growth and catch-ups with advanced industrial countries. The slowdown in growth rates from the mid-1970s to their virtual stagnation in the 1980s, along with environmental abuse, attested to central planning's ineptitude in dealing with a complex industrial economy's need for constant adjustments.

Monopolistic producers and risk-averse managers lacked impetus to innovate, which led to technological backwardness. Full employment guarantees disguised hidden unemployment, causing increased labor-intensive production. Soft budget constraint policy produced wasteful resource use when the costs of nonprofitable production were borne solely by the state. Domestic production had limited exposure to international trade and became noncompetitive except for raw materials and some military goods exports. State provision of public goods and subsidized staples masked consumer goods shortages and poor quality of public goods used by the population compared to the ruling elite.

The treadmill of reforms left central planning unreformed, failed to question state ownership, and died at the end of the 1980s after reenactment of the 1965 self-accounting enterprise reforms (the Law on Enterprise adopted in the summer of 1987), last of the ''command reforms.'' But the late 1980s produced legal recognition of a variety of proprietary arrangements from cautious introduction of cooperatives to individual proprietorships. The move from full state ownership was not fully applied in agriculture where the parties compromised with long-term leases of land still owned by the state.

During the late 1980s reforms acquired momentum, the legal groundwork for reform was put in place, and opposition to reforms lost political weight. After the August 1991 coup d'état attempt the focus shifted to reform implementation determined by objectives. With the monopoly of the Communist Party gone and no truly democratic political institutions to express popular

---

[37]Paul J. Welfens, ''The Socialist Shadow Economy: Causes, Characteristics, and Role for Systemic Reforms,'' *Comparative Economic Systems* 16 (1992), p. 116.

interests, pluralism of opinions and strategies led to stalemate. Reform decisions were made at the top of the postcoup government in pursuit of the political goals of establishing President Boris Yeltsin's reform reputation and the leading role of Russia in reforms. As a result of this situation, aggravated by the disintegration of the Soviet Union, shock therapy was adopted (see Chapter 12) that involved price decontrol in January 1992, followed by dramatic privatization schemes.

Summary and Conclusions

The Soviet model of command economy was brought about by a combination of internal economic underdevelopment and the international political discontinuity of the aftermath of World War I when workers' revolution threatened many nations. The Soviet model was designed to accommodate a speedy transition of relatively backward Russia to industrial society. The Soviet command economy persisted well beyond the attainment of industrialization, serving as an economic basis for the totalitarian regime of the Communist Party. This regime produced a mythology about the system's performance. Central planning was supposedly a superior tool for balancing economic proportions and maximizing the use of resources, whereas in reality it produced disproportionate and inflexible economic outcomes at the expense of abused human and natural resources.

The model produced a lot of problems, Soviet agriculture being a crying example. But problems were not recognized, they were labeled as temporary difficulties,[38] and they were attributed to the aggressive designs of world capitalists and spy-inspired "wreckers" rather than to the malfunctioning of the system itself. The mythology deemed the model a fountainhead of human accomplishment and as such it only needed some perfecting. With isolation of the population from the outside world this mythology took deep root, and when it encountered resistance it was imposed with the threat of physical repression. The reality of the system was revealed as the economy opened to the rest of the world, and the comparison of economic outcomes did not favor the Soviet Union.

Questions for Discussion

1. How did Russian agricultural traditions lay a foundation for socialism?
2. What was the relationship between the geneticist-teleologist debate and the debate over industrialization and agriculture in the late 1920s in the USSR?

---

[38]A Soviet joke noted that temporary problems were permanent.

3. What were successes and failures of Soviet command planning in the 1930s?

4. What was the role of agriculture in the Soviet reform movements?

5. How were Soviet trade relations managed and how did these eventually influence the movement for reform?

6. What was the pattern of Soviet reforms up to the time of Gorbachev?

7. Why and how did the Gorbachev reforms bring about the dissolution of the USSR and the collapse of its economic system?

Suggested Further Readings

Berdyaev, Nikolai. *Russian Thought in the 19th and 20th Centuries.* Amsterdam: Martinus Nijhoff, 1974.

Cohn, Stanley. "Sources of Low Productivity in Soviet Capital Investment." In *Soviet Economy in the 1980's: Problems and Prospects* (Papers submitted to the Joint Economic Committee of the U.S. Congress). Washington: USGPO, 1982, pp. 169–95.

Dobb, Maurice. *Soviet Economic Development since 1917,* 5th ed. London: Routledge & Kegan Paul, 1960.

Ellman, Michael, and Vladimir Kantorovich, eds. *The Disintegration of the Soviet Economic System.* London: Routledge, 1992.

Ericson, Richard E. "The Classical Soviet-Type Economy: Nature of the System and Implications for Reform." *Journal of Economic Perspectives* 5 (1991), pp. 11–29.

Feshbach, Murray, and Alfred Friendly, Jr. *Ecocide in the USSR: Health and Nature under Siege.* New York: Basic Books, 1992.

Goldman, Marshall I. *USSR in Crisis: The Failure of an Economic System.* New York: W. W. Norton, 1983.

Gros, Daniel, and Alfred Steinherr. *Economic Reform in the Soviet Union: Pas de Deux between Disintegration and Macroeconomic Destabilization.* Princeton Studies in International Finance, No. 71. Princeton: Princeton University, 1991.

Grossman, Gregory. "The 'Second Economy' of the USSR." *Problems of Communism* 26 (1977), pp. 25–40.

Kuschpeta, O. *The Banking and Credit System of the USSR.* Leiden: Martinus Nijhoff, 1978.

Kuznets, Simon. "The Share and Structure of Consumption" *Economic Development and Cultural Change* 10 (1962), pp. 68–79.

Levine, Herbert S. "Pressure and Planning in the Soviet Economy." In *Industrialization in Two Systems: Essays in Honor of Alexander Gerschenkron.* ed. Henry Rosovsky. New York: John Wiley & Sons, 1966, pp. 266–85.

McClellan, Woodford. *Russia: A History of the Soviet Period.* Englewood Cliffs: Prentice Hall, 1986.

Nove, Alec. *The Soviet Economic System.* London: Allen & Unwin, 1986.

Ofer, Gur. ''Soviet Economic Growth: 1928–1985.'' *Journal of Economic Literature* 25 (1987) pp. 1,767–1833.

Schroeder, Gertrude E. ''Soviet Economic Reform Decrees: More Steps on the Treadmill.'' In *Soviet Economy in a Time of Change* (Papers Submitted to the Joint Economic Committee of the U.S. Congress). Washington: USGPO, 1982.

Welfens, Paul J. ''The Socialist Shadow Economy: Causes, Characteristics, and Role for Systemic Reforms.'' *Comparative Economic Systems* 16 (1992), pp. 113–47.

Central Asian Republics: Kazakhstan, Turkmenistan, Uzbekistan, Kyrgyzstan, Tajikistan

Baltic Republics: Estonia, Latvia, Lithuania

Slavic Republics: Belarus, Ukraine, Moldova

Transcaucasian Republics: Georgia, Armenia, Azerbaijan

11

ALTERNATIVE PATHS OF DEVELOPMENT IN THE FORMER SOVIET REPUBLICS

The indestructible union of free republics was consolidated together by Great Russia for all times to come.
—Former Soviet National Anthem

Republics want to be free? Take as much independence as you can swallow!
—Boris Yeltsin, President of the Russian Federation, 1992

Introduction

The disintegration of the Soviet Union created new independent states from the constituent union republics, many joining together as the Commonwealth of Independent States (*CIS*). Becoming sovereign political entities, these new states faced tremendous challenges in defining their economic profiles. The collapse of the Soviet Union was brought about by a systemic crisis of the Soviet economy and by the partial nature of attempted reforms within it.

Historically the Soviet republics were compelled to conform with the economic philosophy and policy produced by the center, namely by the nomenklatura largely of Russian ethnic origin. Moreover the idea of a centralized command economy was conceived to economically consolidate areas and regions with diverse economic, political, and cultural backgrounds.

When the reforms in the USSR under Gorbachev got under way, the ideas of a ''pan-European home'' and increasing internationalization were employed to fight growing nationalist sentiments in the republics. The majority of the former republics faced pressures to continue reforms independently and to redefine their relationships with each other.

Individual reforms in the former Soviet republics depend on their ethnic heritage (see Table 11–1) and economic experience within the USSR and on their dependence on each other.

TABLE 11–1   **Ethnic Mix of the Former Soviet Union (1989)**

	Titular Nationality (%)	*Growth Rate 1979–89 (Per 1000)*	*Main Minorities*
Russia	82	6.91	Tatars 4%
Ukraine	73	3.84	Russians 22%
Uzbekistan	71	25.72	Russians 8%
Kazakhstan	40	11.89	Russians 39%, Ukrainians 5%
Belarus	78	6.48	Russians 13%
Azerbaijan	83	15.36	Russians 6%, Armenians 6%
Georgia	70	8.30	Armenians 8%, Russians 6%, Azeri 6%
Tajikistan	62	29.63	Uzbeks 23%, Russians 7%
Moldova	65	9.51	Ukrainians 14%, Russians 13%
Kyrgyzstan	52	19.55	Russians 22%, Uzbeks 12%
Lithuania	80	8.24	Russians 9%, Poles 7%
Turkmenistan	72	24.76	Russians 9%, Uzbeks 9%
Armenia	93	7.99	Azeri 2%
Latvia	52	6.15	Russians 35%
Estonia	62	7.04	Russians 30%

Source: The Economist August 31, 1991, p. 38, and W. Ward Kingkade. ''Demographic Prospects in the Republics of the Former Soviet Union.'' In *The Former Soviet Union in Transition*, eds. Richard F. Kaufman and John P. Hardt, Joint Economic Committee of the Congress of the United States (Armonk: M. E. Sharpe, 1993) p. 796.

Economic transformation in the newly independent states involves populations of different age and gender composition and increasing at different rates, factors that directly affect the progress and scope of reforms. Urban-rural population splits dictate differences in priorities between agrarian and industrial reforms.

Independence or Interdependence

Economic Background of the Union Republics

A look at the relative weights of the newly independent countries demonstrates the territorial and economic preeminence of Russia[1] and the disparities between the countries in economic performance (Tables 11–2 and 11–3).[2]

---

[1]The Russian Federation incorporated on a national autonomy basis the Bashkir (1919), Tatar (1920), Karelian (1920), Chuvash (1920), Kyrgyz (later Kazakh) (1920), Udmurt (1920), Mari (1920), Kalmyk (1920), Gorskaya (1920), Daghestan (1921), Komi (1921), Kabardinian (1921), the Crimea (1921), Buryat (1922), Chechen (1922), Yakut (1922), and Cherkess (1922) republics and regions.

[2]The Baltic states seceded from the USSR before it became defunct and expressed no interest in joining the agreement of the Commonwealth of Independent States (CIS). However they continue trade relations with the rest of CIS even though they possess new national currencies.

TABLE 11–2   The Former Soviet Union (FSU): Territory and Population (January 1, 1990)

Region	Territory	Population		
	% of Total	*Thousand*	*% of Total*	*% Urban*
FSU	100	288,624	100	66
Slavic				
Russia	76.2	148,041	51.3	74
Ukraine	2.7	51,839	18.0	67
Belarus	0.9	10,259	3.6	66
Baltic/Moldova				
Estonia	0.2	1,583	0.5	72
Latvia	0.3	2,687	0.9	71
Lithuania	0.3	3,723	1.3	68
Moldova	0.2	4,362	1.5	47
Transcaucasia				
Georgia	0.3	5,456	1.9	56
Armenia	0.1	3,293	1.1	68
Azerbaijan	0.4	7,131	2.5	54
Central Asia				
Kazakhstan	12.1	16,691	5.8	57
Turkmenistan	2.2	3,622	1.3	45
Uzbekistan	2.0	20,322	7.0	41
Tajikistan	0.6	5,248	1.8	32
Kyrgyzstan	0.9	4,367	1.5	38

Source: Stanley Fischer, ''Economic Reform in the USSR and the Role of Aid,'' *Brookings Papers on Economic Activity* 2 (1991), p. 291.

The countries that made up the FSU differ tremendously economically, culturally, ethnically, and demographically. These differences underlie the current pursuit of economic and political independence. However the new states share the legacy of having been integrated into a centrally planned economy in which allocative and redistributive economic mechanisms served the purpose of reinforcing the authority of the center (largely Russia) over the periphery (see Chapter 10). The legacy is a vertically integrated industrial and trade structure that shaped an essential asymmetry of interdependence.

Divergence of Economic Cultures in the Former Union Republics

Historically, Soviet economic culture was a superstructure above a traditional older communalism that relied on a paternalist State and obedience to the Orthodox Church.[3] But within this pervasive context were distinctive

---

[3]Other Christian churches and dissident sects within the Orthodox Church, as well as non-Christian churches except within certain designated zones, were not tolerated.

TABLE 11–3   Economic Development Level of Different Soviet Republics in 1990 (% of the USSR average)

		Productivity	
Republic	*National Income per Capita*	*Industry*	*Agriculture*
Russia	117	110	108
Ukraine	93	80	108
Belarus	103	103	128
Estonia	140	115	152
Latvia	122	105	131
Lithuania	108	103	152
Moldova	80	73	83
Georgia	84	90	62
Armenia	82	75	76
Azerbaijan	64	60	68
Kazakhstan	91	90	100
Uzbekistan	50	60	56
Kyrgyzstan	53	65	74
Turkmenistan	67	100	66
Tajikistan	40	75	60

Source: *Vheshniaia torgovlja* 11 (1991), p. 36.

variations, which can be grouped into the following categories. The first encompasses Russia,[4] Belarus, Ukraine, Northern Kazakhstan, and Moldova. In this group, population is more educated and responsive to innovations and change, especially in urban areas.[5] In rural areas of these states spontaneous collectivism and shared responsibility are felt strongly despite a climate of major change. The age composition of the population attests to a high percentage of retirees (retirement age for men is 60 and for women 55). In Russia retirees constitute 18.5 percent; in Ukraine, 21.2 percent; in Belarus, 19.5 percent; and in Moldova, 15.3 percent compared to less than 10 percent in Central Asia.[6] The older population concentrated in the countryside creates conservative resistance to reforms. Urban-rural divisions in this group create political biases in reform movements and a strong drive for reform from above.

The Transcaucasian republics—Georgia, Armenia, and Azerbaijan—represent a very special subgroup. They constituted less than 1 percent of the territory of the FSU, and 60 percent of their land is mountainous. Historically

---

[4]There are Muslim autonomous republics within Russia (Tatarstan and controversial Chechnya among others) and Buddhist areas (Kalmykia) that have distinctive economic cultures.

[5]Moldova is an exception given its 52 percent rural population.

[6]John Dunlop, Marc Rubin, Lee Schwartz, and David Zaslow, ''Profiles of the Newly Independent States: Economic, Social, and Demographic Conditions,'' in *The Former Soviet Union in Transition,* eds. Richard F. Kaufman and John P. Hardt. Joint Economic Committee, Congress of the United States (Armonk: M. E. Sharpe, 1993), pp. 1,038–40.

influenced by the Persian, Russian, and Ottoman empires, these republics share a legacy of alliance with Russia against potential Persian and Turkish assaults.[7] Prior to 1917 these republics were virtual colonies of the Russian empire, providing raw materials (manganese, copper, and oil) as well as products of subtropical agriculture (fruits, cotton, silk, tobacco). The historical experience of being objects of aggression and colonization produced strong nationalist longings for independence.

All three states are distinctive in their ethnic composition, religious beliefs, and economic practices. Ethnically diverse Georgia neighbors ethnically homogeneous Armenia. Distinctive varieties of Gregorian Georgian Orthodox and Monophysite Armenian Christianity are in conflict with Shi'i Islam in Azerbaijan and Abkhazian Islam in Georgia. Economically better off Armenia faces perpetual discontent from worse off Azerbaijan: 29.7 percent of the Azeri population were below the lowest income level of 75 rubles per month whereas only 5.4 percent fell below that level in Armenia at the end of the 1980s.[8] In 1990 Azerbaijan ranked fourth from the bottom in per capita income above Tajikistan, Uzbekistan, and Turkmenistan with 1,476.8 rubles compared to 2,149.7 rubles in Armenia.[9]

Georgia and Armenia are part of the quasi-Slavic group due to their reliance on Russia, higher levels of education and professionalism of the urban population, and higher incomes than Azerbaijan, a fundamental source of ethnic strife. Income inequality in this region is higher than in the Slavic republics, making the Christian Transcaucasian republics less disposed to egalitarian reforms. This income differentiation resulted partly from the developed second economy in all three republics, which became even more influential with progressing reforms. Corruption reinforced by the Soviet economic system became a political force when the system started falling apart.[10]

Economically these republics are predominantly agrarian. Oil resources in Azerbaijan make it a special case. Agriculture is extremely varied due to different climate and soil conditions, which has resulted in small specialized farms connected through markets. Industrialization and urbanization came with the Soviet model of fostering the development of the working class, but the terrain sets geographical limits to urban growth. The combination of Soviet-inspired industry and indigenous agriculture that recognized individual initiative and the importance of markets led to economic contradictions in the region and the development of the second economy. Disregard for Soviet

---

[7]Before 1917 the majority of population in Armenia was Muslim. The alliance with Russia contributed to Armenian self-determination and national homogenization.

[8]Michael Alexeev, ''Income Distribution in the U.S.S.R. in the 1980s,'' *Review of Income and Wealth* 39 (1993), p. 25.

[9]Kaufman and Hardt, eds., *The Former Soviet Union in Transition,* p. 1,064.

[10]Economic mafias in Georgia and Azerbaijan were the initial force behind demands to de-Russify and introduce native languages into schools in the 1970s, demands that highlighted nationalist sentiments long before they were openly manifested elsewhere.

economic and general laws in Transcaucasia became blatant and contributed to a mentality of graft and embezzlement.

The Baltic group[11] has a greater orientation toward individualism and respect for private property as well as a longer historical exposure to market economies because of both historical relations with the West and independence from 1920 to 1940. Having access to nonfreezing Baltic sea ports, the Baltic states served as a gateway for Russia's trade with the West. High educational standards, professional competence and the highest per capita incomes in the FSU ease integration with Western market economies. However the substantial Russian population there—30 percent in Estonia, 34 percent in Latvia, and 9.4 percent in Lithuania—coupled with low rates of indigenous population growth produce internal tension and external pressure to conform with Russian policies.[12]

The Muslim group is characterized by archaic forms of economic culture, the lowest per capita incomes in the FSU, a tendency to accept authoritarian rule, and greater gender inequality. A large rural population[13] and relatively low levels of education make this group less likely to adopt swift changes or social and technological innovations from outside. The nationalization of land in the FSU and the subsequent collectivization contributed to slowing urbanization of Central Asia compared to Iran and Turkey where landlessness and impoverishment drove peasants away from the land. Kazakhstan and the other states of Central Asia have never had private ownership of land due to the largely nomadic nature of their populations. Land was allotted to extended nomadic families and within the boundaries of the area owned by their tribe. The communal tradition and the revival of Islam make these states responsive to the redistributive practices of theocratic new traditional economies, such as Iran.

The Economics of Interdependence

The asymmetry among the former republics of the FSU (see Tables 11–2 and 11–3) produces two effects. The centripetal forces are maintained by still unchanged intraindustrial trade between Russia and the ''near abroad'' (the post-Soviet euphemism for the former republics) serviced by the ruble zone, as well as by the former republics' dependence on Russia's oil and other raw materials. Centrifugal impact is brought about by the erratic reform moves in Russia, which oscillate between shock therapy and gradualism amidst political squabbles, as well as by surging nationalism and regionalism, which lead to rejection of whatever originated in Russia.

---

[11]Estonia and Latvia were integrated into the Russian empire after the Northern War with Sweden (1700–1721). Lithuania was partitioned between Poland and Belarus. Its different parts were integrated into the Russian empire during the 18th century.

[12]The situation in Lithuania is aggravated because of the republic's dependence on nuclear power, which accounts for 45 percent of energy consumption. The nuclear plant of the Chernobyl design in Ignalina is largely operated by ethnic Russians.

[13]Compared to Iran and Turkey the Central Asian republics are behind in urbanization and industrialization: Urban population in the region accounted for 41 percent of the total compared to 54 percent in Iran and 53 percent in Turkey at the end of the 1980s. See Alastair McAuley in *The Disintegration of the Soviet Economic System,* eds. Michael Ellman and Vladimir Kontorovich (London: Routledge, 1992), p. 138.

Box 11–1

Estonia and Its New Currency

Estonia's decision to introduce its national currency, the kroon, and to peg it to the deutsche mark serves as a vivid example of attempted monetary independence from Russia. Instead of allowing the Bank of Estonia to control emission of kroons the government kept the exchange rate at 1 kroon to 1/8 DM. Additional issue of kroons was permitted only on condition of a positive hard currency trade balance.

At the end of 1992 Estonian exports to Europe constituted 55 percent (25 percent of which went to Finland) and to the CIS 33 percent (22 percent of which went to Russia) of all exports. Despite Estonia having a positive trade balance until fall 1992, the volume of its trade has fallen dramatically from preindependence days. In 1991 Estonia ranked sixth in the world in the export of scrap metal, much of it copper from melted down old soviet kopecks, at best only a temporary source of export earnings.

Among the individual countries only Russia, Kazakhstan, and Turkmenistan can pursue self-subsistent policies of economic development based on available raw materials. Kazakhstan accounts for 5.2 percent of the oil and 20.7 percent of the coal produced in the former Soviet Union. Turkmenistan accounts for 10.4 percent of natural gas production and Russia produces 79.3 percent. For the rest of the FSU autarkic reforms are impossible. Options are to refocus external trade and economic relations from the near abroad to the West, the Middle East, or the Far East. The most resolute refocus has happened in the Baltic States (particularly Estonia) where departure from the USSR meant returning to a natural association with Scandinavian nations.

Except for Russia and the maritime Baltics, the past experience of the other former republics with foreign trade has been marginal because of the history of state monopoly on foreign trade operations by union institutions located in Russia (Table 11–4).

Insulation from world prices and planned allocation of resources made the manufactured goods of the former republics largely uncompetitive. In the short run, deindustrialization is not under consideration because of fears of massive unemployment. Hence the focus has been on raw materials trade and possibly agriculture, the latter specifically by the Central Asian republics where the majority of population is still rural. In recent trade talks between the Central Asian republics and the countries of the Organization of Economic Cooperation in Asia (Iran, Turkey, and Pakistan) proposals have been made to trade industrial and infrastructure equipment for cotton and dried fruit from the Central Asian republics except for Kazakhstan.

The countries of the FSU are increasingly aware that restructuring their foreign economic relations is contingent on the progress of market reforms,

TABLE 11–4   Interrepublican Exports in 1988 (percentage of net material product)

Republic	To Other Republics	To Other Countries
Russia	29.3	7.5
Ukraine	39.1	6.7
Uzbekistan	43.2	7.4
Kazakhstan	30.9	3.0
Belarus	69.6	6.5
Azerbaijan	58.7	3.7
Georgia	53.7	3.9
Tajikistan	41.8	6.9
Kyrgyzstan	50.2	1.2
Moldova	62.1	3.4
Lithuania	60.9	5.9
Turkmenistan	50.7	4.2
Armenia	63.7	1.4
Latvia	64.1	5.7
Estonia	66.5	7.4

Source: Olekh Havrylyshyn and John Williamson, *From Soviet disUnion to Eastern Economic Community?* (Washington: Institute for International Economics, 1991), p. 20.

which would eventually make their economies compatible with world markets. Three possibilities for post-Soviet interrepublican relations are

- Full economic independence with separate currencies, fiscal and monetary institutions, customs regulations, and memberships in international organizations (IMF, WTO, etc.) with no fiscal ties to the old union.
- Concentric circles of association in which a core of countries maintains a high degree of economic unity comprising a monetary union and a common market and others associate themselves by selecting from a menu of economic cooperation measures.
- Full economic union, involving a common market and a monetary union controlled by a single central bank (allowing republics to print separate currencies pegged to a common currency) with political independence.[14]

Following choices two or three would necessitate concertation of economic reforms, presuming that the participants can find common ground. Option one is not open-ended either because outward reorientation requires substantial progress in marketization and an export promotion strategy involving external assistance to stabilize national currencies, thus bearing the

---

[14]Havrylyshyn and Williamson, *From Soviet disUnion to Eastern Economic Community,* p. 13.

TABLE 11–5   Loss from Disruption of Bilateral Trade (percent of net material product)

	Republic	*Russia*
Russia	11.5	—
Kazakhstan	12.5	1.3
Ukraine	24.2	4.8
Uzbekistan	26.6	1.0
Turkmenistan	28.2	0.2
Tajikistan	31.7	0.2
Georgia	35.9	0.5
Azerbaijan	36.4	0.5
Kyrgyzstan	38.3	0.2
Moldova	45.0	0.4
Lithuania	46.2	0.4
Armenia	50.3	0.3
Estonia	51.1	0.2
Latvia	52.1	0.3
Belarus	52.9	1.2

Source: Holger C. Wolf, *"The Economics of Disintegration in the Former Soviet Union,"* (New York: Department of Economics and International Business, New York University, 1993), p. 13. The first column is the percent of net material product lost if trade with other republics ceases. The second column is the percent loss of Russian net material products from a disruption of trade with the republic in question.

implications of conditionality.[15] Currently the most likely choices for inter-republican relations are between the first and the second options without a monetary union.

Since the dissolution of the USSR all former republics have instituted national currencies, responding to nationalist and political pressures. Some of these are in parallel use with the ruble, which services interrepublican trade.

The interrepublican trade structure exhibits considerable dependence of the republics on trade with Russia and each other as shown in Table 11–5.

Disproportionate reliance on Russian oil (Russia accounted for 89.5 percent of USSR oil production in 1991)[16] is widespread. Only Kazakhstan shows a low degree of dependence and hence could possibly become a center of regional reforms. Because 37.8 percent of the population in Kazakhstan is Russian the chance of regional separatism led by Kazakhstan is slim.

Russia is the major importer of agricultural products and accounted for 66 percent of total intraunion agricultural imports at the end of the 1980s,

---

[15]All of the former Soviet republics except for Azerbaijan (because of internal turmoil) joined the IMF on April 27, 1992. IMF prerequisites to qualify for economic aid and loans, however, require sweeping reforms, elimination of state subsidies, price decontrol, reduction of budget deficits, and general stabilization measures. Only the Baltic states qualified for immediate full-scale aid. Considerable parts of the economic assistance packages for other republics await approval on the basis of inconsistent reform policies.

[16]"Ekonomika Sodruzestva Nezavisimikh Gosudarstv," *FIN*, 1992, p. 12.

complementing the net food exports of Ukraine. The Central Asian republics (Uzbekistan, Kyrgyzstan, Tajikistan, and Turkmenistan) exported electric power (one-fourth of total intraunion exports).[17]

Another factor contributing to dependence within the FSU is monopolism by certain republics in producing individual goods. Russia produced 58 percent of USSR automobiles, 97 percent of street cars, and 100 percent of sewing machines. Ukraine provided 100 percent of corn harvesting machines and 96 percent of diesel locomotives. Thus reducing interrepublican trade risks considerable declines in production. But continuing this trade while different republics establish currencies and pursue reforms at different paces has created tension, as the disintegration of the ruble zone, symbolic of general disintegration, reveals.

Monetary disUnion

The collapse of the interrepublican trade resulted in a reduction of production bsequent supply-push inflation, which added to unleashed repressed demand-pull inflation. Further demand-pull inflationary pressure came from persistent subsidies to enterprises fearing mass unemployment. Individual republics feared the impact of inflation in Russia, which undertook resolute price decontrol at the beginning of 1992, and they chose to drop the ruble in domestic circulation.

The breakup of the union ruble zone started in December 1991 when some republics' new currencies or surrogates of domestic exchange for internal circulation paralleled circulation of the ruble. With the disintegration of the USSR Central Bank, the central government stopped controlling monetary emission, leading to "regionalization" of money expansion. Money in circulation between 1990 and 1991 increased by 10.8 times in Kyrgyzstan, 5.7 in Turkmenistan, 4.8 in Russia, 4.6 in Kazakhstan, 3.3 in Azerbaijan, and 2.2 in Uzbekistan.[18]

Nevertheless the Central Bank of Russia remained the main currency issue institution. The ruble continued to be the medium of multilateral trade accounts settlements. Introducing national currencies did not solve the problem of financing republics' trade with Russia because of their trade deficits and their lack of convertible currency reserves for settlement. Russia faced the dilemma of discontinuing subsidies to the independent states in bilateral trade to contain inflation or of maintaining trade and indirect transfers to the former republics to prevent further reductions in production because of specialized interdependence.

Credit expansion by national banks in surrogate rubles was a method of subsidizing domestic producers and became a potential channel of imported

---

[17]Roy J. Langhammer, *Aussenwirtschaft* 47 (1992), pp. 258–59.

[18]Igor Filatochev and Roy Bradshaw, "The Soviet Hyperinflation: Its Origins and Impact throughout the Former Republics," *Soviet Studies* 44 (1992), p. 745.

Box 11–2

Convoluted Paths of the Byelorussian Ruble

The monetary situation in Belarus was very complex. Instituting a separate currency in May 1992 was a response to the shortage of FSU ruble bank notes because of continuing subsidies to enterprises. It also served as a rationing device to prevent arbitrage of state-subsidized food products outside the country. The currency notes have pictures of hares on them and are known by the Byelorussian name for them, ''Zaichiks.''

By May 1994 Belarus exhausted its credit limits with Russia, causing the Belorussian ruble (Brub) to float. Belarus needed an extension of its bilateral monetary agreement with Russia that formally exchanged Russian rubles (Rrub) and Belorrusian rubles at a one-to-one exchange rate, whereas the actual market rate was 7 Brub to 1 Rrub. Implementation of the April 1994 monetary unification agreement has been stalled because of Russia's unwillingness to finance slower budget reforms in Belarus.

---

inflation into Russia. Initiated in early 1992, price liberalization in Russia exceeded the pace of similar reforms in most other CIS countries. It resulted in differences between republics in price and wage levels leading to arbitrage that further destabilized interrepublican relations. In the periphery of the ruble zone independent reforms required national sovereignty over macroeconomic policy during the transition and those former republics began to consider withdrawal from the zone. This process accelerated after the Russian Bank decision to raise the interest rate from 50 percent to 80 percent, causing angry protests by Ukraine, Belarus, and Kazakhstan.

Ukraine was the first to declare a currency ''divorce.'' Russia responded favorably given the resulting ruble stabilization and arrest of the increasing amount of dollars in domestic circulation. Ukraine was fully determined to establish its currency, the grivna. The two countries signed a protocol wherein rubles issued by the former republic to cover budget needs (subsidies and wage indexation) were to be credits with the Central Bank of Russia at a favorable interest rate of 21 percent. Economic difficulties encountered by Ukraine because of an ill-conceived reform caused a partial ''restoration of socialism'' and the introduction of the grivna was postponed.

In mid-1992 the chairmen of the central banks of most of the former republics (Lithuania as an observer, Turkmenistan and Azerbaijan without voting rights) negotiated an agreement on an interbank union. This agreement was supposed to provide equal representation, coordinated monetary policy, effective control over national credit expansions and interventions by national banks, and acceptability of national currencies with concerted determination of their exchange rates relative to third country currencies. This interbank union agreement was doomed from the start because equal representation did not reflect the different responsibilities of the parties. Russia proposed to set vote quotas depending on relative weights of the banks in the ruble zone, a proposal assuming other republics' recognition of asymmetry in favor of Russia.

At the end of 1992 Kazakh President Nazarbaev proposed a compromise: to delegate authority of currency issue to a supranational body that would create a common currency above the existing national ones. The idea was rejected and the centrifugal forces accelerated. The republics were reluctant to give up sovereignty over monetary policy and to subject themselves to outside control over budget deficits. In addition, stronger economies were apprehensive about becoming importers of inflation from weaker economies. Reorientation of trade in some republics towards regional partners outside the ruble zone dictated freedom of currency policy. The Bishkek summit in Kyrgyzstan in October 1992 failed to agree on the issue of an interbank. The republics split into two contingents: the countries that recognize the ruble as a Russian national currency and intend to remain in the ruble zone (Belarus, Armenia, Kazakhstan, Kyrgyzstan, Uzbekistan, and Russia) and the remaining republics, which sought to disassociate themselves from this zone.

The evolution of the ruble zone shows a widening gulf between the desire of the new states for self-determination and their ability to pursue independent reforms. Their dependence on interrepublican trade cuts two ways. First, reliance on this trade is an impediment to transition to a genuine market economy with freely fluctuating prices. Prices in interrepublican trade are still distorted and subsidized. Ratios of world to domestic prices range from world prices 2.7 times higher than domestic ones in oil and gas, to overpriced domestic light industries where world prices are only 33 percent of domestic ones.[19]

Second, any attempt to further reduce this trade risks reducing production and increasing unemployment, thereby constituting a social deterrent to market reforms.

Divergence or Convergence of the Pace of Reforms

Economic decline began in 1989 before dissolution of the USSR and continued into 1992 when the GNP of the CIS was 82 percent of its 1970 level. But the distribution of this decline shows divergences among the countries, as presented in Table 11–6.

---

[19]Lucjan T. Orlowsky "Indirect Transfers in Trade among Soviet Union Republics: Sources, Patterns and Policy Responses in the Post-Soviet Period," *Europe-Asia Studies* 45 (1993), p. 1,003.

TABLE 11–6   **GNP of the Commonwealth of the Independent States in 1992: Percentage of 1985 level (1990 prices)**

	1992	*1991*	*1990*	*1985*
CIS	55	67	78	100
Russia	53	65	80	100
Ukraine	61	72	78	100
Belarus	61	69	77	100
Moldova	47	64	78	100
Azerbaijan	43	61	78	100
Armenia	33	57	82	100
Kazakhstan	60	69	78	100
Uzbekistan	58	67	77	100
Kyrgyzstan	48	63	80	100
Turkmenistan	62	70	78	100
Tajikistan	38	58	76	100

Note: These data were compiled before Georgia's reentry into CIS.

Source: Calculated from Andrei Sizov, ''Ekonomika Rossiji i drugikh stran SNG v nachale 90kh godov,'' *Mirovaia economika i mezdunarodnyie otnoshenja* 7 (1993), p. 21.

The general synchronicity of the economic decline manifests the interdependence of the economies and a reduction of interrepublican trade from 1991 to 1992 by about 50 percent. Hopes that external trade would compensate were futile in the short run. In 1992 Russian exports were at the level of Denmark, Ukrainian were one-fifth those of Finland, Kazakhstan and Uzbekistan exported respectively one-thirtieth and one-fortieth of Finland's level.[20]

Different rates of republic production decline have changed their relative economic rankings within the CIS. In GDP per capita Russia has yielded leadership to Belarus as presented in Table 11–7. From 1991 to 1993 GDP has fallen in Belarus by 21 percent compared to 37.2 percent in Russia, 37.3 percent in Ukraine, and 34.1 percent in Kazakhstan.[21] The better performance of Belarus appears related to its slower reforms and persistence of administrative measures such as allocating energy and preferential credit to priority sectors.

The uneven pace of reform in the former republics of the USSR has aggravated social and national tensions, producing winners and losers in the environment of asymmetric interdependence. Under the circumstances the disintegrative drive in the intermediate run has prevailed.

[20]Andei Sizov, ''Ekonomika Rossiji i drugikh stran SNG v nachule pokh godov,'' *Mirovaia economika i mezdunarodnyie otnoshenja* 7 (1993), p. 22.

[21]''Belarus,'' *IMF Survey* 11 (1994), Washington: International Monetary Fund, p. 69.

TABLE 11–7   GDP in CIS Countries: Total and Per Capita in 1992 (computed in U.S. dollars using purchasing power parity of the national currencies)

	GNP (total)		GNP (per capita)	
	$ (bn)	*% of U.S.*	*$ (bn)*	*% of U.S.*
CIS	1,275	21.5	4,574	19.5
Russia	775	13.0	5,225	22.3
Ukraine	240	4.0	4,600	19.6
Belarus	58	1.0	5,625	24.0
Moldova	14	0.25	3,250	14.0
Azerbaijan	20	0.33	2,700	11.5
Armenia	10	0.15	2,800	12.0
Kazakhstan	80	1.35	4,675	20.0
Uzbekistan	55	0.9	2,572	11.0
Kyrgyzstan	8	0.13	1,700	7.3
Turkmenistan	8	0.13	2,050	8.7
Tajikistan	6.5	0.1	1,250	5.3

Note: These data were compiled before Georgia's reentry into CIS.

Source: Andrei Sizov, ''Ekonomika Rossiji i Drugikh Stran SNG v Nachale gokh Godov,'' *Mirovaia economika i mezdunarodnyie Otnoshenja* 7 (1993), p. 23.

Agrarian Reforms

Legacies of Soviet Agriculture and Reform Readiness

Readiness for market reforms differs tremendously across the FSU. Industrial republics with higher exposure to foreign economic relations were the first to reform. For republics with a majority rural population market reforms are not recognized as immediately important compared with agrarian reforms,[22] Kyrgyzstan being an exception to this generalization.

Historically the Soviet economic system was in constant conflict with agriculture, the least suited sector for command administration. The centrally planned economy brought successful industrialization, whereas agriculture collapsed the system. Even though agriculture underwent significant evolution from the basic Stalinist model to a moderately reformed one in the 1960s and 1970s, its performance was never satisfactory relative to its potential.

[22]Hasty attempts at decollectivization in Russia have led to disinterest in marketing agricultural products. In addition a new ''scissors crisis'' with agricultural prices held at artificially low levels and decontrolled prices for manufactured goods and agricultural equipment rising has produced devastating reductions in production and withdrawals from market operations. Humanitarian food aid from the West in major cities (Moscow, St. Petersburg, Ekaterinburg) has undercut agricultural producers in adjacent rural areas who had higher costs compared to free products from the West.

The Stalinist model used administrative commands for what and how to produce, setting delivery prices, suppressing private agricultural activity, offering low labor rewards, and setting low investment. Land was nationalized and there was no direct economic valuation of lots. Agriculture was isolated from foreign markets with the exception of government-sponsored grain and caviar exports and forage imports in some years. Compulsory rules of delivery, the absence of material incentives, and the memory of Stalin's elimination of the kulak (well-off) farmers, severely damaged entrepreneurship in agriculture and its productivity. Political-economic deemphasis of agriculture caused a critical flight from the countryside to the cities, contributing to the inability of the overindustrialized economy to subsist on domestically produced food.

In the 1950s state-owned machine tractor stations were liquidated, and the kolkhozy received their equipment. In the 1960s reforms granted wage guarantees to peasants and in the 1970s these guarantees closed the gap in wages between industrial and agricultural workers. In the same years agriculture enjoyed increased investment channeled to accommodate micromanagement in different regions. That regionalization of management allowed the Baltic republics and Georgia and Armenia to reshape their agricultural practices closer to their traditional family farms. But given planned output levels and controlled prices these reforms did not lead to improved overall productivity, thus contributing to suppressed inflation and regional corruption. The infamous cotton scandal saw local authorities in Uzbekistan taking advantage of government investment by reporting fraudulent numbers about dramatically increased productivity.[23]

With land remaining state property and without markets determining differential rents, the country suffered from land misallocation and immense waste of land resources, causing environmental damage.[24] Though yield numbers in specific crops were not bad compared to European averages, Soviet agriculture was extremely cost and investment inefficient. Moreover the policy of stable food prices with increasing wages produced food lines and burdened the state budget.

The agricultural sector could have been a source of radical economic reform if the changes of the 1960s were complemented with reform of land ownership and freeing of prices. Instead Soviet agriculture became disinterested in radical reforms. Adjustments in financial and price policies in the 1980s increased the irrationalities in prices and softened the budget constraint.[25] This produced weak linkage between labor productivity and

---

[23]The fraud was unveiled under Brezhnev's successor, Yuri Andropov, with the aid of space satellites!

[24]A comprehensive program of marsh drainage in Belarus caused underground waters to rise and flood fertile lands.

[25]Edward C. Cook, ''Agriculture's Role in the Economic Crisis,'' in *The Disintegration of the Soviet Economic System,* eds. Michael Ellman and Vladimir Kontorovich (London: Routledge, 1992).

remuneration; two-thirds of farms operated with profitability levels less than 25 percent and experienced no change in remuneration. Only when profitability exceeded 40 percent did labor compensation exceed that for unprofitable farms.[26] Thus complacency grew in farming, destroying incentives for individual entrepreneurship and responsibility.

Other factors contributed to disinterest in decollectivization. First, the reforms of the 1960s and 1970s reversed the urban-rural distribution of income, providing a higher noncash living standard in successful collective farms. The symbiosis of individual plots with collective farm equipment provided a favorable subsidized environment for making additional income on top of guaranteed wages. This symbiosis also produced a new professional farm worker with a taste for urban life in the countryside.[27] This view undermines the naive beliefs of urban intellectuals that the source of the national communal tradition is a conventional peasant. On the other hand, less successful collective farms and less fortunate peasants produced a depressing picture of primitive subsistence agriculture, which led to overexploitation of land and labor.[28]

Second is the survival and revival of religious communes (Baptist, Mennonite, Pentecostal) that kept the communal tradition alive, promoted a high work ethic, and maintained environment-friendly agrarian practices.[29] However the influence of religious communities varies in different republics depending on experience with collectivization, degree of urbanization, and agrarian culture.

Third, agrarian reform was restarted under unfavorable political and economic conditions. In Russia the collapse of administrative control and the resulting institutional chaos coincided with hyperinflation and price disparities. With a June 1991 price level equaling 100, the June 1992 index of prices of agricultural products was 540, whereas the index of input prices used by agriculture was 1,470. In 1992, after price liberalization with industrial monopolies and ambivalent privatization, price scissors (a gulf between the purchasing power of agricultural goods and their industrial inputs) rose to the extent that peasants stopped buying machinery, fertilizers, and pesticides.[30] The subsequent reduction in agricultural production created a tense economic and social situation.

---

[26]Cook, "Agriculture's Role," p. 205.

[27]Robert McIntyre, "Collective Agriculture in Eastern Europe and the Former Soviet Union," *Monthly Review* 45 (December 1993), pp. 2–4.

[28]See Lev Timofeev, "Tekhnologiya chernogo rynka ili krestyanskoye iskustvo golodat." (Technology of Black Markets or Peasants' Art of Starvation) (Vilnius: VIMO, 1993), p. 41–44.

[29]E. Rashkovsky, "Opyit totalitarnoi modernizatsyi Rossyi (1917–1991) v. svete sotsiologyii razvitiya", *Mirovaia ekonomika i mezdunarodnyie* otnoshenja 3(1993), p. 112.

[30]Alexander Nikonov, "Agricultural Transition in Russia and the Other Former States of the U.S.S.R." *American Journal of Agricultural Economics* 74 (1992), p. 1,159.

FIGURE 11–1   **Reorganization of Collective and State Farms in Russia**

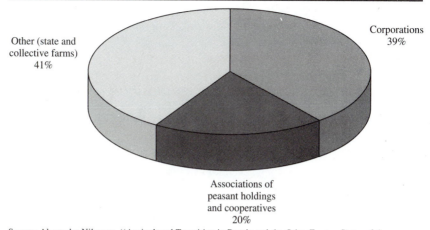

Other (state and
collective farms)
41%

Corporations
39%

Associations of
peasant holdings
and cooperatives
20%

Source: Alexander Nikonov, "Agricultural Transition in Russia and the Other Former States of the
U.S.S.R." *American Journal of Agricultural Economics* 74 (1992), p. 1,160.

The Progress of Agrarian Reforms in the Individual States

The course of agrarian reform in the different FSU states has followed peculiar
patterns. The Law on Land Reform of 1990 in Russia abolished the state
monopoly on land ownership, providing for subsequent land repartitioning
and lifetime leases. However, overseeing repartitioning was delegated to local
authorities, who set conditions for the secession of families from collective or
state farms. The conditions included limits to the size of plots and a land-sales
moratorium for the first 10 years. Even though the Russian government decreed later the right to sell land, local authorities continue to resist the
peasants' use of this nominal right.[31]

In 1992 24,000 Russian collective and state farms (93 percent of all farms)
were reregistered. Of those 8,100 farm collectives decided to maintain their
previous status whereas 11,300 farms became corporations or partnerships.
The initial stage of agrarian reforms thus produced denationalization without
decollectivization.

By November 1, 1993, there were 268,000 individual family farms with
an area of 11.2 million hectares (42 hectares per farm on average). In 1991
the number was 191,000. However the process of forming these farms visibly
slowed and over 9,000 farms ceased to operate by the end of the year.[32] But
urban dwellers are increasingly interested in getting land for residences, and
in 1990 three-fourths of new farms were set up by urban dwellers.[33] Russia

---

[31]Don Van Atta, "Agrarian Reform in Post-Soviet Russia," *Post-Soviet Affairs* 10 (1994),
p. 172.

[32]*Ekonomika i zizn* 49 (1993), p. 24.

[33]Victor Khlystun, "Agrarnaya Reforma v 1993 godu," *Ekonomist* 4 (1994), p. 18.

has instituted the Land Fund to allot land drawn from nonutilized but arable land of collective and state farms to new agrarian units. About 10 percent of their total acreage has been allocated in this way. Individual subsidiary farmer holdings for orchards, vegetable gardens, and animal production were set up on these lands. At the end of 1993 18 million such holdings accounted for 30 percent of agricultural production, approximately the same level as before.[34]

The current scene in Russian agriculture reflects a pluralistic picture. A survey of farmers' attitudes toward private enterprise shows that only 12 percent of peasants wanted to be private farmers, 63 percent expressed negative attitudes towards farming, and the remainder were undecided.[35]

Private ownership of land is now legally recognized in all FSU states except for Kazakhstan, Uzbekistan, Kyrgyzstan, Tajikistan, and Turkmenistan. These countries have had insignificant experience with private ownership of land because of their nomadic economic heritage and the late arrival of settled agriculture when land was allotted to extended families. Agrarian reforms in Central Asia are conditioned by the availability of arable (irrigated) lands.[36] The most advanced in irrigation, Uzbekistan is expanding individual peasants' subsidiary plots for vegetable gardening while maintaining large collective farms for cotton and cereal production. Unprofitable state farms were reorganized into cooperatives and leased enterprises. In Kazakhstan farmer holdings began to pick up, but specialized and breeding units are still owned by the state.

In Armenia privatization of farming was the most developed after the Baltic states, where reversal from collectivization took the sharpest turn. Armenia is encouraging small parcel farming, which has gained very strong momentum. In Georgia both private and state possession of land are legally recognized, and sale and purchase of land are permitted.

The Baltic states had an extensive history of peasant holdings between 1870 and 1940. Agricultural reform here accommodates small family farms, large-scale shareholding companies, and partnerships. The pace of reforms varies among the Baltic states. In Lithuania formal dissolution of all collective and state farms in 1991 led to spontaneous and chaotic redivision and privatization of land with a high incidence of graft of formerly state-owned machinery and equipment. Numerous claimants for land property decreased the size of individual allotments to the frequently economically unviable; average plot size in 1993 was 8.8 hectares.[37] Agricultural privatization in Latvia and

---

[34]*Ekonomika i zizn*, p. 24.

[35]Nikonov, ''Agricultural Transition in Russia,'' p. 1,160.

[36]The diversion of river water for irrigation of Fergana valley in Uzbekistan caused the disaster of Aral Sea, which is progressively disappearing, risking the extinction of its natural habitat.

[37]S. Girnius, ''Economika gosudarstv Baltii v 1993 godu,'' *Voprosy ekonomiki* 8 (1994), p. 112.

TABLE 11–8   **Index of Agricultural Production in 1992 as a Percent of 1991 in Selected Countries**

	Russia	*Belarus*	*Ukraine*	*Armenia*	*Lithuania*
Agricultural production	92	87	85	60	40

Source: "Reformirovanije ekonomiki stran SNG: Belarus," *Rossiisky ekonomichesky zhurnal* 4 (1993), p. 31, and Sizov, "Ekonomika Rossiji," p. 22.

Estonia developed more slowly, new private farms coexisting with collective farms reorganized into agrarian cooperatives.

In Ukraine the nationalist agenda restrained agrarian privatization, fearful of following Russia's ill-conceived reforms. Legislation on land reform and independent family farming allowed private ownership, subject to restrictions on size, resale, and employment of hired labor. In 1992 about 5,000 private farms occupied about 1 percent of the agricultural land with household plots of collective and state farmers and garden plots assigned to city workers taking up an additional 9 percent of the area of private farms. Private plots employed over 90,000, compared with 4.6 million employed on state and collective farms.[38] Private farmers operate in an overbureaucratized environment—the farmer must work for three years under draconian taxation before getting title to the land. Duties (starting from 80 percent of the price and reduced proportionately every year) were imposed on land sold during the first six years of ownership. The sale of land was permitted at the end of 1992, restricted to small cultivation enterprises. Hired seasonal labor was forbidden, and private farmland allotment was not to exceed 10 percent of arable land.[39] In 1995 Ukraine declared its determination to radicalize agrarian reforms and promote privatization.

Belarus exhibits a moderate approach to agricultural reforms in which an overall reform agenda is absent and the authorities of the republic, guided by others' experience, pursue a policy of stabilization and maintain trade relations with the former republics.

A paradoxical picture emerges as a result of different approaches and policies in agriculture: The states that progressed the most in decollectivization have experienced the strongest shock in reduction of agricultural production, as seen in Table 11–8.

This picture reflects how the inertia of institutional arrangements in agriculture fed into antireform sentiment. Such inertia also produces a strong force in favor of government special treatment of agriculture and an increasing

[38]"Ukraine," *International Monetary Fund Survey* 10 (1993), Washington: International Monetary Fund, pp. 58–59.

[39]*Finvest* 21 (1992), p. 2.

belief in reform from above. Success of agrarian reforms is contingent on the success of overall market reforms. However at the current stage the situation in agriculture contributes to slowing reform processes.

Privatization: Reform Panacea?

Transition from command socialism made privatization a central issue of economic reform. Implementing privatization has proven to be highly complex, raising fundamental questions of ultimate destination regarding systemic transformation.

At the early stages of reform initiated from above, replacement of planning by market forces was viewed as sufficient to make economic incentives work. As reform progressed it became clear that transition to a market economy is a self-regulated process that necessitates disaggregating the economy and instituting new property relations. The role of the state becomes that of legal guardian of individual, cooperative, and corporate forms of property.

The transition to a postsocialist economy can be implemented in different ways. The genetic approach[40] accounts for the legacies of the socialist economy and their hysteretic effects.[41] This approach offsets the inertia of the *ancien régime,* gradually freeing the economy of socialist institutions.

The normative approach is the opposite of the genetic approach, based on preconceived models of the ultimate goals of reforms. It seeks to emulate the economic performance of other economies. Specificity of individual cultural, ethnic, and economic environments is neglected.

The evolutionary approach seeks to create institutional boundaries for spontaneous transformation where the role of the microeconomic agents is emphasized.

The development of reforms in the FSU has shown movement from the genetic approach to the normative one in the debate on privatization. Privatization has political implications when the state is politically wary of independent economic agents. Another nuance is recognizing the comprehensive nature of systemic transformation. Readiness for privatization varies tremendously among the republics. The republics where privatization has proceeded the fastest are Russia and the Baltic states.

Privatization in Russia clearly breaks with a long history of associating private economic activity with economic crime and of public resentment of entrepreneurs. The USSR Law on Individual Labor Activity adopted in 1986 articulated rules for operating private enterprise, but its thrust was not to encourage entrepreneurship. Subsequent legislation on cooperatives subjected them to extensive control by central and local governments. The legitimation of private enterprise came only in 1991 with the Law about Enterprise and Entrepreneurship followed by the Law on Principles of Entrepreneurship and

---

[40]See the discussion of geneticists versus teleologists in Chapter 10.

[41]A hysteresis effect is an institutional memory of preexisting economic practices underlying resistance to change.

TABLE 11–9   **Size Distribution of Industrial Enterprises in the Soviet Union (1988)**

	Number of Employees					
	1–99	*100–499*	*500–999*	*1000–4,999*	*5,000–9,999*	*10,000+*
Enterprises (%)	1.8	13.2	11.7	36.2	15.6	21.5

Source: Stanley Fischer, *"Russia and the Soviet Union Then and Now,"* NBER Working Paper No. 4077 (1992), p. 32.

in July 1991 by the Law of the Destatization and Privatization of Enterprises, which specified target dates of state decontrol of enterprises.

Eight FSU states signed the October 1991 agreement committing them to privatization and market reforms. Enjoying the limited economic autonomy granted the Baltic republics in November 1989, Estonia pioneered partial price liberalization in 1989 and introduced private enterprise legislation in 1990. The pace of private property recognition in Latvia and Lithuania was more consonant with Russia's reforms, which took off with price liberalization at the beginning of 1992.[42] In Ukraine, where price liberalization was introduced simultaneously with Russia, privatization was torpedoed by the nomenklatura, which led to a partial restoration of socialism.

In 1991 state property worth 2 billion rubles was privatized according to the head of the Committee of State Property in Russia, Anatoly Chubais. During the first three months of 1992 privatization accelerated, reaching 40 percent of the 1991 level.[43] Russia's privatization program initially contained two elements: small businesses (less than 200 employees) sold or auctioned off and large businesses to be converted into joint stock corporations with subsequent offerings of stock on the open market. The relative weight of the latter part of this program can be seen from the data in Table 11–9.

This program produced individual proprietorships and partnerships instead of small state enterprises. Privatization of large businesses was more complex. The distribution of stock among management, collectives of workers, state representatives in charge of state property to be privatized (State Committee of State Property), and potential foreign investors[44] became a target of political struggle. Populists insisted on closed auctions in which majority ownership is retained by worker collectives. At the other end of the political spectrum the directors' corps associated with the Civic Union accused

---

[42]Roman Frydman, Andrzej Rapaczynski, John S. Earle, eds., *The Privatization Process in Russia, Ukraine and the Baltic States,* (Budapest: Central European University Press, 1993), pp. 5, 132, 196, 235.

[43]Lynn D. Nelson, Lilia V. Babaeva, and Rufat O. Babaev, "Perspectives on Entrepreneurship and Privatization in Russia: Policy and Public Opinion," *Slavic Review* 51 (1992), p. 276.

[44]Curiously, foreign private property was permitted in the FSU before domestic private property was legalized.

the state of deliberately undermining national industry. This lobby pressed for the third variant of privatization in which chief managers are given the option to purchase 20 percent of voting stock with full ownership in a year.

Most shares were to be purchased with vouchers designed to give access to property to every Russian citizen. The specifics of vouchers were that after being distributed freely to the populace they could be invested or traded on the market. But without information on profitability of individual enterprises rational decisions about their use were difficult to make. This fact is reflected in that the market price of vouchers stayed below the nominal 10,000 rubles despite an estimated value of 200,000 to 300,000 rubles in mid-1992. Coupled with soaring inflation, voucher privatization was compromised, although it has continued.[45]

Current privatization in Russia mostly takes the form of quasi-holdings managed by nomenklatura bureaucrats and technocrats paralleled by worker collective holdings of the ESOP type without, however, Western ESOP efficiency. Small privatization has taken off, given the opportunity to purchase businesses for cash and the introduction of three-year deferrable investment tax credits. But successful functioning of privatized holdings was impeded by underdevelopment of a trade and banking infrastructure. A more important problem for the development of private land ownership is the absence of a middle class with sufficient savings for purchasing businesses and the absence of viable commercial banks able to mobilize individual savings into investment funds. Small private businesses burgeon immediately after liberalization of private property, but they cluster in basic consumer goods sectors, such as retail, restaurants, and rudimentary manufacturing, and they rely on self-finance.[46] Large-scale enterprises, which prevail in Russia (Table 11–9), lean toward corporatist organization,[47] based on labor-intensive technology without restructuring.

Privatization remains controversial. One element in privatization is regionalization and decentralization of management, which promote political decentralization and disintegrative trends, which in turn destabilize the macroeconomic environment of reforms. In response, privatization proposals for pocket or target privatization are being advanced in Russia to coordinate institutional change with industrial reorganization. These proposals are strongly related to government-sponsored reforms. Opponents of statist reforms advocate "spontaneous" privatization and the removal of state institutions from the process. The latter scenario, even if given a green light, is unlikely to outweigh the presence and influence of state holdings of various sorts.

---

[45]Yuri Kochevrin, "Privatizatsia v Rossiji," *Mirovaia ekonomika i mezdunarodniye otnoshenja* 6 (1993), p. 9.

[46]Peter Murrell and Yijiang Wang, "When Privatization Should Be Delayed: The Effect of Communist Legacies on Organizational and Institutional Reforms," *Journal of Comparative Economics* 7 (1993), p. 387.

[47]Corporatist approach is a type of coordinated private or semiprivate organization in a specific industrial sector that includes strong representation of labor interests. See Chapter 8.

Summary and Conclusions

The former Soviet republics are experiencing a vast array of difficulties that lead to questioning the successful reforms of the former command socialist economies. The initiation of reforms responded to increasing internationalization of market economies, which demonstrated an impressive ability to efficiently operate in ever-changing economic and technological environments. The attempt at integration with the world economy questioned the systemic compatibility and economic competitiveness of socialism. Reforms were undertaken to make socialism work in the open economy environment but it became increasingly clear that the centrally planned economy would yield to market forces. Systemic transformation became imperative.

In the FSU systemic transformation is complicated by the political disintegration of the economy, which includes varied regions and cultures. The dissolution of the union challenged the new independent states to identify their national goals in reforms and to take responsibility for their respective policies. The legacies of the Soviet economy make this identification and independent decision making problematic given the high degree of economic interdependence and reliance on the former core. Synchronous reforms reinforce the supremacy of Russia; asynchronous reforms are barely feasible in many states.

Russia itself has largely stopped sponsoring other republics' reforms, given its preoccupation with political strife and intrafederation ethnic conflicts. Land reform remains the cornerstone of transition and is not given adequate attention due to the public perception that it would come after industrial privatization, thereby pleasing foreign countries sponsoring economic assistance. So far republics with a moderate pace of reform are better off than ones that went through shock therapy, with some exceptions. The distribution of gains from reforms and the burden of reforms is perceived as unfair, contributing to nationalist sentiments and the popularity of policy extremism. Nevertheless, evidence abounds that at least reforming Russia's urban economy has begun to rebound.

Questions for Discussion

1. What proved to be an obstacle in republics' integration with Western trade?
2. What factors contributed to strong interdependence of the republics of the FSU?
3. Explain the divergence of economic cultures of the Baltic states and the Central Asian republics.
4. Why are reforms in agriculture progressing at a slower pace?
5. Why didn't Russian denationalization of land lead to decollectivization?
6. What are the differences in agrarian reforms in Lithuania and Estonia?
7. Which republics have had the most success in privatization and why?

Suggested Further Readings

The Economist, ''Unruly Child: A Survey of Ukraine,'' May 7, 1994.

The Economist,. ''A Silent Revolution: A Survey of Russia's Emerging Market,'' April 8, 1995.

Ellman, Michael, and Vladimir Kantorovich, eds. *The Disintegration of the Soviet Economic System.* London: Routledge, 1992.

Fischer, Stanley. ''Economic Reform in the USSR and the Role of Aid,'' *Brookings Papers on Economic Activity* (1991), pp. 289–301.

Frydman, Roman, Andrzej Rapaczynski, and John S. Earle, eds. *The Privatization Process in Russia, Ukraine and the Baltic States.* Budapest: Central European University Press, 1993.

Havrylyshyn, Olekh, and John Williamson. *From Soviet disUnion to Eastern Economic Community.* Washington: Institute for International Economics, 1991.

Schroeder, Gertrude E. ''Regional Economic Disparities, Gorbachev's Policies, and the Disintegration of the Soviet Union.'' In *The Former Soviet Union in Transition,* eds. Richard F. Kaufman and John P. Hardt. Joint Economic Committee, Congress of the United States. Armonk: M. E. Sharpe, 1993, pp. 121–46.

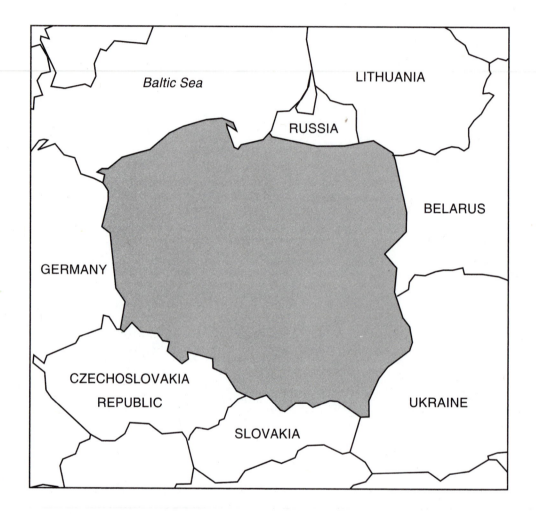

12 POLAND: THE PERIL AND PROMISE OF SHOCK THERAPY

What has decided me definitely for Poland, on the basis of my latest studies of Polish history, is the historical fact that the intensity and vitality of all revolutions since 1789 can be gauged pretty accurately by their attitude to Poland. Poland is their 'external' thermometer.

—Karl Marx, December 1856, Letter to Friedrich Engels[1]

Communism does not fit the Poles. They are too individualistic, too nationalistic. Poland's future economy should be based on private enterprise. Poland will be a capitalistic state.

—Joseph Stalin[2]

Introduction

Poland's geographical and historical misfortune has been to be located between Germany and Russia. It was conquered and ruled by each of them in the 20th century, as well as in earlier centuries. Thus it takes a strong Western orientation in culture, politics, and economics and seeks alliances with Western powers such as France. This longing for Western-oriented national independence underlay the decision of the first post-Communist Polish government in 1989 to undertake economic transition rapidly through ''big bang'' or ''shock therapy'' policy.

---

[1]Quoted in Terry R. Kandal, ''Marx and Engels on International Relations, Revolution and Counterrevolution,'' in *Studies of Development and Change in the Modern World,* eds. M. T. Martin and T. R. Kandal (New York: Oxford University Press, 1989), p. 45.

[2]To Stanislaw Mikoxajczyk, October 1944. Quoted in Stanislaw Mikoxajczyk, *The Rape of Poland: The Pattern of Soviet Aggression,* (New York: Whittlesey House, 1948), p. 100.

Known as the *Balcerowicz Plan,* after then Finance Minister Leszek Balcerowicz, it was implemented in January 1990 and involved immediate decontrol of most prices, devaluation and then pegging of the Polish currency (złoty) to the U.S. dollar, removal of all foreign exchange controls, and legalization of all forms of private enterprise. The plan was to involve privatization of state-owned enterprises (SOEs), but privatization was not fully implemented before a political backlash emerged against the program.

Poland's experience shows both the peril and the promise of such a shock therapy approach. Output declined sharply and a significant rise in unemployment followed, leveling off in late 1993 at around 16 percent. A sharp upward spike in prices following triple digit inflation also occurred. But inflation rapidly declined to a much lower level, although it was still running at 33 percent per year in early 1995. Sharper income inequalities also emerged. These unpleasant economic facts led to the election in September 1993 of a parliament (*Sejm*) dominated by neo-Communists, albeit of a proreform sort. They follow a more gradualistic approach without abandoning reform.

Poland was the first East European economy to bottom out and begin growing again. It was the only European, postsocialist economy to have positive growth of industrial production in 1992, indeed for any of the years from 1990 to 1992, and the highest economic growth rate in all of Europe for 1993 at around 4 percent, maintained in 1994, although growth began from a very low base after the economy's initial decline.

This growth was led by a strong export performance tied to complete currency convertibility at a credible rate. Much of it has been in a rapidly expanding private sector based on native Polish entrepreneurship, despite the slowness of privatizing existing SOEs. By late 1993 a majority of the labor force and about 45 percent of economic activity were in the private sector.

Following the premise of peril or promise, the outcome of economic shock therapy in Poland can be viewed as both failure and success. The failure is that the original goal was to go to full market capitalism, which has not happened because the SOEs have not been privatized. Privatization has not occurred because of political divisions in the parliament (Sejm) where many parties and changes in governments, reflecting a tradition of vigorous democracy and intense individualism in Polish politics, led to fragmentation and indecisiveness. It also reflects fear of more unemployment, the ''shock'' part of the therapy.

But the promise is there also. The actual outcome corresponds with earlier proposals made by Balcerowicz[3] that called for enterprise autonomy with major structural reforms, but only privatization of small and medium-sized SOEs. His 1989–1990 plan achieved the more modest goal of his 1981 plan. It may have been necessary to push a more radical plan to achieve significant changes before the politicians could slow things down. Although the rapidity

---

[3]Leszek Balcerowicz, *Reforma Gospodardarcza. Propzycje, tendencje, kierunki dyskusji* (Warsaw: PWE, 1981), pp. 279–373.

of the plan probably triggered the reaction that slowed it down, the recent growth of the Polish economy shows the possibility of ultimate success of the plan.

Historical Background to 1947[4]

Occupying the original homeland of the Slavic peoples, Poland in 1024 crowned its first king after swearing special fealty to Rome and the Pope, thus initiating a deep tradition of intense adherence to Roman Catholicism.[5] The Polish kingdom achieved great power under Casimir (Kazimierz) the Great (1330–1370), who established traditions of democracy and tolerance long associated with Poland. Democracy came with electing kings by a group of nobles. Tolerance was symbolized by Casimir's invitation to Jews in Western Europe to settle in Poland when they were persecuted during the Black Plague of the mid-1300s. Poland would become the most important center of Jewish life in the world for hundreds of years.[6]

Poland was a major center of the Renaissance, experiencing a flowering of science, art, literature, and economic growth during the 1500s.[7] The Thirty Years War initiated a long economic and political decline. This decline was exacerbated by the *liberum veto,* which allowed a single member of the Sejm to dissolve it by a veto, the ultimate in Polish democratic indecisiveness. Thus little got done during the 1700s and the Polish military decayed. The result was partition of Poland by its three absolutist neighbors, Russia, Prussia, and Austria, culminating in 1795 when Poland ceased to exist as an independent nation.

Desire for independence surfaced repeatedly in revolutionary upheavals in 1830, 1846, 1848, 1863, and 1905. Although there was some industrialization in Russian Poland, the country remained primarily agricultural. Austrian Poland was extremely poor and totally agricultural. The most significant

---

[4]For more detail see W. F. Reddaway, J. H. Penson, O. Halecki, and R. Dyboski, eds., *The Cambridge History of Poland,* vol. 1 and vol. 2 (Cambridge: Cambridge University Press, 1941 and 1950 respectively).

[5]This is exemplified by the Polish Pope, John Paul II. Adherence to Catholicism as part of Polish national identity was enhanced when Poland was ruled by Lutheran Germans from the West or by Orthodox Russians from the East (and most recently by the officially atheist Soviets).

[6]See Chmien Abramsky, Maciej Jachimczyk, and Antony Polonsky, *The Jews in Poland* (Oxford: Basil Blackwell, 1986). Today there are only a few thousand Jews left in Poland, most of them elderly. Hitler killed most of those who did not successfully flee. His deadliest camps were in Poland, notably Auschwitz. Jewish emigration from Poland began in the 1880s when much of the country was ruled by Russia. Anti-Semitic pogroms began there after the assassination of Tsar Alexander II by anarchists. Further emigration occurred after World War II, especially in 1968 during anti-Semitic purges under the Communist regime.

[7]The contrast with Russia to the East was especially sharp then, with Tsar Ivan the Terrible resisting such influences.

development, including expanded mining, occurred in Prussian Poland. Polish independence was won militarily against the Germans and the post-1917 Soviets when Poland's military leader and first Head of State, Marshall Piłsudski, defeated a Soviet siege of Warsaw in 1920.

The parliamentary government succeeding Piłsudski allowed hyperinflation related to large budget deficits as in Poland's neighbors. The economic situation led Piłsudski to carry out a coup in 1926, and he ruled as dictator until his death in 1935, when he was succeeded by a group of colonels. The economic policies of Piłsudski and his successors involved state intervention along authoritarian corporatist lines, and industrial output tripled between 1922 and 1939, although this was only about 5 percent higher than the prewar 1913 level.[8] Poland was still predominantly agricultural when World War II began.

Germany invaded Poland on September 1, 1939, starting World War II in Europe. This followed the Molotov-von Ribbentrop pact between the USSR and Germany. The USSR soon invaded from the East, taking areas that would be annexed after the war when Poland was given former German territory westward. Poland had the highest percentage of its population killed of any nation[9] during the war.

After Germany invaded the USSR in 1941, Stalin set up the Polish Workers' Party, which dominated a multiparty government that took power after the Red Army removed the Germans in early 1945. The United States and Britain supported a Polish government-in-exile in London, but they let Stalin have his way at the Yalta Conference in 1945 for assurances that he would respect Polish independence and that free elections would be held soon.[10]

In early 1947 elections were held, manipulated by the Polish Workers' Party. After this, opposition leaders fled; parties such as the Social Democrats were "amalgamated" with the Polish Workers' Party, many members being purged; "national Communists" such as Władysław Gomułka were purged from the ruling party, and the leadership was taken over by hard-line Stalinists. Poland had gone from the grip of Adolf Hitler to that of Joseph Stalin.

---

[8]See J. Taylor, *The Economic Development of Poland, 1919–1950* (Westport: Greenwood Press, 1952), p. 91, and Ivan T. Berend and György Ránki, *Economic Development in East-Central Europe in the 19th and 20th Centuries* (New York: Columbia University Press, 1974), p. 299.

[9]See George Kolankiewicz and Paul G. Lewis, *Poland: Politics, Economics and Society* (London: Pinter, 1986), p. 11. More Soviets and by some accounts Germans were killed, but out of larger population bases. A larger percentage of the global Jewish and Byelorussian populations were killed than Polish, but they did not have formal nations then.

[10]This decision, and the failure to support the government-in-exile earlier when Stalin might have been more agreeable, has been widely and severely criticized. By the time of Yalta the Red Army was already in Poland and not much could be done.

Economic Policies of the Communist Regime

The Periods of Communist Rule

The 1947–1989 period of Communist rule had four subperiods: 1947–1956, 1957–1970, 1971–1981, and 1982–1989. The 1947–1956 period was characterized by standard Stalinism emphasizing heavy industrialization under socialist command central planning, deviating only in a failed effort to collectivize agriculture.

After Khrushchev's destalinization speech at the 20th Soviet Party Congress, riots erupted in Poznán and many people were killed, wounded, or arrested. The riots triggered a party-government upheaval, and Władysław Gomułka was brought back from disgrace to lead the party and the nation. A "thaw" period ensued, marked by stopping efforts to collectivize agriculture[11] and reducing persecution of the Roman Catholic Church. But then came more repressive policies, culminating in an anti-Semitic purge of the leadership in 1968[12] shortly before Polish troops participated in crushing the reformist Czechoslovak regime.[13]

An effort to raise food prices in 1970 led to strikes and riots that caused Gomułka's replacement by Edward Gierek. He pushed rapid growth, and the early 1970s saw the most rapid growth of the Polish economy ever. But the growth was unbalanced and unsustainable. Gierek encouraged the formation of large enterprise units similar to the East German Kombinate. These units engaged in wasteful gigantomaniac investment projects, which created bottlenecks in the economy.

These projects were financed by foreign borrowing after the signing of a mutual recognition pact between Poland and West Germany at the end of 1970. The debt-service ratio (interest payments on foreign debt as a percent of hard currency export earnings) rose from 16 percent in 1973 to 42.2 percent in

---

[11]Later the government seized land for unpaid debts. This gradually led to an increase in state farmlands to nearly 30 percent in 1989 (Krystyna Daniel, "Private Farm Ownership in a Changing Poland: Myth and Reality," in *A Fourth Way? Privatization, Property, and the Emergence of New Market Economies,* eds. G. S. Alexander and G. Skąpska [New York: Routledge, 1994], pp. 140–41). In 1956 about 23 percent of land was in collective farms, a figure that went to nearly zero shortly thereafter (Frederic L. Pryor, *The Red and the Green: The Rise and Fall of Collectivized Agriculture in Marxist Regimes,* [Princeton: Princeton University Press, 1992], p. 110).

[12]After that it was joked that "Poland is a country that has traffic jams without cars and anti-Semitism without Jews."

[13]Poland's willingness to support Soviet foreign policy after World War II was due to fear of Germany, especially after Poland was given German territory by Stalin, an acquisition not recognized by Germany until 1990 when it was seeking to reunify.

1976.[14] In an attempt to achieve macroeconomic balance, Gierek tried to raise food prices in 1976 only to trigger another round of strikes and riots that forced him to back off. What followed was more foreign borrowing, and the debt-service ratio soared to 101.2 percent in 1980. Growth ceased and was sharply negative for 1979–1982.

Another effort to raise food prices in 1980 led to the formation of the *Solidarity* (Solidarność) trade union, initially based in the Lenin Shipyard in Gdansk and led by Lech Wałęsa. Of course the very idea of a workers' movement rising up against the state in a "workers' paradise" was a major contradiction. The union was tolerated until the end of 1981 when a military coup was carried out by General Wojciech Jaruzelski, who declared martial law and outlawed Solidarity.[15]

In 1982 the Jaruzelski regime introduced the Reformed Economic System (RES), characterized by the "three S's," *self-management* (*samorzadny*), *self-financing* (*samofinansujacy*), and *independent enterprise* (*samodzielny*). Imitating the market socialism of Hungary and even of Yugoslavia, command central planning was scaled back and given a more long-term and consultative character. Workers' Councils, which were supposed to have authority over the management of enterprises, were given increased power. They had been established in 1945 but had little authority after 1958.

Briefly in the mid-1980s the economy stabilized somewhat and grew. But soon old difficulties reappeared. Subsidies for maintaining low food prices ballooned budget deficits. Foreign borrowing resumed and the debt rose from 26 billion U.S. dollars in 1980 (still only 26.8 in 1984) to 40.8 billion U.S. dollars in 1989.[16] Growth stalled and without central command controls on prices inflation ran into triple digit levels by 1989.

Strikes broke out again in 1988 and in early 1989 a round table conference began with Jaruzelski and Wałęsa as the main negotiators. In August a coalition government was established in which Communists participated but non-Communists were in charge and Leszek Balcerowicz was Finance Minister. At the end of 1990, Jaruzelski was replaced as president by Lech Wałęsa after a democratic election. Poland was the first East European country to shrug off Communism, and it did so peacefully.

---

[14]Urszula Plowiec, "Economic Reform and Foreign Trade in Poland," in *Economic Adjustment and Reform in Eastern Europe and the Soviet Union: Essays in Honor of Franklyn D. Holzman*, eds. J. C. Brada, E. A. Hewett, and T. A. Wolf (Durham: Duke University Press, 1988), pp. 348–51.

[15]This was the only military coup ever carried out in any Communist country, there being a long tradition of disliking "Bonapartism" and of maintaining civilian party control of the state. The Soviets supported Jaruzelski's coup. What remains debated is whether he was just a dictator beholden to a foreign power, or partly a national savior who forestalled a Soviet army invasion by his coup.

[16]Dariusz Olszewski, Grazyna Pruban, Monika Pawilica, Piotr Nojszewski, and Miroslawa Sibilska, "The Polish Economy and Politics Since the Solidarity Take-Over; Chronology of Events and Major Statistical Indicators," PPRG Discussion Paper No. 6, Warsaw University, Table 7 (1991).

FIGURE 12–1   **Economic Growth Rates in Poland**

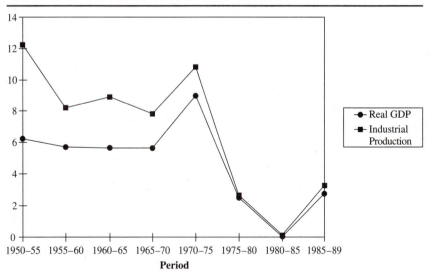

Source: Stanislaw Gomułka, *Growth, Innovation and Reform in Eastern Europe.* Madison: University of Wisconsin Press (1986), p. 191 for 1950 to 1980, and Dariusz Olsewski, Grazyna Pruban, Monika Pawilica, Piotr Nojszewski, and Miroslawa Sibilska, ''The Polish Economy and Politics since the Solidarity Take-Over: Chronology of Events and Major Statistical Indicators,'' PPRG Discussion Paper No. 6, Warsaw University (1991), Tables 3A and 6 for 1980 to 1989.

Overall Economic Performance of the Communist Regime

Economic performance in Poland from 1947 to 1989 resembled that of other East European Communist states. The virtues were these: substantial real economic growth until the late 1970s, a shift from a rural-agricultural society to an urban-industrial one, low unemployment, more equally distributed income than in most market capitalist economies, available public goods, and a generous social safety net, although the quality of medical care deteriorated near the end.

But the usual difficulties were also there: gigantomania, inefficiency culminating in stagnant growth, shortages and poor quality of consumer goods, and severe environmental damage. Peculiar to Poland was a severe disjuncture between agriculture and the rest of the economy, which aggravated Polish inflation. Agriculture was largely market capitalist, but inefficient nonetheless for reasons discussed below. Larger than average foreign debt burdens emerged. Deep-rooted anti-Russian nationalism combined with these difficulties to feed the workers' movement that became Solidarity.

Figure 12–1 shows average annual growth rates of Polish real GNP and industrial production for five-year periods from 1950 to 1989. Industrial production grew fastest during the Stalinist early 1950s whereas overall GNP grew fastest during the early 1970s.

TABLE 12–1   **Social and Consumption Characteristics**

Year	Population Urbanized	Persons per Room	Consumption per Capita
1950	26.6%	1.53	14.44
1980	59.1	1.05	49.50

Source: Figures from Stanislaw Gomulka, *Growth, Innovation and Reform in Eastern Europe* (Madison, WI: University of Wisconsin Press, 1986), pp. 174, 175, and 180.

Table 12–1 shows figures for percent of population urbanized, persons per room in housing, and consumption per capita in thousands of 1977 złotys (Polish currency) for 1950 and 1980. These figures show substantial positive changes.

The Distribution of Income

Poland was about midranked among Soviet bloc countries with respect to income distribution. Decile ratios for per household income (the ratio of the share of the top 10 percent of population to the share of the bottom 10 percent of population) for 1982–85 show Czechoslovakia at 2.4, Hungary at 2.6, Poland at 3.0, the USSR at 3.3, and the United Kingdom at 3.9.[17] These findings generalize to other measures such as Gini coefficients and measures of earnings.

There were some fluctuations and a significant increase in equality both in earnings and in income during the Solidarity period in 1981, which were reversed afterwards.[18] Earnings became more equal during the late 1950s and late 1980s, although this equalization did not show up in income data.

Environmental Degradation in Poland

Poland is paradoxical in containing both some of the most environmentally pristine land in all of Europe, mostly in its northeastern corner, and some of the most polluted, mostly in its southwestern corner. Of Polish land, 8.5 percent is virtually in its natural condition and another 19 percent contains "biological complexes operating on sustainable and ecologically sound principles."[19] At the other extreme, 11 percent of the land area containing

---

[17] Anthony B. Atkinson and John Micklewright, *Economic Transformation in Eastern Europe and the Distribution of Income,* (Cambridge: Cambridge University Press, 1992), p. 114.

[18] Atkinson and Micklewright, *Economic Transformation in Eastern Europe,* pp. 90, 129.

[19] Tomasz Zylicz, "Environmental Policy in Poland," PPRG Discussion Paper No. 12 (Warsaw: Warsaw University, 1991), p. 2.

TABLE 12–2   Environmental Conditions in Poland

Category	Poland	EE-6	EU
Energy intensity of GDP	890	770	230
Water intensity of GDP	116	153	82
Wastewater per GDP	97	83	24
Gases per GDP	47	51	24
Dust per GDP	13	13	1
Solid waste per GDP	1,300	1,000	400

Note: Energy per GDP is in ''ton of oil equivalent'' per U.S. dollar, water intensity per GDP is in cubic meters per $1,000, wastewater is in cubic meters per $1,000, gases are in kilograms per $1,000, dust is in kilograms per $1,000, and solid waste is in kilograms per dollar.

Source: Figures from Tomasz Żylicz, ''Environmental Policy in Poland,'' PPRG Discussion Paper No. 12 (Warsaw: Warsaw University, 1991), p. 17.

one-third of the population is among some of the most polluted and hazardous to health on earth. This southwestern area contains many steel, cement, and chemical plants.[20]

Table 12–2 reports various environmental measures for Poland in the aggregate relative to the Eastern European 6, the EE-6 (Bulgaria, Czechoslovakia, GDR, Hungary, Poland, Romania) and the European Union (EU) for the 1980s as an average. Poland is substantially worse than the EU on all measures and worse than the EE-6 on more measures than is the reverse. Poland's performance is especially bad in the areas of energy intensity per GDP, wastewater per GDP, and solid waste per GDP.

During the later years of the previous regime environmental enforcement was based on a system of fines. But these were weakly enforced and the fines were not very high even when they were collected. With soft budget constraints, such fines made little difference to actual decision making.[21] Current policy prioritizes cleanup of major rivers in major urban areas, but debate continues about appropriate policy tools.

The Curious Case of Polish Agriculture

Conflicts between the interests of the rural and urban sectors of the Polish economy aggravated the difficulties and imbalances that felled the Communist regime. A rural branch of Solidarity was started, but it has gone its separate way since 1990.

---

[20]This area, along with neighboring sections of southeastern former East Germany and northern Czech Republic, is known as the ''Dirty Triangle'' and has very high sulfur emissions from widespread burning of lignite coal.

[21]For further discussion of this problem, see Dietrich Earnhart, ''The Principal-Agent Model in a Centrally Planned and Transitional Market Economy: Environmental Protection in the Czech Republic'' (University of Wisconsin–Madison, 1994, mimeographed).

TABLE 12–3 Agricultural Performance in Various Countries

Country	Output Growth	TFP Growth	Percent Labor	Percent Exports	Percent Imports
Bulgaria	1.41	1.39	22.7	0.0	0.0
Czechoslovakia	2.32	1.93	12.9	4.4	13.5
East Germany	2.09	1.11	10.0	0.0	0.0
Hungary	2.24	1.10	19.9	23.4	11.4
Poland	1.02	0.02	29.8	6.3	16.8
USSR	1.16	0.25	20.0	3.9	26.5
Yugoslavia	1.94	2.77	32.3	11.8	10.4
West Germany	1.46	2.55			
Italy	1.38	1.44			
Spain	2.71	3.21			
United States	1.62	1.76			

Source: Figures are from Frederic L. Pryor, *The Red and the Green: The Rise and Fall of Collectivized Agriculture in Marxist Regimes* (Princeton: Princeton University Press, 1992), pp. 29 and 250.

Poland differed from the rest of the Soviet bloc in that its farms did not become collectivized, although a state farm sector with about 30 percent of the land eventually developed. But part of the problem for the central planners was that Polish agriculture was not very successful in spite of being largely privatized, even relative to the collectivized agricultural systems in the rest of the Soviet bloc.

Table 12–3 provides average annual rates of increase of gross agricultural output and total factor productivity (TFP) in agriculture for 1970–1987 for a set of countries and for the Soviet bloc subset, percent of labor force in agriculture for 1980, and agriculture as a percent of exports and imports.

Poland had the lowest rates of output growth and of total factor productivity growth. It was a close second to Yugoslavia in percent of the labor force on the farm and second to the USSR in the percent of imports that are agricultural.

The comparison with Yugoslavia is worth considering. Both have had mostly private farms, although Yugoslavia's nonprivate sector is in collectives rather than state farms. Both suffer from a problem of too many farms that are of an inefficiently small scale. This is a major reason for Poland's poor performance relative to the collectivized Soviet bloc systems that achieved economies of scale. But Yugoslavia showed the highest rate of TFP growth on the list, a sharp contrast with Poland. Why?

Poland's private farmers worked within a generally centrally planned system that was hostile to them and diverted inputs to their state-owned rivals, no different from them in technical efficiency.[22] In the more decentralized market socialism of Yugoslavia, to be discussed in Chapter 14, farmers were

---

[22]Joseph C. Brada and Arthur E. King, "Is Private Farming More Efficient than Socialized Agriculture?" *Economica* 60 (1993), pp. 41–56.

not discriminated against in this manner and could obtain necessary inputs more easily. Thus their growth and productivity gains resemble the records of the market capitalist economies. Polish farmers had the worst of both worlds, inefficient scale and inefficient input markets.

The Polish Economic Reforms and Their Consequences

The Balcerowicz Plan

In August 1989, a government led by Solidarity activists came into power with vigorously pro–laissez-faire Leszek Balcerowicz as finance minister. Balcerowicz developed a plan for the rapid transformation of the Polish economy with input from foreign advisers, especially from the International Monetary Fund (IMF). Poland had an accelerating hyperinflation so macroeconomic stabilization was the highest priority. The resulting plan resembled those recommended by the IMF to combat hyperinflation in Latin American economies.

The key parts of the plan, which were implemented on January 1, 1990, were the following:

1. Elimination of remaining price controls coinciding with 300 percent to 600 percent increases in still state-controlled energy prices.[23]
2. Sharp devaluation of the złoty to a fixed exchange rate with the U.S. dollar while making it completely convertible both internally and internationally.
3. Tripling the discount rate of the National Bank of Poland, which signaled a tight monetary policy.
4. Reduction of subsidies for SOEs as a share of government expenditures from 36 percent to 10 percent to reduce the budget deficit.
5. Reduction of the rate of wage indexation to inflation from 80 percent to only 30 percent with a confiscatory (500 percent) tax placed on any enterprises that exceeded this goal by more than 5 percent.

These policies drew forth the IMF-organized stabilization fund, but it did not have to be used because Poland rapidly began to run a trade surplus with its competitive exchange rate. Following in the next several months came the introduction of a value-added tax, an income tax, and a stock exchange and moves to allow privatization of small-scale enterprises. The latter occurred rapidly, generally as employee buyouts. What was not implemented due to

---

[23]Overall prices increased more than 70 percent that month alone, the highest rate of increase of any single month. As of the end of 1991 energy prices had increased the most relatively whereas clothing and textiles had decreased the most relatively (*OECD Economic Surveys: Poland,* [Parish: Organization for Economic Cooperation and Development, 1992], p. 86).

political opposition in the Sejm was privatization of large-scale enterprises, despite being a high priority on Balcerowicz's agenda.

The Shock and the Therapy

Tremendous debate exists regarding the results of the Balcerowicz Plan. Initially output plunged, in the neighborhood of 25 percent from December 1989 to January 1990, and a gradual increase in unemployment followed.[24] This immediate decline in output has been argued to have resulted principally from three shocks: reduced consumer demand because of falling real wages, rising costs due to higher taxes, and higher costs of credit, with further declines resulting from a general reduction in the availability of credit.

But the rate of inflation was substantially reduced. Furthermore, a portion of the lost output was essentially nonexistent, either unwanted by anybody or an artifact of the regular falsification of data under the centrally planned economy that ceased to function in January 1990. Official data overstated the initial output decline because many of the officially unemployed entered the private sector where activities were not yet being recorded. Although real wages fell sharply, this followed exorbitant increases in 1989, resulting in little net change. Furthermore, there appears to have been no decline in average consumption flows, and indeed a surge of consumer durables purchases occurred.

The general performance of the Polish economy from 1989 on relative to other CEEC (Central Eastern European countries) economies is portrayed in Table 12–4. During this period of intense change many of these numbers are suspect, although not necessarily more so than previously.[25]

Poland's performance has outpaced that of both Bulgaria and Romania in all categories. It has also outpaced output performance in Hungary and the Czech Republic; indeed it outperformed every nation in Europe in that category in 1993. Its inflation rate remains above that of both Hungary and the Czech Republic, but it shows drastic improvement from 1989 and 1990 when it was by far the highest of any of these countries. Poland's unemployment rate is about the same as that in Hungary—the Czech and Slovak Republics are doing better so far.

The Political and Policy Reactions to Shock Therapy

The severe decline in 1990 and 1991 triggered a political backlash. It began early in 1990 when Solidarity began to fragment over disputes between Lech Wałęsa and the government and between its urban and rural branches as farmers demanded protection and subsidies. Resigning as Solidarity leader in

---

[24]Mark E. Schaffer, ''The Polish State-Owned Enterprise Sector and the Recession in 1990,'' *Comparative Economic Studies* 34 (1992), pp. 58–87.

[25]Communist governments were replaced or significantly altered in all of the countries in this table by the end of 1989.

TABLE 12–4   Postreform Macroeconomic Performance of CEECs

Category/Year	Bulgaria	Czechoslovakia	Hungary	Poland	Romania
Ouput					
1989	−0.4	1.0	−0.2	0.5	−7.9
1990	−13.6	−1.1	−5.0	−12.0	−10.5
1991	−20.0	−10.0	−7.0	−8.0	−9.0
1992	−21.3	−5.3	−7.8	−1.5	−6.4
1993	n.a.	−0.2	−3.3	4.2	0.2
1994	n.a.	3.0	2.0	5.0	n.a.
Unemployment					
1989	0.0	0.0	0.5	0.3	n.a.
1990	1.4	1.0	1.7	6.1	n.a.
1991	1 1.1	7.5	8.0	12.0	6.0
1992	15.2	5.0	13.0	14.0	16.5
1993	16.7	4.8	15.0	16.0	21.6
1994	n.a.	n.a.	n.a.	n.a.	n.a.
Inflation					
1989	9.8	1.4	17.0	251.1	n.a.
1990	64.0	10.0	28.9	553.6	n.a.
1991	400.0	55.0	38.0	65.0	160.0
1992	79.5	12.7	21.6	44.4	199.2
1993	85.3	10.0	22.5	36.9	180.1
1994	n.a.	10.2	21.2	33.5	n.a.

Source: Data for 1989–1991 are from OECD, *Reforming the Economies of Central and Eastern Europe,* (Paris: Organization for Economic Cooperation and Development, 1992, p. 23, for 1992 from OECD, *Short-Term Indicators: Central and Eastern Europe,* (Paris: Organization for Economic Cooperation and Development, (1993), pp. 8, 10. For 1989–1992 rate of change of overall output is used. Figures for output and inflation for 1993 are from *International Financial Statistics,* (Washington: International Monetary Fund, March 1995). 1993 unemployment figures are from OECD, *Short-Term Indicators.* 1994 figures are from *The Economist* (February 4, 1995), p. 98.

Note: Inflation rates are based on consumer price index changes. For 1989–1991 combined Czech and Slovak numbers are presented, whereas for 1992–1993 they are purely Czech. The corresponding Slovak numbers were industrial production declines of 6.4 percent for 1992 and 16.3 percent for 1993, inflation rates of 8.8 percent for 1992 and 21.7 percent for 1993, and unemployment rates around 10 percent in both years (OECD, *Short-Term Indicators,* pp. 8, 10).

November 1990, Wałęsa defeated Prime Minister Tadeusz Mazowiecki of Solidarity in the presidential election. The new government appointed by Wałęsa retained Balcerowicz as finance minister out of a need to keep the IMF and foreign bankers happy.

In October 1991 elections for the Sejm, candidates backed by remnants of the fragmented Solidarity did poorly. In a classic manifestation of Polish democracy, 67 parties contested the race and 28 of them obtained seats, 11 with more than one representative. But no party had more than 13 percent of the seats and a period of instability emerged during which revolving governments and decision-making gridlock were reminiscent of the days of the liberum veto. Balcerowicz did not run in 1991 and thus was out of office. Further movement on economic reform substantially slowed, but Balcerowicz's handiwork was not reversed.

Box 12–1

The Czech Republic: A Transition Success Story?

Compared to Poland and other CEECs, the Czech Republic sticks out for the considerably smoother pattern of its transition. How has the Czech program differed? The Czech Republic liberalized prices almost as rapidly, if somewhat later, than other CEECs. It had a successful and fairly rapid privatization based on a mass distribution of nontradeable vouchers, which have tended to be used to buy stocks of holding companies. Ten holding companies own around 50 percent of all privatized assets;* however, these holding companies are managed by state-owned banks. Compared to Poland, the Czech currency (koruna) is not freely convertible internationally and the Czechs retain considerable foreign exchange controls.

The Czech and Slovak Republics separated on January 1, 1993. The Czechs generally have a higher standard of living, more internationally competitive industries, and a greater commitment to rapid economic reform.† Czech success at keeping unemployment low is something of a mystery given the levels of inflation and output decline, but some speculate that rising interenterprise debts have been responsible, backed up by the state-owned banks managing the holding companies—in other words, de facto subsidies constituting a continuing soft budget constraint.‡

Relative to Poland and Hungary, the former Czechoslovakia had a very strict command economy with stable prices, no unemployment, and few foreign debts. Thus the Czechs started from a position of greater macroeconomic stability. Also they had a higher income base and past experience of industrial market capitalism, the only nation besides the former GDR to have extensively industrialized prior to becoming socialist. Finally they have greater access to the German market because of greater geographic proximity, actually bordering the former West Germany, unlike any other former CMEA state except the former GDR.

---

*OECD, *Trends and Policies in Privatization* 1 No. 2, (Paris: Organization for Economic Cooperation and Development, 1993), p. 18.

†Divisions over the pace of reform were a factor in the separation. In late 1994, Slovakia was undoing a previously passed privatization plan under a government controlled by neo-Communists and extreme nationalists. Czech Prime Minister, Vaclav Klaus, is strongly committed to pro–laissez-faire policies.

‡See Richard Portes, "Transformation Traps," *Economic Journal* 104 (1994), pp. 1178–89.

In September 1993 another Sejm election was held. The outcome was a victory for parties derived from the former Communist party and a substantial reduction in the number of parties in the Sejm. These parties formed a government, although the anti-Communist Wałęsa was in the presidency. Their policies have not been substantially different from those of their immediate predecessors.

Box 12–2

An IMF Adviser's Perspective

Perhaps the most influential foreign adviser to Balcerowicz was Jeffrey Sachs of Harvard University, representing the IMF, who argued for the Latin American–style shock therapy program. After the neo-Communist victory, Sachs speculated in an address to the American Economic Association in January 1994 that the victory reflected increased inequality and increased feelings of insecurity.* In particular, the unemployment rate had continued to rise and 50 to 60 percent of Polish workers expressed fear of job loss in polls. Gainers from the economic transition have been the urban educated young. Losers have been the rural less-educated elderly.

Besides the neo-Communists, who promised increased pensions,† the rural-based Peasant Party did well and is in the ruling coalition. Sachs notes that 93 percent of farmers say things are generally bad whereas two-thirds of them say that personally they are doing all right. ''I don't know why they are unhappy,'' Sachs complains. He argues that consumption levels have held up and that unemployment is not as high as official figures say. Sachs is no longer advising the Polish government.

---

*Another factor was a dramatic decline in representation by strongly pro-Catholic parties. The government immediately before the election was dominated by them and had enacted unpopular social legislation backed by the Church, such as severe restrictions on access to abortions. The backlash may have been as much against domination by the Church as against domination by the IMF.

†Sachs argues that concern over pensions is misplaced, their levels having risen from 10 percent of GDP in 1990 to 21 percent in 1993. As of the end of 1993 there were half as many pensioners as employed workers, one of the highest such ratios in the world.

The Problem of Privatization in Poland

In July 1990 Poland established the Ministry of Privatization (MOP). Several mechanisms for privatizing enterprises were established, including (1) management or employee buyouts, (2) liquidation of assets, (3) trade sales to a specific buyer, and (4) offering stock on public capital markets. As of the end of 1992, out of 8,200 SOEs in Poland, 513 had been bought out by management or employees and another 237 were nearing completion of such a sale, 130 had been liquidated and another 720 were nearing completion of that process, 37 had been disposed of in trade sales, and 12 had been sold through public stock offerings.[26]

---

[26]OECD, *Trends and Policies in Privatization,* p. 45. Another possible method is restitution to previous owners. But this has not been seriously discussed in Poland except possibly for some real estate.

Although a majority of the original state-owned enterprises remain publicly owned, the proportion of the Polish economy produced by the private sector is above 45 percent and the proportion of workers in the private sector is now a slight majority. This is because agriculture was already mostly privatized before 1990. Indeed in 1989 the privately produced share of GDP was already at 29 percent, which increased to over 40 percent by 1991. The other source of explanation for the high proportion of the economy attributed to the private sector is the creation of small businesses. By late 1993 about 1.7 million private firms operated in Poland,[27] far in excess of the remaining 7,000 or so SOEs, which tend to be much larger scale.

The slowness of the privatization process led the MOP in 1991 to propose a voucher scheme for mass privatization. Citizens would have received vouchers allowing them to buy shares in holding companies, which would in turn take possession of the SOEs. What exactly these holding companies would do then was never clearly stated. However, the Sejm refused to accept the plan. Unlike in Russia, the Czech Republic, and Mongolia, the voucher scheme for mass privatization in Poland has remained stalled.

Why has there been so much opposition? One reason is fear of unemployment. In 1982 Workers' Councils were established in the SOEs as part of Jaruzelski's attempts to reform the economy and satisfy the workers. Those councils have actually been functional and fairly influential in running Polish SOEs. However, the first step in privatizing a company is to ''commercialize'' it, which involves eliminating the Workers' Council and putting the enterprise under the control of professional management. In the increasingly common case of outright liquidation, the manager often sells off the assets, obtaining wealth for himself, while the workers are laid off. This is a variation on *nomenklatura privatization,* which has aroused much anger in former CMEA countries.

Yet another source of opposition has to do with fear of foreign buyers, especially Germans, obtaining control of the holding companies and thus of the assets of the economy as a whole on the cheap. Foreign participation has occurred in some privatizations, but there has been much less foreign direct investment in Poland than in either Hungary or the Czech Republic. Generally both workers and managers have resisted buyouts by ''outsiders'' whether foreigners or not, leading to very few trade sales or stock offerings.

Although the majority of foreign advisers urge the Poles to resume a push for rapid privatization, the issue must be faced as to whether or not this is really necessary. In counterpoint some[28] argue that such a push may not be so

---

[27]''Poland: Europe's Tiger,'' *The Economist,* August 28, 1993, p. 48. Some of these private firms were small SOEs that were privatized by management-employee buyouts in 1990, whereas others are newly formed firms reflecting the entrepreneurial vigor of the Poles.

[28]Peter Murrell and Yijang Wang, ''When Privatization Should Be Delayed: The Effect of Communist Legacies on Organizational and Institutional Reforms,'' *Journal of Comparative Economics* 17 (1993), pp. 385–406.

wise and that a gradualistic approach to the privatization of the large-scale SOEs may be better in the long run. One example that is successful so far is China, to be discussed in Chapter 15. Despite differences in levels of industrialization and per capita income, China and Poland are similar in having both agriculture and small enterprises largely out of the control of the central state while still having many large-scale enterprises under central state ownership and control. In 1993 China had the world's highest economic growth rate and Poland had Europe's highest.

Those taking this view say that privatization should proceed, but that caution and gradualism are desirable for the large-scale sector. More important is building up markets and the appropriate institutional structures to support markets. Having functioning markets in agriculture and small-scale enterprises provides this foundation and the experience that creates the environment in which eventually suitable enterprises may be privatized and operate optimally. The difficulties occurring in some rapidly privatized countries such as Russia suggest that mass privatization without the appropriate markets and institutional framework may be problematical.

Poland might have few further privatizations and might impose hard budget constraints on the remaining worker-managed firms, which will then function reasonably efficiently although some argue that the expectation of future privatization induces efficient behavior in SOEs. This would require eliminating remaining subsidies to SOEs, which already have been sharply reduced. Or privatization might continue or accelerate after a period of time, moving toward the liquidation form (already the current trend) as the remaining SOEs become the halt, the lame, and the infirm. The result of this process would be the acquisition of formerly state-owned assets by new private enterprises. Either way, Poland, the prophet of drastic change and shock therapy, has become the voice of an evolutionary gradualism regarding privatization.

Whither Poland in the World Economy?

Following the reforms of 1990 significant changes have occurred in Poland's economic and diplomatic relationships with the rest of the world. An immediate outcome in 1990 was a surge of exports to the EU, led by manufactured goods such as chemicals, steel, and transportation equipment, which continued into 1991.[29] This was followed by an Association Agreement in December 1991 with the EU.

---

[29]Bartlomeij Kamiński, Andrzej Kwieciński, and Jan J. Michalek, ''Competitiveness of the Polish Economy in Transition,'' PPRG Discussion Paper No. 20, (Warsaw: Warsaw University, 1993). Although a rising proportion of Polish exports are from its private sector, the worker-managed SOEs have proven surprisingly agile and were responsible for much of this surge, still maintaining a substantially higher share of exports than of GDP.

This export surge followed the shift of the CMEA to hard currency dealings on January 1, 1991, and its dissolution of the Warsaw Pact in mid-1991. 1991 saw a sharp decline in Polish trade with its former CMEA partners, after an increase in 1990, although trade continued to increase with the former USSR, contrary to widespread impressions in the West.

Poland has formally asked to join both the EU and the NATO alliance. Interest in the latter increases with the increase in nationalism in Russia, which revives primordial fears of partition. Much to the frustration of the Poles these moves have been put off by such devices as the proposed Partnership for Peace by NATO and a wait-and-see attitude by the EU, clearly in no hurry to admit Poland.

Five reasons have been put forward by EU governments for this reluctance.[30] One is fear of migration. Wages in Poznán are a tenth of those in Berlin, a mere 200 miles westward. Germany already suffers from anti-immigrant problems. Another is fear of competition from low-cost producers in Poland. The EU has some trade restrictions on steel and coal and very serious ones on agricultural commodities from Poland. Another complaint is that Poland is not ready to meet the Maastricht conditions for full European unification. But as of the end of 1993, only Luxemburg met those conditions among EU members. EU members fear that their institutions will be unable to handle additional members. Finally they fear the cost of subsidies and other supports that may be called for if Poland and its neighbors join.

This EU failure to admit Poland, combined with ongoing EU protectionism, suggests that the export surge of Poland driving its growth might run into limits. Then the former CMEA partners finally may be beginning to recover themselves and resume growth. If the EU continues to be intransigent and closed it might be that a Central European version of the CMEA might be an alternative. Indeed the core of such a system already exists in the Visegrad group of Poland, Hungary, and the Czech and Slovak Republics.

One other possible problem between Poland and the West is in borrowing and investing. Despite its rapid reforms, reduction of inflation, and rapid growth rate, Poland has not been very successful at obtaining direct foreign investment from the West. During 1991 and 1992 Hungary received about three times as much foreign investment as Poland, despite being a smaller country and economy, and the then-Czechoslovakia also received more than Poland. This imbalance may be due to attitudes towards their foreign debts.

Whereas strict command socialist Czechoslovakia ran up few debts before 1989, market socialist–oriented Poland and Hungary both did so with abandon. As of 1990 their debt service ratios were respectively 25 percent, 71 percent, and 65 percent.[31] Poland and Hungary were in similar straits. Whereas the Hungarian government reacted by accepting the debt burden incurred by its

---

[30]"Rejoined: A Survey of Eastern Europe," *The Economist,* March 13, 1993.

[31]OECD, *Reforming the Economies of Central and Eastern Europe,* p. 65. The debt service ratio is the ratio of interest payments on foreign debt to export earnings.

predecessors and pays in full its obligations, the Polish government reacted by complaining about its situation and requesting a reduction of its burden. Lech Wałęsa made the request in an emotional speech[32] to the U.S. Congress, which responded favorably by cutting Poland's formal debts to the United States in half. The upshot was a perception of Poland as a land of debt repudiators in contrast to its neighbors, thereby reducing substantially the enthusiasm of potential investors.

Despite receiving a favorable response to this appeal and experiencing rapid economic growth, Poland still has ended up with a neo-Communist government. This certainly leaves it uncertain where Poland will ultimately end up.

Summary and Conclusions

Poland has suffered a difficult and at times tragic history. After a glorious period in the late Middle Ages and the Renaissance, Catholic and Slavic Poland suffered in the Thirty Years War and eventually was partitioned by its powerful neighbors in 1795. Regaining independence after World War I, it experienced economic difficulties only to be partitioned again by Germany and the USSR in 1939. Then it was completely conquered by the Germans, and then conquered yet again at the end of the war by the Soviets, falling under their domination until 1989.

Under Soviet rule a Stalinist command socialist system was imposed that pushed heavy industrialization, although the deeply religious and anti-Russian Polish peasantry successfully resisted agricultural collectivization. After uprisings in 1956 the system was relaxed. Poland compiled a standard record for an East European system, achieving substantial growth prior to the late 1970s with reasonable income equality and low unemployment. But accumulating tensions led to the formation of the Solidarity trade union in 1980, which was suppressed by martial law in 1981. The martial law regime attempted marketization, decentralization, and workers' management, but accelerating inflation and foreign indebtedness were the main results. As internal tensions mounted in 1989, a Solidarity-led government came to power in Poland.

A shock therapy or big bang plan to transform the Polish economy into market capitalism rapidly was implemented in 1990, freeing prices, devaluing the złoty and making it freely convertible, and moving towards strict monetary and fiscal policies to combat inflation. The plan succeeded largely in the latter effort. However, a dramatic fall in output was followed by a substantial increase in unemployment. Even though Poland later became the most rapidly

---

[32]For the gist of his argument, see Lech Wałęsa, *The Struggle and the Triumph: An Autobiography* (New York: Arcade Publishing, 1992), pp. 11–12. He invoked a heavy guilt trip for the United States over its role at the Yalta Conference.

growing economy in Europe, there was a political backlash against shock therapy and movement towards market capitalism slowed down.

Privatizing the Polish economy was incompletely implemented. Agriculture and most small enterprises are private, producing about half the GDP, whereas most large-scale enterprises remain state owned. Most privatized firms have been bought out by management-employee combinations or have been liquidated and sold off for their assets. A plan for a mass voucher-based privatization was rejected by the parliament.

Poland seeks to join the EU and has been granted Associate status. But the EU blocks many Polish exports. Trade has broken down with its former CMEA trading partners but may be revived. Partly because of getting its foreign debts reduced, Poland remains somewhat unattractive to foreign investors compared with some of its neighbors. Ultimately its place in a dangerous world remains uncertain and insecure.

Questions for Discussion

1. How has Poland's history affected its approach to economic reform?
2. What are the implications of the problems in Polish agriculture for reform of agriculture in the republics of the former Soviet Union?
3. What have been the greatest successes and failures of the shock therapy approach in Poland?
4. How has Poland's approach differed from that of the Czech Republic?
5. How did the introduction of limited workers' management under martial law affect the later privatization program?
6. Why have neo-Communists returned to power in Poland?
7. Why does the European Union appear to be reluctant to allow Poland and its neighbors to join?

Suggested Further Readings

Alexander, G. S., and G. Skąpska, eds. *A Fourth Way? Privatization, Property, and the Emergence of New Market Economies.* New York: Routledge, 1994.

Berend, Ivan T., and György Ránki. *Economic Development in East-Central Europe in the 19th and 20th Centuries.* New York: Columbia University Press, 1974.

Blanchard, Olivier Jean, Kenneth A. Froot, and Jeffrey Sachs, eds. *The Transition in Eastern Europe,* Volumes I and II. Chicago: University of Chicago Press, 1994.

Bornstein, Morris. "Privatization in Eastern Europe." In *Comparative Economic Systems: Models and Cases,* 7th ed., ed. Morris Bornstein. Burr Ridge: Irwin, 1994, pp. 468–510.

"Poland's Economic Reforms: If It Works, You've Fixed It." *The Economist.* January 23, 1993, pp. 21–23.

Goodwyn, Lawrence. *Breaking the Barrier: The Rise of Solidarity in Poland.* New York: Oxford University Press, 1991.

Kamiński, Bartlomeij. *The Collapse of State Socialism: The Case of Poland.* Princeton: Princeton University Press, 1991.

Lipton, David, and Jeffrey Sachs. ''Creating a Market Economy in Eastern Europe: The Case of Poland.'' *Brookings Papers on Economic Activity,* no. 1 (1990), pp. 75–147.

Portes, Richard. ''Structural Reform in Central and Eastern Europe.'' In *Comparative Economic Systems: Models and Cases,* 7th ed., ed. Morris Bornstein. Burr Ridge: Irwin, 1994, pp. 511–19.

Pryor, Frederic L. *The Red and the Green: The Rise and Fall of Collectivized Agriculture in Marxist Regimes.* Princeton: Princeton University Press, 1992.

Sachs, Jeffrey. *Poland's Jump to the Market Economy.* Cambridge, MIT Press, 1993.

Winiecki, Jan. ''The Polish Transition Programme: Underpinnings, Results, Interpretations.'' *Soviet Studies* 44 (1992), pp. 809–35.

HUNGARY: GRADUAL TRANSFORMATION OF MARKET SOCIALISM

Now, Comrade Kádár,[1] perhaps you could tell us your opinion.''
''Thank you, Comrade Chairman. Well, Marx once wrote . . . ''
''Yes, Comrade Kádár, we know what Marx wrote. It's your opinion we want.''
''Of course, of course, Comrade Chairman. Well, according to Lenin . . . ''
''Please, Comrade Kádár, please; your own thoughts please.''
''Oh, very well, Comrade Chairman, of course comrade, but before I state my own opinion I should like to make very clear in advance that I do not agree with it.''
—Old Budapest joke[2]

Despite the State socialism and the presence of Soviet troops, phrases like 'the country of revolt', 'reform-country', and 'the country of goulash-socialism' strengthened the national identity of Hungarians. Now Hungary and the Hungarians struggling with the transformation are faced with signs of pity, contempt and abandonment.
—Éva Ehrlich and Gábor Révész[3]

Introduction

If Poland is the former Soviet satellite that has engaged in shock therapy, Hungary is the former Soviet satellite that has engaged in gradual transformation. It has been suited to doing so because it underwent a gradual movement toward a market economy since introducing its *New Economic*

---

[1] János Kádár, Hungary's Communist leader, 1956–1988.
[2] William Shawcross, *Crime and Compromise: Janos Kádár and the Politics of Hungary Since Revolution.* (New York: E. P. Dutton, 1974), frontispiece.
[3] Éva Ehrlich and Gábor Révész, *Hungary and its Prospects 1985–2005* (Budapest: Akadémiai Kiadó, 1995), p. 120.

309

Mechanism (NEM) in 1968. This market socialist foundation allows it to move gradually without a sudden leap across a vast abyss. Hungary shows both the advantages and the disadvantages of this approach to systemic transformation compared with the shock therapy approach.

Hungary has many similarities with Poland. Both are East-Central European nations caught between Germany and Russia in this century, although in past centuries Hungary was caught between Germanic Austria and Ottoman Turkey. Both are proudly nationalistic with Western orientations. They were the two most rebellious members of the Soviet bloc in Europe, and both experimented with market-oriented reforms prior to the general loosening during Gorbachev's perestroika. Both slipped away from communism peacefully in 1989.

But they have notable differences. Whereas Poland contains a Slavic population and neighbors on other Slavic nations, the Hungarians stand alone linguistically and culturally—their language is not Indo-European and they are [4] surrounded by Slavs, Germanic Austrians, and Latinic Romanians, which gives an acute particularism to their nationalism. They spent a longer time under outside rule than did the Poles, which may explain their more authoritarian tradition.[5] Like the Poles they have had periodic outbursts of nationalist revolt, such as their failed anti-Soviet uprising in 1956. But they also learned to pragmatically and passively resist a conqueror. After 1956 they trod a careful middle ground going further towards a market economy than any other Soviet bloc country while staying within bounds acceptable to the Soviets.

Hungary contains some of the most fertile soil in Europe and became the breadbasket of the Soviet bloc, with probably the most successful collective farms anywhere, in contrast to the unproductive small family farms of Poland. An unfortunate outcome of the efforts to privatize these farms has been a drastic drop in agricultural production.

Compared to Poland and the rest of the former Soviet bloc, Hungary's gradualist approach led to a less sharp decline in output. It hit bottom later and bounced back more slowly, although it also suffers from negative spinoffs of the war in neighboring former Yugoslavia.[6]

Hungary may have a more solid foundation for future growth than Poland. It makes interest payments on its foreign debts despite having the highest per capita burden in Europe. The resulting confidence by foreign investors has Hungary far outpacing its neighbors in receiving direct foreign investment. It has adopted a ''full value'' privatization process for industry that, while

---

[4]The closest relatives to Magyar, the Hungarian language, are Finnish and Estonian, not spoken nearby.

[5]Another possible explanation is the extreme inequalities in landholdings in Hungary, which persisted to the end of World War II.

[6]Besides receiving many refugees, the embargo against Yugoslavia has reduced Hungarian exports, with losses in the first half of 1993 equaling about 1 billion U.S. dollars. Eva Ehrlich and Gábor Révesz, *Hungary and Its Prospects 1985–2005* (Budapest: Akadémiai Kiadó, 1995), p. 40.

gradual, assures that new owners have sufficient financing to make needed improvements and long-run investments. Also the experience of its citizens with markets is significant.

There are two major flies in the ointment. One it shares with Poland—and arises from the apparent unwillingness of the European Union to allow imports from Eastern Europe or to move rapidly in allowing these Western-oriented nations to join. Given the collapse of the former CMEA trade bloc, this policy of the EU slows their economies.

The other is that unlike Poland, but like Russia and Serbia, Hungary is a nation with many of its ethnic cohorts living in neighboring countries where they are discriminated against. This fires an irredentist nationalism that drags Hungary into conflicts with these neighbors that could yet sabotage economic reform.

Historical Background

Originating in Central Asia, the nomadic Magyars migrated west to settle in Hungary in 896 where they intermarried with the preexisting population while imposing their distinctive language.[7] On Christmas Day, 1000, the Pope granted St. Stephen (István) a crown, which remains the mystical symbol of Hungarian nationhood.[8] Hungary's power peaked during the Renaissance in the late 1400s. In 1526 the Hungarians lost their independence to the Ottoman Turks. The Austrian Hapsburgs drove out the Turks and took control in 1687.

After 1830 movements for autonomy spread, culminating in 1848–49 in a nationalist uprising put down by the Hapsburgs who vigorously suppressed the Hungarians.[9] After defeat by Prussia, the Hapsburgs decided to ally with the second largest group in their empire, and in 1867 the Dual Monarchy was created in which Hungary shared power, the Austro-Hungarian Empire.

Whereas Austria industrialized and democratized, Hungary remained reactionarily feudalistic. Juridically the serfs were freed in 1848, but they remained dominated by the nobility. About four-fifths of the rural population owned too little land to be self-sufficient in food, whereas about one-fifth of the land was held by only 324 estates.[10]

---

[7]A sign of the earlier Slavic farming population is that most farming words in Magyar are of Slavic origin. The term *Magyar* refers to the ethnic group whereas the term *Hungarian* refers to a citizen of the country. Out of a current population of about 10 million, about 90 percent are Magyar, with the major minority groups being Gypsies, Germans, Jews, and Slovaks.

[8]The U.S. government kept this crown from 1945 to 1978. Most Hungarians are Roman Catholic, but lack Polish fervor.

[9]This policy was summed up as being implemented by ''a standing army of soldiers, a sitting army of officials, a kneeling army of priests, and a creeping army of denunciators'' (Oscar Jászi, *The Dissolution of the Habsburg Monarchy* [Chicago: University of Chicago Press, 1929], p. 102).

[10]Oscar Jászi, *The Dissolution of the Habsburg Monarchy,* pp. 222–23.

The Magyars were at best barely a majority of the population in their zone and Magyar landlords ruled over Croatian, Serbian, Romanian, Ruthenian, and Slovak peasants. When World War I came,[11] Hungary was on the losing side and hated by the emerging nationalists among these groups.

Upon Austro-Hungarian surrender in October 1918, Count Mihály Károlyi declared Hungarian independence and called for the creation of an "Eastern Switzerland," but the formerly oppressed nationalities withdrew, supported by the victorious allies. The Károlyi government resigned in March 1919 to be replaced by a revolutionary Bolshevik regime led by Béla Kun who promised to resist the allies and defend Hungarian territory. He was forced to back down and was out of power by August.

Admiral Miklos Horthy took power as Regent. He signed the 1920 Treaty of Trianon, which reduced Hungary to about a quarter of its previous size. Substantial Hungarian minorities ended up in the Vojvodina section of the new state of Yugoslavia, in the Slovakia and Ruthenia portions of the new state of Czechoslovakia, and in Transylvania (now under Romanian rule). Anger over the treaty fed "revisionism," which sought changes in the treaty and led Horthy and Hungary to ally with Italy and Germany in World War II after being granted or seizing chunks of these territories between 1938 and 1941.

The interwar period saw economic stagnation. In 1920 about 15 percent of the rural land was redistributed to the peasants, but severe inequality continued. By 1941 the portion of the workforce in agriculture was still 49 percent and the portion in mining or industry was only 25 percent.[12] Inflation in the early 1920s was followed by a period of stability and trade with immediate neighbors. The Great Depression brought a trade war and a shift to trading with Austria, Italy, and Germany.

In 1944 as the Soviets entered from the East, Admiral Horthy attempted to surrender but was imprisoned by the Germans and replaced by an outright fascist regime that began killing Jews. In April 1945, after much damage and death, the Nazis were defeated in Hungary, which lost its ill-gotten territories.

A multiparty government came to power in 1945, officially led by the peasant-based Smallholder Party.[13] Led by the Stalinist, Mátyás Rákosi, the Communists held key ministries, but they came in fourth in elections in late 1945 after land redistribution was carried out.[14] Rákosi used "salami tactics"

---

[11]During the war Hungary undermined Austria while trying to dominate the groups in its zone. The upshot was the final dissolution of the Hapsburg empire. Ironically many people in these formerly subject areas are nostalgic for it now.

[12]Ivan T. Berend and György Ránki, *The Hungarian Economy in the Twentieth Century* (New York: St. Martin's Press, 1985), p. 95.

[13]This party reemerged in the 1990 elections to place third in parliamentary seats, but it has since fragmented.

[14]Landless peasants declined from 46.8 percent of the peasant population to only 17 percent while those holding more than 14 hectares declined from 7 percent to 2.8 percent (Berend and Ránki, *The Hungarian Economy,* p. 184).

to slice off and reduce the opposition. The world's worst-ever hyperinflation in 1946 strengthened the Communists.[15] In 1947 they staged a rigged election in which, despite only obtaining 22 percent of the vote, they came out with the largest number of seats in the parliament and clear control. By 1949 the salami was fully sliced and Rákosi declared a one-party "dictatorship of the proletariat."

Hungarian Economic Policies under Communism

The Move to Stalinism, 1945–53

At the end of World War II about one-fourth of Hungary's industrial capacity had been destroyed and the country faced reparations payments to the USSR. The Communists would go to command socialism by the end of the decade.

Nationalization of private property proceeded in stages. By December 1949 only about 20 percent of the nonagricultural workforce was still in the private sector, all in firms with less than 10 employees in retail trade, artisan production, and the service sector. By 1960 this figure was zero.

Aware of the popularity of the 1945 land reform, Rákosi moved slowly in agriculture, pressing for collectivization after 1948. As of 1952 collectivization only involved about one-fifth of the agricultural workforce and one-third of the arable land.

A five-year plan began in 1950 emphasizing heavy industrialization within the CMEA framework. Hungary specialized in and exported to its socialist trading partners transportation equipment and vehicles, especially buses. Electronics was also a specialty and much of Hungary's output was produced by Tungsram, which is now owned by General Electric. Only in the early 1960s did the industrial workforce exceed the agricultural. Fertile Hungary became an important food supplier of the Soviet bloc.

The 1950–53 period saw growth exceeding 8 percent per year, increases in income equality, and reductions in economic discrimination against women and ethnic minorities such as Gypsies.[16] But this period also was marked by intense repression, massive purges, and jailings. Rákosi filled concentration camps with 1½ percent of the population by Stalin's death in March 1953.

---

[15]At its peak in July 1946 the inflation rate was 10 to 12 percent *per hour*. Starvation was prevented by imposing a "calorie-standard" of payment. When the pengo was replaced by the forint, they traded at four trillion pengos per forint (Berend and Ránki, *The Hungarian Economy,* pp. 189–91).

[16]See E. Lynn Turgeon, *State and Discrimination: The Other Side of the Cold War* (Armonk: M. E. Sharpe, 1989), chap. 7, which argues that the economic position of women and Gypsies relative to non-Gypsy males was at its best during the Rákosi regime and deteriorated after the 1968 adoption of the NEM. The position of women has held up better in Hungary than in the rest of East-Central Europe since 1989.

The New Course, the Reaction, and the Revolution, 1953–56

In June 1953 the Soviets replaced Rákosi as Premier, but not as Party Secretary, with the moderate national Communist Imre Nagy. He established the New Course that involved backing off from collectivizing agriculture and redistributing investment funds from heavy to light industry. He also closed the prison camps and rehabilitated purged Party members.

In 1955, power returned to Rákosi. But the New Course set off an intellectual process that would culminate in the New Economic Mechanism of 1968. György Péter published influential papers in Hungarian in 1954[17] calling for decentralized decision making. These influenced such reformers as János Kornai.

Rákosi's efforts to censor intellectuals associated with Nagy generated popular opposition after February 1956 when Khrushchev denounced Stalin. Conflict and tension accelerated after Polish riots in June, and Rákosi was removed in July. On October 23, Nagy was reinstated. Mass street uprisings occurred and on November 1 Nagy announced the withdrawal of Hungary from the Warsaw Pact to neutrality. Soviet troops entered the country and on November 4 the revolt was bloodily put down. Nagy was replaced by János Kádár, who remained in power until 1988.[18]

The Move to the "Soft Dictatorship," 1957–67

Intense repression immediately followed the Hungarian Revolution. Economic policy became mostly orthodox. Kádár imposed full collectivization of agriculture. But in contrast to other Soviet bloc countries peasants were partially paid off and the process proceeded in a fairly voluntary manner, aiding the later success of Hungarian agriculture. Industrialization was more gradually implemented. Annual GDP growth rates averaged 5.7 percent for 1957–1967.

Kádár relaxed the repression in 1963 by issuing a general political amnesty followed by general civil liberalization, including allowing Hungarians limited rights to travel abroad, something forbidden in other Soviet bloc countries except for selected individuals. The economic reformers resurfaced.

Kádár "pushed the envelope" on internal civil and economic reforms while observing certain limits. He avoided workers' management (at least before 1985) as smacking of Titoism. He maintained the one-party state and resisted moves to serious privatization. He slavishly supported Soviet foreign policy, including providing troops for the 1968 Czechoslovak repression. And he followed the line of internal Soviet policy. The NEM coincided with the

---

[17]An English version of one is György Péter, "On the Planned Central Control and Management of the Economy," *Acta Oeconomica* 2 (1967), pp. 23–45.

[18]Nagy was arrested and secretly executed. A crucial actor in these events was Soviet ambassador, later longtime KGB Director, and eventual Soviet leader, Yuri Andropov. The role of Kádár shocked many because he had publicly expressed anti-Soviet views during the uprising. This reversal is behind the "Old Budapest joke" at the beginning of this chapter.

Kosygin Reforms in Moscow, the backlash in late 1972 coincided with a backlash in Moscow, the return to reform in 1979 with its Western trade focus coincided with a peak of United States–USSR détente, and the acceleration of reforms after 1985 coincided with Gorbachev's perestroika.

Introduction of the New Economic Mechanism, 1968–72

In 1968 Hungary ended short-term central commands. Command planning was limited to infrastructure investments in high-priority sectors, administrative regulation of defense industries, supervision of domestic supply responsibilities for certain key products, and fulfilling CMEA obligations.

Other aspects of decentralization included firm-specific rewards for profitability such as managerial bonuses and profit sharing for employees, allowing approximately one-quarter of prices to be set by market forces, allowing contracting for production of producer goods by producer and user firms in many industries, allowing some firm-level autonomy over investment out of retained profits, and allowing some managerial discretion in setting wages and in hiring and firing.

This package went further towards market mechanisms than in any other avowedly socialist economy except for Yugoslavia, which had mostly eliminated command central planning in the 1950s and had adopted workers' management. The initial reception of the plan in Hungary was favorable and the economy grew at an annual rate of 6.1 percent between 1968 and 1972. This ''goulash communism'' made Kádár a semipopular leader.

A Period of Retrenchment, 1973–78

After 1972 portions of the NEM involving firm-level control over the distribution of profits and the setting of wages and investment were weakened. Pressure came from the largest firms[19] and the trade unions, the major gainers from the NEM being smaller and medium-sized firms. Subsidies increased to large, unprofitable firms.

This began the *soft budget constraint,* first identified by János Kornai and discussed in Chapter 3 as the principal systemic Achilles heel of market socialism. Firms have freedom but no incentive to behave efficiently because the government will always bail them out.

Also pushing the government towards retrenchment were a worsening trade deficit after the first oil price shock and an antireform mood in Moscow. Annual growth rates averaged 5.2 percent in 1972–78, but slowed down with

---

[19]Hungary suffers from an especially top-heavy distribution of firm sizes (Éva Ehrlich, ''The Size Structure of Manufacturing Establishments and Enterprises: An International Comparison,'' *Journal of Comparative Economics* 9 [1985], pp. 267–95). This continues to be a problem—increased monopoly power has emerged as marketization and privatization proceed.

a worsening trade deficit and foreign debt burden as the government borrowed recklessly from abroad to finance its soft-budget-constrained enterprises.

The Return to Reform, 1979–84

By 1979 Hungary achieved the highest per capita level of foreign debts of any CMEA nation, triggering a return to reform. Hungary became the first Soviet bloc nation to join the IMF and the World Bank since the late 1940s. In line with IMF policies, Hungary adopted monetary tightness and restrictions on imports while trying to stimulate exports, policies that temporarily halted increases in foreign indebtedness. Hungary also eased restrictions on partnerships with foreign firms.

During this period efforts occurred to streamline the government bureaucracy, to remove central control over about 50 percent of prices, to break up some of the larger enterprises into smaller units, and to relax restrictions on some small-scale private enterprises, especially cooperatives, subsidiaries, and domestic joint ventures. A significant private nonagricultural sector reemerged and many citizens worked extra jobs in the *second economy,* an increasing source of income. Given austerity, overall growth was an anemic 1.1 percent per year for this period.

The Acceleration of Reform, 1985–89

In 1985 an admirer of Hungarian market socialism came to power in the USSR, Mikhail Gorbachev.[20] His glasnost and perestroika allowed the Hungarians to lay the basic groundwork for outright market capitalism.

One policy change was to allow leasing of land and certain equipment and structures for private use by members of collective farms. Agriculture had been the first sector freed from central orders in 1965 and had experienced solid output growth with a much larger share of exports being agricultural than for any other European CMEA country (see Table 12–3). Another change was allowing election of enterprise managers by workers, limited workers' management, and a move towards cooperatives. Further loosening of restrictions on foreign trade were enacted as well as loosening of controls on prices.

In 1987 commercial banking was separated from the Central Bank and a decentralized system of financial intermediaries was established with bond and eventually stock markets. In these areas Hungary preceded its neighbors and established the basis for its later gradualistic path.

---

[20]In 1985 he was in a policy debate over whether to follow the East German model of tightened central planning or the looser Hungarian model. His favoring Hungary reflected the influence of his mentor, Yuri Andropov, who became a great fan of the country and its system, despite his role in crushing the 1956 uprising.

The annual growth rate picked up slightly to 1.3 percent, accompanied by renewed accumulation of foreign debts and accelerating inflation that would reach double digit rates in 1988,[21] the last year of positive output growth until 1994.

Intensified policy debates culminated in a party conference in May 1988. Kádár was replaced as Party Secretary by Károly Grósz and all of Kádár's close associates were removed from the Politburo. In two more years the Communists were voted out of power after allowing other parties to operate starting in 1989. But the 1988 party leadership was already committed to moving towards market capitalism. The 1988 Act on Enterprises triggered a wave of ''spontaneous privatizations.'' Market socialism was ending.

An Evaluation of Market Socialism in Hungary

Was It Really Market Socialism?

As discussed in Chapter 3 the most influential theorist of market socialism was Oskar Lange who theorized that state-owned firms would operate in competitive markets adjusted by the central planner to correct for market failures such as externalities. Lange did not posit workers' management, but that developed in the first self-proclaimed market socialist economy, that of Yugoslavia discussed in the next chapter. The goal was to seek a ''middle way'' different from the social market economies like Sweden or West Germany, in which the virtues of both markets and socialism would be manifested, the efficiency and flexibility of the former with the egalitarianism and macrostability of the latter.

During the 1968–88 period Hungarian leaders claimed to be following a market socialist model. But were they? In important ways they were. Ownership of the means of production remained overwhelmingly in state hands, many prices were decontrolled, and short-term command central planning was inoperative. Nevertheless many prices remained controlled and the central government used many methods to bureaucratically coordinate enterprise behavior.

One way Hungary deviated from the Lange model was in its high degree of monopolization. There have been two market socialist traditions: *Manchesterian,* which emphasizes reliance on reasonably competitive markets and is the Langean version, and *anti-Manchesterian,* which came out of the mainstream of late 19th- and early 20th-century German Social Democratic Party

---

[21]It can be argued that Hungary experienced endogenous monetary expansion after the legalization of commercial banking in 1987 (Shirley J. Gedeon, ''Failure of Monetary Restriction in Hungary and Yugoslavia: A Post Keynesian Interpretation,'' in *Socialist Economies in Transition: Appraisals of the Market Mechanism,* eds. M. Knell and C. Rider [Aldershot: Edward Elgar], pp. 154–69).

Box 13–1

The Soft Budget Constraint and the Instability of Market Socialism

János Kornai argues that the "middle way" is fundamentally an unstable system that tends ultimately to revert to a system of state control or to move the other way towards market capitalism.* Central to his argument is the soft budget constraint and its role as the main mechanism of continued state interference and control of the economy. Ultimately the soft budget constraint involves subsidies that allow firms to ignore market signals.

But the soft budget constraint can take a multitude of forms and it did in Hungary: individualization of rules emphasized by continuing bureaucratic control over managerial promotions, tax breaks, uncertainty and negotiability with the appropriate government ministries using political connections, manipulation of prices, low-interest loans with no deadlines for repayment, generous central allocations of investment funds, and outright monetary transfers. "The naive reformer does not recognize the conflicts between indirect bureaucratic control and the market," Kornai wrote.†

---

*János Kornai, *The Socialist System: The Political Economy of Communism* (Princeton: Princeton University Press, 1992), chap. 24.

†János Kornai, "The Hungarian Reform Process: Visions, Hopes and Reality," *Journal of Economic Literature* 24 (1986) p. 1,728.

---

theorizing.[22] The latter school argues that economies of scale should be taken advantage of and that competition is no guarantee of optimality. Given the high concentration in the Hungarian economy, Hungary followed the second rather than the first approach.

Among Hungarian reformers and theorists a distinct evolution of thought developed, a transition from being "naive reformers" as in the early writings of Péter and Kornai to being either "radical reformers" (Manchesterians) or "Galbraithian socialists" (anti-Manchesterians). Eventually the radical reformers, including Kornai, supported full market capitalism.

Macroeconomic Performance

By the late 1980s Hungary was ahead of most of the rest of the socialist world in living standards, with only those having industrialized prior to becoming socialist, the GDR and Czechoslovakia, clearly ahead of it.

---

[22]See Alberto Chilosi, "Market Socialism: A Historical View and a Retrospective Assessment," *Economic Systems* 16 (1992), pp. 171–85, for a discussion of the roots of these schools.

TABLE 13–1   **Inflation Rates in Market Socialist Economies**

Year	Hungary	China	Poland	Yugoslavia
1980	9.1	6.0	9.1	n.a.
1981	4.6	2.4	24.4	46
1982	6.9	1.9	101.5	30
1983	7.3	1.5	23.0	39
1984	8.3	2.8	15.7	57
1985	7.0	8.8	14.4	76
1986	5.3	6.0	18.0	88
1987	8.6	7.3	25.3	118
1988	15.5	18.5	61.3	199
1989	17.0	17.8	244.1	1,256

Source: Data from János Kornai, *The Socialist System, The Political Economy of Communism* (Princeton: Princeton University Press, 1992), p. 550.

One problem with market socialisms wracked by soft budget constraints is a tendency to inflation. Inflation became very serious in Poland after its move to market socialism in the early 1980s and also in Yugoslavia in the 1980s. But it was not so serious in Hungary, which did not experience double digit rates until 1988 and passed a peak rate of 38 percent in 1991. Comparative macro data for Bulgaria, Czechoslovakia, Hungary, Poland, and Romania for 1989–93 are in Table 12–4. Although Hungary was in recession in 1989, its unemployment rate was then a mere 0.5 percent. Table 13–1 shows inflation rates for Hungary, China, Poland, and Yugoslavia for 1980–89.

Thus, until just at the end of Hungary's market socialist period it had fairly steady growth with single-digit inflation and very low unemployment.

The system also exhibited microeconomic virtues for consumers compared with command socialism. There were few lines in Hungary for reasonably available consumer goods, in sharp contrast with the situation in the USSR where the average consumer spent several hours per day in lines and many goods were in short supply. This favorable situation for consumers coincided with a generally more relaxed atmosphere regarding civil liberties relative to the rest of the Soviet bloc countries throughout this period.[23]

The Distribution of Income and Broader Social Indicators

Moving towards markets often leads to increased income inequalities. But Hungary's income distribution not only was more equal than those of most of its cohorts, it also reached its greatest equality around 1982, deep in the market socialist period.

---

[23]This is only relative to the Soviet bloc. There were still restrictions on political and other activities unseen in the West and the ability to buy the available goods increasingly depended on working in the second economy due to poor first economy wages. Hoarding and a shortage mentality persisted.

Decile ratio data for income for 1986 is listed in Chapter 12, "The Distribution of Income." It shows that Hungary had more income equality than Poland, the USSR, and the United Kingdom, but less than Czechoslovakia. This ranking is reinforced by decile ratio data on earnings that includes each of the former Soviet republics individually.[24] Hungary had more income equality than any of those republics and is again surpassed only by Czechoslovakia.

However Hungary had not eliminated poverty. Between 1977 and 1987 the proportion of the population below "minimum subsistence" was between 11 percent and 17 percent, depending on the method of estimation, and a minimum of poverty had been achieved around 1982.[25] Much of the poverty was concentrated among the Gypsies. These poverty rates were below those in Poland. Hungary had a very generous social safety net. For example, it had the highest family benefits of any European country, 25 percent of average earnings compared to 20 percent in second-place Czechoslovakia in 1989.[26]

A measure of inequality calculated as the ratio of the average income earned by those above the overall average income to the average income of those below the overall average income correlates with decile ratios results. This measure of inequality increased after the prereform year of 1967 from 1.92 to 1.96 in 1972, fitting with the preconception, but then declined to 1.84 in 1977 and even further to 1.82 in 1982.[27]

Despite generally favorable economic results, Hungary experienced some unfavorable social trends. Although life expectancy for females steadily increased until 1991, reaching 73.8 years only to decline to 73.7 years in 1992, life expectancy for men peaked in 1970 at 66.3 years and steadily declined to 64.6 years in 1992.[28] This trend may reflect a near quintupling of per capita beer consumption and a near tripling of per capita wine and brandy consumption between 1960 and 1984.[29]

It may also reflect the mystery of Hungary possessing the world's highest suicide rate, which rose quite sharply from a low of 17.7 per 100,000 population in 1954 to a high of 45.6 per 100,000 population in 1981.[30] There has been much speculation about this phenomenon, including a cultural-linguistic theory based on Finland having the world's second highest rate and the two countries speaking related languages. It is unlikely that this high suicide rate

---

[24]Anthony B. Atkinson and John Micklewright, *Economic Transformation in Eastern Europe and the Distribution of Income* (Cambridge: Cambridge University Press, 1992), p. 103.

[25]Atkinson and Micklewright, *Economic Transformation,* pp. 231, 234.

[26]Atkinson and Micklewright, *Economic Transformation,* p. 217.

[27]Kornai, "The Hungarian Reform Process," p. 1,725. Unreported second economy income was increasing as a proportion of the total throughout this period, which could easily nullify these results. Also, "nomenklatura perks" are not counted, making the numbers overstate the degree of equality, although this probably does not affect comparisons over time or within the Soviet bloc.

[28]Ehrlich and Révész, *Hungary and Its Prospects 1985–2005,* p. 107.

[29]Hans-Georg Heinrich, *Hungary: Politics, Economics and Society* (Boulder: Lynne Rienner Publishers, 1986), p. 135.

[30]Heinrich, *Politics, Economics and Society,* p. 137.

or the lowered male life expectancy were caused by the economic system; but they are precautionary signals that one cannot infer social happiness from apparently favorable economic data.

The Post-1989 Transition

General Political and Policy Changes

When a democratically elected, non-Communist government came to power under József Antall in May 1990, most of the framework for the subsequent economic transition policies was already in place. The Antall regime actually slowed down the by-then highly accelerated process of reform and reinforced Hungarian gradualism, without reversing or halting the reforms.

The post-Kádár Communist governments engaged in dramatic policies, including allowing East Germans to emigrate through Austria to West Germany in September 1989.[31] This set in motion the process culminating two months later in the fall of the Berlin Wall and the subsequent political upheavals throughout Eastern Europe. In March 1990, during elections, the government established the State Property Agency (SPA) to oversee privatization and agreed with the USSR on troop withdrawals.

The leading party in that election was Antall's Democratic Forum, a rural-based conservative party with a nationalist bent.[32] Second was the urban-based Free Democrats who supported Polish-style shock therapy; third was the revived Smallholder Party, which supported restitution of agricultural land to former owners or their heirs; and fourth was the successor to the Communists, the Socialist Party of Hungary. The Democratic Forum, the Smallholders, and the fifth-place Christian Democrats formed the government. The Smallholder Party has splintered and Antall died in 1993. After an election in the summer of 1994, the Socialists under Gyula Horn won and formed a government with the Free Democrats.[33]

Antall formally moved in June 1990 to dissolve the Warsaw Pact. The dissolution happened a year later, along with the dissolution of the CMEA.

---

[31]The barbed wire along the border was taken down in May 1989. Now it is Austria and other Western nations that are trying to keep immigrants from the East out, rather than the Eastern nations trying to keep their citizens in.

[32]Antall upset his immediate neighbors by declaring after becoming Prime Minister that he was the ''protector'' of their Hungarian minorities: two million in Romania, 600,000 in Slovakia, and 400,000 in Yugoslavia. Relations with the quasi-Communist regime in Romania are especially tense because of serious anti-Hungarian discrimination in Transylvania. Relations worsened with Slovakia after it became independent in 1993 and began to mistreat its Hungarian minority. The Serbians became upset at reports of Hungary arming Croatia, long a province of Hungary. The Horn government has been less bellicose with its neighbors, but tensions continue.

[33]This result is difficult to interpret. Doubtless some of those voting for the Socialists were hurt by reform and nostalgic for the Kádár era. But the Communists were more rapid reformers than the Democratic Forum and so are the Free Democrats. If anything, the election accelerated reform.

Hungary joined the Visegrad Group, initially Poland, Czechoslovakia, and Hungary, and now including the Czech Republic and Slovakia as separate members. Along with those nations Hungary has achieved Associate status with the European Union and has also asked to be part of the NATO-associated and United States–led Partnership for Peace. It was one of the first nations to recognize the independence of the former Soviet republics, including its neighbor, Ukraine. Also it has sought good relations with Germany and its immediate neighbor, Austria,[34] the two nations that lead foreign direct investment in Hungary.

The Hungarian Approach to Privatization

Whereas Poland has emphasized worker-management buyouts,[35] the Czech Republic has emphasized voucher distribution schemes, and Russia has used both, Hungary has followed a more deliberate policy somewhat resembling the caution of the British privatizations under Margaret Thatcher. The Antall government insisted on this approach, undoing a series of spontaneous "nomenklatura privatizations" that had occurred after 1988 by initially renationalizing those firms.

The State Property Agency (SPA) sells firms at full value to cash-paying buyers, many of them foreign firms, either on the stock market, in open auctions, or after negotiations with the SPA. Although not encouraged, worker-management buyouts have not been prevented and some have occurred. Also, as in Poland, there has been considerable formation of new enterprises by domestic entrepreneurs, many of whom surfaced from the hidden second economy.

Despite gradualism, Hungary has accomplished substantial privatization to the point that a majority of the economy is probably now in private hands if second economy activity is counted. Data on the pace of Hungary's privatization process are presented in Figure 13–1.

Whereas the voucher schemes of the Czech Republic, Russia, and Mongolia have resulted in more rapid shifts to official private ownership than in Hungary, the Hungarian approach has its advantages. One is evidence of continuing state-bureaucratic interference and control in those countries through soft-budget constraint devices such as subsidies. Subsidies to Hungarian enterprises from the state declined from 12.3 percent of GDP in 1987 to only 2.3 percent of GDP in 1992.[36]

---

[34]Observers note in Hungary a nostalgia for the Austro-Hungarian Empire. When Zita, the last empress, died at age 96 in 1989, her Vienna funeral was broadcast live on Hungarian TV and 100,000 Hungarians crossed the border to witness the event live.

[35]For a comparison of Polish and Hungarian privatization schemes see Kálman Miszei, "Privatization in Eastern Europe: A Comparative Study of Poland and Hungary," *Soviet Studies* 44 (1992) pp. 283–96.

[36]János Kornai, "The Evolution of Financial Discipline under the Postsocialist System," *Kyklos* 46 (1993), p. 317.

FIGURE 13–1   Public–Private Balance of GDP in Hungary

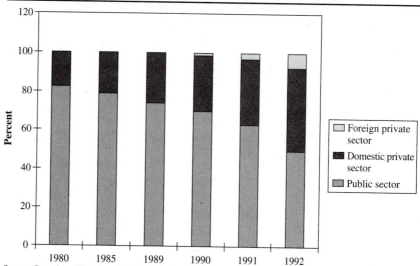

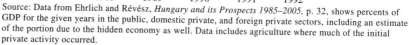

Source: Data from Ehrlich and Révész, *Hungary and its Prospects 1985–2005,* p. 32, shows percents of GDP for the given years in the public, domestic private, and foreign private sectors, including an estimate of the portion due to the hidden economy as well. Data includes agriculture where much of the initial private activity occurred.

Having cash-paying buyers has meant that the buyers are able to make capital investments and productivity improvements. However Hungarians have been disappointed that many foreign buyers have not acted as expected and have in some cases downgraded their Hungarian facilities.

Despite considerable success at reducing the state sector in Hungary, Kornai describes limits to this process.[37] Whereas the bureaucracy of the Communist Party has been disbanded, the new political parties have created professional staffs to work with the new legislative bodies. Whereas the planning bureaucracy has closed, new agencies for regulating the market economy have been created such as for banking, insurance, and antitrust activities. Whereas the former secret police have been disbanded, soaring crime has caused a greater need for regular police. Whereas formerly disputes were settled by party secretaries, now a court and legal system has appeared and expanded to resolve such matters.

Post–1989 Macroeconomic Performance

Overall macroeconomic performance data was presented in Table 12–4 of the previous chapter. Hungary's output declined from 1988 through 1993, but less than most other former Soviet bloc countries, and inflation was moderate and

---

[37]János Kornai, ''The Postsocialist Transition and the State: Reflections in the Light of Hungarian Fiscal Problems,'' *American Economic Review Papers and Proceedings* 82 (1992), pp. 1–21.

improving, although unemployment was at uncomfortable double-digit levels. The high unemployment rates reflect the hardened budget constraint combined with a clearer and stricter bankruptcy law than in most other former CMEA countries. The 1992 overall GDP was 81.2 percent of the 1989 level, although industrial production declined to 71 percent, agriculture and forestry to 75.5 percent, and services to 96.9 percent.[38] Hungarian GDP is growing again, but with a flatter J-curve than some of its neighbors.

The Collapse of Agriculture

A great shock has been declining Hungarian agricultural production, which in turn hit animal production hard—the numbers of cattle and pigs in 1992 dropped to only about two-thirds what they were in 1985.[39]

Hungarian agriculture was a major export earner and was dominated by cooperatives which controlled well over 50 percent of production.[40] Cooperatives exhibit more control by farmers over management than simple collectives. Properly managed collective farms in Eastern Europe were generally more productive than small-scale family farms, although family plots associated with cooperatives were the most productive of all because the collective farms provided many public goods and achieved economies of scale through shared machinery.[41] After 1965 marketization allowed great flexibility and eventually allowed individual farmers to lease cooperative property, an arrangement somewhat resembling the "family responsibility" system in China described in Chapter 15.

Part of the decline of agriculture resulted from bad weather and part from the breakup of the CMEA and the resulting loss of foreign markets that were not replaced by Western ones because of the protectionist stance of the EU. But more devastating has been the emergence of complete uncertainty regarding property rights in agriculture, described in Box 13–2.

The Distribution of Income

As in other postsocialist economies, the distribution of income in Hungary has become substantially more unequal. The percent of the population below the official poverty line approximately doubled between 1989 and 1992.[42] Table 13–2 shows shares of household income going to the bottom and top

[38]Ehrlich and Révész, *Hungary and Its Prospects 1985–2005*, p. 148.
[39]Ehrlich and Révész, *Hungary and Its Prospects 1985–2005*, p. 150.
[40]Frederic L. Pryor, *The Red and the Green: The Rise and Fall of Collectivized Agriculture in Marxist Regimes* (Princeton: Princeton University Press, 1992), p. 417.
[41]On this point see Robert McIntyre, "The Phantom of Transition: Privatization of Agriculture in the Former Soviet Union and Eastern Europe," *Comparative Economic Studies* 34 (1992), pp. 81–95. For the general productivity issue see E. Lynn Turgeon, "A Quarter Century of Non-Soviet East European Agriculture," *ACES Bulletin* 15 (1983), pp. 27–41.
[42]Ehrlich and Révész, *Hungary and Its Prospects 1985–2005*, p. 99.

Box 13–2

Privatization Pitfalls: Hungarian Agriculture

Many charge uncertainty over property rights as the main culprit in the collapse of Hungarian agricultural output. The main source of this uncertainty is demands for restitution to previous owners by the Smallholder Party, demands that apparently would largely benefit urbanites who would suddenly become absentee landlords.

Cooperative lands were assigned to individual owners and compensation vouchers were distributed to previous owners or their heirs. This led to abandonment or destruction of commonly held equipment such as machinery and storage facilities as well as killing of livestock in a reverse parallel of the Soviet agricultural collectivization of the 1930s. Recipients of vouchers include current farmers wanting higher wages, pensioners wanting higher rents, and urban heirs wanting to be able to sell their plots. The voucher system has led to conflict, confusion, and a general paralysis that has been very damaging.

TABLE 13–2   **Hungarian Distribution of Household Income**

Year	Share Bottom 10%	Share Top 10%	Decile Ratio
1962	3.9	20.2	5.2
1972	4.0	19.7	4.9
1982	4.9	18.6	3.8
1992	3.9	24.3	6.2

Source: Figures from Eva Ehrlich and Gábor Révész, *Hungary and Its Prospects 1985–2005,* (Budapest: Akadémiai Kiadé, 1995), p. 157.

10 percent of the population and decile ratios at 10-year intervals from 1962 to 1992. The increased inequality from 1982 to 1992 is sharp, although partially mitigated by the elimination of unreported nomenklatura perks.

Foreign Trade and Investment

Hungary's situation has similarities to Poland's. Both are trying to join the EU after the dissolution of the CMEA and the collapse of former markets. Both countries had high foreign debt burdens, but, as noted in Chapter 12, whereas Poland demanded debt reductions Hungary has not. Hungary has begun to reduce its indebtedness gradually, both in absolute and net terms, while attracting the largest amount of foreign direct investment of any former

TABLE 13–3   Sectoral Composition of Exports in 1989

Sector	Socialist	Nonsocialist
Agricultural products	19.2	22.5
Machinery and transport equipment	46.0	16.1
Miscellaneous manufactured articles	12.2	12.6
Manufactured goods	8.9	24.3
Chemicals	10.7	13.8
Raw materials	2.1	6.0
Mineral fuels	0.9	4.6

Source: Data from Sandor Richter, ''Hungary's Changed Patterns of Trade and Their Effects,'' *Soviet Studies* 44 (1992), p. 967. Figures are the percent of exports to the country group from the sector.

CMEA country. Hungarian exports in 1992 were 93 percent of those in 1989, an increase from 1991 after previous declines.[43]

The redirection of trade has been dramatic. Whereas in 1988 45.5 percent of exports and 44.3 percent of imports were with CMEA countries, by 1991 those proportions had declined to 18.9 percent and 21.2 percent respectively.[44] This shift had major implications for the sectoral structure of Hungarian exports as quite different goods were exported to the socialist countries compared with the nonsocialist countries. Table 13–3 shows this sectoral breakdown for 1989.

The biggest shift was in the machinery and transport equipment sector, long dominated by Hungary's famous buses produced by Ikarus. Bus production and export has sharply declined because of protected markets in the West and the collapse of markets in the East.

Hungarian sectors can be placed into four groups for analyzing foreign investment.[45] One is heavily tied to ongoing trade with the former CMEA, such as the professional electronics, petrochemicals, and oil and gas equipment industries. These industries have attracted investors interested in gaining access to the former Soviet market. The second group is the genuinely high-tech sectors led by politically connected individuals, such as pharmaceuticals and plastics. These industries tended to be privatized early and have attracted substantial foreign investment designed to acquire access to their R&D. The third group had markets in the former CMEA that have largely disappeared, including steel, textiles, and consumer electronics. There has been some investment in this area in the hope of creating EU-competitive exports based on

---

[43]Ehrlich and Révész, *Hungary and Its Prospects 1985–2005,* p. 150.

[44]Sándor Richter, ''Hungary's Changed Patterns of Trade and Their Effects,'' *Soviet Studies* 44 (1992), p. 973.

[45]See Ádám Török, ''Trends and Motives of Organizational Change in Hungarian Industry—A Synchronic View,'' *Journal of Comparative Economics* 17 (1993), pp. 366–84.

low wages or protected domestic industries. The final group is dominated by cultural factors such as food, furniture, and the building industry. This area has attracted less investment except in selected firms, such as Nagykanizsa Furniture Factory, which was bought out by IKEA of Sweden.

For the future of the Hungarian economy the second group is especially important. Hungary has had a strong tradition of education, research, and high-technology development in several areas. Besides pharmaceuticals and plastics, Hungarians have long been at world class levels in mathematics and physics, and have the possibility of expanding into computer software development.[46]

But recently there have been cutbacks in funding for the Academy of Sciences and various research institutes. The crucial question is whether or not foreign investors will support continued development of Hungarian R&D or whether they will just milk recently purchased high-tech firms for existing technologies and then leave them to wither on the vine. A disturbing trend in the latter direction has triggered a brain drain. Whether in the long run Hungary surges forward to high income status or falls into a pathetic state may hinge on this issue.

Summary and Conclusions

Hungary is a nation with a distinctive language and culture that has been surrounded by hostile neighbors throughout most of its history, with long periods of foreign domination and an intense nationalism. Poised between East and West, Hungary declared independence at the end of the Austro-Hungarian Empire in 1918. It was ruled by a conservative authoritarian government that allied with Hitler in World War II in order to reacquire territories lost at the end of World War I. After 1945 it fell under Soviet domination.

After only a few years of following the Stalinist economic model Hungary moved toward more decentralized, market-oriented forms. This movement was cut short by the failed anti-Soviet uprising in 1956, but it resumed with the New Economic Mechanism (NEM) in 1968. The NEM ended command central planning and granted considerable decision-making autonomy to individual enterprises while keeping ownership in state hands. After a period of backsliding to centralized control in the 1970s, the movement to markets accelerated in the 1980s, laying the groundwork for the later gradualist approach to transforming to market capitalism.

---

[46]Two of the century's leading mathematicians were born and educated in Hungary; John (János) von Neumann and Paul Erdös. The "father of the H-bomb" in the United States, Edward Teller, was born in Hungary. A recent Hungarian mathematician-entrepreneur is Rubik, inventor of the popular Cube. In economics Hungary has produced Nobel Prize winner John Harsanyi and the much-cited János Kornai.

Until its abandonment in the late 1980s the market socialist system of Hungary compiled a fair record. It offered a less politically repressive atmosphere than other Soviet bloc states and avoided consumer goods shortages with the attendant lines. Agricultural production, based on cooperatives with flexible leasing and marketing arrangements for both inputs and outputs, made Hungary the breadbasket of the CMEA. Hungary had low unemployment and a fairly equal income distribution.

Nevertheless large foreign debts accumulated as a result of the soft budget constraint as firms still owned by the state were propped up by a variety of devices. Bureaucratic coordination still fundamentally dominated the economy and as time wore on growth stagnated and inflation began to accelerate.

With market experience and an already-existing financial system in place, Hungary was able after 1989 to approach transition in a gradualist manner not based on shock therapy. This led to smaller declines in output than in most other former CMEA countries, although it also meant a slower turnaround. However a confused and misguided approach to land redistribution seriously damaged the previously successful agricultural sector.

Taking a disciplined approach to paying its existing foreign debts and adopting a rigorous bankruptcy law has attracted more direct foreign investment than has gone to any other former CMEA country. Some of this funding has gone into high-technology sectors where Hungary has considerable potential. It seeks to join the European Union and NATO, but continues to have difficulties with some of its neighbors over their treatment of Hungarian minorities. However Hungary's experience with markets bodes well for its eventual adjustment and future prospects.

Questions for Further Discussion

1. Evaluate the successes and failures of Hungarian market socialism as it existed before 1989, especially in comparison with the command socialisms of the GDR and the USSR.

2. Why did the soft budget constraint lead to large foreign indebtedness in Hungary?

3. How did Hungarian market socialism compare with the model of Oskar Lange?

4. Evaluate János Kornai's argument that market socialism is unstable.

5. What are the lessons to be learned from the privatization of Hungarian agriculture?

6. Evaluate the effects of the strict bankruptcy laws in Hungary.

7. Evaluate the gradualistic transition policies of Hungary in comparison with those of the former GDR, Russia, Poland, and the Czech Republic.

Suggested Further Readings

Berend, Ivan T., and György Ranki. *The Hungarian Economy in the Twentieth Century.* New York: St. Martin's Press, 1985.

Csaba, László, ''Transition to the Market: Theory and Evidence.'' In *Comparative Economic Systems: Models and Cases,* 7th ed., ed. Morris Bornstein. Burr Ridge: Irwin, 1994, pp. 520–36.

Ehrlich, Éva and Gábor Révész. *Hungary and Its Prospects 1985–2005.* Budapest: Akadémiai Kiadó, 1995.

Jászi, Oscar. *The Dissolution of the Habsburg Monarchy.* Chicago: University of Chicago Press, 1929.

Kornai, János. ''The Hungarian Reform Process: Visions, Hopes and Reality.'' *Journal of Economic Literature* 24 (1986), pp. 1,687–1,737.

———. *The Road to a Free Economy, Shifting from a Socialist System: The Example of Hungary.* New York: W. W. Norton, 1990.

———. ''The Postsocialist Transition and the State: Reflections in the Light of Hungarian Fiscal Problems.'' *American Economic Review Papers and Proceedings,* 82 (1992), pp. 1–21.

———. ''Transformational Recession: The Main Causes.'' *Journal of Comparative Economics* 19 (1994), pp. 39–63.

Kun, Joseph C. *Hungarian Foreign Policy: The Experience of a New Democracy.* Westport: Praeger, 1993.

Révész, Gábor. *Perestroika in Eastern Europe: Hungary's Economic Transformation, 1945–1988.* Boulder: Westview, 1990.

Van Ness, P., ed. *Market Reforms in Socialist Societies: Comparing China and Hungary.* Boulder: Westview, 1989.

WORKER-MANAGED MARKET SOCIALISM: THE TRAGIC CASE OF YUGOSLAVIA

One day—it must have been in the spring of 1950—it occurred to me that we Yugoslav Communists were now in a position to start creating Marx's free association of producers . . . I soon explained my idea to Kardelj and Kidrić while we sat in a car parked in front of the villa where I lived . . . Tito paced up and down, as though completely wrapped up in his own thoughts. Suddenly he stopped and exclaimed: ''Factories to the workers— something that has never been achieved!'' With these words, the theories worked out by Kardelj and myself seemed to shed their complications, and seemed to find better prospects of being workable.

—Milovan Djilas, *The Unperfect Society: Beyond the New Class*

So in the . . . battle of Kosovo [Polje] the Serbs learned the meaning of defeat, not such defeat as forms a necessary proportion of all effort, for in that they had often been instructed during the course of their history, but of total defeat, annihilation of their corporate will and all their individual wills . . . The night fell for four centuries, limbo became Hell, and manifested the anarchy that is Hell's essential character.

—Rebecca West, *Black Lamb and Grey Falcon: A Journey Through Yugoslavia*

Introduction

On June 28, 1914, in Sarajevo, capital of Bosnia-Herzegovina, a Bosnian Serb named Gavrilo Princip assassinated Archduke Franz Ferdinand, heir to the throne of the Austro-Hungarian Empire. It was the bitter anniversary of the Serb defeat by the Turks in 1389 at Kosovo Polje. Austria-Hungary had taken Bosnia-Herzegovina from the Turks in 1878 and annexed it in 1908 against the opposition of the Serbs. The assassination led Austria-Hungary to declare war against Serbia, thus beginning World War I. Out of this war would emerge the new nation of Yugoslavia, Land of the South Slavs. In the early 1990s this nation would fragment and Sarajevo would be at the center of the most violent warfare in Europe since World War II, warfare marked by horrors such as "ethnic cleansing" and concentration camps.

Prior to this tragedy, Yugoslavia had seen a fascinating economic experiment. After 1950 under the leadership of Josip Broz, known as Marshall Tito, it became the only nation to implement a worker-managed market socialist system with the theoretical aspects that were discussed in Chapter 3. This system achieved successes in its early years. But it also suffered serious difficulties, notably a tendency to inflation, which accelerated after Tito's death in 1980.

At first, the Yugoslav system seemed to combine the best of capitalism and socialism. But after 1980 it increasingly seemed to combine the worst of both worlds. As inefficiencies mounted, output fell, unemployment and foreign indebtedness rose, inflation became hyperinflation, and severe regional economic inequalities grew worse. This latter trend fed the festering ethnic and religious tensions seething beneath the surface of Yugoslav society, which had been held in check by Tito's charismatic leadership. Following an upsurge of nationalism by the most numerous ethnic group (which remained less than a majority), the Serbs, in the late 1980s, these tensions led to secessions by various republics and the outbreak of war.

Variations on the Yugoslav model seem to appeal to other postsocialist economies undergoing systemic transformations, especially the idea of workers' management, albeit in conjunction with workers' rather than state ownership. If the economic system is unworkable it should be avoided. But elements may be salvageable for use elsewhere.

The relationship between Yugoslavia's worker-managed market socialism and its regional conflicts was complex. The existence of these conflicts stimulated adoption of the system because its decentralized emphasis on markets rather than command central planning fit with desires of the republics for local autonomy. But the conflicts undermined the system, particularly as decentralization included a decentralization of control over monetary policy, which aggravated inflationary tendencies. It is an open question whether the inflation was inherent in labor-managed market socialism, was an artifact of regionalized macroeconomic control, or arose from both as local governments pumped money into local worker-managed firms to prop them up, a Yugoslav variation on the soft budget constraint problem discussed in the previous chapter.

The trend to regional inequality accelerated as central control over the economy weakened. The central government long maintained control over investment and reallocated resources from the richer republics in the northwest to the poorer ones in the southeast. The secessions began with the richest republics, which resented these regional reallocations.[1] But the poorer republics increasingly demanded reallocations as the economy overall deteriorated. It is unclear whether the country collapsed because the economy collapsed,

---

[1]That ethnic politics was probably the most important factor in the secessions is seen in that wealthy Vojvodina, an autonomous region of Serbia, did not secede.

the economy collapsed because the country collapsed, or both just collapsed together.

The regional inequality problem was substantially due to the rapid growth of the richer republics. In particular, Slovenia has the highest per capita income of any post-Communist country in the world. It has largely stabilized its macroeconomy while still possessing a largely worker-managed market socialist economy, although it is gradually privatizing. Its success may argue for the system that failed in Yugoslavia as a whole.

Historical and Cultural Background

Overview of the Republics and Their History to 1918

Within the former Yugoslavia[2] are at least 26 identifiable ethnic groups speaking as many as 18 languages. But it is religion, not language, that lies at the base of the intergroup conflicts in Yugoslavia. The two largest groups, the Serbs and the Croats, share the Serbo-Croatian language[3] but write it with different alphabets—the Roman Catholic Croats use the Latin alphabet and the Eastern Orthodox Serbs use the Cyrillic alphabet.

This deep division dates to 285 A.D. when Roman Emperor Diocletian split the empire into East and West along a line through modern Bosnia-Herzegovina, down the middle of the former Yugoslavia. Diocletian's line divided the Greek-influenced Byzantine world to the East from the Latin-influenced Roman world to the West. After the Great Schism of 1054 this line marked the religious division between the Orthodox East and the Catholic West. Into both zones, Slavs immigrated starting in the fifth century.

In the northwest, bordering Italy and Austria, is mountainous Slovenia, best-off economically of the former republics and the first to secede in 1991. It contains mostly Roman Catholic Slovenes who speak a Slavic language distinct from Serbo-Croatian. Heavily industrialized Slovenia is a successful exporter and was a disproportionate source of the former Yugoslavia's foreign exchange earnings. After being an independent kingdom in the seventh and eighth centuries, it was conquered and Christianized by Catholic Charlemagne and his Holy Roman Empire. It was ruled for centuries by Austria and Germanic influence is strong in its culture.

---

[2]Unlike the Soviet Union, Yugoslavia still officially exists, consisting of the republics of Serbia and Montenegro, the former including the autonomous regions of Vojvodina and Kosovo. The other four republics, Slovenia, Croatia, Bosnia-Herzegovina, and Macedonia, became independent nations during 1991 and 1992.

[3]Nationalistic Serbs and Croats agree that there are distinct Serbian and Croatian languages. Linguists disagree. The boundaries between areas where the subdialects of Serbo-Croatian are spoken do not correspond with the boundaries between the zones dominated respectively by the Serbs, Croats, and the Bosnian Muslims, who also speak Serbo-Croatian. (George Rapall Noyes, ''The Serbo-Croatian Language,'' in *Yugoslavia,* ed. R. J. Kerner [Berkeley: University of California Press, 1949], p. 288).

Southeast of Slovenia lies Croatia, second in per capita income and also strongly Western in cultural orientation, being Roman Catholic as a result of conquest by Charlemagne in 803. Independent in the 10th and 11th centuries, it was ruled by Hungary thereafter. Croatia has significant subregions, Slavonia and Krajina, where Serbs outnumber the Croats, which has led to military conflict. Flat in its north and mountainous in its center, it possesses the major coastline of the former Yugoslavia on the Adriatic Sea. This region, Dalmatia, has a distinctive history with Italian influence, although most of its inhabitants are Roman Catholics who speak Serbo-Croatian and consider themselves to be Dalmatian Croats. Dalmatia contains Yugoslavia's most famous tourist attraction, the former city-state of Dubrovnik, now damaged after Serbian shelling.

In the center of old Yugoslavia lies poor and tragic Bosnia-Herzegovina, the mountainous location of the worst fighting in the recent war. No ethnic group has a majority in this nation, although Bosnian Muslims are the most numerous with around 40 percent of the population. But around 30 percent are Serbs and over 10 are Croats. Both of these groups have declared independent republics within Bosnia-Herzegovina. A higher percentage of the population of this republic identified itself as ''Yugoslavs'' than any other, and pictures of Tito, the symbol of Yugoslav national unity, were long prominent there.[4]

Although briefly independent in the 14th and 15th centuries,[5] Bosnia-Herzegovina was hard fought over militarily and religiously by powers east and west of it. Caught between the Catholics to the west and the Orthodox to the east, the landed aristocracy of Bosnia and much of the rest of the population joined the heretical Bogomil sect,[6] for which they were persecuted. After falling under Ottoman Turkish control in 1521, which lasted until 1878, many Bogomils converted to Islam and were allowed to keep their lands. Their friendliness with the Turks fired the hatred of the Serbs for them.

Southeast of Bosnia-Herzegovina lies poor and even more mountainous Montenegro, smallest in land area and population of any of the republics. The Orthodox Montenegrins are very close to the Serbs and remain with their northeastern neighbor in what is left of Yugoslavia. Containing fierce fighters, Montenegro was the first of the Yugoslav republics to achieve independence in modern times, the Ottoman Turks recognizing this in 1799.

East of Croatia, Bosnia-Herzegovina, and Montenegro, is Serbia, the most populous republic, which contains two autonomous regions. North of the Danube River and bordering on Hungary and Romania is economically well-off Vojvodina, where a Catholic Hungarian minority is almost as numerous as the Orthodox Serbs. This region was under Hungarian rule until World War I.

---

[4]Bosnia was the home base of Tito's partisan guerrillas during World War II.

[5]Ironically this kingdom was the only entity before 1918 to ever approximate the territory of modern Yugoslavia.

[6]*Bogomil* means ''mercy of God'' in Old Church Slavonic. The dualistic Bogomils believed that the visible world was created by Satan, for which they were denounced as ''devil worshippers.'' Certain of their views were compatible with Islam.

Tito allowed Hungarian local domination, but Serb domination has been asserted by the nationalistic Serbian leader, Slobodan Milošević.

In the center is Serbia proper, solidly populated by the most numerous Yugoslav ethnic group, the Orthodox Serbs. Midrange in per capita income, its capital, Belgrade, is the largest city of the former Yugoslavia and served (and still serves) as the Yugoslav national capital. Independent between 1169 and 1459 when it fell under Turkish control, Serbia ruled a large and powerful kingdom in the 1300s. It achieved autonomy in 1831 and full independence in 1878 with the support of Russia. The Serbs' position in the former Yugoslavia resembles that of the Russians in the FSU in that they constituted disproportionate numbers in the ruling Communist Party and in the upper ranks of the military and are numerously located outside their home republic. In the recent warfare as these other republics have seceded, the Serbians have demanded rights and protection for their fellow Serbs in those republics.

Under Turkish rule, rural Serbia developed institutions that some[7] think foreshadowed the later Yugoslav economic system, notably the *zadruga,* or farm communally held by an extended family group led by a strong headman. There was no class structure among the Serbian peasantry, their rulers being foreigners. To the extent that these elements affected the formation of the mixed Yugoslav economic system, we might identify it as being partly a new traditional economy.

South of Serbia proper and bordering Albania and Montenegro is the autonomous region of Kosovo, poorest of any republic or region of the former Yugoslavia. Its population is now around 90 percent non-Slavic and Muslim Albanian with the rest being mostly Serbs. But this is the location of Old Serbia, center of the Serbs' powerful medieval kingdom and site of Peć, headquarters of the autonomous Serbian Orthodox Church and location of the battlefield of Kosovo Polje. Under Tito the local government was run by ethnic Albanians, but in 1987 the Serbian Communist Party chief, Milošević, replaced them with Serbs. This action began his nationalistic assertions that eventually triggered the disintegration of the entire country.

Finally in the southeast is Macedonia, poorest of the republics, although richer than Kosovo. Macedonia was long under Byzantine control and later came under Ottoman Turk control. The Orthodox Macedonian Slavs were the object of fighting several times in this century and great controversies surround their identity. Their language is distinct, being somewhere between Serbo-Croatian and Bulgarian.[8] The Bulgarians eastward long claimed Macedonian

---

[7]Joel M. Halpern and Barbara Kerewsky Halpern, *A Serbian Village in Historical Perspective* (New York: Holt, Rinehart and Winston, 1972).

[8]Both Serbs and Bulgarians have often denied the separate existence of the Macedonian language. Noyes (''The Serbo-Croatian Language,'' p. 281), states ''So today a man may walk from Varna on the Black Sea [east end of Bulgaria] west to Sofia, then down to Bitolj in Southern Macedonia, northward to Belgrade, thence west through Slavonia and Croatia to Zagreb, still further west to Ljubljana and into Slovenian districts annexed by Italy after the First World War; and, if he pay heed to the speech of the peasantry rather than that of the postmasters and the schoolmasters, he will never cross a definite linguistic boundary dividing Bulgarian from Serbo-Croatian or Serbo-Croatian from Slovenian.''

TABLE 14–1   **Data on Former Yugoslav Republics and Regions**

Area	Population	Population Growth Rate	Per Capita Product	Unemployment Rate 1967–75	1976–87
Slovenia	1,948	0.71	5,918	2.5	1.7
Croatia	4,683	0.41	3,230	5.2	6.4
Vojvodina	2,051	0.46	3,061	7.4	12.7
Serbia Proper	5,840	0.64	2,238	9.2	15.1
Montenegro	639	0.87	1,754	8.3	16.8
Bosnia-Herzegovina	4,479	0.84	1,573	7.4	15.7
Macedonia	2,111	1.43	1,499	18.9	21.3
Kosovo	1,939	2.34	662	20.5	29.6
Former Yugoslavia	23,690	0.80	2,480	8.1	12.6

Note: Population and per capita social product are for 1988, the former in thousands and the latter in U.S. dollars. Unemployment rates as percents are shown for both the 1967–75 and 1976–87 periods, emphasizing the increasing disparity between richer and poorer areas, and are from Evan Kraft, ''Evaluating Regional Policy in Yugoslavia.''

Source: Figures from Evan Kraft, ''Evaluating Regional Policy in Yugoslavia,'' *Comparative Economic Studies* 34 (1992), p. 13, except for population growth rates, which are from Martin Schrenk, Cyrus Ardalan, and Nawal El Tatawy, *Yugoslavia: Self-management Socialism and the Challenge of Development* (Baltimore: Johns Hopkins University Press, 1979), p. 360. The latter are annual averages for 1975–80.

territory and fought with Serbia, Greece, and Albania in the Balkan Wars of 1912–1913 (the republic also contains a significant Albanian minority). Serbia won that war and Macedonia was South Serbia until Tito made it into a separate Yugoslav republic after World War II. Because the northern province of Greece is also named Macedonia, Greece refuses to recognize Macedonian independence, has placed it under an economic embargo, and keeps its recognition by the major Western nations incomplete.

Table 14–1 and Figure 14–1 present summary data on population, population growth rate, per capita income, and unemployment rate for each of the former republics and autonomous regions. The gap in per capita income between Slovenia and Kosovo was about 9 to 1 in 1988, a within-nation gap greater than almost anywhere in the world, and an increase from a ratio of 3.3 to 1 in 1947.[9] Generally the poorer republics have had higher population growth rates, so that while their overall economic growth rates were often higher, their per capita incomes fell behind those of the richer republics. The high population growth rate in predominantly Muslim Kosovo contributed to the panic of the Serbs and their implementation of oppressive policies there. There is now a strong movement among Kosovo Albanians to reunite with Albania[10] since the ultra-Stalinist regime there fell, despite Albania being Europe's poorest state.

---

[9]Fred Singleton and Bernard Carter, *The Economy of Yugoslavia* (London: Croom Helm, 1982), p 117.

[10]Kosovo was combined with Albania under Italian rule during World War II and was retaken by force into Yugoslavia in 1946.

FIGURE 14–1   Unemployment rates in Former Yugoslav Republics and Regions

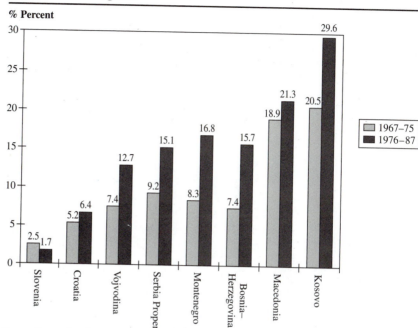

Source: Figures from Evan Kraft, ''Evaluating Regional Policy in Yugoslavia,'' *Comparative Economic Studies* 34 (1992), p. 13, except for population growth rates, which are from Martin Schrenk, Cyrus Ardalan, and Nawal El Tatawy, *Yugoslavia: Self-management Socialism and the Challenge of Development* (Baltimore: Johns Hopkins University Press, 1979), p. 360. The latter are annual averages for 1975–80.

1918 to 1950

On November 24, 1918, right after World War I ended, the Kingdom of Serbs, Croats, and Slovenes was formally declared, with Serbian King Peter I as monarch. This culminated a drive of more than a century for a South Slav nation inspired by intellectuals studying folklore and the Serbo-Croatian language. Initially an ethnically balanced parliamentary democracy, the new state rapidly became dominated by the Serbs. In 1929 King Alexander declared a dictatorship, renamed the nation *Yugoslavia,* and suppressed other ethnic groups. He was assassinated by a Croatian nationalist in 1934.

Economic policy emphasized autarky with high tariffs and state regulation of industries. As the 1930s progressed Yugoslavia engaged in bilateral trade deals engineered by Nazi Germany and its allies. By 1939, 48 percent of Yugoslav imports came from Germany and 70 percent from all the European Axis powers.[11]

In April 1941 the Axis powers invaded and dismembered Yugoslavia. Northern Slovenia was annexed by Germany, which had absorbed neighboring

---

[11]Singleton and Carter, *The Economy of Yugoslavia,* p. 70.

Austria. Southern Slovenia, Dalmatia, Montenegro, and Kosovo were taken by Italy, along with Albania. Hungary retook Vojvodina. Bulgaria took Macedonia. In Croatia and Serbia separate puppet regimes divided Bosnia-Herzegovina.

The Ustashi regime in Croatia, led by Ante Pavelić, was among the most brutal of fascist regimes.[12] It established concentration camps in which hundreds of thousands of Jews, Gypsies, and Serbs perished. The feeling that the Croat Tito insufficiently punished the Ustashis and the bitter memory of these atrocities figure in current Serbian nationalism.[13] Marshall Tito led communist partisan guerrillas against these fascist regimes and liberated Yugoslavia with only minimal outside assistance.

An enthusiastic supporter of Stalin before and during the war, Tito initiated Stalinist policies immediately after the war, except he held a National Assembly election that he and his party won. Among these policies were rapid nationalization of industry during 1946 and introduction of a Five-Year Plan in 1947 that stressed industrialization. Collectivization of agriculture was initiated in 1949, but it was halted and mostly reversed after 1951.[14]

Ironically it was Tito's status as "another Stalin," based on the Yugoslav Partisans' liberating their country from Hitler with minimal assistance from the Red Army, that made Stalin jealous and led to his desire to remove Tito and place Yugoslavia firmly under his personal control.[15] After a series of increasingly hostile letters and discussions over a range of issues, the Cominform[16] formally expelled the Yugoslav Communist Party on June 28, 1948,[17] and called for the overthrow of Tito and his top aides, Kardelj, Djilas, and

---

[12]Among other gruesome practices, Pavelić kept a jar full of eyeballs of his regime's victims in his office.

[13]Fears of new atrocities were aggravated by the newly independent Croatian government in 1991. Croatian President Franjo Tudjman was an anti-Ustashi partisan during World War II, but he has renamed major squares and streets in Croatia's capital, Zagreb, after Ustashi heroes and has adopted uniforms for the Croatian military that the Serbs claim resemble those of the Ustashi.

[14]A small state sector in Yugoslav agriculture remained although the solid majority of farms were privately owned and often uneconomically small. An upper limit for private farms of 10 hectares was imposed in 1951 and removed in 1990.

[15]For detailed accounts of the events surrounding the Stalin-Tito rift of 1948, see Milovan Djilas, *Conversations with Stalin* (New York: Harcourt, Brace and World, 1962), and Vladimir Dedijer, *The Battle Stalin Lost: Memoirs of Yugoslavia 1948–1953* (New York: Viking, 1970).

[16]The Communist Information Bureau was formed in 1947 as successor to the Third Communist International (Comintern), which Stalin formally dissolved in 1943. It would be replaced later by the Warsaw Pact.

[17]Ironically it was the same date as the 1389 Turkish victory over the Serbs and the 1918 assassination of Archduke Franz Ferdinand.

Ranković.[18] A pro-Stalin group tried to carry out this plan, but Tito purged them and asserted his control over the party and the nation.

Despite this political break with Stalin and the resulting economic boycott by East European states, Tito followed a Stalinist economic model for two more years with poor results. Only in 1950, as described in the opening quote to this chapter, did Djilas, Kardelj, and Economic Planning Chief Kidrić convince Tito to move toward worker-managed market socialism.

Worker-Management and Market Socialism in Yugoslavia

Theoretical Issues

Many of the theoretical issues regarding workers' management were presented in Chapter 3. These debates came after the initial implementation of the system in Yugoslavia where, much like the development of central planning in the USSR, it was carried out in an ad hoc and pragmatic manner.

The main criticism of workers' management is the possibility of backward-bending supply curves. This can lead to an unstable general equilibrium or to a gap between goods' market prices and labor market prices, both of which can cause inflation,[19] although actual reductions in output in response to price increases were not observed in the Yugoslav economy until the late 1980s.

Jaroslav Vanek[20] argues that the worker-managed economy can achieve Pareto optimality because factors will be paid their marginal revenue products, and there will be greater stability of employment,[21] high rates of capital accumulation, smaller firms with less monopoly power,[22] no systematic tendency

---

[18]Tito eventually purged two of his three famous aides. The Montenegrin Djilas was out in 1952 for excessive liberalism and would be in and out of jail over the next three decades, a weather vane of Tito's attitudes. His most famous work is *The New Class* (New York: Harcourt, Brace & World: 1957), which attacked nomenklatura perks and powers. The Serbian Ranković was purged in 1966 for supporting excessive central planning and power when Tito decided to decentralize. His removal rankled Serbian nationalists. The Slovenian Kardelj remained in power as Tito's Number Two.

[19]See Gerd Weinrich, ''Instability of General Equilibrium in a Labor-Managed Economy,'' *Journal of Comparative Economics* 17 (1993), pp. 43–69 for the first argument, and Zeljko Bogetić and Dennis Hefley, ''Market Syndicalism and Market Imbalances,'' *Journal of Comparative Economics* 16 (1992), pp. 670–87 for the second.

[20]Jaroslav Vanek, *The General Theory of Labor-Managed Market Economies* (Ithaca: Cornell University Press, 1970).

[21]Surveys of producer cooperatives around the world in capitalist settings support this generalization empirically, based on greater wage flexibility (John P. Bonin, Derek C. Jones, and Louis Putterman, ''Theoretical and Empirical Studies of Producer Cooperative: Will Ever the Twain Meet?'' *Journal of Economic Literature* 31 [1993], pp. 1290–1320).

[22]This did not hold in Yugoslavia where the economy was characterized by large firms and considerable monopoly power, a situation that worsened over time.

to inflation,[23] and a greater tendency to improved productivity. In addition, Vanek says general social harmony will result because of reduced alienation and enhanced democracy. Free riders might reduce productivity, although this can be offset by a greater incentive for workers to monitor each other.[24]

As discussed in Chapter 3, Vanek presents five characteristics of the ideal labor-managed or *participatory* economy: equal participation in management, income sharing, payment for use of capital, free markets, and freedom of .employment. Yugoslavia may have exhibited only three of these, failing to exhibit free markets or payment for the use of capital,[25] and adherence to the three by the Yugoslav economy varied over time.

The above arguments apply to a labor-managed economy that is capitalist, in which workers are owners as well as managers, as in producer cooperatives or ESOPs. This may be where some transforming postsocialist economies are heading. But on top of these issues are the problems associated with market socialism, including the problem of technological stagnation due to worker myopia without property rights[26] and the problem of inefficiency arising from the soft budget constraint.

The latter took a peculiar form in Yugoslavia because of the extreme regional decentralization. Unlike in Hungary there were no explicit firm subsidies. But there were loans made by republic-level or lower banks, often under the control of the firms themselves,[27] at negative real interest rates, especially during the accelerating inflation in the 1980s. Repayment of these loans led to regional redistributions of income from richer to poorer republics and included strong cross-firm subsidizations within republics.[28] This fed the inflation, and the decentralized nature of the process made it more difficult to control the situation.

Stages of Implementation of the System

In 1950 the original Workers' Council Law was passed, directing that the supreme controlling body of an enterprise be a workers' council elected by

---

[23]Certainly the Yugoslav economy was very inflationary. But this may have arisen from aspects of the Yugoslav economy that deviated from the theoretical ideal of a worker-managed economy rather than demonstrating its necessary outcome. If so, this would imply that positive aspects of Yugoslav economic experience do not disprove general arguments against market socialism.

[24]See Samuel Bowles and Herbert Gintis, ''A Political and Economic Case for the Democratic Enterprise,'' *Economics and Philosophy* 9 (1993), pp. 75–100 for elaboration.

[25]John P. Burkett, ''Self-Managed Market Socialism and the Yugoslav Economy, 1950–91,'' in *Comparative Economic Systems: Models and Cases,* 7th ed., ed. M. Bornstein (Burr Ridge: Irwin, 1994), p. 347.

[26]Eirik G. Furobotn and Svetozar Pejovich, *The Economics of Property Rights,* 2nd ed. (Cambridge: Ballinger, 1990).

[27]An extreme example was the Agrokomerc Affair of 1987 in which the Bosnian enterprise sold large volumes of unbacked promissory notes approved by a local bank under the effective control of the managers of Agrokomerc.

[28]Evan Kraft and Milan Vodopivec, ''How Soft Is the Budget Constraint for Yugoslav Firms?'' *Journal of Comparative Economics* 16 (1992), pp. 432–55.

Box 14–1

Ideological Foundations of the Yugoslav System

Tito and his associates were true-believing Marxists and sought to ideologically justify their approach against Stalin's charge that they were anti-Marxist, revisionist deviationists. To avoid being "utopian," Marx and Engels rarely discussed what socialism ought to look like. In fact, the Yugoslav model drew significantly from utopian socialist ideas, as well as from those of the anarcho-syndicalists, more so than from Marx or Engels. So Stalin may have been right.

The problem for Tito and his associates was that although Marx occasionally said something good about producer cooperatives and associations, as in Volume III of *Capital* and in his writings on the Paris Commune, many more of his writings argued that they were a transitional form on the way to socialism and imbued with the problems of capitalism. He especially criticized them when attacking some of their advocates such as the anarchist, Proudhon. Marx did not write about central planning, but Engels strongly advocated it in his 1887 *Anti-Duhring*. Thus, the Yugoslavs had to rely on selected quotations from Marx and Engels and other socialist literature to provide an ideological justification for their model.*

---

*For details of this debate see Milovan Djilas, *The Unperfect Society: Beyond the New Class* (New York: Harcourt, Brace & World, 1969), and Deborah D. Milenkovitch, *Plan and Market in Yugoslav Economic Thought* (New Haven: Yale University Press, 1971).

the workers in an enterprise. It would appoint a management board that would include workers and the enterprise director who would jointly determine organization of production, purchase of inputs, shop-floor conditions, marketing, financing, and wage and salary policy. Control over pricing and investment devolved to these worker-managed enterprises later. Starting in 1952 enterprises elected workers' councils and management boards and moved to the new system, although the fundamental issue remained of whether these bodies could really control a strong director who disagreed with them.

From 1952 into the early-to-mid 1960s the economy was worker-managed with continuing strong central control. It was not yet market socialism. Many prices and most investment were controlled by the central planners. One-year plans directed the economy during the transition to worker-management up to 1957. Then from 1957 to 1961 the Second Five-Year Plan involved much input from the republic level and was viewed as a success as the economy grew rapidly.

A Third Five-Year Plan began in 1961, but it was abandoned the following year as inflation and foreign trade imbalances emerged from the high economic growth. One-year plans operated as debate ensued, and a series of reforms were passed between 1963 and 1966 that resulted in a full shift to market socialism and the reduction of planning to a purely indicative function for the Fourth Five-Year Plan (1966–1970). Price-setting was now in the hands of the enterprises. Control of investment was divided between the firms, the banks, and the local governments. This system continued with the Fifth Five-Year Plan (1971–1975), the period of the Fourth and Fifth FYPs considered by most to be the high water mark of worker-managed market socialism in Yugoslavia.

During the early 1970s debate arose that culminated in the Constitution of 1974 and the Law of Associated Labor in 1976, which shifted the system yet again to one of *integrally planned worker-management*. Behind this shift was a merger wave that reduced the ability of workers to control their managers. In large firms it is difficult for workers to have meaningful input into management decisions. Mergers occurred as an alternative to bankruptcies and soft-budget subsidies in an environment of fierce competition.

Part of that competition came from abroad as Yugoslavia strove to integrate with the world economy. Firms had possessed the right to engage in foreign trade contracts since 1953. In 1961 Yugoslavia unified the exchange rate of the dinar, which became partially convertible. Yugoslav citizens were allowed to travel abroad and many became *gastarbeiters* (guest workers) in Germany, Switzerland, and Scandinavia and sent home their foreign earnings. By 1965 Yugoslavia had joined the IMF and GATT, and had become an associate member of OECD and the CMEA.

Emerging regional differences in rates of economic growth as control of investment was decentralized became entangled in broader political issues of democratization versus central control. Although a one-party state, Yugoslavia was the most liberal of all Communist states in human rights policies. Nevertheless, Tito sometimes felt his control threatened and cracked down on dissent. One such period occurred beginning in 1971 after major separatist uprisings in Kosovo and Croatia. The ones in Croatia were especially violent, involving terrorist bombings and skyjackings.

The 1974 constitution reasserted the leading role of the Communist Party in Yugoslav society. The 1976 Law on Associated Labor went in two directions. On the one hand, it reintroduced planning at the local level that was to be consistent with national level planning, although not on a command basis. On the other, it introduced planning at the level of newly created entities known as *Basic Organizations of Associated Labor* (BOALs). These were groups of related workers within an enterprise who worked on something in common, spinners in a textile mill for example. In some cases BOALs coincided with previously existing firms that had been merged into larger units. Thus this was an effort to revive worker-management in the face of emerging technocratic managerial hierarchies during the high market socialism period. The BOALs could form into *Working Organizations of Associated Labor* (WOALs), which corresponded to existing enterprises, and into *Composite Organizations of Associated Labor* (COALs), which constituted vertically integrated structures across firms.

The Breakdown of Yugoslav Worker-Managed Market Socialism

Economic performance improved during the Sixth Five-Year Plan (1976–1980). But then Tito died in 1980 and national political control went to a rotating collective presidency with little power. Political and economic authority rapidly devolved to the republics. Economic performance deteriorated steadily on all measures and interregional tensions escalated. After 1986 output declined while inflation wildly accelerated. Inflation led to a wave of strikes in 1987 as workers attempted to make wages keep up with prices.[29]

1989 marked the beginning of Yugoslavia's move toward standard market capitalism. New laws allowed privatization and foreign investment. Four types of enterprises were to be allowed: *socially-owned, cooperatives, private* (owned by individuals, foreigners, or civil legal entities), and *mixed* (any combination of asset ownership of the previous three types). In 1990 efforts were made to increase control by the National Bank over the money supply, unify tax systems and regulate fiscal policy from the center, eliminate ceilings on land holdings, and remove remaining restrictions on prices and foreign exchange transactions. A major anti-inflation drive was implemented, involving wage-price freezes, credit limitations, and a strict linking of the dinar, now fully convertible, to the West German deutsche mark, which succeeded in reducing the record 1,256 percent inflation rate of 1989 to 121.7 percent in 1990.[30]

Then came June 1991. After months of failed interrepublic negotiations following threats by Serbian leader Milošević to impose controls on the rest of the country as he had done in Kosovo in 1987 and in Vojvodina in 1989, Slovenia seceded. It was attacked by the Yugoslav air force. Croatia seceded in quick succession and the Yugoslav army invaded. The war had begun, and it would only worsen with the subsequent secessions of Bosnia-Herzegovina and Macedonia. Tragedy descended and the Yugoslav economy as such ceased to exist.

Performance and Evaluation of the Yugoslav Economy

Was It Really Worker-Managed Market Socialism?

The death of the Yugoslav economic system has only stimulated the debate over its nature, functioning, and consequences. Those who argue that such a system is inherently flawed point to the Yugoslav collapse as the ultimate

---

[29]It might seem that strikes in such a system would be impossible, but they had occurred since the late 1950s. The divisions between BOALs within a firm and between BOALs and WOALs, along with the increase in the power of managers within ever larger firms in a highly oligopolistic environment, made strikes more likely as rising inflation seriously eroded real wages.

[30]Egon Žižmond, ''The Collapse of the Yugoslav Economy,'' *Soviet Studies* 44 (1992), p. 108.

proof. But the doubters and critics of this interpretation argue that it was not worker managed, although it was probably market socialism. Indeed, market socialism fundamentally undermined worker management. This implies that the ultimate argument of the disbelievers in the Yugoslav system is correct: true worker-managed market socialism may be impossible in a complex world.

Casting doubt on the idea that the Yugoslav economy was worker managed[31] is evidence that for a long time enterprise directors were really in control, followed by decision makers in technical units. Following behind these in order were supervisors of economic units, management boards, and only then the workers' councils. Semiskilled and unskilled workers themselves had almost no power. If there ever was workers' management it was in the "glorious" early period when the state retained substantial control over prices and investment. But that era was an industrially primitive one and skeptics can argue that it is the very nature of large-scale, technologically advanced firms that they *cannot* be managed by a bunch of "ignorant" workers.

Another argument is that enterprise decision making was heavily influenced by outsiders, including the Communist Party, trade unions, and local government authorities. Local government influence became especially problematical as republics strove to establish autarky and duplicated facilities existing in other republics, such as electricity production facilities, out of fear of being cut off by a neighbor. But then it can be argued that it is precisely when an economy tries to combine workers' management with market socialism that such interference inevitably occurs.[32]

Output Growth and Inflation

Table 14–2 shows the annual average growth rates of aggregate output for the Yugoslav economy for major subperiods from 1947 through 1989. Inflation rates to 1990 and real GDP per head growth rates for some of these periods are also shown. The ultimate source of these numbers is official Yugoslav data that, although not perfect, have greater credibility than those issued by such command economies as the former GDR, especially given Yugoslavia's long-standing association with the OECD and the IMF.

Prior to its stagnation in the 1980s, Yugoslavia's growth record was reasonably impressive in Europe during the postwar era, not declining in any year prior to 1980.[33] In 1945 Yugoslavia was a poverty-stricken, largely preindustrial, war-damaged economy with a per capita income of only U.S. $100 per year. At its collapse it had achieved a respectable middle-income status.

---

[31]See Janez Prasnikar and Jan Svejnar, "Workers' Participation in Management vs. Social Ownership and Government Policies: Yugoslav Lessons for Transforming Socialist Economies," *Comparative Economic Studies* 34 (1991), p. 32.

[32]A further limit on workers' management was restrictions on entry of new firms, especially those started (and owned) by unemployed workers. This further exacerbated the oligopoly and unemployment problems in the Yugoslav economy.

[33]High growth in the 1950s and 1960s was aided by substantial amounts of foreign aid from Western countries.

TABLE 14–2   Yugoslav Macroeconomic Performance, 1947–1990

Years	Real Output Growth	Inflation Rate	Real Per Capita Growth
1947–52	11.8	n.a.	n.a.
1953–64	8.6	n.a.	n.a.
1965–73	6.2	11.7	5.2
1974–80	6.4	17.9	5.3
1981–89	0.6	138.7	−0.2
1985	0.5	77.0	n.a.
1986	3.6	91.0	n.a.
1987	−1.0	118.0	n.a.
1988	−1.6	199.0	n.a.
1989	−0.8	1256.0	n.a.
1990	n.a.	121.7	n.a.

Source: Data for 1947–52 are from Fred Singleton and Bernard Carter, *The Economy of Yugoslavia* (London: Croom Helm, 1982), p. 116. Data for 1953–64 are from Egon Žižmond, "The Collapse of the Yugoslav Economy," *Soviet Studies* 44 (1992), p. 106. Data for 1965–73, 1974–80, and 1981–89 are from *OECD Economic Surveys: Yugoslavia, 1989/1990* (Paris: Organization for Economic Cooperation and Development, 1990), p. 34. Data for individual years 1985–89 are from Janez Prasnikar and Zivko Pregl, "Economic Development in Yugoslavia in 1990 and Prospects for the Future," *American Economic Review Papers and Proceedings* 81 (1991) p. 192, and the inflation rate for 1990 is from Egon Žižmond, "The Collapse of the Yugoslav Economy," p. 108.

Table 14–3 shows annual averages of aggregate output growth rates, inflation rates, and real per capita growth rates for the same three periods for which these data are presented in Table 14–2 for the OECD as a whole, and for Turkey, Spain, and Portugal, fairly comparable in income and general developmental stage to Yugoslavia. Yugoslavia ran ahead of the OECD as a whole but behind the other three countries during 1965–73, outperformed all of them except on inflation during 1974–80, but was behind all of them during 1981–89 in all categories.

Capital Investment and Labor Employment

A central argument regarding worker-managed economies has been that worker-managers will seek to stabilize employment along with seeking to maximize their income per head. These goals lead to contradictory impulses regarding capital investment. On the one hand, such economies should want capital investment in order to increase labor productivity and thus income per worker. On the other, to the extent that they lack a long time horizon they may prefer immediate wages, thus suppressing capital investment.[34] Concern over the latter possibility enhanced the reluctance of the Yugoslav government to give up control over capital investment during the 1960s. Furthermore the desire to stabilize employment does not mean that employment opportunities will expand for those who are unemployed, only that those who are employed will get job security.

---

[34]Lack of worker ownership contributes to this problem.

TABLE 14–3   Macroeconomic Performance of Comparable Countries

Years	Output Growth	Inflation Rate	Real Per Capita Growth
OECD			
1965–73	5.2	4.9	4.2
1974–80	2.6	9.9	1.9
1981–89	2.9	5.0	2.1
Turkey			
1965–73	6.7	11.5	4.1
1974–80	4.0	42.9	1.8
1981–89	4.8	43.5	2.7
Spain			
1965–73	6.4	6.9	5.3
1974–80	2.1	17.9	1.0
1981–89	2.8	9.5	2.0
Portugal			
1965–73	7.2	3.6	7.4
1974–80	3.3	21.7	1.8
1981–89	2.4	17.9	1.5

Source: Data are from *OECD Economic Surveys: Yugoslavia, 1989/1990* (Paris: Organization for Economic Cooperation and Development, 1990), p. 34.

The Yugoslav economy long exhibited high rates of capital investment and stable levels of employment. However, after the mid-1960s, it also exhibited the socialist tendency to a rising capital-output ratio that is indicative of inefficient patterns of capital investment. Also the unemployment rate gradually rose as shown in Table 14–1. During the 1980s capital investment fell sharply and inflation accelerated as workers shifted toward a ''I want my wages now'' attitude. Along with this came falling output and noticeably rising unemployment.

From 1953 to 1977 capital investment constituted an average of 32.5 percent of total output, about the same as for Japan.[35] However by 1988 this ratio had fallen to 18.3 percent for Yugoslavia.[36] Table 14–4 shows the behavior of the capital-output and labor-output ratios over time. The former declined to 1964 but steadily increased afterward. The labor-output ratio declined to 1974 but remained fairly constant afterwards. Inefficiency in the capital market was probably due to the longtime existence of negative real interest rates and the arbitrary allocation of capital by local authorities.[37] The relatively greater efficiency of the labor market reflected its relatively free operation.

---

[35]Dragomir Vojnić, ''Investment Policy,'' in *The Functioning of the Yugoslav Economy,* ed. R. Stojanović (Armonk: M. E. Sharpe, 1982), pp. 65–66.

[36]OECD *Economic Surveys: Yugoslavia, 1989/1990* (Paris: Organization for Economic Cooperation and Development, 1990), p. 90.

[37]Kraft and Vodopivec, ''How Soft Is the Budget Constraint for Yugoslav Firms?''

TABLE 14–4   **Capital-Output and Labor-Output Ratios**

Year	Capital-Output Ratio	Labor-Output Ratio
1953	2.36	0.41
1964	2.00	0.28
1974	2.37	0.19
1979	2.52	0.17
1988	3.23	0.19

Source: Data from Egon Žižmond, *The Economy of Yugoslavia* (London: Croom Helm, 1982), p. 106.

Distribution of Income

Although payment of productivity-related differential wages within enterprises is accepted, the tendency has been to greater equality of wages within worker-managed Yugoslav firms than in other economies.[38] This led to a high degree of equality of the overall income distribution. In 1978 the ratio of the share of income going to the richest 20 percent of the population to that going to the poorest 20 percent (quintile ratio) in Yugoslavia was 5.86, whereas it was 5.6 for Sweden and 9.5 for the United States in 1972.[39] This high degree of overall equality, comparable to Sweden, is all the more striking given how severe the problem of regional inequality was, as shown in Table 14–1. By 1987 the quintile ratio in Yugoslavia had risen to 7.0 (see Table 1–1). Yugoslavia's income was never as equally distributed as that in the other socialist economies of Central and Eastern Europe.

Foreign Economic Relations

Yugoslavia maintained friendly economic relations with a wide variety of nations, in keeping with its position as a founder of the Nonaligned Movement. It maintained a semiconvertible currency and joined all the major multilateral economic bodies, in both the East and the West, either fully or as an Associate. It traded with both blocs, although generally more with the West than with the East.

Yugoslavia ran chronic trade deficits. Like its market socialist neighbor, Hungary, Yugoslavia developed a foreign indebtedness problem as a result. During the 1980s, however, the current account was in surplus as often as in deficit, despite constant trade deficits,[40] largely because of substantial flows

---

[38]See Howard Wachtel, *Workers' Management and Workers' Wages in Yugoslavia* (Ithaca: Cornell University Press, 1973).

[39]World Bank, *World Development Report* (Oxford: Oxford University Press, 1981), pp. 182–83.

[40]*OECD Economic Surveys,* p. 102.

TABLE 14–5   Interrepublic Trade Flows

FROM: TO:	Bosnia-Herzegovina	Montenegro	Croatia	Macedonia	Slovenia	Serbia
Bosnia-Herzegovina	69.5	5.1	4.3	2.5	3.1	3.7
Montenegro	0.9	65.6	0.7	1.1	0.4	1.2
Croatia	6.0	2.8	68.7	4.4	9.4	4.7
Macedonia	1.1	1.9	1.1	66.5	1.1	2.1
Slovenia	3.3	1.7	6.1	3.2	62.9	3.1
Serbia	8.5	14.5	7.0	12.2	8.1	76.2
Exports outside of Yugoslavia	10.7	8.4	12.1	10.1	14.9	9.0
TOTAL	100.0	100.0	100.0	100.0	100.0	100.0
Trade with other republics	19.8	26.0	19.2	23.4	22.2	14.8

Source: Data from Wei Ding, ''Yugoslavia: Costs and Benefits of Union and Interdependence of Regional Economies,'' *Comparative Economic Studies* 33 (1991), p. 22, represents percentages of output levels in 1988. In this table Serbia includes the autonomous regions of Vojvodina and Kosovo.

from Yugoslav workers abroad, the guest workers. For Yugoslavia these earnings were a double-edged sword: When economic times got bad not only did exports decline, but also the repatriated earnings from these workers fell off sharply as they got laid off in disproportionate numbers.

Yugoslav foreign economic relations were relatively insular and autarkic despite all the memberships in international organizations. This tendency to autarky extended to the republic level also. Each republic wanted to be self-sufficient as much as possible, a phenomenon partly responsible for the wasteful and duplicative patterns of capital investment often carried out at the behest of local republic authorities.

These patterns are apparent in Table 14–5, where interrepublic trade flows as percentages of republic outputs are presented for 1988. Exports outside Yugoslavia are also shown. Unsurprisingly the least autarkic republic was Slovenia, which exported 14.9 percent of its output outside Yugoslavia and 22.2 percent to other republics. The most autarkic was Serbia, exporting only 9.0 percent of its output outside of Yugoslavia and 14.8 percent to the other republics. The strongest republic-to-republic flow was from Montenegro to Serbia, reflecting their close link.

War, Blockade, and Collapse

In June 1991 the Serb-dominated Yugoslav military attacked Slovenia from the air. After the later secession by Croatia, war spread there, and much of the fighting was carried out by unofficial local militias encouraged by the Serbs. In 1992 the UN declared a cease-fire, leaving Serbian forces in control of about 20 percent of the country, but with no permanent settlement, a situation leading to renewed fighting in 1995. In 1992, warfare in Bosnia-Herzegovina started, which has resulted in hundreds of thousands dead and millions driven into refugee status and scattered across neighboring republics and throughout Europe.

With blame placed largely on Serbia, the UN in 1992 placed an economic embargo on Yugoslavia (Serbia and Montenegro), exempting only certain humanitarian goods. Since then the embargo has been partially relaxed as Serbia has blockaded the Bosnian Serbs. The combination of war-induced destruction, death, and flight, along with a collapse of interrepublic and foreign trade arising from the economic blockade, has led to a general economic collapse on a scale difficult to measure.

Croatia's economy is in a shambles. From 1990 to 1993 output declined around 60 percent, a catastrophic amount, and food shortages emerged.[41] But because of the threat of renewed fighting, 40 percent of the budget is spent on defense. Tourism has collapsed. The monthly inflation rate in September 1993 was 30 percent (over 2,000 percent annualized), despite an attempted strict monetary policy that only contributed to the output collapse. Most privatizations have been of the "nomenklatura" variety, with previous managers gaining control of firms at cut-rate prices with allegations of corruption and spreading gangsterism. The situation stabilized only to worsen again with renewed fighting in 1995.

The declines in Macedonia have not been as been as bad, but they have been aggravated by Greece's embargo. Economic declines have certainly been much worse in pathetic Bosnia-Herzegovina.

In Serbia itself conflicting reports emerge regarding the decline in output, but there is little doubt that the blockade has taken a severe toll. In August 1993 the annualized rate of inflation was in the *quadrillions* of percents, the highest seen anywhere in the world since the late 1940s, although that rate was sharply reduced during 1994. In contrast to almost every other country in the world, Serbia has adopted a command socialist approach. Slobodan Milošević may have become a nationalist dictator, but he has also become Europe's last classic communist leader.

Many fear that even if settlements are reached in Bosnia-Herzegovina and Croatia, fighting will start in either Kosovo, where Albanian nationalists plot against Serbian control, or in Macedonia. The latter possibility threatens an internationalized conflict, with Greece, Albania, Bulgaria, and even possibly Turkey getting involved in a revival of the Balkan Wars that preceded World War I.[42]

---

[41]"Croatia's War-Ravaged Economy Near Collapse," *Washington Post,* November 11, 1993, p. A46.

[42]It is disturbing that outside powers have reverted to supporting groups they supported long ago. Thus Germany rushed to recognize the independence of Croatia, thereby exacerbating Serbia's fears, and Hungary has reportedly armed Croatia. France, Greece, and Russia have been sympathetic to Serbia. Radical nationalists in Russia see parallels to themselves in the Serbs' situation. Turkey and much of the Muslim world have strongly supported the Bosnian Muslims. Bulgaria recognized Macedonian independence before any other nation did.

How unnecessary and tragic all this is can be seen by contemplating Sarajevo. It has been under long siege and almost constant bombardment and is divided into neighborhoods along mutually hateful ethnic lines. Yet prior to the war Sarajevo was a cosmopolitan and multicultural city where the various groups lived together in integrated peace, even intermarrying at a significant rate to produce the many self-identified ''Yugoslavs'' in Bosnia-Herzegovina. But this peace has probably been permanently shattered. Groups that did not hate each other before do so now and will probably continue to do so for a long time, even if peace is officially declared tomorrow. Truly, the tragedy of Sarajevo is the tragedy of Yugoslavia.[43]

Summary and Conclusions

What was Yugoslavia has broken up in a tragic ethnic war since 1991. Prior to this it possessed the only worker-managed market socialist economy ever seen. The system was introduced beginning in the early 1950s under the leadership of World War II communist partisan leader, Marshall Josip Broz Tito.

This system involved elected Workers' Councils that functioned like capitalist Boards of Directors, appointing a management board and a director of the enterprise, while the state retained ultimate ownership of the enterprises. During the 1950s and early 1960s central planners retained considerable authority over prices and capital investment, the latter partly to achieve regional equality of growth rates and partly out of fear that the workers would allocate all retained earnings to wages rather than capital investment.

In the mid-1960s control by central planners was removed and the system largely followed market forces. As this policy stimulated a merger wave and increasing regional inequalities, the system was revised again in the mid-1970s to allow for integrated planning by organizations of associated labor within enterprises. Starting in 1989 outright privatization was allowed, thus setting the economy on the road to capitalism, although not necessarily on a path away from worker-management.

The economy grew at a rapid pace, had high rates of capital investment, and a fairly equal overall distribution of income. However growth and capital investment fell in the 1980s, unemployment rose to double-digit levels, and inflation accelerated wildly. Regional income disparities increased as did tensions over religion, power, and ethnicity. Eventually these tensions exploded into war, and now there are five nations where previously there was just one.

Although the breakup of Yugoslavia was ultimately due to its ethnic conflicts, many argue that the combination of soft budget constraints, lack of

---

[43]The embarrassment of the international community with this situation shows in a joke circulating in Europe in late 1993: ''A TV salesman brags that the set he is offering automatically switches channels whenever 'Bosnia' is mentioned.''

Box 14–2

Slovenia: The Success Story That Got Away*

Slovenia is the one that got away, despite being bombed in 1991. Once Croatia declared its independence, Slovenia's lack of a common border with Serbia and its relative lack of Serbs drew Milošević's attention away from it.

Slovenia has suffered economic consequences from the war, including a 20 percent decline in output since 1989 and an increase in unemployment to 13 percent from less than 2 percent, largely due to the collapse of trade with its fellow former republics. But its decline hit bottom and the rate of inflation had fallen to a monthly rate of 1 percent as of April 1993. Exports are rising and its currency, the tolar, is stable internationally.

Slovenia has the highest per capita income of any post-Communist nation in the world, 16 percent ahead of the Czech Republic in purchasing power parity terms as of the end of 1992, although well behind Slovene-inhabited areas in neighboring Austria. Privatization is occurring, but about three-fourths of the capital stock was still state owned in mid-1993. In short, worker-managed market socialism was alive and well in Slovenia. Privatization there involves encouragement to continue the worker-management system, even as ownership changes, and worker-ownership is being encouraged.

Thus, worker-managed market socialism ultimately self-destructed in the former Yugoslavia as a whole. But in Slovenia it has been quite successful. The success of Slovenia represents the case that the self-destruction of Yugoslavia was fundamentally due to its ethnic conflicts and not due to an inevitable failure of the economic system itself.

*See ''Slovenia: The Yugoslav Success,'' *The Economist,* July 26, 1993, p. 55. One problem for Slovenia is that it has been kept from obtaining Associate EU status or joining the Partnership for Peace by Italy which has revived old boundary disputes involving the province of Istria.

centralized macroeconomic control, inefficient capital investment, ongoing interferences by apparatchiks and local authorities in decision making, rising monopoly power, and the frustration of workers no longer able to affect management in ever-larger firms and going on strike, were inherent to the economic system and led to its inevitable collapse into rising unemployment and hyperinflation.

A response to this view may be the recent experience of now-independent Slovenia. Although still possessing a largely worker-managed market socialist economy, it has the highest per capita income of any former Communist state and has achieved reasonable economic stability. Nevertheless Slovenia is privatizing ownership. Thus the slogan for those who like workers' management, but accept shedding the socialist aspect might be, ''Worker-managed market socialism is dead! Long live workers' management!''

Questions for Discussion

1. Compare the functioning of market socialism in Yugoslavia with that in Hungary.
2. Compare and contrast the Yugoslav system with USSR-style command socialism. What were the relative advantages and disadvantages of each?
3. How did the regional issue affect the operation of the soft budget constraint and the emergence of hyperinflation in Yugoslavia?
4. If workers' management leads to stability of employment, why did unemployment steadily rise in Yugoslavia?
5. How can it be argued that Yugoslavia did not really have a system of workers' management and what would this imply?
6. What is the evidence for capital market inefficiency but labor market efficiency in Yugoslavia and why might these have occurred?
7. How can one explain the simultaneous existence of general income equality and extreme regional inequality in Yugoslavia?
8. Was the Yugoslav economic system Marxist?
9. What are the future prospects for workers' management in the world economy and why? What forms might this take?

Suggested Further Reading

Bonin, John P., Derek C. Jones, and Louis Putterman. ''Theoretical and Empirical Studies of Producer Cooperatives: Will Ever the Twain Meet?'' *Journal of Economic Literature* 31 (1993), pp. 1290–1320.

Burkett, John P. ''Self-Managed Market Socialism and the Yugoslav Economy, 1950–91'' In *Comparative Economic Systems: Models and Cases,* 7th ed., ed. Morris Bornstein. Burr Ridge: Irwin, 1994, pp. 322–52.

Djilas, Milovan. *The Unperfect Society: Beyond the New Class.* New York: Harcourt, Brace & World, 1969.

''Slovenia: The Yugoslav Success.'' *The Economist,* July 26, 1993, p. 55.

Horvat, Branko, Mihailo Marković, and Rudi Supek, eds. *Self-Governing Socialism,* vols 1 and 2. White Plains: International Arts and Sciences Press, 1975.

Kraft, Evan. ''Evaluating Regional Policy in Yugoslavia.'' *Comparative Economic Studies* 34 (1992) pp. 11–33.

Lydall, Harold. *Yugoslavia in Crisis.* Oxford: Clarendon Press, 1989.

Phillips, Paul, and Bogomil Ferfila. *The Rise and Fall of the Third Way: Yugoslavia 1945–1991.* Halifax: Fernwood Publishing, 1992.

Praznikar, Janez, and Jan Svejnar. ''Workers' Participation in Management vs. Social Ownership and Government Policies: Yugoslav Lessons for Transforming Socialist Economies.'' *Comparative Economic Studies* 34 (1991), pp. 27–46.

Sacks, Stephen R. ''The Yugoslav Firm.'' In *Comparative Economic Systems: Models and Cases,* 7th ed., ed. Morris Bornstein. Burr Ridge: Irwin, 1994, pp. 300–21.

Shoup, Paul. *Communism and the Yugoslav National Question.* New York: Columbia University Press, 1968.

Stojanović, Radmila, ed. *The Functioning of the Yugoslav Economy.* Armonk: M.E. Sharpe, 1982.

West, Rebecca. *Black Lamb and Grey Falcon: A Journey through Yugoslavia.* New York: Viking, 1941.

Žižmond, Egon. ''The Collapse of the Yugoslav Economy.'' *Soviet Studies* 44 (1992), pp. 101–12.

RUSSIA

MONGOLIA

INDIA

Hong
Kong

TAIWAN

354

CHINA'S SOCIALIST MARKET ECONOMY: THE SLEEPING GIANT WAKES

China is a sleeping giant. When China wakes she will shake the world.
—Napoleon Bonaparte

Our celestial empire possesses all things in prolific abundance and lacks no product within its own borders. There is therefore no need to import the manufactures of outside barbarians.
—Emperor Qianlong (Ch'ien-lung)[1] to the special emissary of King George III of Great Britain, 1793

The mountains are high, the emperor is far away.
—Ancient Chinese Proverb

Introduction

With the world's largest population and most rapidly growing economy,[2] the Peoples' Republic of China (PRC) is an important case of economic transformation. It continues to be ruled by an authoritarian and entrenched Communist Party whereas other nations have gone into economic collapse following the political abandonment of communism. What is China's[3] secret?

---

[1]In 1979 China officially switched from the Wade-Giles system of Latin alphabet transliterations of Chinese words to the Pinyin system. Following current scholarly and journalistic usage this chapter uses the Pinyin except for deeply entrenched cases such as the name of the country itself, *Zhongguo* in Pinyin. The first time a name appears in Pinyin it will be immediately followed by the often more familiar Wade-Giles form in parentheses, as with *Qianlong (Ch'ien-lung)*. Wade-Giles is still widely used in Hong Kong and Taiwan.

[2]During 1980–92 China was third in aggregate GDP growth rate behind Botswana and South Korea and was second in per capita GDP growth rate behind South Korea (World Bank, *World Development Report 1994,* [New York: Oxford University Press, 1994], Tables 1 and 2), but was first in aggregate growth rate in 1994 (*The Economist,* January 28, 1995, p. 102).

[3]The term *China* refers to the People's Republic of China (PRC) and the term *Taiwan* refers to the Republic of China (ROC), each claiming to be the legitimate government of all of China, including Hong Kong, although recently Taiwan has ceased forecasting a reconquest of the Mainland.

There is no simple answer. China has a central position, geographically, historically, and culturally, in East Asia where many countries are experiencing rapid industrial growth. Many of these countries have followed the model of Japan, which has led this group, whereas China long lagged behind. But China has awakened and is asserting its central position to emerge as a regional leader. Its economy may have become the third largest in the world[4] and may surpass Japan's in aggregate terms early next century. Given its growing military might, China reckons to become a superpower.

Under Chairman Mao Zedong (Tse-tung) the PRC pursued egalitarianism and regional self-sufficiency, the latter out of a defense motive from fear of attack by the USSR or the United States. The countryside was organized into large communes corresponding with former town and village clusters, and traditional culture and social values were assaulted during the Great Proletarian Cultural Revolution (GPCR, 1966–69).

Although the communes have been disbanded, a remnant of them persists as *town and village enterprises* (TVEs), rural industrial enterprises owned by local units of government, the towns and villages that formerly comprised the communes, and lower-level brigades. These entities are free from central planning and operate in a competitive market context, many exporting abroad through laissez-faire Hong Kong or via specific foreign capitalist firms. This sector of the economy has been growing rapidly in recent years, outperforming the stagnant, centrally planned state-owned sector as well as the strictly privately owned sector, the latter mostly located in *Special Enterprise Zones* (SEZs).[5] This dynamic TVE form is the unique innovation of the PRC's self-proclaimed *socialist market economy.*

Post-Mao China has seen a revival of *Confucianism,* which emphasizes filial loyalty within families and towards state authorities, hard work, and morality. Confucius was Chinese and Confucianism was long the established official state religion of China before the 20th century. It may be this neo-Confucianism with its New Traditional economy element of familism and groupism that is the characteristic shared by the rapidly growing East Asian economies, as noted in Chapters 5 and 6 and to be discussed further in Chapter 18 on Korea.

Emphasis on family units led to the *household responsibility system* in agriculture after 1978. This resulted in dramatic improvements in food output and increases in rural incomes, which is important given that a majority of China's more than 1.2 billion people still live in the countryside. Despite

---

[4]There is a wide range of estimates of Chinese per capita income. World Bank (World Bank, *World Development Report,* Table 1) figures for 1992 with current exchange rates are U.S. $470 per year, making China the world's eighth-largest economy, whereas World Bank estimates based on purchasing power parity suggest per capita income of U.S. $1,910 (World Bank, *World Development Report,* Table 30), putting aggregate Chinese GDP in third position globally behind the United States and Japan, with some estimates ranging still higher.

[5]In 1994 the private sector growth rate exceeded that of the TVE sector.

slowing growth in the agricultural sector since 1984, China has achieved the ability to feed itself, a historic milestone for a society with a past of regular famines, especially the starvation deaths of up to 30 million people in the Great Leap Forward (GLF, 1959–61) when the communes were first established.

Despite recent successes, China faces severe problems, including these: (1) possible political instability and turmoil after the death of supreme leader, Deng Xiaoping (Teng Hsiao-p'ing, born August 1904); (2) continuing political conflicts over democratization and dissent such as the violently suppressed student uprising in Tiananmen Square in the capital, Beijing (Peking), in 1989; (3) the threat of inflation getting out of control and undermining rapid growth; (4) rising income inequalities both regionally as the reforming coastal areas surge ahead and between urban and rural areas as the latter fall behind and are prevented from adjusting by continuing restrictions on labor migration; (5) the problem of absorbing laissez-faire Hong Kong in 1997 and trying to absorb market-capitalist Taiwan later, both of which are far ahead of the PRC in real per capita income, as well as dealing with separatist minorities such as the Tibetans; and (6) the threat of a major energy/environment crisis in the not-too-distant future if China's growth path continues as it has. Thus China is a land of great hopes but also of genuine fears, and it faces potential pitfalls in its path.

Historical and Cultural Background

Culture and Religion

China exhibits deep continuity of culture over thousands of years despite episodes of revolutionary violence and disorder. This reflects the Taoist conception of universal harmony resting on a balance of conflicting and interpenetrating forces of yin (female) and yang (male), which has pervaded Chinese culture. As in Japan, three major religions have coexisted even within individuals,[6] and the balance of their views has produced the synthesis that is Chinese culture. Two of these religions, Taoism and Confucianism, are of Chinese origin, whereas the third, Buddhism, came originally from India mainly via the Silk Road out of Central Asia.[7]

---

[6]It is said that the Chinese have "worn a Confucian crown, a Taoist robe, and a pair of Buddhist sandals" (William Theodore de Bary, Wing-tsit Chan, and Burton Watson, *Sources of Chinese Tradition* [New York: Columbia University Press, 1960], p. 631).

[7]Hinayana missionaries entered in the first century A.D. from Southeast Asia and Mahayana missionaries entered from Central Asia, the latter gaining dominance and fragmenting into numerous schools. In Tibet and Inner Mongolia, Vajrayana (Lamaist) Buddhism prevails. Islam dominates among the Turkic minorities in the northwestern Xinjiang (Sinkiang) Uygur (Uighur) Autonomous Republic, and also in parts of southern China.

The founders of the two native Chinese religions are reported to have met, Lao-tzu (604–? B.C.)[8] who founded Taoism and Confucius (551–479 B.C.) who founded Confucianism. Their philosophies are the complementary and contrasting foundations of Chinese culture, set forth respectively in Lao-tzu's *Tao Te Ching* and in the *Analects* of Confucius.

The follower of the Tao, "the Way," seeks harmony with nature and immortality. The key to this search is *wu-wei*, "no action," a term used for *nirvana* when Buddhism came to China and was Sinified.[9] The *Tao Te Ching* is famous for paradoxical formulations such as "Do nothing and all will be done." It has been associated with a laissez-faire orientation and was so used at the beginning of the Han dynasty (206 B.C.). Further examples are the following quotes from the *Tao Te Ching:*

> Administer the empire by engaging in no activity. . . The more taboos and prohibitions there are in the world, the poorer the people will be. . . Therefore the sage says: I engage in no activity and the people of themselves become prosperous.

Taoism became formally organized in the second century A.D. It was declared the state religion in 440 and again in 574 and 591. It peaked in official favor in tandem with Buddhism during the early Tang dynasty in the 600s and early 700s but was officially suppressed along with Buddhism in 854 by Confucianism. It became a mass religion with numerous gods and priestly hierarchies, emphasizing divination, alchemy, astrology, and other such practices.[10] By the Communist revolution in 1949 it had mostly disappeared as an organized religion.

If Taoism is the yin of Chinese culture with its anarchistic hermit sages escaping to the wilderness to seek harmony and immortality, then Confucianism is the yang with its moralistic scholar-mandarin-bureaucrats administering the empire from great imperial cities. Confucianism has been the favorite doctrine of the scholar in power whereas Taoism has been that of the scholar out of power.

Chinese Confucianism centers on *jen*, usually translated as *benevolence* or *humaneness*, which society's leaders from the emperor down through his mandarin gentry should practice. The emperor is the "Son of Heaven" who rules benevolently and is owed loyal obedience if he does so. This loyal obedience extends to family relations: The son obeys the father and the wife obeys

---

[8]The date of Lao-tzu's death is unknown. There is debate regarding his existence and authorship of the *Tao Te Ching*.

[9]Other Sinifications of Buddhism in China include eliminating the doctrine of reincarnation and downplaying gender equality because Confucianism asserted patriarchal male supremacy. Buddhism said little about politics or economics and became less influential after its suppression in 854, but it underlay politically active 19th-century sects, notably the Boxers who led a 1900 antiforeigner rebellion.

[10]It is analogous to Shintoism in Japan and Sinkyo in Korea. Taoism shares ancestor worship with Confucianism, a practice predating both religions in China.

the husband. Benevolent imperial conduct is key to celestial harmony and order.[11] If an emperor behaves badly, he loses the "Mandate of Heaven" and can be legitimately overthrown.

Although Confucianism would develop into an authoritarian state-centered doctrine in later dynasties, it advocates a "light touch" by the ruler with almost Taoist, laissez-faire overtones. The *Analects* frequently declare that if the emperor is benevolent and reverent (including carrying out rites necessary for maintaining celestial harmony) then he can practice *wu-wei* (no action) and the state will be well governed.

The truly authoritarian Chinese philosophy was *Legalism*, developed in the reign of the initial unifier of China in the third century B.C., Qin Shi Huang (Ch'in[12] Shi Huang-ti). The Legalists supported absolute power in the hands of the State and the Qin dynasty was harsh and oppressive. It was overthrown in 206 B.C. shortly after Qin Shi Huang's death by the Han, who initially followed laissez-faire Taoism. During the first century B.C. when the Han Emperor Wu nationalized the salt industry, a debate occurred between Legalists who supported nationalization and Confucianists who opposed it. But Legalism faded officially until its only remnants were some of its elements that were incorporated into the neo-Confucian synthesis.

After 854 Confucianism became the official Chinese state religion, absorbing elements of other religions in a synthesis codified in the 1100s. It became ossified and reactionary by the 19th century. Official Confucianism opposed commerce, industrialization, and relations with the outside world and supported the ideal of China as the self-sufficient Middle Kingdom to whose emperor foreign barbarians should kowtow and pay tribute.

Social Structure and Land Tenure in Traditional China

Confucius supported equal division of land among patriarchal families. During the Han period family land ownership with division among all male heirs predominated. The basic social pattern emerged of a town with a group of villages functioning as an essentially self-sufficient unit. This pattern still exists—towns became the communes during Mao's Great Leap Forward, the villages became brigades, subvillage or smaller village groups became production teams, and households were at the bottom.

The Confucian ruling class was the scholar-gentry, following the praise of education by Confucius. Starting in the Han dynasty (206 B.C. to 220 A.D.) civil service examinations for the state bureaucracy appeared, the world's first.

---

[11]Confucianism is less theistic than Taoism or Buddhism—its supreme deity is a remote Heaven. The Confucianist model of a nontheistic benevolent ruler influenced anticlerical European Enlightenment thinkers in the 1700s, notably Leibniz, Voltaire, and the physiocratic economist, François Quesnay, sometimes called "the Confucius of the West."

[12]It is from his name that *China* comes. Generally a reviled figure in Chinese history, Qin was admired as a strong national leader by Mao Zedong.

The fairness of these exams and the fluidity of the class structure varied over time. Fairness was a sign of lack of corruption, and testing was usually fairer early in a dynasty's rule.

The lower levels of the bureaucratic elite ruled the countryside in the small towns as the emperor's agents. Class mobility was reduced because to pass the exam one had to spend much time studying numerous classical writings and the thousands of ideographs in the Chinese alphabet. The son of a scholar-bureaucrat was better positioned for such study than the son of an uneducated peasant.

The Dynasty Cycle

A Chinese idea of their history is that it experiences cycles associated with the rise and fall of ruling dynasties. The Communists are seen as just the latest dynasty. The most important dynasties have been the Han (206 B.C. to 220 A.D.), the Tang (T'ang, 618 to 906), the Song (Sung, 960 to 1275), the Yuan (1276 to 1367), the Ming (1368 to 1644), and the Qing (Ch'ing, 1645 to 1911).

A major dynasty initially attacks corruption, builds up the economy, follows Confucian virtues, and strengthens the country. Gradually corruption increases and imperial attention to government decreases. Taxation levels, famines, rebellions, and local warlord activity increase until the dynasty falls. Sometimes new dynasties are foreign, notably the Mongol Yuan[13] and the Manchu Qing.[14]

This dynasty cycle supposedly proved China to be an unchanging society, an idea popular in 19th-century Europe when China fell behind technologically and economically. As discussed in Chapter 4, Marx explained the Chinese lag by the "Asiatic mode of production," although that idea better pertained to India because China largely had private rather than state ownership of land. But China did have a bureaucracy that managed an agrohydraulic infrastructure of dams and irrigation systems, the basis of Wittfogel's extension of Marx's idea to "hydraulic (oriental) despotism." Marx and Wittfogel both saw state bureaucracy suppressing capitalism and class struggle dynamics, thus leading to a stagnant economy and society.

---

[13]The Mongol Yuan, Khubilai Khan, was emperor in the late 1200s when Marco Polo visited China and then told Europe of its splendors. The gap between China and Europe is seen in that Marco Polo left Europe's largest city, Venice, population of 160,000 and visited the former Song capital, Hangzhou (Hangchow), the world's largest city, with around 6 million people.

[14]The foreignness of the Manchus stimulated the antiimperial nationalist movement in 1912, embittering Pu'yi, the last emperor, who was convinced by the Japanese to lead their puppet state of Manchu'ko in conquered Manchuria in the 1930s. Manchuria has since been broken into the provinces of Heilongjiang, Jilin, Liaoning, and northeastern Nei Monggol.

This theory held in late Qing China after the Opium Wars (1839–42) when Great Britain imposed humiliating port treaties granting Britain Hong Kong[15] and the right to import opium into China,[16] but it does not hold over the longer term. For hundreds of years China was the world's technological leader, peaking as such in the early Tang Dynasty[17] and gradually losing its technological edge by the 1400s. When Emperor Qianlong dismissed the British envoy in 1793, the wealth of China was still close to Europe's.

Periods of expansion and outward orientation alternated with ones of contraction and inward orientation. The Han empire ruled parts of Central Asia, established the Silk Road trade link with Europe, and opened itself to outside influences like Buddhism. The early Tang Dynasty expanded, reconquering portions of Central Asia and allowing Christianity, Manichaeism, and Islam. Expansion halted after the Arabs defeated a Chinese army in 751 in Central Asia. Then China withdrew and disintegrated, despite economic and cultural advances in the Song, until the Mongol conquest in 1276. During the 1400s, the Ming expanded, its ships visiting the east coast of Africa and colonizing Taiwan. In the 1500s, the Chinese allowed Jesuits in and studied their scientific knowledge only to expel them later.[18]

From the End of Empire to the Victory of Communism

After the Opium Wars China experienced one defeat after another. France, Germany, Russia, the United States,[19] and Japan,[20] in addition to Britain,

---

[15]Portugal has ruled tiny Macao near Hong Kong since the 1500s, but sought no further entry and will turn it over to Chinese control in 1999 just as Britain will Hong Kong in 1997.

[16]As late as 1867 a majority of China's export earnings came from silk and silk products. Increasingly the British exported tea to Britain in exchange for opium from India.

[17]Some Chinese discoveries and inventions include paper, gunpowder, the compass, row cultivation of crops, the iron plow, efficient horse harnesses, the crank handle, steel, water power, the chain pump, the suspension bridge, the use of petroleum as a fuel, the wheelbarrow, the fishing reel, the stirrup, porcelain ("china"), the umbrella, matches, the mechanical clock, the circulation of the blood, inoculation against smallpox, the decimal system, negative numbers, the contour transport canal, manned flight with kites, the parachute, the rudder, multiple masts on ships, the crossbow, and the rocket. The Chinese origins of most of these was long unknown in Europe. See Joseph Needham, *Science and Civilization in China* (Cambridge: Cambridge University Press, 1954).

[18]They entered through the southern port of Guangzhou (Canton) from Macao, sponsored by the Portuguese. In the late 1600s their influence peaked. They fell in the 1700s, caught between inward-looking Chinese nationalism and Vatican attitudes opposing their participation in imperial Confucian rituals.

[19]The United States flooded China with Protestant missionaries whose impact was less than that of the Jesuits expelled in the 1700s. At a few million, the Christian population of China is small.

[20]Japan got treaty port rights after defeating China in 1895 when it took Taiwan. It took semiindustrialized Manchuria in 1931 and invaded China outright in 1937. Japan never conquered China during World War II, despite committing major atrocities.

established treaty ports where their national merchants operated free of Chinese jurisdiction. All nations operated in Shanghai, where a park under British control infamously bore the sign, ''No Chinese or dogs allowed.'' Antiforeign, antiimperialist movements and westernizing upheavals against the Qing dynasty erupted.[21]

In 1911 the Qing dynasty was overthrown by Sun Yat-sen, a westernizer soon out of power. A period of warlordism ended when Chiang Kai-Shek led the Nationalist Guomindang (Kuomintang) to power in 1928. Chiang had Soviet and Communist support, but he turned on the Communists, which caused them to follow Mao Zedong in 1935–36 on the Long March to Yan'an (Yenan) in the Northwest. From there they fought a peasant-based guerrilla war.[22]

Chiang was eclectic in his ideology, borrowing from the Soviets, the Americans, and the fascists. During World War II he issued a book forecasting a great future for China if it followed Confucian virtues. This is still the official ideology of the Guomindang regime on Taiwan, one reason Mao was anti-Confucian on the surface.[23]

After the war, despite U.S. aid and advice, Chiang did not carry out land reform. He allowed hyperinflation to get out of control, undermining his support among the urban middle class.[24] With a solid rural base, the Communists defeated the Nationalist forces in Manchuria and swept down out of the Northeast. On October 1, 1949, Chiang's forces had retreated to Taiwan where they still rule while Mao's Communists declared the People's Republic in Tiananmen Square in Beijing.[25]

---

[21]The first major upheaval after the Opium Wars was the 1850s Taiping rebellion against the government. Its leaders led a syncretic sect with Christian elements that supported collective ownership of land and other semicommunist ideas.

[22]For Mao's activities in Yan'an, see Edgar Snow, *Red Star Over China* (New York: Grove Press, 1968). For policies towards peasants then, see William Hinton, *Fanshen* (New York: Monthly Review Press, 1966).

[23]Referring to Mao's regime, John King Fairbank (*The United States and China,* 4th ed. [Cambridge: Harvard University Press, 1983], p. 465) notes ''Dynastic absolutism has been replaced by party dictatorship, the Son of Heaven by the party chairman, the imperial family-clan by the central executive committee, the scholar elite by a party elite, tax-gatherers by cadres in the countryside, Confucian classics by Communist classics, written examination by group discussion, scholarly self-cultivation by guilt-ridden self-criticism.''

[24]The Shanghai cost-of-living index rose from 100 in January 1947 to 897,458 in November 1948 (Frank H. H. King, *A Concise Economic History of Modern China (1840–1961)* [New York: Praeger, 1969], p. 161).

[25]Coinciding with the Soviet explosion of a nuclear bomb, this Communist victory in China triggered an outburst of McCarthyite Cold War hysteria in the United States, including a major purge of State Department ''Old China Hands'' who were blamed for this outcome.

Maoist Economic Policies

The Ideology of Maoism

Maoism was initially discussed in Chapter 3. The May Fourth Movement of 1919 protested turning Chinese territory over to Japan in the Versailles Treaty. From that movement came the Chinese Communist Party (CCP), founded in 1921. Mao Zedong of the southern province of Hunan was a founding delegate.[26] Initial links with the Soviet-based Comintern led the CCP to follow a Soviet-led line until the disaster of 1928 when they retreated from Shanghai to the countryside.

Mao became the effective leader of the party during the Long March and formulated his doctrine of relying upon a mass peasant base. Initially this doctrine emphasized land distribution in the Confucian manner, but in the early 1940s he stressed land distribution as a bridge to full collectivization. The Soviets supported the CCP in 1949 and the USSR and PRC were allied during the Korean War of 1950–53, although Mao resented Stalin's reluctance to actively commit troops.

Mao's views evolved over time as did Chinese policy. Nevertheless by the end of his life a Maoist dogma had emerged that can be compared with Soviet views. When Tito split from Stalin in 1948 and when Khrushchev denounced Stalin in 1956, Mao supported Stalin against their "revisionism," and the ideological split with Khrushchev developed into the Sino-Soviet split.

But Maoism differed from Stalinism in at least five ways: (1) its emphasis on developing the rural economic base and maintaining population in the countryside although actual Maoist policy increased the urban-rural income gap, (2) its emphasis on egalitarianism and use of *moral incentives* rather than material incentives, (3) its antibureaucratic attitude, which peaked during the Great Proletarian Cultural Revolution (GPCR) when Red Guards denounced bureaucrats[27] and sent them to the countryside for "reeducation," (4) greater opposition to traditional culture—Stalin supported maintaining important elements of 19th-century Russian art and culture whereas Mao sought to extirpate the past by campaigning against the "Four Olds" (old customs, old habits, old culture, and old thinking), and (5) emphasis on regional decentralization of economic control, more like Khrushchev than Stalin.

---

[26]Several May Fourth Movement–CCP activists from Hunan and Sichuan operated in France, including Deng Xiaoping. Deng was a military commander in the Long March and the civil war, giving him a military base. His last official position was Chairman of the Supreme Military Commission.

[27]Chinese bureaucracy shows up in CCP structure. Whereas most Communist parties have a Central Committee with a Politburo above it, China has two higher layers than that. Officially there is the Standing Committee of the Politburo. But above it has been a group of Long March veterans unofficially known as the Sitting Committee because they are so old they rarely stand up, the most prominent member of this group being Deng Xiaoping.

Implanting Socialism and the Stalinist Model: 1949–1957

Inheriting a devastated economy and initially relying on support from centrist and liberal groups, the new regime moved slowly, emphasizing ending hyperinflation and redistributing land to individual peasants. Collectivization of agriculture proceeded gradually as did nationalization of industry and trade.

In agriculture, after granting land to all peasants individually, the regime began to establish localized mutual aid teams in 1950. The higher level, village-based brigade cooperatives began to be organized in 1955 and had completely displaced the lower organizational forms by April 1958 when the town-level communes began to be formed. Starting from a base of 34.7 percent of industrial enterprises that were fully nationalized in 1949, the economy included no purely private industry by 1956, although a joint state-private sector still controlled 32.5 percent of industrial enterprises.[28]

Between 1953 and 1957 the First Five-Year Plan followed Stalinist lines, reflecting Sino-Soviet friendship and reliance by the Chinese on Soviet advisers. Command central planning emphasized heavy industrial buildup, especially in northeastern Manchuria where Russia traditionally had interests and a pre-existing industrial base had been expanded by the Japanese. Steel production soared at an annual rate of 31.8 percent, pig iron at 27.7 percent, and cement at 29.3 percent, whereas grain output expanded at only 4.0 percent.[29] Per capita kilocalorie availability rose from 2,048 in 1953 to 2,217 in 1957 as rural per capita pork consumption fell from 5.5 kilograms to 4.4 over the same time period.[30]

The Great Leap Forward: 1958–1961

A cutoff of Soviet aid[31] and a poor harvest in 1957 triggered the Great Leap Forward (GLF) in 1958. A goal was to develop rural-based industrialization using traditional technology to produce inputs and mechanization for agricultural production in decentralized communes, "walking on two legs." The outcome of this approach was not as disastrous for industry as many observers claimed then, but the agricultural outcome was much worse than reported at the time.

---

[28]Carl Riskin, *China's Political Economy: The Quest for Development since 1949* (Oxford: Oxford University Press, 1987) p. 96.

[29]James T. H. Tsao, *China's Development Strategies and Foreign Trade* (Lexington: Lexington Books, 1987), p. 17.

[30]Mark Selden, *The Political Economy of Chinese Development* (Armonk: M. E. Sharpe, 1993), p. 26.

[31]This aid was in the form of loans with short payback periods. Arguments over aid coincided with ideological splits over revisionism, cancellation of the joint nuclear agreement in 1959, and the abrupt removal of all Soviet advisers in 1960. By 1965 Sino-Soviet trade was one-fifth of its late 1950s level and occurred only in Swiss francs after 1970. In 1969 armed border clashes occurred in the northeast. Relations finally eased in the late 1980s.

Communes were established at the level of the traditional market towns, which became the accounting units for income determination and distribution. This communalization included establishing dormitories for men and common dining halls. Although potentially liberating women from housework, this move attacked traditional Confucian notions of the family and was resisted in many areas. By late 1959 retreat began from this type of communalization with the elimination of the dormitories, and in 1960 the accounting unit was transferred back to the brigade (village) level.

Rural industry developed in backyard production facilities, and pig iron and other basic industrial goods output increased in 1958–59, although the quality was generally very poor. Industrial output growth decelerated in 1960 and fell sharply in 1961 as disorganization and catastrophe overwhelmed the economy.

The catastrophe in agriculture caused the worst famine anywhere ever, with somewhere between 15 million and 30 million deaths during 1959–61. The overall death rate in China was twice as high in 1960 as in 1958.[32] Rural foodgrain consumption per capita fell from 201 kilograms per capita in 1958 to 156 in 1960, and per capita pork consumption fell from 4.6 kilograms per capita in 1958 to 1.2 in 1960. Given poor transportation and local self-sufficiency, certain areas experienced much sharper declines than these and many people died there.

The Period of Adjustment: 1962–1965

In 1962 Mao accepted blame for the GLF in a "self-criticism" under pressure from a coalition that included Party General Secretary Deng Xiaoping. Central planning was reinstituted. The unit of rural income accounting was lowered from the brigade to the production team where it remained until 1978. Development priority reversed from heavy industry to agriculture, with light industry ahead of heavy industry.

Both agriculture and industry grew solidly. Between 1961 and 1965 overall agricultural output rose at an annual rate of 9.4 percent and industrial production rose at an annual rate of 7.8 percent.[33] Famine disappeared.

Deng was a crucial figure in this policy shift. During a policy debate in 1962 while advocating expanded use of private family plots he coined his famous aphorism, "It does not matter whether the cat is black or white as long as it catches mice." This saying was used against him during the Great Proletarian Cultural Revolution when he was purged as a "capitalist roader." He was rehabilitated in 1973 but purged again before Mao died in 1976.

---

[32]Vaclav Smil, *China's Environmental Crisis: An Inquiry into the Limits of National Development* (Armonk: M.E. Sharpe, 1993), p. 17.

[33]Alvin Rabushka, *The New China: Comparative Economic Development in Mainland China, Taiwan, and Hong Kong* (Boulder: Westview, 1987) p. 208.

The Great Proletarian Cultural Revolution and the Late Maoist Aftermath: 1966–1978

Again in 1966 Mao threw the country into turmoil. Youthful Red Guards, waving copies of *Quotations of Chairman Mao* (the "Little Red Book"), attacked the party hierarchy led by figures such as Deng. Intellectuals and bureaucrats were sent to the countryside or prison for reeducation. Mao sought pure communism.

A crisis occurred in 1967 when virtual anarchy reined throughout the country. Mao then sent in the People's Liberation Army (PLA) to restore order, although the political campaign against Mao's enemies continued through 1969 and political conflicts and switches continued to his death, including the purge and mysterious death in 1971 of then Number Two, Lin Biao (Lin Piao), in an airplane reportedly flying to the USSR.[34] Mao's economic policies continued for two years after his death until Deng established his power and began to implement the *Four Modernizations:* agriculture, industry, science and technology, and national defense.

A policy emphasis of the GPCR era was national and regional self-reliance. Nationally this led to a decline in foreign trade from 4.245 billion U.S. dollars in 1966 to 3.785 billion U.S. dollars in 1968,[35] paralleling declines in agricultural output by 1 percent and in industrial output by a whopping 20 percent.[36] Then all three areas began steady growth, foreign trade reaching 20.64 billion U.S. dollars by 1978,[37] agricultural output increasing annually at 4.4 percent, and industrial production rising annually at 12.7 percent between 1968 and 1978.[38]

The regional element of self-reliance involved substantial decentralization to local government units of planning administration. Fear of Soviet invasion led to the "Third Front" policy, which emphasized major industrial expansion in southwestern provinces like Sichuan, away from the Soviet border and also the coastal regions vulnerable to U.S. attack. Local areas built input supply systems for industrial production, building upon foundations laid out during the GLF and later used for TVE development. The framework established in this period of multiple hierarchical levels of responsibility with restraint by higher levels allowed flexibility and slackness of planning crucial for the later takeoff into very rapid growth.[39]

---

[34]He opposed the anti-USSR opening to the United States then under secret negotiation, which occurred in 1972. After his death Lin Biao was identified with Confucius and the most extreme anti-Confucius campaign of the Maoist period occurred.

[35]Riskin, *China's Political Economy,* p. 208.

[36]Rabushka, *The New China,* p. 208.

[37]Nicholas R. Lardy, *Foreign Trade and Reform in China, 1978–1990* (Cambridge: Cambridge University Press, 1992), p. 12.

[38]Rabushka, *The New China,* p. 208.

[39]See David Granick, *Chinese State Enterprises: A Regional Property Rights Analysis* (Chicago: University of Chicago Press, 1990).

Dengism and the Move to a Market Economy: 1979 to the Present

The Oscillations of the Reform Process

Mao died in 1976 and in 1977 Deng Xiaoping reentered the leadership with the backing of influential military figures. In 1978 the CCP leadership confirmed his leading role and committed the nation to gradualistic market-oriented reforms. Initial changes affected agriculture and laid the foundation for establishing *Special Economic Zones* (SEZs), which opened China to outside economic influences.

As the Mao era saw sudden shifts of sentiment and policy, so the post-Mao period has seen an ongoing conflict with policy oscillations, albeit trending towards marketization and opening up the economy to the outside world. Most backward shifts had the support of Deng, although he may have been forced to go along in some cases.

The first backlash came in 1981 when ideologues attacked intellectual liberalization. But in 1982 the CCP committed itself to eliminating corruption[40] and reforming itself. In 1983 came the ''anti-spiritual pollution'' campaign against foreign influences. Then in 1984 came major enterprise reforms, followed in 1985 by the removal of many military hardliners from Party positions. In late 1986 student prodemocracy demonstrations triggered the removal of Deng's heir apparent, Hu Yaobang, as General Secretary and the initiation of an ''anti–bourgeois liberalization'' campaign. But in 1987 another reformer, Zhao Ziyang, replaced Hu. Then in 1988 tighter central planning controls were imposed in an antiinflation effort led by hardline Premier, Li Peng.

In 1989 came the dramatic events televised to the whole world when thousands of students occupied Tiananmen Square after the death of Hu Yaobang to demand democracy. This movement was brutally crushed by the military and many Chinese were killed. Zhao Ziyang was replaced by Jiang Zemin because of Zhao's friendliness toward the students. Deng supported the crackdown.

After a period of international disapproval, 1992 saw reforms resume, signaled by Deng's visit to Shenzen, the prominent SEZ adjacent to Hong Kong. Reforms spread to many provinces and rules on private enterprise were loosened. In 1993 the CCP officially declared a market economy the desired form, a *socialist market economy*.[41]

---

[40]The major corruption has been nepotism that places children of Party leaders in charge of private or semiprivate businesses favored by the government. Nepotism reflects traditional attitudes of doing business through *guangxi,* patron-client ''connections,'' especially family links.

[41]In the early and mid-1980s the Chinese admired Hungary's market socialism as a model. But now they assert the uniqueness of their path, the socialist market economy, although what is unique about it may be the TVEs.

In 1994 farmer demonstrations and resurging inflation to 20 percent increased pressure again for scaling back reforms. With Deng increasingly ill in early 1995, President and General Secretary Jiang Zemin began wearing Mao jackets rather than business suits and engaging in trade disputes with the United States. Thus the conflict continues and will intensify "when the black Cadillac comes" for Deng Xiaoping, old Long March veteran and Communist activist since immediately after the Bolshevik Revolution.

Reforms in Agriculture

The agricultural reforms introduced in 1978 included recognition of property rights of production teams, adherence to a principle of "to each according to his work," restoration of the right to private plots and respect for household boundaries, allowance of free market rural bazaars, and increases in state purchases of agricultural commodities with price increases for them. In 1979 came the *household responsibility system* in which households became the principal unit of account along with elimination of the communes and the introduction of a two-tier price system under which households could freely sell anything produced above quota.

This household responsibility system allows households to lease equipment from higher units and to engage in long-term transferable leases for the right to use land, although land remains formally owned by villages, now juridical entities again since the dissolution of the communes, brigades, and teams. The response was a dramatic increase in output, greater between 1978 and 1984 than in the previous 21 years, that provides a base of support for further reforms. However the rate of increase slowed after that, including some actual declines in grain production.[42] By 1994 strikes and protests by farmers occurred in some areas. Figures for agricultural output are in Table 15–1.

The acceleration of output between 1978 and 1984 reflected improved incentives provided by changed pricing policies, loosened restrictions on crop specialization, greater interregional trade because of a relaxation of the self-reliance doctrine, elimination of political meddling in team management, a full shift to material rather than moral incentives, and reductions of monitoring costs within teams.[43] But ultimately why these reforms engendered such productivity improvements in China whereas similar ones have generally failed miserably in Eastern Europe is a mystery.

---

[42]This reflected market forces as production shifted to higher value nongrain commodities. Grain continues to be subject to some central planning and quotas.

[43]Estimates of the effect of monitoring costs range from zero (Justin Yifu Lin, "Collectivization and China's Agricultural Crisis in 1959–1961," *Journal of Political Economy* 98 (1990), pp. 1228–52) through 10 percent (Xiao-yuan Dong and Gregory K. Dow, "Monitoring Costs in Chinese Agricultural Teams," *Journal of Political Economy* 101 (1993) pp. 539–53) to 50 percent (John McMillan, John Whalley, and Lijang Zhu, "The Impact of China's Economic Reforms on Agricultural Productivity Growth," *Journal of Political Economy* 97 (1989), pp. 781–807).

TABLE 15–1   **Urban and Rural Per Capita Food Consumption**

Year	Foodgrain		Edible Oil		Pork	
	Urban	*Rural*	*Urban*	*Rural*	*Urban*	*Rural*
1957	196	205	5.2	1.9	9.0	4.4
1978	205	193	4.1	1.1	13.7	6.4
1984	239	254	11.1	3.2	18.7	11.7
1988	233	253	13.6	4.0	21.2	13.3
Annual Percent Rates of Increase						
1957–78	0.2	−0.3	−0.3	−2.6	2.0	2.1
1978–84	2.6	4.6	16.6	17.8	5.2	10.0
1984–88	−0.6	0.0	5.1	5.6	3.2	3.2

Note: The base is 1957 because it was a good year just prior to the GLF disaster. Annual percent growth rates for each subperiod are also shown. The main foodgrains are wheat and millet in the North and rice in the South.

Source: Figures are from Mark Selden, *The Political Economy of Chinese Development* (Armonk: M. E. Sharpe, 1993), p. 21, in kilograms per person.

Since 1984 output has decelerated as short-run decollectivization gains were achieved and the limits of Chinese agriculture appeared. These include the small size of farms, further dropping as the rural birth rate increased,[44] a disinvestment in infrastructure built and maintained by teams and brigades, unfavorable terms of trade as prices were freed in other sectors and growth began to focus there whereas some price controls on grain continued, and a long-term decline in the amount of cultivated land.[45]

But the improvements were substantial and food consumption patterns in China now resemble those of middle-income countries more than those in poor countries. Ending famine in the world's most populous nation is an outcome of historic proportions.

Enterprise Reforms

After initial moves in 1980, major enterprise reforms came in 1984 when most were allowed to replace plan targets with "responsibility contracts" that enabled them to retain and freely dispose of any surplus beyond a generally small contracted production and financial obligation. The dual price system

---

[44]The Chinese birth rate peaked when Mao advocated large families in the 1960s. China vigorously pushes only one child per family, but rural Confucianist families want a son, desires stimulated by the household responsibility system.

[45]Cultivated land reached a maximum of 112 million hectares in 1956. It was down to 93 million hectares by 1988. See Frederick W. Crook, "Primary Issues in China's Grain Economy in the 1990 Decade," in *China's Economic Dilemmas in the 1990s*, ed. Joint Economic Committee (Armonk: M. E. Sharpe, 1992), p. 406.

FIGURE 15–1

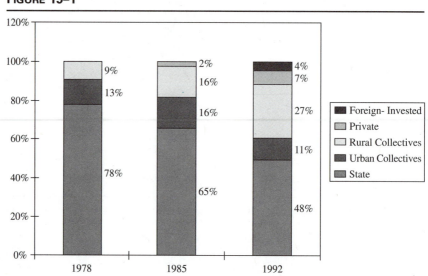

Note: Figures are percentages of industrial production from each category.
Source: Data from Barry Naughton, ''Chinese Institutional Innovation and Privatization from Below,''
American Economic Review Papers and Proceedings 84 (1994), p. 267.

from agriculture was extended to most of the rest of the economy, creating a market economy beyond the contracted portion with a steadily declining share in central state-owned enterprises.

The emerging significance of the *town and village enterprises* (TVEs) has been striking. They are technically known as *rural collectives* and owned by town or village governments. Their managers usually are appointed by the next higher unit of government, usually the county. Many of these entities existed in the Mao era as commune or brigade enterprises, but they have expanded their operations greatly. More so than the centralized SOEs they face hard budget constraints and operate in vigorously competitive markets. In 1989 3 million of these enterprises either went bankrupt or were taken over by other ones.[46]

Figure 15–1 shows percentages of manufacturing output attributable to each type of enterprise. By 1992 the pure SOE was in the minority. Although the strictly private sector has expanded, primarily in the SEZs, the biggest increase in absolute terms has been in the collective sector, especially the rural TVE sector, although the private sector may have begun to grow more rapidly since the 1993 reforms.

---

[46]Yingyi Qian and Chenggang Xu, ''The M-Form Hierarchy and China's Economic Reform,'' *European Economic Review* 37 (1993), p. 547.

Many economists believe such a form should be at a disadvantage because property rights are vague. But this has not been a problem given the often tight oversight by higher level units of government that hire the managers. The earnings of the TVEs go not only to enterprise wages and reinvestment, but also to local public services.

Compared to regular SOEs, TVEs have greater flexibility and freedom from central control, allowing them to fill niches where SOEs were limited, such as light industry. TVEs allow local communities to turn control of assets into income even without asset markets. This applies to labor as well in an environment where labor mobility continues to be limited, despite some recent loosening.

TVEs have had an edge over strictly private firms as well because of lower tax rates, and they have an advantage in negotiating with a still-dominant government. Until 1993, privatization outside of the SEZs continued to be limited. Hence TVEs provided an alternative to privatization where it was unavailable. Thus it has been argued that as privatization and full asset markets and mobility are allowed we shall see a declining importance of the TVEs.[47]

Tremendous variations occur in what TVEs do and how they behave. Many operate as subcontractors for foreign private firms in coastal SEZs or are near to urban areas. But others are the direct extensions of the former suppliers of regionally self-sufficient Maoist rural industrial complexes.

Special Economic Zones and Foreign Trade

In the days of the emperors, it was traditional to restrict foreign traders to specific ports where they kowtowed and paid tribute to the emperor separate from Chinese society at large. The current strategy of establishing selected ports as *Special Economic Zones* (SEZs) with relaxed rules where foreigners are allowed to operate fits this traditional Chinese approach.

A law establishing ground rules for joint ventures was passed in 1979. In 1980 four cities were selected to be SEZs, all along the southeastern coast,[48] including Shenzen adjacent to Hong Kong. Restrictive rules on economic activities were relaxed. In 1984 14 more coastal cities, some in the north, were declared to be ''open cities'' and allowed to have Economic and Technological Development Zones (ETDZs). Foreign investment was encouraged for these areas.

Foreign investment has poured in, exports have poured out, and these cities have boomed. SEZ-rich Guangdong Province, for example, grew at a rate around 25 percent per year in recent years. If it were an independent

---

[47]Since 1993 a privatization wave has occurred among the TVEs, taking various forms in different regions, with *collective shareholding cooperatives,* a form unique to the PRC, the most popular.

[48]There was little industrialization in the Southeast then. The Northeast was industrialized before the 1950s and the Southwest during the Maoist Third Front period.

Box 15–1

The Success of the Shenzen Special Economic Zone

Spectacularly growing Shenzen increasingly resembles its neighbor, wildly successful, laissez-faire Hong Kong, to the point that proposals even have been floated to tie Shenzen monetarily to Hong Kong. Its industrial production in 1979 was 60.61 million yuan, whereas for 1987 it was 5,762.89 million yuan.* Of the 1987 figure, 45.15 percent of production was electronics whereas only 10.30 percent was textiles and clothing.† Between 1985 and 1988, telephone ownership per 100 inhabitants rose from 4.8 to 22.1 whereas in Shanghai, China's largest city and an open city to boot, the number rose from 3.9 to 5.0.‡ Thus, rising living standards increasingly separate Shenzen from the rest of China and regional inequalities of income increase.

---

*Kwan-yu Wong, Yu-you Deng, and Han-xin Chen, ''Shenzen: Special Experience in Development,'' in *China's Coastal Cities,* eds. Y. Yeung and X. Hu (Honolulu: University of Hawaii Press, 1992), p. 280.
†Wong, Deng, and Chen, ''Shenzen,'' p. 285.
‡Wong, Deng, and Chen, ''Shenzen,'' p. 310.

---

nation, it would easily have the world's most rapid growth rate. Much of the foreign investment is from overseas Chinese, often families originally from the southern provinces and operating through Hong Kong.[49]

As of 1989, 61.6 percent of cumulative foreign direct investment was from Hong Kong, much of it in the SEZs of Guangdong, 11.2 percent from the United States and 8.7 percent from Japan. A significant portion of Hong Kong's investment was of Taiwanese origin, enough to put it ahead of both the United States and Japan.[50]

While total PRC trade rose from $20.64 billion in 1978 to $84.05 billion in 1990,[51] exports from Guangdong rose from $1.388 billion in 1978 to

---

[49]Throughout the rapidly growing Southeast Asian economies ethnic Chinese play an important role as merchants, including in Singapore, Malaysia, Thailand, Indonesia, the Philippines, and previously in Vietnam.

[50]Kerry Dumbaugh, ''Hong Kong and China in the 1990's,'' in ''*China's Economic Dilemmas in the 1990s,*'' p. 881.

[51]Nicholas R. Lardy, *Foreign Trade and Reform in China, 1978–1990* (Cambridge: Cambridge University Press, 1992), p. 12. One reason for export growth has been yuan devaluation from 1.50 per U.S. dollar in 1980 to 8.44 in early 1995. This devaluation enters the controversy over measurements of per capita income in the PRC, because the low official numbers reflect this lowered value of the yuan. The surge of exports to the United States has led to a bilateral surplus in China's favor, which exacerbates trade tensions.

$10.370 billion in 1990, and the share of exports from foreign-invested enterprises went from zero to nearly one-third.[52] Thus the SEZs are engines of growth and outward expansion, and they probably have liberalized beyond the point at which the central government could rein them in even if it wanted to. SEZs have become a case of ''the mountains are high, the emperor is far away.''

The Distribution of Income and the Standard of Living

With Dengist marketization has come greater income inequality, although with some countertrends. This issue attracts attention in the PRC because in some ways under Mao it had one of the most equal income distributions ever observed.[53]

The PRC had great class equality within local units, both villages and urban areas. Gini coefficients within eight small rural Chinese communities between 1955 and 1978 range from a highly equal 0.16 to 0.31 compared with an estimate for India of 0.46 in 1981.[54] The overall Gini coefficient for urban income in 1981 was a highly egalitarian 0.16 compared with a range in South and Southeast Asia from 0.36 in Pakistan to 0.52 in Malaysia.[55]

Offsetting this local class equality were urban-rural and broader coast-interior regional inequalities. Overall Gini coefficients on household incomes of 0.33 in 1979[56] and of rural households of 0.37 in 1979[57] are less equal than in several East Asian nations including Taiwan's 0.29 in 1972. But accounting for social services increases the rural PRC equality measure. The Gini coefficient drops to 0.26 for 1979,[58] reflecting the widespread provision of education and medical care in rural areas, a success of Maoist policy.

Stalinist industrialization policies increased urban-rural inequalities during the Maoist period, despite rhetoric about developing the rural base.[59] This inequality decreased during 1979–84 when rural incomes rose sharply, but the former trend toward inequality has reasserted itself with farmers recently engaging in strikes and demonstrations, despite absolutely increasing incomes.[60]

---

[52]Lardy, *Foreign Trade and Reform in China,* p. 126.

[53]Samir Amin, *The Future of Maoism* (New York: Monthly Review Press, 1987).

[54]Selden, *The Political Economy of Chinese Development,* pp. 146–47.

[55]Riskin, *China's Political Economy,* p. 249.

[56]Riskin, *China's Political Economy,* p. 250.

[57]Selden, *The Political Economy of Chinese Development,* p. 155.

[58]Selden, *The Political Economy of Chinese Development,* p. 157.

[59]Kai-yuen Tsui, ''Decomposition of China's Regional Inequalities,'' *Journal of Comparative Economics* 17 (1993), 600–27. An important factor was severe restriction on rural-urban migration, partially relaxed in the early 1990s.

[60]The ratio of per capita urban to rural incomes fell from 2.24 in 1981 to 1.85 in 1983 and then rose to 2.31 in 1989 (Judith Banister, ''China: Population Changes and the Economy,'' in *China's Economic Dilemmas in the 1990s,* Table 1).

Prerevolutionary China exhibited long-entrenched inequality between better-off coastal provinces and poorer interior provinces, which reflected different soil endowments and climate conditions.[61] Maoist policy left more state revenues in poorer provinces and directed investment towards them, especially during the Third Front investment campaign. Regional inequality at the county, provincial, and broader levels has increased since 1978 as investment is directed more at the coastal provinces and especially the rapidly growing SEZs, although this may be changing in the mid-1990s.

Despite broadly increased regional inequality the shift to the household responsibility system raised peasant incomes across the board, even with some recent declines in provision of public services. Despite increased interprovincial inequality between 1980 and 1988, in 1980 17 provinces had per capita incomes below 200 yuan per year whereas by 1988 none were below that figure.[62] In China the rising tide has lifted most ships, although absolute poverty still exists.

A Chinese Energy/Environmental Crisis?

Because the PRC has the world's largest population at just over 1.2 billion and the world's most rapidly growing industrial economy, severe environmental problems have emerged. In the longer run with the deceleration of population growth and time to implement recently enacted environmental protection laws the situation may get under control. In the short run problems ranging from deforestation to declining urban water supplies have become acute.

A focal point of concern has been energy supply. China is well endowed with potential energy sources including substantial coal, oil, and hydropower reserves.[63] However each of these has problems. Most coal has high sulfur content and newer sources are available only through strip mining. Most available onshore oil sources have been utilized already, and China's oil export surplus is likely to become an import deficit. China has a serious ongoing conflict with neighboring countries over control of the Spratley Islands in the South China Sea where oil may be available. China's major new hydropower project in the Three Gorges area of the Yangzi (Yangtze) River will destroy farmland and scenic areas.

Rising electricity demand has led the PRC to rely on massive coal reserves, and it became the world's largest producer by 1990. Nevertheless coal

---

[61]Poorer interior provinces north and west contain minority ethnic groups such as Tibetans in Xizang (Tibet), Mongols in Nei Monggol (Inner Mongolia), and Turkic Muslims in XUAR (Xinjiang). About 95 percent of PRC population are Han Chinese, who in these provinces want more aid from the central government whereas the local minorities, especially the Tibetans, want independence.

[62]John Knight and Lina Song, "The Spatial Contribution to Income Inequality in Rural China," *Cambridge Journal of Economics* 17 (1993), p. 211.

[63]China also has a very limited nuclear power program.

Box 15–2

China Compared with Populous South Asian Economies

China has improved its general living standard, especially compared with other populous Asian nations that had similar poverty levels half a century ago. This improvement reflects both more rapid growth in the Dengist era and the legacy of the redistributionist and public services provision policies of the Maoist era. Summary comparative data for China, India, Indonesia, Bangladesh, and Pakistan are shown in the following table for per capita income, life expectancy, infant mortality, food availability, birth rate,* and overall income distribution. Although official income statistics suggest it is still part of this group, its material quality of life indicators suggest that China is now in the middle-income group of nations worldwide.

Country	General Indicators for Populous Low Income Asia[†]					
	Per Capita GDP	*Life Expectancy*	*Infant Mortality*	*Per Capita Calories*	*Birth Rate*	*Overall Gini*
China	330	69	36	2,620	1.3	0.33
India	340	56	90	2,115	2.2	0.38
Indonesia	440	55	97	2,380	2.1	0.44
Bangladesh	177	50	124	1,864	2.8	0.34
Pakistan	350	51	116	2,205	3.2	0.33

[†]Data on per capita GDPs are for 1988 in U.S. dollars from Mark Selden, *The Political Economy of Chinese Development* (Armonk: M. E. Sharpe, 1993), p. 172. Data for life expectancy at birth in 1988, infant mortality rate per thousand in 1988, calories per person in 1988, and birth rate per thousand over 1980–88 are from the same source. Overall Gini coefficients for households are from Carl Riskin, *China's Political Economy: The Quest for Development since 1949* (Oxford: Oxford University Press, 1987), p. 250, with the China figure for 1979, India for 1975–76, Indonesia for 1976, Bangladesh for 1966–67, and Pakistan for 1970–71.

*The lower Chinese birth rate has been achieved through draconian policies, a one-child-per-family policy at times enforced by forced sterilizations and abortions, but it has risen somewhat recently (see footnote 44).

consumption increased at an annual rate of 6.5 percent whereas production increased at only a 4.5 percent rate during the late 1980s.[64] In the countryside stalks of crops are burned for fuel rather than plowed under for natural fertilization, thus threatening a long-run food and energy crisis.[65]

---

[64]Crook, ''Primary Issues in China's Grain Economy,'' p. 499.

[65]Vaclav Smil, *China's Environmental Crisis: An Inquiry into the Limits of National Development* (Armonk: M. E. Sharpe, 1993), p. 101.

Burning high-sulfur coal with inefficient small burners has led to severe air pollution in industrialized urban areas. Sulfur dioxide levels range from 100 to 2,000 milligrams per cubic meter compared with U.S. urban wintertime levels of 20 to 100, and suspended particulates exceed official Chinese safety standards by 3 to 10 times.[66] Compared to the worst pollution periods in Tokyo in the 1960s, Beijing has four times the level of nitrogen oxide emissions, five times the carbon monoxide emissions, and six times the sulfur dioxide emissions.[67] Given its huge population and projected increasing use of refrigerants that deplete stratospheric ozone, how the PRC deals with its environmental problems has global significance.

Hong Kong, Taiwan, and Mainland China

Development of the Hong Kong Economy

As discussed in Chapter 2, the economy of the British Crown Colony of Hong Kong is one of the world's most laissez-faire. Hong Kong has dramatically succeeded during the last half century as a leading Newly Industrializing Country (NIC) and recently achieved high per capita income status in excess of U.S. $13,000 in 1993.[68] Its laissez-faire policy includes absolute free trade, no regulation of capital flows or labor markets, few regulations on enterprise formation or activity, no government ownership of business, and a low (15 percent) flat income tax rate. Exceptions include major government involvement in infrastructure building and maintenance, some provision of social services, and involvement in housing and real estate because the government owns all land.[69]

After the Opium Wars the island of Hong Kong was ceded in perpetuity to Britain in 1842. In 1860 Kowloon Island was also ceded in perpetuity after another war, and in 1898 the larger New Territories on the mainland were granted for a 99-year lease. Anticipating the impending expiration of this lease, Britain and China in 1984 agreed that the entire Crown Colony would revert to PRC sovereignty and control in 1997.

In this joint declaration China promised *one country, two systems,* a formula the PRC hopes eventually to apply to Taiwan also. For 50 years Hong Kong is to have practical autonomy over local politics and its economic system, but defense and foreign policy are to be controlled by the PRC. This

---

[66]Smil, *China's Environmental Crisis,* p. 117.

[67]Smil, *China's Environmental Crisis,* p. 234.

[68]One estimate accounting for purchasing power parity places it fifth in the world in real per capita income after the United States, Switzerland, Germany, and Japan (World Bank, *World Development Report,* Table 30).

[69]One reason it has low taxes has been its receipt of income from land leaseholder payments.

dual system has created skepticism and anxiety in Hong Kong and its stock market has become highly volatile, responding sharply to every policy wiggle in Beijing. The 1989 Tiananmen Square massacre was an especial shock, and it was followed by an emigration wave of capital and people.

Hong Kong is small, with about 5 million people, and highly urbanized. It long served as an international trade entrepôt between China and the rest of the world, and British-owned banks and trading houses dominated its economy. After 1949 many industrialists and skilled workers came from Shanghai and industrialization took off.[70] China ceased to use Hong Kong as an entrepôt but did not try to retake it.

However after the Sino-Soviet split the PRC used Hong Kong again. This relationship has expanded so that now Hong Kong is China's major trading partner and its major source of foreign capital investment. Between 1963 and 1988 China's share of exports to Hong Kong rose from 1.4 percent to 27 percent.[71] Hong Kong serves four vital functions for the PRC economy: It is China's main (1) trading partner, (2) financier, (3) middleman, and (4) facilitator. This last role is especially important for introducing market capitalist practices and advanced technologies into the PRC.

Despite future uncertainties, the PRC promised to preserve the Hong Kong economic system because it sees many benefits for itself from doing so. Companies under the control of family members of leading members of the PRC regime are engaging in direct investment in Hong Kong, and their total share of market capitalization reached 7 percent as of May 1994.[72]

Finally, Hong Kong is a role model. Its enormous success has influenced post-Mao policymakers in their moves to liberalization, although they fear the virus of political liberalism it potentially represents. Thus Hong Kong is both an allure and a threat that must be controlled "without killing the goose that lays the golden egg."

Development of the Taiwanese Economy

Compared with Hong Kong's, Taiwan's economy more closely resembles those of Japan and South Korea[73] because of its considerable indicative planning and government ownership of enterprises. But Taiwan actually has a largely market capitalist economy with a Confucian tradition that has performed successfully, reaching a per capita income over U.S. $9,000 in 1993.

---

[70]A shift from laissez-faire since 1987 has been encouraging investment in high-tech electronics industries from fear of falling behind other more dirigiste NICs in this area (Robert Wade, *Governing the Market: Economic Theory and the Role of Government in East Asian Industrialization* [Princeton: Princeton University Press, 1990], p. 333).

[71]Marcus Noland, *Pacific Basin Developing Countries: Prospects for the Future* (Washington: Institute for International Economics, 1990), p. 21.

[72]"The Chinese Takeover of Hong Kong Inc.," *The Economist,* May 7, 1944, pp. 35–36.

[73]Both Taiwan and South Korea are NICs with significant agricultural sectors and a history of colonial rule by Japan. See Chapter 18 for more detailed comparisons of these two.

The population of this tropical island was Malayo-Polynesian in the 1500s when the Portuguese established a trading port and named it Formosa. Han Chinese from Fujian province directly across the Straits of Taiwan began to move in, and the Ming dynasty annexed it in the 1600s. It became a separate province under the Qing after the native population became a minority confined to the interior mountains.

Japan took control of Taiwan in 1895 after defeating China in a war and turned it into a source of agricultural output, building transportation infrastructure and some food processing industries. During World War II the Japanese built some light industry, but three-fourths of this capital stock was destroyed by Allied bombing. Per capita income in Taiwan was slightly ahead of that on the mainland in 1945, although well behind that in Hong Kong.

China regained control in 1945, which led to tension between the Fujianese-speaking Taiwanese and the Mandarin-speaking, ruling Guomindang who eventually constituted about 15 percent of the approximately 20 million Taiwanese population after the defeated Chiang Kai-Shek retreated there in 1949.[74] Protected from invasion by the U.S. Seventh Fleet and supported by U.S. economic aid, Chiang Kai-Shek learned from his mistakes and implemented vigorous antiinflation and land reform programs.

Radical land reform was eased because many landlords had been Japanese or their collaborators. Reform proceeded in three stages, the first being rent reduction from pre-1949 levels, which had exceeded 50 percent of total output. Then came a sale of public lands seized from Japanese owners. Finally in 1953 came the *land-to-the-tiller* program in which all landlords were forced to sell to tenants in exchange for government bonds, a plan in accord with ideas of Sun Yat-sen. Agricultural output expanded rapidly although government remained heavily involved during the 1950s. The egalitarian nature of this land reform is a major reason why Taiwan has an extremely equal income distribution.

Up to 1958, when military confrontation with the PRC occurred, indicative plans emphasized import substitution. But then *export processing zones* (EPZs) were established starting in 1966, thought by some to be the models for the PRC's SEZs. Taiwan's exporting success is such that it has the second largest foreign exchange reserves in the world after Japan.

Foreign investment was encouraged and plans emphasized transportation infrastructure development, although a state-owned industrial sector persists. By 1970 full employment was achieved and Taiwan has had low inflationary growth with an income distribution more equal than any other NIC. A six-year plan started in 1990 emphasizes small-firm development of electronics and high-technology exports,[75] especially to Japan, Taiwan's leading trade partner.

Taiwan faces the question of its relations with the PRC. Unlike Hong Kong, the Guomindang government on Taiwan calls itself the Republic of

---

[74]Mandarin is the official dialect of the Chinese language, spoken in Beijing.

[75]The Taiwanese have been accused by other nations, especially the United States, of pirating technologies and violating patents. Signing the 1993 GATT agreement committed them to eliminating this practice, and some of the companies that were engaged in it have shifted their activities to the PRC since then.

China (ROC) and claims to be the legitimate government of all China, a claim relaxed somewhat recently. After the United States-PRC rapprochement of the 1970s, Taiwan was expelled from the UN and lost recognition by the United States and most other nations that chose to recognize the PRC.

Chiang Kai-Shek died in 1975 and was succeeded by his son, who died in 1988 after initiating a liberalization and democratization process. He was succeeded by a native Taiwanese, Lee Teng-hui, although the leadership continues to be dominated by old mainlanders. His election partially pacified the locals, some of whom support an independent Taiwan, an idea opposed by both the Guomindang and the Communists. The PRC has announced that a Taiwanese declaration of independence would cause an invasion.

But PRC leaders would rather absorb Taiwan in the same way as Hong Kong. Such proposals have been made, and they have been resisted. But since 1988 a working relationship has developed between the ROC and the PRC. Groups of Taiwanese businessmen negotiate in Beijing and substantial trade and investment now occurs between the two, mostly via Hong Kong, but increasingly through SEZs in neighboring Fujian province.

The Taiwanese wait to see the outcome of the absorption of Hong Kong and the nature of the post-Deng era in the PRC before they do anything official. However the increasingly close economic links between the three Chinas suggest that probably some day they will be one again.

The Three Chinas Compared

A comparison of the PRC, the ROC, and Hong Kong indicates that the PRC and Hong Kong are the most different geographically, demographically, systemically, and in performance and that Taiwan is between them on most indicators.

Hong Kong is small and urbanized, market capitalist, laissez-faire, and high income, but has a less equal distribution of income. The PRC is huge and rural, still essentially socialist despite marketization, and poorer but more egalitarian despite recent inequality increases. The ROC is closer in size to Hong Kong but with a substantial rural agricultural sector, lies between the two in degree of economic state guidance, and is closer to Hong Kong in income level but even more equal than the PRC in income distribution, although that reflects its relative regional homogeneity. Behind Hong Kong in per capita income, Taiwan is ahead of it in educational levels and the technological level of its exports.

All share Chinese culture, especially Confucianism, but only the PRC has had a Communist revolution, although the other two have been ruled by foreigners for extended periods of time. They all have had authoritarian political systems, although there has been a recent trend to democratization, most marked in the ROC. Unemployment rates are currently low in all three, although the PRC has substantial disguised unemployment.

Table 15–2 compares GDP growth and inflation performances over time and their income distributions as measured by the ratio of the top 10 percent of population to the bottom 40 percent. Per capita incomes from 1966 show

TABLE 15–2   **The PRC, ROC, and Hong Kong Economies Compared**

Category	PRC	ROC	Hong Kong
Per Cap GDP, 1966	88	236	658
GDP Growth, 1970–80	7.9	9.3	9.3
GDP Growth, 1980–90	10.1	8.5	7.1
GDP Growth, 1991–93	9.1	7.0	5.1
Inflation, 1970–80	1.1	11.1	8.7
Inflation, 1980–90	10.1	8.5	7.1
Inflation, 1991–93	10.1	3.4	10.3
Ratio of Top 10%/Bottom 40%	1.22	1.03	1.93

Source: Per capita GDP levels in 1966 are in U.S. dollars from Alvin Rabushka, *The New China: Comparative Economic Development in Mainland China, Taiwan, and Hong Kong* (Boulder: Westview, 1987), pp. 206, 217, and 226. GDP growth rates and CPI inflation rates for 1970–80 and 1980–90 are from Asian Development Bank, *Asian Development Outlook* (Hong Kong: Oxford University Press, 1992), pp. 288 and 296. Figures for 1991–93 are from the same source and ''The Chinese Takeover of Hong Kong, Inc.,'' *The Economist*, May 7 1944, p. 118. The ratio of the top 10 percent of the income distribution to the bottom 40 percent for the PRC is for 1979 from Carl Riskin, *China's Political Economy: The Quest for Development since 1949* (Oxford: Oxford University Press, 1987) p. 250, for the ROC is for 1979 rural areas from Mark Selden, The Political Economy of Chinese Development (Armonk: M. E. Sharpe, 1993), p. 155, and for Hong Kong is for 1980 from World Bank, *World Development Report 1994* (New York: Oxford University Press, 1994), Table 30. Many of these numbers have competing estimates and controversies regarding their true values.

that their respective rankings are unchanged although their relative distances from each other have. Hong Kong and Taiwan did relatively better during the Maoist period, but more recently the PRC has led in growth.

Summary and Conclusions

The world's most populous nation contains its longest continuously existing civilization. Home of the counterbalancing religions of Taoism and Confucianism, reflecting respectively a laissez-faire spontaneity and a contrasting respect for hierarchy and order, China is the cultural fountainhead of the dynamic East Asian regional economy. It has experienced long dynastic cycles of expansion and contraction, innovation and stagnation, cosmopolitan openness and hermitlike isolation. Today it is opening and expanding as the world's most rapidly growing economy.

After more than a century of foreign domination, the Communists led by Mao Zedong came to power on the mainland, the nationalist Guomindang under Chiang Kai-Shek retreated to Taiwan, and the British continued to rule Hong Kong. After initially aping the Stalinist model, Mao's policies went through many changes as he disagreed with Stalin's successors. In the Great Leap Forward and the Great Proletarian Cultural Revolution, Maoism exhibited radical egalitarianism in large rural communes, regional decentralization, opposition to traditional culture, and a search for economic self-sufficiency. But income differences between city and country widened during his rule.

After Mao's death in 1976, Deng Xiaoping came to power and instituted market-oriented reforms. Communes were disbanded and households took responsibility in agriculture. Economic growth focused on local government-owned town and village enterprises and on coastal Special Economic Zones where direct foreign investment was encouraged through loosened rules. Generally successful, the Dengist PRC has experienced increasing income inequalities, rising inflationary pressures, environmental problems, and political dissidence and democracy movements. The future of the Chinese socialist market economy is unclear.

The PRC has been outperformed since 1949 by both Hong Kong and Taiwan, which have had largely market capitalist economies, Hong Kong's highly laissez-faire and Taiwan's with more indicative planning in a consciously Confucianist system. Both have had strong export-led growth, a path now pursued by the PRC as well.

Hong Kong is to be taken over by the PRC in 1997, but it is to continue its economic system, now the PRC's main link to the world economy, for 50 years. Relations between the ROC and the PRC are hostile, because both claim to be the legitimate government of China. But economic relations have expanded since 1988 and eventually some sort of political accommodation will probably create a united China. Such a united China, an awakened giant, could return to its old role as the Middle Kingdom, axis of world history.

Questions for Discussion

1. How does the contrast between Taoism and Confucianism show up in modern discussions of economic policy in China?
2. How did the traditional organization of the rural Chinese economy become transformed in the Maoist period?
3. How did the "dynasty cycle" fit in with the idea of the "Asiatic mode of production"? Is the dynasty cycle of any relevance today, and if so how?
4. How did Maoism resemble and differ from Stalinism?
5. How did the Maoist regional decentralization policy both damage and aid economic development? What has been the pattern of regional development since the Maoist period?
6. What have been the changes in agricultural policy in the Dengist period and why are they reaching their limits?
7. What are the special characteristics of the town and village enterprises and what are their future prospects?
8. Assess the role of the Special Economic Zones in the Chinese economic reform process.
9. How have Dengist reforms changed China's income distribution?
10. What are limits to continued Chinese economic growth?
11. What is the role of the state in the Hong Kong economy?

12. How does the "socialist market economy" differ from "market socialism"?

13. Compare Taiwanese economic policy and performance with those of the PRC and Hong Kong.

14. What are the prospects for the application of the PRC's "one country, two systems" approach in Hong Kong and Taiwan?

Suggested Further Readings

Adshead, S. A. M. *China in World History.* London: Macmillan, 1988.

Chen, Kang, Gary H. Jefferson, and Inderjit Singh. "Lessons from China's Economic Reform." In *Comparative Economic Systems: Models and Cases,* 7th ed., ed. Morris Bornstein. Burr Ridge: Irwin, 1994, pp. 570–90.

Dorn, James A., and Wang Xi, eds. *Economic Reform in China: Problems and Prospects.* Chicago: University of Chicago Press, 1990.

"A Change of Face: A Survey of Taiwan." *The Economist,* October 10, 1992.

Fairbank, John King. *The United States and China,* 4th ed. Cambridge: Harvard University Press, 1983.

Joint Economic Committee, ed. *China's Economic Dilemmas in the 1990's: The Problems of Reforms, Modernization, and Interdependence.* Armonk: M. E. Sharpe, 1992.

Lardy, Nicholas R. *Foreign Trade and Reform in China, 1978–1990.* Cambridge: Cambridge University Press, 1992.

Mao Tse-Tung (Zedong). *Four Essays on Philosophy.* Peking (Beijing): Foreign Languages Press, 1968.

Putterman, Louis. *Continuity and Change in China's Rural Development: Collective and Reform Eras in Perspective.* New York: Oxford University Press, 1993.

Rabushka, Alvin. *The New China: Comparative Economic Development in Mainland China, Taiwan, and Hong Kong.* Boulder: Westview Press, 1987.

Riskin, Carl. *China's Political Economy: The Quest for Development Since 1949.* Oxford: Oxford University Press, 1987.

Selden, Mark. *The Political Economy of Chinese Development.* Armonk: M. E. Sharpe, 1993.

Smil, Vaclav. *China's Environmental Crisis: An Inquiry into the Limits of National Development.* Armonk: M. E. Sharpe, 1993.

Spence, Jonathan D. *The Search for Modern China.* New York: W. W. Norton, 1990.

Wade, Robert. *Governing the Market: Economic Theory and the Role of Government in East Asian Industrialization.* Princeton: Princeton University Press, 1990.

World Bank. "Chinese Economic Reform Experience." In *Comparative Economic Systems: Models and Cases,* 7th ed., ed. Morris Bornstein. Burr Ridge: Irwin, 1994, pp. 537–69.

Yusuf, Shahid. "China's Macroeconomic Performance and Management during Transition." *Journal of Economic Perspectives* 8 (1994), pp. 71–92.

PART

IV

ALTERNATIVE PATHS AMONG DEVELOPING ECONOMIES

The final part presents diverse cases of developing economies and concludes with a summarizing chapter. These cases include new traditional, reforming state-dominated, indicatively planned market capitalist, and the last remaining pure command socialist case in the world. The final chapter also presents detailed material on privatization in Great Britain as well as on the sub-Saharan success story of Botswana.

Chapter 16 presents the case of Iran, the world's leading example of an Islamic fundamentalist economy, both practically and ideologically, and thus of the broader category of a new traditional economy. It is seen to have only partly fulfilled the criteria of such an economy and to be experiencing many problems, some due to the low price of oil and Iran's self-imposed isolation. This chapter includes information about some other Islamic economies, notably Saudi Arabia and Pakistan.

Chapter 17 discusses the Mexican economy, broadly representative of the state-dominated ''technocratic populist corporatisms'' found in Latin America. Its turbulent history of revolution and reform is recounted, with the note that the Latin American reforms became a model for those in the former Soviet bloc. Mexico has moved forcibly to marketize, privatize, and open to the United States with the North American Free Trade Agreement. Recent uprisings in the countryside and crises of the currency have damaged Mexico's efforts. Mexico is also compared with a set of other Latin American economies.

Chapter 18 studies the case of Korea, both South and North, thus closing our case studies with a final direct comparison of capitalism and socialism. South Korea has been one of the most dynamic of the East Asian Newly Industrializing Countries (NICs) and has a strong export-led growth record. Characterized by large industrial groupings somewhat like those in Japan, it has had a strongly market capitalist orientation, albeit with considerable government intervention through indicative planning.

North Korea remains the purest command socialist economy in the world, a virtual fossil of the classic Stalinist model with little reform movement underway. It has fallen far behind the South in overall economic performance, although the living standards of its people are not as far behind as might be expected. Prospects for unification of the Koreas are considered in comparison with the experience of German unification.

Chapter 19 ties up various loose ends and expands further on several themes that thread throughout the book. The first of these is privatization, which is considered by examining in detail the case of Great Britain, which began the modern privatization movement under Margaret Thatcher. The original center of the Industrial Revolution, Great Britain has long been in a state of relative decline. The privatization wave has helped partly to revive its economy, although it now appears to be reaching the limits of this movement.

The second theme is the ''clash of civilizations,'' the idea that Western market capitalism, Islam, and neo-Confucianism are now in a global conflict. This idea is studied by considering the situation in Central Asia where the former Soviet republics are moving out of a command socialist system, but face virtually all three alternatives as possible paths.

The third theme is integration versus disintegration. Examples include the drive to integration in the European Union and for free trade in the World Trade Organization, the North American Free Trade Agreement, and recent initiatives in the Asia Pacific Economic Council. Disintegration is most dramatically manifested by the breakup of the former Soviet Union and of some of the nations allied to it.

The final theme deals with the prospects for economic growth at the global level in light of the deceleration of such growth since the early 1970s. The sub-Saharan success story of Botswana is discussed. Various theories are examined and the chapter and book conclude with a discussion of the role of the environment in this question and the prospects for global cooperation.

IRAN: THE STRUGGLE FOR A REVOLUTIONARY ISLAMIC ECONOMY

A Moslem's belief in the fundamentals of religion must be based upon reason and he may not practice imitation in regards to fundamentals of the religion, that is, accepting someone else's statement without reasoning. But in regards to the precepts (akham) of the religion he must either be an Expert (Mujtahed) and arrive at those precepts by reasoning or he imitates certainty from an Expert, that is, he acts according to his orders.

—Ayatollah Sayyed Ruhollah Mousavi Khomeini, *A Clarification of Questions*

Introduction

The Islamic Republic of Iran is to Islam what the Soviet Union was to communism, the fountainhead of the international revolutionary movement.[1] The 1979 Islamic revolution in Iran was the first overthrow of a modern secular leadership by a popular movement to establish a fundamentalist Islamic system. Its claim to universality inspires similar movements throughout the Islamic world. Furthermore it actively supports such movements with funding, including radical elements who have engaged in terrorist acts such as the Hezbollah in Lebanon.

Thus Iran stands out as an important example of practical Islamic economics, in which intense debates result in policy shifts by the revolutionary regime. Despite controversies, core elements of Islamic economics have been adopted, such as interest-free banking. Poor economic performance has weakened the appeal of the Iranian model to many observers. But supporters of the revolution point to external shocks, from invasion by Iraq, to an economic

---

[1]To compare the 1917 Bolshevik revolution with the 1979 Islamic revolution in Iran see Richard W. Cottam, "The Iranian Revolution," in *Shi'ism and Social Protest,* eds. N. R. Keddie and J. R. I. Cole (New York: St. Martin's Press, 1986), pp. 121–58.

embargo by the United States, to a fall in world oil prices, sources of Iran's economic difficulties.

Despite its image as role model and revolutionary Islamic fountainhead, Iran is atypical of most Islamic nations. It is dominated by the Shi'i (Shi'ite), branch of Islam which differs from the more widespread Sunni branch. Shi'ism has traditionally been more revolutionary precisely because of its underdog position in the Islamic world relative to Sunnism. Some Sunni-dominated societies Islamizing their economies, such as Pakistan, have adopted more gradualist and less radical approaches. Nevertheless, the Iranian revolution influences radical Sunni movements in Algeria, Egypt, Palestine, Central Asia, and the fundamentalist Sunni government in Sudan.

Iran is a major oil producer and member of the Organization of Petroleum Exporting Countries (OPEC), which engineered the oil price shock of 1973.[2] At the time it was second to Saudi Arabia as a producer in OPEC and accumulated vast wealth, which triggered inflation and increased inequalities of income that fueled the revolutionary movement of 1979. Iran's importance in OPEC is clear because the second oil price shock in 1979 was not engineered by OPEC as a whole but resulted from the collapse of Iranian oil production during the revolution.

The Revolutionary Tradition in Shi'i Islam[3]

As recounted in Chapter 5 the Sunnis and Shi'is split over the succession to the Prophet Muhammed as leader of the Islamic community (*umma*). The Shi'is supported members of Muhammed's family, such as his son-in-law, Ali, and his grandson, Husayn, whereas the Sunnis supported nonfamily members for the political position of caliph. After the Shi'i defeat at the Battle of Karbala they developed the notion of a spiritual leader, the *Imam*,[4] to be a direct descendent of Muhammed. The Imam *should* be caliph, but might not be. The Prophet's son-in-law, Ali, was both the fourth caliph and the first Imam. Husayn was the third Imam, succeeding his older brother.

The branch of Shi'ism dominant in Iran and most numerous worldwide recognizes a line of 12 such Imams and thus is known as Twelver Shi'ism.[5]

---

[2]Within OPEC, predominantly Muslim members are Algeria, Nigeria, Libya, Saudi Arabia, Iraq, Iran, Bahrain, Qatar, United Arab Emirates, and Indonesia. Venezuela and Gabon are non-Muslim members. Non-oil producing [there are oil-producing Muslim nations *not* in OPEC such as Oman, Egypt, and Yemen] nations with many Muslims include Bangladesh, India, Pakistan, and Turkey.

[3]For a history of Shi'i Islam see Moojan Momen, *An Introduction to Shi'i Islam: The History and Doctrines of Twelver Shi'ism* (New Haven: Yale University Press, 1985).

[4]In Sunni Islam an *imam* (not capitalized) leads Friday prayers at a mosque. This is distinct from the Shi'i *Imam* (capitalized) who is a supreme religious leader.

[5]The Zaydi Shi'is of Yemen agree on only the first four Imams. The Isma'ili Shi'is recognize the first seven and thus are known as Sevener Shi'is. The Seveners historically generated the most economically redistributionist Muslim movements and societies, such as the Qarmatians of Eastern Arabia in the 900s.

The Shi'i Imams could extend the prophecy of Muhammed, thus making Shi'i law codes subject to ongoing revision by religious authorities in contrast with Sunni ones.

When the 11th Imam died in 874 his infant son, the 12th Imam, went into hiding. For 70 years his proclamations were issued by four successive messengers. Then he was declared to have gone into a state of supernatural suspension (*Occultation*) wherein he waits hidden from the world until the Day of Judgment when he will return and bring about heaven on earth.

This doctrine underpins a messianic tradition in Twelver Shi'ism in which individuals periodically appear claiming to be either the Hidden Imam himself or his special messenger. The latter was the position of Ayatollah Ruhollah Khomeini, leader of Iran's Islamic revolution, although he was called *Imam* after the revolution.[6] As supreme lawgiver he created and took the title *Vilayat al-faqih,* Mandate of the Jurist, a position held by Ayatollah Ali Khamene'i since Khomeini's death in 1989. No one is now called *Imam* in Iran.

Shi'i Islam has a more developed religious hierarchy possessing greater influence over society than does Sunni Islam. The *zakat* goes to the *ulama* (religious authorities) for redistribution. Furthermore, the Shi'is collect an additional 20 percent income tax, the *khums* that also goes to the ulama. In the ulama hierarchy under Imam or Vilayat e-faqih, the next rank is Grand Ayatollah and then Lesser Ayatollah. Below that is Hojjat-el-Islam, the rank held by current President Ali Akbar Hashemi Rafsanjani of Iran.

Another factor in the revolutionary attitude in Shi'ism is the history of oppression by the Sunnis. In Iraq, Bahrain, and Lebanon Shi'is outnumber Sunnis, but the latter are better off economically and are politically dominant. This situation dates from the defeat at Karbala, and the intense focus on martyrdom in memory of that defeat and the martyrdom of Husayn infuses Shi'ism. Thus on Ashura, the 10th of Muharram and the anniversary of Karbala, Shi'is publicly march, cursing the first three caliphs and sometimes flagellating themselves. On Ashura in December 1978, one-fourth of Iran's population was in the streets calling for the overthrow of the Shah and the return of Imam Khomeini, the final blow to the Shah's regime.

In Iran the official view on economic laws is Khomeini's in *A Clarification of Questions.* He agrees with the Sunnis on forbidding interest and supporting zakat, although the latter is to be voluntary and distributed by the ulama. He also supports the one-fifth income tax, or khums, for the ulama. He accepts land rent, sharecropping, and insurance, making him more moderate than some Sunni Islamic economists. In general he accepts private property.

Nevertheless, in 1979 he ordered the confiscation of properties owned by the former royal family and its associates. This signaled the ascension of ''Islamic socialist'' policies in line with those advocated by Ayatollah Taliqani.[7]

---

[6]Khomeini's sending cassette tapes from exile gave him an aura of the Hidden Imam. He exhorted the masses to martyrdom such as occurred at Karbala, and demonstrating crowds called for the return of ''Imam Khomeini.''

[7]See Ayatollah Mahmud Taliqani, *Ownership in Islam,* trans. from Persian by R. Campbell (Berkeley: Mizan Press, 1982).

This fit with Khomeini's call for redistributive justice and his denunciations of corruption in the Shah's regime. He opposed economic domination by foreigners or non-Muslims, especially Americans and Israelis, which he saw as happening under the Shah. Thus the confiscations justly aided the poor ostensibly, and they asserted Muslim Iranian independence from imperialistic domination by foreign non-Muslims. This policy conflicted with the more pro–market capitalist views in much of Khomeini's writings, a conflict played out ever since with a tilt away from the socialist approach emerging over time.

Historical Overview to the Revolution

Iran's territory largely coincides with that of the ancient seat of culture and civilization known as Persia.[8] Just over 2,500 years ago Cyrus founded the Persian empire, core of Alexander the Great's realm later. After Alexander's death, successor states ruled from Persia until the Muslim conquest in 640, after which Persia was ruled from outside for centuries by multinational Muslim empires.

In 1501, Safavid leader Isma'il proclaimed himself Shah and established an empire with the modern borders of Iran. Isma'il was a Shi'i who claimed to be the Hidden Imam. He forcibly converted the previously Sunni Persians to Shi'ism and established the still existing Shi'i ulama hierarchy.

The Qajar dynasty came to power in 1785. Soon after, control of Persia was contested by Great Britain and Russia. The ulama opposed cooperation with these powers, provoking a war with Russia in 1828 that Persia lost. In 1872 the British gained the Reuter concession, which granted them control over mines, the national bank, and railroad construction in Persia. It was cancelled a year later after agitation by the ulama. But there was no opposition to the d'Arcy oil concession in 1901, the first in the Middle East, out of which came the Anglo-Persian Oil Company, now British Petroleum, after oil was discovered in 1908.

In 1906 some ulama combined with Western-oriented intellectuals to remove the Qajar Shah in the Constitutionalist Revolt, which resulted in a constitution modeled on Belgium's. Russian troops reimposed the Qajars in 1911. During World War I both Britain and Russia occupied portions of Persia. This humiliation led to removal of the Qajars in 1925 by the military commander, Reza Shah, who established the Pahlavi dynasty that lasted until 1979.

---

[8]*Persia* became *Iran* in 1935 to emphasize the Aryan, or Indo-European, origins of the Persians. Then leader, Reza Shah, was fascinated with Nazi ideologies of the ''Aryan master race'' and looked to Germany to offset British and Soviet domination. Shi'i Persians are about 60 percent of the population, and Shi'i Turkic Azeris are about 30 percent. Religious minorities include Sunnis, Baha'is, a group founded in Persia in the 1800s and much persecuted today, Christians, Jews, and Zoroastrians, the ancient Persian religion whose New Year is still celebrated in Iran.

Reza Shah followed a secularizing and nationalist course. He forbade women to wear traditional Islamic garb in 1928, stripped the ulama of control of the courts in 1932, and reduced their control over the wealthy religious endowments (*waqfs*) in 1934. He built up a strong military and a strong centralized state that suppressed ethnic minorities.

He also brought in German advisers to offset Britain and the Soviet Union. In 1941 the British and Soviets deposed him in favor of his son, Mohammed Reza Pahlavi, and respectively occupied Iran's south and north. In 1946 the United States pressured the Soviets to withdraw.

British control of the oil industry stimulated reemergence of a nationalist democratic coalition, led by Mohammed Mossadegh, a participant in the 1906 movement. He became prime minister in 1951, nationalized the oil industry, and deposed the Shah. Besides liberal nationalists his supporters included prominent ulama such as Ayatollah Taliqani, the later ''Islamic socialist.'' In 1953 the CIA and British MI6 deposed Mossadegh, restored the Shah, and put the oil industry under the control of British Petroleum and some American companies.[9]

The Shah now followed U.S. foreign policy, joining the anti-Soviet Baghdad Pact of 1955 and maintaining friendly if covert relations with Israel. Internally he established tight dictatorial control enforced by his secret police, SAVAK. He opened the country to foreign investment and angered the ulama by elevating to wealth and power members of religious minorities.

In 1963 the Shah initiated the White Revolution to modernize and westernize Iranian economy and society. A crucial element included land reform involving distribution to peasants from major landowners, including the religious endowments (waqfs). This reform triggered protests led by Ayatollah Khomeini, who was exiled to Iraq and later to Paris from where he became the main opposition leader against the Shah.

In 1973 the Shah supported the OPEC oil price shock, which enormously increased revenues and income for Iran. Much of the money went to state-sponsored industrial development, but also much was siphoned to the Shah's cronies. Inflation soared, resulting in impoverishment of many Iranians while a few became very rich. As broad-based opposition to the regime spread, SAVAK's repression intensified, thus triggering more opposition.

The breadth of opposition to the Shah came to extend from landless peasants and the ulama through the bazaar merchants to government workers and the middle class. In January 1978, police fired on a pro-Khomeini demonstration by students in Qom, the religious center of Iran, and 70 died. This triggered a cycle of demonstrations and strikes every 40 days to memorialize those

---

[9]Known as ''Project Ajax,'' this coup remains a source of controversy. The British government refuses to release documents relating to it. See Kermit Roosevelt, *Countercoup: The Bloody Struggle for Control of Iran* (New York: McGraw-Hill, 1979) and Daniel Yergin, *The Prize: The Epic Quest for Oil, Money and Power* (New York, Simon and Schuster, 1991) chap. 23, for further details.

martyred 40 days before. Civil unrest steadily escalated, even after martial law was declared in September. During Ashura demonstrations in December, millions were in the streets.

The Shah left the country on January 16, 1979, and on February 1 Khomeini returned to Tehran in triumph, welcomed by a crowd estimated at 2 million. The Islamic Revolution had achieved victory over the secularizing monarchy.

Iran's Economy before and after the Revolution

The Revolution after the Revolution

The victory of the Islamic Revolution initiated a period of two and a half years of intense power struggles with serious violence erupting on all sides. Many of those arrested for opposing the regime then were charged with being ''Corrupters of the Earth'' and were executed. Justification for such extreme measures heightened after Iraq invaded Iran in September 1980, beginning a war that lasted until 1988, the bloodiest in the world since World War II.

During 1979 the Revolutionary Council issued many radical economic proposals. Its members included the Islamic socialist, Ayatollah Taliqani, and his ally, Abolhassan Bani-Sadr, who became prime minister two days after Revolutionary Guards seized the U.S. embassy and took those inside hostage in early November 1979.

A month later the Islamic constitution was adopted that mandates the Vilayat-al-faqih concept. A legislative assembly (*Majlis*) was established, which was dominated by Islamic fundamentalists. The constitution also called for a prime minister and a president, and Bani-Sadr was elected to the presidency in January 1980. After more violence he was replaced in 1981 by Ayatollah Ali Khamene'i who was president until Khomeini's death in June 1989, when Khamene'i succeeded Khomeini as Vilayat-al-faqih. Hojjat-el-Islam Ali Akbar Hashemi Rafsanjani was elected president and the position of prime minister was eliminated.

The Islamic constitution also mandates a body of 12 ulama, the Council of Guardians, who pass on the ''Islamicness'' of any legislation. In the struggle over economic policy this body became the bastion of pro–market capitalist forces, blocking a bill to nationalize foreign trade in 1982 and a land reform bill in 1983. It represented the interests of the urban bazaar merchants and also large landlords, including some ulama.[10] As of

---

[10]See Mansoor Moaddel, ''Class Struggle in Post-Revolutionary Iran,'' *International Journal of Middle East Studies* 23 (1991), pp. 317–43. American commentators have been confused by the most anti-American groups in Iran being the most pro-market. Thus the American terminology of ''radicals'' and ''moderates'' has been meaningless.

Khomeini's death, the Council of Guardians had vetoed approximately 48 percent of the bills passed by the assembly.[11]

We can identify four periods in economic policy since the revolution. First is the First Radical Phase, which lasted from 1979 to 1981, or through the main postrevolutionary power struggle. This period saw a wave of nationalizations and confiscations as well as proposals for foreign trade nationalization and land reform, later blocked by the Council of Guardians.

The Second Radical Phase lasted from 1982 to 1984 and was marked by more emphasis on strictly Islamic policies such as implementing interest-free banking rather than the more socialist-oriented policies of the previous phase. The role of the Council of Guardians, supported by Khomeini, was crucial.

From 1985 to 1989 was the First Pragmatic Phase. No major innovations in economic policy came during this period, but Iran opened to the outside world and softened its attitude towards the United States under pressure of the Iran-Iraq war. Real incomes declined and economic crisis set in. Secret arms purchases from the United States culminated in the Iran-contra scandal there.

The Second Pragmatic Phase, from 1989 to the present, coincides with the presidency of Rafsanjani and has been marked by some privatizations of state enterprises and moves towards integrating into the world economy, including obtaining a loan from the World Bank in 1993, while maintaining Islamic economics internally and active support for fundamentalist Islamic movements abroad.

The Economy of Iran under the Pahlavis

In a sense, the Islamic Revolution did not fundamentally alter Iran's economy, which was dominated by the state sector, especially after the oil nationalization in the early 1970s. Iran's economy ran on oil and runs on oil. The ''revolution'' was that a different group came to control this state-run oil machine.

State-led development dated from the 1920s in Reza Shah's nationalist drive for autonomous development. Using modest oil revenues public enterprises were established in textiles, sugar, cement, iron, and steel; infrastructure was built up; and the state loaned money to tariff-protected private sector development in an import substitution industrialization strategy. In 1944 Mohammed Reza Pahlavi established comprehensive indicative central planning. From the late 1950s through the early 1970s capital investment was nearly evenly split between the public and private sectors with the former concentrating on iron, steel, copper, machine tools, aluminum, and petrochemicals, and the latter concentrating on finished metals and specialty steels, synthetic fibers, paper, automobile assembly, and sugar, some of these in joint ventures with foreign capital.

---

[11]Nader Entessar, ''The Challenge of Political Reconstruction in Iran,'' in *Modern Capitalism and Islamic Ideology in Iran,* eds. C. Bina and H. Zangeneh (New York: St. Martin's Press, 1992), p. 229.

The 1973 oil price shock generated a surge of revenues into state coffers and investment shifted towards the state sector. Whereas in the Fourth Development Plan (1968–1972) there were 141 billion rials of private investment and 146 billion rials of public investment, during the Fifth Development Plan (1973–1977) the respective figures were 319 billion rials and 734 billion rials.[12] By 1978 government spending was 43 percent of GNP and military spending was 10 percent of GNP. Of the nonagricultural labor force, 25 percent was on the government payroll.[13]

Despite this industrialization much of the labor force remained in agriculture, which was dominated by sharecropping relationships between landless workers and absentee landlords, often ulama or religious organizations (waqfs).[14] After the Shah's 1963 land reform a major rural-urban migration occurred and a majority of the population was urban by the 1980s.

The dominant feature of Iran's foreign trade was overwhelming dependence on oil exports. Even in the 1960s the percentage of export earnings due to oil exports never fell below 85 percent. After the oil price increase of 1973 this percentage soared to 97 percent and stayed above 94 percent until oil prices dropped in 1986 (see Table 16–2). That the percentage remains high after 1979 contradicts one of the goals of the revolution, which was to reduce the dependence on oil exports. But war with Iraq forced continuing reliance on this source of hard currency. Table 16–1 shows Iranian oil production in relation to OPEC and world production over time, whereas Table 16–2 shows oil exports, their percentage of total exports over time, and the average price of Iranian light crude oil.

The surge in oil revenues after 1973 triggered double-digit real growth rates of GDP but also double-digit inflation rates. Inflation combined with an increasing inequality of income to fuel the fires of revolutionary fervor that exploded in 1978. With strikes, the exodus of foreign technicians, and general upheaval, both oil production and GDP fell in the immediate aftermath of the revolution. Both grew again after 1981, only to decline in 1986. GDP declined again in 1987 under the pressure of the war, but its end saw a return to growth for both oil production and GDP. Inflation has remained at double-digit levels except in 1985. The Gulf War period saw a surge of oil exports and economic growth, which has slowed down since then. Statistics on real GDP growth rates and CPI inflation rates are shown in Table 16–3.

---

[12]H. Razavi and F. Vakil, *The Political Environment of Economic Planning in Iran, 1971–1983* (Boulder: Westview, 1984), p. 66.

[13]Alan Richards and John Waterbury, *A Political Economy of the Middle East: State, Class, and Development* (Boulder: Westview, 1990), p. 207.

[14]There was a tradition dating from the Mongol invasions of insecure land tenure in Iran even among the wealthiest families. This led many to donate land to the waqfs, the charitable organizations controlled by the ulama, so as to avoid seizures by governments.

TABLE 16–1   Iran and OPEC, Shares of World Production

Year	World Total	OPEC	Iran	OPEC Share %	Iran's Share % World	Iran's Share % OPEC
1973	55.7	31.0	5.9	55.6	10.6	19.0
1975	52.8	27.2	5.3	51.5	10.0	19.5
1979	62.5	31.0	3.2	49.6	5.1	10.3
1980	59.4	27.0	1.7	45.4	2.9	6.3
1981	56.0	22.8	1.4	40.7	2.5	6.1
1982	53.2	19.0	2.2	35.7	4.1	11.6
1983	53.0	17.9	2.4	33.8	4.5	13.4
1984	54.2	17.9	2.2	33.0	4.0	12.3
1985	53.6	16.6	2.2	31.0	4.1	13.2
1986	55.9	18.7	2.0	33.4	3.6	10.7
1987	56.3	18.8	2.3	33.4	4.1	12.2
1988	58.5	21.0	2.2	35.9	3.8	10.5
1989	59.5	22.6	2.8	38.0	4.7	12.4
1990	61.2	24.3	3.1	39.7	5.1	12.8
1991	60.1	23.6	3.3	39.3	5.5	14.0
1992	60.2	24.9	3.4	41.4	5.6	13.6
1993	60.1	25.7	3.6	42.8	6.0	14.0
1994	60.4	25.8	3.6	42.7	6.0	14.0

Source: U.S. Department of Energy, *Monthly Energy Review,* November 1994, Tables 10.1a,b, pp. 130–31. 1994 figures are extrapolated from the first eight months. Volume figures are in millions of barrels per day.

Policy and Performance after the Revolution

The Nationalization Question.   The state sector gained in the immediate aftermath of the revolution as the nationalizations and confiscations ordered by Khomeini took place. This ended with the removal of Bani-Sadr from office at the end of the First Radical Phase, when the Council of Guardians asserted the right to private property. The current policy trend in the Second Pragmatic Phase under Rafsanjani sees some privatizing of the state sector and even the opening of a stock exchange in 1990.

Confiscations from the Pahlavi family and their retainers began in March 1979. These confiscations went to a body controlled by the ulama and some bazaar merchants known as the Mustaz'afan Foundation, or ''Foundation of the Oppressed.''[15] The proceeds were to aid the poor, especially in developing low-income housing projects. By 1981 the Mustaz'afan was managing

[15]Scandals involving management of this foundation's funds led Khomeini to wisecrack that ''the foundation for the needy has turned into the foundation for the greedy.''

TABLE 16–2   Iranian Petroleum Exports

Year	Value of Petroleum Exports	Oil as Percent of Total Exports	Price in Dollars per Barrel Iranian Light-34 API
1967	1.75	90.6	n.a.
1970	2.36	98.1	1.36
1973	5.62	90.5	2.11
1974	20.90	97.0	10.63
1975	19.63	97.3	10.67
1976	22.92	97.4	n.a.
1977	23.60	97.3	n.a.
1978	21.68	96.5	n.a.
1979	19.19	96.9	13.45
1980	13.29	94.2	30.00
1981	12.05	95.7	37.00
1982	19.23	99.0	34.20
1983	19.22	99.2	31.20
1984	12.26	98.7	28.00
1985	13.11	98.4	28.00
1986	7.20	88.9	28.05
1987	10.00	90.2	16.15
1988	6.04	n.a.	13.26
1989	9.02	n.a	16.04
1990	13.42	n.a.	20.64
1991	13.64	n.a.	17.37
1992	13.26	n.a.	17.73
1993	11.98	n.a.	14.34

Source: Exports and percentage of exports through 1987 are from Cyrus Bina, "Global Oil and the Oil Policies of the Islamic Republic," in *Modern Capitalism and Islamic Ideology in Iran,* eds. C. Bina and H. Zangeneh, (New York: St. Martin's Press, 1992), p. 129, constructed from *OPEC Annual Statistical Bulletins.* The price of oil though is from Bina, "Global Oil," p. 144, constructed from U.S. Department of Energy reports. The price of oil 1988–93 is from Cyrus Bina, "Oil, Japan, and Globalization," *Challenge* 37, no. 3 (1994), p. 47. Value of petroleum exports for 1988–93 is estimated by multiplying the price by a volume figure from *International Financial Statistics,* International Monetary Fund, December 1994. Exports are in billions of U.S. dollars.

149 industrial units, 64 mining units, 472 agricultural units, 101 construction units, 25 cultural units, 238 commercial units, and 2,786 real estate units.[16] In 1985 the Council of Guardians ordered the return of 180 of these to their original owners.

---

[16]Mehrdad Valibeigi, "Islamization of the Economy: The Post Revolutionary Iranian Experience," Ph.D. thesis, Department of Economics, American University, 1991. Although Mustaz'afan is the largest and wealthiest, there are other such foundations. Some aid the international Islamic revolutionary movement by acts such as offering a bounty of several million dollars for the assassination of novelist Salman Rushdie or by funneling millions of dollars to Muslim opposition groups in Algeria and other countries (Gary Sick, "The Two Faces of Iran: Rafsanjani's Moderation, the Mullahs' Holy Terror," *Washington Post,* April 4, 1993, pp. C1–C2).

TABLE 16–3   Iranian Real GDP Growth and Inflation Rates

Year	Real GDP Growth Rate	CPI Inflation Rate
1974–75	6.9	14.7
1975–76	2.6	12.8
1976–77	12.1	10.9
1977–78	11.1	27.6
1978–79	−16.7	11.7
1979–80	−6.0	10.5
1980–81	−20.8	26.0
1981–82	8.9	22.4
1982–83	14.0	19.2
1983–84	8.8	17.7
1984–85	2.8	10.5
1985–86	4.2	4.1
1986–87	−8.1	20.8
1987–88	−0.1	27.8
1988–89	2.2	28.9
1989	3.3	22.4
1990	11.7	7.6
1991	11.4	28.2
1992	5.7	31.0
1993	0.2	35.8

Source: Data through 1988–89 are from Adnan Mazarei, Jr., "The Iranian Economy Under the Islamic Republic: Institutional Change and Macroeconomic Performance (1979–90)," Working Paper 616s, Department of Economics, UCLA, 1991, Table 4, constructed from data from the Central Bank of the Islamic Republic of Iran. The years are according to the Iranian calendar and begin when astrological ones do, that is on the vernal equinox, March 21. For 1989–93, data are constructed from *International Financial Statistics,* International Monetary Fund, December 1994.

In June 1979 all banks and insurance companies were nationalized. In July a comprehensive nationalization law was passed that established the Organization of Nationalized Industries (ONI), which was to run the nationalized firms. 580 firms were affected in nine categories: food, electricity and appliances, construction equipment, textiles, pharmaceuticals, shoes and leather, paper and wood, chemicals, and cement. Besides firms viewed as crucial to the economy, those nationalized were either set up by families connected to the Shah or had liabilities to the banking system exceeding their assets. In 1990 the government offered minority shares for sale in 400 state-owned firms.[17]

The Islamic constitution, passed in December 1979, mandated public control of all major industries, foreign trade, major mines, banking, insurance, power, dams, major irrigation systems, air, sea, land, and railroad transport. In 1980 the government attempted to nationalize control of foreign trade, of

---

[17]Valibeigi, "Islamization of the Economy," pp. 76–79.

which it already controlled about 40 percent. Legislation mandating such control was passed, but the Council of Guardians declared it to be in nonconformity with Islam because it would take away the rights of merchants and establish a state monopoly. Eventually in 1984 compromise legislation was passed under which the state would import necessary goods and the remaining foreign trade would be privately controlled.

The Land Question.   In late 1979 the Revolutionary Council decreed that confiscated, unclaimed, uncultivated public lands possessed by private agencies and certain scattered woodlands and pastures would be available for redistribution. In 1980 a bill to eliminate leasing and sharecropping passed that limited private farm sizes to three times what was necessary to support a family and that turned large-scale mechanized farms into cooperatives. A committee of seven members was to redistribute land. Between April and November 1980, they redistributed slightly over 1 million hectares of land out of 14 million arable hectares in Iran. Then Khomeini suspended the law and the committee under pressure from the grand ayatollahs and large landlords. A more moderate bill was passed in December 1982, but it was rejected by the Council of Guardians in January 1983.

An urban land law was passed in 1982 that was upheld by the Council of Guardians. It nationalized uncultivated land, land with unknown ownership, and portions of parcels in excess of 3,000 square meters in size. The goal was to develop housing for the poor, and the amount of investment in construction doubled between 1978 and 1983 whereas investment in mining and industry fell sharply during the same period.[18] But this program has not led to expanded housing and has become bogged down in bureaucracy and corruption.[19]

Labor-Management Relations.   Many Islamic economists argue (see Chapter 5) that cooperative workplace relationships are preferable to the standard hierarchical, boss-worker pattern. During the revolution workers' councils spontaneously appeared in some industries. Many called for nationalizing their particular industry, and when nationalization occurred the councils were often disbanded. In some cases, notably oil, the councils supported Marxist opponents of the government and were violently suppressed.

Provisions for Islamic Workers' Councils (*Shourahs*) were promulgated in 1980. But when more restricted legislation was passed in December 1982, it was rejected by the Council of Guardians. A temporary labor law was passed in 1991, but it leaves even less scope for workers' councils. Thus this aspect of Islamic economics has been frustrated in favor of a more standard approach after an attempted beginning.

---

[18]Valibeigi, ''Islamization of the Economy,'' p. 157.

[19]Ali A. Kiafar, ''Urban Land Policies in Post-Revolutionary Iran,'' in Bina and Zangeneh, *Modern Capitalism,* pp. 235–56.

FIGURE 16–1   **Short-Term and Long-Term Bank Accounts in Iran (Billions of Rials)**

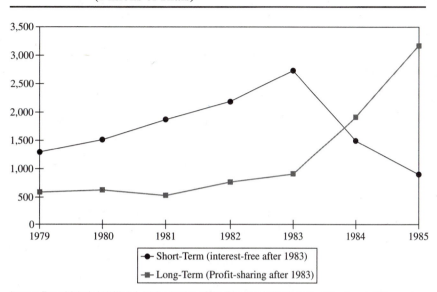

Source: From Mehrdad Valibeigi, "Islamization of the Economy," Ph.D. thesis, Department of Economics, American University, 1991, Table 28, p. 145. The figures are compiled from the Statistical Year Book of Iran for 1985 and 1987. They are in billions of rials.

Interest-Free Banking in Iran.   As noted in Chapter 5, eliminating interest (*riba*) is probably the most distinctive feature of Islamic economics. Iran became the first modern Islamic state to implement nationwide interest-free banking, since followed by Pakistan and Sudan. The elimination of interest was carried out in two stages.

First, in February 1980 the Supreme Council of Money and Credit was formed, and it passed a resolution calling for eventual abolition of all interest. As a preliminary step it replaced interest in banking transactions with "service charges" and set service charge rates for particular kinds of loans and accounts. This was criticized by radical Islamic elements as superficial.

But fears of complete Islamization led to a panic among depositors in late 1980 when Iraq invaded Iran, and long-term savings accounts dropped by about 15 percent from 1980 to 1981.[20] This forced Khomeini to declare that banks' giving prizes to depositors was Islamically legitimate. The policy of prizes implies a varying return because the prizes contain an element of randomness, not unlike many Western bond funds.

The second stage was implemented in 1983 with a comprehensive Law of Interest-Free Banking. Interest on short-term deposits was eliminated. Long-term accounts could share in profits from loans. This policy led to a dramatic shift from short-term to long-term accounts after 1983 as shown in Figure 16–1 above.

---

[20]Valibeigi, "Islamization of the Economy," p. 143.

The 1983 law also granted the Central Bank of Iran the right to determine the overall volume of credit expansion, possible rates of returns for certain kinds of partnerships and lease arrangements, service charge levels, and ranges for credit in the various allowed forms of profit-sharing arrangements. In July 1990 the Central Bank used an increase in the allowed rates of return as a contractionary monetary policy to sop up excess liquidity and combat accelerating inflation.

As noted in Chapter 5, the majority of loans by Iranian banks are of the sort that look more like interest arrangements than of the sort that are clearly profit-sharing arrangements. Many argue this is essentially a semantic issue and that the term *interest* is replaced by the term *profit*. However, the banks are partners rather than lenders under this system, especially given the lack of deposit insurance.

It can be argued that the more important change in Iranian banking was the nationalization of the banks in 1979 and the state direction of investment that resulted. This state direction cut investment in industry and mining and increased it in construction. This shift might have occurred anyway, but it reflects the social emphasis on housing construction and reconstruction as war damage by Iraq escalated. This shift of investment may mean that not only the issue of Islamic banking but more broadly that of Islamic economics is secondary to the conflict between capitalism and socialism (private versus nationalized banking). This continuing conflict is just what some Islamic economists point to in disputing that Islamic economics represents a superior Third Way between capitalism and socialism.

The Distribution of Income.   A driving force of the revolution was resentment of the increasing income and wealth inequalities in the 1970s. This resentment fed the Islamic demand for social justice and supported the ''Islamic socialist'' trend in power in the immediate aftermath of the revolution. Despite the disruptions and economic decline that came out of the revolution, increased equality of income was one initial success. But inequalities have since reemerged, possibly to a greater level than before the revolution.

Table 16–4 presents measures of inequality of household expenditures, accurate data on incomes being unavailable.[21] For both urban and rural households quintile ratios and Gini indexes are presented for selected years. These quintile ratios are the ratio of household expenditures by the richest 20 percent of the population to that by the poorest 20 percent. For the Gini index a higher value indicates greater inequality.

Most reductions in inequality occurred early after the revolution, although in rural areas an initial increase in inequality occurred before a reduction. In urban areas the main factors were sharp reductions in incomes of wealthy individuals because of the confiscations and nationalizations during 1979 to 1981

---

[21]Because such data do not account for savings, they tend to overstate any degree of equality.

Box 16–1

Policies towards Women and Family Planning

The Shah's 1963 White Revolution granted women the right to vote, and their family law rights were strengthened in 1967. Women had not been subject to Islamic dress codes from the 1920s. Women were allowed to enter a variety of professions and many did so. Educational opportunities expanded as female adult literacy rose from 17 percent in 1970 to 30 percent in 1980, compared to 55 percent male adult literacy in 1980.*

With the Islamic Revolution, sexual segregation in education, employment, and public activity was decreed. Birth control and abortion were forbidden. A strict dress code was imposed, violation of which was punishable by up to 74 lashes of a whip.† These restrictions continue with slight relaxations since 1990 in employment, where women may now work in several previously forbidden areas, and in family planning and birth control.

Between 1965 and 1980 the population growth rate of Iran was 3.1 percent per year, a high rate implying that the population doubled every 23 years. Between 1980 and 1990 this rate accelerated to 3.6 percent per year, one of the highest in the world, implying a doubling time of less than 20 years.‡ The increased population growth rate reflects the impact of Islamization on women and the pressure on them to stay home and have children.

It became harder to raise real per capita incomes as the dependency ratio increased. Although real GDP rose in most years since the revolution, real *per capita* income steadily fell. Iran's real per capita income in U.S. 1988 dollars went from 7,988 in 1980 to 7,252 in 1985 to 6,132 in 1988.§ By 1992 its estimated purchasing power parity (PPP) per capita income in 1992 U.S. dollars was 5,280.‖

Policy makers in Iran have decided that rapid population growth contributes to the problem of falling per capita income and have moved towards relaxing family planning policies. However this move is opposed by the stricter ulama and is very controversial. Thus the government hesitates to fully implement family planning and emphasizes study of the issue.ˢ

---

*Alan Richards and John Waterbury, *A Political Economy of the Middle East: State, Class, and Development* (Boulder: Westview, 1990), pp. 88, 113.

†Ann Elizabeth Mayer, ''The Fundamentalist Impact on Law, Politics, and Constitutions in Iran, Pakistan, and the Sudan,'' in *Fundamentalisms and the State: Remaking Polities, Economies, and Militance,* eds. M. E. Marty and R. S. Appleby (Chicago: University of Chicago Press, 1993), pp. 115–16. Traditional Iranian Shi'i clothing for women is the chador, a black garment that completely covers the entire body except for the eyes.

‡World Bank, *World Development Report 1992* (New York: Oxford University Press, 1992), Table 26, p. 269. This rate has declined somewhat since 1990.

§*Statistical Abstract of the United States* (Washington: USGPO, 1991), Table 1446, p. 841.

‖World Bank, *World Development Report 1994* (New York: Oxford University Press, 1994), Table 30, p. 221. This figure may not be comparable with the others.

ˢ1992 personal communication from Ralph Andreano who represented the World Health Organization on a mission to Iran.

TABLE 16–4   **Measures of Household Expenditure Inequalities**

Year	Quintile Ratio—Urban	Gini Index—Urban	Quintile Ratio—Rural	Gini Index—Rural
1977	14.7	0.4998	9.4	0.4375
1979	12.9	0.4702	11.7	0.4789
1980	9.1	0.4040		
1982	10.6	0.4168	8.5	0.4051
1983	12.2	0.4282	10.7	0.4161
1984	11.4	0.4205	11.3	0.4293

Source: Constructed from Sohrab Behdad, ''Winners and Losers of the Iranian Revolution: A Study in Income Distribution,'' *International Journal of Middle East Studies* 21 (1989), pp. 327–58, Tables 5 and 8.

and an increase in income for the working class from an increased minimum wage. Also the income tax code became more progressive. Since the end of the First Radical Phase a trend back towards greater inequality has emerged.

The initial increase in inequality in rural areas coincided with agricultural price hikes in 1978 and 1979, which large-scale farmers took advantage of. These higher relative prices persist, causing a relative improvement of rural incomes relative to urban incomes, although the latter are still about twice the former in per household terms. Less dramatic than in urban areas, the movement towards equality was probably due to the 1980 land reform redistributions before Khomeini and the Council of Guardians halted them. There has been a drift back towards greater inequality in rural areas, as in the urban areas.[22]

The college educated have been noticeable as relative losers whereas the illiterate have been noticeable as relative gainers in the income distribution. An obvious, if unprovable hypothesis is that the highly educated are less devout compared to the illiterate. However, there remains a positive correlation between educational level and income in Iran.[23]

Macroeconomic Imbalance and Rent-Seeking.   Given the fall in oil prices in 1986, pressures of the war with Iraq, trade sanctions by the United States, and general revolutionary upheaval, serious macroeconomic imbalances emerged in Iran. In the late 1980s inflation accelerated (see Table 16–3), the current account balance went into deficit, and the budget deficit sharply increased. Nevertheless, until April 1993, the government refused to devalue the rial against foreign currencies (it was pegged to the IMF's Special Drawing

---

[22]This trend has continued in both areas at least to 1989. Mehrdad Valibeigi (''Distributive Justice Under the Islamic Republic of Iran,'' paper presented at Eastern Economic Association meetings, [Boston, 1994], Tables 1 and 2) finds the percentage share of household expenditures in the richest fifth to have been 69.74 in 1977, 54.43 in 1984, and 60.43 in 1989 in urban areas and 49.83 in 1977, 47.96 in 1984, and 55.17 in rural areas.

[23]Sohrab Behdad, ''Winners and Losers of the Iranian Revolution.''

Right [SDR]) and tried to deal with the external imbalance by ''import compression'' and very strict tariffs and quotas. The outcome of this policy was summarized by Pesaran:

> The result has been rising domestic inflation, a surge in rent-seeking activities at the expense of production, promotion of corruption, misallocation of resources from manufacturing to trade and distribution, and a significant policy bias against investment.[24]

It is inaccurate to blame these disorders upon Islamization of the economy. Rather they arose from pride regarding the value of the rial in the face of shocks and disruptions and hostility of much of the outside world, which beyond a certain point introduced distortions that became self-feeding. Ultimately the problem originates with Iran's history as a major oil exporter and its inability to adjust to lower oil prices and reduced oil markets. Nevertheless, there has been a substantial sectoral reallocation of resources towards trade and away from industry.[25]

A measure of the overvaluation of the rial is the ratio of black market price for U.S. dollars compared to the official price. The gap steadily increased to about 5 to 1 around 1982 and then fell back a bit, but took off again in 1984. In November 1989 it reached a level of almost 20 to 1.[26]

Overvaluation made it difficult for any industry to compete with foreign producers, despite extensive protectionism. This reinforced the dependence of the economy on oil exports for hard currency earnings, even as the market for oil continued to lack strength. Access to imports depended on obtaining appropriate licenses from government officials, allowing a classic setup for corruption and rent-seeking.

The extreme difficulties of 1989 led the Rafsanjani government to introduce multiple exchange rates as the Second Pragmatic Phase began. Combined with the world embargo against Iraq after the 1990–91 Gulf War, which increased Iran's oil export market, economic conditions improved for a while in Iran and inflation fell, per capita income rose, and capital investment rose. This improvement ended by 1993 with a renewed outburst of inflation and continuing weakness in oil prices. The government loosened import restrictions and let the rial float, which led to a loss of more than half its value against the U.S. dollar. But conditions simply worsened and in 1994, restrictions were reimposed on imports, multiple exchange rates were reintroduced, and plans to remove subsidies to various groups and to sell off assets owned by religious foundations were shelved.

---

[24]M. Hashem Pesaran, ''The Iranian Foreign Exchange Policy and the Black Market for Dollars,'' *International Journal of Middle East Studies* 24 (1992), p. 119.

[25]Nations that export large quantities of a primary resource find it difficult to develop or maintain industry because their export earnings drive up the value of their currency, making it difficult for industry to compete and survive. This phenomenon is called the ''Dutch disease'' following events in the Netherlands when major natural gas reserves were discovered there.

[26]M. Hashem Pesaran, ''The Iranian Foreign Exchange Policy,'' p. 116.

Ultimately the policy flip-flops of the Rafsanjani regime reflect an ongoing conflict between radical fundamentalist ulama who seek world revolution and isolation from the world economy and a more pragmatic group seeking renewed economic growth through market-oriented reintegration into the world economy.

Is Iran the Model for the New Traditional Islamic Economy?

Is a new traditional economy really possible and is Iran the model for it? There is no simple answer to this question, as the discussion above should indicate.

For better or for worse, Iran *is* the fountainhead of the international movement for Islamic society and economy, a significant material and spiritual supporter of the most radical factions of this movement. But in the longer run it may not be the role model it is now for those societies that attempt this particular experiment in the future.

A major reason is the Shi'i character of Iran's revolution, which results in at least two peculiar aspects. One is that Iran is ulama dominated—Iran is a theocratic state ruled by the Vilayat-al-faqih, supported by ulama control of the zakat. The Sunni tradition emphasizes more ''separation of church and state.'' Rather than arbitrary promulgations of law codes by Supreme Jurists, the Sunnis accept existing law codes and demand that nonclerical Heads of State, whether hereditary monarchs, usurping military dictators, or democratically elected presidents, adhere to and enforce those codes. If they do not, then they can be overthrown by the Islamic movement. But the Sunni hierarchies, less wealthy and powerful than the Iranian Shi'i one, do not generally demand direct power *for themselves.*

Furthermore the history of oppression and grievance within Islam of the Shi'is has led them to a redistributionist radicalism expressed in the Islamic socialism of the First Radical Phase immediately after Iran's revolution. Given the general discrediting of world socialism and the not-so-aggrieved position of the traditionally dominant Sunnis, Sunnis are less inclined to Iranian-style radicalism.

However, the anti-Western and anti-neocolonialist sentiments felt throughout much of the Islamic world give credence to the strong position taken by Iran and account for the increasing influence of Iran among many Sunni fundamentalist movements. The sense of oppression of the Shi'is allows them to articulate more clearly the frustrations and anger of many throughout the Islamic umma.

But more moderate role models exist, some arguably more Islamic, that may eventually be more influential on Islamic economic experiments in the future. Among these are the predominantly Sunni nations of Saudi Arabia and Pakistan (see Box 16–2). Saudi Arabia is highly influential because of its vast oil wealth, its position as site of the Muslim holy cities of Mecca and Medina, and its long adherence to the strict Hanbali law code. It practices state-gathered zakat but does not enforce interest-free banking.

Box 16–2

Pakistan: The Most Authentic Islamic Economy?

A serious, if less dramatic model, is Pakistan. As noted in Chapter 5, many Islamic economists have been of Pakistani origin. In the modern world Pakistan was the first state specifically established as an Islamic state, although its founders sought a secular system of governance. Its approach to Islamization has been quieter and more gradual than Iran's. But it may have a more truly Islamic economy than Iran. Given its Sunni orientation, these achievements may make it more influential in the long run with the majority of Islamic nations.

Since independence in 1947, Pakistan has alternated between democratically elected governments and military dictatorships. It has experienced wars with neighboring India, the loss of its former province of East Pakistan, now Bangladesh, in 1971, and considerable internal ethnic and religious strife, much of the latter between majority Sunnis and minority Shi'is. Not being an oil producer, Pakistan has remained at a lower level of per capita income and economic development than have either Iran or Saudi Arabia, but it has avoided the wide fluctuations in growth rates those countries have experienced. Its record has been one of real, but slow and steady economic growth.

In 1980, influenced by Iran's revolution, the military dictator, Zia al-Huq, declared Islamization the official policy of the country. Despite backsliding under the rule of Benazir Bhutto, Islamization remains official policy. Its implementation has been more gradual than in Iran, not socialist, but arguably more complete.

In contrast to Iran, Pakistan has a state-managed zakat system. In contrast to Saudi Arabia it has a full-blown Islamic banking system, although subject to the same kinds of subterfuges and superficialities as in Iran. It has not engaged in widespread nationalizations or confiscations. Aside from supporting Islamic fundamentalists in neighboring Afghanistan and Muslim separatists in neighboring Kashmir, Pakistan has largely avoided proselytizing its system abroad.

But Saudi Arabia's wealth and its dependence upon the United States for protection against Iraq make it suspect among Islamic radicals. The Saudi monarchy is antirevolutionary and among the most reactionary regimes in the world. Thus, while it inspires respect among many Muslims, it also inspires contempt in the eyes of global Islamic revolutionaries, and Saudi Arabia faces an internal ultrafundamentalist opposition movement.

Thus Iran is the most prominent global role model for would-be Islamic economics, despite its peculiarities and idiosyncracies. Ultimately the current regime must deal with its own contradictions. It is pulled in the direction of pragmatism, partially released from international ignominy by the shenanigans of Saddam Hussein in Iraq. Its vast oil resources, its base of industry, and its educated entrepreneurs offer great potential for economic growth.

But the pragmatists come into conflict with the now firmly entrenched ulama who adhere to the vision of Khomeini of Iran as the fountainhead of the general Islamic revolution. Any move to seriously reintegrate with the world economy will draw forth opposition from these figures, just as the ulama opposed such policies when they were attempted by the Qajars and the Pahlavis. Furthermore the ongoing effort to support radical and even terrorist Islamic movements around the world keeps Iran in a pariah position with much of the world, including even many Islamic regimes. Its current military buildup and apparent drive for nuclear weapons terrifies its Arab neighbors in the Persian Gulf, including Saudi Arabia whose opposition to the ultimate overthrow of Saddam Hussein at the end of the Gulf War was precisely predicated on the fear that he is all that stands between them and an aggressive and expansionistic Iran, driven by its imperial dreams of glory, made all the more excessive by its aggrieved and impassioned sense of Shi'i martyrdom.

In the end, the more Iran stands out as the antiimperialist, anti-Western, antihegemonist voice of the Islamic Third World, an economic Third Way, and the dispossessed of the world, the more it will thrust itself forward as the definitive role model that all Islamic revolutions must emulate or be overthrown by their discontented radical fringes. At the same time such a stance will undermine its appeal as a model because it will undermine its ability to grow economically. Thus in the competition for influence in newly independent Central Asia it may well ultimately falter and fail as the great alternative to capitalism and socialism.[27]

Summary and Conclusions

Iran is not a typical Muslim state because it is dominated by Shi'ism, the minority branch of Islam, and because it is a major oil producer and exporter. However its Shi'i traditions significantly contributed to the emergence of the Islamic revolution in Iran and as the leading role model of that revolution even among predominantly Sunni nations. These traditions include a sense of aggrieved martyrdom because of long domination by the Sunni majority, the particular strength of the Shi'i ulama based on their independent sources of funding and their ability to order the behavior of followers, and the messianic thrust associated with the idea of the mystical 12th and Hidden Imam who is

---

[27]The Iranian revolution's self-image as the Third Way between the two ''Great Satans'' of the United States and the then-USSR is symbolized by a chant heard on the streets during the revolution. ''Cheerleader: Who took our oil? Crowd: America. Cheerleader: Who took our gas? Crowd: Russia [The Shah sold natural gas to the USSR]. Cheerleader: Who took our money? Crowd: Pahlavi'' (Michael M. J. Fischer, *Iran: From Religious Dispute to Revolution* [Cambridge: Harvard University Press, 1980], p. 190).

to return to save the world. Ayatollah Ruhollah Khomeini's claim to being the special messenger of this Hidden Imam allowed him to become supreme leader and jurist, the Vilayat-al-faqih, of the theocratic revolutionary state in Iran.

After a glorious past as center of ancient empires, the nation was conquered by Islam and ruled by outsiders for centuries. It converted to Shi'ism under the reign of Shah Isma'il after 1501. During the 19th century, Russia and Great Britain contested for Iran with the Shi'i ulama opposing accommodation with either of them diplomatically or economically. In the 20th century, secular nationalist movements arose in the form of the Pahlavi dynasty and in democratic movements such as the Constitutionalist revolt of 1906 and the regime of Mohammed Mossadegh in the early 1950s. After the 1973 oil price shock, inflation, corruption, and increasing inequalities of income and wealth fed discontent and support for Islamic revolution. In 1979 the Shah's regime was replaced by the Islamic regime of Khomeini.

The postrevolutionary period has gone through four phases. The First Radical Phase, 1979–1981, saw an Islamic socialist approach with widespread confiscations and nationalizations. In the Second Radical Phase, 1982–1984, further moves in that direction such as a rural land reform bill and a proposal to nationalize all foreign trade were blocked by the pro–market capitalist Council of Guardians who can declare legislation to be in nonconformity with Islam and therefore invalid. This phase was marked by more traditional Islamic innovations such as the adoption of interest-free banking. This period and the First Pragmatic Phase, 1985–1988, were dominated by the war with neighboring Iraq. The Second Pragmatic Phase emerged after the end of the war and the death of Khomeini. President Rafsanjani has moved towards marketization, privatization, and increased involvement in the world economy while trying to maintain Islamic practices and structures at home.

Economic policies have included nationalization of much of industry as well as of banking and insurance. Interest-free banking is practiced nationwide, although in actual practice it differs little from standard banking—the differences are largely semantic reshufflings. The Islamic taxes, the zakat (wealth tax for the poor), the 'ushr (tithe), and the khums (income tax) are not collected by the state but are voluntarily given to the ulama, thereby reinforcing their power and independence. Furthermore, many confiscated enterprises are owned and run by foundations managed by the ulama. Land reform was carried out in the cities for the purpose of providing housing for the urban poor and homeless. The distribution of income became more equal after the revolution but a trend to greater inequality reemerged later. Rural incomes have improved relative to urban incomes.

After the revolution restrictions were placed on the behavior of women, including dress, labor force participation, and birth control, although the latter issue is being reconsidered by the government because of Iran's high population growth rate.

Iran's currency, the rial, was long fixed in international value, despite being overvalued and despite the accompanying macroeconomic distortions and imbalances of various sorts, including problems of corruption and rent-seeking. The overvaluation of the rial simply reinforced Iran's dependence on oil exports for hard currency revenues, in contrast with the original goals of the revolution.

Thus Iran is the most prominent model in the world for revolutionary New Traditionalism, the attempted combination of a traditional fundamentalist religion with modern high technology in an economy independent of the patterns of either the old capitalist or socialist economies. It stands in contrast to more moderate models such as Saudi Arabia and Pakistan. But Iran faces a choice between pragmatically reintegrating into the world's economy and polity at large, thus probably achieving a greater rate of growth, or pursuing its role as the leading supporter of Islamic revolutions around the world, thus probably achieving a continuing political isolation and economic stagnation. Very likely the struggle between these competing tendencies will go on for a long time to come.

Questions for Discussion

1. Why is the revolutionary tradition stronger in Shi'i Islam than in Sunni Islam?
2. What have been the characteristics of the four phases of economic policy since the 1979 revolution?
3. What has been the role of the oil industry in the economy both before and after the revolution in Iran?
4. What is the role of the religious foundations in the Iranian economy?
5. Has Iran succeeded in eliminating interest from its banking system? What have been the results of its efforts to do so?
6. How does the Shi'i view of zakat differ from the Sunni view and what are the implications of this for Iran?
7. How have economic policies regarding women changed since the revolution?
8. To what extent does the Iranian economy represent a New Traditional Third Way between capitalism and socialism?
9. Compare the Pakistani model of Islamic economics with that of Iran.
10. In its effort to be a role for Islamic economies in the world, what is a fundamental contradiction Iran faces?

Suggested Further Readings

Bakhash, Shaul. *The Reign of the Ayatollahs,* 2nd ed. New York: Basic Books, 1990.

Bayat, Assef. *Workers and Revolution in Iran.* London: Zed Books, 1987.

Bina, Cyrus, and Hamid Zangeneh, eds. *Modern Capitalism and Islamic Ideology in Iran.* New York: St. Martin's Press, 1992.

Keddie, Nikki R., and Farah Monian. "Militancy and Religion in Contemporary Iran." In *Fundamentalisms and the State: Remaking Polities, Economies, and Militance.* eds. Martin E. Marty and R. Scott Appleby. Chicago: University of Chicago Press, 1993 pp. 511–38.

Khomeini, Ayatollah Sayyed Ruhollah Mousavi. *A Clarification of Questions.* Trans. from the Persian by J. Borujerdi. Boulder: Westview Press 1984.

Razavi, H., and F. Vakil. *The Political Environment of Economic Planning in Iran, 1971–1983.* Boulder: Westview Press, 1984.

Richards, Alan, and John Waterbury. *A Political Economy of the Middle East: State, Class, and Economic Development.* Boulder: Westview Press, 1990.

Sanasarian, Eliz. *The Women's Rights Movement in Iran: Mutiny, Appeasement, and Repression from 1900 to Khomeini.* New York: Praeger, 1982.

Valibeigi, Mehrdad. "Islamic Economics and Policy Formulation in Post Revolutionary Iran: A Critique." *Journal of Economic Issues,* 27 (1993), pp. 125–35.

Yergin, Daniel. *The Prize: The Epic Quest for Oil, Money and Power.* New York: Simon and Schuster, 1991.

Zanganeh, Hamid, ed. *Islam, Iran, and World Stability.* New York: St. Martin's Press, 1994.

UNITED STATES

REVOLUTION AND REFORM IN THE MEXICAN ECONOMY

He of the voice confesses that, since having been born, he has conspired against the shadows which cover the Mexican sky . . . that, before being born, being able to possess everything in order to have nothing, he decided to possess nothing in order to have everything . . . that Mexico is something more than six letters and an underpriced product on the international market.

—Subcommandante Marcos, February 16, 1995 (translated by Cindy Arnold and transmitted via Internet on March 7, 1995)

Introduction

On January 1, 1994, two events occurred that captured the conflicts and contradictions of the Mexican economy. One was that the North American Free Trade Agreement (*NAFTA*) went into effect, freeing trade and investment relations between Mexico and the United States and Canada after a long process of marketizing and privatizing reforms in the insular Mexican economy.

The other was the outbreak of an armed rebellion in the poorest state of Mexico, Chiapas, in the far South, by the *Zapatista National Liberation Army* (EZLN),[1] named for the Mexican revolutionary Emiliano Zapata. Led by non-Indians, including Subcommandante Marcos, most soldiers in this group are Tzeltals or other Mayan-related Indians. EZLN leaders declared opposition to NAFTA and timed the uprising to coincide with its implementation. But the Indians were more concerned with ancient conflicts over land control tilted against them by 1992 reforms of then-President Carlos Salinas de Gortari and the long-ruling Revolutionary Institutional Party (Partido Revolucionario

---

[1]The full name in Spanish is Ejercito Zapatista de Liberacion Nacional.

Institucional, or *PRI*). These conflicts reflect the underlying divisions of class, race, and power that have plagued Mexico since the 1521 Spanish Conquest.

In Mexico City at the Plaza of Three Cultures there is a group of Aztec pyramids, behind which stands a Spanish church, behind which in turn stands a group of American-style modern office buildings, thus encapsulating the essential contradictions of Mexico's economy and society.[2] It is a rapidly industrializing and urbanizing, middle-income economy, integrating itself into the world economy while containing pockets of poverty in traditionalist sectors.

On top of the Mexican economy is a mostly Spanish-descended elite who operate successfully within the modern market capitalist economy emerging in Mexico. On the bottom is a somewhat larger minority of poor, mostly pure Indians, many living in a Mexican traditional economy form in village agricultural units known as *ejidos,* many speaking native Indian languages.[3] In the middle are the majority mixed-race *mestizos.*[4] A modern U.S.–related economy sits on top of a colonial Spanish-derived system that in turn sits on top of the remnant of a precolonial traditional economy.

Although it shares characteristics with other Latin American economies, categorizing the Mexican economy is difficult. Since the late 19th century it has had strong market capitalist elements, even during its most inward-looking and "socialist" phases. But Mexico has long had a highly centralized state sector. This tradition was enhanced by the revolution of 1910–1920 and the populist presidency of Lázaro Cárdenas in the 1930s who nationalized the oil industry. It reflects patterns from the Spanish colonial period and even from the Aztec empire. Furthermore the economy includes the traditional remnant of the rural ejidos, reconstructed by revolutionary populism in the 20th century.

This curious system has drawn many labels: *Bonapartist* (after Napoleon III in France);[5] *populist corporatism,* which "activates strategic class groups and incorporates them into the state apparatus, controlling and 'de-radicalizing' their demands";[6] and *state capitalism* manifested as *technocratic populism,*

---

[2]This plaza is in Tlatelolco, site of the main market of the Aztec city of Tenochtitlán. It survived the destruction of that city to become the main Aztec neighborhood of Mexico City. In 1968 at this plaza, a massive student protest was suppressed and hundreds were killed.

[3]Around 50 Indian languages are spoken in Mexico. In the Yucatan in the southeast, around 80 percent of the people speak Mayan languages. In the southern state of Oaxaca, more than 10 percent of the population do not speak Spanish.

[4]Until 1921, 16 different categories of racial mixture were identified in the census and *mestizo* was defined as someone with one pure Spanish parent and one pure Indian parent (Nathan L. Whetten, *Rural Mexico* [Chicago: University of Chicago Press, 1948], pp. 51–2). Racial categories have not been recorded since, but officially then about 10 percent of the population were whites, about 30 percent were Indians, and about 60 percent were mestizos. During the Spanish rule a small number of Africans were brought into certain areas to cut sugar cane.

[5]Martin C. Needler, *Mexican Politics: The Containment of Conflict,* 2nd ed. (New York: Praeger, 1990), p. 130. He confesses that this is no better than labeling it "miscellaneous."

[6]José Luis Reyna, "Redefining the Authoritarian Regime," in *Authoritarianism in Mexico,* eds. J.L. Reyna and R.S. Weinert (Philadelphia: Institute for the Study of Human Issues, 1977), p. 161.

dominated by a politicized and technocratic bureaucracy.[7] Putting these together we might label the Mexican system *technocratic populist corporatism,* while recognizing its recent movement towards a more market capitalist model.

The movement toward market capitalism began after a macroeconomic crisis in 1982, triggered by mounting foreign debt and rising interest rates on that debt, combined with falling oil prices. Mexico exports oil, and by 1982 it received over 74 percent of its export earnings from oil.[8] Based on these earnings the government borrowed massively from abroad, largely to finance rising social expenditures and subsidies for state-owned firms.

By August 1982 the government could not meet its interest obligations and negotiated with the U.S. and the International Monetary Fund (IMF) a program of austerity and import reductions that led to declining output for several years after decades of rapid growth. After 1989 came major efforts to reduce government ownership and control in the economy,[9] as well as opening up to free trade and reducing endemic corruption.[10] The economy grew rapidly again, especially its export manufacturing sector, but it has since gone into recession. Macroeconomic stabilization marked by substantial disinflation was enhanced by the *Pacto,* a corporatist incomes policy established in 1987. But since the sharp devaluation of the peso in December 1994 after a renewal of fighting in Chiapas, inflation has reaccelerated and a new program of austerity has been imposed by President Zedillo.

Although quality of life measures in Mexico have shown improvement, not all have gained. From 1983 to 1988 real wages per worker declined by 41.5 percent and income inequality increased.[11] Signing NAFTA opened President Salinas to charges of putting Mexico under U.S. economic domination similar to that during the Porfirio Díaz dictatorship (1876–1911). Salinas also reformed the ejidos by allowing farmers involved (ejiditarios) to privatize and sell their plots, and he reduced subsidies for corn (maize) production, the principal crop of the ejidos and mainstay of poor Mexicans' diet. Large landowners have gained control of ejido lands, sometimes, as in Chiapas, through violent and corrupt means.

---

[7]Roger Bartra, ''Capitalism and the Peasantry,'' in *Modern Mexico: State, Economy, and Social Conflict,* eds. N. Hamilton and T.F. Harding (Beverly Hills: Sage, 1986), p. 286. The powerful Mexican presidents are picked by their predecessors to serve nonrenewable six-year terms, with nominal elections. For decades they have been ministers in their predecessors' cabinets, rising through the bureaucracy rather than through political offices. Both Salinas and his successor, Ernesto Zedillo, have economics Ph.D.s, from Harvard and Yale, respectively.

[8]*OECD Economic Surveys: Mexico, 1991–1992* (Paris: Organization for Economic Cooperation and Development, 1992), p. 261.

[9]Exceptions to this are in oil where state-owned Petróleos Mexicanos (PEMEX) remains nationalized, although NAFTA allows foreign investment in peripheral parts of the energy industry and in railroads and electricity production.

[10]It has been asserted that the dominant force of the Mexican economy is bribery, *La Mordida* (''the bite''). Recent charges of complicity with drug dealers and assassinations against high figures in the Salinas administration suggest that the effort to reduce corruption was less than successful.

[11]Nora Lustig, *Mexico: The Remaking of an Economy* (Washington: Brookings Institution, 1992), pp. 69, 92.

All these factors converge in the Chiapas uprising. A serious challenge to the reform program has surfaced, with some renationalizing of banks since the December 1994 financial crisis. Significant political and economic changes in Mexico seem possible, the immediate electoral gainer so far being the pro–laissez-faire National Action Party (Partido Acción Nacional, or *PAN*). The ruling PRI is deeply entrenched and practiced at incorporating unhappy groups into the state apparatus and ''deradicalizing'' their demands, but the latest crisis has opened its worst internal splits ever seen.[12] Thus Mexico faces a great drama: Will reform lead to revolution?

Historical Background

From Origins to Independence

Mexico is the original site of Western Hemisphere sedentary agriculture, which originated 6,000 years ago with the domestication of corn (maize). The country contains several independent centers of culture and economic development, with the Mayans in the Yucatán peninsula and a succession of peoples in the temperate and fertile Valley of Mexico most prominent.

In 1325 the Aztecs conquered the Valley of Mexico and established Tenochtitlán. They practiced mass human sacrifice, making them despised by neighboring tribes. Some of these tribes helped the Spanish defeat the Aztecs.

Although possessing horses, guns, and smallpox, the conquest of Mexico by a few hundred Spaniards in 1521 remains a dramatic event in world history.[13] When Hernando Cortés arrived, Tenochtitlán was not only the largest city in the Western Hemisphere at 300,000 people, but was one of the largest in the world, larger than any in Europe.[14] After victory Cortés offered friendship and favors for tribes that surrendered or allied with him, but was brutal to those resisting. Cortés adopted the centralized Aztec tax collection and land tenure systems.

This was New Spain, ruled by viceroys appointed by the kings of Spain. In the center of the country the Spanish controlled vast estates (*encomiendas*) on which Indians were forced to work, initially as slaves and later as debt peons when the encomiendas became *haciendas*.[15] Political and economic domination coincided with a mass, if partially superficial, conversion to

---

[12]A sign of the internal splits is the arrest of the brother of ex-President Salinas on charges related to assassinating a top PRI leader, which led to Salinas leaving Mexico.

[13]A classic account is William H. Prescott, *History of the Conquest of Mexico* (Boston: Phillips, Sampson & Co. 1843).

[14]After its rebuilding by Cortés as Mexico City it would again be the largest in the Western Hemisphere until surpassed by New York in the mid-19th century. Today it has surpassed New York and competes with Tokyo for being the largest city in the world.

[15]The North contained mostly smaller ranchos owned by mestizos. Spanish control in the Mayan Yucatan was less solid with less intermarriage and more native uprisings. The Zapatista upheaval in Chiapas is the latest in a long line.

Roman Catholicism of most Indians.[16] As long as they accepted Catholicism and paid their taxes, Indian villages were generally left to the rule of their own leaders and allowed to control their traditional communal lands, although subject to constant encroachment pressure from neighboring haciendas.[17] Although principally agricultural, New Spain's main export earner (and Mexico's through most of the 19th century) was silver.

From Independence to the Revolution

After Napoleon conquered Spain in 1810,[18] a priest named Miguel Hidalgo led a revolt for Mexican independence, which was initially crushed because it consisted mostly of Indians demanding the distribution of hacienda lands. But independence was achieved in 1821, followed by several decades of economic stagnation, large budget deficits,[19] political instability, severe foreign indebtedness, and in the 1830s and 1840s losses of about half the nation's land area to the United States in wars.

In 1857 a group of liberals led by a Zapotec Indian named Benito Juárez wrote a constitution that forced the sale of all church lands,[20] eliminated special privileges for military officers, and allowed the sale of village ejido lands.[21] This was *La Reforma* (the Reform). After defeating an attempt in the 1860s by the French to impose as emperor on Mexico, Maximilian, the brother of Austrian Emperor Franz Josef, Juárez remained president until he died in office in 1872.

In 1876 a Juárez supporter, Porfirio Díaz, became president. After stepping aside in 1880, he returned to office in 1884 and forbade opposition thereafter, remaining in office until 1911. His tenure can be viewed as an early version of the Salinas presidency in economic policy, with openness to foreign trade and investment, overseen by technocratic advisers known as "científicos." They balanced the budget and oversaw the beginnings of industrialization, mostly in the North, and the development of Mexico's oil industry by U.S. and

---

[16]The vision of an Indian in 1531 that called for a church to be built honoring the Virgin Mary on the site of a temple of the Aztec mother of gods was crucial in extending Catholicism. This became the Shrine of Guadalupe, containing an image of the Virgin as an Indian. The Virgin of Guadalupe became a symbol of Indian Catholicism and a national symbol of Mexico, the independence fighters marching under a banner with her image and even the followers of Zapata in the early 20th century doing so.

[17]Generally the viceroys protected native land holdings against encroachments, recognizing that this eased tax collections. This protection disappeared after independence.

[18]French revolutionary ideas influenced the Mexican revolutionaries. Mexico has a tradition of French intellectual influence, showing up in current economic practices such as the Pacto with its elements of concertation.

[19]Mexico achieved its first balanced budget in 1894.

[20]The church had been a force for extreme conservatism, supporting reestablishment of monarchy. Anticlericalism is still deeply rooted in Mexican politics, although Catholic liberation theologians have supported the Chiapas Zapatista revolt, including the local bishop.

[21]Juárez was a strong supporter of state-run education for Indians and supported assimilation into a market capitalist economy. Many ejido lands were obtained by mestizos after this constitution was adopted.

British investors. The economy grew substantially, but so did landlessness,[22] debt peonage in the countryside, and general inequality and poverty.

From the Revolution to the Present

In 1910 Díaz jailed an opposition candidate in the North whose supporters in Chihuahua, including former bandolero Francisco (Pancho) Villa,[23] rose up in revolt. They were soon supported by a force of mostly Indian peons from Morelos in the South, led by Emiliano Zapata.[24] Díaz resigned in 1911 and Mexico experienced civil war off and on until 1920.

The political party that has ruled Mexico since, the PRI, was victorious in the revolution. Out of the revolution came the constitution of 1917. Article 27 denied the absolute right of private property, thus laying the groundwork for both nationalizing the oil industry and redistributing hacienda lands to peons and villages as reconstructed ejidos. Article 123 guaranteed a variety of labor rights, including the right to organize unions, the eight-hour day, the abolition of child labor and peonage, and compensation for injuries, among other things.

Despite radical and even socialist rhetoric, Mexican policy in the 1920s and early 1930s was moderate, although some land redistribution occurred and unions were allowed. But in 1934 Lázaro Cárdenas, the most populist of all of Mexico's presidents, came to power. He accelerated land redistribution to the ejidos, emphasizing communalism, and organized the peasant CNC as a ruling-party interest group. He also organized a party-related national union federation, the CTM,[25] still the main union federation in Mexico. These are the essential institutions of Mexican corporatism.[26] Most dramatically, he nationalized the oil industry in 1938, establishing Petróleos Mexicanos (PEMEX).

Cárdenas's radicalism triggered a political backlash. PAN, still the main conservative opposition party, was founded in 1938.[27] Cárdenas's land policies were halted after he left office in 1940. After Miguel Alemán became

---

[22]In 1910 well over 90 percent of the population in some states such as Oaxaca were landless, the most extreme such inequality in Mexico's history (George McCutcheon McBride, *Land Systems in Mexico* [New York: American Geographical Society, 1923], p. 154).

[23]In 1914 Villa attacked into New Mexico, thereby triggering U.S. President Wilson to send General Pershing to pursue him. Pershing failed to catch him and withdrew to lead U.S. forces in World War I. Villa laid down arms in 1920 in return for a hacienda and was assassinated in 1923 by a government fearful he might renew his revolt. Despite allying with Zapata, his views on land reform were less radically redistributionist than Zapata's.

[24]Zapata's army mostly worked on sugar-growing haciendas. He was killed in 1919 by government troops after being tricked into coming in for a peace negotiation.

[25]In 1948 its leader, Lombardo Toledano, organized the Socialist Party. The descendent of that party is the main leftist opposition party, the Party of Democratic Revolution (Partido de la Revolucion Democratica, or PRD), now led by Cuauhtémoc Cárdenas, son of Lázaro Cárdenas. Many believe that Cárdenas outpolled Salinas in the 1988 presidential election, but that the corrupt PRI prevented an accurate vote count. He ran a weak third in the 1994 presidential election.

[26]The macrostabilization Pacto of 1987 was negotiated between the government, these two bodies, and business leaders.

[27]Since 1988 PAN has been winning more and more governorships, and it has been allowed to assume them.

president in 1946, policy encouraged privately owned and irrigated farms to adopt Green Revolution technologies developed in the United States that use hybrid seeds and require mechanization. Alemán began an industrial growth policy led by import substitution that continued until 1982. Despite restrictions for some industries, foreign investment was allowed and encouraged. In the 1960s foreign investment took the form of special incentives for investments on the Mexican-U.S. border in *maquiladora* plants.

The period 1940–1970 was marked by strong growth and reasonable macroeconomic stability. Land redistribution resumed after 1958. The student uprising of 1968 triggered a shift to populism and a leftist international stance after 1970.[28] Expanded social spending undermined macroeconomic stability and foreign indebtedness rose.

These problems culminated in the crisis of 1982 and the shift to austerity. After Salinas became president in 1989 came NAFTA, privatizations, and sales of ejido lands. That Salinas opposed much of Lázaro Cárdenas's legacy explains why Cárdenas's son ran against Salinas and his successor, Zedillo, for president, and why Zapatista critics complain that the present is nothing but a return to the past of Porfirio Díaz with foreign domination overseen by local technocratic científicos.

Table 17–1 shows 20th-century economic and population growth in Mexico, population growth having been high for a long time until recently.

The Land Question

Types of Land Tenure

No issue looms more heavily over Mexican history than land. Even today when only 8 percent of GDP and 25 percent of employment are in agriculture,[29] the issue remains controversial as its role in the Zapatista uprising shows. The most serious pockets of poverty are in rural areas.

Traditionally three types of farms existed in Mexico: the hacienda, the rancho, and the ejido. The haciendas mostly derive from royal encomienda land grants to the conquistadores.[30] Many were enormous, containing thousands of people and functioning as self-contained communities. Some haciendas derived directly from estates of the Aztec nobility,[31] some from

---

[28]Mexico maintains an independent international stance from the United States, symbolized by being the only Latin American nation to maintain diplomatic relations with Cuba throughout Castro's rule.

[29]*OECD Economic Surveys,* p. 18. A majority of employment was agricultural as recently as the 1960s.

[30]The encomiendas were abolished in 1720. The shift to the hacienda form involved the Indians assuming debts to the owner that passed from one generation to the next, thus tying them to the land. This debt peonage was abolished in 1917.

[31]Sometimes Aztec nobility and Spanish married coinciding with these land transfers, and a strand of today's Mexican elite descended from this group.

TABLE 17–1   Population and GDP Growth Rates, 1900–1993

	1900–10	*1910–25*	*1925–40*	*1940–54*	*1954–70*	*1970–82*	*1982–89*	*1989–93*
Population	1.1	0.1	1.6	3.0	3.4	3.3	2.3	2.0
GDP	3.3	2.5	1.6	5.8	6.8	6.2	0.6	3.0
Per Capita GDP	2.2	2.4	0.0	2.8	3.4	2.9	−1.7	1.0

Source: Figures for before 1940 are from Clark W. Reynolds, *The Mexican Economy: Twentieth Century Structure and Growth* (New Haven: Yale University Press, 1970), p. 22; for 1940–91 are from *OECD Economic Surveys: Mexico, 1991–1992* (Paris: Organization for Economic Cooperation and Development, 1992) pp. 9, 14, and 19; and since then are from ''Mexico: The Revolution Continues,'' *The Economist,* January 22, 1994, p. 20. All numbers are average annual percent growth rates.

purchases from Indians in tribes allied with Cortés. Many still existing, they have lost their special powers over rural labor. Today there is no legal difference between them and the smaller ranchos with respect to land tenure.

The ranchos, owned by mestizos, tend to be smaller and were favored by the Reform of Juárez. These derived from land grants given to foot soldiers or small farmer immigrants who tended to marry local Indian women, and they differed from the encomiendas in that they did not have vassal laborers attached to them. They were often on poor soil, the haciendas and the Indian villages having the better lands. More numerous in the North, these became the favored base for adopting Green Revolution techniques, especially as they were favored by government investment in road and irrigation systems.

The ejidos derived from communal lands held in preconquest Indian villages. Landholding was based on extended kinship groups identified with certain areas. Although held in common, most of the land would be assigned to individual families for their use. A portion known as the *atlepetalli* would be held for strictly common use, and this would be the basis of the later communal parts of the ejidos.[32]

Prior to 1910 haciendas and ranchos encroached upon ejido lands. Since the 1940s they have been largely ignored in government infrastructure investment and thus left behind technologically. They contain the poorest Mexicans. The 1992 move to allow the sale of ejido lands follows the Juárez policy of trying to turn them into full-blown, rancho-style, capitalist farmers with rising productivities and incomes.

Reestablishment of the Ejidos

Land reform drove the 1910–1920 Revolution. Article 27 of the 1917 Constitution allowed breaking up haciendas and distributing them as ejidos to the former peons. As in the ancient Indian villages this involved both individual

---

[32]The term *ejido* is Spanish from the same root as the word *exit.* In Spain, ejidos were originally lands owned by towns outside of themselves, hence the element of *exit.*

use of collectively owned land and communal farming, the latter encouraged under Cárdenas. Thus now there are three types of land tenure: private farms, individual-use ejido farms, and communal ejido farms.

Prior to Cárdenas, land distribution to ejidos occurred slowly, and no president distributed much over 3 million hectares.[33] In 1930 no region of the country had over 20 percent of cultivated land in ejidos.[34] Cárdenas distributed more than 20 million hectares, more than all presidents before him combined, resulting in 47.4 percent of cultivated land in ejidos in 1940, although state averages ranged from 22.7 percent in southern Baja California to 84.4 percent in Emiliano Zapata's sugar-growing Morelos.[35]

Although Cárdenas's immediate successors focused on helping private farms (the legal distinction between haciendas and ranchos having disappeared in 1917), redistributions resumed between 1958 and 1970 to ''cover their left flank,'' given the otherwise conservative thrust of PRI policies.[36] Although ejido holdings increased, presidents continued to focus infrastructure investment on the increasingly more productive private farms. As of 1988 national shares of agricultural land were 43 percent in private farms, 52 percent in individual-use ejidos, and 5 percent in communal ejido farms.[37]

The Emergence of Dual Agricultural Development

Since Cárdenas a sharp dualism has emerged between private and ejido farms, which triggered the changes in Article 27 passed in 1992. But it is unclear to what extend this dualism reflects the inherent incentive structures of the two kinds of farms and to what extent it reflects population density and government policies favoring private farms. The ejidos are more common in densely populated areas, such as the central Bajío valley. Over half of individual ejido units were less than four hectares in 1960, too small to be efficient under any tenure or technology system, especially for the crop production they engage in.[38]

Whereas ejidos concentrate on traditional corn and beans production, private farms have branched into such commercial crops as soybeans and sorghum, which were not produced in Mexico in 1940 at all. These crops, along with wheat, have experienced larger increases in yields than corn because of

---

[33]John B. Ross, *The Economic System of Mexico* (Stanford: California Institute of International Studies, 1971), p. 3.

[34]Clark W. Reynolds, *The Mexican Economy: Twentieth Century Structure and Growth* (New Haven: Yale University Press, 1970), p. 139.

[35]Whetten, *Rural Mexico,* p. 595.

[36]The ruling PRI attempts to include virtually the entire political and social spectrum of Mexico within its ranks.

[37]*OECD Economic Surveys,* p. 166.

[38]Rodolfo Stavenhagen, ''Collective Agriculture and Capitalism in Mexico: a Way Out or a Dead End?'' In *Modern Mexico,* eds. Hamilton and Harding, p. 264. He argues (pp. 268–73) that communally farmed ejidos have outperformed individually farmed ones because of economies of scale.

the introduction of hybrid Green Revolution varieties and expanded irrigation supporting them.[39]

From 1940 to 1958, the percentage of federal government irrigation investment rose from 4 percent to 53 percent in the North Pacific region, which contains the lowest percent of land in ejidos. In the ejido-laden Center it rose from 3 percent to 9 percent whereas in the poverty-stricken South Pacific region it rose from 0 percent to 1.2 percent.[40] Regional shares of crop production between 1939 and 1959 rose in the North Pacific from 11 percent to 18 percent whereas they declined in the Center from 35 percent to 28 percent. Favoritism towards private farms also extended to government credits and financing.

Whatever caused the problems of the ejidos, in 1992 the reforming government gave up on them. NAFTA removes protection of corn from competition with low-cost U.S. producers, and although the removal will be phased in gradually, observers expect substantial outmigration from current corn-producing ejidos. This follows major reductions of general government subsidies to agriculture during the 1980s austerity period.[41] This is a policy of attacking rural poverty by forcing the poorest farmers off the farms. The response in the poorest state of all has been the Zapatista rebellion.

The Oil Question and the External Debt Crisis of 1982

Development of the Mexican Oil Industry

The first modern[42] oil strike in Mexico was made by Edward L. Doheny of the United States in 1901. By 1916 his Mexican oil holdings made him the second wealthiest oil magnate after John D. Rockefeller. He sold out to Standard Oil of Indiana (Amoco) in 1925. The British Weekman Pearson was building rail lines when he formed an oil company and made a strike in 1906. He sold out to Royal Dutch Shell in 1917 just prior to implementation of the new constitution that granted authority over mineral rights to the government, leading outside investors to view the Mexican environment as unstable.

Nevertheless, many other companies became involved,[43] especially Standard Oil of New Jersey (Exxon), and Mexico became the second largest oil-producing nation in the world during the 1910s, with production peaking in

---

[39]David Barkin, *Distorted Development: Mexico in the World Economy* (Boulder: Westview, 1990), pp. 18–25.

[40]Clark Reynolds, *The Mexican Economy,* p. 156. This reflects that the North is drier than the Center and South Pacific, but the North Pacific also received substantially more road construction than did the Center or South Pacific.

[41]*OECD Economic Surveys,* pp. 160–68.

[42]The Aztecs burned oil to their gods and used it to caulk boats.

[43]The 1938 nationalization affected 17 American and European companies, some small independents. Two companies were not nationalized then because they granted major concessions to their workers.

Box 17–1

The Nationalization of Oil

Nationalization by Lázaro Cárdenas in 1938 resulted from labor disputes—a syndicalist-oriented national oil workers union, the Sindicato de Trabajadores Petróleros de la República Mexicana (STPRM), was founded in 1935. The union wished to control the industry directly as workers had in the recently nationalized railroads. But because of poor performance of the railroads, Cárdenas did not take this route and instead established Petróleos Mexicanos (PEMEX) to run the industry.

The establishment of PEMEX set off a deep conflict that lasted until President Alemán enforced a settlement in 1946. Most of the demands of the STPRM were rejected, but the oil workers gained generous wage and benefit boosts and the union obtained a closed-shop situation which gave it power over hiring. In more recent years this right became a source of massive power and corruption for the union's leadership.*

It has been reported that Mexico's oil reserves are the collateral for the $20 billion loan the United States gave Mexico to support its balance of payments in early 1995, but President Zedillo denies it. Clearly, the issue of oil as Mexico's national patrimony is extremely sensitive.

---
*The union leader after 1962, known as ''La Quina,'' was viewed as the most corrupt man in Mexico—he even had his own private army. President Salinas's most dramatic anticorruption move after taking office in 1989 was to arrest La Quina, which required the use of the regular army.

1921 at 193,398 barrels per day (bpd). Overexploitation combined with a perceived friendlier investment climate in Venezuela led to a decline in production to 32,895 bpd in 1932, after which it increased slightly until 1938 because of the discovery of a major new field.[44]

The 1982 Crisis

After the early 1940s production increased moderately and steadily to 897,000 bpd in 1976,[45] the year López Portillo was elected president. His predecessor had followed a populist policy after the 1968 student uprisings and had sharply increased social spending, resulting in a budget deficit at 9.9 percent of GDP and a foreign debt level of U.S. $27.5 billion. This was the era of oil price shocks and López Portillo decided to have PEMEX borrow massively from

---
[44]George W. Grayson, *The Politics of Mexican Oil* (Pittsburgh: University of Pittsburgh Press, 1980), p. 13.

[45]Grayson, *The Politics of Mexican Oil,* p. 241.

abroad to expand production, which more than doubled by 1980.[46] Combined with 1979 price increases, the share of oil in exports rose from 15.4 percent in 1976 to 74.6 percent in 1982, after which it declined to 33.2 percent by 1990.[47]

The budget deficit as a percent of GDP fell to 6.7 percent for 1977 and 1978.[48] But taken in by overoptimistic forecasts about future oil price increases after 1979, the government engaged in a borrowing binge. Despite surging exports, imports more than quadrupled between 1977 and 1981 with the current account in deficit throughout.[49]

From 1976 to 1981 foreign debt tripled to $74.9 billion and exceeded $100 billion by the mid-1980s. The budget deficit soared to 16.9 percent of GDP by 1982.[50] With oil prices declining and inflation accelerating along with foreign and public sector indebtedness, capital flight exceeded $10 billion in both 1981 and 1982.[51] Double-digit dollar interest rates triggered crisis in August 1982 after the debt service ratio jumped from 42.4 percent in 1980 to 62.2 percent in 1982,[52] and domestic financial capital fled after a bank nationalization carried out by López Portillo.

That August, incoming President Miguel de la Madrid Hurtado sent his incoming finance minister to Washington to negotiate with the IMF and the U.S. government. Mexican default was viewed fearfully by large U.S. banks holding much of the debt. The result was a shift in U.S. macroeconomic policy to lower interest rates and a deal with the IMF imposing strict austerity on Mexico.

Despite another crisis after oil prices plunged in 1986, this austerity combined with later moves to privatization, marketization, tariff reduction, and the corporatist Pacto led inflation to a sustained deceleration after 1987. The current account balance went into surplus; the budget deficit declined to 1.5 percent of GDP by 1991, and the debt service ratio declined to 29.4 percent by 1990.[53] After 1989, Mexicans were on net bringing financial capital back into the country.

However oil remained nationalized, perhaps because Salinas's leading opponent in the 1988 election was the son of the man who originally nationalized the industry.[54] Instead Salinas tightened budgetary controls; imposed

---

[46]Grayson, *The Politics of Mexican Oil.*

[47]Lustig, *Mexico,* pp. 23, 32–33.

[48]Lustig, *Mexico,* p. 23.

[49]Judith A. Teichman, *Policymaking in Mexico: From Boom to Crisis* (Boston: Allen & Unwin, 1988), p. 153. A similar scenario underlay the crisis of late 1994, although in that case the optimism about exports came from implementation of NAFTA, but imports grew more rapidly than exports.

[50]Lustig, *Mexico,* pp. 22, 30

[51]Teichman, *Policymaking in Mexico.*

[52]Lustig, *Mexico,* p. 32.

[53]Lustig, *Mexico,* pp. 30, 33.

[54]Also PEMEX makes money for the government, unlike many of the parastatal companies closed, merged, or privatized under de la Madrid and Salinas. Although Mexico has never joined OPEC, its 1938 nationalization served as a role model for OPEC nationalizations in the early 1970s.

more rational internal pricing; internally restructured PEMEX; arrested La Quina, the oil workers union's corrupt boss; and allowed foreign investment in peripheral parts of the industry through NAFTA. Only Zedillos's U.S. loan at the end of the crisis in 1994 brought the possibility of oil denationalization.

Transformation of the Mexican Economy

Macroeconomic Performance under the Reforms

Mexico is now in its sixth period of macroeconomic policy since 1982. 1982–1985 was the Program for Immediate Economic Reordering (PIRE) under President de la Madrid. Besides rescheduling foreign debts through the IMF, this plan involved massive peso devaluation and sharp cuts in government spending accompanied by tax increases. But by 1985 the economy was nowhere near projected goals for inflation and current deficit reduction, and Mexico fell out of plan compliance during the second period.

A major earthquake hit Mexico City in December 1985, followed by plunging oil prices in 1986. These events triggered a reacceleration of inflation and a run on the peso in 1987. In response, the third period was initiated by adoption of the Pacto by a French-style labor, farmer, business, and government concertation in December 1987. The Pacto set wage and price targets in key sectors, tightened monetary and fiscal policies with tax simplification, and liberalized trade, cutting the maximum tariff rate from 45 percent to 20 percent. This Pacto reduced the rate of inflation substantially.

The fourth stage began in 1989 after Salinas became president. He extended and modified the Pacto using looser wage and price targeting and focused more on a crawling exchange rate peg and foreign debt relief. Salinas renewed this plan six times through the end of his term in September 1994, but increasingly focused on microeconomic reforms such as privatization and trade liberalization over time. By 1993 and the fifth stage, inflation had fallen to a 7.1 percent annual rate and the Mexican economy was in recession. Although the budget was finally in surplus, the current account had fallen into a deep deficit, setting the stage for the crisis at the end of 1994.[55] Since then the sixth stage has emphasized renewed austerity, much as the earlier PIRE did.

Table 17–2 presents several macroeconomic indicators for selected years for the period 1980–1994.

Privatization

Privatization was a major feature of the Mexican reform process from 1982 to 1995. During the PIRE period of 1982–85 privatization focused mostly on liquidating or merging small or unviable enterprises. During the 1986–88

---

[55]See Rudiger Dornbusch and Alejandro Werner, ''Mexico: Stabilization, Reform, and No Growth,'' *Brookings Papers on Economic Activity* 1 (1994), pp. 253–315.

TABLE 17–2   Selected Macroeconomic Indicators, 1980–1994

Category	1980	1982	1984	1986	1987	1989	1991	1993	1994
GDP	8.3	−0.6	3.6	−3.8	1.7	3.3	3.6	−1.2	4.5
Inflation	26.3	58.9	65.4	86.2	131.8	20.0	22.7	8.0	7.1
Current account	−10.7	−6.2	4.2	−1.7	8.4	−0.7	−11.2	−21.5	−27.2
Budget surplus	−7.5	−16.9	−8.5	−15.9	−16.0	−5.5	−1.5	1.0	n.a.

Source: Figures for 1980–91 are from Nora Lustig, *Mexico: The Remaking of an Economy* (Washington: Brookings Institution, 1992), pp. 22–23, 40–41, except for the budget deficits, which are from Pedro Aspe, *Economic Transformation: The Mexican Way* (Cambridge: MIT Press, 1993), p. 15. Figures for 1993 are from Rudiger Dornbusch and Alejandro Werner, "Mexico: Stabilization, Reform, and No Growth," *Brookings Papers on Economic Activity* 1 (1994), Appendix D, and for 1994 from *The Economist,* February 4, 1995, p. 98.

Note: GDP numbers are annual growth rates, inflation rates are for CPI, current account balances are in billions of U.S. dollars, and budget surpluses are percents of GDP.

period there was a shift to selling small to medium-sized enterprises. Later came sales of larger enterprises, following a detailed 12-step process.[56]

The parastatal sector expanded from 15 firms in 1934 to 36 in 1940 to 272 in 1970 to a peak of 1,155 in 1982. Spending on it peaked in 1975 at 18.2 percent of GDP whereas revenues from it peaked in 1984 at 22.33 percent of GDP. As of 1991 parastatal sector spending was down to 9.4 percent of GDP and revenues were down to 14.0 percent, with much of both of those due to PEMEX.[57]

From the maximum number of parastatals of 1,155 in 1982, the number had been reduced to 223 by mid-1992.[58] These privatizations took place as cash sales. During 1989–92 the government accumulated proceeds equal to 6.8 percent of GDP, which compares with Great Britain's 11.9 percent of GDP over the much longer 1979–91 period.[59]

The largest privatization in revenues earned for the government and number of employees involved was the telecommunications company, Teléfonos de México, which was sold in December 1990.[60] Firms selling for more than $50 million included a copper mining company, two airline companies, two sugar refineries, a pasta and vegetable oil company, and a motor vehicles company, most of which went to Mexican buyers. Besides Teléfonos de

---

[56]*OECD Economic Surveys,* p. 88; Pedro Aspe, *Economic Transformation: The Mexican Way* (Cambridge: MIT Press, 1993), chap. 4. Aspe served as Salinas's finance minister for most of his presidency.

[57]Aspe, *Economic Transformation,* pp. 181–3.

[58]*OECD, Economic Surveys,* p. 89. Parastatals have taken four forms in Mexico: decentralized organizations of which 77 were left in 1992, majority-state-owned enterprises of which 106 were left in 1992, public trusts of which 40 were left in 1992, and minority participation companies of which none were left in 1992, down from 78 in 1982.

[59]*OECD Economic Surveys.*

[60]Lustig, *Mexico,* p. 106; Aspe, *Economic Transformation,* p. 218.

México, other companies with more than 10,000 employees include two banks[61] and one of the airline companies.[62]

Since the crisis at the end of 1994 there has been backsliding with scattered renationalizations of banks. Railroads, utilities, and PEMEX remain state owned, although what the future will bring is up in the air.

Maquiladoras, NAFTA, and the Opening of the Mexican Economy

Fear of domination by the United States has been an overriding theme in Mexican political and economic life. Even relatively pro–United States and pro-capitalist, Porfirio Díaz, said, "Poor country, so far from God and so close to the United States".[63] President Alemán after World War II enacted import restrictions for industrial development led by import substitution with minimal U.S. involvement. The most dramatic anti–U.S. moves for economic independence were Cárdenas's oil and railroad nationalizations during the 1930s.

Policy relaxation came in 1965 after U.S. President Lyndon Johnson of Texas settled a long-standing border dispute on terms favorable to Mexico. This policy, known formally as the U.S.-Mexico Border Industrialization Program, was known more generally as the *maquiladora* program. U.S. plants could easily invest on the border and sell output in the United States freely.

This program grew rapidly, drawing investment in numerous industries, to the point that by 1981 1.5 percent of the Mexican labor force was employed in such plants.[64] Rules covering them in Mexico were further liberalized in the mid-1980s, triggering a great expansion of manufacturing output and exports. Controversy over conditions in these plants and border towns erupted during the 1993 NAFTA confirmation fight in the United States. But some found that the lack of potable water, indoor plumbing, and electricity was associated with people in the border towns who did *not* work in the maquiladoras, and that those working in them were generally substantially better off in such matters.[65]

After 1982, Mexico decided to join the world economy, even if mostly as an adjunct to the U.S. economy. Given that in 1982 two-thirds of Mexico's

[61]The largest bank sold was Bancomer of Monterrey, Mexico's third largest city. Located northeast near Texas but not on the border, and thus set to gain from NAFTA, Monterrey has contained powerful entrepreneurial families dating back to the Díaz period known as the Monterrey Group, who have been relatively independent of control by Mexico City elites (Roderic A. Camp, *Entrepreneurs and Politics in Twentieth Century Mexico* [New York: Oxford University Press 1989]).

[62]Aspe, *Economic Transformation*.

[63]Reynolds, *The Mexican Economy*, p. 197.

[64]Barkin, *Distorted Development*, p. 90.

[65]Mitchell A. Seligson and Edward J. Williams, *Maquiladoras and Migration Workers in the Mexico–United States Border Industrialization Program* (Austin: University of Texas Press, 1981), pp. 50–51.

trade was with the United States, that approach seemed inevitable.[66] Although attention has focused on NAFTA and the coincidence of its implementation with the Zapatista uprising, most major moves towards trade liberalization occurred prior to NAFTA. The process began in 1984, when the number of goods requiring import permits fell below 100 percent, a figure that was down to 9.1 percent by 1991.[67] Whereas the maximum possible tariff was 100 percent as late as 1986, when Mexico joined GATT,[68] it was 20 percent by 1989. Tariffs continued to decline as well as nontariff barriers and remaining restrictions on foreign investment.

Along with beginning the NAFTA negotiations in 1990, free trade zones were established with Guatemala in 1989 and with Chile in 1991. NAFTA opens all of Mexico to equal rules for foreign investment, which may reduce activity in the border area and draw investment inward to the rest of Mexico. Foreign investment surged, mostly from the United States.[69] From U.S. $626.5 million in 1982, foreign investment rose to $3.877 billion in 1987, $9.414 billion in 1991,[70] and over $12 billion in 1993.[71]

The Environment

Mexican environmental policy and Mexico's environment were issues in the U.S. NAFTA debate. Mexico suffers from severe environmental problems, but they tend to be concentrated in two main areas: Mexico City and the U.S.–Mexican border area. Considered in the aggregate Mexico has fairly low levels of carbon dioxide emissions compared to most OECD countries.[72]

Mexico City has very severe air pollution, as can be seen by comparing the volumes of various pollutant emissions for the metropolitan area with the aggregate amounts for different countries. At the end of the 1980s Mexico City's particulate emissions equaled those for all of Italy, sulfur dioxide emissions were about the same as for all of Denmark, hydrocarbons emissions somewhat exceeded those of all of Austria as did carbon monoxide emissions, and nitrogen oxide emissions were slightly less than those in all of Switzerland.[73] These emissions aggravate effects because of the city's high

---

[66]*OECD Economic Surveys,* p. 262.

[67]Aspe, *Economic Transformation,* p. 157.

[68]GATT has since been replaced by the World Trade Organization (WTO).

[69]Fear of such investment flows was a concern of labor union critics of NAFTA in the United States. Constraining such investment is the inadequacy of Mexican infrastructure, especially for transportation, and continuing problems with corruption and bureaucratic red tape.

[70]Aspe, *Economic Transformation,* p. 165.

[71]"Mexico: The Revolution Continues," *The Economist,* January 22, 1994, p. 20.

[72]*OECD Economic Surveys,* p. 119.

[73]Mexico City figures are from *OECD Economic Surveys;* the rest are from World Resources Institute, *World Resources 1992–93* (New York: Oxford University Press, 1992), p. 351.

Box 17-2

NAFTA and the Mexican Financial Crisis

Although most estimates suggest major net gains to Mexico from NAFTA* (and minor ones to the United States), certain sectors will be adversely affected in each country. In the United States vulnerable industries include textiles, sugar, and citrus fruits. In Mexico the most vulnerable industry is corn farming, which has also been affected by the abandonment of the ejidos by the Salinas administration and the outbreak of the Zapatista revolt in Chiapas.

One result of trade and investment liberalization has been surging manufacturing output and exports with a major restructuring of Mexico's commodity export profile. Oil's export share peaked in 1982 at 74.6 percent but declined to 26.1 percent in 1991, whereas manufacturing's share rose from 13.7 percent in 1982 to become the majority export sector at 51.3 percent in 1991.[†]

Despite escaping dependence on raw materials exports, Mexico is now dependent on U.S. intermediate goods imports. From 1982 to 1993 exports surged from $24 billion to $52 billion. But imports rose from $17 billion to $65 billion, of which only $8 billion were consumer goods.[‡] This soaring trade deficit triggered the peso crisis at the end of 1994 and the subsequent austerity program, thus questioning NAFTA's benefits for Mexico.

---

*Another issue in the U.S. NAFTA debate involved the high rate of migration from Mexico, driven by Mexico's high population growth rate and lower per capita income. If NAFTA succeeds in creating jobs in Mexico this will lower migration to the United States. Rising incomes and urbanization are lowering the population growth rate (see Table 17-1). Massive migration from the ejidos could alter the migration scenario however.

[†]*OECD Economic Surveys,* p. 261.

[‡]Rudiger Dornbusch and Alejandro Werner, "Mexico: Stabilization, Reform, and No Growth," *Brookings Papers on Economic Activity* 1 (1994), p. 296.

---

elevation (over 7,000 feet) and thermal inversions (like Los Angeles) which trap and concentrate pollutants in a colder layer of air at the bottom of the Valley of Mexico.

The major sources of pollutants have been motor vehicles along with some stationary sources. The Salinas government imposed quantitative controls on motor vehicles in the metropolitan area starting in late 1989 and in 1991 shut down a large polluting oil refinery in the area.[74]

The U.S.–Mexican border problem is due to toxic emissions from maquiladora plants. NAFTA provides U.S. funding for cleaning up these plants,

---

[74]*OECD Economic Surveys,* p. 244.

and the Salinas administration passed new laws and promised stricter enforcement of existing laws. Skeptics abound who doubt these promises will be carried out. The 1994 financial crisis caused reductions in United States–Mexico border cleanup spending.

Generally a nation's polluting pattern varies with its income level. Very poor countries have serious problems with waste water and solid waste, still problems in Mexico City's slums; middle income countries are peak generators of sulfur dioxide emissions; higher income countries generate more carbon dioxide and nitrogen oxide emissions. Mexico is following this pattern, while facing a special challenge in controlling pollution in one of the world's two largest metropolises.

The Distribution of Income and the General Quality of Life

The real standard of living in Mexico has improved for most of the population. Comparing 1970 to 1990, life expectancy has risen from 61 years to 70 years, the infant mortality rate has declined from 68.5 per thousand births to 23.9, the percent of population with access to safe water has risen from 61 percent to 79.4 percent, those who have access to electricity has risen from 58.8 percent to 87.5 percent, and those who have access to sewerage has risen from 41.5 percent to 63.6 percent.[75]

Nevertheless many people have been left behind. Official statistics identify 28.4 percent of the population as being in poverty as of 1989,[76] with most of these in rural areas despite the desperate slums of Mexico City. The distribution of income became more unequal during the early stages of the reform process, after having become more equal up to 1984. Data showing this are presented in Figure 17–1.

The Salinas administration was aware of this trend, especially given the strong showing in the 1988 presidential election by the leftist PRD. The response was the National Solidarity Program, directed mostly at rural infrastructure development, especially roads, health clinics, electricity, and drinking water provision. Social spending rose from a low in 1985 of 5 percent of GDP and 22.6 percent of programmable public sector spending to 7.6 percent of GDP and 43.7 percent of programmable public sector spending in 1991.[77]

But this effort was insufficient to assuage those unhappy with the distributional implications of reform. It is of no solace to the government that it is often when things are getting better that uprisings occur, although Chiapas has been left behind more than any other state. Revolutions of rising expectations can cause reforms to become general revolutions.

---

[75]*OECD Economic Surveys,* p. 112.

[76]*OECD Economic Surveys,* p. 20. Whether the poverty rate increased during the 1980s is controversial, different studies getting different answers depending on different data assumptions.

[77]Aspe, *Economic Transformation,* pp. 119–21.

FIGURE 17–1   Income Distribution in Mexico, 1958–1989

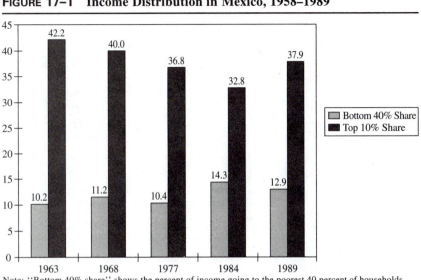

Note: "Bottom 40% share" shows the percent of income going to the poorest 40 percent of households, "Top 10% share" shows the percent of income going to the richest 10 percent of households.

Source: Figures are from Nora Lustig, *Mexico: The Remaking of an Economy* (Washington: Brookings Institution, 1992), p. 92.

The Mexican Economy in Hemispheric Perspective

Mexico reflects common patterns in the nations of Latin America once ruled by Spain. The Spanish colonial legacy left in most of these countries very unequal income distributions associated with the latifundia-hacienda systems of Spaniards owning large estates worked by indigenous peoples.[78] In later political-economic developments, the United States became identified as the resented neocolonial power and populist corporatist governments arose out of unstable conditions broken by periods of military dictatorship.

Mexico's proximity to the United States caused a more intense anticolonial and revolutionary ideological tradition even as the country benefitted from greater exports to the United States relative to other Latin American nations. Mexico was the site of the proudest and most economically advanced indigenous civilizations of the hemisphere—Tenochtitlán was the hemisphere's largest city when Columbus arrived. These advanced civilizations provided a base for the colonial regime both organizationally and in the quality of labor.

Ultimately intermarriage led to a predominantly mestizo population, proud of its nation. The success of Mexican economic development, despite

---

[78]In some the native populations were wiped out by disease, slavery, warfare, or some combination, only to be replaced by African slaves, East Indians, or European immigrants.

TABLE 17–3   Indicators for Western Hemisphere Economies

Country	Per Capita GNP	Inflation Rates	Income Distribution	Life Expectancy	Female Literacy	Social Spending
Guatemala	920	16.5	30.0	64.8	47	4.5
Peru	1,090	311.7	10.5	64.6	79	2.1
Chile	1,770	20.5	17.0	72.1	93	16.4
Costa Rica	1,790	22.5	12.7	75.2	93	16.3
Mexico	1,990	62.4	13.6	70.4	85	5.3
Cuba	2,000	n.a.	3.3	75.7	93	n.a.
Argentina	2,160	402.3	n.a.	71.4	95	8.1
Brazil	2,550	370.2	32.1	66.3	80	11.7
Uruguay	2,620	66.2	n.a.	72.5	96	17.1

Source: Per capita GNP is for 1989 in U.S. dollars from World Resources Institute *World Resources 1992–93* (New York: Oxford University Press, 1992), pp. 236–37; inflation is the average annual rate over 1980–92 from World Bank, *World Development Report 1994* (New York: Oxford University Press, 1994), pp. 162–63; income distribution is the quintile ratio for 1985–90, World Bank, *World Development Report*, pp. 220–21, except for Cuba for which it is for 1978 from Claes Brundenius, *Revolutionary Cuba: the Challenge of Economic Growth and Equity* (Boulder: Westview, 1984), p. 15; life expectancy is for 1990 from World Resources Institute, *World Resources*, pp. 248–49; adult female literacy rate is for 1990 from World Resources Institute, *World Resources*, pp. 254–55, and social spending is the percent of GNP spent on education, health, housing, amenities, social security, and welfare for 1990 from World Bank, *World Development Report 1992*, (New York: Oxford University Press, 1992) pp. 238–39.

its problems, has disproven the standard racist view of Latin American economic development at the end of World War II, which held that only nations such as Argentina and Chile with largely European populations were suitable for industrial development. The success of the East Asian NICs also undermines this notion, but many of those nations revel in their own racial purity. Mexico and Brazil have given the lie to the idea that "miscegenation" is inherently inimical to economic development.

Table 17–3 presents summary snapshots of some Latin American economies. Mexico stands up pretty well, lying between the extremes for most indicators. With the exception of command socialist Cuba, which has suffered severe stagnation since the cutoff of Soviet subsidies while still subject to the U.S. economic embargo, Mexico resembles most of the other Latin American countries in that their reform processes have been similar, except that Chile marketized and privatized sooner than the rest.

But Mexico has had one of the more consistent and vigorous economic reform programs with its move to full trade liberalization under NAFTA.[79] It has been a vanguard reformer, but one with a strong revolutionary tradition because of its proximity to the United States and proud cultural heritage. Thus it has had more dramatic internal conflict than most.[80]

---

[79]See John Williamson, ed., *Latin American Adjustment: How Much Has Happened?* (Washington: Brookings Institution, 1990), for discussion of reform programs in most Latin American economies.

[80]In many of these countries the shift to economic reform came with the reinstitution of political democracy after periods of military dictatorship, whereas technically democratic and civilian rule prevailed in Mexico throughout, if de facto authoritarian and dominated by the PRI.

Guatemala is Mexico's immediate neighbor to the southeast in Central America, bordering on troubled Chiapas, and the site of repressive governments warring against a Mayan-descended population. It has had almost no economic reforms.

Home of the ancient Inca empire in northwestern South America, Peru has suffered deep conflicts between a ruling, mostly Spanish-descended, urban elite and the mostly pure Indians of the rural areas that has involved the Maoist Sendero Luminoso (see Chapter 3). Economic reforms have been inconsistent but more vigorous recently. Democratically elected President Fujimori usurped many parliamentary powers in 1992 but was strongly reelected in 1995.

Long a stable parliamentary democracy in the ''Southern Cone'' of South America, Chile became a military dictatorship under Augusto Pinochet during the 1970s after a brief elected leftist rule. Economic liberalization began under Pinochet prior to the restoration of political democracy and has been more thorough than in any other Latin American country.

Long a continuous political democracy in Central America, Costa Rica is famous for having no standing military, a fact many see as connected to its democracy. It is the first country in the world to have engaged in a ''debt-for-nature'' swap with the World Bank to preserve some of its rain forests.

Caribbean Cuba has had a command socialist economy since soon after Fidel Castro came to dictatorial power in 1959. Like Mexico, Cuba has close proximity to the United States, which has affected it intensely since Cuba achieved its rather late independence from Spain in 1898 during the Spanish-American War.

Argentina in the Southern Cone had by far the highest income of any Latin American country in 1945 only to fall under the populist corporatist rule of Juan Perón whose policies engendered severe stagnation. Saddled with large foreign debts and entrenched hyperinflation, Argentina replaced a military dictatorship with democratic rule in the late 1980s and has followed economic reform policies similar to Mexico's since then.

Brazil is the largest and most multiethnic Latin American nation. This former Portuguese colony, occupying eastern South America, has the largest foreign debt of any nation except the United States, along with high rates of economic growth and income inequality. Having replaced a military dictatorship it has had trouble getting hyperinflation under control.

Except for a period of dictatorship in the 1970s and early 1980s, Uruguay, nestled between Brazil and Argentina, has been fairly quiet and stable with policies imitating those of some social democracies of Western Europe. Its growth has recently stagnated.

Summary and Conclusions

Mexico is opening, marketizing, and privatizing an economy long characterized by a state-dominated, inward-looking policy designed to protect it from U.S. domination. With a long history of centralized state domination dating from the Aztec period, Mexico has been ruled for most of the 20th century by the Institutional Revolutionary Party. Its title indicates its effort to simultaneously include conflicting socioeconomic forces within a corporatist structure, to remain revolutionary in its populist appeal to peasants through land redistribution and to workers through party-related unions, and to protect business through its institutionalized, technocratic bureaucracy.

This technocratic populist corporatism is changing with reform policies developed since the foreign debt crisis of 1982, which was triggered after oil price declines rendered massive borrowings predicated on rising oil prices absurd. Mexico has since escaped from its dependence on raw materials exports and engaged in an industrialization drive fueled by foreign investment, further encouraged by trade liberalization culminating in the NAFTA with the United States and Canada. But these gains were challenged as rising imports of intermediate goods triggered a peso devaluation and austerity program at the end of 1994.

The development and reform policies of Mexico have been mostly successful and influential both regionally and in Central and Eastern Europe. Real living standards have improved for most citizens and urbanization proceeds as Mexico City competes to be the world's largest city with Tokyo.

But as in many other parts of the world, reform has brought increased income inequality and opposition, especially from rural peasants still in traditional ejidos. These grievances exploded at the beginning of 1994 in the armed Zapatista uprising in the poor state of Chiapas. As in Eastern Europe, a possible political backlash might halt or reverse some of the reforms, especially with the new austerity program in place since the peso crisis at the end of 1994. Mexico's path of development continues to be fraught with grand drama.

Questions for Discussion

1. What elements of the modern Mexican economy can be traced to the Spanish colonial and Aztec periods?

2. How do the economic policies of Juárez, Díaz, Cárdenas, Alemán, and Salinas compare and contrast?

3. To what extent are the ejidos a new traditional economy element in Mexico? What is their current status and outlook?

4. Why has President Zedillo denied to the Mexican people that he pledged the oil reserves of PEMEX as collateral for the foreign exchange support loan from the United States in 1995?

5. How might NAFTA undercut the maquiladora plants and what is its impact more broadly on the Mexican economy?

6. How does the Mexican reform program compare with those in Central and Eastern Europe? In what ways has it been more and less successful?

7. How does Mexico compare with other Latin American economies in terms of economic performance?
8. Why did the Zapatista revolt occur?
9. To what extent is the label of the Mexican economy as *technocratic populist corporatism* accurate?

Suggested Further Readings

Aspe, Pedro. *Economic Transformation: The Mexican Way.* Cambridge: MIT Press, 1993.

Barkin, David. *Distorted Development: Mexico in the World Economy.* Boulder: Westview Press, 1990.

Camp, Roderic A. *Entrepreneurs and Politics in Twentieth Century Mexico.* New York: Oxford University Press, 1989.

Dornbusch, Rudiger, and Alejandro Werner. ''Mexico: Stabilization, Reform, and No Growth.'' *Brookings Papers on Economic Activity,* 1 (1994), pp. 253–315.

Grayson, George W. *The Politics of Mexican Oil.* Pittsburgh: University of Pittsburgh Press, 1980.

Hamilton, N., and T. F. Harding, eds. *Modern Mexico: State, Economy, and Social Conflict.* Beverly Hills: Sage Publications, 1986.

Lustig, Nora. *Mexico: The Remaking of an Economy.* Washington: The Brookings Institution, 1992.

Reynolds, Clark W. *The Mexican Economy: Twentieth Century Structure and Growth.* New Haven: Yale University Press, 1970.

Ruiz, Ramón Eduardo. *Triumphs and Tragedy: A History of the Mexican People.* New York: W. W. Norton, 1992.

Seligson, Mitchell A., and Edward J. Williams. *Maquiladoras and Migration Workers in the Mexico-United States Border Industrialization Program.* Austin: University of Texas Press, 1981.

Teichman, Judith A. *Policymaking in Mexico: From Boom to Crisis.* Boston: Allen & Unwin, 1988.

Williamson, John, ed. *Latin American Adjustment: How much has happened?* Washington: Institute for International Economics, 1990.

KOREA: THE LINGERING SHADOW OF THE COLD WAR

Pine and bamboo trees seem to symbolize Koreans. The trees retain green leaves throughout all four seasons, resisting cold temperatures in the winter and hot temperatures in the summer. Similarly, the Korean people have managed to survive periods of suffering and humiliation inflicted upon them by foreign invasions on over 900 occasions.
—Sung Moon Pae[1]

Like one of the ancient and broken down trucks whose corpses litter North Korea's primitive highways, no amount of crashing the gears or cursing from the driver's seat will move the worn-out old vehicle, which is Pyongyang's economy, even a meter further up the steep hill; and now it has started to roll backwards.
—Economist Intelligence Unit[2]

Korean pride assumed many forms . . . it grew into what can only be called a Korean worldview. The scenario goes as follows. For every people there comes a time to rise. The Europeans and Americans became lazy and were replaced by the Japanese. Japan has also become soft. Now it is Korea's turn!
—Jon Woronoff[3]

Introduction

The shadow of the Cold War lingers over the Korean peninsula. Although homogeneous in culture and ethnicity, the Korean people were divided at the end of World War II between a communist North and a capitalist South. They

---

[1]*Korea Leading Developing Nations: Economy, Democracy, and Welfare* (Lanham: University Press of America, 1992), p. 19.
[2]*North Korea Country Report No. 1* (1993), p. 35.
[3]*Korea's Economy: Man-Made Miracle* (1983), pp. 75–76.

fought a bloody war during 1950–53 that involved outsiders and ended in a stalemate with little change in their border, today the most heavily armed on earth.

As South Korea outstripped North Korea economically and diplomatically, North Korea's secretive leadership sought to develop nuclear weapons despite international opposition. Since the death in July 1994 of longtime leader, Kim Il Sung,[4] his son and apparent successor, Kim Chong Il, has agreed to give up the program in return for foreign energy aid, although problems continue with the implementation of this agreement. Still facing 40,000 U.S. troops in the South, North Korea can no longer count on the support of China and Russia, as it could in the early 1950s.

Korea has been a cultural bridge between China and Japan and was invaded frequently by both. This led Korea to adopt extreme isolationism—it was called the "Hermit Kingdom" during the 19th century. The last Asian nation opened to outside influence, it fell under Japanese control that ended in 1945 when the USSR and the United States militarily occupied the North and South respectively, each establishing competing regimes that went to war in 1950.

After the war the North, the Democratic Peoples' Republic of Korea (DPRK), developed an economy that still follows an extreme Stalinist command socialist model. Playing between China and the USSR during the Sino-Soviet conflict, Kim Il Sung developed a self-reliance ideology called *juche*, that led to a modern Hermit Kingdom. Stressing heavy industrialization, North Korea grew more rapidly than South Korea for over a decade after 1953, while developing a wide social safety net and greater income equality. But since the South surpassed it in per capita income in the mid-1970s, the North has stagnated economically and gone into such an outright decline since 1990 that reports have emerged of food shortages and demonstrations.[5]

At the division of Korea the South, the Republic of Korea (ROK), had more agriculture and light industry than the heavy industrial North. After corruption and stagnation in the 1950s a military dictatorship came to power in 1961 under Park Chung-hee that instituted indicatively planned, market capitalist growth. The South integrated with the world economy, following an export-led growth policy like Japan's and evolving its comparative advantage up a technological ladder from textiles through heavy industry to consumer electronics and automobiles. It did so in tandem with the three other "Tigers," or Newly Industrializing Countries (NICs) of East Asia: Taiwan, Hong Kong, and Singapore.[6] With a 1994 per capita income exceeding $7,000 per year,

---

[4]At his death, Kim Il Sung was the world's longest lasting national ruler.

[5]These reports, coming from Koreans living in Japan who visit North Korea, were denied by the North Korean government. But in mid-1993 the North Korean government temporarily stopped such visits despite these visitors bringing needed hard currency. In mid-1995, the North accepted emergency rice shipments from the South.

[6]These are increasingly labeled the Newly Industrializing Economies (NIEs), presumably to defer to the idea that Hong Kong (and perhaps Taiwan) are not "countries."

South Korea has surged far ahead of North Korea with its per capita income of around $1,000 per year. From 1980 to 1992 South Korea had the highest real per capita income growth rate in the world.[7]

As its income rose so did pressures within to democratize. President Park was assassinated in 1979. His successor voluntarily gave up power in 1988 when the Olympic games were held in Seoul, South Korea's capital, to a democratically elected successor. In 1993 an opponent of the previous military regimes, Kim Young Sam, was elected president. He has engaged in an anti-corruption drive that affected the top ranks of both the military and the business communities.[8] South Korean business has been dominated by large conglomerates known as *chaebol,* somewhat similar to the Japanese zaibatsu and keiretsu.

The South Koreans cannot reduce the militarization of their economy with the threat of the world's fourth largest army on their northern border. The long-run solution, supported by both northerners and southerners, is reunification. Despite negotiations in recent years, the northerners resist because they fear peaceful unification will end up like Germany's with the capitalist part dominating the socialist part economically and politically.

The problems of the German unification have made the South Koreans undisposed to rapidly unify. But eventually unification will probably happen, and despite a difficult transition, a unified Korea could be a major world economic power. Koreans work longer hours than any other people in the world and have achieved high levels of education following the claim of some that theirs is the world's most Confucianist society.[9] This combination has already shown its potential in the substantial achievements of South Korea.

Historical and Cultural Background to 1953

Premodern Korea

Koreans have a distinct cultural and ethnic identity—they are related linguistically to the Japanese and Manchurians but are closer culturally to China. Their myths declare they are descended from Tangun, son of a bear and a god,

---

[7]See Table 1–1.

[8]Mark L. Clifford, *Troubled Tiger: Businessmen, Bureaucrats, and Generals in South Korea* (Armonk: M.E. Sharpe, 1994).

[9]Besides Confucianism, another factor in the intensely competitive drive for education by Koreans is an attitude known as *Hahn,* ''a sense of rancor, regret, remorse, revenge, grievance, grudge, and grief,'' possibly due to long, passive suffering under foreign, especially Japanese, conquest. ''Once released *Hahn* has turned into an enormous force inciting and motivating people to find ways to gratify their suppressed needs'' (Kyong Dong Kim, ''Koreans: Who are They?'' in *Doing Business in Korea,* ed. A.M. Whitehall (London: Croom Helm, 1987), pp. 9–11.

founder of the first Korean kingdom in 2333 B.C. There is still a cult that worships him, and recently the North Koreans claim to have found his tomb.[10] The first historical dynasty, founded in 1122 B.C., lasted nearly a thousand years during which Chinese Confucianism penetrated Korea.

In 668 A.D., after more inroads by Chinese culture including Buddhism, the Silla Kingdom conquered two rivals and united Korea for the first time.[11] The Silla kingdom transmitted Chinese cultural influences into Japan. The Silla was replaced in 936 by the Koryo,[12] dominated by increasingly corrupt Buddhist monks and marked by many foreign invasions.

In 1392 the kingdom of Choson established its capital at Seoul. The Kingdom lasted until annexation by Japan in 1910. Initially progressive, it was possibly the world's technological leader in the early 1400s.[13] Choson, with a new aristocratic class, the scholarly bureaucratic yangban, was Confucianized. After a series of invasions at the end of the 1500s, it withdrew upon itself to become the ossified Hermit Kingdom.

The Opening Up of Korea and the Japanese Occupation

After failed efforts were made to open up Korea by various western nations, post-Meiji Japan obtained a commercial treaty in 1876. During the 1880s Korea signed trade treaties with other outside powers and U.S. Protestant missionaries poured in.[14]

An antiforeigner uprising in 1894 triggered a Chinese-Japanese war, won decisively by Japan. In 1905 Russia and Japan fought over Korea and Japan was victorious. In 1910 Japan annexed Korea, resulting in the bitter hostility between Koreans and Japanese that persists today.

Economic growth accelerated and modernizing reforms were carried out to integrate Korea into the Japanese empire in a subordinate position. Among

---

[10]This attempts to legitimize their claim to rule all of Korea. The oldest Korean religion is a disorganized shamanism known as *Sinkyo,* with similarities to Japanese Shintoism and Chinese Taoism. Unlike them it has no priestly hierarchy and is centered on women shamans. The predominance of women in Sinkyo reflects a reaction to the dominant male-oriented Confucianism. See Cornelius Osgood, *The Koreans and Their Culture* (New York: Ronald Press, 1951).

[11]The conflict between the southeastern Silla and the southwestern Paekche continues today in regional dislike between the southeastern Kyongsang provinces and the southwestern Cholla provinces. The 1961–88 military regimes were dominated by officers from Kyongsang, and opposition to them centered in Cholla. A 1980 uprising was suppressed with a massacre of hundreds of students in Kwangju, capital of South Cholla.

[12]Origin of *Korea,* meaning ''land of the morning calm.''

[13]One example was the invention of printing prior to Germany's Gutenberg, who is often given credit as first.

[14]By the late 1980s about 24 percent of the South Korean population was Christian, more than anywhere in East Asia except the Philippines, and 27 percent was Buddhist. Although a few Christian churches and Buddhist temples have recently reopened in North Korea, the main ''religion'' there remains Kim Il Sung worship.

these were the abolition of slavery, the institution of a civil code, introduction of a modern financial system,[15] expansion of the school system, the building of infrastructure in transportation and hydroelectric power, and the initial development of the textile industry.

Koreans revolted in a nonviolent independence movement in 1919, which was suppressed by the Japanese after thousands of Koreans were killed. Koreans opposed the attempt to suppress their language and culture, the takeover of a majority of the most fertile land by Japanese landlords, and the increasing export of food and natural resources to Japan, especially after Japan invaded China in the 1930s.[16] Per capita rice consumption in Korea declined by nearly 50 percent between 1915 and 1938.[17]

In 1919 a Provisional Government was established in exile in Shanghai with a Christian, Syngman Rhee, as president. He was removed in 1925 for embezzlement and moved to the United States. In 1948 the United States installed him as the first president of the Republic of Korea after returning him to the country in October 1945.

Kim Il Sung joined the Korean Communist Party in 1929 and in 1932 joined a group of anti-Japanese guerrillas operating in Manchuko (Japanese-occupied Manchuria). He led a famous cross-border raid in 1937 but retreated into the Soviet Union in 1941 after his Chinese commander died. Although his official biographies have him almost singlehandedly defeating the Japanese in 1945, actually the Soviet military brought him back in October 1945 and installed him as leader of a provisional government in the North in February 1946.[18] Japanese occupation of Korea ended with the Japanese surrender at the end of World War II in August 1945, two months prior to the arrival of either Syngman Rhee or Kim Il Sung.

The Division of Korea and the Korean War

During World War II, the 1943 Cairo Conference between the United States, Great Britain, and China declared that ''The aforesaid three great powers, mindful of the enslavement of the people of Korea, are determined that in due course Korea shall become free and independent.''[19] Korean nationalists interpreted ''in due course'' to mean ''immediately upon liberation from the

---

[15]Before 1876 there was no formal money in Korea. Rent and taxes were generally paid in grain (rice in the South, wheat or millet in the North).

[16]Many Koreans cooperated with the Japanese, and North Koreans charged that the United States elevated many such individuals in the South after 1945. ROK dictator from 1961 to 79, Park Chung-hee, had been an officer in the Japanese army.

[17]Andrew J. Grajdanzev, *Modern Korea: Her Economic and Social Development Under the Japanese* (New York: Institute of Pacific Relations, 1944), p. 118.

[18]There are wildly varying stories about Kim Il Sung's activities prior to 1945. Some South Koreans claim he was not the same Kim Il Sung as the anti-Japanese guerrilla commander in the 1930s, that man having been killed in 1939 (Dae-Sook Suh, *Kim Il Sung: The North Korean Leader* [New York: Columbia University Press, 1988], chap. 3).

[19]Osgood, *The Koreans,* p. 297.

Japanese,'' but President Roosevelt intended an extended postwar trusteeship. Scholars disagree about Stalin's position at Yalta and Potsdam, but he did not declare an official position because the USSR was not formally at war with Japan, although at Yalta in February 1945 he agreed to declare war against Japan three months after German surrender.

On August 8 the USSR did so and fought the large Japanese army in Manchuria. Soviet troops landed in northeastern Korean ports on August 10. On August 15 Japan surrendered and the United States, without troops in Korea, proposed the 38th parallel as a military demarcation line, which was accepted by the Soviets.

Immediately upon surrendering, the Japanese in Seoul turned over power to a local Korean group that established the People's Republic of Korea and set up political action committees throughout the countryside. U.S. troops arrived in September and disbanded this nascent government, establishing a military regime that lasted until 1948. In the North the Soviets allowed the local committees of this government to operate, but increasingly controlled them.

The next three years saw intense and complicated negotiations, disagreements, political maneuverings, assassinations, and a deepening of the Cold War, which prevented the United States and the USSR from agreeing about Korean unification.[20] In August 1948 the ROK was formally established in the South with Syngman Rhee as president and was recognized by the United Nations as the legitimate government of Korea. In September the DPRK was established in the North with Kim Il Sung as its leader. Each leader demanded the overthrow of the other to unify Korea under his own leadership. Cross-border fighting became constant and a guerrilla war began in the South. The USSR and the United States removed their own troops except for some advisers by mid-1949.

Deep disagreements exist regarding the war. Disputed issues include these: (1) Who was really responsible for starting it? (2) Could it have been stopped sooner than it was, and why was it not? (3) What kinds of weapons were used or almost used by each side and what atrocities were committed by each side? and (4) Was Kim Il Sung or Joseph Stalin really in charge on the communist side (or Mao Zedong after the Chinese entry into the conflict)?[21] The question of Stalin's role is central and is related to that of the origins of the Cold War. Most analysts see him as the prime aggressor whereas some see him acting essentially defensively.

---

[20]Scholars dispute the details of this period, when up to 450 different political groups were active at one time or another. For a variety of accounts see Osgood, *The Koreans;* Ellen Brun and Jacques Hersh, *Socialist Korea: A Case Study in the Strategy of Economic Development* (New York: Monthly Review Press, 1976); Bruce Cumings, *The Origins of the Korean War,* vols. I and II (Princeton: Princeton University Press, 1981 and 1989); and Erik Van Ree, *Socialism in One Zone: Stalin's Policy in Korea* (Oxford: Berg, 1989).

[21]For varying discussions of the war see I.F. Stone, *The Hidden History of the Korean War* (New York: Monthly Review Press, 1952); Clay Blair, *The Forgotten War: America in Korea 1950–1953* (New York: Random House, 1987); John Halliday and Bruce Cumings, *Korea: The Unknown War* (London: Penguin Books, 1988); and Van Ree, *Socialism in One Zone.*

The North Korean army invaded South Korea in June 1950, quickly taking Seoul and all but the southeastern corner of the country around Pusan. During a Soviet walkout, the UN condemned the invasion and was formally the combatant on the southern side, although most troops were from the United States and South Korea. In September UN forces under U.S. General Douglas MacArthur landed at Inchon, Seoul's port, far behind North Korean lines. Within two weeks these forces invaded the North across the 38th parallel, going clear to the Chinese border. In November Chinese troops attacked, pushing UN forces south of Seoul to nearly the 37th parallel by January 1951. The war seesawed until armistice was signed in July 1953 with the final military line, and new border, approximating the 38th parallel.

The war devastated both Koreas. More than 10 percent of the Korean population was killed, 3 to 4 million people.[22] Severe damage to cities and infrastructure resulted. GDP in the South declined by 15 percent and in the North by 30 percent, leaving per capita incomes nearly identical at around U.S. $55 per year.[23]

The North Korean Economy

The Ideology of Kim Il Sungism and Juche

The North Korean economy and its relations with the rest of the world developed according to the ideology of "Kim Il Sungism." This ideology arose from struggling against the United States and competing with South Korea while trying to remain independent of the competing USSR and China. These efforts led Kim Il Sung to advocate the doctrine of *juche*,[24] or self-reliance.

Kim Il Sungism is Stalinism with elements of Maoism and Korean Confucianism. Kim Il Sung personally admired Stalin, who put him in power, and tilted towards China when Khrushchev began destalinization in 1956.[25] Classical Stalinist elements include (1) strong central planning without free markets or privatization, (2) emphasis on heavy industry and militarization, (3) de facto "socialism in one country" implied by juche, and (4) a massive Cult of Personality devoted to Kim Il Sung.

---

[22]U.S. deaths were 54,246, similar to those in Vietnam. Chinese deaths were somewhere between 500,000 and 1 million (Halliday and Cumings, *Korea: The Unknown War,* p. 200).

[23]Byoung-Lo Philo Kim, *Two Koreas in Development: A Comparative Study of Principles and Strategies of Capitalist and Communist Third World Development* (New Brunswick: Transaction Publishers, 1992), p. 67.

[24]Frequently transliterated as *chuch'e,* it comes from two words, *ju* meaning *ruler* or *master,* and *che* meaning *body* or *essence* (Byung Chul Koh, "Ideology and North Korean Foreign Policy," in *North Korea in a Regional and Global Context,* eds. R.A. Scalapino and H. Lee [Berkeley: University of California Press, 1986], pp. 20–36).

[25]This anti-Soviet tilt peaked in 1963–64 when the Soviets sharply reduced economic and military assistance. But relations were normalized after Khrushchev's ouster. Periods of anti-Chinese tilt followed in 1967–69 when Chinese Red Guards denounced Kim Il Sung as a "fat revisionist" and 1978–80 at the beginning of China's pro–market economic reforms.

The latter began after Kim Il Sung enunciated juche in 1955 and accelerated after he was criticized by the Chinese in 1967. The extremity of this cult was shown in 1972 when a 66-foot statue of him was erected in Pyongyang and a museum with 92 rooms opened for his 60th birthday. In 1982 an Arch of Triumph larger than that in Paris and a Juche Tower taller than the Washington Monument were built.

Maoist elements showed up in "moral incentives" campaigns to encourage production. Kim Il Sung began the "flying horse" *Chollima* campaign in 1956, calling for a superhuman drive to rebuild industry without outside assistance.[26] Drives in the 1960s emphasized collective management in industry and direct administration by party leaders in agriculture. Agricultural communalization reached levels seen only in China during Mao's Great Leap Forward.

Confucianist elements emphasized filial piety as Kim Il Sung created a cult of his parents and himself, while grooming his son, Kim Chong Il, as his successor. Further elements include disdain of commerce similar to the yangban view, emphasis on hard work, respect for education, and isolationism similar to that during the 19th-century Korean Hermit Kingdom.[27]

Specific elements of juche include political independence (*chaju*), economic self-sustenance (*charip*), and military self-defense (*chawi*). Ironically the search for these elements led to their undermining. To achieve independence from the USSR and China, North Korea reached out to the rest of the world, politically and economically. It became an observer at the UN in 1973, joined the Nonaligned Nations Movement in 1975, and sharply increased its trade and borrowing from capitalist countries during that period.[28]

The upshot of these actions was repudiation of its debts to capitalist countries in 1976, throwing it back upon its old comrades,[29] especially the USSR, which dominated its trade from then to 1991 despite the DPRK's refusal to join the CMEA.[30] With the collapse of the USSR and the recognition of South

---

[26]Stalin had "Stakhanovite" drives in the 1930s, but he also used wage differentials as material incentives much more than either the Chinese under Mao or the North Koreans.

[27]South Korea shares respect for family, hard work, and education, but not disdain for commerce or isolationism. Thus, Confucianism can be associated with either economic dynamism or stagnation.

[28]Between 1971 and 1975, its imports from OECD countries increased tenfold while its exports to them tripled (Sungwoo Kim, "Foreign Trade of North Korea: Analysis and Recommendations," Department of Economics Working Paper No. 73, Northeastern University (1991), p. 14).

[29]A Joint Venture Law was passed in 1984. The main response has been by North Koreans living in Japan, a hotel project with a French company, and a few minor deals with the Chinese and the Russians (Eui-Gak Hwang, *The Korean Economies: A Comparison of North and South* [Oxford: Clarendon Press, 1993], pp. 212–14).

[30]Although the DPRK never joined the CMEA, it was a founding member of the three main suborganizations.

Korea by both Russia and China,[31] North Korea lacks any external supporters and faces the full implications of juche. It must reach out again to a skeptical capitalist world while trying to maintain its isolated and fossilized system, which is in an economic free fall.[32]

Stages of the North Korean Economy

Given how far the DPRK has fallen behind the ROK economically, it is hard to realize that the shoe was on the other foot for a period following the Korean War.[33] This is generally accepted despite the inevitable problems with barely available North Korean data.[34] If East German data were distorted, North Korean data are far worse given their secretive Hermit Kingdom attitudes.[35]

Early economic success for North Korea arose from political consolidation, early equalization through the socialization of all industries and agriculture, mass mobilization strategies, and moral incentive policies. But these measures did not work in the long run because of the lack of incentives to improve productivity and the extreme emphasis on self-reliance.

After taking power in 1946, Kim Il Sung "Sovietized" the North Korean economy.[36] Land was distributed to the peasants and heavy industry was nationalized, most small commodity production remaining private until after the Korean War.[37] During 1953–58 agriculture was completely collectivized as

---

[31]In Moscow one sees large billboard ads for South Korean companies. Recently China has spoken of a "five-way strategic relationship in northeast Asia" that is to involve China, Russia, Japan, the United States, and . . . South Korea (Economist Intelligence Unit, *Country Report: North Korea,* No. 1, 1993, p. 33). This emphasizes how truly isolated the DPRK has become.

[32]North Korea shields its citizens from outside information and influences to an astounding extent. All North Korean students were pulled back from Eastern Europe once the democratization movements took hold there in 1989.

[33]At the peak of this gap, Joan Robinson visited and praised the rebuilding of DPRK capital, Pyongyang, from a city with "not one stone standing upon another" to "a modern city . . . A city without slums" ("Korea, 1964: Economic Miracle," in *Collected Economic Papers,* vol. 3 [Oxford: Basil Blackwell, 1973], pp. 207–15, originally published in *Monthly Review,* January 1965).

[34]At least 10 different agencies have estimated DPRK economic data. DPRK official data report total output two to four times greater than do the other sources (Hwang, *The Korean Economies,* p. 106).

[35]North Korea may join the Asian Development Bank to obtain financing for a special economic zone around Najin-Sonbong, but it has been "troubled by the ADB requirement of exact economic data," since being "used to releasing only figures favorable to itself" (Economist Intelligence Unit, *North Korea,* p. 38).

[36]For accounts of DPRK economic policies before 1970, see Brun and Hersh, *Socialist Korea,* and Joseph Sang-hoon Chung, *The North Korean Economy: Structure and Development* (Stanford: Hoover Institution, 1974).

[37]One reason for this contrast was that heavy industry had been largely in the hands of Japanese owners who were expelled, whereas small commodity production was largely Korean owned.

cooperatives and all remaining private industry was nationalized. Two short-term plans led between 1946 and 1949 to a more than tripling of industrial output and to a 40 percent increase in agricultural production.

Postwar plan targets and actual performance are presented in Table 18–1. The plan for 1954–56 emphasized reconstruction and was successful, beginning North Korea's rapid growth stage. A five-year plan came next, which was completed in three years with 1960 serving as a buffer year afterwards. This plan continued rapid growth, completed the socialization drive, and began the mass mobilization drives.

In 1961 the First Seven-Year Plan was introduced. It was extended to 1970 because of difficulties arising from expanding the juche policy after the Soviets reduced aid. It emphasized heavy industrial development and mechanization of agriculture. Military spending sharply increased from a low of 3.7 percent of the state budget in 1959 to 19 percent in 1960 and to 30.4 percent in 1967, a level it maintained until 1972, after which it gradually declined.[38]

The Six-Year Plan of 1971–76 emphasized technical improvement through importing foreign technologies because the North Koreans realized that South Korea was outstripping them economically. Official statistics claim this plan's targets were fulfilled, but making 1977 a buffer year to delay announcing a new plan suggests otherwise. The 1976 foreign debt crisis implied this underachievement as the DPRK would be cut off from easy access to Western technology.

The Second Seven-Year Plan (1978–84) emphasized modernization and ''scientification'' by North Korean engineers and scientists. This was the first attempt to increase light rather than heavy industry and to increase material incentives for workers. The plan also involved major efforts in energy extraction (especially coal) and large-scale ''nature-remaking'' projects such as massive land reclamation. This plan generally fell somewhat short.

A three year interim without a plan followed, in which an effort was made to reform and decentralize. In 1984 North Korea's Joint Venture Law passed due to Chinese influence. So far it has generated minimal interest (see footnote 29), but it has increased control over accounting and funds by enterprise managers somewhat.

Opponents of reform gained in 1987 when the Third Seven-Year Plan (1987–93) began. This plan was to emphasize modernization and light industry, but its abject failure and the collapse of socialism in the former USSR, formerly North Korea's leading trading partner (40 percent of trade in 1991)[39] and aid supplier, created a crisis. The response during a ''period of adjustment'' projected to 1996 appears to reemphasize heavy industry.[40] North Korea's crisis is the crisis of the last and purest command socialist economy.

[38]Chung, *The North Korean Economy,* p. 180.

[39]Economist Intelligence Unit, *North Korea,* p. 5.

[40]Economist Intelligence Unit, *Country Report: Korea,* Second Quarter, 1994, p. 40.

TABLE 18–1   **Performance of the Post-1953 North Korean Plans**

Plans	National Income		Industrial Production		Grain Production	
Years	Target	Actual	Target	Actual	Target	Actual
1953–56	20.5	30.1	37.5	41.8	10.8	7.1
1957–60	17.1	20.9	21.1	36.6	5.6	7.2
1961–70	15.2	7.5	18.1	12.8	8.2	2.7
1971–76	10.3	n.a.	14.0	16.3	5.8–7.0	8.2
1978–84	9.6	8.8	12.1	12.2	2.3	2.3
1987–93	7.9	−1.8*	n.a.	n.a.	n.a.	−4.5

Note: All figures are average annual percent rates of change. These numbers are certainly positively exaggerated.

*This figure masks the severity of the recent decline. Growth averaged 3 percent through 1989, but has fallen more than 5 percent per year since then (Economist Intelligence Unit, p. 5).

Source: Data from Joseph Sang-hoon Chung, ''Economic Planning in North Korea,'' in *North Korea Today: Strategic and Domestic Issues,* eds. R.A. Scalapino and J.Y. Kim (Berkeley: University of California Press, 1983), p. 17; and ''North Korea's Economic Development and Capabilities,'' in *The Foreign Relations of North Korea: New Perspectives,* eds. J.K. Park and B.C. Koh (Seoul: Kyungnam University Press, 1987), p. 112; Byoung-Lo Philo Kim, *Two Koreas in Development* (New Brunswick: Transaction Publishers, 1992), p. 207; and Economist Intelligence Unit, p. 5.

The South Korean Economy

The Stages of Development and Indicative Planning

The South Korean economy is a global superstar, having experienced the highest rate of real per capita economic growth in the world during 1980–92. Although somewhat slowed more recently, its 7.7 percent aggregate real GDP growth rate in 1994 remains impressive.

The East Asian NICs have much in common: strong emphases on education and traditions of hard work associated with the Confucianist heritage,[41] significant state infrastructure development, and strong market orientations. Nevertheless these economies exhibit major differences, the ROK having more state involvement in its economy and higher levels of corporate concentration in the *chaebol* than the others. South Korea has had one of the most indicatively planned of market capitalist economies, sharply contrasting with laissez-faire Hong Kong. Whereas the chaebol dominate the ROK economy more than do the keiretsu in Japan, Taiwan's economy has a competitive small business market structure in most industries.

The ROK had a pathetic start after 1945. The period of U.S. military rule from 1945 to 1948 was a complete loss and production in most sectors declined. The main achievement of the Syngman Rhee regime (1948–60) was

---

[41]Now a truism, this argument was first made in 1979 (Herman Kahn, *World Economic Development: 1979 and Beyond* [Boulder: Westview, 1979]). Before then the antibusiness aspects of Confucianism were generally remarked upon.

land reform, which laid the groundwork for later increases in agricultural productivity. Whereas GDP grew at an annual rate of about 3 to 4 percent during 1953 to 1960,[42] per capita income barely rose due to rapid population growth[43] and remained under $100 per year. The Rhee regime was corrupt, mismanaged macroeconomic policy, was excessively protectionist with a strong import substitution policy, and began some of the chaebol through political links.

Student demonstrations in 1960 brought down the government, and elections were held. But in 1961 Park Chung-hee took power in a military coup and ruled until his assassination in 1979. His authoritarian regime instituted indicative planning and saw the takeoff into rapid growth. Some argue that the growth occurred *in spite* of planning and that it was currency and exchange rate unification, budget deficit reductions, and the shift from import substitution to export promotion that caused the takeoff.[44] Others argue that the Park regime's manipulation of market prices and investment significantly stimulated the high growth rate.[45] In contrast to both Japan and France, the Economic Planning Board (EPB) in South Korea could force government budgets to be in accord with its plans.

Table 18–2 and Figure 18–1 summarize the performance of the plans. In general, actual performance outstripped planned targets.

Initially came the Nathan Plan, developed in 1954 by a U.S. consulting firm. Not implemented, it underlay Park's First Five-Year Plan (FYP) beginning in 1962.[46] This first plan of *guided capitalism* had little detail and was revised in 1964 to emphasize industrial growth rather than food self-sufficiency at the time of the macroeconomic stabilization. Its goals were to increase energy production, grain production, and import substitution industries. Government provided one-third of investment funds.

The Second FYP (1967–71) resembled the original version of the First FYP, but it emphasized textile exports as a leading sector and increasing the public sector for social overhead capital investment.[47] This plan was more detailed, having been developed from an input-output model of the economy. Actual performance easily exceeded targets for the first two plans.

---

[42]Kim, *Two Koreas in Development,* p. 67.

[43]In mid-1991 ROK population was over 43 million, about twice that of the DPRK. The ROK is the fifth most densely populated country in the world after Singapore, Hong Kong, Taiwan, and Bangladesh. Seoul may now be the fourth most populous metropolitan area in the world (*Statistical Abstract of the United States* [Washington: USGPO, 1991], p. 835).

[44]Marcus Noland, *Pacific Basin Developing Countries* (Washington: Institute for International Economics, 1990), p. 41.

[45]Alice H. Amsden, *Asia's Next Giant: South Korea and Late Industrialization* (New York: Oxford University Press, 1989).

[46]For detailed discussions of South Korean planning see Paul W. Kuznets, *Economic Growth and Structure in the Republic of Korea* (New Haven: Yale University Press, 1977), and "Indicative Planning in Korea," *Journal of Comparative Economics* 14 (1990) pp. 657–76.

[47]Sectors completely owned by the state include postal service and telecommunications, and those partly owned by the state include railways, airlines, electricity, and banks.

TABLE 18–2   Performance of the South Korean Plans

Plans	Years					
	1962	1963	1964	1965	1966	Average
First FYP	5.7	6.4	7.3	7.8	8.3	7.1
Revised FYP	2.8	4.4	5.0	5.0	5.0	4.8
Actual	2.2	9.1	9.6	5.8	12.7	9.3
	1967	1968	1969	1970	1971	Average
Second FYP	7.0	7.0	7.0	7.0	7.0	7.0
Actual	6.6	11.3	13.8	7.6	9.4	10.5
	1972	1973	1974	1975	1976	Average
Third FYP	9.0	8.5	8.5	8.5	8.5	8.6
Actual	5.8	14.9	8.0	7.1	13.6	11.2
	1977	1978	1979	1980	1981	Average
Fourth FYP	10.0	9.0	9.0	9.0	9.0	9.2
Actual	10.3	11.6	6.4	−6.2	6.6	4.3
	1982	1983	1984	1985	1986	Average
Fifth FYP	8.0	7.5	7.5	7.5	7.5	7.6
Revised FYP	5.6	9.3	7.5	7.5	7.5	8.0
Actual	7.2	12.6	9.3	7.0	12.9	10.4
	1987	1988	1989	1990	1991	Average
Sixth FYP	7.1	7.1	7.1	7.1	7.1	7.1
Actual	9.1	11.5	6.2	9.2	8.4	8.9
	1992	1993	1994	1995	1996	Average
Seventh FYP	7.5	7.5	7.5	7.5	7.5	7.5
Actual	5.0	4.5	7.7	n.a.	n.a.	n.a.

Note: Numbers are annual real GDP growth rates.
Source: Data for the first five plans is from Paul W. Kuznets, "Indicative Planning in Korea," *Journal of Comparative Economics* 14 (1990), p. 670, and for the remaining two is constructed from the same source, p. 662; Asian Development Bank, *Asian Development Outlook 1992* (Hong Kong: Oxford University Press, 1992) p. 84; Economist Intelligence Unit, *Country Report: South Korea,* No. 1 (1993), p. 3; and Dilip K. Das, *Korean Economic Dynamism* (New York: St. Martin's Press, 1992), p. 3. Actual growth figures for 1993 and 1994 are from *The Economist,* various issues.

The Third FYP (1972–76) emphasized balanced regional development and improved quality of life for workers,[48] focusing on rural development through the "new village movement" to utilize excess rural labor for rural revitalization. It had a prescriptive rather than indicative drive to build up heavy and chemical industries, which was implemented partly by the government taking over the banks and directly controlling investment, a policy many thought was overdone. Plan performance exceeded targets, despite the first oil price shock, but foreign borrowing left the ROK with a large foreign debt burden that remains today.

---

[48]The latter was Park's follow-up to his banning independent labor unions in 1971 after a series of strikes. In 1972 he declared himself President for Life. The lack of peaceful and equitable labor market dispute-resolution mechanisms is a continuing problem.

The Fourth FYP (1977–81) was the only one completed so far to fall short of its targets. Industrial policy shifted towards electronics, machinery, and shipbuilding, with lower foreign borrowing. The second oil price shock combined with the political upheavals following President Park's assassination by the Korean CIA director in 1979 to sandbag this plan. 1980 was the only year since the Korean War that the ROK had negative economic growth. General Chun Doo-hwan seized power in 1980 and ruled until voluntarily retiring in 1988.

After Park's death planning shifted back towards more indicativeness and less prescriptiveness.[49] The Fifth FYP (1982–87) had similar sectoral goals as the previous plan, adding price stabilization, regional equality and social welfare, and the encouragement of competitive market forces, the latter directed at the powerful chaebol. This plan exceeded its targets aided by declining oil prices, declining world interest rates, and the appreciation of the yen. Japan is the ROK's largest trading partner after the United States and has been its leading source of licensed technology.[50]

The Sixth FYP (1987–91) expanded welfare state programs and emphasized domestic research and development. It also called for liberalization of the financial system, which had been strictly controlled,[51] including partial reprivatization of the banks, while curbing ongoing real estate speculation. It also exceeded its targets.

The Seventh FYP (1992–96) moves further towards high technology and greater free marketization with the new democratic regime of Kim Young Sam in power. During 1992 and 1993 this plan was below its target, but was above it again in 1994.

Debates over the role of indicative planning resemble debates in other countries with such planning. Critics charge that sectoral targets have been wildly off and that outperforming planned targets proves the uselessness of plans rather than their effectiveness. They also point out that when planning had a strong element of command in the 1970s, inefficiencies arose as investment became overly focused on heavy industry and chemicals.[52] Defenders of South Korean planning claim beneficial effects of the information-sharing mechanism arising from the planning process similar to

---

[49]Atsuko Ueda ("Growth Model of 'Miracle' in Korea: An Application of Numerical Analysis," mimeo, Department of Economics, University of Wisconsin-Madison 1993) supports this conclusion, finding that during the 1970s the growth path deviated substantially from that of a competitive equilibrium, but that since then it has been much closer to competitive equilibrium.

[50]Amsden, *Asia's Next Giant,* p. 233.

[51]Changes include partial opening of South Korean financial markets to foreigners while delinking the won from the U.S. dollar. The won and ROK interest rates appear increasingly influenced by the Japanese yen and Japanese financial markets, although the United States still has a greater influence in the ROK than in any of the other NICs where Japan is apparently now completely financially dominant (Jeffrey A. Frankel, "Foreign Exchange Policy, Monetary Policy and Capital Market Liberalization in Korea," Center for International and Development Economics Research Working Paper No. C93–008, University of California at Berkeley, 1993).

[52]Paul W. Kuznets, "Indicative Planning in Korea."

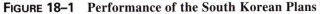

FIGURE 18-1   **Performance of the South Korean Plans**

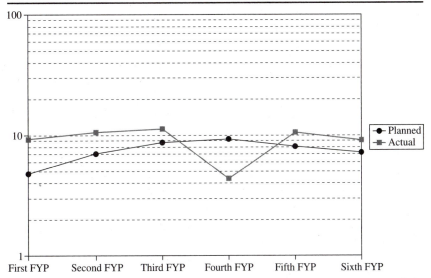

Source: Data for the first five plans is from Paul W. Kuznets, ''Indicative Planning in Korea,'' *Journal of Comparative Economics* 14 (1990), p. 670, and for the remaining two is constructed from the same source, p. 662; Asian Development Bank, *Asian Development Outlook 1992* (Hong Kong: Oxford University Press, 1992) p. 84; Economist Intelligence Unit, *Country Report: South Korea,* No. 1 (1993), p. 3; and Dilip K. Das, *Korean Economic Dynamism* (New York: St. Martin's Press, 1992), p. 3. Actual growth figures for 1993 and 1994 are from *The Economist,* various issues.

that in French-style concertation as discussed in Chapter 8.[53] But the recent trend has been toward looser indicative planning.

South Korea's high degree of state intervention relative to the other NICs reflects its higher levels of industrial concentration due to the chaebol.[54] Domination of the ROK economy by a small number of large firms simplifies gathering information and coordinating between planners and decision-making managers. The chaebol have benefitted from this planning, particularly its industrial policy aspect.

Industrial Policy and the Chaebol[55]

South Korea has followed Japan with respect to industrial policy, viewing imitation as key to competing with the former colonial master. In both, the pattern of exports and imports has evolved as each country climbed a developmental

---

[53]Il KaSong, ''Indicative Planning in South Korea: Discussion,'' *Journal of Comparative Economics* 14 (1990), pp. 677–80.

[54]The average percent of market share in an industry held by the three largest firms (''three firm concentration ratio'') in the ROK in 1981 was 62.0 percent, in Japan in 1980 was 56.3 percent, and in Taiwan in 1981 was 49.2 percent (Amsden, *Asia's Next Giant,* p. 122). Aggregate concentration appears to be rising in South Korea, holding steady in Taiwan, and declining slightly in Japan.

[55]Sometimes transliterated as *jaibul,* which more accurately indicates its pronunciation.

ladder from exporting primary commodities and low-skill labor-intensive products to exporting higher skill, high-technology ones. In both countries infant industry protectionism has been used, often backed by state-directed investment, until the next targeted industry achieved a certain level of development and exports.

The Korean pattern of development has involved decade-long spurts. During 1946–53 the country produced mostly simple commodities and imported many goods. During 1954–62 the import substitution strategy was uppermost. During 1963–72 labor-intensive light industries led export expansion. During 1973–82 emphasis was on capital-intensive heavy industries. During 1983–92 came the shift to technology-intensive industries based on the high technical education of the population—the number of scientists and engineers rose between 1953 and 1986 from 4,157 to 361,330—and from exploding R&D spending, which rose between 1971 and 1986 from 10.67 billion won to 1,523.28 billion won.[56]

From 1963 to 1987 the percentage of food and live animal exports fell from 21.6 to 4.3 and of industrial raw materials exports fell from 28.4 to 1.6, while the percentage of engineering products exports rose from 5.7 to 41.9.[57] The driving engines of this expansion were the chaebol.

The chaebol are more like Japan's prewar zaibatsu than the modern keiretsu. Like the keiretsu they are technically groups of companies[58] rather than a single conglomerate. But all the companies in the group are entirely owned by a single family, thus making them more like the zaibatsu. The major difference between the chaebol and both Japanese forms is that the latter had or have a bank at their base whereas that is not the case for the chaebol. For an extended period of time all the banks in South Korea were state owned, making the chaebol dependent on directing state credit institutions.[59]

The major chaebol developed in two generations. Samsung and Lucky-Goldstar are the largest of the first generation, which began during the Syngman Rhee regime in the 1950s. The second generation began in the 1960s under the Park regime, and Hyundai and Daewoo are its largest members. A few chaebol developed out of old firms founded by Japanese capitalists, Sunkyong being the largest of these. In 1982 these five were the largest chaebol in the ROK by sales, their rank order being Hyundai, Sunkyong, Daewoo, Samsung, and Lucky-Goldstar.

---

[56]E. Willmot and M. Thorpe, "Korean Economic Development: Export Composition and Performance," Curtin School of Economics & Finance Paper 92.16, University of Technology, Perth, 1992, p. 6. High-technology goods that South Korea now produces are supercomputers, fingerprint recognition devices, double video machines, high-volume workstations, HDTV, and satellites.

[57]Marcus Noland, *Pacific Basin Developing Countries,* p. 50.

[58]In 1988 the largest chaebol, Hyundai, consisted of 33 technically independent companies.

[59]Part of Kim Young Sam's anticorruption drive has been to outlaw the use of false names in bank accounts and other financial dealings. Ironically this has dried up the major source of funds for curbside moneylenders who have financed small businesses, thus slowing economic growth. The major state-controlled banks focus their lending on the chaebol.

The share of all exports from the nine largest chaebol trading companies rose from 13 percent in 1975 to 54.2 percent in 1984.[60] The share of GDP attributable to the 10 largest chaebol rose from 15.1 percent in 1974 to 67.4 percent in 1984, the three largest alone responsible for 35.8 percent of 1984 GDP,[61] an almost unheard-of degree of concentration in a market economy.

The chaebol were encouraged under Rhee and Park, especially if they went along with government plans under Park. But concern about concentration led under Chun to pressure to open up ownership to the public and to sell some less related subsidiaries. Pressure on the chaebol has intensified under Kim Young Sam because of links between them and the previous military regimes, especially on Hyundai, largest of them all.[62]

Despite these efforts, domination of the ROK economy by the chaebol is likely to continue. The most likely mechanism for ending chaebol domination would be if they fail to grow while new firms grow faster. This has been the pattern in the United States and other mature industrialized economies where older and larger firms have often lost their dynamism. This pattern represents a possible threat to South Korea's dreams of continued rapid growth, especially relative to other NICs, such as Taiwan, with comparable levels of education but much lower levels of industrial concentration.

South Korea among the NICs

Among the rapidly growing East Asian economies are four subgroups based on relative per capita incomes. These subgroups exhibit a Gerschenkronian relationship with each other: Growth rates tend to decelerate for the highest income East Asian economies and to be higher for the lowest income ones. At the top is Japan, the regional leader, which was recently in an outright recession as discussed in Chapter 6. At the bottom is the world's currently most rapidly growing economy, the People's Republic of China, as discussed in Chapter 15. The second highest group is the upper tier of NICs: Hong Kong, Singapore, Taiwan, and the ROK. The lower tier of NICs, lying below them but above China, includes Thailand, Malaysia, and Indonesia.

Table 18–3 presents data on the characteristics and performance of the seven upper and lower tier NICs. Generally the ROK compares well with its fellow upper tier NICs except for its foreign indebtedness. The growth rate figures for 1981–90 seem to contradict the statement above regarding the Gerschenkronian relationship between them. The higher tier grew more rapidly than the lower tier. However that has not held during the 1990s, and the lower tier, at least Thailand and Malaysia, has recently grown faster than the upper tier.

Within the upper tier of NICs Taiwan and South Korea are closer to each other than to the other members in many ways. Hong Kong and Singapore are

---

[60]Dong Sung Cho, ''Government, Entrepreneurs and Competition,'' in *Doing Business in Korea,* ed. A.M. Whitehall (London: Croom Helm, 1987), pp. 80–93.

[61]Amsden, *Asia's Next Giant,* p. 116.

[62]Hyundai compounds in countries outside of South Korea are run like military compounds. Hyundai has experienced bitter strikes in recent years.

The Evolution of a Chaebol: Lucky-Goldstar

How the growth of the ROK economy has intersected with that of the chaebol can be seen by considering Lucky-Goldstar.* Founded as a cosmetic cream company in the late 1940s, it branched into plastics to supply itself with plastic caps for its cream jars. Plastics led it to produce combs, toothbrushes, and soap boxes, and later to electrical and electronic and telecommunication equipment. To supply inputs it got into oil refining and then tanker shipping. The high insurance costs of oil refining led it to start an insurance company. Energy, chemicals, and electronics will be Lucky-Goldstar's future growth areas with emphasis on fine chemicals, genetic engineering, semiconductor manufacturing, fiber optic communications, and satellite telecommunications. Thus the group evolves through a step-by-step evolution of related businesses.

*Alice H. Amsden, *Asia's Next Giant* (New York: Oxford University Press, 1989), p. 126.

TABLE 18–3   Comparative Economic Data for East Asian NICs

Country	Population	GDP Per Capita	GDP Growth	Inflation Rate	Export Growth	Government Share	Debt Service
ROK	43.2	5,400	9.9	6.4	18.2	16.4	12.0
Hong Kong	5.8	11,540	7.1	8.2	21.9	16.7	0.0
Singapore	2.7	12,310	6.3	2.3	18.3	21.0	0.0
Taiwan	20.5	8,000	8.5	3.1	16.9	15.9	0.0
Indonesia	168.1	550	5.5	8.6	8.8	21.6	28.4
Malaysia	18.2	2,320	5.2	3.2	15.7	30.6	11.0
Thailand	57.5	1,420	7.8	4.4	25.7	14.8	15.1

Note: Population is in millions for mid-year 1991. GDP per capita is in U.S. dollars for 1990. GDP growth is annual average percent rate for 1981–90. Inflation rate is annual average percent rate of change of CPI for 1981–90. Export growth is annual average percent rate of change for 1986–91. Government share is average percent of GDP that is government expenditures for 1991. Debt service is the ratio of foreign debt-service payments to export earnings as a percent for 1991.

Source: Figures from Asian Development Bank, *Asian Development Outlook 1992* (Hong Kong: Oxford University Press, 1992), Statistical Notes.

both almost completely urban with virtually upper income status, whereas Taiwan and South Korea are still middle-income countries with substantial rural sectors. Taiwan and South Korea also share having been Japanese colonies prior to 1945, being the capitalist portions of systemically divided nations, and having recently moved towards democratization of their political systems.

Important differences between them include that relative to Taiwan, South Korea has fewer small businesses, a lower savings rate, a less equal income distribution, more borrowing from abroad, less agricultural production, more state ownership of enterprises, less direct foreign investment, more regulation of industry, a more overvalued exchange rate, a more closed and restricted credit market, more controlled markets, and more real estate speculation.[63]

The Economies of North and South Korea Directly Compared

General Observations

Directly comparing the two Korean economies is very close to being a controlled experiment given the common cultural heritage and fairly similar geographic conditions of the two.[64] Their major differences are their respective economic and political systems. This comparison is hampered by the paucity of reliable data for the secretive North.

Despite a few surprises, notably in the area of agriculture, the generalizations about the two systems apply well to the DPRK and the ROK. Current real per capita incomes and growth rates are much higher in the ROK, as is its volume of exports and general integration into the world economy. The last is unsurprising given the juche isolationism of the DPRK. The ROK has a more diversified economy, with more variety of consumer goods, high-technology goods, and services, whereas the DPRK retains a greater focus on heavy industry and military production.

The DPRK has a more equal distribution of income and greater gender equality. Until recently, material index of living standards in the DPRK compared well with those in the ROK, despite the growing disparity in real per capita incomes and a recent apparent deterioration in the North.

Despite these contrasts the two Koreas have much in common economically, a fact that may yet be important if they unify. They share deep Confucian

---

[63]Sung Moon Pae, *Korea Leading Developing Nations: Economy, Democracy, & Welfare* (Lanham: University Press of America, 1992), p. 106.

[64]There are greater geographical differences between these two than between eastern and western Germany, the former favorite subjects of comparative economists for such studies. The North is more richly endowed in mineral and hydroelectric resources. Because of its colder climate it grows more wheat whereas the South grows more rice. Hence the South has had a much denser population than the North, reaching a rural peak in the long-rebellious, southwestern Cholla provinces. Also, the South has Seoul, far larger than any city in the North.

traditions and the competitive spirit of *Hahn,* the latter stimulated by the decades-long competition between them as well as their shared resentment of Japan. They possess the two hardest working labor forces in the world as measured by average length of work week.[65] Also they share a respect for education that has led to nearly universal literacy as well as very rapid rates of growth of high-tech education among their populations. The ROK in particular has a higher percentage of its student-age population in college (36 percent in 1988, 23 percent in the DPRK) than any countries except the United States and Canada.[66]

Growth of Per Capita GDP

Table 18–4 and Figure 18–2 show per capita GDP for the North and the South respectively for various years from 1945 to 1992. North and South Korea use different measures because in traditional socialist fashion the DPRK does not count services. Correcting ROK numbers for this would reduce them by about a third, still leaving a very large gap between the two in 1992, even presuming that these estimates of DPRK GDP are accurate, which is highly questionable. The two started out fairly equal and were about equal at the end of the Korean War. The North surged ahead for a decade, but then the South moved ahead after 1975, leaving the North in the dust. Given that the ROK has about twice the population of the DPRK, the difference in aggregate GDPs is that much more pronounced.

Composition of Output

The two economies contrast sharply in the composition of their respective outputs between industry, agriculture, and services. Whereas services declined sharply from 33.3 percent of GDP in 1956 to 5 percent in 1982 and industry increased from 40.1 percent to 70 percent of GDP with agriculture holding steady in the DPRK, services rose from 40.3 percent to 53.1 percent and industry increased from 12.5 percent to 30.7 percent for the same years in the ROK with agriculture declining from 47.2 percent to 16.2 percent.[67]

A surprise in available data is the strong performance in agriculture by North Korea relative to South Korea. The UN Food and Agriculture Organization reports an average annual overall rate of growth of agricultural output from 1970 to 1987 of 4.53 percent for North Korea compared with 2.39 percent for South Korea.[68] Even if the DPRK's number is exaggerated as is likely,[69]

---

[65]Amsden, *Asia's Next Giant,* p. 205. This long work week was introduced by the Japanese who had imitated Europe when it first began industrializing. Both in Europe and in Japan work weeks have shortened, but they have not done so in either Korea.

[66]Kim, *Two Koreas in Development,* p. 91.

[67]Kim, *Two Koreas in Development,* p. 75.

[68]Frederic L. Pryor, *The Red and the Green: The Rise and Fall of Collectivized Agriculture in Marxist Regimes* (Princeton: Princeton University Press, 1992), p. 251.

[69]The reports in 1993 of food riots and the 1995 emergency rice imports from the South suggest that not all is well in DPRK agriculture. There are other reports of rising grain imports and "food rations barely above starvation levels" (Economist Intelligence Unit, *North Korea,* pp. 35, 38).

TABLE 18–4   Per Capita GDP in North and South Korea

Year	North	South
1945	36	25–50
1949	72	67
1953	56	55
1960	208	60
1965	292	88
1970	312	264
1975	605	518
1980	1,000	1,553
1985	1,192	2,177
1988	1,260	3,850
1992	1,096	6,897

Source: Figures through 1988 are from Byoung-Lo Kim, *Two Koreas in Development* (New Brunswick: Transaction Publishers, 1992), p. 67, and for 1992 are estimated from Economist Intelligence Unit, *Country Report: North Korea,* No. 1 (1993), p. 5 and *Country Report: South Korea,* No. 1 (1993), p. 3, in current U.S. dollars.

FIGURE 18–2   Per Capita GDP (in current U.S. $) for North and South Korea

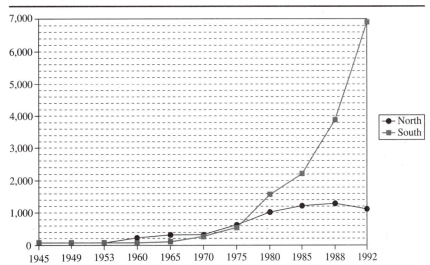

Source: Figures through 1988 are from Byoung-Lo Kim, *Two Koreas in Development* (New Brunswick: Transaction Publishers, 1992), p. 67, and for 1992 are estimated from Economist Intelligence Unit, *Country Report: North Korea,* No. 1 (1993), p. 5 and *Country Report: South Korea,* No. 1 (1993), p. 3, in current U.S. dollars.

collectivized agriculture held its own in the North relative to the free market farming in the South, at least to 1987 . The Marx-Stalin vision of the economies of scale available to collectivized agriculture may have worked there. Another explanation involves respective policy choices—the juche policy in the North stimulated food self-sufficiency whereas the South emphasized exporting manufactures and importing food after 1964.

TABLE 18–5   **Agricultural Output in the North and the South**

Product	North	South
Rice	6,200	5,905
Wheat and rye	893	5
Potatoes	1,950	450
Sweet potatoes	494	542
Beef and veal	41	196
Pork	165	368
Poultry meat	42	183
Fish catch	1,700	3,660

Note: Figures are in thousands of metric tons and are for 1987, except for fish, which are for 1986.
Source: Figures from Byoung-Lo Kim, *Two Koreas in Development* (New Brunswick: Transaction Publishers, 1992), p. 76.

Table 18–5 shows outputs of various agricultural products in 1987 for the two economies. The comparison results in a generalization (which coincides with comparisons between private market and collectivized command agriculture elsewhere) that the North's performance was better in grains, notably in producing some that the South has a natural advantage in such as rice, but that the South's performance has been better in animal products. Thus, although the North had a higher per capita calorie supply than the South,[70] the opposite is almost certainly true with respect to per capita protein supply in 1987. But this was probably the year of the North's best relative performance, as Table 18–1 shows a 4.5 percent annual decline in grain production thereafter, culminating in the 1995 crisis with emergency rice imports from the south.

Social Indicators and the Distribution of Income

Internationally published data suggest few differences in basic social indicators. There are the expected consumption differences: Southerners have many more automobiles, TV sets, and better clothing; northerners have more public transportation, pay less for housing, and have more doctors per capita.[71] Life expectancy in 1988 in the South of 70 years slightly exceeded that in the North of 69 years.[72] Overall, Physical Quality of Life Index estimated by the Overseas Development Council for the World Bank for the two in 1985 were identical at 86 out of a possible 100.[73]

---

[70]Byoung-Lo Philo Kim, *Two Koreas in Development*, p. 90.

[71]Kim, *Two Koreas in Development*, chap. 5.

[72]Hwang, *The Korean Economies*, p. 126.

[73]Sung Moon Pae, *Korea Leading Developing Nations*, Appendix A. Japan received 100. Countries receiving 99 were Sweden, Iceland, France, and Australia. Scores ranged as low as 6 for Sierra Leone.

The distribution of income is reported as more equal in the DPRK than in the ROK. In 1988 the decile ratio for the DPRK was 5.83 and for the ROK was 13.73.[74] Inequality in the South increased as the Gini coefficient indicates—it rose from 0.332 in 1970 to 0.389 in 1980,[75] but has declined somewhat since then, despite apparent continuing increases in property income inequality.[76]

Even lacking definitive data, there is almost certainly greater gender equality in the North than in the South. The ROK in 1980 had the lowest ratio of women's wages to men's of any country in the world, 44.5 percent.[77] This reflects large educational and work experience differences between the sexes in South Korea following a strong paternalistic/sexist element in traditional Korean Confucianist society where husbands have dominated wives to an extreme degree.[78] Although gender inequality persists in the DPRK, there has long been a movement to remove it and the women's labor force participation rate rose from 20 percent in 1956 to 48 percent in 1976.[79]

International Trade

One reason for the growing gap in incomes between the two Koreas is the contrast between the export orientation of the ROK and the juche-based self-reliance of the DPRK. This encourages the technological dynamism of the South compared with the increasing stagnation of the North. Table 18–6 tracks the time path of exports and imports in the two Koreas.

Particularly serious for the North is that Russia and China, its top two trading partners, were letting it run up debts in trade but have ceased to do so. The DPRK must now earn its hard currency. That it will be difficult to do so can be seen by looking at its exports, which in 1985 to its main capitalist market, Japan, were in order, gold, zinc, fresh vegetables simply preserved, iron and simple steel coils, anthracite coal, and shellfish. These are not rapid growth industries in contrast to the high-technology engineering and consumer products that dominate South Korea's export mix.[80]

---

[74]Kim, *Two Koreas in Development*, p. 95. DPRK numbers do not capture nomenklatura perks and income in kind. ''Fat revisionist,'' Kim Il Sung and his son, Kim Chong Il, led lavish lifestyles, and the upper reaches of the party and government are packed with their relatives, Kim Chong Il's rivals for power including his stepmother and half brother. He is reputed to hand out expensive French cognac to allies. But, the false name bank accounts in the ROK mean that the incomes of the most wealthy have not been fully identified there either.

[75]Das, *Korean Economic Dynamism*, p. 104.

[76]Hwang, *The Korean Economies*, p. 136.

[77]Amsden, *Asia's Next Giant*, p. 204.

[78]Osgood, *The Koreans*, p. 47.

[79]Changsoo Lee, ''Social Policy and Development in North Korea,'' in *North Korea Today*, p. 124.

[80]Economist Intelligence Unit, South Korea, Appendix 2.

TABLE 18–6   Foreign Trade of the North and the South

	North		South	
Year	*Exports*	*Imports*	*Exports*	*Imports*
1970	365	396	835	1,984
1975	814	1,093	5,081	7,274
1979	1,150	1,160	15,056	20,339
1985	1,380	1,720	30,283	31,136
1989	1,690	2,900	62,400	61,500
1991	1,400	2,310	71,900	81,500

Source: Figures through 1985 are from Byoung-Lo Philo Kim, *Two Koreas in Development* (New Brunswick: Transaction Publishers, 1992), p. 81, and for 1989 and 1991 are from Economist Intelligence Unit, *Country Report: North Korea,* No. 1 (1993), p. 5 and *Country Report: South Korea,* No. 1 (1993), p. 3, and are in millions of U.S. dollars.

The Threat of War and the Hope for Unification

Although South Korea surges ahead of North Korea economically, the DPRK retains a clear lead in one important area, accumulated military hardware and armed forces. The only hope it has of unifying Korea under its control is through military conquest. Compared to the South, the North has nearly twice the number of men under arms (1,132,000 to 633,000), nearly twice as many tanks and combat aircraft, and far more armed helicopters and submarines. Their forces are deployed in an offensive stance near the border.[81] Combined with the North's possible acquisition of nuclear weapons and the uncertainties arising from the apparent power struggle since Kim Il Sung's death, this increasing disjuncture is the main source of threat of a possible outbreak of war on the Korean peninsula.

But peaceful unification is possible, both Koreas sharing a deep nationalism.[82] Their economies are broadly complementary and could fit together, if the political and economic difficulties of transition could be handled. That the latter would be serious is seen by the high costs in Germany where the income gap was not as great as it is between the two Koreas.

There is also the problem of the profound isolation of the North Korean people and their continuing absorption in the Cult of Personality of Kim Il Sung. Even with him dead, it will take time for them to come out of their trance.

---

[81]Figures from the International Institute of Strategic Studies as reported in *The Economist,* "North Korea's Nuclear Stand-Off," April 3, 1993, pp. 38–39. The South has a slight edge in warships, a general and increasing technological and qualitative edge, and the support of 40,000 U.S. troops.

[82]They were simultaneously admitted to the UN in 1991.

Box 18–2

The South Korean Plan for Unification

The ROK Ministry of Finance has studied what they should do if there is a peaceful unification on the South's terms around the year 2000, drawing on the German experience.*

First, they think the two currencies should not be exchanged at par. The DPRK won currently trades for several hundred times less than the ROK won. An appropriate exchange rate that will not immediately bankrupt all northern industry without utterly degrading the northerners is more difficult to establish than it was in Germany.

Second, they wish to limit migration of northerners to the South. This will be politically and practically very difficult to manage without engendering extreme resentment.

Third, they propose to renationalize all land in the North and then to sell it or lease it as quickly as possible. Land is already nationalized, but they wish to preempt any claims by previous owners like those bogging down real estate privatization in eastern Germany.

Finally, they propose financing the costs of unification by foreign borrowing, problematical given the ROK's continuing large foreign debt burden. Although the domestic savings rate is high, the tax rate is low. The desire to avoid raising taxes led to this proposal. But Chancellor Kohl's promise not to raise taxes had to be embarrassingly rescinded after much havoc was created. That this is a *very* serious issue is seen by the enormous size of the adjustment costs, estimated to be around U.S. $980 billion. No wonder the South Koreans hesitate.

---

*Economist Intelligence Unit, *Country Report: North Korea,* No. 1 (1993), pp. 28–29.

Summary and Conclusions

The two Koreas represent the sharpest continuing contrast between a command socialist economy and a largely market capitalist one. This contrast coincides with the extreme political and military tension that exists between the two, a lingering shadow of the Cold War.

Korea was divided at the end of World War II after being ruled by Japan from 1910 to 1945. Japan had displaced an isolationist Confucianist regime. The division led to war from 1950 to 1953, in which the United States and China significantly participated. The war left both Koreas economically devastated.

Initially after the war the North grew more rapidly than the South economically. The North was ruled during 1946–1994 by Kim Il Sung who instituted Stalinist command socialism, modified by the self-reliance doctrine of juche and Maoist moral incentives campaigns. The South was ruled during 1948–60 by Syngman Rhee, whose postwar regime was marked by corruption and mismanagement.

South Korean growth took off after the introduction of indicative planning combined with a general macroeconomic stabilization under the military dictatorship of Park Chung-hee from 1961 to 1979. With the exception of the tumultuous postassassination year of 1980, the South Korean growth rate has probably exceeded that of the North since around 1963.

Whereas North Korea has pursued an inward-looking isolationist strategy reminiscent of the 19th century Hermit Kingdom, South Korea has pursued an outward-looking, export-led strategy of growth similar to that of Japan and its fellow East Asian NICs. Whereas the North has had a fair agricultural performance until recently and strong heavy industrial output, the South has evolved from exporting simple light manufactures to high-technology electronics and consumer products, largely produced by the giant chaebol. Whereas the North appears to have greater income and gender equality, the South has recently moved towards significant political democratization and is currently carrying out a vigorous anticorruption campaign.

Despite their obvious differences North and South Korea share many characteristics, including a strong nationalism partly rooted in a shared resentment of Japan for its past colonial rule. Both Koreas manifest their deep Confucian heritage in drives to hard work and great respect for education, which both have intensely pursued. Thus, despite their intense competition and the threat of a new Korean War, they may eventually achieve their mutually longed-for reunification.

Unless the unification is achieved by a northern military conquest, it will be carried out on the South's terms, given its overwhelming economic and diplomatic predominance. The South hesitates, observing the difficulties experienced in Germany. Nevertheless, the economic potential of a unified Korea is considerable, although it will remain the smaller brother caught between the Chinese and Japanese giants. Eventual unification on the South's terms may finally end that chapter in human history known as the Cold War.

Questions for Discussion

1. Compare and contrast the Confucian elements in the North and South Korean economies.
2. Compare and contrast North Korean *juche* with the Stalinist and Maoist economic models.
3. Compare and contrast South Korean indicative planning with indicative planning in Japan and France.
4. Compare and contrast the South Korean *chaebol* with the Japanese zaibatsu and keiretsu.

5. How and why is South Korean industrial policy changing?

6. Compare and contrast the South Korean economy with that of Taiwan. What are their positions relative to the other East Asian NICs?

7. How might the democratization movement in South Korea both slow and stimulate economic growth?

8. Why did North Korea surpass South Korea economically in the 1950s and 1960s? Why has it lost that lead and fallen far behind since?

9. Despite recent difficulties, one area where North Korea has done surprisingly well relative to South Korea has been in agriculture. How can the pattern of their respective performances be explained?

10. How does a comparison of the North and South Korean economies resemble and differ from the comparison between the former East and West German economies?

11. How have the South Korean plans for possible unification with North Korea been influenced by the German example?

12. What are the prospects for a unified Korea to become a major world economic power. Why or why not?

Suggested Further Readings

Amsden, Alice H. *Asia's Next Giant: South Korea and Late Industrialization.* New York: Oxford University Press, 1989.

Clifford, Mark L. *Troubled Tiger: Businessmen, Bureaucrats, and Generals in South Korea.* Armonk: M.E. Sharpe, 1994.

Hwang, Eui-Gak. *The Korean Economies: A Comparison of North and South.* Oxford: Clarendon Press, 1993.

Kang, Myoung-Kyu, and Keun Lee. ''Industrial Systems and Reform in North Korea: A Comparison with China.'' *World Development,* 20 (1992), pp. 947–58.

Kim, Byoung-Lo Philo. *Two Koreas in Development: A Comparative Study of Principles and Strategies of Capitalist and Communist Third World Development.* New Brunswick: Transaction Publishers, 1992.

Kuznets, Paul W. ''Indicative Planning in Korea,'' *Journal of Comparative Economics* 14 (1990), pp. 657–76.

Lee, C.-S., and S.-H. Yoo, eds. *North Korea in Transition.* Berkeley: University of California: Institute of East Asian Studies, 1991.

Lee, Keun. *New East Asian Economic Development: Interacting Captialism and Socialism.* Armonk: M.E. Sharpe, 1993.

Nahm, Andrew C. *Korea, Tradition and Transformation: A History of the Korean People.* Elizabeth: Hollym International, 1988.

Noland, Marcus. *Pacific Basin Developing Countries.* Washington: Institute for International Economics, 1990.

Pae, Sung Moon. *Korea Leading Developing Nations: Economy, Democracy, &*

19

FUTURE TRENDS OF THE TRANSFORMING WORLD ECONOMY

Henceforth books on comparative economic systems will be found on the shelves dealing with economic development.
—Yegor Gaidar (1992 address to the International Economic Association, Moscow)

It is better to hang together than to hang separately.
—Benjamin Franklin (1776 during the debate on the Declaration of Independence, U.S. Continental Congress, Philadelphia)

Introduction

This concluding chapter neither attempts to summarize what has been presented so far nor to draw definitive conclusions. Rather it deals with certain general trends and loose ends without a concluding section. The transformation process of the world economy is far too complex and profound for simplistic summaries or statements.

It should be clear that history is not at an end. When Yegor Gaidar made the remarks quoted above he was Acting Premier of Russia in charge of a radical program of moving toward market capitalism in Russia, former fountainhead of world communism. Gaidar is out and his successors are stumbling rather than rushing towards his former goal, and possibly going in reverse. In much of the reforming socialist world, successors to the former Communist parties have been democratically elected with mandates to slow, if not reverse the process. Although China continues to move towards marketization, its most substantial sector is the local market socialist one of town and village enterprises. In East Asia indicatively planned, neo-Confucianist economies thrive, and in the Islamic world fundamentalist movements with uncertain state-market balances continue to spread. The future is less certain than when Fukuyama wrote.

The Trend to Privatization and Its Limits: The Case of Great Britain

Despite hesitations and confusion, the global trend to market capitalism is indisputably entrenched and ongoing in most of the world, including in the mixed market capitalist economies. Transformation towards market-oriented economies has been the easier part and there are now only a few nations left, such as North Korea, where markets are effectively inoperative.

But in nations ranging from Poland to China the process of privatization has proceeded slowly with a variety of problems and difficulties. A few formerly socialist nations have succeeded in implementing mass privatizations, notably the former East Germany, the Czech Republic, Mongolia, and Russia. Except for the German case the others used mass voucher schemes resulting in arrangements of uncertain long-run stability or arrangements that involve large amounts of worker or manager ownership, notably in Russia and Mongolia.[1]

In discussing Poland's economy in Chapter 12, the variety of privatization methods from mass voucher schemes to selling shares of state-owned firms in open stock markets were presented. Selling shares is the standard approach in market capitalist economies with functioning stock markets. Motives for privatizing and limits to the process will be seen by examining the process in Great Britain, the United Kingdom (UK). This privatization drive was part of a broader movement known as *Thatcherism*, after Margaret Thatcher, British prime minister from 1979 to 1990.[2]

The motive of Thatcherism was to reform and revive an apparently moribund and stagnant economy. Although it had generally positive long-term real per capita economic growth after World War II, the UK's performance lagged that of other major market capitalist economies leading to relative decline. Whereas the UK led the world economy in the 19th century as the source of the Industrial Revolution and maintained a lead in both aggregate and per capita GDP as late as the 1870s when the United States and Germany surpassed it, its relative position has steadily declined since to seventh or eighth place in aggregate GDP globally[3] and sixteenth in per capita terms, with even its colony of Hong Kong surpassing it on a purchasing power parity (PPP) basis.[4]

---

[1]Although the Russian scheme was designed to achieve such an outcome, that in Mongolia was not. Vouchers were distributed to the general public who were allowed to buy shares of firms directly. But the Mongolians heavily bought shares of firms in which they or their close relatives worked.

[2]Thatcherism preceded and inspired Reaganomics in the United States under President Ronald Reagan (1981–1989), despite differences in approaches. Reagan's program had less emphasis on privatization because there was little state ownership of enterprises in the United States in 1981 in contrast to the United Kingdom in 1979. Reaganomics has had a second wind since the 1994 U.S. congressional election.

[3]Ahead of it are the United States, Japan, China, Germany, France, Italy, and, if one allows a purchasing power parity accounting, Russia. These are its fellow G-7 members plus China and Russia and minus Canada.

[4]World Bank, *World Development Report 1994* (New York: Oxford University Press, 1994), Tables 1 and 30. The UK is sixteenth in both nominal and PPP per capita measures.

The sources of this relative decline are numerous. Hypothesized causes include a failure of entrepreneurship with accompanying technological slowdown,[5] excessive class conflicts resulting in too many strikes,[6] excessive slowness to join the European Union because of nostalgia for the dead British Empire, and a past special relationship with the United States and the costs of past "imperial overreach."[7]

A theory compatible with the Thatcherite position is that of Mancur Olson,[8] discussed in Chapter 2. Olson argues that the longer a nation goes without a major revolution, defeat, or general shakeup, the stronger will become rent-seeking special interest groups who generate laws and institutions to satisfy their rent seeking, which eventually drains away economic vitality. In the Olson view, the UK has not had a serious shakeup since the 1066 invasion by William the Conqueror, although the English Revolution and Oliver Cromwell's rule in the mid-1600s created a flurry despite the subsequent Restoration. This entrenchment of rent-seeking groups culminated with the Labor Party government of the late 1940s, which nationalized much industry and introduced welfare state elements such as socialized medicine. It was this legacy which Thatcher sought to overthrow after 1979.

Central to this effort was her privatization drive. The most popular part of this was privatizing public housing to current inhabitants.[9] Industrial firms were privatized by selling shares in the existing stock markets, often with vigorous publicity campaigns designed to attract many buyers in the spirit of *popular capitalism,* including some encouragement of workers to buy into their own firms, although with little effort at formal ESOPs until the late 1980s. The largest enterprises sold in this manner were British Telecom, British Gas, Rolls Royce, British Airports Authority, large portions of British Petroleum, Britoil, British Airways, and Cable and Wireless.[10] Overall the share of the public sector in the capital stock declined from 44.1 percent to 30.6 percent between 1979 and 1989 and its share of GDP declined from 27.2 percent

---

[5]This is despite generating the second largest number of Nobel Prize science winners after the United States. A break has developed in the UK between pure and applied science. Some attribute this to cultural trends and social disdain, and Thatcher is thought to have represented a new entrepreneurial class not associated with older aristocratic Tory elites.

[6]Thatcher blamed this on unions possessing too much power, which she moved to reduce.

[7]Paul Kennedy (*The Rise and Decline of Fall of the Great Powers: Economic Change and Military Conflict from 1500 to 2000,* [New York: Random House, 1987]) sees this related to Britain's fall from its past "world hegemonic position," militarily and politically as well as economically. He argues that there is a "hegemony cycle" and that once a nation begins its relative decline, powerful forces are set in motion that reinforce it (see J. Barkley Rosser, Jr., *From Catastrophe to Chaos: A General Theory of Economic Discontinuities* [Boston: Kluwer, 1991]), chap. 16, for further discussion).

[8]Mancur Olson, *The Rise and Decline of Nations: Economic Growth, Stagnation, and Social Rigidities* (New Haven: Yale University Press, 1982).

[9]Despite publicity surrounding this program the share of owner-occupied housing only rose from 54.7 percent to 66.5 percent between 1979 and 1989 (Christopher Johnson, *The Grand Experiment: Mrs. Thatcher's Economy and How it Spread* [Boulder: Westview, 1991], p. 298). But it was a popular success and a political triumph, attracting working class voters to the Conservative Party on the premise of "popular capitalism."

[10]Johnson, *The Grand Experiment,* p. 300.

to 20.3 percent during the same period,[11] a rather undramatic decline compared to some other countries.

Goals of this privatization program included (1) efficiency improvements[12] arising from greater competition, reduced interference in managerial decisions by government ministers,[13] freeing up of prices, and reduced wage pressures with weakened government sector unions, (2) equity improvements as ownership spread widely, the "popular capitalism,"[14] and (3) macroeconomic policy gains as the government received revenues from "selling off the family silver,"[15] along with greater antiinflationary pressure[16] as firm debts were privatized and wage pressures were reduced. Many of these goals were achieved to some degree, and during 1983 and 1985–88 the British economy grew more rapidly than either the EU or OECD averages, although it went into recession thereafter as in the early 1980s.

The major criticism of the program is that many of the major firms privatized were and continue to be natural monopolies. The upshot has been government regulation of them. Also Thatcher eventually began to push privatization of parts of the medical care system and local water supply systems, some of the latter actually occurring. These were unpopular positions that, combined with her attack on local public finance and opposition to the Maastricht Treaty, led to her downfall in late 1990. This slowed, but did not end, the British privatization campaign.

Thus privatization has limits discussed in Chapter 2, despite its apparent global acceleration. This global privatization drive increasingly emphasizes worker ownership in a variety of forms not supported by Thatcher, with the worker takeover of United Airlines in the United States being a dramatic example. Nevertheless it was Thatcher's program that initiated the global agenda in this area, even if it did not completely succeed in reviving the British lion's growth.

---

[11]Johnson, *The Grand Experiment,* p. 302.

[12]Evidence is strong that during the 1970s public sector firms had declined in performance relative to private sector ones, despite efforts to emphasize a commercial approach during that period relative to earlier ones.

[13]An example of this included frequent orders to buy higher-cost British-made inputs rather than imported ones.

[14]The share of the adult population owning some stock rose from 7 percent to 20 percent between 1979 and 1988 (Colin Harbury, "Privatization: British Style," in *Comparative Economic Systems: Models and Cases,* 7th ed., ed. M. Bornstein [Burr Ridge: Irwin, 1994] p. 133).

[15]This phrase is due to former Prime Minister Harold Macmillan. Proceeds from privatization peaked in 1988 at 4.0 percent of government expenditure.

[16]The rate of inflation fell from a 1970s annual average of 12.5 percent to a 1980s 7.4 percent (Johnson, *The Grand Experiment,* p. 72), although global inflation declined during this period and the Thatcher program also included a vigorous monetarist policy. However the UK has had trouble maintaining lower inflation as its being forced to drop out of the ERM in late 1992 suggests.

A Clash of Civilizations?

A theme of this book has been the emergence of the new traditional economic system. This form has no single model, despite focus on the Islamic economic system in Chapters 5 and 16. Less clear is that the East Asian zone of neo-Confucian, partially state-directed economies with their groupism and familism may also fit this mold, although substantially contrasting with the Islamic form.[17] This raises the issue of a possible global ''clash of civilizations,'' centered on economic blocs defined as *western liberal* (market capitalist Western Europe and North America), *Islamic* (largely Middle Eastern and South Asian), and *neo-Confucian* (centered on Japan, Korea, and China). Recently this latter group seems the global ''comer.''

This emerging clash coincides complexly with the remnant of the capitalism/socialism clash, largely in abeyance with the apparent victory of capitalism. In Central Asia all of these economic forces—market capitalist, command socialist, and the two major forms of new traditional—come together.

Some argue that Central Asia is a central cockpit of world history as both a generator and a transmitter between East and West of technology and culture.[18] Recently it was in the command socialist system, whether in the Soviet Central Asian republics, in Afghanistan dominated by the Soviets, or in Chinese Inner Asia (Xinjiang). Now that system has loosened, although the former Soviet republics have a conservative reluctance to change, and the command socialist mode persists there more than in most of the FSU.

Religiously this region is Islamic and linguistically most of it is Turkic or Persian. Islamic fundamentalist movements are on the rise, dramatized by military conflicts in Afghanistan and Tajikistan. Simultaneously, systemic market forces are penetrating, spearheaded by Turkey[19] and U.S. multinational corporations. Although the region is not culturally Confucian, the rapid growth of the Chinese economy offers an allure of Chinese influence through possible close relations between Xinjiang and the former Soviet republics.[20]

World leadership in technological innovation and economic growth has shifted back and forth between Europe and East Asia over the last several thousand years. Many argue that this leadership is shifting again from West back to East. But this is an uncertain outcome given that although China and

---

[17]One major difference is that neo-Confucianism is not a radical fundamentalist movement, but is more subtle in its cultural pervasiveness and influence.

[18]S. A. M. Adshead, *China in World History* (London: Macmillan 1988); Andre Gunder Frank, *The Centrality of Central Asia,* (Amsterdam: VU Press, 1992).

[19]A manifestation of this conflict is the question of alphabets, with traditional pro-Soviets supporting continued use of the Cyrillic in which Russian is written, pro-free market westernizers supporting the Latin as used in Turkey, and Islamic fundamentalists supporting the Arabic. Several of these republics have shifted to the Latin alphabet.

[20]Gaye Christoffersen, ''Xinjiang and the Great Islamic Circle: The Impact of Transnational Forces on Chinese Regional Economic Planning,'' *The China Quarterly,* 1993, pp. 130–51.

Korea are growing very rapidly, the leading candidate for Asian-based leadership, Japan, suffers serious economic problems, as discussed near the end of Chapter 6.

Integration and Disintegration

Another major theme of this book has been how individual nations relate to the larger world economy as it exhibits powerful trends towards expanded international trade and investment. Offsetting trends have been integrative and disintegrative. The former are exemplified by the European Community (EC) becoming the European Union (EU) after the 1991 Maastricht Treaty; the NAFTA between the United States, Canada, and Mexico; the formation of the new Asian-Pacific Economic Community (APEC),[21] and the successful conclusion in December 1993 of the Uruguay Round of GATT negotiations on world trade with over 100 nations signing the agreement in 1994 to establish the World Trade Organization (WTO). The most dramatic counterexample has been the disintegration of the former Soviet Union, the collapse of its CMEA trade bloc, and the splitting up of several other Eastern European states, most bloodily the former Yugoslavia.

But even within the integrative tendencies powerful counterforces can be seen. Although the Maastricht Treaty promised full monetary union by the end of the century, the withdrawal of the UK and Italy from the transitional European exchange rate mechanism (ERM) linking currencies to the dominant deutsch mark within bands has slowed the movement to full union.[22] Nationalism is rearing its head in Europe in various nations and ways, in some as neo-fascist anti-immigrant movements. The drive to expand the EU runs into resistance in some would-be members, such as Norway, and also from existing members, especially towards Eastern Europe.

Passed by the U.S. Congress in late 1993, NAFTA has been associated with upheavals in Mexico as described in Chapter 17. Furthermore it has been undermined by a series of petty trade disputes between the United States and Canada, which have the world's largest bilateral trade flows. These have covered a range of products, engendering considerable bitterness.

Regarding the GATT agreement that established the WTO to adjudicate global trade disputes, many nations claim various exemptions and demand special treatment and authority over various matters A dramatic sign of this was the United States's bypassing of the WTO in its auto parts trade dispute with Japan in 1995. If this effort at global free trade fails, it will recall the

---

[21]In late 1994 this fairly informal group dedicated itself to a long-term goal of complete free trade.

[22]On the other hand, the nascent ''Eurofed'' began in 1994 in the form of the European Monetary Institute. But it has a long way to go to match its U.S. counterpart.

1870s and 1930s when world slowdowns led to abrogations of free trade agreements that had been gradually arrived at among the major trading nations.[23]

Can the Transforming World Economy Sustain Growth?

Among the striking developments of the past quarter century has been the dramatic slowdown in the growth rate of the global economy since the first oil price shock in 1973.[24] This slowdown occurred for most of the nations discussed in this book. It happened for the United States and virtually all of Western Europe, irrespective of systemic variations. It happened in Mexico and throughout all of Latin America after 1980, although Mexico as an oil exporter did very well in the 1970s, as did Iran. It happened in sub-Saharan Africa, where many countries slipped into negative per capita GDP growth.[25] It happened dramatically for the entire Soviet bloc with declines like the Great Depression or worse for many nations.

The main exceptions to this dismal scenario have been the East Asian NICs: China, Thailand, Malaysia, Indonesia, South Korea, Taiwan, Hong Kong, and Singapore. But the upper income members of this group, the last four, have had declining growth rates in the early 1990s, and the leader of the neo-Confucian pack, Japan, experienced the dramatic slowdown described in the previous paragraph. It has gone from double-digit growth rates in the 1950s and 1960s to growing about as rapidly as the United States or even more slowly. This is the Gerschenkron "relative backwardness hypothesis" at work. Furthermore most of these countries have relied on export-led growth. If protectionism erupts in the EU and NAFTA blocs against outsiders,[26] this could crimp even the most rip-roaring NICs, although China has a base for expansion, given the enormous size of its potential market, thus providing a potential alternative engine for continued regional expansion.

Thus, although maybe China will surge forward to lead the world, it is more likely that the East Asian NICs are the exceptional pocket of catch-up growth within the broader stagnationist trend. What is going on?

One important trend indicates that many of the very poorest nations have actually gotten poorer. Not only do they have low per capita incomes, but

---

[23]The most dramatic such example was the U.S. Smoot-Hawley tariff of 1930, enacted to "preserve American jobs," which was followed by the job-destroying Great Depression after a global round of protectionist retaliation.

[24]Although slow growth in the 1970s could be attributed to high oil prices, this no longer flies as an explanation as the real price of oil in 1993–94 had fallen to the 1970 level that preceded the oil price shock.

[25]Data are presented on some of these countries in the tables in Chapter 1. This group includes parts of South Asia, most of sub-Saharan Africa, and several countries elsewhere. Detailed discussion of their problems is in books on economic development.

[26]The 1994 APEC free trade agreement mitigates this. But it is a long way from implementation.

also low life expectancies and literacy rates. To this dismal list can be added high infant mortality rates and high birth rates, high rural populations, little infrastructure, and especially low education of women. Their falling behind has increased the overall global level of income inequality. In 1960 the top 20 percent of the world's people received 70.2 percent of the income while the bottom 20 percent received 2.3 percent, whereas in 1989 these figures had become 82.7 percent and 1.4 percent respectively.[27] The global Gini coefficient measured on national per capita incomes rose from 0.69 to 0.87 over the same period.[28]

There is no single reason for those growing inequities. One theory is the "long wave" Kondratiev cycle, a hypothesized macroeconomic fluctuation of about half a century in length.[29] One problem with this argument is that a clear cause for the cycle is lacking. The most common explanation depends on alternating waves of technological innovation. But whether we are about to experience a round of global growth-inducing innovation soon is impossible to forecast.

Another argument involves the trend to postindustrial, service-oriented economies. It is harder to increase productivity in service sectors than in industrial sectors, the most rapidly growing economies being those undergoing industrialization. The service-oriented nature of most public sectors underlies the "cost disease of the public sector,"[30] which explains the tendency to an increasing share of public sector activities in high-income market capitalist economies ("Wagner's Law"), even those trying to avoid such an increase.

Yet another argument is that a global environmental and resource crisis is slowing growth. Its extreme doomsday version was made by the neo-Malthusian Club of Rome,[31] a study widely criticized on many grounds. But the explosion of environmental concern around the world since the early 1970s has resulted in many nations diverting resources to pollution cleanup or avoidance activities. This alone explains part of the slowdown.

A number of global environmental threats have been identified, the most serious from atmospheric pollution affecting global climate. Despite criticism of the global warming hypothesis,[32] it and the threat to the ozone layer from

---

[27]United Nations Development Program, *Human Development Report 1992* (New York: Oxford University Press, 1992) p. 36.

[28]United Nations Development Program, *Human Development Report,* p. 36.

[29]For an application of this concept to the rise and fall of the Soviet-bloc economies, see J. B. Rosser and M. V. Rosser, "Long Wave Chaos and Systemic Economic Transformation," *World Futures,* 39 (1994), pp. 197–207. Joshua Goldstein (*Long Cycles: War and Prosperity in the Modern Age* [New Haven: Yale University Press, 1988]) uses this to explain the hegemony cycle.

[30]See William J. Baumol and Alan S. Blinder, *Macroeconomics: Principles and Policy,* 6th ed. (Fort Worth: Dryden, 1994), chap. 17.

[31]Meadows, Donella H., Dennis L. Meadows, Jorgen Randers, and William W. Behrens III, *The Limits to Growth* (New York: Universe, 1972).

[32]Patrick J. Michaels, *Sound and Fury: The Science and Politics of Global Warming* (Washington: Cato Institute, 1992).

Box 19–1

Botswana: A Sub-Saharan African Success Story

Poor sub-Saharan Africa contains the world's most rapidly growing economy for 1980–92, Botswana.* Its high growth has been accompanied by low inflation, budget surpluses, and current account surpluses. How has Botswana succeeded?

Some of it is sheer luck. Diamonds were discovered after independence in 1965 and their export has been the main source of the nation's rising income. But other nations in the region also have valuable natural resources, such as Zaire, but have fared poorly.

An important factor is absence of corruption reflecting democratic government. Thus, diamond earnings have been used to expand infrastructure, education, and other underpinnings of growth and development, rather than to line the pockets of a rent-seeking elite.† Another lucky factor is ethnic homogeneity, with most of the population belonging to the Tswana tribe, thus avoiding the tribal wars dragging down many African countries.‡

The economy has been market oriented since independence, and capitalist enterprises have been encouraged. However, a substantial state-owned sector faces little pressure for privatization because of its profitability and accountability. This sector is marked by joint ventures between the state and foreign corporations, the most important being with the De Beers diamond company, Debswana, which generates half of government revenues.§ That this sector continues to be efficient reflects Botswana's non-corrupt and democratic government.

---

*This conclusion is based on aggregate GDP (World Bank, *World Development Report 1994* [New York: Oxford University Press, 1994], Table 2). Because of its rapidly growing population it was fourth in real per capita growth rate at 6.1 percent (see Table 1–1), after South Korea, China, and Bhutan.

†Botswana stands out globally for both its high rate of infrastructure investment and its high growth rate (J. Bradford De Long and Lawrence H. Summers, ''Equipment Investment and Economic Growth,'' *Quarterly Journal of Economics* 106 [1991], pp. 445–502). Botswana has avoided the wasteful ''gigantomaniac'' projects favored by many other African nations.

‡A major minority group are the traditionalist Khoi-San described in Chapter 4. Botswana contains more of them than any other country.

§Keith Jeffries, ''Public Enterprise and Privatization in Botswana,'' in *International Privatization: Strategies and Practices,* ed. T. Clarke (Berlin: Walter de Gruyter, 1994), p. 386.

TABLE 19–1   Greenhouse Gas Emissions by Top 10 Nations

Country	Carbon Dioxide	Methane	CFCs	Total	Percent of World Total
United States	540,000	130,000	350,000	1,000,000	17.6
USSR	450,000	60,000	180,000	690,000	12.0
Brazil	560,000	28,000	16,000	610,000	10.5
China	260,000	90,000	32,000	380,000	6.6
India	130,000	98,000	700	230,000	3.9
Japan	110,000	12,000	100,000	220,000	3.9
Germany (West)	79,000	8,000	75,000	160,000	2.8
UK	69,000	14,000	71,000	150,000	2.7
Indonesia	110,000	19,000	9,500	140,000	2.4
France	41,000	13,000	69,000	120,000	2.1

Note: Gases are measured as thousand metric tons of carbon dioxide equivalents. It has been discovered that CFCs are not greenhouse gases, but they are included because of their threat to the stratospheric ozone layer. Sulfur dioxide emissions may offset global warming and data on them are presented in several other chapters.
Source: Data from Paul Kennedy, *Preparing for the Twenty-First Century* (New York: Random House, 1993), p. 117. Data are for 1987, when the USSR was still a nation.

CFC emissions symbolize what humanity faces. Table 19–1 presents data on atmospheric greenhouse gas pollutants emitted by the world's 10 largest aggregate air polluters as measured by a Greenhouse Index. Carbon dioxide comes substantially from burning fossil fuels, generally a high-income activity, and from deforestation, a poorer tropical countries activity. Methane generally comes from cattle and producing certain crops like rice, thus from both rich and poor countries. The chlorofluorocarbons (CFCs) are used by richer countries and are of strictly industrial, anthropogenic origin.

Consideration of this problem leads to a final note of optimism regarding a possible wave of innovations that could lift the world economy. The most serious transformation of the world economy comes from the relationship between humanity and the environment, the search for an economic system that is ecologically sustainable in the long run. Arguably we have entered a higher stage of evolution of the interacting human-environment system. This is symbolized by the global association between environmental movements and political democratization movements, evident in the breakdown of the former Soviet bloc.

Continued global cooperation is crucial. The 1989 Montreal Accords on CFC emissions and the agreements on carbon dioxide emissions of the 1992 Rio Earth Summit offer grounds for optimism. Furthermore, forward progress on crucial technologies might improve the possibility of long-run sustainable growth. These include solar batteries competitive with fossil fuels in cost and electric cars competitive with fossil fuel–driven cars. Breakthroughs in these and related areas could trigger a globally sustainable, real capital investment boom as the world economy adopts the new technologies and truly transforms itself into a higher stage of evolution within a framework of international peace, democracy, and cooperation. Thus, rather than bringing the end of history, the transforming world economy will transform history.

Questions for Discussion

1. Compare and contrast the British privatization program under Thatcher with those of other countries presented in this book.

2. Evaluate the success or failure of the popular capitalism program in turning around the relative decline of the British economy.

3. Why is Central Asia a major focal point of a potential global clash of civilizations, including of economic systems?

4. What are the sources of the competing pressures for global economic integration and disintegration?

5. Why has Botswana been an exception to the dismal record of sub-Saharan African economic development?

6. What are some of the explanations for the global deceleration of economic growth since the early 1970s and what are the prospects for overcoming this trend?

7. What do you see as the predominant trends in the evolution of economic systems in the coming century and why?

Suggested Further Readings

Aslanbeigui, Nahid, Steven Pressman, and Gale Summerfield, eds. *Women in the Age of Economic Transformation: Gender Impact of Reforms in Post-Socialist and Developing Countries.* London: Routledge, 1994.

Thomas Clarke, ed. *International Privatization: Strategies and Practices.* Berlin: Walter de Gruyter, 1994.

Gerschenkron, Alexander. *Economic Backwardness in Historical Perspective.* Cambridge: Harvard University Press, 1962.

Goldstein, Joshua S. *Long Cycles: War and Prosperity in the Modern Age.* New Haven: Yale University Press, 1988.

Harbury, Colin. "Privatization: British Style." In *Comparative Economic Systems: Models and Cases*, 7th ed., ed. Morris Bornstein. Burr Ridge: Irwin, 1994, pp. 115–36.

Kennedy, Paul. *Preparing for the Twenty-First Century.* New York: Random House, 1993.

Rosser, J. Barkley, Jr. *From Catastrophe to Chaos: A General Theory of Economic Discontinuities.* Boston: Kluwer, 1991.

Stokes, Kenneth M. *Man and the Biosphere.* Armonk: M.E. Sharpe, 1992.

Index

DATE DUE

FEB	9 2001		
			Printed in USA